MW01254750

Constitutional Rights Of
PRISONERS

This updated tenth edition covers all aspects of prisoners' rights, including an overview of the judicial system and constitutional law and explanation of specific constitutional issues regarding correctional populations. It also discusses the federal statutes that affect correctional administration and inmates' rights to bring litigation. Accessible and reader-friendly, it provides a practical understanding of how constitutional law affects the day-to-day issues of prisons, jails, and community corrections programs.

The tenth edition includes a thorough update of relevant case law, and new chapters are included that deliver the latest developments on Search, Seizure, and Privacy, Juveniles and Youthful Offenders, and the Death Penalty. Part II contains the Supreme Court syllabi for the significant Court cases relating to the concepts covered.

This updated edition is appropriate as a primary text for undergraduate or graduate-level correctional law and prisoner rights courses within Criminal Justice, Criminology, and Sociology departments. It is also an invaluable reference tool for law students and correctional agencies.

Shaun M. Gann is an Assistant Professor in the Department of Criminal Justice at Boise State University. He earned his PhD in Criminal Justice from the University of Cincinnati. He has also worked as a Parole Officer for the Arkansas Department of Community Corrections, where he gained extensive experience in the day-to-day operations of the correctional system. He regularly teaches both undergraduate and graduate-level courses in corrections, including Contemporary Issues in Corrections, Correctional Law, and Correctional Counseling. His research interests include correctional programming and policy; juvenile court decision-making; race and delinquency; and the effects of court decisions on criminal justice policy. He is the coauthor of *Correctional Assessment, Casework, and Counseling*. He has published research in leading peer-reviewed journals such as *Youth Violence and Juvenile Justice*, *Journal of Developmental and Life Course Criminology*, *Journal of Crime and Justice*, *Journal of Juvenile Justice*, and *Journal of Criminal Justice Education*.

John W. Palmer served as a Professor of Law at Capital University Law School for close to 30 years. He earned his JD from University of Michigan Law School in 1962 and continued his education in legal advocacy and languages across his career. In addition to practicing law, Palmer held teaching positions at Concordia International University in Estonia, University of Warsaw, Central European University, International University of Germany, American University in Armenia, and Ohio Dominican University. He was a three-time Fulbright Scholar at the University of Stockholm, Sweden, 1962–1963; the University of Warsaw, Poland, 2003–2004; and Estonia, 2004. He has been a frequent speaker on Criminal Justice, International Law, and Labor Law in South America and Europe. Throughout his illustrious career, he has amassed a variety of distinguished honors, including the Ohio Association of Chiefs of Police Award, 1972; Fellow, American Bar Foundation, 1977–Present; Special Commendation from FBI Director William Webster, 1978; Special Recognition Award, National Association for Dispute Resolution, 1979 (shared award with President Jimmy Carter); Ritter Award, Night Prosecutor's Program, Ohio Bar Foundation, 1983; Team Member of Conference with Russian Leadership, Kremlin, 1987; and Special Award, Association International de Droit Penal, Siracusa, Italy, 1991.

Constitutional Rights Of
PRISONERS

10TH EDITION

Shaun M. GANN and John W. PALMER

Routledge
Taylor & Francis Group

NEW YORK AND LONDON

Tenth edition published 2022
by Routledge
605 Third Avenue, New York, NY 10158

and by Routledge
2 Park Square, Milton Park, Abingdon, Oxon, OX14 4RN

Routledge is an imprint of the Taylor & Francis Group, an informa business

© 2022 Taylor & Francis

First edition published by Anderson Publishing 1973
Ninth edition published by Routledge 2010

Library of Congress Cataloging-in-Publication Data
Names: Palmer, John W., 1933– author. | Gann, Shaun M., author.
Title: Constitutional rights of prisoners / Shaun M. Gann, John W. Palmer.
Description: Tenth Edition. | New York : Routledge, 2021. | Includes
    bibliographical references and index.
Identifiers: LCCN 2021001727 (print) | LCCN 2021001728 (ebook) | ISBN
    9780367335120 (hardback) | ISBN 9780367359263 (paperback) | ISBN
    9780429342660 (ebook)
Subjects: LCSH: Prisoners—Legal status, laws, etc.—United States | Prisoners—
    Legal status, laws, etc.—United States—Cases. | Prisoners—Civil rights—
    United States—Cases.
Classification: LCC KF9731 .P3 2021 (print) | LCC KF9731 (ebook) | DDC
    344.7303/56—dc23
LC record available at https://lccn.loc.gov/2021001727
LC ebook record available at https://lccn.loc.gov/2021001728

ISBN: 978-0-367-33512-0 (hbk)
ISBN: 978-0-367-35926-3 (pbk)
ISBN: 978-0-429-34266-0 (ebk)

Typeset in Times New Roman
by Apex CoVantage, LLC

Access the Support Material: www.routledge.com/9780367335120

Shaun M. Gann:
To my Bearcat and Bronco families

John W. Palmer:
To my family

Contents

Chapter 3
Searches, Seizures, and Privacy 57

Chapter 4
Rights to Visitation and Association 71

Chapter 7
Prisoner Legal Services 135

Chapter 8
Additional Constitutional Issues 159

Chapter 9
Isolated Confinement—"The Hole" and Administrative Segregation   193

Chapter 10
Prisoner Disciplinary Proceedings   211

Chapter 14
Juvenile and Youthful Offenders   299

Chapter 15
Legal Remedies Available to Prisoners   309

Chapter 16
Selected Federal Statutes Affecting Prisoners   359

Preface

In 2018, 2,123,100 adults were incarcerated in American prisons and jails.[1] Another 4,399,000 were being supervised in the community on probation or parole. The incarcerated population decreased 8.1 percent from 2008 to 2018, while the community supervision population decreased 13.6 percent. Though we have seen steady decreases in the correctional population over the past decade, 1 in 40 adults are still under some form of correctional supervision in the U.S. Despite these decreases, state and federal government correctional expenditures increased from $79 billion in 2005 to $89 billion in 2016.

Suffice to say, the American correctional system is a massive undertaking. Since the mid-twentieth century, hundreds of Supreme Court cases and thousands of federal appellate court cases have addressed myriad correctional issues. Some cases have provided inmates with constitutional protections that survive incarceration, while others have limited—or completely restricted—inmates' rights that are incompatible with the goals of corrections.

In recent years, the legal framework of our federal judiciary system has become more conservative. Prior to 2018, there essentially was an even split between liberal and conservative justices on the U.S. Supreme Court, with Justice Kennedy frequently serving as the swing vote. As of October 2020, however, there is now a strong conservative majority (6–3) on the Supreme Court with the recent appointments of Justices Gorsuch, Kavanaugh, and Barrett. The ideological split among the members of the Court gives us a hint as to how they may rule, although it is impossible to predict with accuracy what any particular Justice will do in any given case. Only time will indicate how the new conservative justices evolve concerning the constitutional rights of those under correctional supervision.

Since the Ninth Edition of *Constitutional Rights of Prisoners*, the Court has decided a number of important cases regarding correctional issues. Some of the recent cases discussed in the Tenth Edition include:

- *Holt v. Hobbs*, 574 U.S. 352 (2015): A prison policy that prohibits inmates from growing beards violates the Religious Land Use and Institutionalized Persons Act of 2000 insofar as it prevents an inmate from growing a ½-inch beard in accordance with his religious beliefs.

---

[1] Laura M. Maruschak & Todd D. Minton, Bureau of Justice Statistics, Correctional Populations in the United States, 2017–2018 (2020), http://bjs.gov/content/pub/pdf/cpus17 18.pdf.

- *Florence v. Board of Chosen Freeholders*, 566 U.S. 318 (2012): Jail detainees, even those arrested for minor crimes, can be subject to strip searches and body cavity searches upon being booked.

- *Brown v. Plata*, 563 U.S. 493 (2011): Courts can limit a state's correctional population if necessary to remedy violations of prisoners' constitutional rights caused primarily by severe overcrowding.

- *Kingsley v. Hendrickson*, 576 U.S. 389 (2015): Pretrial detainees must show only that the force purposely or knowingly used against him was objectively unreasonable to prevail on an excessive force claim.

- *Hall v. Florida*, 572 U.S. 701 (2014): Florida's requirement that a defendant show an IQ score of 70 or below before being permitted to present any additional evidence of intellectual disability is unconstitutional.

- *Graham v. Florida*, 567 U.S. 460 (2010): Offenders who commit their crime under the age of 17 cannot be sentenced to life in prison without parole for a nonhomicide offense.

- *Miller v. Alabama*, 567 U.S. 460 (2012): The Eighth Amendment forbids a sentencing scheme that mandates life in prison without the possibility of parole for juvenile homicide offenders.

In addition to the thorough update of case law, there are a number of other changes in the Tenth Edition that we believe have improved on previous editions.

1. The death penalty discussion from the Ninth Edition is moved to a new, separate chapter, updated, and expanded to include more detail on death penalty procedures, eligibility, and methods of execution.

2. We added a new chapter on juvenile and youthful offenders that discusses, among other things, the significant Court cases regarding juvenile court proceedings, life without parole sentences, the death penalty, and searches of juveniles.

3. The chapter on the right to medical care was expanded to include transgender inmates and gender reassignment surgery.

4. Discussion of search and seizure is consolidated into a single chapter and expanded.

5. The "Selected Federal Statutes Affecting Prisoners" chapter is expanded to include the 2010 revisions to the Americans with Disabilities Act and the Prison Rape Elimination Act.

6. The section on inmate transfer was updated to include civil commitment for sex offenders.

Another significant change to the Tenth Edition is the addition of myself, Dr. Shaun M. Gann, as a new coauthor. I am an Assistant Professor of Criminal Justice at Boise State University. I have conducted research and taught courses on correctional law, correctional counseling, community corrections, and the death penalty. In addition, I previously worked as a parole officer in Arkansas; as such, I have firsthand experience in how judicial decisions affect the day-to-day operations of both institutional and community corrections. I want to thank John W. Palmer, Ellen Boyne, and the editorial team at Routledge for allowing me to coauthor the new edition of *Constitutional Rights of Prisoners*.

Shaun M. Gann
Boise, Idaho
December 2020

Part I:
Correctional Law

An Overview of the Judicial System and Correctional Law

1

Chapter Outline

§ 1.1 Introduction

Law is the set of rules that governs the conduct of individuals and entities in our society. In the United States, the rules are applied in cases or controversies by the judicial branch of government. There are three principal sources of laws: federal and state constitutions, federal and state statutes, and the common law, or judge-made law. Taken collectively, these sources establish what is known as the *law*.

The federal Constitution is the product of a balance of power between the sovereign states in the late eighteenth century. It established the basic form of the federal government of the United States as we know it today. It divides federal power among three branches of government: the legislative, the executive, and the judicial. Only limited power is granted by the sovereign states to the federal government; all power not expressly or implicitly granted to the federal government is reserved to the states. Congress is given the duty of legislating in areas of national interest, the executive branch carries out the execution of federal laws, and the judicial branch is entrusted with the administration of federal laws and justice. Each branch of government has specifically enumerated functions and powers under the Constitution. Thus, the Constitution is the supreme law of the land; it provides the basic rules for the functioning of the national government. It also governs the relationships between the states and the federal government, between the states themselves, and between states and foreign governments.

State constitutions, on the other hand, are limitations on the power of the states. Whereas the federal government can act only in the areas in which the Constitution specifically or implicitly provides, state governments can legislate in any area, except where state or federal constitutions limit their power. State constitutions also provide for the organization of the state government and for the duties and powers of the members of government that they create.

Federal and state statutes are other sources of law. Congress is entrusted with enacting laws for the national good, while state legislatures provide for the welfare of the citizens of the respective states. The statutes enacted for these purposes become the law, subject only to the limitations of state and federal constitutions. Statutes are enacted to specifically guide the conduct of affected individuals or entities. The courts, both federal and state, apply the rules thus established, which are then enforced by the executive branch of government.

The other major source of law in the United States is a body of rules called the *common law*. Common law, in the sense used here,[1] is the rule of law that has its origins in the courts rather than in the legislatures. Because it is the result of court cases, it is often referred to as *case law*.

Treaties between the United States and foreign countries and international organizations may also be a source of law applicable to state and federal courts.[2] Administrative law is the set of principles that govern the activities of administrative agencies, such as a state Department of Corrections or the Federal Bureau of Prisons. Since the 1930s, there has been an explosion of complex social, economic, and political issues that are subject to administrative regulation. In effect, administrative law brings the rule of law to executive decision-making.

State authorities have increasingly turned to administrative law as a source of prison law. Administrative law is part executive, judicial, and legislative and sometimes has been referred to as the "headless fourth Branch" of government.[3] Most administrative agencies are now subject to state and federal Administrative Procedure Acts. These acts set forth the procedures that govern administrative agencies and provide for limited judicial review.[4]

§ 1.1.1　– The Constitutional Framework

The Constitution of the United States is the supreme law of the land. Further, it has been doctrine since 1803. Any laws, statutes, regulations, or government policies in conflict with the Constitution are unenforceable.[5] It is the standard by which all governmental action is measured.

Individuals are protected under the Constitution and its amendments. The Bill of Rights, adopted at the same time as the Constitution, protects individuals from actions of the federal government. As originally interpreted, the Bill of Rights did not apply to the relationship between individuals and state and local governments. It was not until the passage of the Fourteenth Amendment after the Civil War that rights protected under the Bill of Rights became applicable to the states. For example, if the FBI conducts an unlawful search, it is a violation of the Fourth Amendment. If a local sheriff conducts an unlawful search, it is a violation of the Fourteenth Amendment, which applies the doctrine of the Fourth Amendment through the Due Process Clause of the Fourteenth Amendment. The Constitution does not protect individuals from the actions of individuals acting in their private capacity.

As will be discussed throughout this book, courts have reviewed conduct by prison officials under specific constitutional provisions, such as the Eighth Amendment's ban on cruel and unusual punishments or general principles stemming from the Due Process Clause of the Fourteenth Amendment. Cruel and unusual punishment may thus be reviewed under both Eighth Amendment standards or independently as a violation of due process.

Civil rights may be protected by statutes passed by Congress under its constitutional authority. The commerce clause gives Congress the power to enact legislation that has an effect on interstate commerce. Congress also has the authority to enact legislation to carry out the intent of the Fourteenth Amendment. Section 5 of the Fourteenth Amendment states: "The Congress shall have power to enforce this article by appropriate legislation."

An academic example illustrates these principles. If a professor at a state university conducts an unlawful search or seizure of a student, he violates the student's Fourteenth Amendment rights, as the Due Process Clause of the Fourteenth Amendment applies the Fourth Amendment to the states. The professor is an agent of the state in such a situation. However, if a professor at a private liberal arts college conducts an unwarranted search or seizure of a student, no constitutional rights are involved because the professor is not an agent of a state agency.

Individuals may also be protected under various federal statutes. For example, if private colleges accept federal benefits, such as student aid programs, they are subject to federal regulation. Further, as many private entities are engaged in some form of interstate commerce, they become subject to federal regulation as well. Title VII of the Civil Rights Act, which deals with employment discrimination, is an example. This statute does not apply to employers who are not engaged in interstate practices. It should further be noted that, although the reach of the United States Constitution and federal statutes may not offer protection to individuals, there is nothing preventing state and local governments from enacting protections, either civil or criminal.

§ 1.1.2 — Separation of Powers

Articles I, II, and III of the United States Constitution set out the framework of the federal government. Article I establishes the Congress. Article II establishes the Presidency. Article III establishes the Judiciary. History has shown that it is an act of human nature that the executive branch of government frequently attempts to expand its power, often at the expense of one or the other branches of government.

§ 1.1.3 — Limits on Executive Power

The Supreme Court has frequently intervened to curtail the President of the United States from exercising power that he did not have. President Truman unconstitutionally seized steel mills in an attempt to stop a strike.[6] President Nixon unsuccessfully attempted to exercise Executive Privilege during the Watergate crisis. President Bush unconstitutionally attempted to set up special military tribunals in his fight against terrorism. *Hamdan v. Rumsfeld*[7] held that as the military commissions established by the President were not expressly authorized by any congressional act, they were invalid. Further, the structure and procedures of the military commissions established by the President violated both the Uniform Code of Military Justice[8] and four Geneva Conventions signed in 1949.[9] This is but one example where international law was used to justify a decision of the Supreme Court.

§ 1.2   The American Common Law

The common law is so called because originally it was the law common to all of England. It was the law that the English courts used in deciding cases when there was no legislative enactment. The common law has never been regarded as static. It is "the wisdom, counsel, experience, and observation of many ages of wise and observing men."[10]

The common law for many centuries was oral, and there were no written reports of judicial decisions. Thus, it was often known as the "unwritten law." With the practice of reporting decisions,[11] the written opinions of the judges in deciding actual cases provided a starting point in determining the legal principles applicable to new factual situations that faced the courts. The "old" law was applied when the facts of a "new" case were the same as the facts of the "old" case. If the facts were different, a new rule often developed.

The English common law was transplanted to America through English colonization. The charters of colonies provided for the protection of the rights of free men according to the laws of England.[12] Several state constitutions, such as those of Massachusetts, New York, New Jersey, and Maryland, specifically adopted the English common law as the law in that state except as changed by the state statutes.[13] Other state statutes and court decisions adopted the English common law as the law of the land.[14] Once transplanted, however, American common law was adapted to meet the needs of the American economic and social systems.

§ 1.2.1   — Equity as Part of the Common Law

At the end of the thirteenth century in England, there were three main court systems: the King's courts (including King's Bench, Common Pleas, and Exchequer), the communal courts of the counties and hundreds, and the ecclesiastical courts. The King's courts administered the King's justice common to all of England (common law); the communal courts and ecclesiastical courts administered specialized justice that was not within the jurisdiction of the King's courts.

To secure access to the King's courts, a person had to procure a "writ" from the King's Chancellor, who was the King's Secretary of State for all departments whose office was responsible for any writing done in the King's name."[15] A *writ* was a command from the King to a named person to appear in one of the King's courts to answer a claim. There were certain standardized claims, or forms of action, that could be issued by the Chancellor, although the Chancellor had the authority to frame new writs when the case was similar to cases in which existing writs were issued as a matter of right. For a writ to be valid, it had to follow the rigid patterns set by the common law principles that the King's courts administered. As a result of the rigid rules applied by the King's judges in the common law courts, which had to conform to the writ issued, many people who were wronged were denied adequate relief. It was essentially "no writ, no remedy."

The King, as the source of all justice in England, naturally could fill the void left by the rigidity of the common law. Thus, people could petition the King and his council for redress as a matter of favor, if no relief was available in the common law courts.

The Chancellor, as the King's chief minister and secretary, was delegated the power and authority to grant redress in such cases in the King's name. The Chancellor was generally a cleric, often a bishop. He dispensed the King's justice, also called *equity*, and was strongly influenced by moral and ethical considerations and the justice of the conflict rather than by previous court decisions. The Chancellor became the conscience of the legal system.

The granting of a special favor in a particular case in which no adequate remedy existed at common law became an accepted practice. The relief granted by the Chancellor was popular and much sought-after. Once established, relief given by the Chancellor, known as equitable relief, became an integral part of the law, standing side by side with the common law rather than something granted as a favor of the King. It became more than one man could manage, and this led to the establishment of a Court of Chancery (or court of equity). The body of principles of moral justice applied to individual cases developed into rules of equity by subsequent repetition. Thus, a body of court-made law separate from the traditional common law developed (administered by a separate court of equity). The separation of common law courts and courts of equity remained until fairly recent times (e.g., 1848 in New York, 1873–1875 in Great Britain). Now, in most states, a single court administers both "law," in the sense of common law, as well as "equity."

Distinctions still remain, however, depending upon whether the relief sought was traditionally administered by common law courts or courts of equity. For example, the right to a jury trial attached only when the claim was recognized by the "law" courts, because a claim in the court of equity was decided by the Chancellor without the aid of a jury. In addition, the traditional remedy granted by equity was an order against a person (i.e., an injunction) while the traditional remedy of the common law courts was an order involving property (i.e., damages).

Equity has the power of contempt of court to enforce its orders, because equity relief is directed against the person and not against the person's property. Contempt of court occurs when a person willfully disobeys an order of the court of equity, either in the presence of the court (direct contempt) or when a person obstructs the justice of the court out of the presence of the court (indirect contempt). Thus, one cannot be held in contempt of court for failing to pay a monetary judgment, because that is a judgment at "law." The court can only execute judgment and levy on the property of the defendant.

Equitable relief is discretionary and can only be granted when the remedy at law, or in damages, is inadequate. If monetary damages will adequately compensate a wrong, equitable relief, such as an injunction against future conduct, cannot be obtained.

§ 1.2.2 — Role of Case Law

The legal principles applied in a particular case before a court become part of the common law. It takes its place as a part of the body of court-made rules that will form the basis of future decisions.

With the publication of reports of cases contemporaneous with the decisions in England, published cases were at first merely instructive and informative. However, courts began to cite previously decided cases to support their own conclusions, and ever-increasing weight was placed on reported cases. For the past three centuries, the decisions of judges of higher courts have been precedent for later cases.[16] Precedent is the decision of a court that furnishes authority for an identical or similar case that arises subsequently. The practice of using past case law as the basis for current decisions is called *stare decisis*, which means "let the decision stand." The use of a case as precedent or authority requires that the exact rule or principle of law, known as the *holding*, be determined from the language of the reported decision. Any reasoning or principle of law in a decision that is not part of the holding, or not essential to the determination of the case, is termed *obiter dictum*, or simply *dictum*, meaning words "spoken by the way."

The precise effect of precedent, or the doctrine of *stare decisis*, depends upon the factual similarity between a prior case and a subsequent controversy. The principle of *stare decisis* rests upon the presumption that a previous court determined the law applicable to a factual situation after reasonable consideration and that it provides authority for later decisions made in similar cases.

The reasons for applying the doctrine of *stare decisis* include: (1) certainty and predictability of the law, which is necessary for the regulation of personal conduct and commerce; (2) growth when new issues arise; (3) equality of application; and (4) respect for the prior judgments of an esteemed legal mind.

As an exposition of the applicable law, the prior decision of a court is binding on that court and the inferior courts (courts lower in the hierarchical judicial structure) of that judicial system. Thus, a decision of the Supreme Court of the United States on questions of federal law is binding on all lower federal courts (courts of appeals and district courts). Likewise, the decisions of the highest court of each state are binding on the inferior state courts. However, a decision of the Supreme Court of Ohio is not precedent for a New York court. The New York court may follow the Ohio precedent voluntarily, due to its persuasiveness, but it is not bound to do so.

However, certain handicaps are present in the doctrine of *stare decisis*, such as hardships resulting from rigidity, illogical distinctions on the facts of a case, and the sheer numbers of reported cases that establish law. In addition, the American social and economic systems change with the passage of time. As has been said:

> The life of the law has not been logic: it has been experience. The felt necessities of the time, the prevalent moral and political theories, institutions of public policy, avowed or unconscious, even the prejudices which judges share with their fellow-men, have had a good deal more to do than the syllogism in determining the rules by which men should be governed.[17]

The methods for changing case-made law to meet new demands on the law are distinguishing or overruling previous cases. Distinguishing previous cases occurs when later courts confine prior decisions strictly to their facts and apply a new rule to the facts of the controversy at issue. The effect is to give very limited application to an earlier case. A court overrules a prior rule of law by finding that it was improperly decided or that the social and economic conditions have changed from the time the prior decision was made. Thus, a new rule of law should apply.

§ 1.3   The American Court Structure

The court system of the United States is composed of 51 independent court systems. The federal court system and each of the 50 state systems operate within their own judicial spheres.

The states operate their court systems as one of the powers reserved to them by the Tenth Amendment to the United States Constitution. Each state has its own system, with the structure and jurisdiction of the courts established by the state constitution and statutes. However, all court structures include two types of courts: trial courts and appellate courts.

State trial courts generally include courts of limited jurisdiction and courts of general jurisdiction. The limited jurisdictional courts are the numerous local courts that have the power to hear civil cases involving limited monetary amounts and minor criminal offenses, such as traffic violations. Above the limited jurisdictional courts in the hierarchical structure are the trial courts of general jurisdiction. They generally have the power to hear all civil cases involving any monetary amount greater than that handled by the limited jurisdiction courts and serious criminal cases.

The functions of the trial court are receiving proper evidence, compiling a record of the evidence introduced, finding disputed facts from the evidence introduced, applying the appropriate law to the facts, and granting appropriate relief. The fact-finding function of a trial can be exercised either by the jury—if the right to jury trial exists and is exercised—or by the judge, who then has two separate and distinct duties: fact-finding and applying the proper law.

Every state has at least one level of appellate courts. The highest appellate court in a state is generally called the supreme court, though some states call it the court of appeals (e.g., New York). The supreme court of a state is the "court of last resort" because it is the final, authoritative source of judicial relief in the state court system. In the more populous states, such as California, Florida, Illinois, Ohio, or Texas, there are intermediate appellate courts in the state court system, generally called courts of appeals. These courts handle appeals from the trial courts, and their decisions, in turn, are reviewable by the supreme court of the state. The function of the appellate courts is to review the decisions of trial courts or lower-level appellate courts for errors that might have prejudiced the rights of a party, such as errors in procedure or errors in applying the proper rule of law to the facts established by the evidence. The factual findings of the trial court are generally final. The appellate courts do not receive any evidence when reviewing a case but use the record of the trial court. Whenever there was a dispute at the trial level as to the existence of a particular fact, the decision of the trier of fact (either the judge or jury) is binding upon the appellate court, and the appellate court cannot overturn the trial court's factual findings unless they are clearly erroneous.

The federal court system was created by the Constitution, which expressly provided for the Supreme Court and authorized Congress to create inferior federal courts. As a result of this grant of power to Congress, federal statutes provide for 94 federal trial courts (district courts) and 13 intermediate appellate courts (courts of appeals). Figure 1.1 displays the geographic boundaries of the federal district courts and courts of appeals.

The types of cases that a federal court can adjudicate are limited; that is, the federal courts have limited jurisdiction. The limited jurisdiction of the federal courts is a result of the structure of our federal government. The sovereign states have granted (to the federal government through the Constitution) certain powers to be exercised for the common good, among them the judicial power as specified. The federal judicial power extends to (1) cases arising under the U.S. Constitution, federal laws or treaties, (2) all cases affecting ambassadors, public ministers, and consuls, (3) admiralty and maritime cases, (4) controversies in which the United States is a party, (5) controversies between states, between a state and a citizen of another state, between citizens of the same state claiming lands under grants from different states, and in cases between a state or citizen of a state and foreign countries, their citizens, or subjects.[18]

For a case to be heard in a federal court, it must fall under one of these categories. The greatest number of federal cases are those arising under the Constitution, cases based upon federal statutory rights, and cases between citizens of different states, referred to as "diversity of citizenship" cases. Cases arising under the Constitution are those that enforce the provisions of the Constitution; that is, a right created by the Constitution itself, such as the First Amendment freedom of speech provisions. Controversies arising under federal laws are cases in which a federal statute has specifically provided a procedure for judicial relief, such as the various Civil Rights Acts.

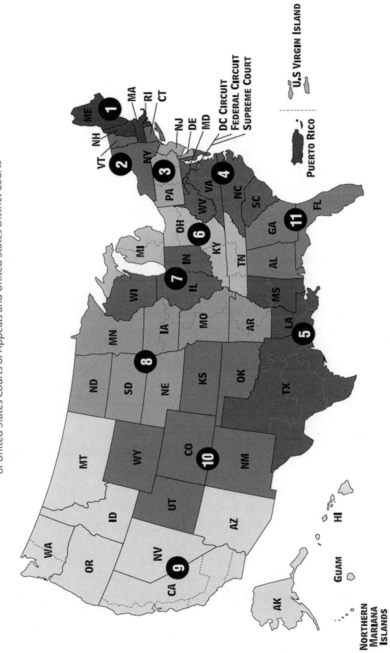

Figure 1.1 Federal Court Map

Diversity of citizenship cases are those in which the cause of action, or right to seek judicial relief, arises under state law, either statutory or common, but is between citizens of different states. In a diversity case, the federal court applies state law. The federal court merely provides a neutral forum for resolving the dispute. Congress has placed a statutory limit on diversity cases by requiring that the controversy involve an amount in excess of $75,000. This was done to limit the number of cases using the federal court system at the expense of the state court systems.

The federal district courts' jurisdictional areas (in a geographical sense) are the result of a division of the nation into 94 judicial districts by population. For example, New York is divided into four districts, while in less populated states, such as Maine or Arizona, the district encompasses the entire state.

The federal district court is a trial court for federal criminal prosecutions and civil actions, with its function being the same as a state trial court. It also has the power to review the decisions of certain federal administrative agencies.

Federal statutes have also created several specialty courts that have the same functions as a district court but that limit the type of cases heard to one subject, such as tax, patents, or military appeals. These courts are created to handle a highly specialized subject so that the judges of the courts will have exceptional knowledge of the complex subject involved.

The federal courts of appeals are the intermediate appellate courts. There are 13 circuits, dividing the country geographically according to the volume of the judicial caseload. One circuit is provided exclusively for the District of Columbia, due to the heavy volume of appeals from federal administrative agencies. The Federal Court of Appeals hears cases involving patents, copyrights, trademarks, and cases from the Court of Claims and Court of International Trade. The function of the federal courts of appeals is similar to that of a state court of appeals. These courts review the decisions of the federal district courts and some federal administrative agencies.

The United States Supreme Court—often referred to as simply "the Court"—serves as the court of last resort for cases from the federal system. The Supreme Court is the ultimate interpreter of the Constitution and federal statutes. It reviews the decisions of the federal circuit courts of appeals and some direct appeals from district courts. The Supreme Court also reviews the decisions of state courts involving matters of federal constitutional rights when the case has been finally adjudicated in the state court system. Besides its appellate function, the Court has original jurisdiction in suits in which a state is a party and in controversies involving ambassadors, ministers, and consuls.[19]

Cases are brought to the Supreme Court for consideration by two methods: (1) appeal as a right and (2) discretion of the court. The appeals of right are appeals that are expressly provided for by statute. The court grants discretionary review by issuing a writ of certiorari, which is an order to review the action of an inferior court. The Court grants few petitions for the writ of certiorari. The Court receives about 7,000–8,000 petitions each term but only grants writs of certiorari to approximately 80.[20]

§ 1.3.1   – The Trial

In the federal system, the parties to a civil lawsuit for damages are entitled to a jury trial under the Seventh Amendment.[21] The Seventh Amendment applies to all civil rights actions for damages. However, if the lawsuit is in equity, asking for injunctive and similar relief, the Seventh Amendment does not apply and the judge decides all factual issues. There is no trial by jury in equity.

A civil suit begins by the filing of a complaint. The defendant then files an answer or a motion to dismiss on the grounds that the complaint filed by the plaintiff does not constitute a legal wrong or that the defendant is protected by a privilege.

After an answer is filed, the parties begin the discovery process. Discovery may take the form of (1) depositions, in which parties and witnesses are examined under oath in a somewhat informal setting; (2) interrogatories, in which parties are asked to provide statements under oath or provide documents; or (3) requests for admissions, in which parties are asked to admit to certain facts or to the genuineness of documents. Interrogatories and requests for admissions can only be used against parties to the lawsuit. They may not be used with witnesses who are not parties to the suit.

At any time during the proceedings, but generally before the trial begins, either party can file a motion for summary judgment, alleging that there are no substantive facts in dispute and that the party filing the motion is entitled to judgment as a matter of law. Motions for summary judgment are supported by the pleadings, written statements under oath called affidavits, and other evidence obtained through the discovery process.

After all pretrial motions and procedures are finished, the jury phase of the trial begins. After selecting a jury—through a process called *voir dire*—and the opening statements by the parties, evidence is presented. Prior to the admission of any evidence, the opposing party has the right to object to particular methods of proof. These questions concerning the admissibility of evidence are for the judge alone to decide, because they involve matters of law as distinguished from matters of fact, which are for the jury to decide.

Evidence may take several forms:

- *Testimony*: A person, called a witness, tells the court what he or she saw, heard, did, or experienced in relation to the incident in question.

- *Documents*: Letters, notes, deeds, bills, receipts, etc. that provide information about the case.

- *Physical Evidence*: Tangible items, such as weapons, drugs, and clothing, that can provide clues to the facts.

- *Expert Testimony*: A professional person, someone not involved in the incident, gives medical, scientific, or similar expert instruction to help the trier of fact understand the evidence presented.

At the end of the plaintiff's case, the defendant will normally make a motion for a directed verdict. The judge will then determine whether the plaintiff has presented sufficient evidence to support each and every element of his or her claim. The judge does not weigh the evidence; that is for the jury. However, if there is a total failure of proof on a substantive issue in the case, the motion will be granted and the lawsuit is over. If the judge overrules the motion, the case proceeds and the defense begins its case.

When all of the evidence has been presented, each side will make a motion for a directed verdict. If there are any substantive facts in dispute, the judge will overrule the motion, and the case will then be submitted to the jury.

Prior to jury deliberations, lawyers for the parties make final arguments, summarizing the evidence that is most favorable to their side. The judge then instructs the jury on the law to be applied to the facts they find to be true and the jury retires to deliberate. When the jury returns, it may return a verdict for either side, decide the amount of damages, if applicable, or be "hung" and unable to reach a verdict. In this event, the trial begins anew with a different jury at a later date.

§ 1.3.2 — The Burden of Proof

In every lawsuit, one or more parties have what is known as the *burden of proof*. In a civil case, the plaintiff has the burden of proof. Plaintiffs must convince the fact finder that they have proved their case by *a preponderance of the evidence*. This means that their proof is slightly more convincing than the defendant's. Some refer to this as meaning that 51 percent or more of the evidence supports the plaintiff's side or that the plaintiff's theory is "more probable than not."

In a criminal case, the burden of proof is much stricter, because the defendant will be punished if the prosecutor proves the state's case. Therefore, the prosecutor must convince the judge or jury *beyond a reasonable doubt* that the accused committed the crime.

In an equity case, the facts are decided by the judge alone. In such cases, the burden of proof is *clear and convincing*, a standard that falls approximately halfway between the civil and criminal standards.

In civil and criminal trials, when the jury decides who wins, the judge then enters a verdict.

§ 1.3.3 — The Appeal

Parties may appeal on questions of law, not questions of fact. Appeals might involve issues concerning the admissibility of evidence, instructions of the judge to the jury, or whether motions made by either party were properly decided.

In principle, an appeal can be made only from a final judgment. However, in certain circumstances, during the trial process itself, a party who loses a motion may file an interlocutory appeal with an appellate court. The trial process stops when there is an interlocutory appeal and resumes when the court of appeals has ruled on the motion. Generally, there is an automatic right to one appeal. After that, appeals to higher courts are discretionary.

Discretionary appeals to the United States Supreme Court are granted by writ of certiorari. This happens when four of the nine members of the Supreme Court wish to hear a case; this is oftentimes referred to as the "rule of four." Denial of the writ does not mean approval of the lower court's ruling. All it means is that a majority of the Supreme Court did not wish to hear the case at that time. Frequently, conflicting decisions for the various courts of appeals are denied certiorari. This conflict permits the rule of law to germinate through time before the Supreme Court decides it is proper to have a uniform rule of law throughout the United States.

Reasons for denial of certiorari are seldom published. However, one example when an opinion was published was in *Moreland v. Federal Bureau of Prisons.*[22] Petitions for writ of certiorari to the United States Court of Appeals for the Third and Fifth Circuits were denied. Mr. Justice Stevens wrote a rare concurring opinion:

> The legal question presented by these certiorari petitions is whether the phrase "term of imprisonment" in 18 U.S.C. § 3624(b) means "sentence imposed," as petitioners argue, or "time served," as the Government contends. The answer to that question determines the actual amount of good-time credits that prisoners serving federal sentences may earn, and therefore how much time they may actually spend in prison. For prisoners who consistently comply with prison regulations, the difference in approaches amounts to about a week for each year of their sentences. The issue, accordingly, is of great importance to such prisoners. Given the numbers affected and the expense of housing prisoners, it surely also has a significant impact on the public fisc.

The fact that a vast majority of the courts of appeals have either agreed with, or deferred to, the government's interpretation provides a principled basis for denying these certiorari petitions.

§ 1.4   Anatomy of a Case

Case law is a major source of law in a common law system of jurisprudence. A great amount of a lawyer's time is spent reading and studying cases to determine the rule of law on a particular point. It is appropriate, then, to describe briefly the anatomy of a decision.

A case is the published report of an opinion indicating the decision of a court on a controversy heard by the reporting court. Generally, only appellate court decisions are published on a national basis, except for decisions of the federal district courts, which are published infrequently. The report contains the *majority opinion* of the court, which is the decision of the court as decided by a numerical majority of the tribunal (court) making the decision. The report is written by a judge of the court who expresses the opinion for the court. If any judge of the court (when more than one judge hears the controversy) disagrees with the majority decision, he or she may write a separate opinion, called a *dissenting opinion*, explaining his or her reasons for holding a view that is different from the majority opinion of the court. A judge may also agree with the results of the decision of the court, but for different or additional reasons not shared by the majority of the court. This opinion is called a *concurring opinion*.

When the opinion, or opinions, are made public, they are kept by the clerk of the court and accumulated along with other opinions until published in a volume. The volumes are numbered consecutively by the clerk; they are called state reports when they involve state court decisions. West Publishing Company also publishes the appellate decisions in a series of reports (called the National Reporter System) that contain the decisions of all state and federal courts. The U.S. government publishes Supreme Court decisions in a series of volumes called the United States Reports.

Most published opinions are now easily accessed via the Internet.

§ 1.4.1   − Citations

In order to find a particular opinion among the staggering number of reported decisions, a reference system has developed, called citations. The following is an example of a citation, or cite, to a state court opinion:

Ford Motor Co. v. London, 217 Tenn. 400, 398 S.W.2d 240 (1966).

The citation indicates the following information: (1) the names of the parties, generally with the plaintiff first (Ford Motor Co.) and the defendant second (London); (2) the volume of the state reporter where the opinion is found (217); (3) the state reporter system (Tenn.); and (4) the page in the state reporter system volume where the opinion begins (400). Then listed is the exact same case in the West National Reporter system: (5) the volume of the West Reporter system (398); (6) the West Reporter where the opinion is found (S.W.2d); (7) the page in the West Reporter where the opinion begins (240); and (8) the date that the court decided the case (1966). In California and New York, the decisions of the state courts may appear in two West Reporters, the regional reporter (Pacific and North Eastern, respectively), and a special supplement reporter that deals exclusively with the cases of that particular state (California Reporter and New York Supplement). An example of a citation of a case from New York is: *Greenburg v. Lorenz*, 9 N.Y.2d 195, 196 N.E.2d 430, 213 N.Y.S.2d 39 (1966).

A citation to a case from a federal district court appears as:

Landman v. Royster, 333 F. Supp. 621 (E.D. Va. 1971).

Table 1.1 West National Reporter System and Respective Jurisdictions

Atlantic (A.)		North Eastern (N.E.)	
Connecticut	New Jersey	Illinois	New York
Delaware	Pennsylvania	Indiana	Ohio
Maine	Rhode Island	Massachusetts	
Maryland	Vermont		
New Hampshire			
District of Columbia			
(Municipal Court of Appeals)			

Southern (So.)		West's California Reporter (Cal.)
Alabama	Louisiana	California Supreme Court
Florida	Mississippi	District Courts of Appeal
Superior Court, Appellate Department		

Pacific (P.)		South Eastern (S.E.)	
Alaska	Montana		
Arizona	Nevada	Georgia	Virginia
California	New Mexico	North Carolina	West Virginia
(Sup. Ct. only)	Oklahoma	South Carolina	
Colorado	Oregon		
Hawaii	Utah	**South Western (S.W.)**	
Idaho	Washington	Arkansas	Tennessee
Kansas	Wyoming	Kentucky	Texas
Missouri			

New York Supplement (N.Y.S.)	North Western (N.W.)	
Court of Appeals	Iowa	North Dakota
Appellate Division	Michigan	South Dakota
Miscellaneous	Minnesota	Wisconsin
	Nebraska	

Federal Supplement (F. Supp.)

U S. District Courts
U.S. Customs Courts

Federal Rules Decisions (F.R.D.)

U.S. District Courts

Federal Appendix (Fed. Appx.)

U.S. District Courts

Federal (F.)

U.S. Court of Appeals
Federal Court of Appeals

U.S. Supreme Court* (S. Ct.)

*Supreme Court decisions are also reported by the government, cited as U.S., and by Lawyers Co-Operative

The citation gives the following information about the case: (1) the parties, plaintiff first and defendant second (*Landman v. Royster*); (2) the volume of the West Federal Reporter where the opinion appears (333); (3) the West Reporter that publishes the case (F. Supp.); (4) the page in the reporter where the opinion begins (621); (5) the court that decided the case (E.D. Va.), the federal district court for the Eastern District of Virginia; and (6) the date of the decision (1971). A citation to a federal court of appeals, for example, *Jackson v. Bishop*, 404 F.2d 571 (8th Cir. 1968), gives the same information (parties, volume, reporter, page, court, and date).

The symbol "2d" or "3d" appearing in many citations indicates that the reporter system has begun a second or third series. The citation may also give a history of the case. Such history is only included in the citation if it is significant to the point of law for which the case is cited. The signals of citation used to indicate history are:

- **aff'd**—affirmed: The decision of the lower court was upheld on appeal.

- **rev'd**—reversed: The decision of the lower court was overruled on appeal.

- **aff'd (or rev'd) on other grounds**: The rule of law cited from the case was unaffected by a subsequent affirmation (or overruling) of the court's decision.

- *cert.* **denied (or granted)**: Petition for writ of certiorari, or grant of discretionary review of a lower court's decision, was denied (or granted).

- **Modified**: The decision of a case was modified by a reviewing court.

- *sub nom.*: The names of the parties of the appellate decision differ from the names of the lower court decisions.

The following is an example of a citation to a Supreme Court opinion in the United States Reports:

Graham v. Florida, 560 U.S. 48 (2010).

The citation indicates the following information: (1) the names of the parties (*Graham v. Florida*); (2) the volume of the reporter where the opinion is found (560); (3) the abbreviation for the United States Reports (U.S.); (4) the page in the reporter system volume where the opinion begins (48); and the date of the decision (2010).

Some cases may include parallel citations such as 44 U.S.L.W. 1000 or 19 Cr. L. 2133. These represent publications that provide judicial decisions to the public before they are printed in the publications mentioned earlier. These publications serve to keep the public current on the most recent decisions from the judiciary. U.S.L.W. stands for *United States Law Week*, and Cr. L. is an abbreviation for *Criminal Law Reporter*.

Citations increasingly include Internet citations. Numerous databases that contain cases, statutes, administrative regulations, and articles, both domestic and foreign, are available via the Internet. 2004 U.S. App. LEXIS 6951 is an example of the Internet citation form used by the Lexis-Nexis subscription service.

§ 1.5   Correctional Law

Until the last 60 years, correctional law was practically nonexistent. Prisoners were regarded as "slaves of the state." The tradition was that upon conviction of a felony, prisoners lost all of their civil rights. Access to the courts was denied, and the treatment of prisoners was left to the uncontrolled discretion of the warden. Indeed, some institutions were in fact run by the prisoners themselves.

Until the 1960s, the courts adopted a hands-off attitude toward prisons. This is no longer true. Upon entering the prison system, it is widely accepted that prisoners retain all of their constitutional rights that are not necessarily withdrawn by virtue of prison security, discipline, and necessity. In short, prisoners take the Constitution into the prison with them.

Litigation over the past 60 years, however, has shown that not every denial of a "right" involves a deprivation of a "constitutional right." As a practical matter, state and federal courts do not wish to become involved in the administration of prisons. They become involved only when there is no other alternative. Given a reasonable alternative, courts will and do defer to the administrative process. This doctrine was mandated by the Prison Litigation Reform Act (PLRA),[23] where prisoners, in general, must exhaust all available administrative remedies before filing federal lawsuits against prison officials. (The PLRA is discussed in detail in Chapter 16.)

In general, courts intervene in the correctional administrative process under three circumstances:

1. The statute or policy under which the prison administrator is acting is unconstitutional or unconscionable;

2. The act of the prison administrator is outside the scope of his authority, or *ultra vires*; or

3. The procedure used by the prison administrator in decisions affecting the status of a prisoner falls below minimum requirements of due process.

Consequently, when prison administrators act within the scope of valid authority and provide at least minimum procedural due process, judicial intervention will be limited, if not avoided altogether.

§ 1.5.1   – Control of Discretionary Power

It is impossible to totally regulate the operating and running of prison systems. Too many dissimilar events occur on a daily basis. Positive law must leave room for resolving the never-ending issues that involve dealing with offenders. In areas not subject to the direct rule of law lies administrative discretion. This can be as simple as a correctional officer ordering a prisoner to pick up a piece of trash to a warden ordering a complete lockdown for security reasons. Decision-making outside the parameters of positive law results in most of the litigation in correctional law.

Decisions of prison administrators form a substantial part of correctional litigation. Many prison administrators have brought this legal deluge upon themselves. Bad judgments, blatant violations of elementary principles of human dignity, and naive concepts and applications of nineteenth-century justice by prison officials have made judicial intervention into the correctional process inevitable.

The judicial process is essential in the American system of governmental checks and balances and in dealing with specific issues calling for the finding of facts and the application of law or policy. However, as a practical matter, many of the issues that prison administrators face daily are beyond the competence of the courts. Few instances of judicial trusteeship over prisons have been successful.

The administrative process requires the exercise of discretion, or making choices between two or more alternatives. The proper exercise of administrative discretion is to be sought; the abuse of discretion is to be prevented. Unfortunately, history has shown that many of our prisons are characterized by the presence of unnecessary discretionary power, resulting in the danger of its abuse and, subsequently, judicial intervention. The alternative to arbitrary litigation is the reasonable exercise of controlled discretion; all discretion need not be eliminated—only unnecessary discretion.

We control discretionary power by keeping it within designated boundaries. In other words, standards are created. This may be accomplished through statutory enactments, administrative rules and regulations, and judicial decisions.

In developing a methodology to control discretion, we must also realize that certain counterbalancing propositions must be considered.

1. Prison officials cannot function without exercising discretion. Controls cannot be so tight and structured that the result is the elimination of discretion.

2. It must be recognized that we are a government of human beings and laws. They are not mutually exclusive. A pure legal system controlled by the "rule of law" alone cannot survive in a dynamic, organic society such as found in prisons. We must recognize that a prison system is administered by human beings.

3. We must not standardize our prison system to such an extent that the flexibility to meet new and changing circumstances is lost. We must recognize that certain policies and determinations should be left to be developed on a case-by-case basis based on changing facts and not an absolute rule.

4. The courts recognize that administrative expertise should be considered whenever there is judicial intervention in the correctional process. For example, objective proof that riots can be prevented by rule making or that an "explosive" situation requires the temporary curtailment of certain procedural safeguards is impossible to obtain. Courts must defer to administrative discretion in such cases and not substitute their uninformed opinion for the expert judgment of professional and competent administrators who are on the front line. The doctrine of exhaustion of administrative remedies goes a long way in this regard.

5. Not every decision should be reduced to writing and subjected to administrative review. Controlled discretion must be tempered by realistic administrative considerations such as available personnel, budgets, intelligence levels, security issues, and economy.

In confining, structuring, and checking administrative discretion, we speak in terms of optimums, not absolutes. Realistically, what is optimum in one prison, or state, may be less than optimum in another. We must avoid universal generalizations. The goal is fundamental fairness in a system of justice that takes into account the human frailties in correctional administration. However, we must be guided by the old adage that unrestricted discretion, like corruption, marks the beginning of the end of liberty.

§ 1.5.2   – Legal Effect

Validly enacted administrative regulations have the force of law. However, agency protocols and procedures, like agency manuals, do not have the force or effect of a statute or administrative regulation. Rather, they provide officials with guidance on how they should perform those duties that are mandated by statute or regulation.[24] Prison administrators must be careful when drafting protocols and procedures that they do not create rights that otherwise would not exist.

Under the *Turner*[25] doctrine, a regulation that would impinge on prisoners' constitutional rights is nevertheless valid if it is reasonably related to the prison's legitimate interests. To prevail on a claim that their statutory rights have been violated, prisoners must show that the challenged prison policy or regulation is unreasonable. The burden on prison administrators is to show the reasonableness of prison policies. An essential condition is whether there is a valid, rational connection between the prison policy and the legitimate governmental interest put forward to justify it.

To uphold a policy, a factual record is necessary to determine the rationality of the policy's overall connection to rehabilitative interests. It is necessary to first identify the specific rehabilitative goals advanced by the government to justify the policy, and then give the parties the opportunity to present evidence sufficient to enable a determination of whether the connection between these goals and the restriction is rational.[26]

Courts should apply the compelling governmental interest standard with due deference to the experience and expertise of prison and jail administrators in establishing necessary regulations and procedures to maintain order, security, and discipline, consistent with consideration of costs and limited resources.[27] In any event, prison administrators must show that the policy furthers a compelling governmental interest by the least restrictive means.[28]

§ 1.6   Conclusion

The first chapter has provided an overview of the American judicial system, including common law, equity, the role of case law, constitutional law, the American court structure, and an illustrative case anatomy. In addition, we provided an introduction to correctional law in the United States and discussed the significance of administrative discretion in the correctional context. To derive the most benefit from this chapter, the reader should review key concepts, giving special attention to the significant terms used by courts. All are essential to understanding the legal system in which we function.

Notes

1   The term *common law* has many meanings, usually depending upon the context. In its broadest sense, common law refers to the entire Anglo-American system of law, in contrast to the civil law (entirely code-based) systems of most non-English-speaking nations. It also can refer to the body of law originating in the courts of common law, as opposed to the law of the courts of equity.

2   See *Hamdan v. Rumsfeld*, 548 U.S. 557 (2006).

3   See *Freytag v. Commissioner of Internal Revenue*, 501 U.S. 868 (1991).

4   The federal Administrative Procedure Act was enacted in 1946. *See* 5 U.S.C. 1001–1011.

5   Marbury v. Madison, 5 U.S. 137 (1803).

6   Youngstown Sheet & Tube Co. v. Sawyer, 343 U.S. 579 (1952).

7   548 U.S. 557 (2006).

8   10 U.S.C. § 801 *et seq.*

9   *See* 6 U.S.T. 3316, T.I.A.S. No. 3364.

10   1 KENT'S COMMENTARIES 472 (12th ed. 1873).

11   Some of the first reports were made during the reign of Henry III (1216–1272), with the first volume of reports, called the Year Books, which began in the latter part of the reign of Edward II (1307–1326) and continued until Henry VIII (1509–1547). However, the Year Books were first printed during the reign of James I (1603–1625) and reprinted in 1679. Parts of the Year Books were incorporated into the treatises of the legal scholars of the times, such as Statham, Fitzherbert, and Brooke. When the practice of reporting cases for the Year

Books was discontinued by the Crown, English lawyers made reports for their own uses. Legal scholars then began to make their commentaries serve the function of the reporter of the common law.

12 *The Law in the Massachusetts Bay Colony*, READINGS IN AMERICAN LEGAL HISTORY 101–102 (M. Howe ed. 1949).

13 1 KENT'S COMMENTARIES 472–473 (12th ed. 1873).

14 *Id.*

15 WILLIAM MARTIN GELDART, ELEMENTS OF ENGLISH LAW 23 (6th ed. 1959).

16 *Id.* at 6–7.

17 OLIVER WENDELL HOLMES, THE COMMON LAW 1 (1881).

18 U.S. CONST., art. III, § 2.

19 *Id.*

20 *Frequently Asked Questions: General Information*, SUPREME COURT OF THE U.S., www.supreme court.gov/about/faq_general.aspx.

21 In criminal cases, an accused is entitled to trial by jury under the Sixth Amendment.

22 547 U.S. 1106 (2006).

23 42 U.S.C. § 1997e.

24 Jackson v. District of Columbia, 541 F. Supp. 2d 334 (D.D.C. 2008).

25 Turner v. Safley, 482 U.S. 78 (1987).

26 Ramirez v. Pugh, 379 F.3d 122 (3d Cir. 2004).

27 Baranowski v. Hart, 486 F.3d 112 (5th Cir. 2007).

28 Sossamon v. Texas, 560 F.3d 316 (5th Cir. 2009).

Religion in Prison 2

Chapter Outline

§ 2.1   Introduction

The First Amendment to the United States Constitution states in part that "Congress shall make no law respecting an establishment of religion, or prohibiting the free exercise thereof."[1] An obvious contradiction exists within the two clauses of this Amendment: the establishment clause and the free exercise clause. This contradiction is particularly apparent when the amendment is applied to the prisoners of correctional systems.

In *Gittlemacker v. Prasse*,[2] the inherent difficulty in applying First Amendment religious freedom to prisoners is pointed out:

> The requirement that a state interpose no unreasonable barriers to the free exercise of a prisoner's religion cannot be equated with the suggestion that the state has an affirmative duty to provide, furnish, or supply every prisoner with a clergyman or religious services of his choice. It is one thing to provide facilities for worship and the opportunity for any clergy to visit the institution. This may be rationalized on the basis that since society has removed the prisoner from the community where he could freely exercise his religion, it has an obligation to furnish or supply him with the opportunity to practice his faith during confinement. Thus, the Free Exercise Clause is satisfied.

But to go further and suggest that the free exercise clause demands that the state not only furnish the opportunity to practice but also supply the clergy is a concept that dangerously approaches the jealously guarded frontiers of the establishment clause.

The existence of this conflict between the free exercise clause and the establishment clause provides one explanation for the recognition by the courts of a need to balance the interests of the state with the interests of the prisoner. Although the state interest in avoiding the establishment of religion is a problem of constitutional proportions, this interest has not negated the equally significant right of the prisoner to the free exercise of his or her religious beliefs.

Despite the difficulty in balancing these two fundamental and conflicting rights, courts have given increasing attention to the needs of prisoners in this area. The traditional reluctance of the judiciary to interfere in the management of a prison[3] is no longer apparent. Rather than simply dismissing an action, as in the past, the courts are now giving recognition to the existence of First Amendment rights behind prison walls. Furthermore, they have required prison officials to provide a reasonable explanation for any attempt to limit such rights.

The requirement for prison officials to explain their rationale for impeding the free exercise of religion was pointed out in *Barnett v. Rodgers*,[4] where the court stated:

> To say that religious freedom may undergo modification in a prison environment is not to say that it can be suppressed or ignored without adequate reason. And although "within the prison society as well as without, the practice of religious beliefs is subject to reasonable regulation necessary for the protection and welfare of the community involved," the mere fact that government, as a practical matter, stands a better chance of justifying curtailment of fundamental liberties where prisoners are involved does not eliminate the need for reasons imperatively justifying the particular retraction of rights challenged at bar. Nor does it lessen governmental responsibility to reduce the resulting impact upon those rights to the fullest extent consistent with the justified objective.[5]

In *Employment Division, Department of Human Resources of Oregon v. Smith*,[6] two Native Americans were fired by a private drug rehabilitation organization because they ingested peyote, a hallucinogenic drug, for sacramental purposes at a ceremony of their Native American Church. The Supreme Court held that the free exercise clause permitted the state to prohibit sacramental peyote use and to deny unemployment benefits to persons discharged for such use. Although it is constitutionally permissible to exempt sacramental peyote use from the operation of drug laws, it is not constitutionally required. However, a prison chaplain who engages in inherently ecclesiastical functions, even if a full-time state employee, is not a "state actor" for purposes of the Civil Rights Act.[7]

§ 2.2 Restrictions on the Free Exercise of Religion

In response to demands of the courts, prison officials have provided a number of explanations for the restrictions they have placed upon prisoners' free exercise of religion. Among these are (1) the maintenance of discipline or security, (2) proper exercise of authority and official discretion, (3) the fact that the regulation is reasonable, and (4) economic considerations. Frequently, these explanations are used interchangeably by the courts, and it is sometimes difficult to determine which justification was the basis of the decision. However, in most cases, if prison officials are able to show that restrictions on religious practices are actually based upon one or more of these reasons, the courts will allow the restrictions to continue. In addition to providing explanations for the restrictions placed upon the prisoners' free exercise of religion, prison officials and the courts have attempted to define what a "religion" is and what "religious practices" are for purposes of First Amendment protection. Unfortunately, few precise guidelines have emerged.[8]

Restrictions on access to "religious opportunities"—whether group services, chapel visits, or meetings with religious advisers—are reviewed in light of four factors: (1) whether there is a "valid, rational connection" between the regulation and a legitimate government interest put forward to justify it; (2) "whether there are alternative means of exercising the right that remain open to prisoners;" (3) whether accommodation of the constitutional right would have a significant impact on guards and other prisoners; and (4) whether available alternatives are absent, bearing on the reasonableness of the regulation.[9]

§ 2.2.1   – Restrictions Based on the Maintenance of Discipline or Security

Prison officials are obligated to maintain security and discipline within the institution. For this reason, the courts analyze restrictions of religious freedom within the prison setting in the framework of that obligation. A proper justification by prison officials of the need for such restrictions will frequently result in its approval by the courts. Indeed, the duty of prison officials to maintain security within an institution is the most frequently cited justification for limiting a prisoner's religious freedom.

In *Jones v. Willingham*,[10] the court, concerned with the trouble allegedly caused by Black Muslims in the early 1960s and the fact that the prisoner was confined at the maximum-security U.S. Penitentiary in Leavenworth, Kansas, held that the warden had a duty to prevent disruptions and thus concluded that there was no religious discrimination under the facts of the case. In *St. Claire v. Cuyler*,[11] the court held that a reasonable relationship to security interests justified the denial of a prisoner's request to attend religious services. The prisoner had the burden to prove by substantial evidence that the security concerns were unreasonable or exaggerated.

In *Wojtczak v. Cuyler*,[12] a Pennsylvania court held that prisoners confined in segregation for their own safety may not be unduly restricted in the rights held by prisoners in the general population. However, the prisoner bears the heavy burden of disproving a claim that different treatment is based upon genuine security considerations. This rationale likewise was applied in *McDonald v. Hall*.[13] The appellate court took notice of an affidavit, filed by prison officials, which indicated that allowing segregated prisoners to attend services outside of their unit would pose a safety threat. The court upheld the officials' decision because it was neither arbitrary nor capricious.

In *Cooper v. Pate*,[14] the court allowed prison officials to restrict the religious freedom of certain individuals where the officials showed that such free exercise had been abused at a prior time. It held that, although a complete ban on religious services was discrimination, precautions that were necessary for security would be sanctioned. Prisoners with records of prior misconduct "which reasonably demonstrates a high degree of probability that the individual would seriously misuse the opportunity for participation with the group"[15] could be excluded from religious services at the authorities' discretion.

The use of the "clear and present danger" test enunciated by the Supreme Court[16] as a valid reason for limiting First Amendment freedom of speech was utilized by analogy in *Knuckles v. Prasse*.[17] Certain infringements of religious freedoms were permitted because they presented a "clear and present danger of a breach of prison security or discipline or some other substantial interference with the orderly functioning of the institution."[18] The court further stated that prison officials had the right to be present and to monitor religious services and if the services became nonreligious, the authorities could cancel them."[19] The court further found that its "task is not to evaluate plaintiffs' religious wisdom but rather to determine whether regulations of that religion in a prison context are reasonable."[20]

Female prisoners unsuccessfully contended that a Washington State prison policy subjecting fully clothed female prisoners to random "pat searches" by male as well as female correctional officers infringed their religious freedom.[21] The female prisoners' beliefs prohibited them from being touched by men other than their husbands. The majority of the court concluded, however, that the policy was reasonably related to prison officials' legitimate interests in institutional security and that it therefore passed muster under the standard set in *Turner v. Safley*.[22] The majority relied on the testimony of prison officials that the same-sex searches would conflict with the officers' collective bargaining agreement, create security problems by requiring female guards to leave their posts to conduct the searches, and make the searches more predictable.[23]

§ 2.2.2 — Restrictions Based on the Exercise of Authority and Official Discretion

The argument that control over religious freedom in prison is a proper subject for the exercise of authority and official discretion is a carryover from the historical approach of noninterference by the judiciary. Although this argument is now subject to closer court scrutiny, it has not been completely abandoned. *Knuckles v. Prasse* again pointed out that constitutional standards for the practice of religion in prison must be analyzed in the realistic context of the prison situation. The process requires a balancing of broad discretionary powers vested in prison officials with the right of prisoners to practice religion in a prison.[24]

The noninterference approach was further evidenced in *Kennedy v. Meacham*,[25] a case involving the free exercise of the "Satanic religion." The court recognized that matters of prisoner regulation and discipline are to be left to the discretion of prison authorities as long as the officials' conduct does not involve the unreasonable deprivation of constitutional rights and is not clearly capricious or arbitrary. The court held that the state's interest in the proper administration of its penal system outweighs a prisoner's right to organize a branch of his or her sect within the prison. The prisoner's request to hold meetings was denied in view of his inability to provide the name of a sponsor or information relating to the proposed activities of the group. Safety considerations also justified the denial of the use of candles or incense in a cell. Denial of the right to borrow library books for group use was consistent with general prison policies, and, in any event, the prisoner was not prejudiced because he owned many of the books himself.[26]

Another case in which the significance of unlimited discretion exercised by prison officials was reviewed is *Belk v. Mitchell*.[27] The prisoner was placed in solitary confinement for 30 days, and his request to attend Sunday services was denied. The court held:

> If the solitary confinement itself is justifiable, then it would seem entirely reasonable to allow some discretion to the prison authorities whether to allow or not allow the Sunday morning commingling of solitary prisoners with the others. Prison authorities of course have no right to restrict the prisoner's freedom of religious beliefs and convictions. However, absent a showing of prolonged and unjustifiable discrimination, his "public" exercise of his religious beliefs and his access to publicly provided chaplains during temporary punitive solitary confinement would seem to be matters within the reasonable discretion of the prison authorities.[28]

Similarly, in *Mims v. Shapp*,[29] the denial of congregational prayer to prisoners in a segregation unit was held not to have been an improper denial of the right to practice religion but rather a proper exercise of official discretion. Another case in which the significance of unlimited discretion exercised by prison officials was reviewed was *Wojtczak v. Cuyler*.[30] The court held:

> Prisoners confined for their own safety in segregation may not be unduly restricted in the rights held by prisoners in the general population. However, the prisoner bears a heavy burden to disprove a claim that different treatment is based upon genuine security considerations. . . . The state must permit the prisoner in segregation to receive both a chaplain and communion in his cell . . . but need not escort him to the prison chapel.[31]

Sweet v. Department of Corrections[32] recognized the need for broad official discretion in light of the peculiar problems necessary to the maintenance of a prison. Because prison society is both sensitive and explosive, it is necessary for those with experience to make decisions in light of their particular knowledge. For this reason, prison authorities may adopt any regulation dealing with the prisoners' exercise of religion that may be reasonable and substantially justified by consideration of prison administrative requirements. The court rationale in the *Sweet* decision is significant in that, like most courts, it demonstrates a certain hesitancy to interfere with the internal management of a prison.

Another relevant and closely related issue in discussing official discretion arises when arguments are made that prison rules and regulations are capricious and arbitrary. This was pointed out in *In re Ferguson*,[33] in which the court discussed the reasonableness of a regulation restricting the activities of Black Muslims. The court stated:

> [I]n the instant circumstances, the refusal to allow these petitioners to pursue their requested religious [activities] does not appear to amount to such extreme mistreatment, so as to warrant the application of whatever federal constitutional guarantees which may exist for the protection of prisoners in state prisons. *** We are . . . reluctant to apply federal constitutional doctrines to state prison rules reasonably necessary to the orderly conduct of the state institution.
>
> *** Even conceding the Muslims to be a religious group it cannot be said under the circumstances here presented that the Director of Corrections has made an unreasonable determination in refusing to allow petitioners the opportunity to pursue their claimed religious activities while in prison.[34]

The court then determined that in view of the inflammatory nature of the Black Muslims' interpretation of the Koran, the officials were under no obligation to retract a restriction on its use.

§ 2.2.3 — Restrictions Based on Economic Considerations

Although carefully constrained, economic considerations are another factor cited by prison administrators as justification for controlling prisoners' free exercise of religion. In *Gittlemacker v. Prasse*,[35] a Jewish prisoner alleged a violation of the First Amendment because the state did not provide him with a rabbi. The court stated that the requirement that a state interpose no unreasonable barriers to the free exercise of a prisoner's religion could not be equated with the suggestion that the state had the affirmative duty to provide, furnish, or supply every prisoner with clergy or with religious services of his or her choice. The court pointed out that it was no great burden on the institution or on prison officials to provide facilities of worship and the opportunity for clergy to visit the institution. This requirement could be rationalized on the basis that, because society had removed the prisoner from the community where he could freely exercise his religion, the state had an obligation to furnish or supply the prisoner with the opportunity to practice his faith. But to go further and suggest that the free exercise clause demands that the state not only furnish the opportunity to practice but also supply the clergyman is a concept that dangerously approaches the jealously guarded frontiers of the establishment clause.[36]

The court pointed out that the sheer number of religious sects was a practical consideration. It suggested that there were perhaps 120 distinct established religious denominations in the state. To the court, it became readily apparent that to accept the prisoner's contention was to suggest that each state prison have an extravagant number of clergy available. Although the court did not address this question, it did recognize that explicit in the First Amendment were two separate and distinct concepts designed to guarantee religious liberties: (1) the establishment clause and (2) the free exercise clause. The court also recognized that under the circumstances of the case, a slavish insistence upon a maximum interpretation of rights vested in one clause would collide with the restrictions of the other clause. Using the analogy of school prayer cases, the court approved the language:

> It is no defense to urge that the religious practices here may be relatively minor encroachments on the First Amendment. The breach of neutrality that is today a trickling stream may all too soon become a raging torrent, and, in the words of Madison, "it is proper to take alarm at the first experiment on our liberties."[37]

In *Gittlemacker*, the prisoner alleged that the officials denied Jewish prisoners a rabbi in regular attendance, although they provided Catholic and Protestant chaplains. The response of the prison superintendent was: "The small number of Jewish prisoners at Dallas, usually two or three, makes the use of a full-time rabbi economically unfeasible and unwarranted."[38] The court also found that the superintendent had, on numerous occasions, attempted to secure the services of a rabbi for Jewish prisoners. It was asserted that the official intended to have him come to the institution on a fee basis. The court concluded that the prisoner's claim of religious discrimination was effectively and conclusively refuted.

In *Walker v. Blackwell*,[39] Muslim prisoners proposed that they be provided with a special meal during Ramadan, their religious period, and that it be served after the normal dinner time, but at a time that would not interfere with their work schedules. Prisoners asserted that the cost of purchasing the special foods would not be prohibitive and that, under present conditions, they could not make adequate selections from the menus prepared because pork was included. The prison officials' argument was that they could not afford to buy the various special items within the limits of the existing budget. They further pointed out that while once-a-year special purchases were made for Passover, the Muslims were requesting 30 days of special menus.

With respect to the after-sunset meals, the court felt that supplying such meals could only be done at a prohibitive cost. It held further that there were problems of security and additional staff involved in serving Muslims after all other prisoners had eaten. In the court's opinion, considerations of expense and security outweighed "whatever constitutional deprivation petitioners may claim. In this regard . . . the government has demonstrated a substantial compelling interest."[40]

The same analysis has been applied to the kosher food cases brought by Jewish prisoners. Represented by the holding in *Kahane v. Carlson*,[41] the attitude of the courts appears to be that there is no obligation to provide all Jewish prisoners with kosher food on a full-time basis. However, the Ninth Circuit held that a policy of serving only one kosher meal per day to Orthodox Jewish prisoners imposes an impermissible burden on the free exercise of religion. In place of expensive frozen dinners, prison authorities could supply foods such as whole fruits, tinned fish, and kosher cereals that met kosher standards.[42]

A significant U.S. Supreme Court case concerning prisoners who were members of the Islamic faith was *O'Lone v. Estate of Shabazz*.[43] Prisoners argued that prison policies prevented them from attending Jumu'ah, a congregational service held on Friday afternoons, and thereby violated their rights under the free exercise clause of the First Amendment. The first policy required prisoners in the prison's custody classifications to work outside the buildings in which they were housed and in which Jumu'ah was held, while the second prohibited prisoners assigned to outside work from returning to those buildings during the day.

The Court held that there was no burden on prison officials to disprove the availability of alternative methods of accommodating prisoners' religious rights. The Constitution allows respect for and deference to the judgment of prison administrators. The policies were reasonably related to legitimate penological interests and therefore did not offend the free exercise clause of the First Amendment. Both policies had a rational connection to the legitimate governmental interests in institutional order and security invoked to justify them. One was a response to critical overcrowding and was designed to ease tension and drain on the facilities during the part of the day when the prisoners were outside. The policy was necessary because returns from outside work details generated congestion and delays at the main gate, a high-risk area. Decisions involving return requests placed pressure on officers supervising outside work details. Rehabilitative concerns also supported the policy as corrections officials sought to simulate working conditions and responsibilities in society. Although the policies may have prevented some Muslim prisoners from attending Jumu'ah, they did not deprive the Muslims of all forms of religious exercise. There were no obvious, easy alternatives to the policies because both of the suggested accommodations would, in the judgment of prison officials, have adverse effects on the prison institution. Placing all Muslim prisoners in inside work details would be inconsistent with the legitimate prison concerns, while providing weekend labor for Muslims would require extra supervision that would be a drain on scarce human resources. Both proposed accommodations would also threaten prison security by fostering "affinity groups" likely to challenge institutional authority, while any special arrangements for one group would create a perception of favoritism on the part of other prisoners.

Although prison officials argued that even if the prison's policies of punishing Muslim prisoners for one hour of weekly Jumu'ah attendance imposed a substantial burden on their exercise of religion, the state had a compelling interest in administering a work incentive program. The program provided for safety and security in prisons and prevented prison conditions from deteriorating. The absence of the prisoners for about one hour on Fridays would not disrupt the operation of work incentive programs, and even assuming that the state's asserted interests in keeping prisoners occupied and using their labor for prison upkeep were sufficiently compelling, prison officials did not demonstrate that the policy with respect to Jumu'ah, in particular, was the least restrictive means to achieve those interests.[44]

§ 2.3   Religious Discrimination: The Equal Protection Clause

The cases dealing with religious freedom frequently refer to the Equal Protection Clause of the Fourteenth Amendment.[45] Section I of that amendment provides in part: "Nor shall any state . . . deny to any person within its jurisdiction the equal protection of the laws."[46]

The application of the Equal Protection Clause is particularly relevant in cases dealing with minority religions. This was apparent in *Newton v. Cupp*,[47] in which the court stated: "If members of one faith can practice their religious beliefs and possess religious materials, equivalent opportunity must be available to members of another faith."[48]

The soundness of this decision is apparent from the Supreme Court's subsequent decision in *Cruz v. Beto*,[49] holding that Texas prison officials had discriminated against a prisoner by denying him a reasonable opportunity to pursue his Buddhist faith comparable to that offered other prisoners adhering to conventional religious precepts. Similarly, in *People ex rel. Rockey v Krueger*,[50] the court found that because an orthodox Jew would be allowed to retain his beard without being placed in solitary confinement, a Muslim who had been placed in solitary confinement for not shaving his beard was entitled to be released. Thus, because prison policy permitted orthodox Jews to wear beards, other religious beliefs requiring beards could not be suppressed even in the face of a Commissioner of Correction's Regulation, which required that prisoners be "clean-shaven."

In *Konigsberg v. Ciccone*,[51] a prisoner alleged the denial of the right to exercise his religion. He claimed that while he was confined in close custodial supervision, he was not permitted to attend any religious services. Further, when he was transferred from such custody, his attendance at Jewish religious services was conditioned upon a pass, issued specifically for that purpose. On the other hand, Protestant and Catholic prisoners in close custody confinement were allowed to attend services. The prison officials established that the Protestants and Catholics did not need passes to attend services because those services were held at a time when no other activity was in progress. Thus, the destination of people moving through the corridors could be easily identified. Also, it was proved that sufficient staff were available to guarantee security at that time. However, prison officials stated that prisoners who attended services at times other than Sunday needed passes to move through the corridors just as any other prisoner would at the same time.

The court would not accept as reasonable the prison officials' basis for denying minority religions the right to attend services while at the same time permitting Protestants and Catholics to do so. The court said that it was unrealistic to take the position that sufficient escorts were not available to conduct them to services "in view of the high importance the law places on the right to worship and [on] the right to be free of religious discrimination."[52] The court then directed that such a prisoner be allowed to attend religious services unless: (1) his physician certified medical reasons, (2) there was proof that the prisoner was a dangerous security risk, or (3) his attendance would substantially and adversely affect security.

In *Cooper v. Pate*,[53] the court stopped prison officials from preventing a prisoner's communication (by mail and visitation) with ministers of his faith, subject to usual prison regulations. The court felt that such communication did not present a clear and present danger to prison security and that to grant it to one faith but deny it to another was religious discrimination. However, the prisoner also wished to purchase Swahili grammar books. He pointed out that prisoners were allowed to purchase foreign language books. The lower court held that these books were not necessary for the practice of the prisoner's religion and that the denial was based on staff and facility limitations. The court of appeals affirmed the holding that this involved no impairment of a constitutional right.

§ 2.4   Specific Areas of Constitutional Concern

While the right of Black Muslims to practice their religious beliefs dominated the litigated cases in the past, controversy over this right has declined. Issues such as the right to attend services, to obtain literature, and to wear religious medals were usually raised by Black Muslims because, unlike Protestant or Catholic prisoners, the Black Muslims had been denied the right to engage in such practices. The threshold question was the recognition of the Black Muslim faith as a religion. It has been recognized as a religion in several cases[54] and, for this reason, it can now be asserted—at least in theory—that a Black Muslim prisoner retains the same constitutional protection offered to members of other recognized religions.

Despite the general recognition of the Black Muslim faith as a religion, certain specific problems remain relative to the free exercise of its beliefs. Those problems, although usually presented by Black Muslim petitioners, are common among all prisoners seeking to exercise religious freedoms. For this reason, it must be assumed that the rights accorded by the judiciary to the Black Muslim prisoner must also be rendered to all recognized religions. The general applicability of these decisions to all recognized religions practiced within penal institutions is consistent with the constitutional mandate of the First Amendment and the Equal Protection Clause.

§ 2.4.1   — Right to Hold Religious Services

Numerous cases have recognized the Black Muslims' right to hold some sort of religious service.[55] However, the cases in which this right was not extended were usually based upon the belief that a congregation of Black

Muslim prisoners would result in some security risk. This was apparent in the decisions of *Jones v. Willingham*[56] and *Cooke v. Tramburg*.[57] In the first of these decisions, *Jones*, the court refused to grant the Black Muslims the right to assemble for worship. The court based its decision on the duty of the warden to prevent breaches of security. It asserted that, in view of the possibility of disruptions resulting from a congregation of Black Muslims, the restriction was a valid exercise of the warden's duty. In *Cooke*, the court also denied the right to hold religious services because of the danger it believed was inherent in such assemblage. According to *Cooke*, the freedom to exercise religious beliefs is not absolute but is subject to restriction for the protection of society as a whole.

However, *Banks v. Havener*[58] held that a prison could not prohibit the practice of an established religion unless it could prove that the teaching and practice of the Act created a clear and present danger to the orderly functioning of the institution. Absent such evidence, the court in *Battle v. Anderson*[59] found that the policy of prison officials of denying to all prisoners, including Muslims, the opportunity to gather together for religious services, was unjustified.

Examples of cases concerning the right of nontraditional religious groups to hold services are *Theriault v. Carlson*[60] and *Remmers v. Brewer*,[61] both dealing with a prisoner-created religion based on the Eclatarian faith and organized around The Church of the New Song of Universal Life. In *Theriault*, the prisoner who created the religion and who was head of the newly developed church was confined in punitive segregation for attempting to hold religious services to promote the new belief. Although the district court ordered his restoration to the general prison population and directed prison officials to permit the prisoner to hold religious services, this ruling was overturned on appeal and remanded for an evidentiary hearing.[62] On remand, a different district court concluded that the Eclatarian faith was not a "religion" entitled to First Amendment protection, but was rather "a masquerade designed to obtain protection for acts which otherwise would have been unlawful and/or reasonably disallowed by various prison authorities."[63]

While failing to provide a precise definition of what a "religion" is for purposes of First Amendment protection, the court declared that such protection does not extend to so-called religions "which tend to mock established institutions and are obviously shams and absurdities and whose members are patently devoid of religious sincerity."[64]

Essentially the same issue was present in *Remmers*, but the court in that case, while aware of the holdings in *Theriault*, nevertheless decided that the Eclatarian faith was a "religion" and that members of such religion were entitled to protection under the free exercise clause. However, the court declared that if it were subsequently proved that the Eclatarian faith, as practiced at the prison, was in fact a sham, then the prison administrators and the court could deal with the eventuality. These two decisions highlight the continuing legal problem facing prison administrators when apparently inconsistent decisions are rendered by different federal courts, and the United States Supreme Court is either unwilling or unable to resolve the conflict.

A number of courts have adjudicated petitions that have alleged that religious liberties were denied when authorities prohibited attendance at general services while the petitioner was confined in a maximum-security unit (correctional cell).[65] A majority of these courts dismissed the complaint and distinguished between one's freedom to believe and one's freedom to exercise one's belief. Such a restriction on the free exercise of beliefs is justified on the basis of maintaining both security and correctional discipline.[66]

A Mississippi court[67] indicated that full access to a minister of one's denomination while confined in a correctional cell satisfies the constitutional right to free exercise of religion. This case could be cited for two propositions: (1) that it is not necessary to release prisoners from maximum-security cells to attend services with the general population, or (2) that it is not necessary to conduct formal services for prisoners confined in correctional custody. Note, however, that this court held that full access to a minister of one's denomination satisfied the constitutional requirements. Another court,[68] however, ruled that the petitioner who was being held on death row be permitted to attend midweek services in the chapel instead of having to receive communion and services in a shower room.

Prison rules and policies prohibiting prisoners from leading religious services and requiring that all services be conducted in an interfaith chapel do not violate the Equal Protection Clause.[69] Further, a prison regulation prohibiting prisoners from leading religious groups is valid under the First Amendment if it is reasonably related to legitimate penological interests.[70]

Although a prisoner espoused a religion that included a belief in Caucasian supremacy and asserted that prison officials unlawfully refused to allow television programming concerning his religion while allowing other religious programming, there was no First Amendment violation because there was no showing that the prison's religious television programming favored any particular religion. The same result applied when the prisoner was denied group worship rights when other religions that practiced segregation were permitted group worship. The prisoner was not similarly situated to members of the other religions because other religions did not have separatism as a central religious tenet.[71]

A prison policy required that disqualification from participation in one religious exercise (the fast) meant that normal avenues for communal worship (group services and prayers) at the prison became unavailable automatically. When this broad disqualification aspect of policy was applied to a Muslim prisoner, he was forced to modify significantly his religious behavior, and his right to religious exercise was substantially burdened. The prison officials failed to show that its Ramadan policy was the least restrictive means of furthering a compelling governmental interest.[72] However, prison rules that prohibited Muslim prisoners from engaging in Friday afternoon prayer services were reasonable as the prisoners were allowed to participate in other weekly religious services and to have free access to the prison's imam.[73]

Religious exercise is not only a prisoner's ability to practice his religion as a whole but his ability to engage in group worship.[74] Prisoners in "punitive segregation and keeplock" could not be denied participation in chapel services simply on the basis of their classification. Individualized determinations of the "necessity of their exclusion" were required.[75]

§ 2.4.2   —Wearing of Religious Medals

In general, the courts have recognized that Black Muslims have a right to possess and wear religious medals.[76] This recognition has, in at least two cases,[77] been based upon the fact that prisoners practicing other religions had been given such a right by prison officials. However, the issue of internal security has been asserted in this area as well as in the other areas concerning religious freedoms. In *Rowland v. Sigler*,[78] the court thought that, in view of the possibility of a prisoner using a medallion as a weapon, prison officials could justifiably prohibit the prisoner from wearing the medallion. Any possible infringement of First Amendment rights was justified by the state interest in regulating the nonspeech aspect, i.e., the use of a medallion as a weapon. This case would not, of course, support the denial (by prison officials) of medallions to Black Muslims where officials permitted medallions to be worn by those of other religions.

§ 2.4.3   —Right to Correspond with Religious Leaders

Numerous prisoners have petitioned the court for the right to correspond with Elijah Muhammad, a Black Muslim leader. Some institutions have a general restriction pertaining to correspondence with heads of religious groups. This regulation is based on the theory that such communications are not "meaningful contacts."[79] Occasionally, courts have accepted this rationale and have held that because the policy applies to all religions, it does not result in religious discrimination. However, in *Walker v. Blackwell*,[80] when prison officials gave as their reasons for not allowing such correspondence the fact that Elijah Muhammad had a prison record and that the prison had a general policy not to allow Catholics to correspond with the Pope, the court held that Elijah Muhammad's confinement had occurred more than 25 years earlier, that a criminal record was only one factor to be considered in approving a correspondence according to the Bureau of Prisons, and that "[t]he prohibition against Catholics' correspondence with the Pope is of questionable constitutional merit."[81] Nevertheless, both *Theriault* and *Remmers* expressly declare that prison authorities may ascertain the contents of such correspondence with religious leaders in order to make certain that what is sought is spiritual guidance and advice and that such correspondence is not used for anything other than religious purposes.[82]

§ 2.4.4 — Right to Proselytize

Although there is no case that recognized an absolute right of a prisoner to proselytize, members of all religions share the same right to proselytize in prison. This right does not extend, however, to such activity that would create a disturbance or interfere with the privacy rights of other prisoners.[83] Furthermore, when the purpose of proselytizing is "to cause or encourage disruption of established prison discipline for the sake of disruption," such activity enjoys no First Amendment protection because it is not based on an underlying "religion."[84] In *Fulwood v. Clemmer*,[85] prison authorities presented evidence to show that the prisoner's "field preaching" had resulted in a disturbance among the other prisoners. As a result, he had been placed in solitary confinement for six months, excluded from the prison population for two years, and denied the use of rehabilitation and recreational facilities. The court held that this punishment was not reasonably related to the infraction.

Proselytizing can also be done by prison employees. In a Ninth Circuit case, a guard's unauthorized religious proselytizing while on the job did not violate a county jail prisoner's rights under the First Amendment.[86]

Preaching is a form of religious exercise. In *Spratt v. Rhode Island*,[87] the court held that a prisoner's religious exercise had been substantially burdened where prison officials would not allow him to preach anytime or anywhere, threatening that if he did so, he would be subject to disciplinary sanctions. Prison officials failed to show that the blanket ban on all preaching was the least restrictive means available to achieve its interest.

§ 2.4.5 — Free Access to Ministers

The cases dealing with the right of a prisoner to have access to a minister have been inconsistent. In two of these cases, *Jones v. Willingham*[88] and *Coleman v. Commissioner*,[89] the courts held that the prison officials could exclude Muslim ministers for protection or for security in the institution. In *Cooper v. Pate*,[90] however, the court enjoined the administration from refusing to permit a prisoner to communicate through the mail or personal visitation with the ministers of their faith. As such communication did not constitute a clear and present danger to prison security and such communication was permitted for other religious denominations, the restriction against the Black Muslims was discriminatory.

There can be little doubt, irrespective of the controversy regarding security within the institution, that Muslim ministers, once admitted to the institution, must be permitted to wear such religious robes and raiment as they desire.[91] Furthermore, they must be paid at an hourly rate comparable to that paid to chaplains of other faiths.[92]

§ 2.4.6   — Restrictions of Diet: Muslims

As a general rule, the courts have refused to order prisons to provide Muslims with pork-free meals, despite the fact that such dietary restraint is an essential doctrine found in that faith. The rationales for such refusal have been diverse. For example, in *Northern v. Nelson*,[93] in which the Muslim prisoner sought special meals during the period of Ramadan, the court asserted that budgetary restrictions constituted a justifiable reason for refusing to serve pork-free meals. The court found that, despite the constitutional deprivations claimed, the government had demonstrated a substantial compelling interest and, for that reason, dismissed relief.

Childs v. Pegelow[94] justified the failure to provide pork-free meals by finding that a prisoner could acquire adequate nourishment by avoiding pork foods. In view of this fact, the prison was under no obligation to provide specified meals. The court simply found that no constitutional issue was involved and that, essentially, the Muslims were demanding special privileges rather than constitutional rights.

A unique approach to the issue of pork-free meals is found in *Barnett v. Rodgers*.[95] The District of Columbia Circuit Court held that the lower court erred in dismissing the prisoner's complaint without determining whether the government had compelling justification and purposes for denying their request. The court believed that the prison officials had not adequately demonstrated a budgetary constraint that would prevent the use of pork and had not shown why they could not post a menu or why they could not distribute pork meals more evenly throughout the week. "To say that religious freedom may undergo modification in a prison environment is not to say that it can be suppressed or ignored without adequate reason."[96] On remand, however, final judgment was entered in favor of the prison superintendent.[97]

In *McEachin v. McGuinnis*,[98] the court ruled that a seven-day restrictive diet imposed upon on prisoner as discipline impinged upon his observance of Ramadan. The diet deprived him of properly blessed food with which to break his daily fast. Further, the discipline was a product of religious discrimination by a correctional officer who intentionally ordered the prisoner to return his tray and cup during the prisoner's prayer, knowing that his beliefs would not permit him to respond to such a command before he had finished making salat.

In *Williams v. Bitner*,[99] a Muslim prisoner refused to handle pork in his job as a prison cook. The prisoner did not act improperly or disruptively, and he completed all other tasks he had been assigned in the kitchen. He objected only when officials directed him to assist in activities that violated his sincere religious beliefs, and his protests were limited to simple refusal and explanation, without threat or show of disrespect. As punishment, he was issued a misconduct citation, placed on cell restriction, and reassigned to a lower-paying job. The Third Circuit agreed with decisions from the Fifth, Seventh, and Eighth Circuits that prison officials were required to accommodate a Muslim prisoner's religious beliefs regarding the handling of pork and that the actions of prison officials in this case were not the least restrictive means of maintaining institutional order and security.

§ 2.4.7 — Restrictions of Diet: Jews

Though the analysis employed in the Muslim food cases generally has been echoed in the Jewish kosher food cases, cases out of New York have added much to the discussion of the kosher food question. Within two days of one another, two federal district courts in New York came to apparently opposite conclusions. Both cases involved Jewish prisoners who had asked the court for orders directing the Bureau of Prisons to make kosher foods—meeting the requirements of Jewish orthodox dietary laws—available to them during their incarceration.

In the first case, *United States v. Huss*,[100] the court ruled that the prison was not obligated to provide kosher food. In arriving at this conclusion, the court relied on four primary considerations: (1) the extra cost of providing kosher foods to Jewish prisoners on a regular basis; (2) the obvious problems that would arise from special treatment given to such prisoners; (3) the security risk involved, given the relative ease of smuggling contraband to a prisoner when it is known that the food is for a designated prisoner; and (4) the availability of substitute foods to ensure a sufficient diet. On appeal, this judgment was vacated on procedural grounds.[101]

The second case, *United States v. Kahane*,[102] involved the kosher food requests of an orthodox rabbi. In this case, the court decided that the prisoner was entitled to receive kosher meals. It was reasoned that comparatively simple administrative procedures—i.e., a combination of pre-prepared frozen kosher meals and suitable dietary alternatives—would result in a nutritionally sound diet consistent with kosher requirements. In the court's opinion, the government had shown no serious reasons why providing a kosher diet for the prisoner would affect prison security or discipline.

The conflict arising from these two cases is somewhat settled by *Kahane v. Carlson*.[103] In this decision, the Second Circuit Court of Appeals affirmed and modified *United States v. Kahane*. The court agreed that the finding of deep religious significance for a practicing orthodox Jew was justified and was entitled to constitutional protection. It was explained that the difficulties encountered by the prisons were surmountable in view of the small number of practicing orthodox Jews in federal prisons (approximately 12).[104] The court clarified and modified the district court's decision by explaining that the use of frozen prepared kosher foods, while helpful, was not constitutionally required. Rather, the prison was required to provide the incarcerated orthodox rabbi with a diet sufficient to sustain his good health without violating Jewish dietary laws. However, the court did not mandate specific items of diet.

While the court ordered the provision of a kosher diet in this instance, it should be noted that this does not necessarily apply to all Jewish prisoners. The application of this decision seems to require a situation involving a practicing orthodox Jew before a prison is required to provide a kosher diet.

§ 2.4.8   — Access to Religious Literature

Prisoner access to religious literature remains a controversial issue. The justification for suppressing religious literature that prison administrators frequently advance is that the material is inflammatory and will cause disruptions and breaches in security. Consequently, the decisions usually turn on when the court believes that the material requested is of a nature tending to incite disruptions or security problems. A case finding no such tendency is *Northern v. Nelson*.[105] Here, the court held that the prison library was under an obligation to make available copies of the Koran. Further, the court ordered that prisoners be allowed to receive the publication *Muhammad Speaks* unless it could be clearly demonstrated that a specific issue would substantially disrupt prison discipline.

In *Walker v. Blackwell*,[106] although the district court held that issues of *Muhammad Speaks* were inflammatory, the Fifth Circuit Court of Appeals reached a conclusion similar to *Northern* and reversed the district court. The basis of its decision is found in the following:

> First, taken as a whole, the newspapers are filled with news and editorial comment, a substantial portion of which generally encourages the Black Muslim to improve his material and spiritual condition of life by labor and study. Nowhere, including the supposedly inflammatory portions described by the court below, does there appear any direct incitement to the Black Muslims to engage in any physical violence.

This court thus concluded that *Muhammad Speaks* was not inflammatory and ordered that Black Muslims be allowed to receive the newspaper. The court qualified this, however, by saying that they were not holding that exclusion of the newspaper could not take place, if it became inflammatory. The order was merely to direct that the warden not arbitrarily deny Black Muslims the right to read *Muhammad Speaks*.[107]

While *Northern* and *Walker* held that, taken as a whole, the Muslim publications presented no threat to prison security, other courts have come to the opposite conclusion. In *Knuckles v. Prasse*,[108] the district court found that it was not mandatory that prison officials make available Muslim books and periodicals. The court held that, without proper guidance and interpretation by trained Muslim ministers, these materials might be misinterpreted by a prisoner. An uninformed prisoner could read the material as an encouragement to defy prison authorities. Thus, the literature could constitute "a clear and present danger of a breach of prison security or discipline or some other substantial interference with the orderly functioning of the institution."[109]

Another decision following this basic rationale is *Abernathy v. Cunningham*.[110] In that case, a prisoner desired to obtain a copy of "Muhammad's Message to the Black Man in America" and to subscribe to *Muhammad Speaks*. The Fourth Circuit held that the prison's decision denying access to this literature, so far as the record disclosed, was not motivated by religious prejudice and that the particular materials in question contained recurring themes of black superiority and hatred for the white race. It was the prison authorities' opinion that such materials would be inflammatory and subversive to discipline. The court thought that it should not attempt to substitute its judgment on the nature of the publication for that of the prison authorities. For this reason, the court denied relief.

In spite of the courts' determination as to whether material is inflammatory, most courts place the burden of proving that the deprivation of constitutional rights is justified upon the prison. In *Burns v. Swenson*,[111] prison officials were ordered to return the plaintiff's Koran. The court believed that deprivation of his holy book would interfere with his right to freely practice his religion, particularly because the prison officials had given no explanation of why this book should not be returned to the prisoner. Similarly, in *Long v. Parker*,[112] the Third Circuit Court of Appeals placed the burden on prison authorities who wished to suppress *Muhammad Speaks*. The court found that the administration must show that "[t]he literature creates a clear and present danger of a breach of prison security or discipline or some other substantial interference with the orderly functioning of the institution."[113] However, it also required the Muslims to establish that it was basic religious literature essential to their belief and understanding of their religion.

In *Sasnett v. Department of Corrections*,[114] Wisconsin state prisoners challenged several internal management procedures, emergency rules, and permanent administrative rules regulating the types and amounts of personal property they may possess while in prison. Rules regulating prisoner personal property and clothing, which included limiting the amount of personal and state-issued property a prisoner may possess, were issued. As a result, a prisoner was forced to relinquish approximately 11 religious books, including *The Amplified Bible*, volumes one through three of the *Jamison, Fauset Brown Commentary*, the *Inductive Study Bible*, the *NIV Interliner Greek–English New Testament*, and the *NIV Interliner Hebrew–English Old Testament*. These religious books were sent out of the prison to or with Sasnett's pastor. Because of the new rules, one prisoner was forced to dispose of several Jehovah's Witnesses pamphlets.

After holding that the prisoners had no property interest that was protected under the Due Process Clause, it granted the prisoners relief. Unlike property interests, liberty interests can arise from the Constitution. The right to "liberty" guaranteed by the Fourteenth Amendment denoted a freedom to worship God according to the dictates of one's own conscience, as well as the right to petition the courts for redress.[115]

§ 2.4.9   — Classification on Religious Grounds

It is a frequent practice in various correctional institutions to require that a prisoner specify his or her religious preference upon entering the prison. The prisoner is then forbidden to alter this choice during his or her period of confinement. For the most part, such practices have been upheld by courts.

For example, in *Long v. Katzenbach*,[116] the court sustained the classification procedure as a valid means of controlling the proselytizing that had been a source of disruption within the institution. A similar finding was handed down in *Peek v. Ciccone*,[117] in which prison officials had refused to permit a non-Jewish prisoner to attend Jewish services. The prison allowed prisoners to attend any service connected with their specified religious affiliation. The court found that such a restriction was not unreasonable in that it did not curtail religious belief. This was especially true in light of the fact that the rabbi in the institution had a policy of refusing conversion of prisoners to the Jewish faith. The court found that religious practices, as distinguished from religious beliefs, may properly be the subject of administrative control.

Although the issue is not entirely clear, religious classification would appear to be supportable as long as equal treatment is afforded to all religious groups and there is a rational basis for such classification.

§ 2.4.10   — Beards and Haircuts

Both *Brown v. Wainwright*[118] and *Brooks v. Wainwright*[119] held that regulations requiring shaves and haircuts were proper and were not a source of religious discrimination. However, the court in *People ex rel. Rockey v. Krueger*[120] heard evidence from the prisoner that he was being held in solitary confinement because he had refused to shave his beard. The prison administration justified the regulation as one for the protection of health. The jail supervisor also testified that there was no formal regulation about hair but that the order to the staff was that prisoners were only permitted to wear neatly trimmed mustaches. He said that an orthodox Jew would not be required to shave his beard. The court held that, on the basis of the treatment afforded orthodox Jews, the prisoner was the subject of religious discrimination.

In cases concerning prison haircut regulations as applied to Native Americans, at least three courts have held that where a long hairstyle is motivated by indisputably sincere religious beliefs, then such regulations impermissibly infringe on the prisoner's right under the First Amendment to the free exercise of his religion.[121] However, in *Proffitt v. Ciccone*,[122] the court upheld prison haircut regulations, despite the prisoner's contention that he was thereby forced to violate religious vows he had taken. In this area, in order to restrict prisoner conduct based upon religious motivations, prison authorities face a heavy burden.

In *Cleveland v. Garner*,[123] a prisoner alleged that the prison's grooming regulations interfered with the free exercise of his Rastafari religion in violation of the First Amendment.[124] Based on the Biblical vow of the Nazarite, Rastafari practices include never cutting or combing one's hair, instead allowing it to grow in dreadlocks.[125] Diametrically opposed to that tenet of the Rastafari religion is the aspect of the prison grooming regulations that prohibits long hair and beards. The rule is well established that prisoners retain their First Amendment right to the free exercise of religion.[126] The right, however, is subject to reasonable restrictions and limitations necessitated by penological goals.[127] It was conceded that, as a general proposition, the prisoner's religious practices conflicted with penological interests, such as prison security and ease of prisoner identification. However, it was contended that an exception should be made on the basis that confinement in administrative segregation and segregation from the general prison population so significantly reduces the importance of these penological interests that they serve no valid purpose. The prisoner had no desire to return to the general prison population and, in his unique confinement situation, being forced to comply with the grooming regulations both interfered with his religious beliefs and served no actual penological interests.

The court held that, as a general principle, prison grooming regulations, including specifically the requirement that a prisoner cut his hair and beard, are rationally related to the achievement of valid penological goals, such as security and prisoner identification.[128] Consequently, the prisoner's First Amendment claim was denied.

The Supreme Court finally addressed the issue of beards grown for religious reasons in *Holt v. Hobbs*.[129] The Arkansas Department of Corrections' grooming policy stated that "no inmates will be permitted to wear facial hair other than a neatly trimmed mustache that does not extend beyond the corner of the mouth or over the lip."[130] Holt was a devout Muslim who wished to grow a half-inch beard on religious grounds;[131] prison officials denied his request, arguing that beards compromised prison safety because (1) they could be used to conceal contraband and (2) an inmate could shave his beard to disguise his identity. The Court rejected these arguments and ruled in favor of the inmate:

> While the [prison officials] have a compelling interest in regulating contraband, its argument that this interest is compromised by allowing an inmate to grow a ½-inch beard is unavailing, especially given the difficulty of hiding contraband in such a short beard and the lack of a corresponding policy regulating the length of hair on the head.[132]

§ 2.5   Religious Freedom Restoration Act

Congress passed The Religious Freedom Restoration Act (RFRA) in direct response to the Supreme Court's decision in *Employment Division, Department of Human Resources of Oregon v. Smith*.[133] In *Smith*, the Supreme Court upheld a free exercise challenge to Native American Church members who objected to a state law of general applicability criminalizing the use of peyote. The case involved members of the church who lost their jobs because of using peyote in their church services. The *Smith* Court declined to apply the balancing test of *Sherbert v. Verner*,[134] which mandated the "compelling government interest" standard in religious practices cases and applied a lower standard. Congress reacted by "overruling" the Supreme Court and required courts to use the "compelling government interest" standard that was rejected by *Smith*.

However, the legislative history of the RFRA indicated that the required test had to be construed in the prison context, giving due deference to the expert judgment of prison administrators. The legislative history of RFRA also indicated that, while Congress intended for the same compelling interest test in the statute to apply to prisoners as well as nonprisoners, the outcome of the analysis would depend upon the context.

Many cases wrestled with religious practices under the RFRA and its application to prisons. However, in 1997, the Supreme Court held in *City of Boerne v. Flores*,[135] that the RFRA was not a proper exercise of Congress's power because it contradicts vital principles necessary to maintain separation of powers and the federal–state balance. According to *Boerne*, the RFRA attempted a substantive change in constitutional protections, proscribing state conduct that the Fourteenth Amendment itself does not prohibit. Its restrictions applied to every government agency and official and to all statutory or other laws, whether adopted before or after its enactment. Requiring a state to demonstrate a compelling interest and show that it has adopted the least restrictive means of achieving that interest is the most demanding test known to constitutional law. However, *Boerne* was limited to the impact of the RFRA on state systems and had no effect on the federal system. As a result, there were two standards by which to measure judicial review of prison religious practices: one for federal prisons and one for state and local prisons and jails.

§ 2.6   Religious Land Use and Institutionalized Persons Act

This impossible situation was finally resolved by Congress in 2000, with the enactment of the Religious Land Use and Institutionalized Persons Act (RLUIPA).[136] Congress enacted the RLUIPA in response to the Supreme Court's holding in *City of Boerne v. Flores*. The statute provides:

> No government shall impose a substantial burden on the religious exercise of a person residing in or confined to an institution . . . even if the burden results from a rule of general applicability, unless the government demonstrates that imposition of the burden on that person—

(1) is in furtherance of a compelling governmental interest; and

(2) is the least restrictive means of furthering that compelling governmental interest.

Under the RLUIPA, once a prisoner produces prima facie evidence to support a free exercise violation, the prisoner bears the burden of persuasion on whether the regulation substantially burdens his exercise of religion, and the state then bears the burden of persuasion on all other elements.[137] This shifting of the burden of proof makes it easier for district courts to dismiss frivolous claims while placing the burden of proof on the state in legitimate claims.

By its terms, the RLUIPA is to be construed to broadly favor protection of religious exercise.[138] The statute defines religious exercise as "any exercise of religion, whether or not compelled by, or central to, a system of religious belief."[139] This reflects an extension of the definition provided for in the statute, which defines exercise of religion as "the exercise of religion under the First Amendment to the Constitution."[140] The Act does not elevate accommodation of religious observances over an institution's need to maintain order and safety. An accommodation is necessary so that it does not override other significant interests. Congress was mindful of the importance of discipline, order, safety, and security in penal institutions. The Court expected that lower courts would apply the Act's standard with due deference to prison administrators' experience and expertise. Further, the RLUIPA does not differentiate among bona fide faiths. It confers no privileged status on any particular religious sect.

The constitutionality of the RLUIPA came up for Supreme Court review in 2005. In *Cutter v. Wilkinson*,[141] prisoners alleged that prison officials had violated the Act by failing to accommodate their exercise of nonmainstream religions. *Cutter* held that the RLUIPA does not impermissibly advance religion by giving greater protection to religious rights than to other constitutionally protected rights. A state is permitted to accommodate traditionally recognized religions by providing chaplains and allowing worship services. The Supreme Court did not believe that there was any reason to anticipate that abusive prisoner litigation would overburden state and local institutions. However, the Court cautioned that, should prisoner requests for religious accommodations become excessive, impose unjustified burdens on other institutionalized persons, or jeopardize an institution's effective functioning, the facility would be free to resist the imposition.

The RFRA was declared unconstitutional as its mandates for state systems were beyond the constitutional power of Congress. The constitutional basis of the RLUIPA is the power of Congress to spend money. As a result, the RLUIPA applies only to programs or activities that receive federal financial assistance. States have the right to avoid the Act's requirements by refusing federal aid. As a result, the statute does not impermissibly "control" state legislatures in violation of the Tenth Amendment and is constitutional.[142]

§ 2.6.1   — Cases Decided Under the RLUIPA

Since it was enacted, numerous cases have been decided using the standards set by the RLUIPA. For example, *Hamilton v. Schriro*[143] concerned a Native American prisoner who was denied access to a "sweat lodge," an instrumental aspect of many Native Americans' religion. The correctional facility provides cross-denominational religious facilities inside prison buildings. Native Americans are allowed to pray, to gather together for regularly scheduled services, to meet with outside spiritual leaders, and to obtain religious reading material from the library. They are also allowed to carry medicine bags containing ceremonial items and have access to a ceremonial pipe and kinnikinnik (a ceremonial "tobacco" consisting of willow, sweet grass, sage, and cedar). However, authorities did not allow a sweat lodge, sweat lodge ceremony, or fires on the premises, which the prisoner argued would prevent him from practicing any other aspect of his religion.

Relying on the RLUIPA, the Eight Circuit ruled in favor of prison administrators. First, prohibiting prisoners from meeting in a completely enclosed area is rationally connected to preventing the type of harm prison officials fear would occur in the sweat lodge. Second, alternative means remain open to prisoners for exercising their religion, including carrying a medicine bag containing ceremonial items, having access to a ceremonial pipe and kinnikinnik, and praying with other Native American prisoners. Third, accommodating the request for a sweat lodge would have an adverse impact on prison staff, other prisoners, and prison resources, due to the risk of assaulting participants in the ceremony, as well as possible resentment resulting from the construction of an exclusive religious facility. As such, prison officials met their burden under the RLUIPA and established as a matter of law that prohibiting a sweat lodge was in furtherance of a compelling governmental interest. Denying the prisoner's request was the least restrictive means by which to further the institution's compelling interest in safety and security.

In *Baranowski v. Hart*,[144] a prisoner claimed that prison officials failed to provide weekly Sabbath and other holy day services for Jewish prisoners and failed to comply with kosher dietary requirements. The prison policies passed constitutional review. Despite being denied weekly Sabbath and holy day services, the prisoner retained the ability to participate in alternative means of exercising his religious beliefs. Further, prison officials did not need to respond to particularized religious dietary requests. Meeting those requirements would place undue costs and administrative burdens on the prison system. The prison actions regarding religious services did not place a substantial burden on the prisoner's free exercise of his faith. On the days that services were not provided, no rabbi or approved religious volunteer was available to lead the services. The dietary policy of not providing kosher meals was the least restrictive means of furthering a compelling government interest of maintaining good order and controlling costs.

§ 2.7 Conclusion

The primary emphasis of decisions concerning a prisoner's religious freedom has been on the fact that the prison is a closed environment. It is because of this fact that courts frequently invoke the "noninterference" logic so prevalent in early cases dealing with prisons. The state interest in maintaining security within the institution, together with the need for administrative discretion in handling disciplinary problems, has been held sufficient reason for limiting a prisoner's First Amendment rights.

One of the few restrictions placed upon the prison administrator in his or her dealings with the First Amendment rights of prisoners has been that of equal protection—that is, treating all classes of prisoners equally. Courts have consistently held that when one religious group is permitted to engage in a particular activity, the same right must be accorded all other religious groups within the institution. Thus, it would appear that although prison officials have a right to regulate religious activity in order to promote valid institutional interests, the regulation must, in all cases, be equally applied to all groups. Likewise, where one group is permitted to manifest its religious beliefs in a certain manner, all other religious groups must be accorded the same privilege.

The Religious Land Use and Institutionalized Persons Act will continue to have a substantial impact on state institution management, as will the Religious Freedom Restoration Act on federal institutions. In any event, the "compelling government interest" standard is the same in both Acts.

Notes

1 U.S. CONST., amend. I; *see* Appendix I.
2 428 F.2d 1 (3d Cir. 1970).
3 Wright v. McMann, 257 F. Supp. 739 (N.D.N.Y. 1966), *rev'd on other grounds*, 387 F.2d 519 (2d Cir. 1967).
4 410 F.2d 995 (D.C. Cir. 1969).
5 *Id.* at 1000–1001.
6 494 U.S. 872 (1990).
7 Montano v. Hedgepeth, 120 F.3d 844 (8th Cir. 1997). *See* Chapter 15.
8 Theriault v. Sibler, 391 F. Supp. 578 (W.D. Tex. 1975), vacated and remanded, 547 F.2d 1279 (5th Cir. 1977). The court of appeals held that the requirement of a belief in a supreme being as a criterion to determine whether a practice constitutes a religion within the protection of the First Amendment is too narrow. The court stated: "When reconsidering what constitutes a religion, a thorough study of the existing case law should be accompanied by appropriate evidentiary exploration of philosophical, theological, and other related literature and resources on this issue." *Id.* at 1281. In a subsequent case, Theriault v. Sibler, 453 F. Supp. 254 (W.D. Tex. 1978), a Texas federal court ruled that an inmate-created religion was not entitled to First Amendment protection, because it was not a true "religion" for purposes of federal law. After reviewing the facts in the case, the court concluded: "The professed views of Mr. Theriault that he 'would have established a New World order' with Harry W. Theriault as the head of the Order . . . are, in the opinion of the Court more closely akin to

the megalomania of Adolph Hitler and the Nazis or Charles Manson and his 'family' than any 'belief . . . that occupies a place parallel to that filled by the orthodox belief in God.'"; Remmers v. Brewer, 396 F. Supp. 145 (S.D. Iowa 1975), rev'd on other grounds, 529 F.2d 656 (8th Cir. 1976); cf. Ron v. Lennane, 445 F. Supp. 98 (D. Conn. 1977); cf. Loney v. Scurr, 474 F. Supp. 1186 (S.D. Iowa 1979) (the Church of the New Song was a religion entitled to the protection of the First Amendment); Africa v. Commonwealth of Pennsylvania, 662 F.2d 1025 (3d Cir. 1981). (On the facts of the case, an inmate belief was not a religion within the purview of the First Amendment. His organization did not address fundamental and ultimate questions. It was not comprehensive in nature and did not have the defining structural characteristics of a traditional religion.)

9   Turner v. Safley, 482 U.S. 78 (1987) and Beard v. Banks, 548 U.S. 521 (2006).

10   248 F. Supp. 791 (D. Kan. 1965).

11   634 F.2d 109 (3d Cir. 1980); Montoya v. Tanksley, 446 F. Supp. 226 (D. Colo. 1978).

12   480 F. Supp. 1288 (E.D. Pa. 1979).

13   McDonald v. Hall, 576 F.2d 120 (1st Cir. 1978).

14   382 F.2d 518 (7th Cir. 1967).

15   *Id.* at 523.

16   Brandenburg v. Ohio, 395 U.S. 444 (1969).

17   302 F. Supp. 1036 (E.D. Pa. 1969), *aff'd*, 435 F.2d 1255 (3d Cir. 1970).

18   *Id.* at 1049, citing Long v. Parker, 390 F.2d 816, 822 (3d Cir. 1968).

19   *Id.* at 1058.

20   *Ibid.*

21   Jordan v. Gardner, 986 F.2d 1521 (9th Cir. 1993).

22   Turner v. Safley, 482 U.S. 78 (1987).

23   *See* Chapter 3.

24   302 F. Supp. 1036 at 1048 (E.D. Pa. 1969), *aff'd*, 435 F.2d 1255 (3d Cir. 1970).

25   Kennedy v. Meacham, 382 F. Supp. 996 (D. Wyo. 1974), *vacated and remanded on appeal*, Kennedy v. Meacham, 540 F.2d 1057 (10th Cir. 1976). The court of appeals ruled that the district court improperly dismissed the complaint and the case would be remanded to determine whether the practice of a religious belief was involved, whether there were restrictions imposed upon it, and whether such restrictions were justified.

26   Childs v. Duckworth, 705 F.2d 915 (7th Cir. 1983).

27   Belk v. Mitchell, 294 F. Supp. 800 (W.D.N.C. 1968).

28   *Id.* at 802.

29   Mims v. Shapp, 399 F. Supp. 818 (W.D. Pa. 1975), *vacated and remanded on appeal*, Mims v. Shapp, 541 F.2d 415 (2d Cir. 1976). The court of appeals held that the inmates' affidavits sufficiently alleged personal bias of the judge and that the district judge erred in denying the inmates' refusal motion.

30   480 F. Supp. 1288 (E.D. Pa. 1979); Nadeau v. Helgemoe, 423 F. Supp. 1250 (D.N.H. 1976), *modified*, 561 F.2d 411 (1st Cir. 1977); 581 F.2d 275 (1st Cir. 1978).

31   Wojtczak v. Cuyler, 480 F. Supp. 1288 (E.D. Pa. 1979).

32   529 F.2d 854 (4th Cir. 1974).

33   361 P. 2d 417 (Cal. 1961).

34   *Id.* at 421.

35   428 F.2d 1 (3d Cir. 1970).

36   *Id.* at 4.

37   *Id.* at 5.

38   *Ibid.*

39   411 F.2d 23 (5th Cir. 1969).

40   *Id.* at 26.

41   527 F.2d 492 (2d Cir. 1975).

42   Ashelman v. Wawrzaszek, 111 F.3d 674 (9th Cir. 1997).

43   482 U.S. 342 (1987).

44   Mayweathers v. Terhune, 328 F. Supp. 2d 1086 (E.D. Cal. 2004).

45   *See* Appendix I.

46   U.S. CONST., amend. XIV, § 1.

47   474 P. 2d 532 (Or. App. 1970).

48   *Id.* at 536.

49   405 U.S. 319 (1972).

50   306 N.Y.S.2d 359 (Sup. Ct. 1969); *see also* Maguire v. Wilkinson, 405 F. Supp. 637 (D. Conn. 1975).

51   285 F. Supp. 585 (W.D. Mo. 1968), *aff'd*, 417 F.2d 161 (8th Cir. 1969), *cert. denied*, 397 U.S. 963 (1970).

52   *Id.* at 595.

53   382 F.2d 518 (7th Cir. 1967).

54   *See* Howard v. Smyth, 365 F.2d 428 (4th Cir. 1966); Lee v. Crouse, 284 F. Supp. 541 (D. Kan. 1968), *aff'd*, 396 F.2d 952 (10th Cir. 1968); Fulwood v. Clemmer, 206 F. Supp. 370 (D.C. Cir. 1962); State v. Cubbage, 210 A.2d 555 (Del. Super. Ct. 1965).

55   *See* Knuckles v. Prasse, 435 F.2d 1255 (3d Cir. 1970); Sewell v. Pegelow, 304 F.2d 670 (4th Cir. 1962); Banks v. Havener, 234 F. Supp. 27 (E.D. Va. 1964).

56   248 F. Supp. 791 (D. Kan. 1965).

57   43 N.J. 514, 205 A.2d 889 (1964).

58   234 F. Supp. 27 (E.D. Va. 1964).

59   376 F. Supp. 402 (E.D. Okla. 1974).

60   339 F. Supp. 375 (N.D. Ga. 1972), *vacated and remanded*, 495 F.2d 390 (5th Cir.), *cert. denied*, 419 U.S. 1003 (1974).

61   361 F. Supp. 537 (S.D. Iowa 1973), *aff'd*, 494 F.2d 1277 (8th Cir. 1974), *cert. denie*d, 419 U.S. 1012 (1974).

62   Theriault v. Carlson, 495 F.2d 390 (5th Cir. 1974).

63   Theriault v. Sibler, 391 F. Supp. 578 (W.D. Tex. 1975), *vacated and remanded*, 547 F.2d 1279 (5th Cir. 1977).

64   *Ibid.*

65   *See* Sharp v. Sigler, 408 F.2d 966 (8th Cir. 1969); Belk v. Mitchell, 294 F. Supp. 800 (W.D.N.C. 1968); Konigsberg v. Ciccone, 285 F. Supp. 585 (W.D. Mo. 1968), *aff'd*, 417 F.2d 161 (8th Cir. 1969), *cert. denied*, 397 U.S. 963 (1970); Morgan v. Cook, 236 So. 2d 749 (Miss. 1970).

66   *See* Sharp v. Sigler, 408 F.2d 966 (8th Cir. 1969); Belk v. Mitchell, 294 F. Supp. 800 (W.D.N.C. 1968); McBride v. McCorkle, 44 N.J. Super. 468, 130 A.2d 881 (App. Div. 1957).

67   Morgan v. Cook, 236 So. 2d 749 (Miss. 1970).

68   Gunn v. Wilkinson, 309 F. Supp. 411 (W.D. Mo. 1970).

69   Samad v. Ridge, U.S. Dist. LEXIS 6348 (E.D. Pa. 1998).

70   Anderson v. Angelone, 123 F.3d 1197 (9th Cir. 1997).

71   Murphy v. Mo. Dep't of Corr., 372 F.3d 979 (8th Cir. 2004).

72   Lovelace v. Lee, 472 F.3d 174 (4th Cir. 2006), *criticized in*, Washington v. Klem, 497 F.3d 272 (3d Cir. 2007).

73   Turner. Cf. O'Lone v. Estate of Shabazz, 482 U.S. 342 (1987).

74   Greene v. Solano County Jail, 513 F.3d 982 (9th Cir. 2008).

75   Mawhinney v. Henderson, 542 F.2d 1 (2d Cir. 1976).

76   *See* Knuckles v. Prasse, 302 F. Supp. 1036 (E.D. Pa. 1969), *aff'd*, 435 F.2d 1255 (3d Cir. 1970).

77   *See* Coleman v. District of Columbia Commissioners, 234 F. Supp. 408 (E.D. Va. 1964) and State v. Cubbage, 210 A.2d 555 (Del. Super. Ct. 1965).

78   327 F. Supp. 821 (D.C. Neb. 1971).

79   *See* Knuckles v. Prasse, 302 F. Supp. 1036 (E.D. Pa. 1969), *aff'd*, 435 F.2d 1255 (3d Cir. 1970); Long v. Katzenbach, 258 F. Supp. 89 (M.D. Pa. 1966); Desmond v. Blackwell, 235 F. Supp. 246 (M.D. Pa. 1964).

80 411 F.2d 23 (5th Cir. 1969).

81 *Id.* at 29.

82 Theriault v. Carlson, 339 F. Supp. 375 (N.D. Ga. 1972), *vacated and remanded*, 495 F.2d 390 (5th Cir. 1974), *cert. denied*, 419 U.S. 1003 (1974); Remmers v. Brewer, 361 F. Supp. 537 (S.D. Iowa 1973), *aff'd*, 494 F.2d 1277 (8th Cir. 1974), *cert. denied*, 419 U.S. 1012 (1974).

83 *See* Evans v. Ciccone, 377 F.2d 4 (8th Cir. 1967); Sewell v. Pegelow, 304 F.2d 670 (4th Cir. 1962); Long v. Katzenbach, 258 F. Supp. 89 (M.D. Pa. 1966).

84 Theriault v. Sibler, 391 F. Supp. 578 (W.D. Tex. 1975), *vacated and remanded*, 547 F.2d 1279 (5th Cir. 1977). The court of appeals held that the requirement of a belief in a supreme being as a criterion to determine whether a practice constitutes a religion within the protection of the First Amendment is too narrow. The court stated that: "When reconsidering what constitutes a religion, a thorough study of the existing case law should be accompanied by appropriate evidentiary exploration of philosophical, theological, and other related literature and resources on this issue." *Id.* at 1281.

85 206 F. Supp. 370 (D.D.C. 1962).

86 Canell v. Lighter, 143 F.3d 1210 (9th Cir. 1998).

87 482 F.3d 33 (1st Cir. 2007).

88 248 F. Supp. 791 (D. Kan. 1965).

89 234 F. Supp. 408 (E.D. Va. 1964).

90 382 F.2d 518 (7th Cir. 1967).

91 *See* Samarion v. McGinnis, 314 N.Y.S.2d 715 (N.Y.A.D. 1970).

92 *See* Northern v. Nelson, 315 F. Supp. 687 (N.D. Cal. 1970).

93 *See also* Young v. Robinson, 29 Cr. L. 2587 (M.D. Pa. 1981) (Muslim inmates are not required to be furnished with diets that conform to their religious beliefs).

94 Childs v. Pegelow, 321 F.2d 487 (4th Cir. 1963), *cert. denied*, 376 U.S. 932 (1964); cf. Muhammad-D.C.C. v. Keve, 479 F. Supp. 1311 (D. Del. 1979) (Muslim inmates have a constitutional right to a pork-free diet).

95 410 F.2d 995 (D.C. Cir. 1969).

96 *Id.* at 100.

97 Unreported decisions HC 174–66 and HC 66–66 (S.D.N.Y. 1975).

98 357 F.3d 197 (2d Cir. 2004).

99 285 F. Supp. 2d 593 (M.D. Pa. 2003), *aff'd*, 445 F.3d 186 (3d Cir. 2006).

100 United States v. Huss, 394 F. Supp. 752 (S.D.N.Y.), *vacated*, 520 F.2d 598 (2d Cir. 1975).

101 United States v. Huss, 520 F.2d 598 (2d Cir. 1975).

102 396 F. Supp. 687 (E.D.N.Y.), *modified sub nom.*, Kahane v. Carlson, 527 F.2d 492 (2d Cir. 1975).

103 527 F.2d 492 (2d Cir. 1975).

104 *Id.* at 495.

105 315 F. Supp. 687 (N.D. Cal. 1970).

106 411 F.2d 23 (5th Cir. 1969).

107 *Id.* at 28–29.

108 302 F. Supp. 1036 (E.D. Pa. 1969).

109 *Id.* at 1049.

110 393 F.2d 775 (4th Cir. 1968).

111 288 F. Supp. 4 (W.D. Mo. 1968), *modified*, 300 F. Supp. 759 (W.D. Mo. 1969).

112 390 F.2d 816 (3d Cir. 1968).

113 *Id.* at 822.

114 Sasnett v. Department of Corrections, 891 F. Supp. 1305 (W.D. Wis. 1995).

115 Williams v. Lane, 851 F.2d 867, 881 (7th Cir. 1988), *cert. denied*, 488 U.S. 1047 (1989).

116 258 F. Supp. 89 (M.D. Pa. 1966).

117 288 F. Supp. 329 (W.D. Mo. 1968).

118 419 F.2d 1376 (5th Cir. 1970).

119   428 F.2d 652 (5th Cir. 1970).

120   People ex rel. Rockey v. Krueger, 306 N.Y.S.2d 359 (Sup. Ct. 1969).

121   Teterud v. Gillman, 371 F. Supp. 282 (W.D. Mo. 1973), *aff'd*, 506 F.2d 1020 (8th Cir. 1974); Teterud v. Gillman, 385 F. Supp. 153 (S.D. Iowa 1974), *aff'd*, 522 F.2d 357 (8th Cir. 1975), and Crowe v. Erickson, 17 Cr. L. 2093 (D.S.D. 1975); Gallahan v. Hollyfield, 516 F. Supp. 1004 (E.D. Va. 1981), *aff'd*, 670 F.2d 1345 (4th Cir. 1982).

122   371 F. Supp. 282 (W.D. Mo. 1973), *aff'd*, 506 F.2d 1020 (8th Cir. 1974).

123   69 F.3d 22 (5th Cir. 1995).

124   *See* § 2.4.11.

125   Numbers 6:6–1. Verse five of that vow reads: "All the days of the vow of his separation there shall no razor come upon his head: until the days be fulfilled, in the which he separateth himself unto the Lord, he shall be holy, and shall let the locks of the hair of his head grow."

126   Powell v. Estelle, 959 F.2d 22 (5th Cir.) (*per curiam*), *cert. denied sub nom.*, Harrison v. McKaskle, 506 U.S. 1025 (1992).

127   *Id.* (citing Turner v. Safley, 482 U.S. 78 (1987)).

128   *See* Powell, 959 F.2d at 25 (holding that the prohibition on long hair and beards is rationally related to legitimate state objectives); Scott v. Mississippi Dep't of Corrections, 961 F.2d 77 (1992) (Hair-grooming regulation that required short hair was reasonably related to legitimate penological concerns of identification and security).

129   574 U.S. 352 (2015).

130   *Id.* at ___ (slip op., at 4).

131   Holt argued that his faith required him not to trim his beard at all, but he proposed a compromise under which he would be allowed to maintain a ½-inch beard.

132   *Ibid.*

133   494 U.S. 872(1990).

134   374 U.S. 398 (1963).

135   521 U.S. 507 (1997).

136   42 U.S.C. 2000cc-1(a).

137   42 U.S.C. 2000cc-2(b). *See* Appendix II for the full Act.

138   42 U.S.C. 2000cc-3(g).

139   42 U.S.C. 2000cc-5(7)(A).

140   42 U.S.C. 2000bb-2(4).

141   544 U.S. 709 (2005).

142   Williams v. Bitner, 285 F. Supp. 2d 593 (M.D. Pa. 2003), *aff'd*, 445 F.3d 186 (3d Cir. 2006).

143   74 F.3d 1545 (8th Cir. 1996).

144   486 F.3d 112 (5th Cir. 2007).

Searches, Seizures, and Privacy

3

Chapter Outline

Section

§ 3.1   Introduction

The Fourth Amendment to the U.S. Constitution states:

The right of the people to be secure in their persons, houses, papers, and effects, against unreasonable searches and seizures, shall not be violated.[1]

This protection is entrenched in American society. It is intended to prevent government officials from conducting unlawful searches and seizures, as well to avert violations of our right to privacy in our day-to-day lives. Many court cases have addressed different aspects of the Fourth Amendment, such as which areas and items are protected under the amendment[2] and whether a particular search and/or seizure is considered reasonable.[3]

Searches of both inmates and their living areas are common—and necessary—in prisons to prevent escape and to discover contraband such as weapons, drugs, and cell phones. Furthermore, visitors and employees, persons who are not incarcerated in the prison, are routinely searched upon entering the facility. In this chapter, we discuss how the Fourth Amendment applies—if at all—in correctional institutions. The Fourth Amendment's application to probationers and parolees will be discussed in Chapter 13.

§ 3.2   Searching Inmates and Their Cells

A state's right to incarcerate offenders includes the right to limit or extinguish prisoners' constitutional rights that are inconsistent with the goals of incarceration. In *Olsen v. Klecker*,[4] the Fourth Amendment prohibition on unreasonable searches and seizures was held not to restrict warrantless searches of prison cells. The basic point of this case is not that the Fourth Amendment does not apply to prisoners but that the reasonableness of prison searches and seizures is to be assessed in light of the institutional needs of security, order, and rehabilitation.

In *Hudson v. Palmer*,[5] the Supreme Court finally addressed whether a prison inmate has a reasonable expectation of privacy in his prison cell, which would grant him protection against unreasonable searches and seizures under the Fourth Amendment. Prison officials conducted a random "shakedown" search of Palmer's cell for contraband and discovered a ripped pillowcase in a trashcan. Palmer was charged with violating prison policy (destroying state

59

property) and found guilty of the charge after a disciplinary hearing. Palmer filed suit under 42 U.S.C. § 1983[6] claiming that the prison officials conducted an unreasonable search of his prison cell.

On appeal from the Fourth Circuit, the Supreme Court ruled in favor of the prison officials:

> A prisoner has no reasonable expectation of privacy in his prison cell entitling him to the protection of the Fourth Amendment against unreasonable searches. While prisoners enjoy many protections of the Constitution that are not fundamentally inconsistent with imprisonment itself or incompatible with the objectives of incarceration, imprisonment carries with it the circumscription or loss of many rights as being necessary to accommodate the institutional needs and objectives of prison facilities, particularly internal security and safety. It would be impossible to accomplish the prison objectives of preventing the introduction of weapons, drugs, and other contraband into the premises if inmates retained a right of privacy in their cells.[7]

Certain factors, however, can counterbalance the institutional needs of security, order, and rehabilitation and can make the search or seizure unreasonable and therefore unconstitutional. Clearly established prisoner rights, such as the right to possess legal and religious material, can clash with the state's right to search and seize prisoner property. For example, in *Bonner v. Coughlin*,[8] a prisoner was awarded damages for the seizure by prison guards of his copy of his trial transcript. Also, in *O'Connor v. Keller*,[9] a prisoner was awarded punitive damages from a prison official who made an unreasonable seizure of personal property from the prisoner's cell. In such cases, it is not an inherent right to be free from searches and seizures that allows recovery but the constitutional protection that surrounds and flows from the property seized.

§ 3.3 Strip Searches and Body Cavity Searches

In *Hodges v. Klein*,[10] the court held that a prison policy that requires prisoners to submit to anal searches not only upon leaving or entering the institution but following contact visits with other prisoners or friends and relatives as well is constitutional. The state's interest in the prevention of contraband transmission into and within the prison is very strong, and private contact with an individual from outside the prison presents an excellent opportunity for the introduction of all types of contraband into the prison community. Prison officials must be able to completely shut off this port of entry for contraband. To do so, an anal examination, degrading though it is, as part of a strip search, is not, in view of the state's compelling interest, an unreasonable requirement. However, the court held that mandatory anal searches were not permissible as applied to prisoners who are entering or leaving solitary confinement. There is no compelling state interest that can justify anal examinations prior to or following a segregated prisoner's transfer within the segregation area or anywhere in the prison while under escort or observation. The court believed that metal detectors provide the necessary security.[11]

In *Bell v. Wolfish*,[12] the Supreme Court approved both body cavity searches and living quarters searches (among other constitutional issues). Inmates at the Metropolitan Correctional Center (MCC) in New York City filed a class action lawsuit claiming that multiple conditions of confinement and practices at MCC were unconstitutional. Among these were the practice of body cavity searches of inmates following contact visits with persons from outside the facility and the requirement that inmates remain outside their rooms during routine cell searches. The Court held:

> Simply because prison inmates retain certain constitutional rights does not mean that these rights are not subject to restrictions and limitations. . . . [T]he room search rule does not violated the Fourth Amendment, but simply facilitates the safe and effective performance of the searches, and thus does not render the searches 'unreasonable' within the meaning of that Amendment. . . . [T]he body cavity searches do not violated [the Fourth] Amendment. Balancing the significant and legitimate security interests of the institution against the inmates' privacy interests, such searches can be conducted on less than probable cause and are not unreasonable.[13]

There are still some situations, however, in which strip searches may be considered unreasonable. For example, in 2020, the Seventh Circuit heard a case regarding mass strip searches at a female prison in Illinois.[14] Prison officials held a random cadet training exercise that simulated a mass shakedown, where guards search inmates' living areas and perform strip searches to find contraband. There was no emergency or security concern that prompted the shakedown; the exercise was held solely to train the cadets. Inmates were strip searched in groups of four to ten. After removing their clothing, the inmates were forced to "raise their breasts, lift their hair, bend over, spread their buttocks and vaginas, and cough several times."[15] Two hundred current and former inmates of the prison filed a class action suit against prison officials claiming the mass strip search violated their Fourth Amendment rights. The Seventh Circuit agreed, holding that the Fourth Amendment protects a right to bodily privacy for convicted prisoners, albeit in a significantly limited way, including during visual bodily inspections. The training exercise was not a "significant and legitimate security interest"[16] to warrant the intrusion of the inmates' bodily privacy interests.

§ 3.4   Cross-Sex Searches

Though the Supreme Court has not ruled on the topic, several appellate court cases discuss the problems associated with cross-sex searches. One case also raised the religious issue in cross-gender searches.[17] In support of their claim that the searches violated their First Amendment rights, two female prisoners testified that their religion prohibited them from being touched by men who are not their husbands. The inmates also argued that the cross-sex searches were unreasonable and violated the Fourth Amendment. It was recognized that requiring female employees to perform all searches would have an adverse effect on the institution and that a single-sex search policy created a number of labor problems and conflicted with the requirements of the collective bargaining agreement. Further, requiring female employees to perform all searches made the "pat" searches more predictable and less effective for controlling the movement of contraband through the facility. Under the facts, it was determined that pulling female employees off their posts to perform searches in other areas of the prison would create additional security problems in terms of leaving that post vacant and also by creating delays in moving prisoners through the facility.

The Ninth Circuit in *Grummett v. Rushen*[18] rejected a constitutional challenge to a prison policy that permitted female guards to perform pat-down searches on clothed male prisoners and occasionally view naked prisoners. Although the searches included the groin area, they were done briefly and while the prisoners were fully clothed. There was no intimate contact with the prisoners' bodies.

In another case, *Canedy v. Boardman*,[19] two female correctional officers strip-searched a prisoner during a shakedown of his housing unit. Ten male officers were nearby while the two female officers conducted the search. It was also alleged that female officers regularly observed male prisoners in a variety of settings typically considered private, including while they dressed, showered, defecated, and slept in various states of undress. The Seventh Circuit first stated that the right to privacy is firmly ensconced among the individual liberties protected by the Constitution and one of the clearest forms of degradation in western society is to strip a person of his or her clothes. The right to be free from strip searches and degrading body inspections is basic to the concept of privacy. At the same time, prisons must be allowed to utilize female correctional officers to the fullest extent possible. But that does not mean that prisoners are without constitutional protection against invasion of their privacy by members of the opposite sex.[20] The Court recognized the right of one sex not to be discriminated against in job opportunities within the prison because of gender but concluded that prisoners do have some right to avoid unwanted intrusions by persons of the opposite sex. Where it is reasonable, taking account of a state's interests in prison security and in providing equal employment opportunity for female officers—to respect a prisoner's constitutional privacy interests, doing so is not just a palliative to be doled out at the state's indulgence. It is a constitutional mandate.[21]

Canedy was distinguished in *Johnson v. Phelan*,[22] in which female officers at the Cook County Jail were assigned to monitor male prisoners' movements and could see men naked in their cells, the shower, and the toilet. The Seventh Circuit stated that there are two justifications for cross-sex searches and monitoring. First, it makes good use of the staff, because it is more expensive for a prison to have a group of officers dedicated to shower and toilet monitoring than to have all officers serving in each role in the prison. If female officers cannot perform this task, the prison must have more officers on hand to cover for them. It is a form of featherbedding. Similarly, an interest in efficient deployment of the staff supports cross-sex monitoring.[23]

Second, cross-sex monitoring reduces the need for prisons to make sex a criterion of employment and therefore reduces the potential for conflict with Title VII of the Equal Employment Opportunity Act and the Fourteenth Amendment's Equal Protection Clause. Cells and showers are designed so that guards can see in in order to prevent violence and other offenses. Prisoners dress, undress, and bathe under watchful eyes. Guards roaming the corridors are bound to see naked prisoners. A prison could comply with the rule that Johnson proposed and still maintain surveillance only by relegating women to the administrative wing, limiting their duties, or eliminating them from the staff, none of which are appropriate or constitutionally permissible.

§ 3.5   Searching Jail Inmates and Pretrial Detainees

Pretrial detainees constitute a special category of prisoners. It generally has been held that pretrial detainees are entitled to the same rights as free citizens except to the extent necessary to assure their appearance at trial and the security of the institution.[24] Although a pretrial detainee may be subject to some of the same restrictions as convicted prisoners, the restrictions are not unconstitutional unless they amount to punishment.[25]

In *Illinois v. Lafayette*,[26] the Supreme Court addressed whether police can perform a warrantless search of an arrestee's bag while he or she is being booked. The Court ruled that an arrestee's personal bag may be "inventoried" without violating the Fourth Amendment. It is reasonable for police to search the personal effects of a person under lawful arrest as part of the routine administrative procedure at a police station incident to the booking and jailing of persons arrested. It is entirely proper for police to remove and list or inventory property found on the person or in the possession of an arrested person who is to be jailed.

Reasons justifying the search are considerations of orderly police administration, protection of a suspect's property, deterrence of false claims of theft against the police, security, and identification of the suspect. The fact that the bag could have been secured otherwise does not make the search unreasonable. Even if some less intrusive means existed, it would be unreasonable to expect police officers in the everyday course of business to make subtle distinctions in deciding which containers or items may be searched and which must be sealed without examination. As a caution, the Court stresses that it is important as to whether the suspect was to be incarcerated or released after being booked. If the suspect was to be released, there is arguably no reason to inventory his or her property.[27]

Cases have been filed in numerous jurisdictions in which plaintiffs challenged a policy or custom of conducting strip searches of pre-arraignment jail detainees without grounds for reasonable suspicion.[28] For example, in a 2003 First Circuit Court of Appeals case,[29] the court ruled that a department cannot constitutionally conduct strip and visual body cavity searches of pre-arraignment detainees that are not based upon reasonable suspicion that a particular detainee is concealing weapons or contraband. The court additionally held that strip and visual body cavity searches of arrestees for minor offenses without reasonable suspicion that the arrestees carried weapons or contraband was unconstitutional.

Another court ruled that an Indiana county jail's policy of subjecting arrestees to an "observed clothing exchange procedure" during which a female arrestee was required to remove her street clothing down to her underwear and change into a jail-issued uniform under the observation of a female jail officer did not violate the Fourth Amendment.[30] Further, forcing a pretrial detainee to stand naked for 20 minutes as part of a random drug-testing policy was permissible.[31]

In 2012, the Supreme Court stepped in to address the disparities in lower courts' rulings regarding the issue of strip searching jail detainees. In *Florence v. Board of Chosen Freeholders of the County of Burlington*,[32] Florence was arrested for failure to appear at a hearing to enforce a fine. Two separate New Jersey jails had blanket policies that all arriving detainees had to be searched for scars, tattoos, and contraband. This included the requirement that detainees remove their clothing while an officer looked in their ears, nose, mouth, hair, scalp, fingers, hands, armpits, and other body openings. Florence filed suit under 42 U.S.C. § 1983 alleging Fourth and Fourteenth Amendment violations in that persons arrested for minor offenses cannot be subjected to invasive searches unless officers have reason to suspect the offender is concealing weapons, drugs, or other contraband. On appeal, the Supreme Court ruled that correctional officials have a significant interest in conducting a thorough search as a standard part of the intake process to (1) screen for medical issues, (2) screen for evidence of gang affiliation such as scars, tattoos, or brands, and (3) detect the possession of weapons, drugs, and other contraband. As such, the policy requiring strip searches of all new detainees did not violate the Fourth Amendment ban on unreasonable searches. This applies to those arrested for minor offenses as well: "The seriousness of an offense is a poor predictor of who has contraband, and it would be difficult to determine whether individual detainees fall within the proposed exemption [for those charged with minor offenses]."[33]

§ 3.6 Searches of Visitors

Though prison visitors are not inmates, they are nonetheless subject to certain restrictions upon entering the facility. Most correctional facilities have clearly posted signage stating that all visitors—including employees—and their belongings are subject to search prior to entering the prison. These searches are conducted for essentially the same reason as inmate searches: to prevent contraband from entering and circulating throughout the facility. The unauthorized use of narcotics is a problem that plagues virtually every penal and detention center in the country,[34] and a detention facility is a unique place, fraught with serious security dangers. The smuggling of money, drugs, weapons, and other contraband is an all too common occurrence.

Courts have ruled that prison visitation may be conditioned on the willingness of the visitors to submit to reasonable searches of their property and person. Visiting pursuant to reasonable regulations would trigger the "consent exception" to the Fourth Amendment's search warrant requirement. However, without an adequate basis to believe that contraband is being smuggled into the facility, no forcible search may be made. The sanction would be to immediately terminate visiting rights, subject to appropriate due process hearings.

Strip searches raise different issues.[35] Strip searches of prison visitors are considered unreasonable when based solely on anonymous tips that were not investigated to confirm their validity. To justify a strip search of a visitor, prison officials must point to specific objective facts and rational inferences drawn from those facts, which indicate that the visitor will attempt to smuggle contraband into the prison on his or her person. Individualized suspicion is essential.[36]

Several decisions of the Sixth Circuit Court of Appeals concerned such searches. In *Long v. Norris*,[37] it was held that a Tennessee prison regulation created a constitutionally protected liberty interest in visitation. Thus, an official's threats to remove visitation rights in retaliation for visitors' refusal to submit to strip and body cavity searches in the absence of probable cause was contrary to the prison regulation. The relevant provisions of the Tennessee prison regulation stated that prisoners "shall" have visitation rights, that visits "shall be limited only by the institution's space and personnel resources," and that visitation rights may not be suspended absent a showing of good cause.

In another case, a woman wanted to visit a Kentucky prisoner, but the prison staff refused to allow her to visit unless she submitted to a strip and body cavity search. They also refused to allow her to leave without a similar search. The Sixth Circuit[38] recognized the search to be "an embarrassing and humiliating experience." However, the court held that the Fourth Amendment does not afford a person seeking to enter a penal institution the same rights that a person would have on public streets or in a home. A citizen simply does not have the right to unfettered visitation of a prisoner that rises to a constitutional dimension. In seeking entry to such a controlled environment, a visitor simultaneously acknowledges a lesser expectation of privacy.[39]

The Sixth Circuit recognized that prison authorities have greater leeway in conducting searches of visitors, such as a pat-down or a metal detector sweep, merely as a condition of visitation, absent any suspicion. However, because a strip and body cavity search is the most intrusive type of search, courts have attempted to balance the need for institutional security against the remaining privacy interests of visitors. Even for strip and body cavity searches, prison authorities need not secure a warrant or have probable cause. However, the residual privacy interests of visitors in being free from such an invasive search requires prison authorities to have at least reasonable suspicion that the visitor is carrying contraband before conducting such a search.

In the First Circuit,[40] a woman sued prison authorities because of a strip search to which she was subjected before being permitted to visit her father. She had been a regular visitor since she was very young. She had never violated a prison visitation rule or presented any threat to institutional security. Prior to a visit, the woman was informed that she would not be allowed to visit her father that day, or ever again, until she submitted to a strip search. She was presented with a form containing a consent to search, which she signed. Two female correctional officers then led her into a bathroom, where she was told to remove her clothing. A correctional officer checked her hair and her ears. She was instructed to squat, hold her head to her chest and cough, while two female correction officers stood behind her. No contraband was discovered and the appellant was permitted to visit her father. The woman was emotionally shaken by the experience. The First Circuit recognized that a prison visitor retains the Fourth Amendment right to be free from unreasonable searches and seizures. It was also recognized that a strip search, by its very nature, constitutes an extreme intrusion upon personal privacy, as well as an offense to the dignity of the individual.[41] The court also rejected the argument that the daughter's signing of the consent form rendered moot any question as to whether there was a reasonable basis for the strip search. A prison visitor confronted with the choice between submitting to a strip search or foregoing a visit cannot provide a legally cognizable consent.[42]

In a state case, *Gadson v. Maryland*,[43] the question presented was the constitutional right of a state to detain a prospective visitor long enough to conduct a canine "sniff" inspection of the visitor's motor vehicle after the visitor, upon being told of the procedure, objected and expressed a desire to leave without entering the prison. While it is proper to require the visitor to submit to such a detention as a condition of entry, the court held that absent some reasonable, articulable suspicion of criminal activity, it was unreasonable under the Fourth Amendment to detain visitors who, prior to entering the prison, indicated a preference to leave rather than submit to the detention.

Similarly, courts have ruled that correctional facilities can conduct random, suspicionless searches of visitors' vehicles to combat the entry of contraband into the facility. For example, in *Neumeyer v. Beard*,[44] the Third Circuit addressed the plaintiffs' claim that the practice of subjecting prison visitors' vehicles to random searches violated the Fourth Amendment. The court based their ruling on the "special needs" exception to the Fourth Amendment's warrant requirement,[45] which states that there are instances when a search furthers a "special governmental need" beyond that of normal law enforcement such that the search, although not supported by the typical quantum of individualized suspicion, can nonetheless still be found constitutionally reasonable. Relying on this doctrine, the *Neumeyer* court held that prison officials' need to maintain security and safety makes the relatively minor inconvenience of the vehicle searches valid.[46]

In a 2020 Ninth Circuit case,[47] Cates went to visit her boyfriend who was incarcerated in a Nevada prison. Prison officials believed that she intended to smuggle drugs into the facility, so a female officer took the Cates into a bathroom and instructed her to disrobe and remove her tampon. Believing she had no choice, Cates complied, and the officer performed a visual body cavity search. Another officer searched Cates's car. Though no contraband was found in either search, Cates was not allowed to visit her boyfriend, and her visiting privileges at the prison were terminated. Cates filed a 42 U.S.C. § 1983 suit against prison officials claiming that the strip search violated her Fourth Amendment rights. The federal district court granted summary judgment for the prison officials, but on appeal the Ninth Circuit reversed in part. The court held that "a strip search of a visitor is permissible only if it can be justified by a legitimate security concern. That justification does not exist when the visitor is not in a position to introduce contraband into the prison,"[48] as was the case here. As such, the court ruled that the search was a Fourth Amendment violation but also that the prison officials were protected by qualified immunity.

§ 3.7   Conclusion

The Fourth Amendment's prohibition against unreasonable searches and seizures is a hallmark of American society. But like many constitutional guarantees discussed throughout this book, Fourth Amendment protections are severely curtailed in correctional facilities as a means of maintaining safety and security and confiscating contraband. Inmates do not have a reasonable expectation of privacy in their cells, and thus prison officials can conduct suspicionless searches of these areas. The Supreme Court has also approved strip and body cavity searches in many situations, such as after contact visits. Most of these search-related practices apply to jail inmates and pretrial detainees as well.

Notes

1 U.S. CONST., amend. IV.
2 *See*, e.g., Carroll v. U.S., 267 U.S. 132 (1925); California v. Greenwood, 486 U.S. 35 (1988); City of Ontario v. Quon, 560 U.S. 746 (2010).
3 *See*, e.g., U.S v. Katz, 389 U.S. 347 (1968); Terry v. Ohio, 392 U.S. 1 (1968); Wyoming v. Houghton, 526 U.S. 295 (1999).
4 642 F.2d 1115 (8th Cir. 1981); Clifton v. Robinson, 500 F. Supp. 30 (E.D. Pa. 1980); Becket v. Powers, 494 F. Supp. 364 (W.D. Wis. 1980); Brown v. Hilton, 492 F. Supp. 771 (D.N.J. 1980); State v. Pietraszewski, 283 N.W.2d 887 (Minn. 1979); Butler v. Bensinger, 377 F. Supp. 870 (N.D. Ill. 1974).
5 468 U.S. 517 (1984).
6 *See* Chapter 15.
7 Hudson v. Palmer, 468 U.S. 517, 518 (1984).

8   517 F.2d 1311 (7th Cir. 1975).
9   510 F. Supp. 1359 (D. Md. 1981); Steinburg v. Taylor, 500 F. Supp. 477 (D. Conn. 1980); Digiuseppe v. Ward, 514 F. Supp. 503 (S.D.N.Y. 1981); cf. Roque v. Warden, Conn. Corrections, 434 A.2d 348 (Conn. 1980).
10 412 F. Supp. 896 (D.N.J. 1976); see also United States v. Lilly, 599 F.2d 619 (5th Cir. 1979); Coleman v. Hutto, 500 F. Supp. 586 (E.D. Va. 1980); Vera v. State, 29 Cr. L. 2409 (Fla. Dist. Ct. App. 1981); Williams v. State, 400 So. 2d 988 (Fla. Dist. Ct. App. 1981); but cf. Sims v. Brierton, 500 F. Supp. 813 (N.D. Ill. 1980); Arruda v. Berman, 522 F. Supp. 766 (D. Mass. 1981) (Repeated rectal cavity searches accompanied by abusive and insulting comments and beatings stated a cause of action under the Civil Rights Act).
11 Cf. Lee v. Downs, 641 F.2d 1117 (4th Cir. 1981) (Where a female prisoner was possibly suicidal, it was proper for correctional officers to forcibly remove her clothes in the presence of male officers).
12 441 U.S. 520 (1979).
13 Bell v. Wolfish, 441 U.S. 520, 522 (1979).
14 Henry v. Hulett, 969 F. 3d 769 (2020).
15 Id. at 775.
16 Bell v. Wolfish, 441 U.S. 520 (1979).
17 Jordan v. Gardner, 953 F.2d 1137 (9th Cir. 1992); see also Chapter 2.
18 779 F.2d 491 (9th Cir. 1985).
19 Canedy v. Boardman, 16 F.3d 183 (7th Cir. 1994).
20 See Forts v. Ward, 471 F. Supp. 1095 (S.D.N.Y. 1979), vacated in part, 621 F.2d 1210 (2d Cir. 1980), in which the court ordered that adjustments be made either in scheduling or in the physical structure of the facilities to protect the women prisoners from male surveillance while they were dressing or undressing, showering, using the toilet facilities, or sleeping in the housing units.
21 Canedy, at 17.
22 69 F.3d 144 (7th Cir. 1995).
23 See Timm v. Gunter, 917 F.2d 1093 (8th Cir. 1990), which concluded that opposite sex surveillance of male prisoners, performed on the same basis as same sex surveillance, is constitutionally permissible.
24 Bell v. Wolfish, 441 U.S. 520 (1979); Rhem v. Malcolm, 396 F. Supp. 1195 (S.D.N.Y.), aff'd, 527 F.2d 1041 (2d Cir. 1975).
25 Occhino v. United States, 686 F.2d 1302 (8th Cir. 1982).
26 462 U.S. 640 (1983).
27 Illinois v. Lafayette, 462 U.S. 640 (1983).
28 Tardiff v. Knox County, 2004 U.S. App. 6951 (1st Cir. 2004); Blihovde v. St. Croix County, 219 F.R.D. 607 (W.D. Wis. 2003); Bynum v. District of Columbia, 217 F.R.D. 27 (D. D.C. 2003); Dodge v. County of Orange, 209 F.R.D. 65 (S.D.N.Y. 2002).
29 Savard v. Rhode Island, 320 F3d 34 (1st Cir. 2003), op withdrawn and on reh'g, en banc, substituted op, by split decision, 338 F.3d 23 (1st Cir. 2003).
30 Stanley v. Henson, 337 F.3d 961 (7th Cir. 2003).
31 Whitman v. Nesic, 368 F.3d 931 (7th Cir. 2004).
32 566 U.S. 318 (2012).
33 Florence, 556 U.S. at 320.
34 Block v. Rutherford, 468 U.S. 576 (1984).
35 Cf. Bell v. Wolfish, 441 U.S. 520 (1979).
36 Hunter v. Auger, 672 F.2d 668 (8th Cir. 1982).
37 929 F.2d 1111 (6th Cir.), cert. denied, 502 U.S. 863 (1991).
38 Spear v. Sowders, 71 F.3d 626 (6th Cir. 1995).
39 Blackburn v. Snow, 771 F.2d 556, 565 (1st Cir. 1985).
40 Cochrane v. Quattrocchi, 949 F.2d 11 (1st Cir. 1991).
41 See Burns v. Loranger, 907 F.2d 233 (1st Cir. 1990); Arruda v. Fair, 710 F.2d 886 (1st Cir. 1983); Hunter v. Auger, 672 F.2d 668, 674 (8th Cir. 1982).

42 Blackburn v. Snow, 771 F.2d 556, 563 (1st Cir. 1985). Pretermitting the question of whether a visitor possessed a constitutional right or merely a privilege to visit the prison, *Blackburn* concluded that conditioning (access to the Jail upon sacrifice of [the visitor's] right to be free of an otherwise unreasonable strip search)" was "dispositive of the consent issue." *Id.* at 568. *Blackburn* rejected the argument that the visitor's right to leave rather than submit to search, or to decline to return after the first strip search, in any way affected the issue; "for it is the very choice to which she was put that is constitutionally intolerable."

43 341 Md. 1 (Md. Ct. App. 1995).

44 421 F.3d 210 (3d Cir. 2005).

45 *See* Vernonia School District 47J v. Acton, 515 U.S. 646 (1995); Michigan Department of State Police v. Sitz, 496 U.S. 444 (1990).

46 Neumeyer v. Beard, 421 F.3d 210 (3d Cir. 2005).

47 Cates v. Stroud, 976 F. 3d 972 (9th Cir. 2020).

48 *Id.* at 980.

Rights to Visitation and Association

4

Chapter Outline

§ 4.1 Introduction

Humans are by nature social beings. Our biology drives us to associate with other humans. We naturally gravitate towards others, especially family members and social groups. For most people, frequent association with our loved ones is as common as breathing. This need for human interaction and contact is no different for prison and jail inmates; it does not disappear when the prison doors are closed behind those entering the facility.

This chapter focuses on inmates' rights to visitation and association under the First Amendment. We first discuss the case law regarding whether visitation is a liberty interest under the Due Process Clause. The remainder of the chapter concentrates on some specific types of associations, such as communications among inmates at different institutions, conjugal visits, media interviews, and meetings with attorneys.

§ 4.2 Visitation as a Liberty Interest

Traditionally, the right of prisoners to have visitors while incarcerated has been strictly limited by prison officials. Many states permit a prisoner to see only those persons who have been approved by the prison administrators. Cases concerning prisoners' rights to have visitors generally hold that controlling this activity is within the prison officials' discretion and that such control is not subject to judicial intervention unless a clear abuse of discretion is shown.[1] Further, any restrictions imposed by prison visitation policies must merely be reasonably related to a legitimate government interest.[2]

Although visitation privileges are considered matters within the scope of internal prison administration, this fact does not permit discriminatory application of visiting regulations.[3] For example, refusal to permit visitation privileges because the visitor and prisoner are of different races constitutes racial discrimination under the Fourteenth Amendment.[4]

Visiting regulations that set forth procedures under which visitors "may" be refused admittance or have visitation privileges suspended do not give state prisoners a liberty interest in receiving visitors that is entitled to the protection of the Due Process Clause. In order to create a protected liberty interest in the prison context, state regulations must use "explicitly mandatory language" in connection with the establishment of "specific substantive predicates" to limit official discretion and thereby require that a particular outcome be reached upon a finding that the relevant criteria have been met.[5]

Although regulations provide certain "substantive predicates" to guide prison decision makers in determining whether to allow visitation, regulations have no protected federal constitutional interest unless they are worded in such a way that a prisoner could reasonably form an objective expectation that a visit would necessarily be allowed, absent the occurrence of one of the listed conditions, or could reasonably expect to enforce the regulations against prison officials should that visit not be allowed.[6]

The question has been raised as to whether the right to visitation may be restricted for disciplinary reasons. In *Agron v. Montanye*,[7] prisoners challenged the practice of barring visits from family and friends to prisoners who refused to shave. The court granted a preliminary injunction because there was a New York policy not to bar visitation to prisoners as punishment. The court, citing *Pell v. Procunier*,[8] drew attention to the constitutional dimensions of a prisoner's right to visitation with reference to rights of association as well as the interests of family members who need and want to visit with the prisoner. Because most courts defer to the authority of prison officials, it is doubtful that the case would have been decided similarly, absent the preexisting state policy.

§ 4.2.1   — *Overton v. Bazzetta*

In 2001, Michigan prisoners and prospective prison visitors challenged regulations that restricted prison visitation rights. The visits at issue were "contact visits," which customarily take place in a "visitation room" or other area set aside for this purpose and permit "innocent-only" physical contact between prisoner and visitor. Noncontact visits, on the other hand, take place in small booths or cubicles, and no physical contact is permitted.

Prisoners were graded on the basis of their dangerous propensities. The grades were numbered I through VI. The most dangerous prisoners were placed in either grade V or grade VI. With rare exceptions, contact visits were not permitted in either of these two grades. This restriction was not at issue. The issue for decision was whether the no-contact rule could be applied broadly to all classification grades.

Michigan officials attempted to accommodate, to some extent, the visitation desires of prisoners in the lower grades, but security problems developed. The liberal visitation policy opened institutions to drugs, weapons, and other contraband. Visitors could easily conceal contraband and pass it to a prisoner. Aside from these security considerations, there were also additional expenses associated with the allowance of contact visitation. As a result of these concerns, contact visits were prohibited.

A Michigan district court upheld the revised prison regulations. The court reasoned that the benefits of the blanket prohibition outweighed the costs (financial and otherwise) of any alternative method. Otherwise, jail personnel who were free from the complicated, expensive, and time-consuming processes of interviewing, searching, and processing visitors would have to be reassigned to perform these tasks. The hiring of additional personnel would be required. Intrusive strip searches after contact visits would be necessary. Finally, as the district court noted, at the very least, "modest" improvements of existing facilities would be required to accommodate a contact visitation program if the prison authorities did not purchase or build a new facility elsewhere. The Sixth Circuit Court of Appeals affirmed the district court's decision.[9]

In reaching these conclusions, the Sixth Circuit also approved an Administrative Code promulgated by the Michigan Department of Corrections. Briefly summarized, the Code provided that a visitor younger than 18 had to be a prisoner's child, stepchild, or grandchild and had to be accompanied by an immediate family member or legal guardian. Prisoners could not visit with their natural children if their parental rights had been terminated. Prisoners could have only ten nonfamily individuals on their approved visitors list. Members of the general public could be on only one prisoner's visitation list. A former prisoner could visit a current prisoner only if the former prisoner was an immediate family member or a person with special qualifications such as a lawyer, clergy member, or government representative.

In upholding the regulations, the Sixth Circuit cited numerous decisions of the Supreme Court that stressed that problems of prison administration were best resolved by prison authorities and that their resolution should be accorded deference by the courts. Moreover, when a federal court reviews the constitutionality of a state penal system, federal courts should, wherever possible, defer to the appropriate prison authorities. The important word, one that appears specifically or by implication in all the pertinent Supreme Court opinions, is *deference*.

The court further held that when prison regulations were reasonably related to and supportive of legitimate penological interests, there should be no federal intervention. The decision followed the well established principle that there is no inherent, absolute constitutional right to contact visits with prisoners. The restrictions in this case did not constitute cruel and unusual punishment under the Eighth Amendment, because the rules applied only to contact visits. Moreover, to the extent that they could be construed as "punishments," they were punishments that were imposed upon every prisoner at the time of sentencing. They were the "rules of the game," pursuant to which the Michigan penal system operated.[10]

In 2003, Michigan's new noncontact visitation regulations reached the Supreme Court in *Overton v. Bazzetta*.[11] Prisoners and their potential visitors sued state correctional officials, alleging that the state prison regulations restricting noncontact prison visitation violated their constitutional rights. The regulations restricted noncontact visits with prisoners. With the exception of qualified members of the clergy and attorneys on official business, all visitors were required to be on an approved visitors list. The list could include an unlimited number of members of the prisoner's immediate family and ten other individuals the prisoner designated, subject to some restrictions. Minors under the age of 18 could not be placed on the list unless they were children, stepchildren, grandchildren, or siblings of the prisoner. A child authorized to visit had to be accompanied by an adult who was an immediate family member of the child or of the prisoner or who was the legal guardian of the child. If the prisoner's parental rights were terminated, the child could not be listed as a visitor. A prisoner could not place a former prisoner on the list unless the former prisoner was a member of the prisoner's immediate family and the warden gave prior approval. Finally, prisoners who committed multiple substance-abuse violations were not permitted to receive any visitors except attorneys and members of the clergy. A prisoner subject to this restriction could apply for reinstatement of visitation privileges after two years, subject to the warden's discretion.

The regulations were in response to prison security problems caused by an increasing number of visitors to Michigan's prisons and substance abuse among prisoners. *Overton v. Bazzetta* held that the regulations bore a rational relation to legitimate penological interests. This was enough to sustain them regardless of whether the prisoners and their potential visitors had a constitutional right of association that has survived incarceration. *Overton* gave substantial deference to the professional judgment of prison administrators, who bore a significant responsibility for defining the correctional system's legitimate goals and determining the most appropriate means to accomplish them. The regulations satisfied each of the four factors used to decide whether a prison regulation affecting a constitutional right that survives incarceration withstands constitutional challenge under *Turner v. Safley*.[12]

First, the regulations must bear a rational relationship to a legitimate penological interest. In *Overton*, the restrictions on children's visitation were related to the prison's valid interests in maintaining internal security and protecting child visitors from exposure to sexual or other misconduct or from accidental injury. They promoted internal security, arguably the most legitimate penological goal, by reducing the total number of visitors and by limiting disruption caused by children. Under *Overton*, it is also reasonable to ensure that the visiting child is accompanied and supervised by adults charged with protecting the child's best interests. Prohibiting visitation by former prisoners bears a self-evident connection to the state's interest in maintaining prison security and preventing future crime. Restricting visitation for prisoners with two substance abuse violations serves the legitimate goal of deterring drug and alcohol use within prison.

Second, prisoners have alternative means of exercising their asserted right of association with those prohibited from visiting. They could send messages through those who are permitted to visit and could communicate by letter and telephone. Visitation alternatives do not have to be ideal, only available. Third, accommodating the right to association would have a considerable impact on correctional officers, other prisoners, the allocation of prison resources, and the safety of visitors by causing a significant reallocation of the prison system's financial resources and by impairing correctional officers' ability to protect all those inside the prison's walls. Finally, the prisoners asserted no alternatives that could fully accommodate the asserted right while not imposing more than a minimal cost to valid penological goals.

Although *Overton v. Bazzetta* did not specifically address whether prison regulations suspending certain prisoners' visitation privileges violated the Fourteenth Amendment's procedural due process guarantee, the Sixth Circuit later held that no due process claim can survive in light of the ruling in *Overton*.[13]

The next year, in 2004, the Tenth Circuit reviewed visiting restrictions placed on a sex offender who refused to participate in a treatment program requiring the admission of guilt. This prevented the prisoner from visiting with his child under a prison policy that prohibited inmates from visiting their children if they fail to comply with the sex offender treatment program. Relying heavily on the Supreme Court's recent *Overton* decision, the Tenth Circuit held that this policy did not violate the prisoner's First Amendment right of intimate association, nor did it constitute compelled self-incrimination in violation of the Fifth Amendment.[14]

§ 4.2.2 — *Block v. Rutherford*

There have been a number of cases that have dealt with the particular rights of visitation for pretrial detainees. One such case is *Rhem v. Malcolm*,[15] in which pretrial detainees demanded a minimum number of visitors per visit (three), as well as a minimum number and length of visits per week (two hours daily). The court reasoned that the detainees did not have a constitutional right to receive a minimum number of visitors at any one time. Another is *Jordan v. Wolke*,[16] in which the Seventh Circuit Court of Appeals ruled that if jail officials' blanket refusal to allow contact visits for pretrial detainees is not intended as punishment, is rationally related to the goal of maintaining order and security in the jail, and is not excessive in relation to that goal, it does not constitute "punishment" forbidden by the Fourteenth Amendment Due Process Clause. Further, under a standard of reasonableness, the number of visitors allowed at any one time was a function of the capacity of the facility. The court also ruled that pretrial detainees had no constitutional right to any minimum number and length of visits.

The Supreme Court addressed the issue a few years later in *Block v. Rutherford*.[17] In 1979, pretrial detainees being held in the Los Angeles County Central Jail filed a class action suit against the county sheriff and other officials challenging a number of conditions and practices at the jail. Among the challenges was the jail's policy of denying pretrial detainees contact visits with their spouses, relatives, children, and friends. The district court ruled in favor of the inmates and ordered that low risk detainees incarcerated for more than a month must be allowed contact visits. On appeal, the Ninth Circuit Court of Appeals affirmed the district court's ruling.[18]

The Supreme Court granted certiorari in *Block v. Rutherford*.[19] The Court first reiterated its view that, when considering whether a specific policy or practice is reasonably related to security interests, courts should play a limited role since such policies and practices are within the professional expertise of correctional officials.[20]

Regarding the jail's policy of not allowing contact visits for pretrial detainees, the Court ruled that the "blanket prohibition on contact visits is an entirely reasonable, nonpunitive response to legitimate security concerns, consistent with the Fourteenth Amendment."[21] Contact visitation allows the introduction of drugs, weapons, and other contraband into the facility. "Totally disallowing contact visits is not excessive in relation to the security and other interests at stake."

§ 4.3   Communication Among Prisoners and Union Formation

In *Brooks v. Wainwright*,[22] a federal district court in Florida dismissed a prisoner's complaint that he was deprived of his First Amendment freedoms and his right to equal protection when his custody classification was changed after he had attempted to organize a prisoners' union. The court believed that the opposition by prison officials to the formation of this union was not a deprivation of the prisoner's constitutional rights. The court stated:

> Prisons are not motels or resorts where prisoners can check in or out at their liberty. Neither is a prison a public forum providing open access to citizens to freely express their beliefs. The full range of constitutional freedoms that ordinary members of society enjoy must be curtailed in order to achieve the legitimate purposes of imprisonment. So long as the restrictions and limitations are not patently unreasonable, the discretionary decisions of prison officials will be given deference by the courts.[23]

The court found that the prison officials' argument (that organizing a prisoners' union carried with it inherent dangers and threats to the security of the prison) was reasonable.

Two California courts, however, did not go so far in some respects. They held that, while prisoners have no constitutional right to participate in a prisoners' union meeting,[24] their right to freedom of speech was unlawfully restricted by prison officials' denial of permission for the prisoners to wear prisoner union lapel buttons.[25]

The Supreme Court addressed the issue of inmate unions in *Jones v. North Carolina Prisoners' Union*.[26] The prison administration permitted inmates to join the union, which had a stated goal of "the promotion of charitable labor union purposes."[27] At issue here were the prison rules forbidding (1) members from soliciting other prisoners to join the organization, (2) union meetings, and (3) bulk mailings concerning the union from outside sources. The district court saw little sense and even less legality in this rule and held that because union membership was already permitted, solicitation for membership was also to be permitted. In addition, the district court held that union members had the right to hold meetings like all other inmate organizations.

The Supreme Court, however, reversed on all issues. The Court ruled that the prohibition on union members soliciting other inmates does not unduly abridge inmates' right to free speech and that such a prohibition is both reasonable and necessary. In addition, the Court held that prohibiting bulk mailing and meeting rights does not violate the Equal Protection Clause: "The prison does not constitute a 'public forum,' and [prison officials] demonstrated a rational basis for distinguishing between the Union (which occupied an adversary role and espoused a purpose illegal under North Carolina law) and the service organizations (which performed rehabilitation services)."[28]

§ 4.4   Conjugal Visitation

Many foreign countries and several states have provided facilities in their penal institutions for conjugal visits, that is, visits by a prisoner's spouse with an opportunity for intimate sexual relations.[29] The Supreme Court has not ruled on any cases regarding conjugal visitation. However, the Circuit Courts of Appeals have long held that prisoners do not retain the right to contact visits.[30] For example, a D.C. Circuit case, *Payne v. District of Columbia*,[31] held that such visits are not constitutionally required. The holding in *Payne* was reinforced in the Fifth Circuit case *Tarlton v. Clark*,[32] in which the court said that a prisoner's claim to a right to conjugal visitation "would not come up to the level of a federal constitutional right so as to be cognizable as a basis for relief in the federal court."[33] The cases of *Polakoff v. Henderson*[34] and *Lyons v. Gilligan*[35] indicate the continuing refusal of the federal courts to recognize conjugal visitation as a constitutional right of prisoners. *Polakoff* declared that the denial of conjugal visitation did not constitute cruel and unusual punishment prohibited by the Eighth Amendment. In *Lyons*, the court denied the prisoner's assertion that failure to provide conjugal visits violated a married couple's right to privacy. Even assuming that such a right of privacy could be implied from the Supreme Court's decision in *Griswold v. Connecticut*[36] to apply to a prison setting, the Court explained: "The rub of *Griswold* was restraint on governmental intrusion. It cannot be extended to impose an affirmative duty on the government."[37]

Even within those states that do allow conjugal visitation, state prison regulations authorizing conjugal visits create no enforceable rights. In *Champion v. Artuz*,[38] a prisoner's conjugal visits were revoked after prison guards found that the wife, herself an ex-offender, was carrying various items that they viewed as potential instrumentalities for escape, including a wig, a camouflage handkerchief, and a man's identification card. The Second Circuit held that the state regulations permitting correctional facilities to allow conjugal visits to prisoners did not give the prisoner a liberty interest in such visits that would rise to constitutional protection.

The same federal appellate court that decided *Tarlton* indicated the firmness of its position in a subsequent case, *McCray v. Sullivan*,[39] when it said: "Failure to permit conjugal visits does not deny a prisoner a federal constitutional right."[40] However, the visiting rights of a wife cannot be summarily suspended after she and her prisoner husband were caught together in an unauthorized area of the prison during visiting hours.[41]

§ 4.5   News Media Interviews

In *Seattle-Tacoma Newspaper Guild v. Parker*,[42] a federal appellate court held that a regulation of the Federal Bureau of Prisons that completely denied press interviews with individual prisoners did not violate the prisoners' First Amendment freedom of speech. The regulation was also seen as not unduly restricting the flow of information to the public through the news media. Recognizing that the Director of the Bureau of Prisons and the warden at the federal prison must be given wide discretion in formulating rules to govern prison life, the court observed that there were sufficient alternative means of communication that would ensure that "any real complaint about the treatment of the prisoner or the administration of the prison"[43] would not go unrectified. The court also noted that the challenged regulation would not affect a prisoner's right to confer freely with his or her counsel, to conduct unlimited confidential correspondence, to visit with relatives and friends, to counsel with the clergy of his or her faith, and to have free access to the courts. In view of the damaging consequences of a policy permitting press–prisoner interviews, such as increased disciplinary problems and the creation of "big wheel" status for certain prisoners, who often become less subject to constructive rehabilitation, the court said it was convinced that any burden imposed on the media's ability to report caused by the interview ban was more than justified.[44]

The companion cases of *Pell v. Procunier*[45] and *Saxbe v. Washington Post Company*[46] presented the United States Supreme Court with the question of the constitutionality of the same federal regulation at issue in *Seattle-Tacoma*, along with a similar provision from the California Department of Corrections Manual. In *Pell*, the court answered the claim of four prisoners and three professional journalists that the state prison regulation violated their First Amendment freedom of speech by declaring that neither the prisoners nor the press had a freedom of speech right to specific personal interviews. Alternative channels of communication were seen to be open to prisoners and would be protected by the court's ruling in *Procunier v. Martinez*,[47] which established standards for the review of prisoner correspondence by prison officials.[48] So long as the restriction on interviews operated in a neutral fashion, without regard to the content of expression, it was seen as falling within the appropriate rules and regulations to which prisoners are necessarily subject.[49] As to members of the press, the Court said that because such interviews were not available to members of the general public, they need not be made available to the media on a privileged basis.

In *Saxbe*, the challenge to the federal prison regulation prohibiting personal interviews by the news media and individually designated prisoners was made only by news media representatives. Referring to its decision in *Pell*, the Court declared that the regulation did not violate any First Amendment guarantees because it "does not deny the press access to sources of information available to members of the general public" but is merely a particularized application of the general rule that nobody may enter the prison and designate a prisoner whom he would like to visit, unless the prospective visitor is a lawyer, clergy, relative, or friend of that prisoner.[50]

In *Main Road v. Aytch*,[51] a federal district court and a federal appellate court applied the holdings of *Pell* and *Saxbe* in a suit brought by pretrial detainees of the Philadelphia prison system. Inmates of the Philadelphia prisons had, on two separate occasions, sought permission from the superintendent to hold press conferences in which they desired to express to the public their concern about problems encountered by them in dealings with a public defenders' association that represented many of the inmates in their criminal cases and to allege improprieties in probation procedures. Both requests were denied, although the district court found that the superintendent had authorized other large gatherings of prisoners and outsiders, particularly other group press conferences.[52] The decisions in *Pell* and *Saxbe* were announced while *Main Road* was under consideration by the district court, and although the evidence presented indicated that permission to hold the press conferences had been denied on the basis of their expected content, contrary to the neutral approach mandated by *Pell*, the trial judge denied injunctive or declaratory relief on the ground that he believed such censorship was unlikely to recur.[53]

On appeal, the appellate court also observed that the ban had not been applied in a neutral fashion without regard to the content of the expression and declared that the criteria the superintendent applied in determining whether to permit a news conference provided too much occasion for subjective evaluation, thus enabling him to act as a censor.[54] Whether subjects were "explosive" or "sensitive" were said to be standards lacking the constitutionally indispensable "narrowly drawn limitations" on administrative discretion, which therefore ran afoul of the tests of valid prison regulations prescribed in *Procunier v. Martinez*.[55] The case was remanded, and the district court was directed to determine whether the superintendent intended to continue to grant some but not all prisoner requests for interviews and press conferences. If such were the case, the superintendent was to develop proposed regulations governing the issuance of such permission, which delineated precise and objective tests, on the basis of which permission may be denied. Additionally, the district court was directed to implement a review process that would assure a fair determination of the facts upon which a prison administrator denied permission to hold a news conference.[56]

The case of *Houchins v. KQED*[57] dealt further with the issue of the standards followed by prison authorities in denying media access to prisons and prisoners. A sheriff refused to allow the anchors of an educational radio-television station to inspect the grounds of a county jail after a program by the station reported the suicide of a prisoner there, together with certain allegations made by a staff psychiatrist as to jail conditions. The exclusion was justified as a matter of "policy," but subsequently a limited program of monthly public tours of the facility was implemented. The federal district court read *Pell* as standing for the proposition that a prison or jail administrator may curtail media access upon a showing of past resultant disruption or present institutional tension but found that the sheriff had not made such a showing in this case.[58] The inadequacy of the policy in question was more apparent in view of the fact that officials at two neighboring facilities testified that media interviews of prisoners had proved neither unduly disruptive nor dangerous to prison security. A preliminary injunction was issued prohibiting the sheriff from excluding, as a matter of general policy, responsible representatives of the news media from the jail facilities.

The decision was appealed to the United States Supreme Court. The Court reversed the lower court's decision and held that the news media has no constitutional right of access to a county jail, over and above that of other persons, to interview prisoners and make sound recordings, films, and photographs for publication and broadcasting by newspapers, radio, and television. There is no requirement that prison officials provide the press with information. The Supreme Court saw the issue as involving the question of whether the news media has a constitutional right of access to a county jail, over and above that of other persons, to interview prisoners and gather other information. It held that the degree of openness of a penal institution is a question of policy that a legislature, and not a court, must resolve.[59]

§ 4.6   Attorney Representatives

It is impermissible for prison officials to arbitrarily limit a prisoner's right to an attorney's assistance in crafting appeals of conviction or protesting prison conditions. But what about legal paraprofessionals, investigators, or law students working for an attorney or legal clinic? Does the prisoner have a constitutional right to meet with these people?

In *Souza v. Travisono*,[60] a court recognized that a corollary to the right of access to the courts was the right of access to reasonably available, competent legal assistance. The warden's arbitrary decision to exclude a student legal assistant was held unconstitutional. Although prison officials may not arbitrarily limit access to nonattorney legal assistance, they may place reasonable regulations on such visits. The time, place, and manner of visits may be regulated to further the governmental interests of security, order, or rehabilitation.[61]

The Court of Appeals affirmed the district court ruling but refused to decide whether prisoners must be given reasonable access to law students for the resolution of such issues as divorce, bankruptcy, or probate. The Supreme Court addressed this issue—among many others—in *Procunier v. Martinez*.[62] The California Department of Corrections had a policy prohibiting the use of law students and paralegals to conduct attorney–client interviews with inmates. The federal district court ruled that these policies were unconstitutional under the First and Fourteenth Amendments. On appeal, the Supreme Court affirmed. The Court held: "The ban against attorney–client interviews conducted by law students or legal paraprofessionals . . . constituted an unjustifiable restriction on the inmates' right of access to the courts."[63]

§ 4.7   Conclusion

Though the freedom of association is guaranteed by the First Amendment, courts have placed some limitations on this right as it applies to prison inmates. Most correctional institutions have policies that outline who can visit inmates, as well as the conditions of visitations. Due to prison officials' valid interests in maintaining safety and security within the facility, courts have allowed certain restrictions on visitation, including conjugal visits and media visits and interviews.

Notes

1 Walker v. Pate, 356 F.2d 502 (7th Cir. 1966), *cert. denied*, 384 U.S. 966 (1966).
2 James v. Wallace, 406 F. Supp. 318 (M.D. Ala. 1976).
3 Underwood v. Loving, 391 F. Supp. 1214 (W.D. Va. 1975) was reversed in part on appeal with no published opinion. Underwood v. Loving, 538 F.2d 325 (4th Cir. 1976).
4 Martin v. Wainwright, 525 F.2d 983 (5th Cir. 1976).
5 Kentucky v. Thompson, 490 U.S. 454 (1989). Due to the 1995 decision of the Supreme Court in *Sandin v. Conner*, state regulations may not necessarily create constitutionally protected liberty interests.
6 *Id.*
7 392 F. Supp. 454 (W.D.N.Y. 1975).
8 417 U.S. 817 (1974).
9 Bazzetta v. McGinnis, 124 F.3d 774 (6th Cir. 1997).
10 Subsequent to the *Bazzetta* decision, the Michigan Department of Corrections applied the opinion to noncontact visitations. The Sixth Circuit then issued a Supplementary Opinion solely for the purpose of clarification. The opinion emphasized that the Court's earlier decision only concerned limitations on contact visitation and did not apply to noncontact visitation. Bazzetta v. McGinnis, 133 F.3d 382 (6th Cir. 1998).
11 539 U.S. 126 (2003).
12 482 U.S. 78 (1987); *see* Chapter 5 and Chapter 6.
13 Bazzetta v. McGinnis, 430 F.3d 795 (6th Cir. 2005).

14 Wirsching v. Colorado, 360 F.3d 1191 (10th Cir. 2004).

15 396 F. Supp. 1195 (S.D.N.Y.), *aff'd*, 527 F.2d 1041 (2d Cir. 1975).

16 615 F.2d 749 (7th Cir. 1980); In re Smith, 169 Cal. Rptr. 564 (Cal. App. 1980) (a jail policy that prohibited the visitation of minor children with their incarcerated parents was a denial of the incarcerated parents' rights); Valentine v. Englehardt, 492 F. Supp. 1039 (D.N.J. 1980).

17 468 U.S. 576 (1984).

18 Rutherford v. Pitchess, 710 F. 2d 572 (9th Cir. 1983).

19 468 U.S. 576 (1984).

20 *See* Bell v. Wolfish, 441 U.S. 520 (1979).

21 Block v. Rutherford, 468 U.S. 576 (1984).

22 439 F. Supp. 1335 (M.D. Fla. 1977).

23 *Id.* at 1340.

24 In re Price, 158 Cal. Rptr. 873, 600 P. 2d 1330 (Cal. 1979).

25 In re Reynolds, 157 Cal. Rptr. 892 (Cal. 1979).

26 433 U.S. 119 (1977).

27 *Id.* at 122.

28 *Id.* at 120.

29 *See* NORMAN ELLIOT KENT, *The Legal and Sociological Dimensions of Conjugal Visitations in Prisons*, 2 NEW ENG. J. ON PRISON L. 47 (1975).

30 *See* Toussaint v. McCarthy, 801 F.2d 1080 (9th Cir. 1986), *cert. denied*, 481 U.S. 1069 (1987) (prisoners have no right to contact visits); Hernandez v. Coughlin, 18 F.3d 133 (2d Cir. 1994) (prisoners have no right to conjugal visits because "rights of marital privacy . . . are necessarily and substantially abridged in the prison setting"); Bellamy v. Bradley, 729 F.2d 416, 420 (6th Cir. 1984), *cert. denied*, 469 U.S. 845 (1984) ("prisoners have no absolute constitutional right to visitation"); Ramos v. Lamm, 639 F.2d 559, 580 n. 26 (10th Cir. 1980), *cert. denied*, 450 U.S. 1041 (1981) ("weight of present authority clearly establishes that there is no constitutional right to contact visitation . . . we agree with this view"); Lynott v. Henderson, 610 F.2d 340, 342 (5th Cir. 1980) ("convicted prisoners have no absolute constitutional right to visitation"); Peterkin v. Jeffes, 661 F. Supp. 895, 913–914 (E.D. Pa. 1987) (the weight of authority concludes that a ban on contact visits for convicted persons does not run afoul of the Eighth Amendment"), *modified*, 855 F.2d 1021 (3d Cir. 1988). Cf., Block v. Rutherford, 468 U.S. 576 (1984) ("That there is a valid rational connection between a ban on contact visits and internal security of a detention facility is too obvious to warrant discussion").

31 253 F.2d 867 (D.C. Cir. 1958).

32 441 F.2d 384 (5th Cir.), *cert. denied*, 403 U.S. 934 (1971).

33 Id. at 385.

34 370 F. Supp. 690 (N.D. Ga. 1973), *aff'd*, 488 F.2d 977 (5th Cir. 1974).

35 382 F. Supp. 198 (N.D. Ohio 1974). *See also* Hernandez v. Coughlin, 18, F.3d 133, 137 (2d Cir. 1994).

36 381 U.S. 479 (1965) (a Connecticut statute forbidding use of contraceptives violates the right of marital privacy).

37 Lyons v. Gilligan, 382 F. Supp. 198, 200 (N.D. Ohio 1974).

38 76 F.3d 483 (2d Cir. 1996).

39 509 F.2d 1332 (5th Cir.), *cert. denied*, 423 U.S. 859 (1975).

40 *Id.* at 1334.

41 McKinnis v. Mosley, 693 F.2d 1054 (11th Cir. 1982).

42 480 F.2d 1062 (9th Cir. 1973).

43 *Id.* at 1066.

44 *Id.* at 1067.

45 417 U.S. 817 (1974).

46 417 U.S. 843 (1974).

47 416 U.S. 396 (1974).

48   Pell v. Procunier, 417 U.S. 817, 824 (1974).

49   *Id.* at 828.

50   Saxbe v. Washington Post Co., 417 U.S. 843, 849 (1974).

51   385 F. Supp. 105 (E.D. Pa. 1974), *vacated and remanded*, 522 F.2d 1080 (3d Cir. 1975).

52   *Id.* at 1084.

53   *Id.* at 1090.

54   *Id.* at 1089.

55   *Id.* at 1090.

56   *Id.*

57   438 U.S. 1 (1978).

58   *Id.*

59   *Id.* at 12.

60   368 F. Supp. 459 (D.R.I. 1973), *aff'd*, 498 F.2d 1120 (1st Cir. 1974); *see also* Dreher v. Sielaff, 636 F.2d 1141 (7th Cir. 1980); United States v. Blue Thunder, 604 F.2d 550 (8th Cir. 1979).

61   *See* Shakur v. Malcolm, 525 F.2d 1144 (2d Cir. 1975); Reed v. Evans, 455 F. Supp. 1339 (S.D. Ga. 1978), *aff'd*, 592 F.2d 1189 (5th Cir. 1979).

62   416 U.S. 396 (1974).

63   *Id.* at 397.

Rights to Use of Mail, Internet, and Telephone   5

Chapter Outline

§ 5.1 Introduction

Detention in a penal institution necessitates a limitation on full enjoyment of constitutional rights. But exactly which rights are completely terminated and which are retained is usually unclear. Even rights not forfeited by incarceration are often retained in a diminished form. These general statements are illustrated by an analysis of the prisoner's specific right to use the telephone, Internet, and the mail system to send and receive various items such as letters, legal materials, books, and magazines.

Article I, § 8 of the Constitution vests power in Congress to establish post offices. This power has been interpreted by the Supreme Court as granting to Congress and the U.S. Postal Service the exclusive right to regulate the postal system of the country.[1] That a prisoner has at least a qualified federal right to use the mail system would thus seem clear. However, a long line of cases has established the principle that prison officials may place reasonable restrictions on this right.[2] Restrictions include limiting the number of persons with whom a prisoner can correspond, opening and reading incoming and outgoing material, deleting sections from both incoming and outgoing mail, and refusing to mail material for a prisoner or to forward correspondence to a prisoner subject to important exceptions discussed here. For purposes of this chapter, the phrase "mail censorship" will be used to denote deletion of material from prisoner mail.

Two general reasons have been advanced by both prison administrators and the judiciary to justify placing restrictions on a prisoner's right to use the mail system. First, prison security requires such restrictions. Contraband must be kept out of the prisons. Escape plans must be detected. Material that might incite the prison population must be excluded. The second rationale for mail restrictions—that the orderly administration of a prison requires them—is closely related to the first. Correctional systems do not have unlimited funds that can be used to hire employees to enforce the restrictions placed on sending and receiving mail. However, because prison security may reasonably demand that prisoner mail be opened, inspected for contraband, read, and some sections deleted, some limit on the amount of mail to be checked must be established. Thus, prison officials have justified rules limiting the quantity of mail that an individual can send and receive.

A third reason—rehabilitation of prisoners—is sometimes used to justify mail restrictions. Thus, although the requirements of security and administration may justify limiting the amount of mail each prisoner may send or receive, neither requirement will justify the establishment of a mail list whereby a prisoner can send or receive mail only from sources approved by the prison authorities. However, the goal of rehabilitation has been advanced by penal administrators to justify such action.[3]

§ 5.2   The General Right to Control a Prisoner's Use of the Mail System — The Traditional Approach

This section, together with the following sections, will discuss the general right of prison authorities to regulate prisoner mail, as well as several of the specific procedures they use to accomplish this regulation.

As a starting point, it may be stated that a myriad of previous cases have established and maintained the proposition that control of prisoner mail is an administrative matter in which the courts will not interfere, unless it is shown that an independent constitutional right is being infringed.[4] This may be called, for lack of a better phrase, the "traditional view" of the courts on prisoner mail regulation. The reason most often advanced to support the traditional view is that courts will not become involved in the normal management of a prison system.

In retrospect, we can see that in cases in which the courts did interfere with prison mail rules, another constitutional right was involved. Thus, communication between a prisoner and a court involved the right of access to the court system. Communication between a prisoner and his or her attorney involved both the right of access to courts and the Sixth Amendment's guarantee of counsel for inmates. The First Amendment right to petition the government for redress of grievances justified court intervention in correspondence to and from nonjudicial public officials and agencies. The cherished American freedoms of speech and press were involved in regulations concerning access to news media. These rights also were involved in attempts by prison officials to exclude newspapers, magazines, and books from an institution.

If, however, a prisoner could not couple his or her complaint of undue restriction on use of the mail with an allegation that a separate constitutional right was thereby infringed, he or she was, under the "traditional view," doomed to failure in the courts. Thus, in *Dayton v. McGranery*,[5] a prisoner's allegation that he was prevented from writing to a young woman was dismissed because he did not state a cause of action. *Stroud v. Swope*[6] affirmed the dismissal of a prisoner's complaint that sought to restrain a federal prison warden from refusing to mail the prisoner's manuscript to a publisher. Such allegations, the court held, did not constitute a deprivation of any of the petitioner's rights. Several federal appellate courts also refused to inquire into the reasons for not allowing a prisoner to take a correspondence course. Such decisions are "simply an exercise of administrative discretion."[7]

§ 5.3   The New Approach

Reading and inspection of prisoner mail serves two purposes: (1) It prevents contraband from being smuggled into or out of an institution, and (2) it enables the prison authorities to detect plans for illegal activity—namely escape. Thus, such action, at least for incoming mail, has uniformly been upheld by the courts.[8] However, the administrators' refusal to mail correspondence that does not contain contraband or details of illegal schemes has been subject to judicial criticism. Under the traditional view, described in the preceding section, such a refusal is normally considered unreviewable. Under what we call the "new approach," prison officials are judicially required to justify such actions. Thus, in *McNamara v. Moody*,[9] prison officials were held to have violated a prisoner's constitutional rights by refusing to mail a letter to the prisoner's girlfriend. The court held that censorship must be limited to concrete violations such as escape plans, plans for disruption of the prison system or work routine, or plans for importing contraband.[10]

§ 5.3.1   —*Procunier v. Martinez, Turner v. Safley,* and *Thornburgh v. Abbott*

The new approach to regulation of prisoner mail is best illustrated by contrasting *Procunier v. Martinez*[11] with *Turner v. Safley*[12] and *Thornburgh v. Abbott*.[13] In *Procunier*, prisoners filed suit attacking the validity of a California prison mail regulation that authorized prison officials to refuse to send prisoner mail and to refuse to distribute mail to prisoners. The Supreme Court held the regulation void due to vagueness and overbreadth. In doing so, the Court recognized that the First Amendment rights of the "free world" correspondent were at issue. Guidelines for regulating prison mail were established.

According to the Court's ruling in *Procunier*, censorship of prison mail is justified if the following criteria are met. First, the regulation must further a substantial governmental interest that is unrelated to the suppression of expression. Prison officials may not censor prisoner correspondence simply to eliminate unflattering or unwelcome opinions or factually inaccurate statements. Rather, they must show that the regulation authorizing censorship furthers one or more of the substantial government interests of security, order, and rehabilitation. Second, the limitation of First Amendment freedoms must be no greater than is necessary or incidental to the protection of the particular government interest involved.[14]

In addition to providing the criteria for censorship, *Procunier* enunciated the minimum procedure that must be followed when prison officials censor or withhold mail. The prisoner must be notified of the rejection of his or her letter, the letter's author must be allowed to protest the refusal, and the complaint must be decided by an official other than the one who made the original decision to refuse delivery.[15]

In 1987, a different standard was used in *Turner v. Safley*. The Supreme Court held that lower courts had been in error in holding that *Procunier* required the application of a strict scrutiny standard of review for resolving prisoners' constitutional complaints. Rather, a lesser standard is appropriate when an inquiry is made into whether a prison regulation that impinges on prisoners' constitutional rights is "reasonably related" to legitimate penological interests. In determining reasonableness, relevant factors include: (1) whether there is a "valid, rational connection" between the regulation and a legitimate and neutral governmental interest put forward to justify it, and the connection cannot be so remote as to render the regulation arbitrary or irrational; (2) whether there are alternative means of exercising the asserted constitutional rights that remain open to prisoners, and the alternatives, if they exist, will require a measure of judicial deference to the corrections officials' expertise; (3) whether and the extent to which accommodation of the asserted right will have an impact on prison staff, on prisoners' liberty, and on the allocation of limited prison resources, and whether the impact, if substantial, will require particular deference to corrections officials; and (4) whether the regulation represents an "exaggerated response" to prison concerns, the existence of a ready alternative that fully accommodates the prisoner's rights at minimal costs to valid penological interests being evidence of unreasonableness.[16]

Prisoner correspondence regulations that permitted correspondence between immediate family members who were prisoners at different institutions within a jurisdiction and between prisoners "concerning legal matters" but that allowed other prisoner correspondence only if each prisoner's classification was reasonable and factually valid, passed constitutional review.[17] The regulations were logically related to the legitimate security concerns of prison officials. It was thought that mail between prisons could be used to communicate escape plans, to arrange violent acts, and to foster prison gang activity. The regulation did not deprive prisoners of all means of expression but simply barred communication with a limited class of people—other prisoners—with whom authorities have particular cause to be concerned. The regulation was entitled to deference on the basis of the significant impact of prison correspondence on the liberty and safety of other prisoners and prison personnel. Such correspondence facilitates the development of informal organizations that threaten safety and security at penal institutions. Nor was there an obvious, easy alternative to the regulation, because monitoring prisoner correspondence imposed more than a minimal cost in terms of the burden on staff resources required to conduct item-by-item censorship. It also created an appreciable risk of missing dangerous communications. The regulation was content-neutral and did not unconstitutionally abridge the First Amendment rights of prison prisoners.

Two years later, in *Thornburgh v. Abbott*,[18] the Supreme Court reviewed Federal Bureau of Prisons regulations that generally permitted prisoners to receive publications from the "outside" but authorized wardens, pursuant to specified criteria, to reject an incoming publication if it is found "to be detrimental to the security, good order, or discipline of the institution or if it might facilitate criminal activity." Wardens could not reject a publication solely because of its religious, philosophical, political, social, sexual, unpopular, or repugnant content, or establish an excluded list of publications, but were required to review each issue of a subscription separately.

The Court held that mail regulations that affect sending publications to prisoners must be analyzed under the standard set forth in *Turner v. Safley* and are valid if they are reasonably related to legitimate penological interests. Prison officials are due considerable deference in regulating the delicate balance between prison order and security and the legitimate demands of "outsiders" who seek to enter the prison environment. The less deferential standard of *Procunier*—whereby prison regulations authorizing mail censorship must be "generally necessary" to protect one or more legitimate government interests— was limited to regulations concerning outgoing personal correspondence from prisoners, i.e., regulations that are not centrally concerned with the maintenance of prison order and security. In addition, *Procunier* was overruled to the extent that it might support the drawing of a categorical distinction between incoming correspondence from prisoners (to which *Turner* applied its reasonableness standard) and incoming correspondence from nonprisoners.

The regulations under review were factually valid under the *Turner* standard. Their underlying objective of protecting prison security was legitimate and was neutral with regard to the content of the expression regulated. The broad discretion that the regulations accorded wardens was rationally related to security interests. Further, alternative means of expression remained open to the prisoners, because the regulations permitted a broad range of publications to be sent, received, and read, even though specific publications were prohibited. Finally, the prisoners established no alternative to the regulations that would accommodate their constitutional rights at a minimal cost to valid penological interests.

The "new approach" to prisoner mail advanced by *Procunier*, *Turner*, and *Thornburgh* did not eliminate mail censorship but only regulated it. When the screening of mail is done pursuant to regulations that are reasonably related to legitimate government interests, the prison official's right to read, inspect, and stop prisoner correspondence remains intact.

Mail issues are subject to the exhaustion requirement. In addition, a prisoner has a due process right to have the prison's decision to exclude incoming publications reviewed by a prison official other than the one who made the initial exclusion decision.[19]

§ 5.4   Communication with the Courts

It has been the law of the land since 1941 that a state and its officers may not abridge or impair a prisoner's right to apply to a federal court for a writ of habeas corpus.[20] In *Ex parte Hull*,[21] a prisoner was confined in the Michigan State Prison. He had prepared a petition for a writ of habeas corpus to be filed in the Supreme

Court, but a prison official refused to mail it, pursuant to a prison regulation requiring legal papers to go through the institutional welfare officer. The regulation provided that if the writ were favorably acted upon, it would be referred to the legal section of the parole board, and then if found to be properly drawn, it would be directed to the appropriate court. The Supreme Court held this regulation invalid, declaring that a state and its officers may not abridge or impair a prisoner's right to apply to a federal court for a writ of habeas corpus. Whether the writ is properly drawn is a question for the court to determine, not prison officials.

Since the decision in *Ex parte Hull*, federal courts have closely scrutinized any prison regulation that allows prison administrators to refuse to forward prisoner mail. For example, in *Bryan v. Werner*,[22] a federal court struck down a prison regulation that permitted officials to refuse to mail legal matters for prisoners if the officials thought the form used was improper.

Although there would seem to be no rational basis for distinguishing between legal material that pertains to the prisoner's conviction and legal material that involves other matters, at least one federal appellate court has sustained such a distinction. *Kirby v. Thomas*[23] involved a regulation of the Kentucky Department of Corrections that forbade the mailing of legal papers unless they pertained to the validity of the prisoner's conviction. The court stated only one reason for upholding the regulation: the state prison administrator's need for discretion in maintaining discipline. However, the vast majority of courts now recognize that a prisoner has the right to petition the courts concerning not only his or her conviction but also the constitutionality of the conditions of his or her confinement. Access to the courts is a fundamental right and "all other rights of a prisoner are illusory without it."[24]

Similarly, mail from a court to a prisoner is "legal mail" entitled to constitutional protection and may not be opened outside the presence of the prisoner if he has specifically requested that he be present at the opening of his legal mail. However, a prisoner's correspondence from a county clerk, a register of deeds, or the American Bar Association is not "legal mail."[25]

In *Smith v. Shimp*,[26] the Seventh Circuit stated that privileged mail, i.e., mail between a prisoner and attorneys, government officials, or news media personnel, can be opened only in the presence of the prisoner and only to verify the addressee. Emphasizing the prisoner's right of access to the courts, the Eighth Circuit held that legal mail that is identified as such cannot be opened for inspection for contraband except in the presence of the prisoner.[27]

The clear state of the case law is to allow incoming mail from the courts to be inspected for contraband, but with prohibitions against reading the correspondence.

§ 5.5   Communication with Attorneys

A basic corollary to the right of access to the courts is the prisoner's right to communicate with an attorney concerning the validity of his or her conviction or the constitutionality of conditions within the detention facility.[28] If the prisoner is not represented by counsel, he or she has the right to correspond with an attorney in an attempt to secure legal representation, and this communication may set forth factual elements of his or her claim, even though critical of the prison administration.[29] The right to seek legal representation extends not only to the right to communicate with individual members of the bar but also to the right to seek advice and possible representation from legal organizations such as the American Civil Liberties Union.[30]

However, the right to communicate with an attorney has been limited to communication involving legal matters. For example, in *Rhinehart v. Rhay*,[31] Washington state prison officials refused to mail several letters from an inmate to his attorney. The officials claimed, and the court agreed, that the purpose of the letters in question was to express the plaintiff's belief that homosexual acts among consenting prisoners ought to be legalized. There was no evidence that the plaintiff was denied access to his attorney for the purpose of perfecting an appeal of his conviction.

§ 5.5.1   —Censorship of Communication with Attorneys

The right of a prisoner to communicate with his or her attorney concerning pending or contemplated legal action is recognized by all courts today. Of more importance, however, is the authority of prison authorities to open, read, and censor such communications. Prisoners often complain that such conduct interferes with their right to counsel as guaranteed by the Sixth Amendment.

Generally, the cases concerning censorship of prisoner letters to their attorneys fall into three groups. In the first group are cases that recognize that the censoring of prisoner mail, including correspondence to attorneys, is a matter of internal prison administration with which the courts hesitate to interfere.[32] These cases hold that inspection of prisoner mail is necessary to detect contraband or to discover escape plans, and as long as the contents of the communications are not disclosed to the prosecuting attorney, and the prisoner is afforded ample time to confer privately with his or her attorney in the institution, there is no infringement on the prisoner's Sixth Amendment right to counsel.[33] An extreme application of this reasoning is found in *Cox v. Crouse*.[34] In that case, the prisoner was being tried on a criminal charge, and the warden systematically opened and read the prisoner's correspondence with his attorney and then communicated the contents to the state attorney general. The prisoner argued that prejudice could be presumed from such disclosure. The court rejected this claim, stating that the prisoner must show actual prejudice in order to be entitled to relief.

In the second group, *Sostre v. McGinnis*[35] represents a compromise between the position of no censorship of correspondence between a prisoner and an attorney and the position of treating such correspondence like any other type of mail and allowing it to be censored. In *Sostre*, the court held that officials could open and read such letters but could not delete anything from them or refuse to forward them unless the prisoner was clearly abusing the privilege. Two examples of clear abuse of the privilege, the court stated, would be mailing or receiving contraband and mailing plans for an illegal activity.

Smith v. Robbins,[36] another federal appellate decision, sought to give even more protection to prisoner–attorney correspondence than did *Sostre*. In *Smith*, the warden was enjoined from reading the correspondence, and he could open such material to inspect for contraband only in the presence of the prisoner involved.

The third group of cases represents the current view, which is a significant break with the past. These cases hold that prison officials are permitted to open attorney correspondence in the presence of the prisoner to check for contraband, but the contents may not be read. This procedure of checking for contraband neither constitutes censorship, nor does it have a chilling effect on the correspondence.[37] However, reasonable regulations of the correspondence are permitted. Such regulations may require that the attorney first identify himself or herself in a signed letter or that the prisoner supply prison officials with the name and business address of his or her attorney.[38]

In another case falling within the third group, the Arizona Department of Corrections had a policy wherein prison officials could quickly scan and inspect for contraband a prisoner's letter to his or her lawyer. An inmate claimed that on one occasion a guard actually *read* a letter to the inmate's lawyer, in violation of his First and Sixth Amendment rights. In a 2014 case, the Ninth Circuit agreed, holding that "*inspecting* letters and *reading* them are two different things. . . . [P]rison officials don't have the right to . . . read a confidential letter from an inmate to his lawyer."[39]

Prisoners who are serving sentences need the assistance of counsel to perfect appeals of their convictions and to initiate and litigate civil actions. Many prisoners of detention facilities, however, are not convicted of any crime but are being held pending trial on charges filed against them. The pretrial detainee's need for counsel is crucial. Therefore, it is not surprising that multiple cases recognize the right to uncensored correspondence between pretrial detainees and their legal counsel.

Prisoners have a constitutionally protected right to have their properly marked attorney mail opened in their presence. However, a prisoner does not have the requisite actual injury required to overcome the Prison Litigation Reform Act[40] when he makes only a conclusory allegation that the mail opening compromised his case and does not identify how any legal matters specifically were damaged.[41] A prisoner's legal materials purchased for him by a third party who had ties to another prisoner was intercepted. The prisoner's right to receive mail claim was properly dismissed where the prison officials asserted and substantiated a set of legitimate penological interests rationally related to the restriction under review; specifically, the penological purposes of the restriction were to prevent unauthorized bartering, extortion, and contraband smuggling inside the prison facilitated through the assistance or exploitation of third parties outside the prison. The prisoner had alternative means of exercising his right, and the burdens of accommodation indicated the absence of any obvious and easy alternative security measures.[42]

§ 5.6　Communication with Nonjudicial Public Officials and Agencies

One of the rights specified in the First Amendment is the right to petition the government for the redress of alleged grievances. This right is especially important to prisoners when they complain of conditions of confinement. Quite often, however, an administrative complaint to the department of government ultimately responsible for the management of the prison is both faster and more effective than seeking judicial review. Thus, the courts have generally protected the right of prisoners to utilize the mail system to communicate with nonjudicial public officials and agencies. *LeVier v. Woodson*[43] prevented state prison officials from stopping letters complaining of prison conditions to the state governor, attorney general, and the attorney working for the state's pardon agency.

Reading and censoring prisoner correspondence became more restricted after the *Procunier* and *Wolff* decisions. The rationale of these two cases was relied upon in *Taylor v. Sterrett*[44] and applied to prisoner correspondence with government agencies. Emphasizing the prisoner's First Amendment right to petition the government for redress of grievances and finding the reading of government agency correspondence not substantially related to jail security, the court enjoined prison officials from reading the correspondence. The decision, however, allowed prison officials to continue opening incoming mail to check for contraband.

Punishing a prisoner for communicating his or her complaints to higher administrative levels is as much a denial of the right to petition government as is the outright refusal to mail such letters. This principle is exemplified by *Cavey v. Williams*,[45] in which a warden was ordered to pay compensatory and punitive damages to the prisoner plaintiff because the warden violated the prisoner's First Amendment rights by punishing him for a letter he wrote criticizing prison policies.

The few cases that are cited in support of the proposition that prisoners do not have the right to use the mails to voice complaints to government officials are either devoid of legal reasoning or simply do not involve a petition seeking redress of prison grievances. For example, the prisoner in *McCloskey v. Maryland*[46] sought to enjoin state penal officials from refusing to mail letters from him to his elected state and federal legislators. However, the letters did not complain of conditions of confinement but were expressions of the prisoner's anti-Semitic views. In such a case, the court held, refusal to mail the letters was not an abuse of the prison officials' control over prisoners' mailing privileges. *McCloskey*, therefore, is not authority for the view that prison administrators may arbitrarily refuse to forward a letter from a prisoner to the state director of corrections, complaining of conditions within the prison, even though it has been cited as such.[47]

A case similar to *McCloskey* is *United States ex rel. Thompson v. Fay*,[48] in which a federal district court held that a state prisoner had no right to mail a letter, seeking legal advice, to a federal committee that was investigating the problems of indigent defendants accused of federal crimes. The committee was not rendering legal aid to indigents, and, furthermore, the prisoner had not been charged or convicted of a federal crime. Thus, not only did the correspondence fail to complain of conditions of confinement but was entirely frivolous.

In *Davidson v. Skully*,[49] prison rules for mailing nonprivileged matter required mailing a form to the addressee with whom the prisoner wanted to correspond. The form had to be mailed back by the addressee. The prisoner then requested permission to mail his "correspondence request" mail sealed. The rules did not permit the prisoner to state on the form his reasons for requesting permission to correspond. The rule was held to be irrational and unconstitutional as applied to three letters to public officials or agencies and one to the American Civil Liberties Union.

Since 2004, there has been a nationwide increase in the number of filings by prisoners of unsubstantiated liens and Uniform Commercial Code financing statements against state or federal officials involved with their incarceration designed to harass and intimidate government officials in the performance of their duties. The Michigan Director of Corrections established a policy that restricted the prisoners from obtaining access to such statements and declared the related materials to be "contraband" subject to seizure because prisoners could use those materials to facilitate criminal activity:

> Prisoners are prohibited from receiving mail that is a threat to the security, good order, or discipline of the facility, may facilitate or encourage criminal activity, or may interfere with the rehabilitation of the prisoner. The following pose such risks within a correctional facility under all circumstances and therefore shall be rejected. . . . Mail regarding actions that can be taken under the Uniform Commercial Code (UCC). This does not include legal materials which set forth the statute or provide a scholarly legal analysis of the UCC.

On appeal, the Sixth Circuit in *Caruso*[50] held that the policy was too broad and violated the prisoner's First Amendment rights, and it upheld an injunction that prevented enforcement of the policy.

In *Caruso*, the court held that the Michigan mail policy was a rational means by which to achieve the legitimate goal of preventing prisoners from engaging in fraudulent and illegal behavior. While the policy prevents prisoners from possessing books, pamphlets, forms, or other material regarding actions that can be taken under the UCC, prisoners were still permitted to possess publications in the law library, such as Michigan Compiled Laws Annotated, that set forth the statute or provide a scholarly legal analysis of the UCC. There was, therefore, a valid, rational connection between the policies at issue and a legitimate government interest.

Caruso analyzed the Michigan regulation under the *Turner* standards. The failure to satisfy the first factor—whether there is a valid, rational connection between the regulation and a legitimate governmental interest—renders a regulation unconstitutional without regard to the remaining three factors. If the first factor is satisfied, the remaining factors are considered and balanced together as "guidelines" by which the court can assess whether the challenged actions are reasonably related to a legitimate penological interest.

With respect to the third *Turner* factor, *Caruso* considered the impact that accommodation would have on guards and other inmates and on the allocation of prison resources generally. The officials' argument that an injunction against the policy would drain prison resources and distract prison staff from their responsibilities by requiring them to attend to inmates' fraudulent liens was rejected on the basis that there are reasonable alternatives at a minimal cost to the prison administration. Effective rules have been developed that allow prisoners to receive a broad range of UCC-related materials while still limiting fraudulent filings.

The Supreme Court has made it clear that prison inmates retain all First Amendment rights not incompatible with their status as prisoners or with the legitimate penological objectives of the corrections system.[51] The Court has recognized that receiving mail from an outside source, an interest in communication shared by prisoners and their correspondents, is such a First Amendment right.[52]

However, prisoners' First Amendment protection does not encompass "general communications" with public officials that do not implicate the right to petition for grievances and the right of access to the courts. A prisoner does not have the right to send communications to any public officials throughout the United States, making requests for general information and numerous federal and state statutory sections, chapters, codes, procedural rules, and court decisions.[53]

§ 5.7   Use of the Mail to Contact News Media

The First Amendment prohibits governmental interference with freedom of speech and freedom of the press. Although the judiciary has construed the amendment to allow reasonable restraints on these freedoms, it is still true that these rights occupy a preferred position in the American system of government. Thus, the courts generally require that any restriction on First Amendment rights be based upon a "substantial and controlling" state interest that requires such restriction[54] and that the restriction be the least drastic method of accomplishing the state goal.[55]

A prison ban on prisoners sending letters that complain of internal conditions in the institution to the news media—radio, television, and the press—restricts First Amendment freedoms in two ways. First, the prisoner's right to free speech is curtailed. Second, the public's right to know what is happening within the prison system, a right that can only be fulfilled through an informed press, is restricted.

Regardless of the degree of restriction on the actual flow of information between prisoner and reporter, however, prisoners would seem to have an interest in communication with the public through the press that is distinctive from and in addition to their interest in simply communicating with the news media.[56]

In *Nolan v. Fitzpatrick*,[57] prisoners contested the legality of a Massachusetts state prison regulation that totally banned letters from prisoners to the news media. The right of prison officials to read such letters and to inspect them for contraband or for escape plans was not challenged. The prison officials advanced various reasons in support of the rule: that such communications would inflame the prisoners and thus endanger prison security; that complaint letters would create administrative problems because they would encourage the news media to seek personal interviews with prisoners; and that complaint letters would inhibit the rehabilitation of both the writer and other prisoners. The district court found these reasons to be either unsupported by evidence or insufficient to require a total ban on letters to the press.

The rationale of *Procunier v. Martinez* and its applicability to all classes of prisoner correspondence becomes evident. Applying the *Procunier* rationale to prisoner contact with the media, a federal court invalidated prison regulations on the grounds that they "provide too much occasion for subjective evaluation, thus enabling the licensing official to act as a censor."[58] Similarly, in *Taylor v. Sterrett*,[59] the court recognized the prisoner's right to communicate with the press under *Procunier* guidelines:

> [T]he interest of jail security necessitates that incoming mail from the press be inspected for contraband. . . . And the distinctive ethical standards attorneys are held to cannot apply to the press. We cannot say, therefore, that the reading of outgoing prisoner correspondence to the press does not further a substantial governmental interest. Transmitting unread mail to supposed members of the press could be used as a subterfuge for discussing illegal activities.
>
> . . . Since the free expression and petition interests of the prisoner-plaintiffs are operative in this case, the practice of reading this mail must be essential to jail security.

The decision further stated that the prisoner–press correspondence should be treated under procedures similar to those applying to prisoner–attorney mail.[60]

§ 5.8 Communication with Prisoners in Other Institutions

The courts have generally given prison administrators unfettered discretion in refusing to allow one prisoner to correspond with another prisoner. The reason most often given to justify such action is that the control of prisoner mail is an administrative function in which the courts refuse to intervene. Thus, in *Schlobohm v. United States Attorney General*,[61] a federal district court held that a prison policy of prohibiting correspondence between prisoners of different institutions was permissible. The court stated that indefinite mail restriction imposed as a punishment was a legitimate exercise of disciplinary power when a prisoner had violated existing prison mail regulations.[62]

The Supreme Court case *Johnson v. Avery*[63] held that prison officials who fail to provide adequate legal assistance cannot forbid a jailhouse lawyer from rendering legal assistance to a fellow prisoner. The case left open the interesting question concerning correspondence between prisoners. Even though prison officials might have the general power to prevent such correspondence, would the *Johnson* rationale prevent the refusal to allow a prisoner to engage in legal correspondence with a prisoner in another institution? The Ninth Circuit Court of Appeals held that the complete prohibition of a prisoner's correspondence with his jailhouse lawyer in another institution was a violation of that prisoner's rights.[64]

In *Shaw v. Murphy*,[65] the Supreme Court held that prisoners do not possess a special First Amendment right to provide legal assistance to fellow prisoners that enhances the protections otherwise available under *Turner v. Safley*.[66] Prisoners' constitutional rights are more limited in scope than the constitutional rights held by individuals in society at large. The Supreme Court commented that some First Amendment rights are simply inconsistent with the correctional system's legitimate penological objectives. Moreover, because courts are ill equipped to deal with the complex and intractable problems of prisons, the Supreme Court has generally deferred to prison officials' judgment in upholding regulations against constitutional challenge. *Turner* reflects this understanding, setting a unitary, deferential standard for reviewing prisoners' claims that does not permit an increase in the constitutional protection whenever a prisoner's communication includes legal advice.

To increase the constitutional protection based upon a communication's content first requires an assessment of that content's value. But the *Turner* test simply does not accommodate valuations of content. On the contrary, it concerns only the relationship between the asserted penological interests and the prison regulation. Moreover, prison officials are to remain the primary arbiters of the problems that arise in prison management. Seeking to avoid unnecessary federal court involvement in prison administration affairs, the Supreme Court rejected an alteration of the *Turner* analysis that would involve additional federal court oversight.[67] Even if the Supreme Court were to consider giving special protection to particular kinds of speech based on content, it would not do so for speech that includes legal advice. Augmenting First Amendment protection for such advice would undermine prison officials' ability to address the complex and intractable problems of prison administration. The legal text could be an excuse for making clearly inappropriate comments, which may circulate among prisoners despite prison measures to screen individual prisoners or officers from the remarks.

§ 5.9　Receipt of Inflammatory Material

The Supreme Court has held that the First Amendment freedoms of speech and press encompass the "right to receive information and ideas."[68] These rights are not absolute, however, but are subject to two important qualifications: (1) Pornographic material is not protected by the First Amendment, and (2) the First Amendment does not protect activity that involves a clear and present danger of inciting or producing imminent lawless action.[69] This section will discuss the authority of prison administrators to exclude material, mainly magazines and books, from the institution because they constitute a clear and present danger of disrupting prison security.

Although the "clear and present danger" test did not originate in prison litigation, it applies as a general principle of law to that specific environment. In fact, due to the tense atmosphere that often exists in such institutions, prison officials may be able to exclude material using this test, even though such material is clearly protected by the First Amendment outside of the prison walls. The application of the clear and present danger test in a prison setting was explained in the case of *Sostre v. Otis*:

> We accept the premise that certain literature may pose such a clear and present danger to the security of a prison, or to the rehabilitation of prisoners, that it should be censored. To take an extreme example, if there were mailed to a prisoner a brochure demonstrating in detail how to saw prison bars with utensils used in the mess hall, or how to provoke a prison riot, it would properly be screened. A magazine detailing for incarcerated drug addicts how they might obtain an euphoric "high," comparable to that experienced from heroin, by sniffing aerosol or glue available for other purposes within the prison walls, would likewise be censorable as restraining effective rehabilitation. Furthermore, it is undoubtedly true that in the volatile atmosphere of a prison, where a large number of men, many with criminal tendencies, live in close proximity to each other, violence can be fomented by the printed word much more easily than in the outside world. Some censorship or prior restraint on inflammatory literature sent into prisons is, therefore, necessary to prevent such literature from being used to cause disruption or violence within the prison. It may well be that in some prisons where the prisoners' flash-point is low, articles regarding bombing, prison riots, or the like, which would be harmless when sold on the corner newsstand, would be too dangerous for release to the prison population.[70]

Even though all courts previously accepted the proposition that prison officials can exclude literature that presents a clear and present danger to prison security, the judiciary was often called upon to review the procedure that administrators use to make the determination that a certain book or newspaper is a clear and present danger to the institution's security. This aspect of judicial review is crucial; if the courts routinely sanction the officials' decision, with little or no analysis of the process and standards used to reach that decision, the First Amendment rights of the prisoners are likely to be lost. This loss can be illustrated by two cases decided by the federal courts. In the first case, *Abernathy v. Cunningham*,[71] the prisoner-plaintiff sought court permission to obtain a book titled *The Message to the Black Man in America* and to subscribe to the newspaper, *Elijah Muhammad Speaks*. Both publications pertained to the Black Muslim religion. The appellate court upheld the prison officials' refusal to comply with the requests, stating that the evaluation of the literature by the officials as to its probable effects on the prison population must be given great weight.

In the later case of *Battle v. Anderson*,[72] the court recognized that a prisoner retains some of his or her First Amendment rights even while incarcerated and that the prison officials had the burden of proving to the court that the publications *Elijah Muhammad Speaks* and *The Message to the Black Man in America* present a threat to security, discipline, and order within the institution.

Battle was written to conform to *Procunier* standards for protecting the prisoner's right to receive literature, delineating the restrictions and procedures under which mail may be censored. Accordingly, "censorship of these publications is permissible only if it furthers the prison's substantial interest in security, order, or rehabilitation, and no less restrictive means would suffice to protect the prison's interest."[73] Recognizing the significant contributions of *Procunier* to prison mail regulation, later decisions have refined the holding to fashion the law concerning inflammatory material.[74] Publications containing enlarged views of the inner mechanisms of guns may be withheld.[75]

§ 5.10 Receipt of Obscene Material

In 1957, the Supreme Court held that obscene literature is not within the domain of constitutionally protected freedoms of speech or press.[76] Therefore, obscene material can be regulated by both federal and state governments. Federal regulation is usually effected by prohibiting the mailing of obscene material. State regulation is accomplished by confiscating such material and by criminally punishing those who sell it. In a prison environment, however, pornography is controlled by refusing to forward such literature to the prisoner. Because pornographic material is not protected by the First Amendment, such refusal by prison administrators is not unconstitutional.[77] At least one case has stated that obscene material can also be excluded from a prison because of its tendency to incite homosexual activity, which in turn often leads to violence.[78]

Sexually explicit material may be kept from prisoners on the grounds that the material is detrimental to rehabilitation and leads to deviate sexual behavior by some prisoners.[79] Regulations excluding such material must not be overbroad so that "nudes," not designed primarily to arouse sexual desires, are unconstitutionally excluded.[80] However, the Court of Appeals for the District of Columbia held that a law banning sexually explicit materials in federal prisons violated the First Amendment.[81]

The problem in excluding pornography from the prisons is similar to the problem encountered in excluding allegedly inflammatory literature: Is the decision to exclude made under safeguards that protect the prisoners' rights to receive constitutionally protected material? If the decision to exclude literature as obscene is left to a prison censor, without meaningful administrative or judicial review, the prisoners' rights will often depend on highly subjective decisions. This is not necessarily the fault of the censor; although he or she may be judicially ordered to exclude only those "books or periodicals which would come clearly within the definition of pornography established by the decisions of the Supreme Court."[82] The definition of "pornographic" is nebulous at best.

The Supreme Court first sanctioned the following test in *Roth v. U.S.*:[83] material is obscene if "to the average person, applying contemporary community standards, the dominant theme of the material taken as a whole appeals to the prurient interest." Subsequent cases, however, led to various interpretations of this definition by different members of the Court. Two justices believed "community standards" meant varying local standards;[84] others felt it meant a uniform national standard.[85] Another justice found it impossible to define obscenity, but stated "I know it when I see it."[86]

In 1973, the Supreme Court decided *Miller v. California*[87] and held that contemporary community standards were not necessarily a national standard. However, no case has held, or could reasonably be expected to hold, that the "community" is the prison itself.

With this variety of definitions, a prison censor must be fully informed as to the current legal definition of pornography. Memoranda from the institution's legal advisor could accomplish this. One court, however, decided to relieve the censor of such worries by allowing him to use the *Roth* guidelines, without regard to post-*Roth* decisions.[88] In any event, minimum due process and opportunity to appeal the censor's decision would seem to be required.

§ 5.11   Receipt of Racially Oriented Newspapers and Magazines

The Fourteenth Amendment to the Constitution forbids the states to deny any person "equal protection of the laws"; that is, the state must treat all similarly situated persons in an identical manner. Black prisoners at several institutions have successfully used the Equal Protection Clause to contest the refusal of prison officials to allow them to subscribe to nonsubversive periodicals published primarily for blacks (for example, national magazines such as *Ebony* and *Sepia*). *Jackson v. Godwin*[89] is illustrative of such cases. Petitioner Jackson, a prisoner in the Florida State Prison, alleged that although one-half of the institution's population was black, nonsubversive newspapers and magazines written primarily for blacks were systematically kept off the approved list of periodicals, while numerous white-oriented publications were approved for receipt. The administrators claimed that the establishment of an approved periodicals list was a function of prison management that was not reviewable by the courts and that the literature in question would harm prison security.

The court held that a prisoner retains his or her Fourteenth Amendment right to equal protection even while he or she is incarcerated and that the exclusion of all black-oriented periodicals at a prison in which the receipt of many white-oriented publications is permitted violated the Equal Protection Clause. The penal officials were ordered to allow black inmates to subscribe to nonsubversive black newspapers and magazines.

The case of *Aikens v. Lash*,[90] relying on *Procunier* standards, held that prison officials must afford prisoners minimal due process when publications are prohibited. The "liberty interest" required the following form of review: (1) written notice to the prisoner of the denial and reason for denial of the publication, (2) opportunity to object to the denial, and (3) prompt review by a prison official other than the one who made the original denial to forward the publication.

In a Third Circuit case, magazines addressed to a prisoner were rejected as either being sexually explicit or featuring nudity. The court ruled that to uphold the policy, a factual record was necessary to determine the rationality of the policy's overall connection to rehabilitative interests. In addition, a district court is required to first identify the specific rehabilitative goals advanced by the government to justify the restriction and then give the parties the opportunity to offer evidence sufficient to enable a determination as to whether the connection between these goals and the restriction was rational.[91]

While incarcerated, a prisoner placed in the outgoing mail a letter addressed to a company that sold politically oriented products, including T-shirts, posters, and stickers. The prisoner's letter encouraged the company to develop a line of small posters targeted at prisoners who were prohibited by prison regulations from possessing stickers and large posters. Several designs were included as attachments. One was a drawing of a swastika textured with the image of cell bars. Above the swastika was the slogan "The Department of Corruptions," and below it was the slogan "Keeping Kids in Kages" written with enlarged, stylized capital Ks. The letter was not sent because it violated an administrative code,[92] which prohibited the swastika and the letters KKK. The fact that the regulation provided some latitude to prison officials in defining gang symbols did not render it void for vagueness.[93]

§ 5.12   Use of Mail Lists

One method commonly used by prison authorities to control correspondence between a prisoner and the outside world is the requirement that a prisoner send mail to and receive mail from only those persons approved by the prison authorities. Names can be added to and deleted from the mail list at any time. Administrators justify the use of mail lists on two grounds: (1) that the time-consuming task of reading and inspecting prisoner mail requires a limit on the number of persons with whom a prisoner can correspond and (2) that the rehabilitation of prisoners requires controls upon the people with whom a prisoner corresponds.

Generally, the few cases that have considered the legality of mail lists have held that the establishment and maintenance of such lists is a necessary aspect of prison administration that does not violate any federal right.[94] *Jones v. Wittenberg*[95] prohibited county jail officials from placing limitations on the persons to whom pretrial detainees could write. However, in another case involving pretrial detainees, a federal district court sanctioned the use of an approved addressee list of seven persons to whom a detainee could write.[96] Such a regulation, the court stated, "is a reasonable method of maintaining prison security without undue restriction on the First Amendment rights of prisoners."[97]

The use of mail lists has been closely scrutinized by the courts. Prison officials have been required to justify mail list regulations with evidence that such rules are "necessary to protect a substantial government interest unrelated to the suppression of expression and the limitations imposed were no greater than necessary to accomplish that objective."[98] Thus, *Finney v. Arkansas Board of Corrections* enjoined prison officials from enforcing a broad regulation concerning mail lists until the tests of *Procunier* had been met. Prohibiting prisoners from corresponding with minors to whom they were not related by blood or marriage, without the prior consent of the minor's parents, violates the First Amendment.[99]

In *Lindell v. O'Donnell*,[100] prison officials were enjoined from enforcing a rule that allowed prisoners to receive published materials only from a publisher or from a commercial source. However, the prison officials violated the plaintiff-prisoner's First Amendment rights by applying a "publishers only" rule to ban clippings of published articles or photocopies of such clippings.

§ 5.13   Receipt of Books and Packages from Outside Sources

The Supreme Court approved special institutional regulations regarding the receipt of books and packages in *Bell v. Wolfish*.[101] The Court recognized that prisons have a legitimate government purpose to provide security and order. This permits placing restrictions on a prisoner's receipt of books and packages. The institution's regulations prohibited the prisoners and pretrial detainees from receiving any books that did not come directly from a publisher. The Court held that the regulation was a rational response by officials to the contraband smuggling problem.[102]

Likewise, the Court upheld a regulation prohibiting the receipt of packages from the outside. The fact that packages are easily used for smuggling contraband justified the prohibition and served the government interest of maintaining institutional security and order. Therefore, under this decision, prisoners, including pretrial detainees, have no constitutional right to receive packages from outside sources. Institutions may restrict or completely prohibit the flow of incoming packages to prisoners because of their overriding interest in protecting the security and order of the institution.[103]

In *Parratt v. Taylor*,[104] mailed materials were lost when the normal procedure for receipt of mail packages was not followed. It was held that there was no deprivation of a right, privilege, or immunity secured by the Constitution or laws of the United States.

In *Morrison v. Hall*,[105] prison mail regulations prohibited prisoners from receiving bulk rate, third-, and fourth-class mail. This was unconstitutional as applied to for-profit, prepaid, subscription publications, where prison officials failed to demonstrate that banning the incoming mail based on postage rates was rationally related to legitimate government objectives. However, a rule requiring the complete return address was justified as necessary for facilitating investigations in prison.

According to the Ninth Circuit, a Washington state prison mail policy that prevents prisoners from receiving nonsubscription bulk mail and catalogs they have requested was not reasonably related to a legitimate penological interest and, thus, violates the First Amendment. Prisoners have a constitutionally protected right to receive subscription nonprofit and for-profit bulk mail.[106]

§ 5.14 Mail in Maximum-Security Prisons

A group of prisoners sued the Pennsylvania Department of Corrections, alleging that a prison regulation that prohibited prisoners housed in the most restrictive level of the state's long-term segregation unit from having access to newspapers, magazines, and personal photographs violated the First Amendment. The long-term segregation unit housed 40 prisoners guilty of assaults, possession of weapons or implements of escape, being a sexual predator, or other violent or disruptive behavior and were the most dangerous in the system. There was an internal progression in the unit, and eligible prisoners were given some access to newspapers and magazines. Justifications for the prison's policy included the need to motivate better behavior on the part of particularly difficult prisoners, the need to minimize the amount of property they control in their cells, and the need to assure prison safety by diminishing the amount of material a prisoner might use to start a cell fire. The regulation was upheld by the Supreme Court in *Beard v. Banks*[107] as necessary to motivate better behavior on the part of particularly difficult prisoners who had already been deprived of almost all privileges. Further, deference to the professional judgment of prison officials must be given.

Turner v. Safley[108] and *Overton v. Bazzetta*[109] contain the basic substantive legal standards that are applicable here. In *Beard*, the Supreme Court recognized that while imprisonment does not automatically deprive a prisoner of constitutional protections, the Constitution sometimes permits greater restriction of such rights in a prison than it would allow elsewhere. The judicial system owes substantial deference to the professional judgment of prison administrators, and restrictive prison regulations are permissible if they are reasonably related to legitimate penological interests.

§ 5.15   Use of the Internet and e-Mail

In 2004, the Ninth Circuit held that a California policy that prohibited prisoners from receiving mail containing material downloaded from the Internet violated the prisoner's First Amendment rights. A statewide injunction against enforcing the policy was justified because it was sufficiently narrow to avoid unnecessary disruption to the state's normal course of proceeding, did not require court supervision, enjoined only the enforcement of an unconstitutional policy, and did not interfere with prison mail security measures.[110]

The Federal Bureau of Prisons uses the Trust Fund Limited Inmate Computer System (TRULINCS) program to, among other things, provide e-mail access to federal prisoners. An inmate was barred from using the e-mail program because (1) he had prior computer expertise and (2) he was punished at a previous prison for misusing the program to tamper with other inmates' legal work. The inmate filed a *Bivens* action,[111] claiming that his prohibition from using e-mail violated his rights under the First Amendment, the Due Process Clause, and the Equal Protection Clause. In the 2013 case *Solan v. Zickfoose*,[112] the Third Circuit ruled in favor of prison officials. The court stated that while e-mail can be a means of exercising one's First Amendment rights, the inmate's claims did not rise to constitutional violations under the *Turner v. Safley* standard. Most importantly, barring the inmate from using the TRULINCS program did not prevent him from all communications with family and friends as he was still able to communicate with them via phone calls, in-person visits, and the regular mail system. In 2018, the Seventh Circuit heard a similar case regarding the BOP's TRULINCS program and reached the same conclusion.[113]

§ 5.16   Use of the Telephone

Prison walls do not form a barrier that separates prisoners from the protections of the Constitution,[114] nor do they bar free citizens from exercising their own constitutional rights by reaching out to those on the "inside."[115] Prisoners retain their First Amendment rights to communicate with family and friends.[116] Courts have determined that there is no legitimate governmental purpose to be achieved by not allowing reasonable access to the telephone, and such use is protected by the First Amendment.[117]

However, a prisoner does not have the right to unlimited telephone use,[118] and his or her right to telephone access is subject to rational limitations in the face of legitimate security interests of the penal institution.[119] The exact nature of telephone service to be provided to prisoners is generally to be determined by prison administrators, subject to court scrutiny for unreasonable restrictions.[120]

Washington v. Reno[121] involved replacing the collect-call telephone system available to federal prison prisoners with a direct-dial system monitored by correctional facility employees. In 1994, the Bureau of Prisons changed a rule concerning telephone use by prisoners in federal correctional institutions.[122] That rule altered the previously existing prisoner telephone system (ITS) procedures and requirements in response to many prisoner concerns. Specifically, the final rule amended the phone list requirement that accompanied the advent of the ITS system. Under the rule, a prisoner may ordinarily place up to 30 numbers on the call list—a 50 percent increase from the former total of 20 numbers. In addition, "[T]he Associate Warden may authorize the placement of additional numbers on a prisoner's telephone list based on the prisoner's individual situation, e.g., size of family."[123]

The rule abandoned the controversial Request for Telephone Privilege Form that required private information from potential call recipients outside the prison system. In place of the form, the rule provides that the prisoner must acknowledge "to the best of the prisoner's knowledge, the person or persons on the list are agreeable to receiving the prisoner's telephone call and that the proposed calls are to be made for a purpose allowable under Bureau policy or institution guidelines."[124] Ordinarily, all such numbers listed by the prisoner will then be placed on the call list. When numbers of individuals other than the prisoner's immediate family and prison visitors are listed, however, the Bureau of Prisons sends a notice to the additional individuals informing them that they have been designated as telephone call recipients of the prisoner. If a recipient desires to be deleted from the call list, a written request to the Bureau will suffice.

In response to concerns raised regarding potential discrimination against indigent prisoners in the operation of the direct-dial system, the rule also provided that a minimum of one collect call per month (exclusive of legal calls to an attorney) may be made by prisoners without funds.[125] Additionally, the wardens of the federal institutions are authorized by the rule to increase the number of collect calls available to such indigent prisoners "based upon local institution conditions (e.g., institution population, staff resources, and usage demand)."[126]

In response to concerns that the ITS tie-in with the prisoner financial responsibility program would place an undue hardship on prisoners and their families because additional funds sent to the prisoners for phone calls would be used for increased program payments, the rule created a limited exemption for such outside funds. Prison officials developing a prisoner's financial responsibility plan "shall exclude from its assessment $50 a month deposited into the prisoner's trust fund account. . . . This $50 is excluded to allow the prisoner the opportunity to better maintain telephone communication under the prisoner Telephone System (ITS)."[127] The regulation also increased the number of calls allowed to a prisoner who refuses to participate in the financial responsibility program. Whereas the previous policy of the Bureau of Prisons was to limit such nonparticipants to one telephone call every three months, the regulation (28 C.F.R. § 545.11(d)(10)) provided that, effective January 3, 1995, the prisoner "will be allowed to place no more than one telephone call every month."

Prison authorities argued that prisoner use of a telephone is not a right at all but merely a privilege extended by the correctional facility to foster continued communication with family and friends outside the prison walls. They further argued that implementation of a direct-dialing system did not violate a right of free expression and association because any restrictions imposed are "reasonably related" to legitimate penological interests, because the restrictions are content-neutral and are unrelated to the purpose of suppressing expression and because prisoners may still communicate with family and friends through alternate means of expression such as prison visits and letters.

It should be remembered that regulations of the Federal Bureau of Prisons have no direct effect on state prison systems. They only apply to the federal prison system. Caution should also be used when relying on any state or federal administrative regulation or rule. The amendment process is rather simple, and they change as circumstances and time dictate.

§ 5.17 Conclusion

Prison administrators may place reasonable restrictions on mail, subject to the prisoner's qualified right to use the mail system. Formerly, many federal courts refused to intervene in prisoner suits that alleged undue restriction on mail rights unless the prisoner alleged that restrictions infringed upon another federal right, such as the rights of free speech and press, the right to petition the government for the redress of grievances, the right to communicate with an attorney, and the right to receive information.

Following *Procunier*, *Turner*, *Thornburgh*, and *Beard*, prison officials have great discretion in allowing prisoners to send and receive mail and publications. As long as they act "reasonably," their actions will not be reviewed by the federal courts. The standards to determine "reasonableness" include whether there is a "valid, rational connection" between the regulation and a legitimate and neutral governmental interest put forward to justify it; the existence of alternative means of exercising the asserted constitutional rights that remain open to prisoners; the extent to which accommodation of the asserted right will have an impact on prison staff, on prisoners' liberty, and on the allocation of limited prison resources; and whether the regulation represents an "exaggerated response" to prison concerns.

The extent to which state prisoners may use the Internet, e-mail, and telephones is unsettled. The federal prison system controls the use of telephones through administrative regulations that are not of constitutional significance.

Notes

1 Public Clearing House v. Coyne, 194 U.S. 497 (1904).

2 Adams v. Ellis, 197 F.2d 483 (5th Cir. 1952); Numer v. Miller, 165 F.2d 986 (9th Cir. 1948);

Medlock v. Burke, 285 F. Supp. 67 (E.D. Wis. 1968).

3 Sherman v. MacDougatt, 656 F.2d 527 (9th Cir. 1981); Parnell v. Waldrep, 511 F. Supp. 764 (D.N.C. 1981).

4 *E.g.*, Brown v. Wainwright, 419 F.2d 1308 (5th Cir. 1969); Ortega v. Ragen, 216 F.2d 561 (7th Cir. 1954); Medlock v. Burke, 285 F. Supp. 67 (E.D. Wis. 1968); Zaczek v. Hutto, 642 F.2d 74 (4th Cir. 1981).

5 201 F.2d 711 (D.C. Cir. 1953); Carwile v. Ray, 481 F. Supp. 33 (E.D. Wash. 1979).

6 187 F.2d 850 (9th Cir. 1951), *cert. denied*, 342 U.S. 829 (1951).

7 Diehl v. Wainwright, 419 F.2d 1309 (5th Cir. 1970); Carey v. Settle, 351 F.2d 483 (8th Cir. 1965); Numer v. Miller, 165 F.2d 986 (9th Cir. 1948); Cook v. Brockway, 424 F. Supp. 1046 (N.D. Tex. 1977), *aff'd*, 559 F.2d 1214 (5th Cir. 1977).

8 Sostre v. McGinnis, 442 F.2d 178 (2d Cir. 1971), *cert. denied*, 405 U.S. 978 (1972); Jones v. Wittenberg, 330 F. Supp. 707 (N.D. Ohio 1971) (incoming parcels or letters addressed to prisoners awaiting trial can be inspected for contraband, but letters cannot be read); Palmigiano v. Travisono, 317 F. Supp. 776 (D.R.I. 1970) (all incoming mail may be read and inspected, but no outgoing mail may be read without a search warrant); Smith v. Shimp, 562 F.2d 423 (7th Cir. 1977).

9 606 F.2d 621 (5th Cir. 1979); Carothers v. Follette, 314 F. Supp. 1014 (S.D.N.Y. 1970).

10 McNamara v. Moody, 606 F.2d 621 (5th Cir. 1979).

11 416 U.S. 396 (1974).

12 482 U.S. 78 (1987).

13 490 U.S. 401 (1989).

14 Procunier v. Marinez, 416 U.S. at 413 (1974).

15 *See* Padgett v. Stein, 406 F. Supp. 287 (M.D. Pa. 1975); Gates v. Collier, 525 F.2d 965 (5th Cir. 1976).

16 Turner v. Safley, 482 U.S. at 89–90 (1987).

17 *Id.*

18 490 U.S. 401 (1989).

19 Krug v. Lutz, 329 F.3d 692 (9th Cir. 2003).

20 *See* § 8.9, ex post facto.

21 Ex parte Hull, 312 U.S. 546 (1941).

22 516 F.2d 233 (3d Cir. 1975).

23 336 F.2d 462 (6th Cir. 1964).

24 McCray v. Sullivan, 509 F.2d 1332, 1337 (5th Cir.), *cert. denied*, 423 U.S. 859 (1975); *cf.*, Coleman v. Crisp, 444 F. Supp. 31 (W.D. Okla. 1977).

25 Sallier v. Brooks, 343 F.3d 868 (6th Cir. 2003).

26 562 F.2d 423 (7th Cir. 1977); Frazier v. Donelon, 381 F. Supp. 911 (E.D. La. 1974), *aff'd*, 520 F.2d 941 (5th Cir. 1975).

27 Jensen v. Klecker, 648 F.2d 1179 (8th Cir. 1981); Ramos v. Lamm, 639 F.2d 559 (10th Cir. 1980); Jones v. Diamond, 594 F.2d 997 (5th Cir. 1979); Taylor v. Sterrett, 532 F.2d 462 (5th Cir. 1976).

28 Sostre v. McGinnis, 442 F.2d 178 (2d Cir. 1971), *cert. denied*, 405 U.S. 978 (1972); Blanks v. Cunningham, 409 F.2d 220 (4th Cir. 1969); Marsh v. Moore, 325 F. Supp. 392 (D. Mass. 1971); Thibadoux v. LaVallee, 411 F. Supp. 862 (W.D.N.Y. 1976).

29 Bounds v. Smith, 430 U.S. 817 (1977).

30 Burns v. Swenson, 430 F.2d 771 (8th Cir. 1970), *cert. denied*, 404 U.S. 1062 (1971), *reh'g denied*, 405 U.S. 969 (1971); Nolan v. Scafati, 430 F.2d 548 (1st Cir. 1970).

31 314 F. Supp. 81 (W.D. Wash. 1970).

32 Brabson v. Wilkins, 19 N.Y.2d 433, 280 N.Y.S.2d 561 (1967); Frazier v. Donelon, 381 F. Supp. 911 (E.D. La. 1974), *aff'd*, 520 F.2d 941 (5th Cir. 1975).

33 Ramer v. United States, 411 F.2d 30 (9th Cir. 1969), *cert. denied*, 396 U.S. 965 (1969); Haas v. United States, 344 F.2d 56 (8th Cir. 1965).

34 367 F.2d 824 (10th Cir. 1967).

35   442 F.2d 178 (2d Cir. 1971), *cert. denied*, 405 U.S. 978 (1972).

36   454 F.2d 696 (1st Cir. 1972).

37   Wolff v. McDonnell, 418 U.S. 539 (1974); Jensen v. Klecker, 648 F.2d 1179 (8th Cir. 1981).

38   Taylor v. Sterrett, 532 F.2d 462 (5th Cir. 1976).

39   Nordstrom v. Ryan, 762 F. 3d 903 (2014).

40   *See* Chapter 16.

41   Smith v. Al-Amin, 511 F.3d 1317 (11th Cir. 2008).

42   Wardell v. Maggard, 470 F.3d 954 (10th Cir. 2006).

43   443 F.2d 360 (10th Cir. 1971).

44   532 F.2d 462 (5th Cir. 1976).

45   435 F. Supp. 475 (D. Md. 1977), *aff'd*, 580 F.2d 1047 (4th Cir. 1978); Fulwood v. Clemmer, 206 F. Supp. 370 (D.C. Cir. 1962).

46   337 F.2d 72 (4th Cir. 1964).

47   Belk v. Mitchell, 294 F. Supp. 800 (W.D.N.C. 1968).

48   197 F. Supp. 855 (S.D.N.Y. 1961).

49   694 F.2d 50 (2d Cir. 1982).

50   Jones v. Caruso, 569 F.3d 258 (6th Cir. 2009).

51   Pell v. Procunier, 417 U.S. 817, 832 (1974).

52   Procunier v. Martinez, 416 U.S. 396, 417 (1974).

53   *See* Lee v. Tahash, 352 F.2d 970 (8th Cir. 1965). *See also* Witherow v. Paff, 52 F.3d 264 (9th Cir. 1995), holding that prison regulation requiring that mail sent from prisoners to certain public officials be visually inspected did not violate First Amendment rights. *See also* Monroe v. Beard, 536 F.3d 198 (3d Cir. 2008).

54   Jackson v. Godwin, 400 F.2d 529, 541 (5th Cir. 1968).

55   Shelton v. Tucker, 364 U.S. 479 (1960); Vienneau v. Shanks, 425 F. Supp. 676 (W.D. Wis. 1977).

56   THE SUPREME COURT, *1973 Term*, 88 HARV. L. REV. 165–173 (1974).

57   451 F.2d 545 (1st Cir. 1971), *rev'g*, 326 F. Supp. 209 (D. Mass. 1971).

58   Main Road v. Aytch, 522 F.2d 1080 (3d Cir. 1975).

59   532 F.2d 462 (5th Cir. 1976).

60   *See* § 5.4.1.

61   Schlobohm v. United States Attorney General, 479 F. Supp. 401 (M.D. Pa. 1979); Lawrence v. Davis, 401 F. Supp. 1203 (W.D. Pa. 1979).

62   *Id.*

63   393 U.S. 483 (1969).

64   Storseth v. Spellman, 654 F.2d 1349 (9th Cir. 1981).

65   532 U.S. 223 (2001).

66   *See* 5.3.1 *supra*.

67   Shaw v. Murphy, 532 U.S. 223 (2001).

68   Stanley v. Georgia, 394 U.S. 557, 564 (1969).

69   Brandenburg v. Ohio, 395 U.S. 444 (1969).

70   Sostre v. Otis, 330 F. Supp. 941, 944–945 (S.D.N.Y. 1971).

71   393 F.2d 775 (4th Cir. 1968).

72   376 F. Supp. 402 (E.D. Okla. 1974).

73   Carpenter v. South Dakota, 536 F.2d 759 (8th Cir. 1976).

74   *E.g.*, Chiarello v. Bohlinger, 391 F. Supp. 1153 (S.D.N.Y. 1975) (refusal to mail prisoner's manuscript); Morgan v. LaVallee, 526 F.2d 221 (2d Cir. 1975) (refusal to allow prisoner to receive specific publication); Aikens v. Jenkins, 534 F.2d 751 (7th Cir. 1976) (regulations concerning publications must not be overbroad); Blue v. Hogan, 553 F.2d 960 (5th Cir. 1977) (regulations must be governed by the test in *Procunier*).

75   Sherman v. MacDougatt, 656 F.2d 527 (9th Cir. 1981).

76   Roth v. United States, 354 U.S. 476 (1957).

77 In re Van Geldern, 14 Cal. App. 3d 838, 92 Cal. Rptr. 592 (1971).
78 *Ibid.*
79 Carpenter v. South Dakota, 536 F.2d 759 (8th Cir. 1976).
80 Aikens v. Jenkins, 534 F.2d 751 (7th Cir. 1976).
81 Amatel v. Reno, 156 F.3d 192 (D.C. Cir. 1997).
82 Jones v. Wittenberg, 330 F. Supp. 707, 720 (N.D. Ohio 1971), *aff'd*, 456 F.2d 854 (6th Cir. 1972).
83 354 U.S. 476 (1957).
84 Jacobellis v. Ohio, 378 U.S. 184 (1964) (Warren, C.J. and Clark, J., dissenting).
85 *Id.* at 192–195 (Brennan and Goldberg, JJ.).
86 *Id.* at 197 (Stewart, J. concurring).
87 413 U.S. 15 (1973).
88 Palmigiano v. Travisono, 317 F. Supp. 776, 790 (D.R.I. 1970).
89 400 F.2d 529 (5th Cir. 1968); *accord*, Owens v. Brierley, 452 F.2d 640 (3d Cir. 1971); *see also* Martin v. Wainwright, 525 F.2d 983 (5th Cir. 1976).
90 390 F. Supp. 663 (N.D. Ind. 1975), *modified in*, 514 F.2d 55 (7th Cir. 1975); Hopkins v. Collins, 548 F.2d 503 (4th Cir. 1977).
91 Ramirez v. Pugh, 379 F.3d 122 (3rd Cir. 2004).
92 WIS. ADMIN. CODE, § 303.20.
93 Koutnik v. Brown, 456 F.3d 777 (8th Cir. 2006).
94 Lee v. Tahash, 352 F.2d 970 (8th Cir. 1965) (number of persons with whom prisoner could correspond limited to 12); Labat v. McKeithen, 243 F. Supp. 662 (E.D. La. 1965) (Louisiana statute limiting death row prisoner's correspondence to specific persons).
95 330 F. Supp. 707 (N.D. Ohio 1971).
96 Palmigiano v. Travisono, 317 F. Supp. 776 (D.R.I. 1970).
97 *Id.* at 791.
98 Finney v. Arkansas Board of Corrections, 505 F.2d 194, at 210–211 (8th Cir. 1974).
99 Hearn v. Morris, 526 F. Supp. 267 (E.D. Cal. 1981).
100 135 Fed. Appx. 876 (7th Cir. 2005).
101 441 U.S. 520 (1979).
102 *Id.* at 550, 551; Rich v. Luther, 514 F. Supp. 481 (W.D.N.C. 1981).
103 *Id.* at 554, 555; Jones v. Diamond, 594 F.2d 997 (5th Cir. 1979).
104 451 U.S. 527 (1981).
105 261 F.3d 896 (9th Cir. 2001).
106 *Ibid.*
107 Beard v. Banks, 548 U.S. 521 (2006).
108 482 U.S. 78 (2003).
109 539 U.S. 126 (2003).
110 Clement v. Cal. Dep't of Corr., 364 F.3d 1148 (9th Cir. 2004).
111 *See* Chapter 16.
112 530 Fed. Appx 109 (3d Cir. 2013).
113 Sebolt v. Samuels, 749 Fed. Appx. 458 (7th Cir. 2018).
114 Turner v. Safley, 482 U.S. 78 (1987).
115 *Id.*; Thornburgh v. Abbott, 490 U.S. 401 (1989).
116 Morgan v. LaVallee, 526 F.2d 221 (2d Cir. 1975).
117 Johnson v. Galli, 596 F. Supp. 135 (D. Nev. 1984).
118 Benzel v. Grammer, 869 F.2d 1105, 1108 (8th Cir.), *cert. denied*, 493 U.S. 895 (1989), *citing* Lopez v. Reyes, 692 F.2d 15 (5th Cir. 1982).
119 Strandberg v. City of Helena, 791 F.2d 744 (9th Cir. 1986).
120 Fillmore v. Ordonez, 829 F. Supp. 1544, 1563–1564 (D. Kan. 1993), *aff'd*, 17 F.3d 1436 (10th Cir. 1994), and citing Feeley v. Sampson, 570 F.2d 364, 374 (1st Cir. 1978), and Jeffries v. Reed, 631 F. Supp. 1212, 1219 (E.D. Wash. 1986).

121 35 F.3d 1093 (6th Cir. 1994).

122 59 Fed. Reg. 15812–15825 (Apr. 4, 1994).

123 59 Fed. Reg. 15824 (Apr. 4, 1994); 28 C.F.R. § 540.101(a).

124 59 Fed. Reg. 15824 (Apr. 4, 1994); 28 C.F.R. § 540.101(a)(1).

125 59 Fed. Reg. 15824 (Apr. 4, 1994); 28 C.F.R. § 540.105(b).

126 *Id.*

127 28 C.F.R. § 545.11(b); 59 Fed. Reg. 15825 (Apr. 4, 1994).

Rights to Rehabilitation Programs and Medical Care

6

Chapter Outline

§ 6.1   Introduction

This chapter discusses two important issues within correctional institutions: rehabilitation programs and medical care. Both of these topics have far-reaching effects on the well-being of both offenders and the "outside" community. Rehabilitation programs aim to reduce offenders' criminal propensity. The benefits of this reduction once an offender is released from prison are self-evident. Medical care for incarcerated offenders is vital in achieving the prison's goal of safety and security. Because inmates are not free to seek medical care outside of the prison while they are incarcerated, courts have ruled that prison officials must supply at least basic medical care for all inmates. However, this seemingly straightforward edict becomes more complex when considering topics such as whether inmates have a right to refuse medical treatment or to obtain gender reassignment surgery.

§ 6.2   Right to Rehabilitation Programs

Many state constitutions and statutes encourage the rehabilitation of prisoners.[1] Such programs are considered essential by virtually all penologists if incarceration is to reduce the incidence of crime. For example, the American Correctional Association has stated that "prison serves most effectively for the protection of society against crime when its major emphasis is on rehabilitation."[2] Similarly, a commission appointed by President Lyndon Johnson to study the crime problem in the United States concluded that "rehabilitation of offenders to prevent their return to crime is, in general, the most promising way to achieve this end (reduction of crime)."[3]

§ 6.2.1   —Judicial Decisions

Despite the view that rehabilitation programs should be the core of any correctional system, the courts have refused to hold that there is an absolute right to rehabilitation during incarceration. In *Padgett v. Stein*,[4] prisoners of a county prison sought enforcement of a consent decree entered into with prison authorities to remedy allegedly unconstitutional conditions of confinement. The prisoners contended that convicted prisoners have a constitutional right to receive meaningful rehabilitative treatment and that the failure of the prison authorities to afford prisoners rehabilitation programs constituted cruel and unusual punishment. The court rejected the prisoners' contentions on the ground that there is no constitutional duty imposed on a governmental entity to rehabilitate prisoners. The court went on to state that:

> whether penal institutions should undertake to rehabilitate prisoners at all— in view of the serious questions which exist with respect to the effectiveness of rehabilitation programs—is a social policy question which should be resolved by the representative branches of government—i.e., the legislative and executive branches—and not by the courts.[5]

Courts have repeatedly stated that prisoners have no constitutional right to rehabilitative treatment.[6] One court has characterized the duty owed to a prisoner by prison officials as the duty "to exercise ordinary care for his protection and to keep him safe and free from harm."[7] In *Holt v. Sarver*,[8] however, a district court did state that when examining the totality of conditions within a penal institution, a federal court should consider the lack of any meaningful rehabilitation programs as a factor "in the overall constitutional equation before the court."[9] But because that court had previously stated that lack of rehabilitative opportunities was not, by itself, a defect of constitutional magnitude, it was evident that the prison administrators could remove the absence of rehabilitative programs from federal judicial consideration. They could do so by rectifying the other major deficiencies in the institution. The court tacitly recognized this by omitting lack of rehabilitative services from its list of defects that had to be corrected. The court that decided *Holt v. Sarver* has since required that an overall program for treatment and rehabilitation of the prisoners be submitted to the court.[10]

Lack of meaningful rehabilitative opportunities is one of the grounds upon which several state prison systems have been declared to be unconstitutional.[11] In *James v. Wallace*,[12] it was noted that courts have not made a positive rehabilitative program a constitutional right. It is clear, however, that a penal system cannot be operated in such a manner that it impedes the ability of prisoners to attempt their own rehabilitation or simply to avoid physical, mental, or social deterioration. A federal district court's opinion in *Alberti v. Sheriff of Harris County, Texas*[13] was more specific when it ordered officials who were responsible for the operation and maintenance of a county jail to provide adequate vocational and educational programs to foster the prisoners' rehabilitation. However, a prisoner has no constitutional right to participate in community programs, to enroll and attend classes in college outside the prison, or to visit with relatives outside the prison.[14]

Another aspect of the rehabilitation program is the extent of a state's right to rehabilitate its prisoners without the consent of the prisoners. Aversion therapy—the so-called Clockwork Orange technique—has been held to be cruel and unusual punishment, not rehabilitative treatment, and thus unconstitutional.

In *Knecht v. Gillman*,[15] severely nauseating injections were used to produce what the officials called a "Pavlovian" aversion to minor infractions of prison rules. The court prohibited the treatment program, holding such sanctions to be cruel and unusual punishment, in violation of the Eighth Amendment, and not treatment. In such cases, the courts look to the substance of a program, not its name or label. Labeling a program as treatment rather than punishment makes no difference in terms of the constitutional requirements that must be met.[16]

Short of aversion therapy, courts have been sympathetic toward state requirements that prisoners be enrolled, either voluntarily or involuntarily, in education-oriented rehabilitative programs. In *Rutherford v. Hutto*,[17] a state was held to have a sufficient interest in the elimination of illiteracy among its convicts, including adults, to justify its requirement that illiterate convicts attend classes that were designed to bring them up to at least a fourth grade reading level. More than mere attendance at such classes can be required; meaningful participation can be encouraged by using sanctions for nonparticipation. In *Jackson v. McLemore*,[18] a disciplinary action that arose from a prisoner's refusal to comply with a teacher's instruction to spell in a compulsory educational program class was held not to violate the prisoner's constitutional right to be let alone.

In conjunction with the discussion of involuntary rehabilitative programs, it should be noted that the basically coercive nature of prison life severely undercuts any notion that a prisoner's consent to treatment is motivated primarily by the prisoner's desire to be rehabilitated or, in other words, is not coerced. In *McGee v. Aaron*,[19] the Seventh Circuit recognized implicitly that consent may not always be genuine but is merely choosing the least of several evils. That case involved the sufficiency of the reasons given for denial of parole. One of the reasons given was the parole board's estimation of the need for the prisoner to complete his high school equivalency and to complete a training program that would provide him with a marketable skill. The court upheld the decision, thus giving the prisoner a concrete goal to work toward; not some ideal form of rehabilitation, but freedom in the form of early parole.

The voluntariness of a prisoner's consent to participation in therapeutic medical experimentation and research is also suspect. Modern medical research and drug testing techniques require the participation of large numbers of subjects for substantial periods. Prisons provide an excellent source for such volunteers. However, due to the indigency of most prisoners and the emphasis that parole boards place upon cooperative activity by prisoners, there is a real question as to whether true consent is ever obtainable from prisoners for their participation in sometimes painful or dangerous medical experimentation.[20]

The scope and nature of rehabilitation are left largely to the discretion of prison authorities. In *Sellers v. Ciccone*,[21] which involved rejection of long-term prisoners for admission to an X-ray technician training program, the court stated that, absent arbitrariness or caprice, the balance between individual benefit and institutional benefit is for prison officials to determine. The court declined to intervene in order to meet the desires of the individual prisoner. However, in certain situations courts will order specific rehabilitative opportunities to be made available to specific individual prisoners or classes of prisoners. For example, in *Cudnik v. Kreiger*,[22] pretrial detainees were held to be entitled to continue with the methadone treatment program in which they had been involved prior to their detention.

§ 6.2.2   – Analogy of Right to Treatment in Other Areas

In the past few decades, several courts have recognized that certain groups of persons who have been deprived of their liberty have a right to treatment. These cases were based, however, on statutory interpretation and not on any constitutional right. Thus, in *Rouse v. Cameron*,[23] a federal appellate court held that the District of Columbia's Hospitalization of the Mentally Ill Act required treatment programs for persons who were involuntarily committed to a mental health facility after their acquittal by reason of insanity. Minnesota's Hospitalization and Commitment Act has been interpreted to confer a statutory right upon persons who are involuntarily civilly committed to state institutions to receive minimally adequate treatment while so institutionalized.[24] In *New York State Association for Retarded Children, Inc. v. Carey*,[25] an expansion of current notions of the right to treatment of involuntarily civilly committed mental patients occurred when prisoners of state mental facilities were held to have a constitutional right to some treatment, regardless of whether their confinement was voluntary or involuntary.

In *O'Connor v. Donaldson*,[26] the Supreme Court made specific note of its refusal to decide whether mental patients have a constitutional right to treatment as a consequence of their detention by the state. The Fifth Circuit Court of Appeals had concluded[27] that where a nondangerous patient was involuntarily committed to a state mental hospital under a civil commitment procedure, the only constitutionally permissible purpose of such confinement was to provide treatment and that such confinement must involve rehabilitative treatment or minimally adequate habilitation and care where rehabilitation was impossible, in order to justify the confinement. The Court of Appeals made a careful distinction between the rights of those who are civilly committed for an indefinite term and those who are adjudged guilty of a specific offense and who are sentenced for a fixed term. The Supreme Court's refusal to affirm even this relatively simple distinction suggests that the Court will not require, at least upon a constitutional basis, rehabilitative treatment for ordinary prisoners in the near future.

The Supreme Court has held, however, that involuntarily committed mentally deficient persons have, under the Fourteenth Amendment's Due Process Clause, constitutionally protected liberty interests in reasonably safe conditions of confinement, freedom from unreasonable bodily restraints, and such minimally adequate training as reasonably may be required by such interests. The proper standard for determining whether the state has adequately protected such rights is whether professional judgment has been exercised. The judgment of a qualified professional is entitled to a presumption of correctness. Liability may only be imposed when the decision is such a substantial departure from accepted professional judgment as to demonstrate that the decision was not based on professional judgment.[28]

One of the consequences of conviction under a habitual sex offender statute, which usually carries a sentence of from one day to life, seems to be a right to rehabilitative treatment. In *People v. Feagley*,[29] the California Supreme Court ruled that a statutory scheme that provides for confinement of mentally disordered sex offenders for an indefinite period in prison without treatment violates the cruel and unusual punishment clauses of the state and federal constitutions. However, judicial expansion of the indefinitely sentenced prisoner's right to treatment[30] has motivated the New York legislature to alter its habitual sex offender statute so as to eliminate such a right.[31]

In *Ohlinger v. Watson*,[32] the Ninth Circuit held that the goal of the Oregon statutory scheme for sex offenders is rehabilitation. Consequently, sex offenders in Oregon have a right to individual treatment that will afford them a reasonable opportunity to be cured or to improve their mental condition. Further, such treatment is also required by due process.

As noted, many state statutes and constitutions say that rehabilitation is an objective of their correctional systems.[33] As such, it is possible that courts in the future will demand that prison administrators implement, with specific programs, the state's statutory and constitutional requirement of rehabilitation programs. Judge David Bazelon[34] has written that:

> The rationale for the right to treatment is clear. If society confines a man for the benevolent purpose of helping him ... then its right to so withhold his freedom depends entirely upon whether help is in fact provided. ... When the legislature justifies confinement by a promise of treatment, it thereby commits the community to provide the resources necessary to fulfill the promise.[35]

§ 6.2.3   – Administrative Review

An administrative hearing was held for prisoners in Washington who refused to be treated with antipsychotic drugs. The panel was comprised of a psychiatrist, a psychologist, and the associate superintendent of the special unit. The Washington state prison system had a special unit in which felons with severe mental disorders were housed. None of the panel members was involved in the prisoner's treatment or diagnosis at the time of the hearing, in order to assure independence. Among many other procedures, the prisoner had the right to attend, present evidence, cross-examine witnesses, and be assisted by a lay advisor. Further, a decision to medicate involuntarily was subject to periodic review. As with most administrative hearings, the prisoner was not afforded a right to counsel, and adherence to evidentiary rules was not required.

The Supreme Court held in *Washington v. Harper*[36] that a state may conclude, with good reason, that a judicial hearing will not be as effective, as continuous, or as probing as administrative review using medical decision-makers. The Court observed that a prisoner has a protected liberty interest in being free from the arbitrary administration of antipsychotic drugs through the state's policy and the Fourteenth Amendment's Due Process Clause. However, the Court applied the test of *Turner v. Safley*[37] and found that a state's interest in prison safety and security is sufficiently great to justify subordinating the prisoner's liberty interest in the proper case. Justice Kennedy, writing for the majority, commented that the *Turner* test applies to all circumstances in which the needs of prison administration implicate constitutional rights.

§ 6.3   Right to Medical Care

Prisoners in state and federal institutions have sought redress in the federal court system for medical treatment they have received and failed to receive. Complaints about medical treatment have included claims about the adequacy and nature of the medical care received, allegations of a total denial of medical care, improper care, inadequate care, and conduct of prison officials attendant to the medical care.

The power of the federal courts to adjudicate a prisoner's complaint about medical treatment requires that a federal right be involved in the medical treatment.[38] The prisoner must allege the presence of a federally protected right. Several federally protected rights have been named by the federal courts in medical treatment cases:

1. *Right to due process of law under the Fifth or Fourteenth Amendment:*[39] The due process right has been couched in terms of the prisoner's right to be free from an abuse of discretion on the part of prison administrators,[40] protection from unconstitutional administrative action,[41] protection of a prisoner's life and health from administrative action.[42]

2. *Right to be free from the infliction of cruel and unusual punishments as guaranteed by the Eighth Amendment:*[43] Violation of Eighth Amendment rights has been found when there is an intentional denial of needed medical care or when a prison official's conduct indicates deliberate indifference to the medical needs of prisoners.

Despite the willingness of federal courts to hear cases that involve the federally protected rights of prisoners to medical aid, there are limits to what prisoners can expect to accomplish through the courts. For example, in *Priest v. Cupp*,[44] the court explained that neither federal nor state constitutional prohibitions of cruel and unusual punishment guarantee any prisoner that he or she will be free from or cured of all real or imagined medical disabilities while in custody. What is required is that the prisoner be afforded such medical care, in the form of diagnosis and treatment, as is reasonably available under the circumstances of his or her confinement and medical condition.

Just as prison officials cannot deny all medical aid, prisoners cannot expect a flawless medical services system. Consequently, litigation involving the medical rights of prisoners has now focused upon the nature of so-called adequate or reasonable medical care.

What amount of medical care is adequate depends largely upon the facts of each case. In *Gates v. Collier*,[45] the Fifth Circuit reviewed the medical treatment that was available at the Mississippi State Penitentiary. With more than 1,800 prisoners, the prison administration relied upon one full-time physician, several prisoner assistants, and a substandard hospital to provide medical care. The court ruled that the services and facilities were inadequate and ordered the prison administration to: (1) employ such additional medical personnel as necessary so that the prison's medical staff would consist of at least three full-time physicians, one of which must be a psychiatrist and another the prison's chief medical officer;[46] two full-time dentists; two full-time trained physicians' assistants; six full-time registered or licensed practical nurses; one medical records librarian; and two medical clerical personnel, and obtain the consultant services of a radiologist and a pharmacist; (2) comply with the general standards of the American Correctional Association relating to medical services for prisoners; (3) have the prison hospital and equipment brought into compliance with state licensing requirements for a hospital and infirmary, including adequate treatment for the chronically ill; (4) refrain from punishment of prisoners who seek medical aid unless the superintendent makes an express finding that the prisoner sought medical care unnecessarily and for malingering purposes; and (5) refrain from the use of prisoners to fill any of the civilian medical staff just described but to encourage the use of trained and competent prisoners to supplement the minimal civilian medical staff.[47]

As in most "treatment" cases, the lack of funds has not been recognized as a defense or excuse. However, in *Miller v. Carson*,[48] a federal court approved a Florida county prison's medical services staff, which included one full-time physician, a licensed physician's assistant, and 13 nurses, because their work schedule allowed a crisis intervention desk to be staffed 24 hours per day, with the physician or the licensed physician's assistant on call at the jail 24 hours a day as well. The proximity to the jail of a university hospital for emergency treatment made such a minimal staff feasible. This Florida county prison had a maximum capacity of 432 prisoners.[49]

Other states have also grappled with this personnel problem. In *Craig v. Hocker*,[50] the court found that medical care was adequate and reasonable based on the presence of a full-time physician and a full-time dentist in the prison, as well as two registered nurses, a psychiatrist, a part-time pharmacist who gave reasonably prompt attention to genuine complaints from prisoners, a prison hospital ward to which sick prisoners could be removed when so directed by a doctor, and provisions for taking prisoners under guard to local hospitals for diagnostic or treatment procedures not available in the prison. The prison contained 854 prisoners prior to trial.

Once the courts have assured themselves that adequate or reasonable medical care is available to a prisoner, the historic hands-off doctrine is again evident. What constitutes necessary and proper medical care of a prisoner, in the absence of allegations of intentional negligence or mistreatment, must be left to the medical judgment of the prison physician and cannot form the basis for a civil rights complaint.[51] Prisoners cannot be the ultimate judges of what medical treatment is necessary or proper, and courts must place their confidence in the reports of reputable prison physicians.[52]

An apparent difference of opinion between a prisoner and his or her physicians as to what treatment is necessary and proper does not give rise to a legal cause of action against the physician.[53] Medical mistreatment or nontreatment must be capable of characterization as cruel and unusual punishment in order to present a claim under a civil rights statute.[54]

The standard for what treatment rises to cruel and unusual punishment was set forth in the Supreme Court case *Estelle v. Gamble*.[55] In that case, the Court reasoned that there must be facts and evidence to show a deliberate indifference to serious medical needs. Thus, simple negligence will not be sufficient to obtain a judgment against prison medical or security staff for inadequate treatment as a constitutional violation. The lack of medical treatment must be intentional; an accident or inadvertent failure to provide proper medical care is insufficient to meet the Court's standard of deliberate indifference to serious medical needs. It should be noted, however, that negligence may be actionable in state courts under state law.

§ 6.3.1 — Violation

The deliberate indifference test of *Estelle v. Gamble*[56] embodies both an objective and a subjective prong. First, the alleged deprivation must be, in objective terms, "sufficiently serious."[57] Second, the charged official must act with a sufficiently culpable state of mind. Deliberate indifference requires more than negligence but less than conduct undertaken for the very purpose of causing harm.[58] More specifically, a prison official does not act in a deliberately indifferent manner unless that official knows of and disregards an excessive risk to prisoner health or safety; the official must be aware of facts from which the inference could be drawn that a substantial risk of serious harm exists, and he or she must also draw the inference. Following are examples of cases in which courts found a violation of inmates' constitutional rights concerning medical care.

In *Hathaway v. Coughlin*,[59] the Second Circuit applied the *Estelle* standards and held that a prison doctor was deliberately indifferent to the prisoner's serious medical needs in that he knew of and disregarded an excessive risk to his health. The doctor never informed the prisoner that he had two broken pins in his hip.

The prisoner did not learn of his condition for one year after an X-ray. The presence of broken pins in a hip is information that would cause most people to consider surgery. Nonetheless, the doctor never shared this information with the prisoner nor raised the possibility of surgery with him following the discovery of the broken pins. Deliberate indifference was also present in a delay of more than two years between the discovery of the broken pins and the time the doctor asked that the prisoner be reevaluated for surgery. Despite requests for further evaluation and additional treatment and the prisoner's constant complaints, the doctor did not take the prisoner's condition seriously.

In *Ricketts v. Ciccone*,[60] the court held that when a federal prisoner was in need of medical treatment due to chronic rhinitis caused by allergic sensitivity to an identified mold, the director of the prison and the Bureau of Prisons were legally required to provide the most suitable medical treatment reasonably available. In determining a claim for lack of medical treatment, the standard is whether needed or essential, as opposed to desirable medical treatment is being denied. The court held that denial of the request by the prisoner, suffering from chronic rhinitis, to be transferred to a federal prison in a relatively dry climate as treatment for his illness, was arbitrary and unreasonable. Such action was held to be a denial to the prisoner of the best reasonably available medical treatment, when at least one federal prison was available in a climate beneficial to the prisoner, given his illness.

In *Comstock v. McCrary*,[61] a prison psychologist subjectively perceived a risk of serious harm to a prisoner but displayed deliberate indifference to the prisoner's serious medical needs. The psychologist took the prisoner off the suicide watch he had placed him on just the day before. He did not make a thorough assessment of the prisoner's emotional state or make a reasoned assessment or evaluation of the prisoner's suicide risk. The psychologist knew that the prisoner was concerned about possibly being harmed by other prisoners.

A commissioner rejected a prison medical staff's recommended transfer of a disabled prisoner to another facility with appropriate accommodations. The failure to maintain the prison in accordance with federal standards of accessibility was contrary to a clearly established requirement that the state not act in deliberate indifference to a prisoner's serious medical needs.[62]

A deliberate indifference to serious medical needs claim was shown where a prisoner alleged numerous problems and symptoms he suffered without proper glasses in the fluorescent lighting of his cell. Prison officials ignored the orders of two doctors that the prisoner be provided with tinted glasses with side shields.[63]

Prison officials were held deliberately indifferent to a prisoner's medical needs when his dentures were not given to him. This resulted in an inability to chew or eat properly, as well as bleeding, headaches, and disfigurement. Also, he was not given his heart medication, resulting in heart "fluttering" due to the lapse in medication and severe chest pain.[64]

A prisoner stated a valid claim where it was shown that a prior gunshot injury to his leg was so severe that he required reconstructive surgery and was unable to walk without the assistance of a cane or crutches. An officer denied him use of the cane and crutches and forced him to walk without assistance, resulting in unnecessary pain and suffering.[65]

A prisoner experienced frequent, sometimes unbearable, pain in his left hip. He was diagnosed with avascular necrosis of his left femoral head and was recommended for a bone graft procedure in August 1998. He received no surgery by August 1999, when, following further X-rays, a decision was made to cancel the surgery. The lengthy delay raised the issue of deliberate indifference to a serious medical need.[66]

The failure to arrange for dental treatment until about six weeks after a prisoner's written request for it, causing him to suffer further pain and infection, violated the Eighth Amendment.[67]

The Eighth Amendment is violated where a prisoner's s hernia surgery was delayed for four years, in the face of continual "complaints of intense pain, anxiety, and limited mobility."[68]

Deliberate indifference to a prisoner's medical needs occurred when correctional officers failed to provide him with medical treatment after he was pepper sprayed. The state's medical examiner credited the spray as contributing to the prisoner's death from asphyxia. Even a layperson would have inferred from the prisoner's collapse in the medical room that he was in need of medical attention. The use of force directive gave officers actual knowledge of the risk posed by the use of pepper spray. Officers were present when the prisoner was repeatedly sprayed during cell extraction. Facts showed that the prisoner was nonresponsive to a nurse's inquiries, then collapsed in plain sight, but was never given medical treatment.[69]

A jury determined that a psychiatrist's deliberate indifference and medical malpractice caused a prisoner's death from severe dehydration after being held for several days in a 90- to 100-degree observation room was awarded $1.5 million in compensatory damages and $3 million in punitive damages.[70]

§ 6.3.2   — No Violation

Following are examples of cases in which courts ruled the prison and/or medical officials did not act with deliberate indifference to an inmate's medical concerns.

In *Gutierrez v. Peters*, a prisoner suffered from a cyst on his back that became infected and caused severe pain and a high fever. His medical needs were "serious." Serious medical needs include not only life-threatening illnesses but also conditions that when left untreated cause needless pain and suffering. However, the treatment that the prisoner received, although not prompt, was sufficient to preclude a finding of "deliberate indifference" to his medical needs.[71]

Segregated confinement may be used for health needs. A form of confinement called "tuberculin hold" for prisoners who refuse to submit to testing for latent tuberculosis did not amount to cruel and unusual punishment.[72]

Jail officials were not deliberately indifferent to the risk of a decedent's suicide where the jail was in compliance with the state's minimum standards for suicide prevention although the intake officers had only general training in recognizing a suicide risk and the intake form was inadequate. The decedent acted as if he were joking when he spoke of a prior suicide attempt.[73]

A deliberate indifference to medical needs claim failed in *Bout v. Bolden*, even though the prisoner alleged that he was forcefully held down and subjected to dental work without benefit of anesthesia. The prisoner needed tooth repair, and the treatment was successful. The decision to drill without anesthesia rather than further delay treatment—given the minor nature of repair and relatively brief period of pain—did not amount to a constitutional violation.[74]

A doctor treated a prisoner's hepatitis C virus with interferons before his release from state prison. The doctor referred the prisoner to a specialist who became his primary care physician. This justified the doctor's decision to leave the interferon treatment decision to the specialist. The specialist believed that he could not or should not act unilaterally in administering the interferon treatment without approval of the procedure by the state health department. The apparent confusion or miscommunication between the physician and the specialist was, at most, negligence.[75]

A prison doctor misdiagnosed a prisoner's need for surgery. However, the doctor made extensive efforts to diagnose, monitor, and control the prisoner's hernia symptoms and did not disregard any risk of harm of which he was aware. Consulting other physicians disproved any contention that his diagnosis, even if incorrect, was somehow deliberate or indifferent. The doctor's classification of the prisoner's potential surgery as elective—rather than as an emergency— did not violate the prisoner's Eighth Amendment rights. A delay with respect to hernia surgery does not necessarily constitute deliberate indifference, absent some resultant harm or a worsened condition.[76]

A prisoner's claim that medical personnel were deliberately indifferent to his health and safety did not allege any physical harm. His allegation did not rise to a constitutional violation.[77] Similarly, where a prisoner did not allege that his medical condition was aggravated or that he suffered any injury or harm as result of his work assignment, he failed to show "deliberate indifference" in connection with his work assignment.[78]

During pretrial detention, a detainee contracted tuberculosis after being exposed to other detainees with tuberculosis. As the policies for tuberculosis diagnosis and treatment in force at the facility complied with state statutes and were formulated with input from the director of health care services, no reasonable fact finder could find that the sheriff had acted with deliberate indifference to the serious health risk posed by tuberculosis.[79]

§ 6.3.3 — Right to Refuse Medical Care

The right to medical aid also includes the right of refusal. A competent person has a constitutionally protected liberty interest to refuse unwanted medical treatment, as was stated in *Cruzan v. Director, Missouri Dept. of Health*.[80] Similarly, a patient has the right to refuse drug treatment. The right is adequately protected by hospital regulations that provide a series of informal consultations and interviews to determine, from a medical standpoint, whether compelled administration of drugs is necessary. It is not necessary to provide the patient with a due process hearing, a system of "patient advocates," or an independent decision-maker.[81]

In the case of a prisoner, the state has an important interest in maintaining the confinement of prisoners. The integrity of a correctional system must also be considered.[82] Courts will not condone a prisoner's manipulation of his or her medical circumstances to the detriment of a state's interest in prison order, security, and discipline. The "purpose" for refusing unwanted medical treatment is a factor that prison officials may legitimately consider in determining whether the refusal is likely to be a disruptive influence on or otherwise detrimental to the effective administration of the prison system[83] because the state's interest in orderly prison administration is the controlling factor.[84]

There are certain situations in which prison officials can require involuntary medical care. For example, in *North Dakota ex rel. Timothy Schuetzle v. Yogel*,[85] a prisoner was required to submit to diabetes monitoring of his blood sugar and, if ordered by a physician, to forcibly submit to food, insulin, and other medications to prevent deterioration of his health or premature death.

In 2004, the Seventh Circuit held that jail officials had a legitimate interest in preventing the prisoner population and staff from being exposed to lice. Their policy with respect to the required use of delousing shampoo by incoming prisoners did not amount to an unreasonable intrusion on the prisoner's constitutional right to refuse medical treatment. Permitting the prisoner to reject delousing shampoo would place the health and sanitation of other prisoners and jail staff at risk and give any prisoner exposed to lice potential grounds for a lawsuit.[86]

In a Second Circuit case two years later, a prisoner was diagnosed with Hepatitis C. He underwent a liver biopsy to verify the diagnosis and then was treated with two separate medications. Although this treatment was successful, the prisoner complained that he was not warned about its serious side effects and that had he known of them, he would have refused treatment. The Fourteenth Amendment right to refuse medical treatment also contains a concomitant right to information necessary to make an informed decision. The prisoner established a violation of this right by showing that the failure to provide him with necessary information caused him to undergo treatment that he would otherwise have refused and that such failure to inform was taken with deliberate indifference to his rights.[87]

§ 6.4   Transsexual and Transgender Inmates

Recently, an emerging body of litigation has focused on transgender inmates and gender reassignment surgery while incarcerated. However, none of the cases have reached the Supreme Court, and only a handful of cases have reached federal Courts of Appeal. Furthermore, because there is no consensus among the rulings from the federal appellate courts, the constitutional applications of this body of case law is far from settled.

In a federal district court case, a gender dysphoric inmate was incarcerated in an all-male facility. The inmate was born with male genitalia yet identifies as a woman. From a young age, she had taken estrogen treatment to "slow hair growth, soften skin, develop her breast implants, and further develop female characteristics." The Michigan Department of Corrections denied her request to continue the estrogen treatment while incarcerated, even after she stated she would pay for it herself. The inmate filed a 42 U.S.C. § 1983 lawsuit claiming that prison officials had been deliberately indifferent to her serious medical needs by not allowing the continued estrogen treatment, a violation of the Eighth Amendment's ban on cruel and unusual punishment. The court agreed and granted a preliminary injunction ordering correctional officials to provide her with estrogen therapy.[88]

In a similar case heard by the Eight Circuit, an inmate who was born male but identified as female filed suit against prison officials for refusing to provide hormone-replacement therapy for Gender Identity Disorder (GID), claiming it amounted to deliberate indifference to her serious medical needs.[89] The court granted summary judgment for prison officials, holding that the Eighth Amendment does not require hormone-replacement therapy.

Since 2014, five cases have reached federal Courts of Appeal concerning sex reassignment surgery for incarcerated offenders. Though the specific details of the five cases differ slightly, the similarity found among the cases is that a transgender inmate filed suit against state officials arguing that male-to-female sex reassignment surgery was the only available treatment for their gender dysphoria and that prison officials' refusal to provide said surgery equated to deliberate indifference. In three of the cases,[90] the court ruled that a state does not inflict cruel and unusual punishment by declining to provide sex reassignment surgery to a transgender inmate and thus that prison officials were not deliberately indifferent to serious medical needs. One of the courts further stated that the prisoner offered no evidence that the medical community universally accepted the necessity and efficacy of sex reassignment surgery as treatment for gender dysphoria. In the other two cases, *Rosati v. Igbinoso*[91] and *Edmo v. Corizon, Inc.*,[92] the courts concluded exactly the opposite and ruled in favor of the inmates.

§ 6.5   Right to Confidentiality

In *Anderson v. Romero*,[93] a prisoner was discovered to be infected with HIV (human immunodeficiency virus). The superintendent of the cell house at which the prisoner was placed told a correctional officer, in the presence of another officer, to make sure that he was put in a cell by himself because he was HIV positive. The officer told at least one other officer that the prisoner was HIV positive. Later the officer noticed a prisoner sleeping on the floor of the prisoner's cell. The officer told the prisoner that the prisoner was a homosexual and that the prisoner could catch AIDS from him and so had better stay away from him. The officer told a prisoner barber not to cut the prisoner's hair because he had HIV. His yard privileges were denied for several months because of his HIV-positive status.

The Seventh Circuit could not find any cases holding that prisoners have a constitutional right to the confidentiality of their medical records. The closest was *Harris v. Thigpen*,[94] which involved a challenge to the compulsory testing of prisoners for HIV and the segregation of those who tested positive. The challenge was based in part on a claimed constitutional right to the confidentiality of one's HIV status. The *Thigpen* court refused to go further than to assume, for the sake of argument, that seropositive prisoners enjoy some significant constitutionally protected privacy interest in preventing the nonconsensual disclosure of their HIV-positive diagnosis to other prisoners, as well as to their families and other outside visitors to the facilities in question. This was not believed to be a holding that prisoners have such a right.

However, it was recognized that certain disclosures of medical information or records would be actionable under the Cruel and Unusual Punishments Clause of the Eighth Amendment rather than the Due Process Clause of the Fourteenth Amendment. If prison officials disseminated humiliating but penologically irrelevant details of a prisoner's medical history, their action might conceivably constitute the infliction of cruel and unusual punishment; the fact that the punishment was purely psychological would not excuse it.[95]

The *Anderson* court conceded that the law is not clearly established that a prison cannot, without violating the constitutional rights of its HIV-positive prisoners, reveal their condition to other prisoners and to officers in order to enable the other prisoners and officers to protect themselves from infection.[96] The Seventh Circuit had previously held that the knowing failure to protect a prisoner from the danger posed by an HIV-positive cellmate with a propensity to rape violated the prisoner's right not to be subjected to cruel and unusual punishments.[97]

The Eighth Amendment only forbids cruel and unusual punishments; it does not require the most intelligent, progressive, humane, or efficacious prison administration. The *Anderson* court held that warnings to endangered prisoners or staff did not violate the Constitution just because they are ad hoc. The duty to protect prisoners from lethal encounters with their fellows is derived from the Eighth Amendment. The officer could not be criticized for having warned the other prisoner that the prisoner in whose cell he was seen sleeping was HIV positive or even for having warned the prisoner barber about the prisoner. It was recognized that a barber, especially if he uses a razor, may cut the skin of the person whose hair he is cutting and if the person's blood makes contact with a part of his skin where he has a cut or abrasion, he may become infected.

However, it is one thing to warn other prisoners that a prisoner is an HIV carrier; it is another to "punish" him or her for being a carrier by refusing to allow him or her to get a haircut or to exercise in the prison yard. *Anderson* was the first appellate case in which these specific modalities of punishing HIV carriers have been alleged. The Eighth Amendment forbids the state to punish people for a physical or medical condition, as distinct from illegal *actions*.[98] The Equal Protection Clause forbids the state to treat one group, including a group of prisoners, arbitrarily worse than another. If the only reason the prison officials denied haircuts and yard privileges to the prisoner was that he was HIV positive, and there was no conceivable justification for these as AIDS-fighting measures, the denial was improper.

§ 6.6   Conclusion

Penologists argue that effective rehabilitation programs are the key to success from any correctional system. Judicial concern for penal reform, coupled with the fact that many state statutes and constitutions specifically make rehabilitation an objective of incarceration, raise the probability that treatment programs may soon be judicially required in penal facilities, although *O'Connor v. Donaldson* and *Sandin v. Conner* have slowed, if not reversed, this trend.

It should be recognized that the main objective to "treatment" or "medical experimentation" is the reality that no "voluntary" program in prison is truly free from coercion. Perhaps innovative techniques, such as the appointment of legal guardians for the prisoners concerned, or prior judicial review or approval may answer the problem of "free and voluntary consent" within the prison context.

Judicial intervention in medical treatment cases has increased markedly in recent years. Unfortunately, however, federal courts are divided as to when a complaint alleging inadequate medical treatment is sufficient to state a cause of action for deprivation of a federal right. The Supreme Court has not yet rendered a decision clarifying the law in this area.

Notes

1   *E.g.*, *see* R.I. GEN. LAWS ANN. 13–3–1 (1956).
2   THE AMERICAN CORRECTIONAL ASSOCIATION, MANUAL OF CORRECTIONAL STANDARDS 10 (3d ed. 1966).
3   THE PRESIDENT'S COMMISSION ON LAW ENFORCEMENT AND ADMINISTRATION OF JUSTICE, TASK FORCE REPORT: CORRECTIONS 16 (1967).
4   Padgett v. Stein, 406 F. Supp. 287 (M.D. Pa. 1976).
5   *Id.* at 296; Pace v. Fauver, 479 F. Supp. 456 (D.N.J. 1979), *aff'd*, 694 F.2d 860 (4th Cir. 1981); Bresolin v. Morris, 558 P. 2d 1350 (Wash. 1977); State v. Damon, 20 Cr. L. 2530 (Wash. Ct. App. 1977).

6 Russell v. Oliver, 392 F. Supp. 470 (W.D. Va. 1975); Lunsford v. Reynolds, 376 F. Supp. 526 (W.D. Va. 1974); Wright v. Rushen, 642 F.2d 1129 (9th Cir. 1981); Rucker v. Meachum, 513 F. Supp. 32 (W.D. Okla. 1980).

7 Wilson v. Kelley, 294 F. Supp. 1005 (N.D. Ga. 1968), *aff'd per curiam*, 393 U.S. 266 (1969); Graham v. Vann, 394 So. 2d 180 (Fla. Dist. Ct. App. 1981); Layne v. Vinzant, 657 F.2d 468 (1st Cir. 1981); Leonardo v. Moran, 611 F.2d 397 (1st Cir. 1979).

8 Holt v. Sarver, 309 F. Supp. 362 (E.D. Ark. 1970), *aff'd*, 442 F.2d 304 (8th Cir. 1971).

9 *Id.* at 379.

10 Finney v. Arkansas Board of Corrections, 505 F.2d 194, 209 (8th Cir. 1974).

11 Miller v. Carson, 401 F. Supp. 835, 900 (M.D. Fla. 1975); Battle v. Anderson, 376 F. Supp. 402 (E.D. Okla. 1974); Prisoners of Allegheny County Jail v. Pierce, 612 F.2d 754 (3d Cir. 1979).

12 406 F. Supp. 318 (M.D. Ala. 1976); Morris v. Travisono, 499 F. Supp. 149 (D.R.I. 1980).

13 406 F. Supp. 649 (S.D. Tex. 1975); Ohlinger v. Watson, 652 F.2d 77 (9th Cir. 1980).

14 Breedlove v. Cripe, 511 F. Supp. 467 (N.D. Tex. 1981).

15 488 F.2d 1136 (8th Cir. 1973).

16 Clonce v. Richardson, 379 F. Supp. 338 (W.D. Mo. 1974).

17 377 F. Supp. 268 (E.D. Ark. 1974).

18 523 F.2d 838 (8th Cir. 1975); Mukmuk v. Commissioner, 529 F.2d 272 (2d Cir. 1976).

19 523 F.2d 825 (7th Cir. 1975).

20 Comment, *Non-Therapeutic Prison Search: An Analysis of Potential Legal Remedies*, 39 Alb. L. Rev. 799 (1975); Bailey v. Talley, 481 F. Supp. 203 (D. Md. 1979).

21 530 F.2d 199 (8th Cir. 1976); Yusaf Asad Madyun v. Thompson, 657 F.2d 868 (7th Cir. 1981) (in order to maintain an action based upon insufficient opportunities for vocational and educational training, it is necessary to show that the prison environment threatens a prisoner's mental and physical well-being).

22 392 F. Supp. 305 (N.D. Ohio 1974); Gawreys v. D.C. General Hospital, 480 F. Supp. 853 (D.D.C. 1979); cf. Holly v. Rapone, 476 F. Supp. 226 (E.D. Pa. 1979) (there is no constitutional right to receive methadone); United States ex rel. Walker v. Fayette County, Pennsylvania, 599 F.2d 573 (3d Cir. 1979) (state law did not require the establishment of methadone maintenance facilities at correctional institutions—therefore, the county was not obligated to provide methadone to its prisoners).

23 373 F.2d 451 (D.C. Cir. 1966).

24 Welsch v. Likins, 373 F. Supp. 487 (D. Minn. 1974).

25 393 F. Supp. 715 (E.D.N.Y. 1975).

26 422 U.S. 563 (1975); *see* Mills v. Rogers, 457 U.S. 291 (1982) (The United States Supreme Court reversed a lower court decision that mental patients who are involuntarily committed have a federal constitutional right to refuse treatment with antipsychotic drugs. The decision must be reexamined by the lower court in light of an intervening state supreme court decision concerning noninstitutionalized mental patients).

27 Donaldson v. O'Connor, 493 F.2d 507 (5th Cir. 1974), *vacated and remanded*, 422 U.S. 563 (1975).

28 Youngberg v. Romeo, 457 U.S. 307 (1982).

29 14 Cal. App. 3d 338, 535 P. 2d 373 (Cal. 1975).

30 People v. Wilkins, 23 App. Div. 2d 178, 259 N.Y.S.2d 462 (N.Y. App. Div. 1965).

31 People v. Hutchings, 74 Misc. 2d 14, 343 N.Y.S.2d 845 (Cortland County Court 1973).

32 652 F.2d 775 (9th Cir. 1980).

33 *See* n. 1.

34 Author of several right-to-treatment decisions from the Federal Circuit Court of Appeals for the District of Columbia.

35 David L. Bazelon, *Implementing the Right to Treatment*, 36 U. Chi. L. Rev. 742, 748–749 (1969).

36 494 U.S. 210 (1990).

37 Turner v. Safley, 482 U.S. 78 (1987).

38 A federal prisoner complaining about medical treatment in the institution utilizes the federal habeas corpus procedure. A state prisoner may use a Civil Rights Action (42 U.S.C. 1983) or the federal habeas corpus procedure. *See* Chapter 15 for a discussion of the prisoner's remedies.

39 *See* Chapters 10 and 13 for a discussion of due process of law.

40 Shannon v. Lester, 519 F.2d 76 (6th Cir. 1975); Derrickson v. Keve, 390 F. Supp. 905 (D. Del. 1975); Nickolson v. Choctaw County, Alabama, 498 F. Supp. 295 (S.D. Ala. 1980); Lareau v. Manson, 507 F. Supp. 1177 (D. Conn. 1980), *modified in*, 651 F.2d 96 (2d Cir. 1981).

41 Clements v. Turner, 364 F. Supp. 270 (D. Utah 1973).

42 Hoitt v. Vitek, 497 F.2d 598 (1st Cir. 1974); Runnels v. Rosendale, 499 F.2d 733 (9th Cir. 1974); Johnson v. Harris, 479 F. Supp. 333 (S.D.N.Y. 1979).

43 Bishop v. Stoneman, 508 F.2d 1224 (2d Cir. 1974); Russell v. Sheffer, 528 F.2d 318 (4th Cir. 1975). *See* Comment, *The Eighth Amendment: Medical Treatment of Prisoners as Cruel and Unusual Punishment*, 1 CAP. U. L. REV. 83 (1972). Estelle v. Gamble, 429 U.S. 97 (1976); Burks v. Teasdale, 492 F. Supp. 650 (W.D. Mo. 1980); Hampton v. Holmesburg Prison Officials, 546 F.2d 1077 (3d Cir. 1976); Kelsey v. Ewing, 652 F.2d 4 (8th Cir. 1981); Prisoners of Allegheny County Jail v. Pierce, 612 F.2d 754 (3d Cir. 1979); Duncan v. Duckworth, 644 F.2d 653 (7th Cir. 1981).

44 Priest v. Cupp, 545 P. 2d 917 (Or. Ct. App. 1976).

45 501 F.2d 1291 (5th Cir. 1974).

46 Gates v. Collier, 390 F. Supp. 482, 488 (N.D. Miss. 1975).

47 Gates v. Collier, 501 F.2d 1291, 1303 (5th Cir. 1974).

48 401 F. Supp. 835 (M.D. Fla. 1975).

49 *Id*. at 898; *see also* Brown v. Beck, 481 F. Supp. 723 (S.D. Ga. 1980).

50 405 F. Supp. 656 (D. Nev. 1975); *see also* Jackson v. State of Mississippi, 644 F.2d 1142 (5th Cir. 1981).

51 United States ex rel. Hyde v. McGinnis, 429 F.2d 864 (2d Cir. 1970).

52 Fore v. Godwin, 407 F. Supp. 1145 (E.D. Va. 1976).

53 Ray v. Parrish, 399 F. Supp. 775 (E.D. Va. 1975); Jackson v. Moore, 471 F. Supp. 1068 (D. Colo. 1979).

54 Boyce v. Alizadun, 595 F.2d 948 (4th Cir. 1979); Shepard v. Stidham, 502 F. Supp. 1275 (M.D. Ala., 1980); DiLorenze v. United States, 496 F. Supp. 79 (S.D.N.Y. 1980); Campbell v. Sacred Heart Hospital, 496 F. Supp. 692 (E.D. Pa. 1980); Estelle v. Gamble, 429 U.S. 97 (1976).

55 429 U.S. 97 (1976).

56 Id.

57 Wilson v. Seiter, 501 U.S. 294 (1991).

58 *See* Farmer v. Brennan, 511 U.S. 825 (1994).

59 37 F.3d 63 (2d Cir. 1994).

60 371 F. Supp. 1249 (W.D. Mo. 1974); Commissioner of Corrections v. Meyers, 399 N.E.2d 452 (Mass. 1979).

61 273 F.3d 693 (6th Cir. 2001).

62 Navedo v. Maloney 172 F. Supp. 2d 276 (D.C. Mass. 2001).

63 Shelton v. Angelone, 148 F. Supp. 2d 670 (W.D. Va. 2001).

64 Wynn v. Southward, 251 F.3d 588 (7th Cir. 2001).

65 Castellano v. Chicago P.D., 129 F. Supp. 2d 1184 (N.D. Ill. 2001).

66 Palermo v. Corr. Med. Servs., 133 F. Supp. 2d 1348 (S.D. Fla. 2001).

67 Hartsfield v. Colburn, 371 F.3d 454 (8th Cir. 2004).

68 Garrett v. Elko, 1997 U.S. App. LEXIS 21271 (4th Cir. 1997).

69 Iko v. Shreve, 535 F.3d 225 (4th Cir. 2008).

70 *See* Gibson v. Moskowitz, 523 F.3d 657 (6th Cir. 2008).

71 Gutierrez v. Peters, 111 F.3d 1364 (7th Cir. 1997).

72 Word v. Croce, 169 F. Supp. 2d 219 (S.D.N.Y. 2001).

73 Estate of Boncher v. Brown County, 272 F.3d 484 (7th Cir. 2001).

74 Bout v. Bolden, 22 F. Supp. 2d 646 (E.D. Mich. 1998), *aff'd*, 225 F.3d 658 (6th Cir. 2000).

75 Bender v. Regier, 385 F.3d 1133 (8th Cir. 2004), *reh'g denied, reh'g en banc denied*, 2004 U.S. App. LEXIS 23040 (8th Cir. 2004).

76 Webb v. Hamidulla, 281 Fed. Appx. 159 (4th Cir. 2008).

77 Newland v. Nafrawi, Fed. Appx. 390 (5th Cir. 2007).

78 Winston v. Stacks, 243 Fed. Appx. 805 (5th Cir. 2007).

79 Butler v. Fletcher, 465 F.3d 340 (8th Cir. 2006).

80 497 U.S. 261 (1990).

81 Rennie v. Klein, 653 F.2d 836 (3d Cir. 1981), *vacated and remanded* in light of Youngberg v. Romeo, 457 U.S. 307 (1982).

82 Washington v. Harper, 494 U.S. 210 (1990). The extent of a prisoner's right under the Due Process Clause to avoid the unwanted administration of antipsychotic drugs must be defined in the context of the prisoner's confinement. *See also* Sandin v. Conner, 515 U.S. 472 (1995).

83 Jones v. North Carolina Prisoners' Labor Union, Inc., 433 U.S. 119 (1977).

84 *See* Zant v. Prevatte, 248 Ga. 832, 286 S.E.2d 715 (1982), in which the Supreme Court of Georgia held that a hunger-striking prisoner, who began fasting to obtain transfer out of the Georgia prison system for fear of his safety, had the right to die by refusing food and medical treatment.

85 537 N.W.2d 358 (N.D. 1995).

86 Russell v. Richards, 384 F.3d 444 (7th Cir. 2004).

87 Pabon v. Wright, 459 F.3d 241 (2d Cir. 2006).

88 Phillips v. Michigan Department of Corrections, 731 F. Supp. 792 (W.D. Mich. 1990).

89 Reid v. Griffin, 808 F. 3d 1191 (8th Cir. 2015).

90 Kosilek v. Spencer, 774 F. 3d 63 (1st Cir. 2014); Gibson v. Collier, 920 F. 3d 212 (5th Cir. 2019); Williams v. Kelly, 818 Fed. Appx. 353 (5th Cir. 2020).

91 791 F. 3d 1037 (9th Cir. 2015).

92 935 F. 3d 757 (9th Cir. 2019).

93 72 F.3d 518 (7th Cir. 1995).

94 941 F.2d 1495 (11th Cir. 1991).

95 *See, e.g.*, Thomas v. Farley, 31 F.3d 557 (7th Cir. 1994); Joseph v. Brierton, 739 F.2d 1244 (7th Cir. 1984); Williams v. Boles, 841 F.2d 181 (7th Cir. 1988); Northington v. Jackson, 973 F.2d 1518 (10th Cir. 1992). It was also suggested that branding or tattooing HIV-positive prisoners (the branding of persons who are HIV positive was once seriously proposed as a method of retarding the spread of AIDS), or making them wear a sign around their neck that read "I AM AN AIDS CARRIER!" would constitute cruel and unusual punishment. So, too, if employees of the prison, knowing that a prisoner identified as HIV positive was a likely target of violence by other prisoners, yet are indifferent to his fate, gratuitously revealed his HIV status to other prisoners, and a violent attack upon him ensued. Cf. Bowers v. DeVito, 686 F.2d 616 (7th Cir. 1982).

96 Cf. Camarillo v. McCarthy, 998 F.2d 638 (9th Cir. 1993).

97 Billman v. Indiana Department of Corrections, 56 F.3d 785, 788–789 (7th Cir. 1995).

98 *See* Robinson v. California, 370 U.S. 660 (1962); Despears v. Milwaukee County, 63 F.3d 635 (7th Cir. 1995).

Prisoner Legal Services 7

Chapter Outline

§ 7.1 Introduction

The Supreme Court has repeatedly affirmed that one of the fundamental rights within the Due Process Clause of the Fourteenth Amendment is the right of access to the courts. Essential to the concept of due process of law is the right of an individual to have "an opportunity . . . granted at a meaningful time and in a meaningful manner,"[1] "for [a] hearing appropriate to the nature of the case."[2]

The right of a prisoner to exercise this basic constitutional right was established in the 1940 case of *Ex parte Hull*.[3] In *Hull*, a state prison regulation required that all legal documents in a prisoner's court proceedings be submitted to a prison official for examination and censorship before they were filed with the court. The Supreme Court found this regulation invalid on the ground that "the state and its officers may not abridge or impair petitioner's right to apply to a federal court for a writ of habeas corpus."[4]

In spite of the rule of law established in *Hull*, courts have hesitated to interfere with the exercise of discretion by prison administrators in matters concerning institutional control. The courts have frequently stated that prison administration was a function relegated to the executive branch of government, and for this reason the judiciary would interfere only where the wrongs committed by institution officials were of monumental proportions.[5] This judicial reluctance offers insight as to why various prison practices (although they may violate the prisoners' constitutional rights) have gone uncontested in the past.

Bounds v. Smith[6] opened the courtroom doors to prisoners in 1977 by requiring meaningful access to the courts. The *Bounds* principle can be satisfied in various ways, and state legislatures and prison administrators were given "wide discretion" to select appropriate solutions from a range of complex options.[7]

Bounds did not create an abstract, freestanding right to a law library or legal assistance program. The right that *Bounds* acknowledged was the right of access to the courts. To establish a *Bounds* violation, the "actual injury" that a prisoner must demonstrate is that the alleged shortcomings in the prison library or legal assistance program have hindered or are presently hindering his or her efforts to pursue a nonfrivolous legal claim. The doctrine of "standing"[8] is a constitutional requirement for a federal court to exercise jurisdiction and decide a case. Thus, an actual injury was required. Although *Bounds* made no mention of an actual injury requirement, it did not eliminate that constitutional prerequisite.

The access of prisoners to the courts was cut back in a 5–4 decision by the Supreme Court in *Lewis v. Casey*.[9] Inmates at various prisons operated by the Arizona Department of Corrections brought a class action lawsuit alleging that state prison officials were furnishing them with inadequate legal research facilities and thereby depriving them of their right of access to the courts. A broad, system-wide injunction was issued by the district court, which found the restrictions to be unconstitutional. The Supreme Court reversed, holding that any systemic challenge to the Arizona system was conditioned on the prisoner's ability to show widespread actual injury. The district court failed to identify anything more than isolated instances of any actual injury. The Supreme Court held in *Lewis* that any statements in *Bounds* suggesting that prison authorities must also enable the prisoner to discover grievances or to litigate effectively once in court find no precedent in the Court's pre-*Bounds* cases and were rejected. Moreover, *Bounds* does not guarantee prisoners the right to file any and every type of legal claim but required only that they be provided with the tools to attack their sentences, directly or collaterally, and to challenge the conditions of their confinement.

Lewis held that the findings of the Arizona district court as to actual injury did not support a system-wide injunction. A remedy must be limited to the inadequacy that produced the injury-in-fact that the prisoner had established. Only one named prisoner was found to have suffered an actual injury. This was a result of the failure to provide the special services he would have needed, in light of his particular disability of illiteracy. Eliminated from the proper scope of the injunction, therefore, were any provisions directed at special services or facilities required by non-English speakers, by prisoners in lockdown, or by the prisoner population at large. Furthermore, the Supreme Court held that the inadequacy that caused any actual injury to illiterate prisoners was not sufficiently widespread to justify system-wide relief.

After *Lewis*, the prisoner must show that the officials actually prevented him or her from taking some meritorious legal action. However, the door to the courthouse remains open. A district court decision holding that this standard does not apply to retaliation cases was vacated.[10] In the Sixth Circuit, in order to support a civil rights action based on a claim that prison officials retaliated against the filing of a lawsuit by interfering with a prisoner's access to the courts, the prisoner does not have to show any injury beyond that which results from the retaliation. The Sixth Circuit stated that it is well established that prisoners have a constitutional right of access to the courts. This is not a generalized "right to litigate" but a carefully bounded right, as Justice Scalia makes clear in *Lewis*:

> *Bounds* does not guarantee prisoners the wherewithal to transform themselves into litigating engines capable of filing everything from shareholder derivative actions to slip-and-fall claims. The tools it requires to be provided are those that the prisoners need in order to attack their sentences, directly or collaterally, and in order to challenge the conditions of their confinement. Impairment of any other litigating capacity is simply one of the incidental (and perfectly constitutional) consequences of conviction and incarceration.[11]

Thus, a prisoner's right to access the courts extends to direct appeals, habeas corpus applications, and civil rights claims only. The importance of this right to incarcerated individuals is evident and can hardly be overstated:

> The right to file for legal redress in the courts is as valuable to a prisoner as to any other citizen. Indeed, for the prisoner it is more valuable. Inasmuch as one convicted of a serious crime and imprisoned usually is divested of the franchise, the right to file a court action stands . . . as his most "fundamental political right, because preservative of all rights."[12]

§ 7.2 The Nature of Legal Services in Prison – Prevailing Practices

Many of the practices that prevailed in prisons throughout the country until recent times have amounted to impairments of the prisoners' right of access to the courts. Disciplinary actions for prisoners pursuing legal remedies, censorship or wholesale confiscation of a prisoner's legal documents, and other such practices were common in many of America's prison systems.

Further restriction on access to the courts was seen in the fact that prison officials seldom provided prisoners with any services related to legal needs. In most cases, only a few outdated law books and, occasionally, the services of a notary public were supplied. As a result of this lack of legal assistance, prisoners were frequently forced to accept the aid of a self-proclaimed "jailhouse lawyer" or "writ-writer." A jailhouse lawyer is a prisoner who, through self-education, has acquired minimum legal skills and, notwithstanding prison restriction, offers legal advice and counseling to fellow prisoners, either with or without compensation. These individuals have been subject to a great deal of restriction and regulation by prison officials. It is on the restriction of jailhouse lawyers and alternatives to them that judicial concern has focused in the modern cases.

Restrictions on the legal practice of jailhouse lawyers, in light of the unique position of an incarcerated individual, place an impossible burden on the prisoner seeking legal relief. These restrictions, coupled with the unavailability of legal assistance in the outside world, had resulted in the complete loss of a basic constitutional right. This loss and difficulty was finally acknowledged and partially resolved by the Supreme Court in 1969.

§ 7.3 The Rule of *Johnson v. Avery*

The 1969 Supreme Court case of *Johnson v. Avery*[13] has had a profound effect upon the power of prison officials to regulate or prohibit a prisoner's right of access to the courts. The case involved the constitutionality of a Tennessee prison regulation that provided: "No prisoner will advise, assist or otherwise contract to aid another, either with or without a fee, to prepare Writs or other legal matters. Prisoners are forbidden to set themselves up as practitioners for the purpose of promoting a business of writing Writs."[14]

In analyzing this prison rule, the Supreme Court emphasized that prisoners, a great percentage of whom are illiterate, were frequently unable to obtain assistance in preparing requests for postconviction relief from any source other than one available within the prison walls. Therefore, because the necessary legal assistance was usually available only in the form of a jailhouse lawyer or prisoner writ-writer, the Supreme Court reasoned that a regulation that effectively cut off this assistance amounted to a denial of access to the courts. For this reason, together with the "fundamental importance of the writ of habeas corpus in our constitutional scheme,"[15] the Supreme Court declared the Tennessee regulation invalid.

Although *Johnson v. Avery* has played a prominent role in bringing about prison reform, the ruling itself was very narrow in scope. Essentially, the only "right" guaranteed by this decision was that of an illiterate prisoner to receive legal aid from a fellow prisoner in the preparation of petitions for writs of habeas corpus. This right was not absolute but was restricted to prisoners incarcerated in a prison system that had failed to provide a "reasonable alternative" by which access to the courts (i.e., competent legal assistance) could be gained. The Supreme Court further limited this right by allowing prison authorities to: (1) place reasonable restrictions upon the time and place where the prisoners' legal counseling could be given and (2) impose punishment or discipline for any exchange of consideration or payment for the services rendered. Thus, a prison rule that provided for the discipline of a jailhouse lawyer who charges for his or her services or receives anything of value in return for such services is authorized under *Johnson v. Avery*.

§ 7.3.1   —Judicial Interpretation of *Johnson v. Avery*

Johnson v. Avery recognized the existence of two competing interests in the area of corrections: (1) the legitimate exercise of control by prison officials and (2) the constitutionally protected rights retained by prisoners. As a result of these dual concerns, lower courts applying the rule of *Johnson v. Avery* have attempted to balance the proper state concern with the concern of the prisoner in obtaining the legal assistance necessary to gain access to the courts. The state has the choice of providing prisoners with access to the courts by making available either adequate law libraries or persons trained in the law.[16] A clear test is found in a decision of the Supreme Court of California,[17] in which the court established three governing principles to guide future decisions. First, the court must determine the extent to which the institutional regulations impede or discourage mutual prisoner legal assistance. Second, the court is to decide, from the standpoint of legitimate custodial objectives, how undesirable the conduct is that the particular regulation sought to avoid. Third, the court must determine whether there are alternative means of dealing with the undesirable conduct—means that do not result in significant restrictions on mutual prisoner aid.[18] However, it should be noted that, consistent with the ruling of *Johnson*, emphasis is placed upon the needs of the prisoner rather than on those of the institution. In effect, the court stated that where an irreconcilable conflict exists, the prison officials, rather than the prisoner, must alter their practices.

Although other courts have not enumerated so specific a test as California, they have nevertheless maintained the same theoretical approach in dealing with the conflict existing in a prison setting.[19] There is a tendency for the courts to retain the same noninterference rhetoric used by the pre-*Johnson* cases, but an obvious change in attitude has occurred.

In *Cruz v. Hauck*,[20] the Fifth Circuit held that a broad rule that prohibited prisoners from giving or receiving legal assistance on habeas corpus or other general civil legal matters in jail was invalid. It approved, however, reasonable rules governing the time and place for prisoners to obtain legal assistance. The court said that the officials have a duty to maintain security in the cellblock and can restrict the storage of law books in prisoners' cells for security purposes. If prisoners cannot safely store legal materials in their cells, arrangements for storage of these materials in a readily available area with reasonable procedures for their use are required. To maintain a proper balance between competing interests of prison control and prisoner rights, the court held that a prisoner should be permitted to obtain legal materials from sources other than attorneys or publishing houses, subject to screening only for security purposes. Courts would no longer defer to administrative discretion but would more closely scrutinize the fact situation in order to prevent possible violation of constitutional rights.

Johnson v. Avery opened a new area of concern for the judiciary in its recognition of the necessity for mutual prisoner legal assistance in the preparation of writs. Five primary concerns of the courts deal with the issue of mutual prisoner legal assistance:

1. Which prisoners are permitted to receive legal assistance from a jailhouse lawyer?
2. Who may act as a jailhouse lawyer?
3. How may prison authorities reasonably restrict the jailhouse lawyer?
4. What type of legal assistance may be received from the jailhouse lawyer?
5. What is a reasonable alternative to the jailhouse lawyer?

§ 7.4 Which Prisoners Are Permitted to Receive Legal Assistance from the Jailhouse Lawyer?

The emphasis in *Johnson v. Avery* was on recognition of the need for an illiterate or functionally illiterate prisoner to receive legal assistance in the preparation of legal documents to be filed with the courts. The federal courts that have dealt with this issue, however, have refused to restrict the *Johnson* doctrine to its narrow confines.

Restrictions that forbid the receipt of legal assistance by anyone but illiterate prisoners have been invalidated as contrary to the Supreme Court ruling. Where there is no "reasonable alternative," all prisoners in the institution must be permitted to seek legal counsel from the jailhouse lawyer.[21] However, a paroled state prisoner was found to be in the same situation as any other *pro se* plaintiff who had the choice of representing him- or herself or finding an attorney. A parolee was not entitled to be represented by the jailhouse lawyer who had initially prepared the pleadings in the prisoner's civil rights action against a prison physician.[22] The uncontrolled discretion of a prison official as to who may or may not receive legal counseling has been invalidated when official approval is not subject to established standards.[23]

An exception to the broad statement that all prisoners must be permitted assistance from the jailhouse lawyer occurs when prisoners have been temporarily confined in isolation. As long as the confinement is not for an extended period—thereby hindering access to the courts—isolated prisoners need not be afforded assistance from the jailhouse lawyer.[24]

Jailhouse lawyers may also play a role in internal prison matters. In *Kirby v. Blackledge*,[25] prison officials were required to allow the assistance of a fellow prisoner, or some designated staff member, to be part of proceedings to transfer an illiterate and disadvantaged prisoner to maximum security. In *Clutchette v. Enomoto*,[26] the Fourth Circuit held that prison discipline procedures must permit a prisoner who is illiterate or who faces complex issues to have adequate assistance in lieu of counsel. The reason for counsel substitute was that the prisoner might not have the capacity to collect and present necessary evidence for an adequate presentation of the case.

It must be stressed here that *Johnson v. Avery* applies only when a prison system has no meaningful alternative to the jailhouse lawyer.

§ 7.5 Who May Act as the Jailhouse Lawyer?

Related to the issue of who may receive legal assistance from a jailhouse lawyer is the problem of who among the prisoner population may function as the jailhouse lawyer. The courts have stressed that the right asserted in *Johnson v. Avery* was not the privilege of the jailhouse lawyer to practice law. Rather, it was the right of a prisoner to receive legal assistance from a fellow prisoner.[27] This principle is most clearly expressed in cases in which jailhouse lawyers have attempted to send legal material to a prisoner in another prison and, as a result, have been subjected to disciplinary action. The rule that has emerged from these cases has been that the "client" prisoner could receive legal assistance from prisoners in his or her own prison. Because his or her rights could be protected there, there was no necessity that legal assistance be furnished to him or her by a prisoner confined in another prison. Therefore, because no prisoner needed legal assistance from a particular prisoner in another prison, the jailhouse lawyer could be restricted accordingly,[28] in the absence of evidence that alternative means of obtaining legal assistance were unavailable.[29]

§ 7.6   May Prison Officials Restrict the Jailhouse Lawyer?

In *Johnson v. Avery*, the Supreme Court stated that the activities of the jailhouse lawyer could be restricted as to time and place. Furthermore, an absolute prohibition on the jailhouse lawyer receiving fees was also enunciated. As a result of the "reasonableness" requirement, the interpretation given this rule by the lower courts has been varied.

One of the most litigated issues involving restrictions upon mutual prisoner legal assistance has concerned the proper exercise of discretion by prison officials. Courts have asserted that the uncontrolled discretion of prison officials in restricting the practice of the jailhouse lawyer is unconstitutional under *Johnson v. Avery*. This discretion, according to these courts, must be subject to established guidelines or standards in order to assure that they are reasonable.[30] Another related issue is the validity of a rule that required all legal work to be conducted in a special writ room. The courts, both before and after the *Johnson* ruling, have approved such a rule, as long as prison officials were not unduly restrictive[31] in the hours of use they permitted.

The right of a jailhouse lawyer to have the legal papers of another prisoner in his or her possession is unclear. In one case, in order for jailhouse lawyers to function effectively, the court held that they must be able to have in their possession papers that pertain to their "client's" case.[32] Another court interpreted a prison regulation as authorizing the papers to be kept by the jailhouse lawyer only until such time as the petition was complete, after which the papers had to be returned to the "client."[33] At a minimum, it would appear that a prison regulation could not forbid the jailhouse lawyer from having the papers of another prisoner in his or her possession on that ground alone.

The Supreme Court of California, in the case of *In re Harrell*,[34] dealt extensively with the type of restrictions permissible under the *Johnson* ruling. The regulations discussed were typical of many institutions. One regulation invalidated by the court forbade the jailhouse lawyer to file with a court an application for relief on behalf of, or as "next friend" of, his client. The court held that the *Johnson* rule authorized legal assistance in writ-writing, not in representation before the courts. Although an application submitted by a "next friend" will not generally be accepted by a court unless there are exceptional circumstances, this judicial policy did not, according to *Harrell*, give prison officials the right to examine such applications to determine whether the request for relief had merit. This determination is a decision for the courts, not prison officials. Therefore, prison officials may not refuse to forward a document to the courts on the grounds that it is improperly prepared.[35]

Another disputed restriction dealt with the right of a prisoner to correspond on legal matters with prisoners in other institutions. The prisoner in *Harrell* sought to give legal advice through use of the mail. The court found that the prison rule restricting this practice was valid under *Johnson*. The *Johnson* rule, stated the court, guaranteed the right to be assisted but did not give the "client" the right to be assisted by a particular jailhouse lawyer. No infringement upon that right necessarily resulted from a restriction on the activities of a particular prisoner "lawyer." The restriction placed on the jailhouse lawyer in this area is valid because the prisoners of another prison can seek assistance from jailhouse lawyers at their own prison.[36]

A third regulation attacked by the prisoner involved the number of books that could be retained by the jailhouse lawyer in his own cell. The court found that such restrictions on the jailhouse lawyer:

> impinge upon the rights enumerated in *Johnson* only to the extent it is shown that the ability of other prisoners seeking legal assistance to gain such assistance is affected. Unless and until it is demonstrated that other sources of legal assistance—e.g., other prisoners who use the library—cannot provide assistance to disadvantaged prisoners, the state of any prisoner's personal library is of no significance.[37]

Under the facts, the California regulation was upheld.

In a case that eventually reached the Supreme Court, a prisoner (Murphy) learned that a fellow inmate had been charged with assaulting a correctional officer. Murphy decided to assist the inmate with his defense and sent him a letter. Prison officials confiscated the letter and sanctioned Murphy for violating prison rules prohibiting insolence and interfering with due process hearings. Murphy filed suit, alleging that the disciplinary action violated his First Amendment rights, including the right to provide legal assistance to other inmates. In 2001, the Supreme Court held in *Shaw v. Murphy*[38] that prisoners do not possess a special First Amendment right to provide legal assistance to fellow prisoners that enhances the protections otherwise available under the *Turner v. Safley* standard. Furthermore, "Augmenting First Amendment protection for [legal] advice would undermine prison officials' ability to address the complex and intractable problems of prison administration."[39]

§ 7.7   What Type of Legal Assistance May a Prisoner Receive from the Jailhouse Lawyer?

The issue before the Supreme Court in *Johnson v. Avery* was concerned with habeas corpus petitions. It was because of the vital necessity to protect the right of a prisoner to file this writ that the Supreme Court heard the case. The lower federal courts, however, have again refused to restrict themselves to such narrow applications of constitutional rights. They have, on the contrary, expanded the right to include other legal petitions besides habeas corpus petitions. Two cases have held that the theoretical basis of *Johnson* was protection of the prisoner's right of access to the courts and that, for this reason, the *Johnson* ruling must be extended beyond habeas corpus petitions. Similarly protected, the court said, was the right of a jailhouse lawyer to aid in preparing a specific type of petition outside of habeas corpus, such as a civil rights action under 42 U.S.C. § 1983.

In *Nolan v. Scafati*,[40] a prisoner alleged that his constitutional right of access to the courts was violated when prison officials refused to mail his letter to the American Civil Liberties Union. This letter sought advice and assistance on his constitutional rights in a prison disciplinary hearing. The court found that the rule of *Johnson v. Avery* stood for "the general proposition that a prisoner's right of access to the courts involves a corollary right to obtain some assistance in preparing his communication with the court."[41] In view of this "general proposition," the court refused to confine the *Johnson* rule exclusively to prisoners seeking postconviction relief. The court believed that to so limit that rule would allow prison officials to silence—and perhaps to punish—prisoners seeking vindication of constitutional rights clearly held by prisoners.[42] The findings of the *Nolan* case were cited with approval by the court in *Cross v. Powers*.[43] The result of these two cases was to extend to all prisoners the right to assistance in their preparation of civil rights actions against prison officials.

Subsequent cases have expanded the type of aid that may be given. In *Williams v. Department of Justice*,[44] the Fifth Circuit went one step beyond the *Nolan* and *Cross* cases. *Williams* held that *Johnson* stood for the proposition that a prison regulation prohibiting prisoner assistance in the drafting of *pro se* legal papers constituted a "deprivation of due process of law, where no 'reasonable alternative' was available to furnish legal advice."[45] This would appear to be an assertion that, at least to this court, prisoners must be permitted the assistance of a jailhouse lawyer in the preparation of all of their legal petitions.

Finally, in *Wolff v. McDonnell*,[46] the Supreme Court held that the doctrine of *Johnson v. Avery* was not limited to cases involving the preparation of habeas corpus petitions but also applied to civil rights actions. Therefore, unless the state provides a reasonable alternative to the "jailhouse lawyer" in the preparation of civil rights actions, prisoners cannot be barred from furnishing such assistance to one another. In compliance with *Wolff v. McDonnell*, *Graham v. State Dept. of Corrections*[47] held that a counsel substitute must be available whenever the prisoner is unable to competently handle his or her case in a prison reclassification proceeding. If a counsel substitute is requested by a prisoner on such grounds, and the request is denied, the record of the reclassification proceeding should contain findings to support the denial.

§ 7.8　What is the Reasonable Alternative to the Jailhouse Lawyer?

The main thrust of *Johnson v. Avery* was that a state may not restrict the practices of the jailhouse lawyer unless a "reasonable alternative" to legal services is available to the prisoners. In the cases relating to this issue, it is clear that some measure of professional assistance must be made available if prison officials wish to suppress the activities of the jailhouse lawyer. In reality, this "professional assistance" means the services of an attorney or a law school assistance program. It should be noted, however, that the courts have differed as to the adequacy of legal assistance programs. Courts dealing with this issue have expressed little concern over the adequacy of the reasonable alternative provided by a prison.[48]

In *Ayers v. Ciccone*,[49] a single attorney working 12 hours per week was held to be a reasonable alternative to the jailhouse lawyer. It should be apparent, however, that an attorney working for such a limited period could not effectively meet the legal needs of many prisoners. A similar decision was *Novak v. Beto*.[50] In that case, a Texas district court upheld an absolute restriction against a jailhouse lawyer because the state had provided the services of two full-time attorneys to assist the 13,000 prisoners in the Texas correctional system. The failure of the district court to question the effectiveness of such a program in assuring the availability of assistance resulted in a reversal on appeal.[51] That this court found it necessary to inquire into the adequacy of the existing program is not unusual. This is evidenced by other cases dealing with the issue.

Beard v. Alabama[52] held that an absolute restriction against jailhouse lawyers "might well be sustained if the state were to make available a sufficient number of qualified attorneys or other persons capable and willing to render voluntary assistance in the preparation of petitions for habeas corpus relief."[53] This court asserted that the state must provide a "sufficient" legal services system, implying that the courts have the obligation to inquire into the effectiveness of the legal services provided.

In *Noorlander v. Ciccone*,[54] the Eighth Circuit remanded the case to the trial court to determine the adequacy of the prison law library and to see whether adequate alternatives to legal publications for prisoners existed. The court rejected the prisoner's claim that his right to self-representation required a law library at the institution. The reasoning of the court was that the public defender program was sufficient and that the prisoner was provided reasonable opportunity for access to the courts. However, he was not entitled to access by all available means.

Two other cases that have given careful scrutiny to the legal services provided to prisoners are *Williams v. Department of Justice*[55] and *Cross v. Powers*.[56] Both cases dealt with the use of a law school clinic program in prisons. It should also be noted that, as previously mentioned, both cases expanded *Johnson* to legal actions beyond habeas corpus petitions. *Williams* included all *pro se* petitions, and *Cross* allowed prisoners filing civil rights actions to receive the assistance of a jailhouse lawyer. The crucial similarity between these cases is the fact that both courts found the clinic programs inadequate to meet the reasonable alternative requirements of *Johnson v. Avery*. The petitioner in *Williams* claimed that there was an 18-month delay between the time a prisoner requested aid and the time he received it from the student clinic.[57] The court held that such a delay was inconsistent with the goals of the Supreme Court ruling.

Cross v. Powers[58] invalidated an absolute restriction against jailhouse lawyers because the law school clinic did not assist prisoners who wished to file civil rights actions against prison officials. The effect of this decision is to require legal services programs to provide prisoners with assistance not only in habeas corpus actions but also in cases in which a prisoner seeks civil rights relief, if the prison officials wish to suppress jailhouse lawyers.

Prison officials act on questionable grounds if they attempt to restrict a law clinic from conducting full legal services. In *Bryan v. Werner*,[59] the Third Circuit held that restrictions preventing a law clinic from assisting prisoners in suits against the prison were valid only if there were reasonable alternatives to the clinic for obtaining assistance in such suits. The prison could prohibit the clinic from using its title in suits that were not authorized under clinic rules, but it could not prevent the clinic from notarizing or mailing legal papers relevant to such suits. Such practice would be invalid as impeding access to the courts.

Although few prison officials will voluntarily open their prisons to law school clinics so that legal services will be provided to prisoners suing them for monetary damages, it seems clear that such legal services must be provided if the jailhouse lawyer is prohibited. To not provide these legal services has been held a violation of the prisoner's rights to legal representation and access to the courts. In *Cruz v. Beto*,[60] the former director of the Texas Department of Corrections was held personally liable in money damages to a group of indigent prisoners for depriving them of the opportunity to continue consultations with their attorney. The director alleged that the attorney was causing trouble and consequently prohibited her from visiting the state prisons. At trial, the allegations were never substantiated. The court noted that no criminal charges were ever filed against the attorney, nor was any complaint ever made to the state bar association.

In *Procunier v. Martinez*,[61] the Supreme Court considered a California prison regulation that provided in part:

> [i]nvestigators for an attorney-of-record will be confined to not more than two. Such investigators must be licensed by the State or must be members of the State Bar. Designation must be made in writing by the Attorney.[62]

This regulation restricted access by the prisoners to members of the bar and licensed private investigators and imposed an absolute ban on the use of law students and legal paraprofessionals by attorneys to interview prisoner clients. Attorneys were also prohibited from delegating to such persons the task of obtaining prisoners' signatures on legal documents. However, law school clinical programs were permitted in the prison. Citing *Johnson v. Avery*, the Supreme Court held the regulation void because it created an artificial distinction between law students employed by practicing attorneys and those associated with law school programs providing legal assistance to the prisoners. Further, the regulation was overbroad. Its prohibition was not limited to prospective interviewers who posed some colorable threat to security or to prisoners thought to be especially dangerous. Nor was it shown that a less restrictive regulation would unduly burden the administrative task of screening and monitoring visitors.[63]

§ 7.9   Access to Legal Materials

Prior to *Johnson v. Avery*, the courts, with few exceptions, staunchly deferred to official discretion as to what legal materials could be kept by a prisoner in his or her own cell. Their rationale was the right of a state to impose reasonable restrictions upon the times and places where a prisoner could engage in legal work.[64] It was thought that there was in fact no interference with access to the courts as a result of these types of reasonable restrictions.[65] Restrictions as to the possession of any law books or limitations on numbers were treated in much the same manner. It was thought that the prisoner had no constitutional right to possess law books where no one had alleged a lack of access to the courts.[66] Therefore, where a limitation upon the number of books prisoners could possess was not found to be arbitrary, unreasonable, or discriminatory, discretion of the officials was valid and controlling.[67]

Although a majority of the courts took the conservative approach, later decisions have taken a contrary view. For example, a California court concluded that the constitutional right of a prisoner of access to the courts:

> includes not only the right to place a petition for relief in the mails, . . . but also the right to possess in his cell the legal materials which the prisoner desires to include in such a document while they are being collated into mailable form.[68]

This right, however, was not interpreted to mean that prisoners could collect in their cells all-purpose compendiums that could substitute for law books from the library. This decision did not prevent prison officials from restricting legal research to a certain area and from forbidding the storage of legal notes in a prisoner's cell.

A county jail rule prohibiting storage of hardcover law books in prisoners' cells and restricting storage of nonhardcover materials so as not to limit the "floor or wall space dimensional of the jail cell block" was held to be reasonable, in light of the duty of jail authorities to maintain security and to protect against the dangers of fire.[69]

In *United States ex rel. Mayberry v. Prasse*,[70] a district court found that the right of access to the courts included "the right of a prisoner to prepare, serve, and file legal papers and prosecute legal actions affecting his personal liberty."[71] The court held that, although there was no constitutional right to be supplied with a law library, the prisoner could not be restrained from effectively prosecuting his appeal. Based upon the facts of that case, and in view of the absence of effective counsel to assist him in prosecuting his legal action, the prisoner was permitted, through court order, to acquire the rules of procedure of Pennsylvania. Without these rules, access to the courts would be unconstitutionally restrained.

Another court ruled that, although prison officials may regulate the manner in which a prisoner conducts his or her research, they may not engage in wholesale confiscation of significant legal documents. The court further suggested that the prison officials should consult the prisoner about the relevance of legal materials in his or her possession before any action is taken to remove them.[72]

Johnson v. Avery did not substantially affect the law in this area. Courts have permitted prison officials to restrict the number of books kept by a prisoner. Regulations forbidding the accumulation of a law library within the confines of a prisoner's cell have been held valid for two reasons. First, the state has the right to reasonably restrict the time and manner in which legal research may be done, as long as no unconstitutional impediment of access to the courts arises.[73] Second, the condition of a prisoner's personal law library carries no constitutional significance, as long as the prisoners have other sources of assistance available, such as other jailhouse lawyers who use the prison law library. A prison regulation that does not impede access to the courts will be held valid.[74]

Thus, a prisoner was not prejudiced by the inability to do his own research to supplement that of his legal counsel. A warden's policy of returning ordered law books to the publisher was upheld under such circumstances. The prison had a procedure for receiving books by mail, and the prisoner failed to follow the procedure.[75]

On the other hand, in *Sigafus v. Brown*,[76] the Seventh Circuit held that confiscation of materials necessary to afford reasonable access to the courts resulted in a denial of constitutional rights. Prison officials may not prevent a prisoner from possessing his or her own legal material while permitting him or her to possess other articles, on the grounds that the legal material might serve as incendiary matter during future, although unanticipated, disturbances.[77]

It would thus appear that in cases both before and after *Johnson*, the majority of courts have allowed the state to have the discretion of determining where legal research may take place. As a result, prison officials may enforce a rule forbidding the possession of personal legal materials and books in a prisoner's cell.

The application of this rule, however, led to inconsistent results. The confusion arises in cases in which a jailhouse lawyer has in his possession papers pertaining to another prisoner's case. *In re Harrell*[78] held that a rule permitting confiscation of those papers prevented meaningful aid in the preparation of legal documents by the jailhouse lawyer. It was there asserted that the chief purpose of the rule of *Johnson v. Avery* was to permit prisoners to assist one other in the drafting of legal documents. In view of this purpose, the court believed that prison officials were forbidden to impose a rule that prohibited prisoners from possessing legal documents that pertained to another prisoner's case. Similarly, *Gilmore v. Lynch*[79] considered the identical prison regulation addressed in *Harrell*. It stated: "One prisoner may assist another prisoner in the preparation of legal documents, but . . . all briefs, petitions, and other legal papers must be and remain in the possession of the prisoner to whom they pertain."[80] This court applied a somewhat different rule to this regulation than that found in the *Harrell* decision. The court held that if the rules were applied only to completed documents, that application would be valid. Thus, the jailhouse lawyer may retain possession of another prisoner's papers while preparing a brief or petition. However, upon their completion, he or she must deliver them to his or her client without accepting payment.

The inconsistent results of these cases leave a double standard. A prisoner may be restricted from having in his or her possession legal documents pertaining to his or her own case, while at the same time a prisoner doing legal work for a fellow prisoner may keep with him or her legal materials pertaining to the other prisoner's case.

Fortunately, the source from which personal legal materials may be obtained is better defined. Prison officials may restrict a prisoner from ordering law books from any source other than that which is approved by them,[81] as long as this does not amount to a restriction of the type of book that may be ordered.[82]

A delay in delivery of books to a prisoner does not necessarily infringe upon his or her access to the courts.[83] Requiring a prisoner to wait, on one occasion for ten days, to have a document notarized does not unconstitutionally deprive the prisoner of access to the courts.[84] The justification for such a decision has been that prison officials have a legitimate right to prevent introduction of contraband through the prisoners' mail.[85]

A prisoner was not denied a reasonably adequate opportunity to prepare his habeas motion where he was incarcerated in a facility without access to a law library for only 22 days of a one-year period in which he had to file his motion. He had access to a law library at the jail and correctional facility when he was transferred from the original facility 12 days before his motion was due. He admitted on appeal that he had delayed writing his motion until the *U.S. Sentencing Guidelines Manual* was amended.[86]

A prisoner's legal materials purchased for him by a third party who had ties to another prisoner were intercepted. The prisoner's right to receive mail claim was properly dismissed where the prison officials asserted and substantiated a set of legitimate penological interests rationally related to the restriction under review; specifically, the penological purposes of the restriction were to prevent unauthorized bartering, extortion, and contraband smuggling inside the prison facilitated through the assistance or exploitation of third parties outside the prison. The prisoner had alternative means of exercising his right, and the burdens of accommodation indicated the absence of any obvious and easy alternative security measures.[87]

§ 7.10   Legal Materials That Must be Supplied by Prison Officials

The traditional view as to what legal materials prison officials must supply to prisoners was expressed in the 1961 case of *Hatfield v. Bailleax*,[88] in which the court stated:

> State authorities have no obligation under the federal Constitution to provide library facilities and an opportunity for their use to enable a prisoner to search for legal loopholes in the judgment and sentence under which he is held, or to perform services which only a lawyer is trained to perform. All prisoners are presumed to be confined under valid judgments and sentences. If a prisoner believes he has a meritorious reason for attacking his, he must be given an opportunity to do so. But he has no due process right to spend his prison time or utilize prison facilities in an effort to discover a ground for overturning a presumptively valid judgment.

The view expressed by the *Hatfield* decision, however, was repudiated by the Supreme Court in the 1971 case of *Gilmore v. Lynch*.[89] *Gilmore* was decided by a three-judge panel in California and subsequently affirmed by the Supreme Court.[90] The district court stated that access to the courts is a right that encompasses "all the means a defendant or petitioner might require to get a fair hearing from the judiciary on all charges brought against him or grievances alleged by him."[91] In affirming, the Supreme Court, citing *Johnson v. Avery*, approved the invalidation of a regulation that had established, as a standard for prison libraries, a highly restrictive list of law books. The decision has set a new precedent by asserting that prison officials have a duty to take affirmative action in assuring prisoners the right of access to the courts. The state must make available, notwithstanding economic difficulties, sufficient legal materials to assure that the prisoner is able to file petitions that contain at least some legal proficiency.

In *Bounds v. Smith*,[92] the Supreme Court took an affirmative view toward the responsibility of prison authorities to provide prisoners with adequate law libraries or some other viable source of legal knowledge. The Court did not mandate the use of law libraries if a sufficient alternative program for legal services is in operation. Law libraries were held to be one constitutionally acceptable method to ensure prisoners meaningful access to the courts. Other alternatives mentioned in the decision included the training of prisoners as paralegal assistants to work under lawyers' supervision; the use of paraprofessionals and law students either as volunteers or in formal clinical programs; the organization of volunteer attorneys through bar associations or other groups; the hiring of lawyers on a part-time consultant basis; and the use of full-time staff attorneys working either in new prison legal assistance programs or as a part of a public defender or legal services office.

Several decisions have stressed the necessity of supplying prisoners with sufficient material for legal research by listing exactly what state statutes and volumes of the court reporters the prison law library must contain.[93] For example, a plan for Georgia prison law libraries was approved with the following mandatory revisions: The library must be kept open for a minimum of nine hours per week, and for such additional hours as may be needed to afford each prisoner wishing to use the facility the equivalent of one full day (eight hours) of research time every three weeks; the library must contain certain reference materials; prisoners must be permitted to receive and use appropriate volumes from the county library, subject only to a requirement that these materials be returned in good order within reasonable periods. The use of paralegals was not required.[94]

In an Eleventh Circuit case, a state prisoner maintained that the denial of his request for free photocopies of legal precedents to use in preparation for a hearing on his motion for postconviction relief had deprived him of his right of free access to the courts. The court held that because he had access to the law library at the county jail and had made no allegations of inadequacy of the facility, his complaint failed to state a cause of action.[95]

As shown by the previous cases, *Casey v. Lewis*[96] has had a substantial impact on all aspects of legal services as well as on the legal materials that must be made available to prisoners.

§ 7.11   The Prisoner's Right to Counsel

An individual accused of a crime has a fundamental right to counsel and the right to be represented by an attorney of his or her choice, if the attorney indicates a willingness to represent him or her. If the individual is indigent and unable to afford counsel when he or she has a right to counsel, the state must appoint an attorney.[97] This right is protected by the Fifth and Sixth Amendments and may not be unreasonably limited by state officials.[98] This right is not altered when the individual is incarcerated. Prison officials may not unreasonably prevent legal counsel from meeting with their prisoner clients as long as the attorney observes all of the rules of the institution.[99] Nor may officials infringe upon a prisoner's right to communicate with his or her attorney by placing undue restrictions on his or her correspondence[100] or visitation rights.[101] However, a prisoner who has exercised his or her right to proceed without counsel in pursuing his or her appeal does not have the right to receive for his or her use an adequate law library, where the state has offered to appoint counsel.[102]

Prisoners in a federal prison were placed in administrative detention in individual cells during the investigation of the murder of a fellow prisoner. They were held in administrative detention for 19 months before they were indicted and counsel was appointed. The Supreme Court held that the prisoners had no constitutional right to counsel while in administrative segregation and before any adversary proceedings had been initiated against them. The right to counsel attaches only at or after the initiation of adversary judicial proceedings.

Further, providing a defendant with a preindictment private investigator is not a purpose of the right to counsel.[103]

Associated with the right to counsel is the right to call expert witnesses. In *McKinney v. Anderson*,[104] the Ninth Circuit held that a federal district court has the discretion to appoint expert witnesses and to assess the cost of an expert's services entirely to one party.[105] In this case, a prisoner claimed that compelled exposure to environmental tobacco smoke amounted to cruel and unusual punishment. The district court was directed on remand to consider appointing an expert witness who could provide scientific information on health effects of environmental tobacco smoke and on concentration levels of the smoke in the prison in which the prisoner was incarcerated.

§ 7.12   Restrictions on Access to the Courts

The *in forma pauperis* statute[106] is designed to ensure that indigent litigants have meaningful access to the federal courts.[107] However, Congress was also concerned that indigent persons could abuse this cost-free access to the federal courts. As a result, Congress empowered the courts with the right to dismiss the abusive filings that could result from the absence of a cost barrier by including § 1915(d), which authorizes a court to dismiss an *in forma pauperis* complaint if satisfied that the action is frivolous or malicious.

A prisoner appealed an order that dismissed his *in forma pauperis*[108] complaint as "frivolous or malicious."[109] The relief sought—$4.20 for loss of the prisoner's pens—was considered by the court to be a "trifle" and not worthy of adjudication. According to the ruling in *Deutsch v. United States*, the court may dismiss an *in forma pauperis* claim as frivolous if, after considering the contending equities, the court determines that the claim is: (1) of little or no weight, value, or importance; (2) not worthy of serious attention; or (3) trivial.[110]

According to *Deutsch*, to find that an *in forma pauperis* litigant's claim is trivial, a court must be satisfied that the record supports a finding that a reasonable paying litigant would not have filed the same claim after considering the costs of suit. A court must first find the actual amount in controversy under the claim presented and determine whether the amount in controversy is less than the expense of the court costs and filing fees. If the court so determines, then the claim may be dismissed as frivolous under § 1915(d).

A court must next determine whether the litigant has a meaningful nonmonetary interest at stake under the claim, such that service of the complaint and an allocation of the court's resources for its adjudication is warranted, despite the fact that the claim is economically trivial. If, in addition to finding that the amount of damages in controversy is less than the court costs and filing fees, and the court is satisfied that there is no other meaningful interest at stake, then the suit is frivolous within the meaning of § 1915(d).

Deutsch recognized that emotions are intensified in the insular life of a correctional facility and that prisoners often must rely on the courts as the only available forum to redress their grievances, even when those grievances seem insignificant to one who is not so confined. A court is obligated to take into account the unique nature of each claim presented and the extent to which the claim is "meaningful" to the one in the litigant's situation. Thus, in determining whether a claim is meaningful, a court must protect the right of indigent persons to have access to the courts.[111]

A court must also consider whether the prisoner is filing the suit to pursue a nonmeaningful activity, such as harassment or entertainment, or merely to hone litigation skills.[112] A court must balance the equities and dismiss the claim only if it is satisfied that the claim is of little or no weight, worth, or importance; not worthy of serious attention; or trivial.

The Supreme Court has barred abusive prisoners from relief at the Supreme Court level from receiving *in forma pauperis* status.[113]

A prisoner cannot rely on another plaintiff's injury in support of his own denial of access claim. As the prisoner had no right to judicial relief distinct from another prisoner's claim, his affidavit in support of the other prisoner's litigation was not a constitutionally protected exercise of his right to access the courts.[114]

§ 7.13   Conclusion

In view of the very liberal interpretation given the *Johnson* decision by many lower courts, the prison administration is confronted with an extremely difficult task. In order to comply with constitutional standards and to avoid possible court action, prison officials must either allow jailhouse lawyers to practice or implement an effective legal services program. Whichever alternative is selected will inevitably result in numerous difficulties. To allow the virtually unrestricted practice of prisoner writ-writers would result in the continuation of long-recognized abuses. The alternative, to provide a judicially acceptable legal service program, presents equally difficult problems. The program must provide professional assistance sufficient to meet the needs of the prisoner population without undue delay. Furthermore, it must provide assistance to any prisoner wishing to file habeas corpus, civil rights, or *pro se* petitions. Only by providing such complete legal services can the prison administration protect itself against court action. The fact that this burden could be overwhelming in most states is irrelevant to the courts.

Casey v. Lewis has clarified many of the issues involving legal services for prisoners. It represents a conservative retrenchment of what legal services and materials must be provided to prisoners in their quest for access to the courts.

Notes

1   Armstrong v. Manzo, 380 U.S. 545, 552 (1965).

2 Mullane v. Central Hanover Tr. Corp., 339 U.S. 306, 313 (1950).

3 312 U.S. 546 (1941); *see also* Webb v. State, 412 N.E.2d 790 (Ind. 1980).

4 Ex parte Hull, 312 U.S. 546 (1941).

5 *See* Lee v. Tahash, 352 F.2d 970 (8th Cir. 1965); United States v. Marchese, 341 F.2d 782 (9th Cir. 1965); *see also* Webb v. State, 412 N.E.2d 790 (Ind. 1980); Johnson v. Teasdale, 456 F. Supp. 1083 (W.D. Mo. 1978); Miller v. Stanmore, 636 F.2d 986 (5th Cir. 1981).

6 430 U.S. 817 (1977).

7 Murray v. Giarratano, 492 U.S. 1 (1989).

8 Federal courts may only decide cases that involve actual cases or controversies and may not issue abstract advisory opinions.

9 578 U.S. 343 (1996).

10 Thaddeus-X v. Blatter, 175 F.3d 378 (6th Cir. 1997). *See* § 7.6.

11 Lewis, 518 U.S. at 355.

12 Hudson v. Millian, 503 U.S. 1, 15 (1992) (Blackmun, J., concurring in the judgment).

13 393 U.S. 483 (1969).

14 *Id.* at 484.

15 *Id.* at 485.

16 Carter v. Kamka, 515 F. Supp. 825 (D. Md. 1980).

17 In re Harrell, 470 P. 2d 640 (Cal. 1970).

18 *Id.*

19 *See* Gittlemacker v. Prasse, 428 F.2d 1 (3d Cir. 1970); Gilmore v. Lynch, 319 F. Supp. 105 (N.D. Cal. 1970), *aff'd sub nom.*; Younger v. Gilmore, 404 U.S. 15 (1971); Jordan v. Johnson, 381 F. Supp. 600 (E.D. Mich. 1974), *aff'd*, 513 F.2d 631, *cert. denied*, 423 U.S. 851 (1975); McKinney v. DeBord, 507 F.2d 501 (9th Cir. 1974).

20 515 F.2d 322 (5th Cir. 1975).

21 Wolff v. McDonnell, 418 U.S. 539 (1974); *see* Wainwright v. Coonts, 409 F.2d 1337 (5th Cir. 1969); United States ex rel. Stevenson v. Mancusi, 325 F. Supp. 1028 (W.D.N.Y. 1971); State v. Williams, 595 P. 2d 1104 (Kan. 1979); Carter v. Kamka, 515 F. Supp. 825 (D. Md. 1980); Storseth v. Spellman, 654 F.2d 1349 (9th Cir. 1981).

22 Rizzo v. Zubrik, 391 F. Supp. 1058 (S.D.N.Y. 1975).

23 *See* Sostre v. McGinnis, 442 F.2d 178 (2d Cir. 1971), *cert. denied*, 405 U.S. 978 (1972); Williams v. Department of Justice, 433 F.2d 958 (5th Cir. 1970); Carothers v. Follette, 314 F. Supp. 1014 (S.D.N.Y. 1970); Prewitt v. State ex rel. Eyman, 315 F. Supp. 793 (D. Ariz. 1969).

24 *See* In re Harrell, 470 P. 2d 640 (Cal. 1970).

25 530 F.2d 583 (4th Cir. 1976).

26 471 F. Supp. 1113 (N.D. Cal. 1979); Moore v. Smith, 390 N.E.2d 1052 (Ind. Ct. App. 1979); cf. Lamb v. Hutto, 467 F. Supp. 562 (E.D. Va. 1979) (a prisoner does not have a right to counsel at a prison transfer hearing).

27 *See* Guajardo v. Luna, 432 F.2d 1324 (5th Cir. 1970); In re Harrell, 470 P. 2d 640 (Cal. 1970); Bounds v. Smith, 430 U.S. 817 (1977); Delgado v. Sheriff of Milwaukee County, 487 F. Supp. 649 (E.D. Wis. 1980); Rhodes v. Robinson, 612 F.2d 766 (3d Cir. 1979); State v. Williams, 595 P. 2d 1104 (Kan. 1979).

28 *See* McKinney v. DeBord, 324 F. Supp. 928 (E.D. Cal. 1970); Putt v. Clark, 297 F. Supp. 27 (N.D. Ga. 1969); In re Harrell, 470 P. 2d 640 (Cal. 1970); Storseth v. Spellman, 654 F.2d 1349 (9th Cir. 1981).

29 Boehme v. Smith, 378 N.Y.S.2d 170 (N.Y. App. Div. 1976); Webb v. State, 412 N.E.2d 790 (Ind. 1980).

30 *See* Sostre v. McGinnis, 442 F.2d 178 (2d Cir. 1971), *cert. denied*, 405 U.S. 978 (1972); Carothers v. Follette, 314 F. Supp. 1014 (S.D.N.Y. 1970); Prewitt v. State ex rel. Eyman, 315 F. Supp. 793 (D. Ariz. 1969); Wolff v. McDonnell, 418 U.S. 539, 71 Ohio Op. 2d 336 (1974).

31 *See* Novak v. Beto, 320 F. Supp. 1206 (S.D. Tex. 1970), *rev'd on other grounds*, 453 F.2d

661 (5th Cir. 1972); Brown v. South Carolina, 286 F. Supp. 998 (D.S.C. 1968); Ex parte Wilson, 235 F. Supp. 988 (E.D.S.C. 1964); Corpus v. Estelle, 409 F. Supp. 1090 (S.D. Tex. 1975); Ford v. LaVallee, 390 N.Y.S.2d 269 (1976); Cruz v. Androd, 15998B Opinion (5th Cir. 1980); cf. Jensen v. Satran, 303 N.W.2d 568 (N.D. 1981).

32   *See* In re Harrell, 470 P. 2d 640 (Cal. 1970).

33   Gilmore v. Lynch, 319 F. Supp. 105 (N.D. Cal. 1970), *aff'd sub nom.*, Younger v. Gilmore, 404 U.S. 15 (1971).

34   470 P. 2d 640 (Cal. 1970).

35   In re Harrell, 470 P. 2d 640, 649.

36   *Id.*; Boehme v. Smith, 378 N.Y.S.2d 170 (N.Y. App. Div. 1976).

37   *Id. See* Storseth v. Spellman, 654 F.2d 1349 (9th Cir. 1981).

38   Shaw v. Murphy, 532 U.S. 223 (2001).

39   *Id.* at 224.

40   430 F.2d 548 (1st Cir. 1970).

41   *Id.* at 551.

42   *Ibid.*

43   328 F. Supp. 899 (W.D. Wis. 1971).

44   433 F.2d 958 (5th Cir. 1970).

45   *Id.* at 959. The term *pro se* is used to mean any petition filed by an individual for him or herself; Corpus v. Estelle, 409 F. Supp. 1090 (S.D. Tex. 1975).

46   418 U.S. 539 (1974).

47   392 F. Supp. 1262 (W.D.N.C. 1975).

48   *See* Novak v. Beto, 320 F. Supp. 1206 (S.D. Tex. 1970); Ayers v. Ciccone, 303 F. Supp. 637 (W.D. Mo. 1969); Collins v. Haga, 373 F. Supp. 923 (W.D. Va. 1974). *But see* Bounds v. Smith, 430 U.S. 817 (1977).

49   303 F. Supp. 637 (W.D. Mo. 1969).

50   320 F. Supp. 1206 (S.D. Tex. 1970).

51   Novak v. Beto, 453 F.2d 661 (5th Cir. 1969).

52   413 F.2d 455 (5th Cir. 1969).

53   *Id.* at 457.

54   489 F.2d 642 (8th Cir. 1973).

55   433 F.2d 958 (5th Cir. 1970).

56   328 F. Supp. 899 (W.D. Wis. 1971).

57   *But see* Ramsey v. Ciccone, 310 F. Supp. 600 (W.D. Mo. 1970), in which the court asserted that some delay must necessarily accompany any new program and for this reason found a three-month delay acceptable.

58   328 F. Supp. 899 (W.D. Wis. 1971).

59   516 F.2d 233 (3d Cir. 1975).

60   19 Cr. L. 2094 (S.D. Tex. 1976); *see* Cruz v. Beto, 453 F. Supp. 905 (S.D. Tex. 1977) for the issue of attorney's fees in the earlier case.

61   416 U.S. 396 (1974).

62   *Id.* at 419.

63   *Id.* at 420.

64   *See* Hatfield v. Bailleaux, 290 F.2d 632 (9th Cir. 1961); Edmundson v. Harris, 239 F. Supp. 359 (W.D. Mo. 1965); Austin v. Harris, 226 F. Supp. 304 (W.D. Mo. 1964).

65   *See* Taylor v. Burke, 278 F. Supp. 868 (E.D. Wis. 1968).

66   Williams v. Wilkins, 315 F.2d 396 (2d Cir. 1963), *cert. denied*, 375 U.S. 852 (1963); *see* Roberts v. Pepersack, 256 F. Supp. 415 (D. Md. 1966), *cert. denied*, 389 U.S. 877 (1967).

67   *See* Walker v. Pate, 356 F.2d 502 (7th Cir. 1966), *cert. denied*, 384 U.S. 966 (1966); People v. Matthewes, 46 Misc. 2d 1054, 261 N.Y.S.2d 654 (Sup. Ct. Crim. Term, 1965); Cruz v. Hauck, 515 F.2d 322 (5th Cir. 1975).

68   In re Schoingarth, 425 P. 2d 200, 207 (Cal. 1967).

69   Cruz v. Hauck, 515 F.2d 322 (5th Cir. 1975).

70   225 F. Supp. 752 (E.D. Pa. 1963).

71 *Id.* at 754.

72 *See* Konigsburg v. Ciccone, 285 F. Supp. 585, *aff'd*, 417 F.2d 161 (8th Cir. 1969), *cert. denied*, 397 U.S. 963 (1970); *see* Hiney v. Wilson, 520 F.2d 589 (2d Cir. 1975), in which the confiscation of inmates' legal papers may constitute a denial of access to the courts.

73 *See* Gittlemacker v. Prasse, 428 F.2d 1 (3d Cir. 1970); McKinney v. DeBord, 324 F. Supp. 928 (E.D. Cal. 1970).

74 *See* In re Harrell, 470 P. 2d 640 (Cal. 1970). *But see* Sigafus v. Brown, 416 F.2d 105 (7th Cir. 1969), in which the court found that confiscation of legal materials necessary to afford reasonable access to the courts results in denial of due process for which damages may be claimed.

75 Russell v. Hendrick, 376 F. Supp. 158 (E.D. Pa. 1974); United States v. Wilson, 690 F.2d 1267 (9th Cir. 1982). There is no absolute right for an inmate to conduct his or her own legal research when he or she has appointed counsel to assist in preparing his or her defense. The services of a lawyer cannot be rejected as a means of achieving access to a law library.

76 416 F.2d 105 (7th Cir. 1969).

77 Adams v. Carlson, 352 F. Supp. 882 (E.D. Ill. 1973), *rev'd and rem'd on other grounds*, 488 F.2d 619 (7th Cir. 1973).

78 470 P. 2d 640 (Cal. 1970).

79 319 F. Supp. 105 (N.D. Ca. 1970), *aff'd sub nom.*, Younger v. Gilmore, 404 U.S. 15 (1971).

80 *Id.* at 112.

81 *See* McKinney v. DeBord, 324 F. Supp. 928 (E.D. Cal. 1970); Wakely v. Pennsylvania, 247 F. Supp. 7 (E.D. Pa. 1965).

82 *See* In re Harrell, 470 P. 2d 640 (Cal. 1970).

83 Russell v. Hendrick, 376 F. Supp. 158 (E.D. Pa. 1974).

84 Hudson v. Robinson, 678 F.2d 462 (3d Cir. 1982).

85 *See* Lockhart v. Prasse, 250 F. Supp. 529 (E.D. Pa. 1965).

86 Mathison v. Swenson, 143 Fed. Appx. 730 (8th Cir. 2005).

87 Wardell v. Maggard, 470 F.3d 954 (10th Cir. 2006).

88 290 F.2d 632 (9th Cir. 1961).

89 319 F. Supp. 105 (N.D. Cal. 1970), *aff'd*, 404 U.S. 15 (1971).

90 Gilmore v. Lynch, 404 U.S. 15 (1971).

91 Gilmore v. Lynch, 319 F. Supp. 105, 110 (N.D. Cal. 1970).

92 430 U.S. 817 (1977); *see* Morales v. Schmidt, 340 F. Supp. 544, 548 (W.D. Wis. 1972), in which Judge Doyle recognized that access by inmates "to a certain minimum of legal books and materials" was a constitutionally protected right; United States v. West, 557 F.2d 151 (8th Cir. 1977); Dreher v. Sielaff, 636 F.2d 1141 (7th Cir. 1980); State v. Simon, 297 N.W.2d 206 (Iowa 1980); State v. Ahearn, 403 A.2d 696 (Vt. 1979); Wojtczak v. Cuyler, 480 F. Supp. 1288 (E.D. Pa. 1979).

93 *See* Gaglie v. Ulibarri, 507 F.2d 721 (9th Cir. 1974); White v. Sullivan, 368 F. Supp. 292 (S.D. Ala. 1973); Craig v. Hocker, 405 F. Supp. 656 (D. Nev. 1975).

94 Mercer v. Griffin, 29 Cr. L. 2058 (D.C. Ga. 1981).

95 Wanninger v. Davenport, 697 F.2d 992 (11th Cir. 1983); Johnson v. Parke, 642 F.2d 337 (10th Cir. 1981).

96 518 U.S. 343 (1996).

97 Argersinger v. Hamlin, 407 U.S. 25 (1972).

98 Sander v. Russell, 401 F.2d 241, 247 (5th Cir. 1968); State ex rel. McCamie v. McCoy, 276 S.E.2d 534 (W. Va. 1981).

99 Lynott v. Henderson, 610 F.2d 340 (5th Cir. 1980).

100 Jones v. Diamond, 594 F.2d 997 (5th Cir. 1979).

101 *See* § 4.6.

102 Bell v. Hooper, 511 F. Supp. 452 (S.D. Ga. 1981).

103 United States v. Gouveia, 467 U.S. 180 (1984).

104 McKinney v. Anderson, 924 F.2d 1500 (9th Cir.), *vacated sub nom.*, Helling v. McKinney, 502 U.S. 903 (1991).

105 *See* Federal Rule of Evidence 706.

106   28 U.S.C. § 1915.

107   Neitzke v. Williams, 490 U.S. 319 (1989). Specifically, Congress enacted the *in forma pauperis* statute to ensure that administrative court costs and filing fees, both of which must be paid by everyone else who files a lawsuit, would not prevent indigent persons from pursuing meaningful litigation.

108   A legal term that refers to the ability of an indigent person to file a lawsuit or appeal without having to pay the typical court fees and filing costs.

109   § 1915(a) provides, in pertinent part, that any court of the United States may authorize the commencement, prosecution or defense of any suit, action, or proceeding, civil or criminal, or appeal therein, without prepayment of fees and costs or security therefor, by a person who makes affidavit that he is unable to pay such costs or give security therefor. This section was extensively amended by the Prison Litigation Reform Act. *See* Chapter 16.

110   Deutsch v. United States, 67 F.3d 1080 (3d Cir. 1995). On the facts of the case, the prisoner, Deutsch, had filed 20 civil actions since 1992.

111   *See* In re Oliver, 682 F.2d 443, 446 (3d Cir. 1982).

112   *See* Cruz v. Beto, 405 U.S. 319 (1972) (*per curiam*) (Rehnquist, J., dissenting) ("[Inmates are] in a different litigating posture than persons who are unconfined. The inmate stands to gain something and lose nothing from a complaint stating facts that he is ultimately unable to prove. Though he may be denied legal relief, he will nonetheless have obtained a short sabbatical in the nearest federal courthouse."); Lumbert v. Illinois Dep't of Corrections, 827 F.2d 257, 259 (7th Cir. 1987) ("the problem of [frivolous litigation] is even more acute when the indigent plaintiff is a prison inmate, because the costs of a prisoner's time are very low"); Savage v. Central Intelligence Agency, 826 F.2d 561, 563–564 (7th Cir. 1987) ("No rational system of government burdens its highest courts with a class of litigation dominated by petty cases typically brought for their nuisance value by persons on whose hands time hangs heavy").

113   *See, e.g.*, In re Whitaker, 513 U.S.1 (1994) (*per curiam*) (barring abusive petitioner from proceeding *in forma pauperis* when seeking extraordinary relief); In re Anderson, 511 U.S. 364 (1994) (*per curiam*) (same); In re Sassower, 510 U.S. 4 (1993) (*per curiam*) (barring abusive petitioner from proceeding *in forma pauperis* in noncriminal matters when seeking extraordinary relief and certiorari review); Martin v. District of Columbia Court of Appeals, 506 U.S. 1 (1992) (*per curiam*) (barring abusive petitioner from receiving *in forma pauperis* status to file petitions for writs of certiorari); Zatko v. California, 502 U.S. at 18 (1991) (denying *in forma pauperis* status to two abusive petitioners); In re Demos, 500 U.S. 16 (1991) (*per curiam*) (barring abusive petitioner from proceeding *in forma pauperis* when seeking extraordinary relief); In re Sindram, 498 U.S. 177 (1991) (*per curiam*) (same).

114   *Id.*

Additional Constitutional
Issues 8

Chapter Outline

§ 8.1   Introduction

There are many legal issues of constitutional magnitude affecting prisoners that do not readily fit into any of the preceding chapters. The topics noted here do not, of course, exhaust the differences between free people and prisoners. They do, however, point out the fact that incarceration is much more than merely a change in location. It is a change in constitutional status.

§ 8.2   Classification

Classification is the assessment, for rehabilitative and security purposes, of a prisoner's personality, background, and potential and the assignment of the prisoner to a specific status or setting that is commensurate with these findings. Classification occurs at numerous times during a prisoner's involvement with the criminal justice system. This section, however, is concerned only with the narrow area of classification by prison authorities—that is, administrative classification. That prison authorities have the right and duty to classify prisoners has been clearly determined by the courts.[1] The assessment aspect of administrative classification is usually fulfilled by committees of prison officials.[2] Such bodies are frequently called adjustment committees, because their initial goal is to enable new prisoners to adjust to the rigors of incarceration. Administrative classification committees, however, have a mission beyond intake assessment and assignment. Behavioral changes in prisoners, which occur as time is served, demand constant reassessment and reassignment.[3]

In *Meachum v. Fano*,[4] the Supreme Court held that the transfer of a prisoner from one prison to another, although arguably to a prisoner a "grievous loss," did not require a due process hearing. This decision, by analogy, applies to the classification of prisoners. However, lower federal courts that have considered the classification issue have determined that some degree of procedural due process is applicable to prison classification hearings. In *Kirby v. Blackledge*,[5] an informal hearing procedure that was used to assign prisoners to maximum-security cellblocks was found to violate due process. Illiterate or otherwise disadvantaged prisoners, for whom the complexity of issues may foreclose the needed capacity to collect and present the evidence necessary for an adequate comprehension of the case, were allowed the assistance of fellow prisoners or a designated staff member. Other courts have specified the form of intake classification to be undertaken. In

Alberti v. Sheriff of Harris County, Texas,[6] the court held that a sufficient number of classification officers should be employed so that at least one is on duty at all times to interview incoming prisoners. Prisoners are to be classified and segregated on the basis of the danger that they pose to others, based on their prior criminal record, the danger posed to the new prisoner by the existing prison population, and the likelihood of successful rehabilitation by proper placement.

The proposed imposition or assignment of certain classifications can trigger a need for more substantial due process safeguards. In *Cardopoli v. Norton,*[7] the Second Circuit held that inasmuch as classification of a prisoner as a special offender hinders or precludes eligibility for social furloughs, work-release, transfer to community treatment centers, and the opportunity for early parole, changes in a prisoner's status that accompany the designation create a "grievous loss" and may not be imposed in the absence of basic elements of rudimentary due process. When a special offender classification is contemplated, the prisoner must be given at least ten days' notice in writing, specifying the reason or reasons for the proposed designation and providing a description of the evidence to be relied upon. The prisoner must be afforded a personal appearance before a neutral decision maker and must be permitted to call witnesses and present documentary evidence. If the hearing officer determines that the classification is warranted, he or she must support that decision with written findings submitted within a reasonable time after the hearing.

Beyond the procedural considerations of classification hearings, there exists the problem of the permissibility of certain types of classifications or statuses. In *McDonald v. McCracken,*[8] a court held that if a prisoner is placed in lockup status for the protection of other prisoners and prison employees rather than for the imposition of punishment, in this case for 13 months, and such classification is not arbitrary, abusive, or capricious, the hearing requirements of *Wolff v. McDonnell*[9] for rule infraction board proceedings do not apply. Classification based upon a discriminatory basis such as race or religion will usually be held to be unconstitutional. However, classification on the basis of sex or age is permissible.

The use of the "level system," a mandatory behavior modification system employed by the Kentucky Correctional Institute for Women to govern the access of female prisoners to certain prisoner privileges, was declared unconstitutional. The system resulted in grossly unequal treatment of female, as opposed to male, prisoners in the availability of prisoner privileges. In addition, the imposition of the system on the prison population as a whole violates the prisoners' substantive due process rights. Behavior modification was found to have a unique effect upon each individual. Officials of the Kentucky Correctional Institute for Women were cited by the district court for failing to fulfill their obligation to provide equal programs and facilities for women, especially in the areas of prison industries, institutional jobs, vocational education and training, and community release programs.[10]

Associated with classification is administrative segregation of prisoners. The state cannot place a detainee in segregation for no reason,[11] but maintaining jail security comprises an appropriate justification for inflicting restrictions on pretrial detainees. The same principle should apply to convicted prisoners.

In *Zarnes v. Rhodes*,[12] a pretrial detainee argued with other prisoners about the selection of the television channel. The fight did not include any physical contact, but upon hearing from one prisoner that Zarnes was to blame, the officer in charge at the time placed Zarnes in "lockdown." He did not give Zarnes any reason for his action. Zarnes remained segregated from the general population for 19 days without receiving any explanation.

The correctional officer was held to have put Zarnes in administrative segregation for her protection and the protection of other prisoners, following Zarnes's verbal confrontations with other prisoners. The officer's action was pursuant to the Sheriff's Department's policies and procedures that allow placement in segregation only when housing a prisoner in the general population would pose a serious threat to life, property, self, staff, or other prisoners or in order to secure orderly operations of the facility. The court found that these declarations adequately established that the officer assigned Zarnes to segregation for a legitimate reason, thereby making the officer's conduct constitutional.

§ 8.3   Transfer

Incident to all classifications, whether initial or review, is transfer. This topic has generated much litigation. Federal district courts and courts of appeals that have dealt with the need for due process safeguards in conjunction with intra-prison and inter-prison transfers of prisoners and have specified substantial safeguards. A typical case is *Fano v. Meachum*,[13] in which the First Circuit held that whether a prisoner's transfer is thought of as punishment or as a way of preserving institutional order, its effect on the prisoner is the same. The appropriateness of the transfer depends upon the accuracy of the official allegation of misconduct. Under normal circumstances, notice and a hearing must be afforded to a prisoner prior to a transfer from a medium-security to a maximum-security prison and, at the very least, must state the time and place of the alleged offense with reasonable accuracy.

However, the decision was reversed by the Supreme Court. In *Meachum v. Fano*[14] the Court held that, absent a state law or practice that conditions the transfer of prisoners between institutions upon proof of serious misconduct or the occurrence of other specified events, the Fourteenth Amendment's Due Process Clause in and of itself does not entitle a prisoner to a fact-finding hearing prior to his or her transfer from one penal institution to another, even if the conditions of the recipient institution are substantially less favorable than those in the institution from which he or she was transferred, provided that such conditions are within the sentence imposed upon him or her and do not otherwise violate the Constitution.

The Supreme Court further considered prisoners' transfer rights in *Montanye v. Haymes*,[15] a companion case to *Meachum*, and held that the Fourteenth Amendment's Due Process Clause does not, on its face, require a hearing prior to the transfer, for whatever reason, of a prisoner from one institution to another in the same penal system, provided that the conditions or degree of the confinement to which the prisoner is thus subjected are within the sentence imposed upon him or her and do not otherwise violate the Constitution.

According to the Supreme Court in *Olim v. Wakinekona*,[16] a state prisoner has no justifiable expectation that he or she will not be transferred to a prison in another state, where state prison regulations create no constitutionally protected liberty interest against such a transfer. The regulation under review in this case provided for a pretransfer hearing but left prison administrators with unfettered discretion over transfers. Confinement in another state is within the normal limits or range of custody that the conviction has authorized the transferring state to impose.[17]

Taken together, *Meachum, Montanye*, and *Olim* eliminate the constitutional underpinnings of the argument that minimal procedural due process must be provided to prisoners before they are transferred. As mentioned in the preceding section, beyond the narrow scope of the prisoner transfer issue, these decisions suggest a possible reexamination by the Supreme Court of the constitutional validity of the "grievous loss" argument that has required minimal procedural due process requirements for administrative classification hearings in general. The standard is now whether "liberty interests" are involved.[18]

The Interstate Agreement on Detainers creates uniform procedures for lodging and executing a detainer—a legal order that requires a state to hold a currently imprisoned individual when he has finished serving his sentence so that he may be tried by a different state for a different crime. The Agreement provides that a state that obtains a prisoner for purposes of trial must try him within 120 days of his arrival, and if it returns him to his original place of imprisonment prior to that trial, charges shall be dismissed with prejudice. In *Alabama v. Bozeman*,[19] while a prisoner was serving a federal prison sentence in Florida, an Alabama district attorney sought temporary custody of him to arraign him on firearms charges and to appoint counsel. When taken to Alabama, he spent one day in Alabama and was returned to federal prison that evening. About one month later, he was brought back to the county for trial. His counsel moved to dismiss the state charges on the ground that, because he had been returned to the original place of imprisonment, the federal prison, prior to trial on state charges being had, in violation of Article IV(e), the local court had to dismiss the charges with prejudice in light of Article IV(e)'s command as to remedy. The prisoner was convicted, but the conviction was reversed. The Supreme Court held that the literal language of Article IV(e) bars any further criminal proceedings when a defendant is returned to the original place of imprisonment before trial.

The statutory right of a prisoner to a hearing under Article IV(d) of the Interstate Agreement on Detainers before he or she is transferred to another jurisdiction was upheld in the Supreme Court case *Cuyler v. Adams*.[20] However, according to the Court in *Vitek v. Jones*,[21] the involuntary transfer of a convicted felon from a state prison to a mental hospital violates a liberty interest that is protected by the Due Process Clause of the Fourteenth Amendment. The stigmatizing consequences of a transfer to a mental institution for involuntary psychiatric treatment, including mandatory behavior modification, require the following procedure:

1. A written notice to the prisoner that a transfer to a mental institution is being considered;

2. A hearing, sufficiently after the notice to permit the prisoner to prepare, at which disclosure to the prisoner is made aware of the evidence being relied upon for the transfer and at which an opportunity to be heard in person and to present documentary evidence is given;

3. An opportunity at the hearing to present testimony of witnesses by the prisoner and to confront and cross-examine witnesses called by the state, except upon a finding, not arbitrarily made, of good cause for not permitting such presentation, confrontation, or cross-examination;

4. An independent decision-maker;

5. A written statement by the fact finder as to the evidence relied on and the reasons for transferring the prisoner;

6. Availability of legal counsel, furnished by the state, if the prisoner is financially unable to furnish his or her own; and

7. Effective and timely notice of all the foregoing rights.

With respect to the appointment of legal counsel, the ruling was indecisive. Four of the nine Justices believed:

> The District Court did go beyond the requirements imposed by prior cases by holding that counsel must be made available to prisoners facing transfer hearings if they are financially unable to furnish their own. We have not required the automatic appointment of counsel for indigent prisoners facing other deprivations of liberty . . . but we have recognized that prisoners who are illiterate and uneducated have a greater need for assistance in exercising their rights. A prisoner thought to be suffering from a mental disease or defect requiring involuntary treatment probably has an even greater need for legal assistance, for such a prisoner is more likely to be unable to understand or exercise his rights. In these circumstances, it is appropriate that counsel be provided to indigent prisoners whom the State seeks to treat as mentally ill.

The issue of transferring prisoners from state custody to the federal system for service of sentence was addressed by the Supreme Court in *Howe v. Smith*.[22] A high-risk Vermont prisoner was transferred to a federal prison because Vermont had closed its only maximum-security prison. It was held that the transfer was authorized and proper, even though no particularized, specialized treatment program was available in the federal system to meet the needs of the prisoner. The plain wording of the statute[23] authorizes transfers not simply for treatment, but also for the custody, care, subsistence, education, and training of state prisoners in federal institutions. However, a prisoner was deprived of an independent decision-maker guaranteed by Hawaii regulations. The same committee that recommended his transfer to a California prison also initiated the transfer. A valid claim under 42 U.S.C. § 1983 was stated.[24]

Although a prisoner has no right to a hearing before being transferred and can be transferred for no reason at all, a prisoner may nevertheless establish a civil rights claim if the decision to transfer him was made by reason of his exercise of constitutionally protected First Amendment freedoms.[25] For example, a corrections officer violated a prisoner's rights when he wrote false disciplinary reports against a prisoner in retaliation for grievances filed against him. The prisoner was transferred 250 miles from his home after he questioned the corrections officer regarding prisoners' rights to legal assistance.[26] Similarly, an officer made repeated death threats to a prisoner resulting in his transfer to worse conditions of confinement. The prisoner had a pending civil rights suit against the officer's brother. These allegations state a viable claim of retaliation for filing the lawsuit.[27]

However, a prison policy of restricting a prisoner's privileges and transferring him to a maximum-security prison if he refused to disclose his sexual history as required by a sex offender treatment program did not violate the Fifth Amendment's protection against compelled self-incrimination.[28]

Finally, the Supreme Court has held that there is no constitutionally protected right to placement in any particular facility. Once an offender is convicted and sentenced to incarceration, he or she may be placed in any prison within that jurisdiction pursuant to the terms of the sentence. However, this may not apply to "supermax" prisons. These prisons have highly restrictive conditions and are designed to segregate the most dangerous prisoners. Supermax inmates are deprived of almost all environmental or sensory stimuli and of almost all human contact. The conditions were so restrictive that the district court and the Sixth Circuit held that Ohio inmates have a protected liberty interest in avoiding placement to the supermax prison. In *Wilkinson v. Austin*,[29] the Supreme Court agreed that the inmates had a protected liberty interest, but held that Ohio's informal, nonadversarial procedures for placement of inmates in the supermax prison were adequate to safeguard the inmates' liberty interest.

§ 8.3.1   – Extradition

One aspect of prison litigation that occasionally arises is the transfer of prisoners to other states or to foreign countries, either to serve their sentences or by extradition. Article IV of the United States Constitution § 2, cl.2. provides:

> A person charged in any State with Treason, Felony, or other Crime, who
> shall flee from Justice, and be found in another State, shall on Demand of the

Executive Authority of the State from which he fled, be delivered up, to be removed to the State having Jurisdiction of the Crime.

The Federal Extradition Act[30] provides the procedures by which this constitutional command is carried out.

In a case involving interstate extradition of a parole violator,[31] a parolee was sentenced to a term of 25 years for armed robbery involving drugs and was paroled from the Ohio correctional system in 1992. In 1993, the parolee was told that Ohio planned to revoke his parole status. Before the scheduled date of his meeting with his parole officer, he fled from Ohio to New Mexico.

Ohio sought extradition, and the governor of New Mexico issued a warrant directing the extradition of the parolee. He was arrested in October 1994 and later that year sought a writ of habeas corpus from the New Mexico State District Court. He claimed he was not a "fugitive" for purposes of extradition because he fled under duress, believing that Ohio authorities intended to revoke his parole without due process and to cause him physical harm if he were returned to an Ohio prison. The state courts in New Mexico ruled in his favor and ordered his release.

According to established case law,[32] once a governor has granted extradition, a court considering release on habeas corpus can do no more than decide: (a) whether the extradition documents on their face are in order; (b) whether the petitioner has been charged with a crime in the demanding state; (c) whether the petitioner is the person named in the request for extradition; and (d) whether the petitioner is a fugitive.

The Supreme Court of New Mexico held that the respondent was not a "fugitive" from justice but rather was a "refugee from injustice,"[33] that the parolee fled Ohio because of fear that his parole would be revoked without due process, and that he would be thereafter returned to prison where he faced the threat of bodily injury. According to the New Mexico court, this "duress" negated his status as a fugitive under Article IV.

The United States Supreme Court reversed, citing *Sweeney v. Woodall*.[34] The parolee was extradited to Ohio. *Woodall* held that extradition does not contemplate an appearance by the demanding state in the asylum state to defend against the claimed abuses of its prison system. Ohio did not make an appearance in New Mexico to protest the failure of New Mexico to extradite the parolee. According to the Supreme Court, claims relating to what actually happened in Ohio, the law of Ohio, and what may be expected to happen in Ohio when the fugitive returns are issues that must be tried in the courts of Ohio and not in those of New Mexico.[35]

The Supreme Court's reasoning was based on practical considerations. In a brief filed by 40 states as "friends of the court," the Court was advised that in 1997, Ohio made 218 extradition requests from its sister states and returned 209 prisoners to other states. California in that same year had a total of 685 demands and returns, New York 490, Texas 700, and Pennsylvania 543. The burden on Ohio of producing witnesses and records in New Mexico, or any other state, to counter allegations such as those of the parolee in New Mexico would make the system virtually unworkable.

In *Marquez-Ramos v. Reno*,[36] a Mexican national imprisoned in Colorado filed a petition with the United States Attorney General, requesting that he be transferred to a Mexican prison pursuant to a treaty.[37] On February 15, 1994, "after considering all appropriate factors," the Attorney General denied the transfer on the basis of the seriousness of the offense and prisoner's significant ties to the United States.

Article IV of the Treaty delineates the procedures for initiating the international transfer of a prisoner. Section (2) states that "if the Authority of the Transferring State finds the transfer of an offender appropriate, and if the offender gives his express consent for his transfer, said Authority shall transmit a request for transfer, through diplomatic channels, to the Authority of the Receiving State." The "first clause of this section sets forth a necessary precondition to a prisoner transfer under the Treaty whether the Attorney General finds a transfer appropriate." In deciding upon the transfer of an offender, all factors bearing upon the probability that the transfer will contribute to the social rehabilitation of the offender—including the nature and severity of the offense and his or her previous criminal record, if any, his or her medical condition, the strength of his or her connections by residence, presence in the territory, family relations and otherwise to the social life of the transferring state and the receiving state—must be taken into consideration. The Treaty on its face makes the decision to transfer a prisoner a discretionary one, so relief was properly denied in *Marquez-Ramos*.

Similarly, in *Bagguley v. Bush*,[38] an English national asked to be sent home to England to serve his American sentence. In 1985, the United States and the United Kingdom ratified the Convention on the Transfer of Sentenced Persons,[39] which provides for the transfer of foreign prisoners to their home countries. The Transfer of Offenders to and from Foreign Countries Act[40] authorizes the Attorney General to implement the Convention. Relief was denied on the same grounds as in *Marquez-Ramos*.

§ 8.3.2   — Civil Commitment of Sex Offenders

Most states have civil commitment statutes where certain sex offenders can be indefinitely committed to a mental health facility following completion of their prison sentence. For example, Kansas's Sexually Violent Predator Act, passed in 1994, allows for the civil commitment of persons who, due to a "mental abnormality" or a "personality disorder," are likely to engage in "predatory acts of sexual violence."[41] The Supreme Court upheld such laws in two cases: *Kansas v. Hendricks*[42] and *Kansas v. Crane*.[43]

In *Kansas v. Hendricks*, inmate Hendricks, who had a long history of sexually molesting children, was scheduled to be released from prison soon after the Kansas law was enacted. Kansas filed a petition under the Act to commit Hendricks upon his prison release. Hendricks testified at a hearing that he suffered from pedophilia and that he continued to harbor sexual desires for children that he cannot control when he becomes stressed. Finding that pedophilia qualifies as a mental abnormality under the Act, the court ordered him committed. On appeal, the Kansas Supreme Court invalidated the Act on the ground that the pre-commitment condition of a "mental abnormality" did not satisfy the substantive due process requirement that involuntary civil commitment must be predicated on a "mental illness."

The U.S. Supreme Court reversed, thus upholding the Act. The Court relied on prior cases in which it had upheld involuntary commitment statutes that detain people who are unable to control their behavior and thereby pose a danger to the public health and safety, provided the confinement takes place pursuant to proper procedures and evidentiary standards.[44] The Court also held that the Act does not violate the Constitution's prohibition against double jeopardy or ex post facto legislation because involuntary confinement is not a criminal issue leading to punishment; rather, it is a civil issue.

In *Kansas v. Crane*, the Court provided some clarification of its *Hendricks* ruling. In *Hendricks*, the Court held that the statutes' words "mental abnormality or personality disorder" satisfied substantive due process. The Kansas Supreme Court interpreted *Hendricks* as requiring a finding that the defendant cannot control his dangerous behavior, even if problems of emotional, and not volitional, capacity prove the source of behavior warranting commitment.[45] The U.S. Supreme Court reversed, holding that *Hendricks* did not require a "total or complete lack of control" but rather only an abnormality or disorder that makes it "difficult, if not impossible" for the offender to control his dangerous behavior.

Thus, the Court has approved civil commitment statutes for sex offenders. It should be noted, however, that the *Hendricks* case was decided with only a slight 5–4 majority, indicating that the issue of the constitutionality of these statutes may not be a settled matter in the future.

§ 8.4   Overcrowding

For a variety of reasons, overcrowding is a major problem at almost all penal institutions. Overcrowding has not, in itself, been declared unconstitutional. However, overcrowding has been viewed as a causal factor that, when other conditions are present, may be enough to declare a prison's conditions to be unconstitutional.[46] While overcrowding itself may not be a violation of the Eighth Amendment, overcrowding can, under certain circumstances, cause unsanitary conditions or high levels of violence, which violate the Eighth Amendment.[47] Furthermore, constitutional treatment of human beings who are confined to penal institutions does not depend upon the willingness or the financial ability of the state to provide decent penitentiaries,[48] especially when the legislature has had ample opportunity to provide for the state to meet its constitutional responsibilities.[49]

In 2011, the Supreme Court addressed severe overcrowding in California's prison system. This case, *Brown v. Plata*,[50] represented the Court's most ambitious step toward addressing overcrowding to date. California's prisons were designed to house roughly 80,000 inmates, but at the time, the prison population was almost double that. Inmates filed two class action suits claiming that the overcrowding was so severe that prisoners with serious mental illnesses were not able to receive even minimal care, which violated their Eighth Amendment rights. For example, documents presented to the court showed backlogs of up to 700 prisoners waiting to see a doctor for care. The inmates also claimed that overcrowding led to unsafe and unsanitary conditions, promoted unrest and violence, and caused some prisoners with latent mental illnesses to worsen and develop overt symptoms.

The Supreme Court upheld a lower court's ruling that required California to reduce its prison population to 137 percent capacity—from about 160,000 inmates to 110,000—over the course of two years. The Court believed that overcrowding was the primary cause of the violations and that if a prison deprives inmates of basic sustenance, including adequate medical care, the courts have a responsibility to remedy the resulting Eighth Amendment violation.[51] As of late 2020, California's prison population sits at roughly 115,000.

§ 8.5   Conditions of Confinement

Most aspects of prison life are dictated by the needs of institutionalization. Prison authorities have wide discretion to regulate or prohibit prisoners' comforts, including the keeping of pets,[52] permissible clothing,[53] plumbing,[54] and checking accounts.[55] At the same time, courts have a duty to protect prisoners from unlawful and onerous treatment of a nature that, in itself, adds punitive measures to those legally meted out by a court.[56] While the federal courts continue to recognize the broad discretion that state prison officials require in order to maintain orderly and secure institutions, constitutional deprivations of such a magnitude as to allow the maintenance of facilities that are wholly unfit for human habitation cannot be tolerated.

As shown in *Brown v. Plata*, the courts are under a duty to—and will—intervene to protect incarcerated persons from such infringements of their constitutional rights.[57] However, federal courts are limited in their intervention into the operations of institutions to the issue of whether there are constitutional violations. In *Bell v. Wolfish*,[58] the Supreme Court said:

> There was a time not too long ago when the federal judiciary took a completely "hands-off" approach to the problem of prison administration. In recent years, however, these courts largely have discarded this "hands-off" attitude and have waded into this complex arena. The deplorable conditions and draconian restrictions of some of our Nation's prisons are too well known to require recounting here, and the federal courts rightly have condemned these sordid aspects of our prison systems. But many of

these same courts have, in the name of the Constitution, become increasingly enmeshed in the minutiae of prison operations. Judges, after all, are human. They, no less than others in our society, have a natural tendency to believe that their individual solutions to often intractable problems are better and more workable than those of the persons who are actually charged with and trained in the running of the particular institution under examination. But under the Constitution, the first question to be answered is not whose plan is best, but in what branch of the Government is lodged the authority to initially devise the plan. This does not mean that constitutional rights are not to be scrupulously observed. It does mean, however, that the inquiry of federal courts into prison management must be limited to the issue of whether a particular system violates any prohibition of the Constitution, or in the case of a federal prison, a statute. The wide range of "judgment calls" that meet constitutional and statutory requirement[s] are confided to officials outside of the Judicial Branch of Government.

Similarly, in *Rhodes v. Chapman*,[59] the Supreme Court reinforced its holding in *Bell v. Wolfish*. It admonished the lower federal courts that in determining whether prison conditions constitute cruel and unusual punishment under federal standards, federal courts cannot assume that state legislatures and prison officials are insensitive to the requirements of the Constitution or to the sociological problems of how best to achieve the goals of the prison in the criminal justice system.

Although federal courts may lack the power to order public or governmental entities, which represent the public, to expend funds to build new facilities, they do have the power to order the release of persons who are being held under conditions that deprive them of rights guaranteed to them by the Constitution, unless such conditions are corrected within a reasonable period.[60] Some courts have gone so far with the conditions-of-confinement argument that they have allowed escapees to raise the criminal defenses of necessity and duress to criminal charges of prison escape. Such cases usually involve threats of rape as the mitigating condition of confinement.

As a result of the increase in conditions-of-confinement suits, the Supreme Court has added to the obstacles that prisoners face in filing such suits. In *Wilson v. Seiter*,[61] a civil rights action was filed against an Ohio facility where the prisoner was housed. The complaint alleged overcrowding, mixing of healthy prisoners with physically and mentally ill prisoners, excessive noise, inadequate heating and cooling, and lack of sanitation. In such cases, prisoners must prove a culpable mental state on the part of prison officials. Such proof is an essential element in a claim that prison conditions violate the Eighth Amendment's prohibition of cruel and unusual punishment. *Estelle v. Gamble*,[62] *Rhodes v. Chapman*,[63] and *Whitley v. Albers*[64] were observed by the Supreme Court as showing that a mental element is implicit in the Eighth Amendment's language. The cases require a prisoner to show "deliberate indifference" on the part of the official.

The Supreme Court indicated that there is no distinction between cases involving prison-wide conditions of confinement and cases alleging unconstitutional acts or omissions directed at particular prisoners. This idea—

that no distinctions will be made between the two types of cases—was reiterated, but in a different context, in the Federal Magistrates Act.[65] The Act allows suits brought by prisoners to be referred to a magistrate without the consent of the parties. The wording of the Act makes specific reference to petitions challenging conditions of confinement.

In the Supreme Court case *Rufo v. Prisoners of Suffolk County Jail*,[66] state officials sought to modify a consent decree previously entered into, which had resulted from constitutionally deficient conditions at the facility known as the Charles Street Jail. The terms of the program set out in the decree were designed to include 309 single-occupancy rooms. By the time construction began in 1984, the prisoner population had outpaced population projections. State officials were then ordered to build a larger jail. The number of cells was later increased to 453 with construction beginning in 1987. In 1989, the sheriff moved to modify the consent decree to allow double-bunking in a portion of the cells to raise the capacity of the new jail to 610 male detainees. The federal district court supervising the consent decree applied the standard of *United States v. Swift & Co*:[67]

> Nothing less than a clear showing of grievous wrong evoked by new and unforeseen conditions should lead us to change what was decreed after years of litigation with the consent of all concerned.[68]

The district court stated that because a separate cell was an important element of the original relief sought, a more flexible standard would not be available to the sheriff. In moving to modify the decree, the sheriff relied on Federal Rule of Civil Procedure 60(b)(5) and (6), which in part provides that a court may relieve a party from a final judgment, order, or proceeding for the reason that the judgment has been satisfied, or that it is no longer equitable that the judgment should have prospective application, or any other reason justifying relief from the operation of the judgment.

The sheriff asserted that modification of the decree would improve conditions by cutting down on transfers of detainees away from the area where their family members and legal counsel were located. Further, in the transfer facilities, the detainees would be double-celled in less desirable conditions. Finally, the public interest would be served by such modification because fewer releases and transfers to halfway houses would be necessary and thus fewer escapes would occur.

On appeal, the Supreme Court held that the *Swift* "grievous wrong" standard does not apply to requests to modify consent decrees that stem from institutional reform litigation. The Court then adopted a much more flexible standard that a party seeking modification of a consent decree must establish: a significant change in facts or law must be present in order to warrant revision, and the proposed modification must be suitably tailored to the changed circumstances. The Court further directed the lower court on remand to consider whether the increase in the prisoner population was foreseeable.

This ruling may in fact lead to delay on the part of state officials who are working under consent decrees as a result of prison conditions. The prison system is constantly changing, and it could be argued that most of those changes are foreseeable. The lasting effect of consent decrees in conditions-of-confinement cases is yet to be known.

In *Del Raine v. Williford*,[69] a prisoner claimed that in the period following a lockdown, he was forced to inhabit a cold cell and was not given adequate clothing or blankets. The prisoner alleged:

> Every few days I'm strip-searched in my cell (notwithstanding the bitter cold resulting from the open window above my cell), cuffed behind my back, pulled backwards from my cell, put in an empty cell while cuffed, from fifteen to thirty minutes, while my cell is ransacked, i.e., personal property is stolen, legal papers mixed up, scattered, walked on, towels and sheets thrown on the floor. This practice continues to the present time. On December 23, 1983 while the chill factor was minus 40 degrees to 50 degrees below zero, according to the radio weather reports, I was strip-searched and placed in an empty cell while my cell was ransacked. No hats, jackets, or gloves were allowed, nor could we put a blanket over our cell bars to warm the cell. Many other days were also bitterly cold. Repeated requests to . . . close the windows and fix broken ones were futile.

Applying *Farmer v. Brennan*,[70] the Seventh Circuit held that a prison official is not liable under the Eighth Amendment for denying a prisoner humane conditions of confinement unless the official knows of and disregards an excessive risk to prisoner health or safety. The official must both be aware of facts from which the inference could be drawn that a substantial risk of serious harm exists, and he must also draw the inference. The Eighth Amendment does not outlaw cruel and unusual "conditions." It outlaws cruel and unusual "punishments." An act or omission unaccompanied by knowledge of a significant risk of harm might well be something society wishes to discourage, and if harm does result, society might well wish to assure compensation. The common law reflects such concerns when it imposes tort liability on a purely objective basis.

The Court concluded that the prisoner was entitled to have a jury determine whether the conditions of his administrative confinement, principally with regard to the cell temperature and the provision of hygiene items, violated the minimal standards required by the Eighth Amendment. However, the Court also concluded that the right of a prisoner not to be confined in a cell at so low a temperature as to cause severe discomfort and in conditions lacking basic sanitation was well established. The prison officials therefore were not entitled to summary judgment on the basis of qualified immunity.

Other circuits have recognized the temperature factor in assessing conditions of confinement. The Second Circuit reversed the dismissal of a prisoner's complaint of exposure to extreme cold.[71] Subsequently, it affirmed on the merits a finding of cruel and unusual punishment in confining a prisoner for 11 days, naked, without soap, towels, or toilet paper, and without bedding of any kind, forcing the prisoner to sleep on the floor, the temperature being sufficiently cold to cause extreme discomfort.[72] The Fourth Circuit[73] found two sets of conditions of confinement involving the same prisoner to violate the Eighth Amendment. In the first, the prisoner was confined for two days in a cell where a concrete slab was initially the prisoner's bed. A mattress was furnished later during the first night, but no blankets were supplied. Although the record did not disclose the temperature in the cell, it was so cold that the prisoner tore open the mattress and nestled inside. The prisoner also was denied personal hygiene items. The court held that in the case of an ordinary prisoner, these conditions violated the Eighth Amendment; the only justification would be such mental derangement on the part of the prisoner that self-harm was a real danger, in which case immediate contact with a psychologist/psychiatrist was required. The second set of conditions included another two-day confinement in a cell without clothing, blanket, or mattress, where the prisoner claimed sleep was impossible and that he had to stand up most of the first night. He was also denied articles of personal hygiene. The court held that these conditions also violated the prisoner's Eighth Amendment rights in the absence of mental derangement.

§ 8.5.1   — Conditions Above Constitutional Minimum Standards

In *Anderson v. County of Kern*,[74] prisoners challenged as unconstitutional the use of safety cells for suicidal and mentally disturbed prisoners. Safety cells are padded cells that are used to temporarily confine violent or suicidal prisoners so they cannot hurt themselves. The claims were evaluated under the Eighth Amendment, and the pretrial detainees' challenge was evaluated under the Fourteenth Amendment. Under the Eighth Amendment, the pertinent inquiry is whether placement of mentally disturbed or suicidal prisoners in safety cells constitutes an infliction of pain or a deprivation of basic human needs, such as adequate food, clothing, shelter, sanitation, and medical care, and if so, whether prison officials acted with the requisite culpable intent such that the infliction of pain is "unnecessary and wanton."[75]

On the basis of testimony, the district court rejected prisoners' challenge to the use of safety cells, finding that nothing suggested that the safety cells had been inappropriately used as more than a temporary measure to control violent prisoners until they "cooled down" sufficiently to be released from those cells. The experts agreed that the cells could appropriately be used for this purpose. The district court's ruling was affirmed. Safety cells are a very severe environment but are employed in response to very severe safety concerns.

It was recognized that prison officials must have some means of controlling violent or self-destructive prisoners temporarily until the episode passes, and as the plaintiffs' own expert testified, it is difficult to distinguish between violent, mentally healthy prisoners and violent, mentally disturbed ones. Similarly, in an emergency, prison officials are not culpable when they put a prisoner who imminently threatens or attempts suicide temporarily in a place where he or she cannot hurt him- or herself. In light of the safety concerns underlying use of the safety cell, there was no inference that the prison officials were knowingly and unreasonably disregarding an objectively intolerable risk of harm and would continue to do so in the future.

Also at issue in *Anderson* was an order by the district court requiring jail officials to develop a policy allowing prison officials to exercise discretion in determining whether certain prisoners housed in administrative segregation can safely exercise or have day room access together. The law is clear that the transfer of a prisoner to less amenable and more restrictive quarters for nonpunitive reasons is well within the terms of confinement ordinarily contemplated by a prison sentence.[76] Thus, the hardship associated with administrative segregation, such as loss of recreational and rehabilitative programs or confinement to one's cell for a lengthy period, does not violate the Due Process Clause because there is no liberty interest in remaining in the general population.[77] Administrative segregation, even in a single cell for 23 hours per day, is within the terms of confinement ordinarily contemplated by a sentence. Further, prison officials have a legitimate penological interest in administrative segregation, and they must be given wide-ranging deference in the adoption and execution of policies and practices that in their judgment are needed to preserve internal order and discipline and to maintain institutional security. Here, prisoners in administrative segregation retained all prisoner privileges such as family visits, telephone access, and exercise. They were all single-celled, however, and had no contact with any other prisoner, either for exercise, day room access, or otherwise.

In an Eighth Circuit case, corrections officers were entitled to qualified immunity in a civil rights action by the mother of a prisoner who died from heat exhaustion after collapsing while on a work squad in 72-degree weather. The court held that the supervisor did not compel prisoners to perform physical labor in disregard of known serious medical needs, the prisoner displayed no signs of physical difficulties prior to his collapse, and corrections officers promptly responded to the emergency and transported the prisoner to the prison infirmary.[78]

The Sixth Circuit held that a prisoner who was deprived of a lower bunk, subjected to a flooded cell, and deprived of a working toilet did not state a claim under the civil rights act. The claims, although not frivolous, referred to temporary inconveniences and did not demonstrate that conditions fell beneath the minimal civilized measure of life's necessities as measured by a contemporary standard of decency.[79]

In *Overton v. Bazzetta*,[80] the Supreme Court held that visitation restrictions for all prisoners with two or more substance abuse violations were not a cruel and unusual confinement condition violating the Eighth Amendment.

Withdrawing visitation privileges for a limited period in order to effect prison discipline is not a dramatic departure from accepted standards for confinement conditions. Further, the restrictions did not create inhumane prison conditions, deprive prisoners of basic necessities, or fail to protect their health or safety, nor did the restrictions involve the infliction of pain or injury or deliberate indifference to their risk.

A male prisoner failed in his claim that his equal protection rights were violated in prison because privacy partitions were installed in bathrooms to protect the privacy of female prisoners and cross-gender monitoring and surveillance of females was not allowed, but similar partitions and prohibitions of cross-gender monitoring were not used to protect male prisoners' privacy. The Fifth Circuit held that the female and male prisoners were not similarly situated. The male prisoners were violent felons and the female prisoners had been convicted of the lowest level of felonies, and the male units had a higher incidence of violent gang activity and sexual predation.[81]

The use of a restraint chair for eight hours did not violate the Eighth Amendment rights of a convicted prisoner awaiting sentencing. Even if prison officials overreacted to a disturbance that the prisoner caused, the prison officials did not act maliciously and sadistically to cause harm. The prisoner's physical condition was checked every 15 minutes, he was released every two hours for a 10-minute relief period, and the prisoner was properly fed and examined by a nurse at the end of the eight-hour confinement.[82]

The Eleventh Circuit ruled that a constant temperature between 80 and 86 degrees in a prison was not unconstitutionally excessive. The prison was equipped with a ventilation system that effectively managed air circulation and humidity. Numerous conditions in the prison alleviated heat, including the fact that cells were not exposed to any direct sunlight, the prisoners were not required to wear many clothes, every cell had a sink with hot and cold running water, each prisoner had a drinking cup, prisoners were generally sedentary, they were not compelled to perform prison labor, and they had limited opportunities to gain relief in air-conditioned areas.[83]

In a 2005 federal district court case, a county had been previously found in contempt for failing to implement specific steps to correct unconstitutional conditions at its jail. The county purged itself of contempt by implementing a new remedial scheme, which included direct supervision in cell blocks, improved population management, collection and utilization of data, installation of an objective classification system, improved control of gang members through creation of a Gang Intelligence Unit, improved prisoner discipline and prosecution of prisoner crimes committed within the jail, creation of a Disturbance Response Team, a provision for adequate prisoner services, creation of an effective grievance procedure, improved staff training, improved security, efforts to achieve certification and accreditation, creation of programs and activities to reduce prisoner idleness, and improved leadership.[84]

§ 8.5.2   — Conditions Below Constitutional Minimum Standards

In *Maxwell v. Mason*,[85] the Eighth Circuit affirmed a finding of cruel and unusual punishment in the confinement of a prisoner to 14 days in a solitary cell with no clothing except undershorts and no bedding except a mattress. Correctional officers had testified that the temperature would have been at least 70 degrees, but the prisoner had testified that he huddled in the corner of his cell to stay warm. The court stated that prisoners in punitive solitary confinement should not be deprived of basic necessities, including light, heat, ventilation, sanitation, clothing, and a proper diet, and affirmed a denial of qualified immunity for two prison officials.

The Seventh Circuit[86] reversed the dismissal of a prisoner's complaint that alleged being placed in solitary confinement for three days without a mattress, bedding, or blankets and without articles of personal hygiene. It also set aside summary judgment in *Lewis v. Lane*,[87] in which two state prisoners alleged that the heat in their cells was maintained at an unreasonably low temperature during December and January and that the lack of heat was severe enough to produce physical discomfort. Consequently, an allegation of inadequate heating may state an Eighth Amendment violation.[88]

A county was liable to jail prisoners who were beaten by other jail prisoners based on deliberate indifference to a substantial risk of serious harm. The county failed to maintain the jail building. Sewage leaked from pipes, sinks and toilets were dilapidated and inoperable, windows could not be closed, shards of broken glass lay on window sills, and vermin entered the jail through windows and wall cracks. The prisoners could and did fashion weapons by vandalizing the dilapidated physical structure. Cell locks on the second floor were broken and jailers did not have a surveillance system. The jail was grossly understaffed and had no system for segregating prisoners with mental illness or for other reasons.[89]

An Eighth Amendment claim was shown where a prisoner suffered a six-month deprivation of all out-of-cell exercise due to a lockdown to conduct an extensive shakedown of a prison and to implement new security measures. Reasonable officials should have known that such complete and lengthy deprivation of exercise was constitutionally questionable.[90]

A pretrial detainee slipped in a shower and injured himself. The defendants failed to repair the shower in his unit for more than nine months even though they were alerted to the conditions in the shower area several times. The exposure of the detainee to the unsanitary and hazardous showering area for more than nine months was "sufficiently serious" to meet an objective element of a due process claim based upon conditions of his confinement.[91]

§ 8.5.3   — Exercise

Exercise is one of the basic human necessities protected by the Eighth Amendment.[92] The Fourteenth Amendment requires that pretrial detainees be granted adequate opportunities for exercise. Denial requires a legitimate governmental objective. Determining what constitutes adequate exercise requires consideration of the physical characteristics of the cell and jail and the average length of stay of the prisoners.[93]

The Seventh Circuit held that failure to provide prisoners confined for more than a very short period with the opportunity for at least five hours a week of exercise outside the cell raises serious constitutional questions.[94] Similarly, jail officials who fail to provide each prisoner at least one hour per day of exercise outside the cells create a constitutionally intolerable condition.[95]

In a California jail, pretrial detainees in administrative segregation and other restrictive classifications, such as protective custody, were typically afforded, at best, only 90 minutes weekly in a space equipped for exercise.[96] Providing the equivalent of slightly less than 13 minutes of exercise a day does not give meaningful exercise.[97] Curtailment of exercise to 90 minutes weekly for prisoners who otherwise spend the bulk of their time inside their cells reduces the amount of exercise to a point at which there is no meaningful vindication of the constitutional right to exercise for this entire category of detainees. Given the severity of these restrictions and their application across an entire category of detainees, the Ninth Circuit concluded that 90 minutes of exercise per week constitutes punishment for purposes of §1983.

§ 8.5.4   — Failure to Protect

A significant Supreme Court pronouncement on Eighth Amendment claims arising from unconstitutional conditions of confinement is *Farmer v. Brennan*,[98] which involved the rape of a prisoner. A preoperative transsexual was transferred from a Federal Correctional Institute to a penitentiary and raped soon after his arrival. He claimed that the wardens and officials in the two prisons acted with deliberate indifference to his safety in violation of the Eighth Amendment because they knew that the penitentiary had a violent environment and a history of prisoner assaults and that the plaintiff would be particularly vulnerable to sexual attack if placed in the general prisoner population. The Supreme Court held that a prison official cannot be found liable under the Eighth Amendment for denying a prisoner humane conditions of confinement unless the official knows of and disregards an excessive risk to prisoner health or safety. The official must both be aware of facts from which the inference could be drawn that a substantial risk of serious harm exists, and he or she must also draw the inference.

The Sixth Circuit pointed out that, in 1910, Winston Churchill coined a phrase and recognized an obvious truth when he said that the "treatment of crime and criminals is one of the most unfailing tests of civilization of any country."[99] In *Farmer*, the Supreme Court applied the same idea to prison rapes, saying that "gratuitously allowing the beating or rape of one prisoner by another serves no 'legitimate penological objective,' any more than it squares with 'evolving standards of decency.'" Prisons are dangerous places because they house dangerous people in congested conditions. But the Eighth Amendment to the Constitution mandates that prison officials maintain humane conditions of confinement and take reasonable measures to guarantee the safety of prisoners. Their duty includes protecting prisoners from violence at the hands of other prisoners: "Having stripped [prisoners] of virtually every means of self-protection and foreclosed their access to outside aid, the government and its officials are not free to let the state of nature take its course."[100]

After assaults of female prisoners by male detention officers, a sheriff was aware of prison conditions that were substantially likely to result in the sexual assault of female prisoners and a serious deprivation of prisoners' rights. Given that knowledge, the sheriff was under a duty not only to take reasonable measures to remedy the circumstances that directly led to sexual assaults but to cure his own lack of attention and unresponsiveness to prisoner complaints and other indicators of serious problems with his detention staff. The assaults on prisoners were caused by those dangerous conditions.[101]

The Eighth Circuit held that a supervisor at county jail was deliberately indifferent to a substantial risk that a prisoner would be sexually assaulted by a correctional officer. The deputy conceded that no one was supposed to go into a prisoner's cell after lockdown, but he knew that a trainee went to a female detainee's cell three times after lockdown within the space of an hour. When this happened, the detainee's constitutional right to be protected from being sexually assaulted by a guard was clearly established.[102]

In *Ware v. Jackson County*,[103] the county was liable to a jail prisoner who was raped. Rampant sexual misconduct of employees toward female prisoners was shown. The director of the jail was the final policymaker for the county and had notice of sexual incidents. In violation of the Eighth Amendment, he failed to investigate incidents or to take disciplinary action. The failure of the director to address sexual misconduct by jail personnel was the moving force behind the violation of the raped prisoner's rights. On the other hand, a suit by female residents of a state detention facility for juveniles who were sexually assaulted by a youth development aide at the facility against the executive director of the facility was dismissed. The claim was that the policies and procedures approved by him created an unreasonably unsafe environment that allowed abuse. The court held that the director was not aware of any pattern of known injuries and was not deliberately indifferent to a great and obvious risk of safety to the residents.[104]

§ 8.6   Correctional Personnel

Several unique problems affect correctional personnel. As free people they are entitled, of course, to the full measure of liberty accorded all other persons. However, two counterforces may circumscribe the exercise of such liberty. First, prison employees who are also police officers are subject to the same occupationally generated need for uniformity and discipline as regular civil police forces. There is a paramilitary aspect to prison employment, and certain sacrifices must be made by the employees so that the police power of the state may be most efficiently used and effectively displayed. In *Kelley v. Johnson*,[105] the Supreme Court upheld a county regulation that specified its police officers' hair length. The Court concluded that whether a state or local government's choice to have its police in uniform reflects a desire to make police officers readily recognizable to the public or to foster the *esprit de corps* that similarity of garb and appearance may inculcate within the police force itself, the justification for the hair length regulation is sufficiently rational to defeat a claim based upon the liberty guarantee of the Fourteenth Amendment.[106]

The second counterforce to the unrestrained exercise of the constitutional liberties of correctional personnel applies equally to uniformed and nonuniformed employees. The institutional needs of security, order, and rehabilitation provide the basis for certain limitations upon such employees' liberties. Limitations upon the right to be free from searches and seizures and upon the exercise of the rights to free association are examples of the numerous daily adjustments that correctional personnel must make when they physically cross the barriers between prison society and free society. The smuggling of contraband into prisons is so dangerous to institutional order that its prevention outweighs the probable cause requirement that normally limits searches and seizures in free society. Rehabilitative considerations can dictate that correctional personnel limit or minimize their personal associations with prisoners.

As previously stated, prison employees are also subject to search. The Fourth Circuit held that a visual body cavity search of a prison employee was constitutionally permissible where the search was within the scope of a warden's authority. The warden had a particularized and individualized tip from an informant that the employee was bringing contraband into the prison hidden in a tampon on a specific occasion.[107] However, in *Armstrong v. Newark State Comm. of Corrections*,[108] a federal district court ruled that there was no justification in subjecting a correctional officer to a body cavity search where there was only a bare assertion that officials had received information that the officer was involved in smuggling contraband, and there were no other facts shown to support the allegation.

Another aspect of corrections work is the standard prohibition against the use of armed trusties, or prisoner assistants, as correctional officers. Once quite prevalent, this practice is now limited[109] to areas such as medical services. Medically trained prisoner assistants are encouraged in addition to, although not as total fulfillment of, the prison's medical services staff.[110]

§ 8.7 Retaliation Claims

Numerous cases litigate the allegation that prisoners have suffered retaliation by prison officials when the prisoners exercise their constitutional rights or file grievances against correctional personnel. The right to be free from retaliation for a prisoner's exercise of his First Amendment rights was "clearly established" by the 1980s.[111]

The necessary elements of a retaliation claim are: (1) a prison official acting under color of state law and (2) intentional retaliation for the exercise of a constitutionally protected activity. The law is clearly established that a prison official may not retaliate against or harass a prisoner for exercising the right of access to the courts.[112] Even the prison officials candidly conceded that this was a claim of constitutional proportions that is actionable. Further, the court determined that there was no immunity defense.

To state a claim of retaliation, a prisoner must allege the violation of a specific constitutional right and be prepared to establish that, but for the retaliatory motive, the incident would not have occurred.[113] This places a significant burden on the prisoner. Mere conclusory allegations of retaliation will not withstand a summary judgment challenge.[114] The prisoner must produce direct evidence of motivation or, the more probable scenario, allege a chronology of events from which retaliation may plausibly be inferred.

In a 1995 case, a corrections officer warned a prisoner that if he did not become an informant, bad things would happen to him, including transfer to a less desirable part of the prison. The prisoner reported the alleged threat by a letter addressed to a United States District Judge who was presiding over pending prison litigation. As a result, the prisoner was issued a disciplinary charge for defiance. The constitutional right of access to the courts was violated by this retaliation.[115] The Fifth Circuit in *Woods v. Smith* remained fully supportive of the proposition that although prison officials must have wide latitude in the control and discipline of prisoners, such latitude does not encompass conduct that infringes on a prisoner's substantive constitutional rights. However, the court agreed with the Fourth Circuit when it cautioned that the prospect of endless claims of retaliation on the part of prisoners would disrupt prison officials in the discharge of their most basic duties and that claims of retaliation must therefore be regarded with skepticism, lest the federal courts embroil themselves in every disciplinary act that occurs in state penal institutions.[116]

In the 2019 Sixth Circuit case *Berkshire v. Beauvais*,[117] an inmate filed suit claiming that he was removed from a residential treatment program in retaliation for bringing other inmates' complaints to the attention of prison staff, thus violating his First and Eighth Amendment rights. The court agreed, holding that the facts of the case met the two necessary elements of a retaliation claim. First, the inmate was engaged in conduct protected by the First Amendment when he filed complaints for other inmates. Second, prison officials intentionally retaliated against the inmate for the exercise of this constitutionally protected activity.

The Seventh Circuit held that a prisoner suffered retaliation through delays in his incoming and outgoing mail, harassment by a guard kicking his cell door, turning his cell light off and on, and opening his cell trap and slamming it shut in order to startle him when he was sleeping, unjustified disciplinary charges, and improper dismissal of his grievances. Such acts constitute retaliation for the exercise of a constitutionally protected right.[118]

A prison official's serious threats of substantial retaliation against a prisoner for lodging a good faith grievance make any administrative remedy unavailable. There is no exhaustion requirement under the PLRA where: (1) the threat actually did deter a prisoner from lodging a grievance or pursuing a particular part of process, and (2) the threat is one that would deter a reasonable prisoner of ordinary firmness and fortitude from lodging a grievance or pursuing the part of the grievance process that the prisoner failed to exhaust.[119] Threats from prison officials and withholding of grievance forms rendered exhaustion inapplicable.[120]

§ 8.7.1   — Retaliation Not Shown

In a Seventh Circuit case, a prisoner claimed that prison officials had retaliated against him by removing him from his position cochairing a prison-approved group called the Paralegal Base Committee (which assisted prisoners with legal research and preparing legal documents) and then transferring him to another facility. The retaliation occurred after he wrote a letter, written on an official Committee letterhead and sent to various prison officials, requesting that all security staff involved in filing negative conduct reports against a certain prisoner be given polygraph examinations prior to the prisoner's disciplinary hearing. He also offered to pay for the examinations from the funds of the Committee. Under the prison's regulations, the prisoner should have requested permission from the Committee's advisor prior to sending the correspondence. He also should have had the Committee's advisor cosign the request, because it purported to authorize spending of Committee funds. The prisoner did neither. As a result, he was removed from the Committee and transferred to another prison. The prisoner did not satisfy his burden to demonstrate that the prison officials, in reacting to his violation of the regulations, exaggerated their response to preserving the legitimate penological objectives of the prison environment.[121]

In another case, a prisoner's conduct amounted to a public rebuke of the prison chaplain and members of the prison administration's staff and was intended to, and did, incite about 50 other prisoners in a walkout from a church service. The manner of the prisoner's statement was inconsistent with his status as a prisoner. He was thus not entitled to any First Amendment protection in a claim alleging that he was transferred in retaliation for exercising his First Amendment rights.[122]

§ 8.8   Smoking

A prisoner has a clearly established constitutional right to be free from levels of secondhand smoke that pose an unreasonable risk of future harm.[123] Smokers seldom win in contemporary life, but secondhand smoke cases often fail on procedural or proof issues.

A prisoner alleged deliberate indifference to his medical needs regarding exposure to secondhand smoke. The case was dismissed because he failed to allege that the level of smoke in the prison created an unreasonable risk of serious damage to his future health or to show a serious medical condition necessitating a smoke-free environment. He did not complain to the officials about his shortness of breath or chest pains. Even if he had a serious medical need for a smoke-free environment, he failed to show a deliberate indifference to that need. Although he alleged that the nonsmoking policy was not fully enforced, he failed to allege any single incident in which the officials were aware that a smoking violation was occurring but did not act.[124]

In *Helling v. McKinney*,[125] the Ninth Circuit held that a nonsmoking prisoner's compelled exposure to environmental tobacco smoke (ETS) can amount to cruel and unusual punishment prohibited by the Eighth Amendment. The Supreme Court eventually vacated and remanded the case.[126]

The Nevada state prisoner claimed that his involuntary exposure to ETS from his cellmate's and other prisoners' cigarettes posed an unreasonable risk to his health, thus subjecting him to cruel and unusual punishment in violation of the Eighth Amendment. A federal magistrate granted petitioners' motion for a directed verdict, but the Court of Appeals reversed in part, holding that McKinney should have been permitted to prove that his ETS exposure was sufficient to constitute an unreasonable danger to his future health.

The Supreme Court held that by alleging that the prison officials had, with deliberate indifference, exposed him to ETS levels that posed an unreasonable risk to his future health, the prisoner had stated an Eighth Amendment claim on which relief could be granted. An injunction cannot be denied to prisoners who plainly prove an unsafe, life-threatening condition on the ground that nothing yet has happened to them.[127]

However, as the Court could not rule that the prisoner could not possibly prove an Eighth Amendment violation based on ETS exposure, the Court held that it would be premature to base a reversal on the argument that the harm from ETS exposure is speculative, with no risk sufficiently grave to implicate a serious medical need, and that the exposure is not contrary to current standards of decency. The lower court, on remand, was directed to give the prisoner the opportunity to prove his allegations, which would require that he establish both the subjective and objective elements necessary to prove an Eighth Amendment violation. With respect to the objective factor, it was pointed out that he may have difficulty showing that he is being exposed to unreasonably high ETS levels, because he has been moved to a new prison and no longer has a cellmate who smokes, and because a new state prison policy restricts smoking to certain areas and makes reasonable efforts to respect nonsmokers' wishes with regard to double-bunking. He was required to also show that the risk of which he complained is not one that today's society chooses to tolerate. The subjective factor, deliberate indifference, was to be determined in light of the prison authorities' current attitudes and conduct, which, as evidenced by the new smoking policy, might have changed considerably since the Court of

Appeals' original judgment. The inquiry into this factor also was deemed to be an appropriate vehicle to consider arguments regarding the realities of prison administration.

In a lower court case subsequent to *Helling*,[128] a prisoner was "roomed up" with a heavy smoker. He informed a prison official that he suffered various medical problems, severe headaches, dizziness, nausea, vomiting, and breathing difficulties when roomed with a smoking prisoner. The prisoner's room was designated a "nonsmoking" room. However, his roommate continued to smoke and a "shakedown" revealed that the "smoking conditions were still the same." Although the prisoner personally showed the orders to the prison officials, the officials made no attempts to enforce the orders. The prisoner filed a second grievance, and the Director of Correctional Services responded by reiterating that the room was nonsmoking and by indicating that if the prisoner continued to experience problems, he should contact unit management staff for an investigation or a room change. The prisoner did so and asked that either he or his roommate be moved to another room, but no move was forthcoming. Finally, the prisoner asked to see the prison doctor, who ordered that he be switched to a room with a nonsmoking roommate immediately. The prison officials complied with the doctor's orders. The prisoner then filed suit.

The district court found that the prisoner, like the prisoner in *Helling*, had alleged that the prison officials were deliberately indifferent to the future health risks posed by his continued exposure to environmental tobacco smoke. However, the Court of Appeals read the complaint differently and found that *Helling* was not on point. In this case, the prisoner did not allege that prison officials showed deliberate indifference to his future health. Rather, he alleged deliberate indifference to his existing ill health. As portrayed in the complaint, environmental tobacco smoke was the catalyst for his existing health problems. *Helling*, in contrast, did not involve deliberate indifference to existing medical needs. However, the Eighth Circuit concluded that the deliberate indifference to his existing serious medical needs was a violation of a constitutional right.

There are few smoking-related cases brought today, however, because every state, as well as the Federal Bureau of Prisons, now prohibits smoking indoors. About half of the states have banned smoking outdoors as well.

§ 8.9   Ex Post Facto

Prisoners often attack laws and regulations that affect them adversely on the ground that the application of the law or regulation to them violates the ex post facto clause of the Constitution. A state violates the ex post facto clause if it attempts to punish as a crime an act that was not criminal when done, removes a defense that was available when the act was committed, or increases the punishment for a crime after it was committed.[129] For a law to run afoul of this ban, it must be retrospective—that is, it must apply to events that occurred before its enactment, and it must disadvantage the offender affected by it.[130]

An example is *Dominique v. Weld*.[131] A sentenced prisoner was returned to confinement after he had been allowed to participate in a work-release program for almost four years. It was asserted that the administrative action violated the ex post facto clause[132] based on a new state regulation governing the treatment and movement of sex offenders from commitment to release. The regulation became effective in October 1994, at which time the prisoner was incarcerated at the medium-security facility to which he had been transferred following his removal from work-release earlier that year. He did not dispute the Commonwealth's contention that, under the regulation, he was ineligible to participate in the work-release program. The prisoner was an identified sex offender who could not be moved to a minimum-security facility, with associated privileges, unless and until he successfully completed a treatment program, admitted his offense, and otherwise obtained approval for a transfer. The policy required identified sex offenders to complete a four-phase treatment program at a medium-security facility as a precondition for transfer. It outlined further transition phases and evaluation processes as well.

According to the Supreme Court, the proper focus of an ex post facto inquiry is whether the relevant change "alters the definition of criminal conduct or increases the penalty by which a crime is punishable."[133] *California Department of Corrections v. Morales*[134] examined a California statutory amendment that authorized the Board of Prison Terms to defer for up to three years parole suitability hearings for multiple murderers. The Supreme Court found no ex post facto violation, because the amendment created only the most speculative and attenuated possibility of producing the prohibited effect of increasing the measure of punishment for covered crimes. The Supreme Court did not develop a precise formula. It said that these judgments must be a matter of "degree." The regulation did not increase the penalty by which the prisoner's crime was punishable. The change in the conditions determining the nature of his confinement while serving his sentence was held to be an allowed alteration in the prevailing "legal regime" rather than an "increased penalty" for ex post facto purposes. Further, the change did not affect the length of the prisoner's sentence or his parole options.

Another example is *Williams v. Lee*.[135] After the prisoner, who was confined at the South Dakota State Penitentiary, violated his parole, the state of South Dakota, acting on the authority of legislation enacted after Williams had committed the offense that resulted in his conviction and sentence, revoked his accumulated good-time credits. The application of the statute to the prisoner violated the ex post facto clause.[136]

§ 8.10   Funding and Costs

As costs of incarceration increase, legislative bodies often enact legislation that passes on part of the costs to the prisoners. For example, it is permissible to allow a state jail in which a pretrial detainee was held to charge prisoners up to $1 per day to defray the costs of confining them, even though the prisoners confined in the facilities operated by the state Department of Corrections were not charged the same fee.[137]

A lawsuit was filed by present and former prisoners, who claimed that state officials committed an unconstitutional taking by failing to pay interest on funds deposited in prisoner trust accounts. Interest earned on prisoner trust accounts had been deposited into the prisoner welfare fund for the benefit of the entire prison population. This program violated the Fifth Amendment because it appropriated interest earned by prisoner trust accounts and allocated it for public use.[138]

However, the Eleventh Circuit thought otherwise. A prison policy bans interest on prisoner accounts deposited in a bank. There is no taking of property under the Fifth Amendment. The common law rule that interest follows principal does not apply in the absence of a property right. Prisoners have no such right either at common law or by statute.[139]

§ 8.11 Tax Returns

Prisoners have filed false tax returns involving millions of dollars. As a result, in 2008, Congress passed the Prisoner Tax Fraud Prevention Act of 2008[140] as an amendment to the Internal Revenue Code. The Act authorizes the Secretary of the Treasury to disclose to the head of the Federal Bureau of Prisons tax return information of prisoners whom the Secretary has determined may have filed or facilitated the filing of a false tax return. For privacy purposes, the Act prohibits the head of the Federal Bureau of Prisons from disclosing any prisoner tax return information to any person other than an officer or employee of the Bureau. The Act also restricts the use of tax return information to preventing the filing of false and fraudulent tax returns. It may not be used for other purposes. Prisoner tax returns may not be disclosed to state prison officials.

§ 8.12 Conclusion

Incarceration is much more than merely a change in location or an obstacle to physical mobility. It is a fundamental change in one's constitutional status. There is one final consideration that is relevant in this regard. There is a grain of truth to the oft-repeated aphorism that a society is best judged by its prisons and the treatment of its outcasts. Certainly the accomplishments of science and the arts are a good measure of the character of a people. However, a society's ethics, as manifested by its treatment of those who have offended it, may be a more telling characteristic. Beyond considerations such as, "There but for the grace of God go I," a society's treatment of its prisoners can be viewed as the constitutional floor below which society will tolerate no variations in condition.

The treatment of prisoners may be characterized as a society's moral lowest common denominator.

In a pluralistic society such as America, there can be no moral ceiling. This is the essence of our theory and practice—people are and of right ought to be free to realize their potential, to reach their own level. However, given our society's relatively haphazard processes of socialization and values internalization, failure, though somewhat less prevalent than success, is still rather commonplace. Thus, the need for some externally dictated minimum standard is felt. Our criminal codes fill this need but create the problem of defining the constitutional status of the resultant prisoners. The evolving solution to this problem is that prisoners retain all the rights of free people except those that are inconsistent with the institutional needs of security, order, and rehabilitation and of necessity must be withdrawn during incarceration. The determination of which rights are restricted and which are guaranteed is at the root of the explosive increase and frenzied pace of prison-related litigation today. As our society evidences the evolving standards of decency that mark the progress of a maturing society, reassessment of prior determinations will be necessary, and, thus, the need for prison-related litigation will be constant.

Notes

1　Marchesani v. McCune, 531 F.2d 459 (10th Cir. 1976); McGruder v. Phelps, 608 F.2d 1023 (5th Cir. 1979); Jones v. Diamond, 594 F.2d 997 (5th Cir. 1979); Jennings v. State, 389 N.E.2d 283 (Ind. 1979) (State only needs to show a reasonable basis for the classification).

2　James v. Wallace, 406 F. Supp. 318 (M.D. Ala. 1976); Zaczek v. Hutto, 642 F.2d 74 (4th Cir. 1981); French v. Hevne, 547 F.2d 994 (7th Cir. 1976).

3　Fitzgerald v. Procunier, 393 F. Supp. 335 (N.D. Cal. 1975).

4　427 U.S. 215 (1976); cf. Cuyler v. Adams, 449 U.S. 433 (1981); Vitek v. Jones, 445 U.S. 480 (1980).

5　530 F.2d 583 (4th Cir. 1976); In re Westfall, 162 Cal. Rptr. 462 (Cal. Ct. App. 1980); United States v. Swift & Co., 286 U.S. 106 (1932); Cobb v. Aytch, 643 F.2d 946 (3d Cir. 1981) (in which the court distinguishes between the transfer rights of sentenced and pretrial prisoners).

6　406 F. Supp. 649 (S.D. Tex. 1975).

7　523 F.2d 990 (2d Cir. 1975); see also Raia v. Arnold, 405 F. Supp. 766 (M.D. Pa. 1975); People ex rel. Williams v. Ward, 423 N.Y.S.2d 692 (N.Y. App. Div. 1980); Makris v. United States Bureau of Prisons, 606 F.2d 575 (5th Cir. 1979).

8　399 F. Supp. 869 (E.D. Okla. 1975); Wojtczak v. Cuyler, 480 F. Supp. 1288 (E.D. Pa. 1979).

9　418 U.S. 539 (1974).

10　Carterino v. Wilson, 546 F. Supp. 174 (W.D. Ky. 1982), 562 F. Supp. 106 (W.D. Ky. 1983).

11　Hawkins v. Poole, 779 F.2d 1267, 1269 (7th Cir. 1985).

12　Zarnes v. Rhodes, 64 F.3d 285 (7th Cir. 1995).

13　520 F.2d 374 (1st Cir. 1975).

14　427 U.S. 215 (1976).

15　427 U.S. 236 (1976).

16　456 U.S. 1005 (1983).

17　Olim v. Wakinekona, 456 U.S. 1005 (1983); Shango v. Jurich, 681 F.2d 1091 (7th Cir. 1982) (A state prison prisoner has no liberty interest in remaining in any particular prison that is protected by the United States Constitution).

18 Sandin v. Connor, 515 U.S. 472 (1995).

19 533 U.S. 146 (2001).

20 449 U.S. 433 (1981).

21 445 U.S. 480 (1980).

22 452 U.S. 473 (1981).

23 18 U.S.C. § 5003(a).

24 Wakinekona v. Olim, 664 F.2d 708 (9th Cir. 1981), *rev'd on other grounds*, 456 U.S. 1005 (1983).

25 McDonald v. Hall, 610 F.2d 16 (1st Cir. 1979), *criticized in* McGrath v. Johnson, 155 F. Supp. 2d 294 (E.D. Pa. 2001).

26 Farver v. Schwartz, 255 F.3d 473 (8th Cir. 2001).

27 Wilson v. Silcox, 151 F. Supp. 2d 1345 (N.D. Fla. 2001).

28 McKune v. Lile, 536 U.S. 24 (2002).

29 545 U.S. 209 (2005).

30 18 U.S.C. § 3182 (1998).

31 New Mexico ex rel. Ortiz v. Reed, 524 U.S. 151 (1998).

32 Michigan v. Doran, 439 U.S. 282 (1978).

33 124 N.M. at 146.

34 344 U.S. 86 (1952).

35 *See* Drew v. Thaw, 235 U.S. 432 (1914); Sweeney v. Woodall, 344 U.S. 86 (1952); Michigan v. Doran, *supra*, Pacileo v. Walker, 449 U.S. 86 (1980).

36 69 F.3d 477 (10th Cir. 1995).

37 Treaty on the Execution of Penal Sentences, November 25, 1976, U.S.–Mexico, T.I.A.S. No. 8718, and its implementing legislation, the Transfer of Offenders to and from Foreign Countries Act, 18 U.S.C. 4100 to 4115.

38 953 F.2d 660 (D.C. Cir. 1991).

39 T.I.A.S. No. 10824, 22 I.L.M. 530 (1983).

40 18 U.S.C. § 4100 *et seq.* (1988).

41 Kansas v. Hendricks, 521 U.S. 346 (1997).

42 *Id.*

43 534 U.S. 407 (2002).

44 Kansas v. Hendricks, 521 U.S. 346, 347 (1997).

45 Kansas v. Crane, 534 U.S. 407 (2002).

46 Wichman v. Fisher, 629 P. 2d 896 (Utah 1981); Benjamin v. Malcolm, 495 F. Supp. 1357 (S.D.N.Y. 1980). In Bell v. Wolfish, the Court held that double-bunking does not deprive pretrial detainees of liberty without due process and that a particular restriction is valid if it is reasonably related to a legitimate, nonpunitive government objective. The Court emphasized that regulations or practices must be rationally related to a legitimate, nonpunitive government purpose and must not appear excessive in relation to that purpose. Maintaining security and order is a nonpunitive objective that may necessarily infringe upon or cause many restrictions to the rights of prisoners or pretrial detainees. Bell v. Wolfish, 441 U.S. 520 (1979). In *Rhodes v. Chapman*, the Supreme Court held that double-celling at Ohio's maximum-security prison did not amount to cruel and unusual punishment prohibited by the Eighth and Fourteenth Amendments. In order for conditions of confinement to constitute punishment, they must involve the wanton and unnecessary infliction of pain or be grossly disproportionate to the severity of the crime warranting imprisonment. The fact that overcrowding falls below contemporary standards does not make the overcrowding unconstitutional. The Supreme Court recognizes that to the extent that such conditions are restrictive and even harsh, they are part of the price that criminals must pay for their offenses against society. *Ruiz v. Estelle*, 679 F.2d 1115 (5th Cir. 1982) (A district court decree requiring single-celling in Texas prisons and at least 60 square feet per prisoner in dormitories was set aside. The district court's requirements go beyond that which is necessary for the elimination of unconstitutional prison conditions. Also, the district court

acted properly within its discretion in prescribing certain exercise requirements for the Texas Department of Corrections. Although the deprivation of exercise is not per se cruel and unusual punishment, in certain circumstances such a denial may constitute an impairment of health forbidden under the Eighth Amendment); *Smith v. Fairman*, 690 F.2d 122 (7th Cir. 1982) (A prison practice of housing two prisoners in a single cell did not violate the Eighth Amendment. The lower court's ruling was reversed).

47 *See* Hoptowit v. Ray, 682 F.2d 1237 (9th Cir. 1982).

48 Smith v. Sullivan, 611 F.2d 1039 (5th Cir. 1980); Williams v. Edwards, 547 F.2d 1209 (5th Cir. 1977); Gates v. Collier, 407 F. Supp. 1117 (N.D. Miss. 1975).

49 Clay v. Miller, 626 F.2d 345 (4th Cir. 1980); Battle v. Anderson, 594 F.2d 786 (10th Cir. 1979); James v. Wallace, 406 F. Supp. 318 (M.D. Ala. 1976).

50 563 U.S. 493 (2011).

51 *Id.*

52 Sparks v. Fuller, 506 F.2d 1238 (1st Cir. 1974).

53 *Id.* at 1239; *see also* State v. Rouse, 629 P. 2d 167 (Kan. 1981).

54 Mims v. Shapp, 399 F. Supp. 818 (W.D. Pa. 1975), *vacated and remanded on appeal*, Mims v. Shapp, 541 F.2d 415 (2d Cir. 1976). The court of appeals held that the prisoners' affidavits sufficiently alleged personal bias of the judge and that the district judge erred in denying the prisoners' recusal motion; *see also* Freeman v. Trudell, 497 F. Supp. 481 (E.D. Mich. 1980) and Jefferson v. Douglas, 493 F. Supp. 43 (D. Okla. 1979) (Whether a prisoner has a proper diet is a question wholly within the discretion of the prison administration). Herring v. Superintendent, Danville City Jail, 387 F. Supp. 410 (W.D. Va. 1974).

55 Nix v. Paderick, 407 F. Supp. 844 (E.D. Va. 1976).

56 Stickney v. List, 519 F. Supp. 617 (D. Nev. 1981).

57 Jordan v. Arnold, 472 F. Supp. 265 (M.D. Pa. 1979); Taylor v. Sterrett, 600 F.2d 1135 (5th Cir. 1979); Robson v. Biester, 420 A.2d 9 (Pa. Commw. Ct. 1980); James v. Wallace, 406 F. Supp. 318 (M.D. Ala. 1976).

58 441 U.S. 520 (1979).

59 452 U.S. 337 (1981).

60 Clay v. Miller, 626 F.2d 345 (4th Cir. 1980); Battle v. Anderson, 594 F.2d 786 (10th Cir. 1979); James v. Wallace, 406 F. Supp. 318 (M.D. Ala. 1976).

61 501 U.S. 294 (1991).

62 429 U.S. 97 (1976).

63 452 U.S. 337 (1981).

64 475 U.S. 312 (1986).

65 28 U.S.C. § 636(b)(1)(B).

66 502 U.S. 367 (1992).

67 286 U.S. 106 (1932).

68 Prisoners of the Suffolk County Jail v. Kearney, 734 F. Supp. 561, 564 (D.C. Mass. 1990).

69 32 F.3d 1024 (7th Cir. 1994).

70 Farmer v. Brennan, 511 U.S. 825 (1994).

71 Wright v. McMann, 387 F.2d 519 (2d Cir. 1967).

72 Wright v. McMann, 460 F.2d 126 (2d Cir. 1972).

73 McCray v. Burrell, 516 F.2d 357 (4th Cir. 1975).

74 45 F.3d 1310 (9th Cir. 1994).

75 *See* Farmer v. Brennan, 511 U.S. 825 (1994).

76 Hewitt v. Helms, 459 U.S. 460 (1983).

77 Toussaint v. McCarthy, 801 F.2d 1080, 1091–1092 (9th Cir. 1986) (applying Hewitt v. Helms), *cert. denied*, 481 U.S. 1069 (1987).

78 Mays v. Rhodes, 255 F.3d 644 (8th Cir. 2001).

79 Dellis v. Correctional Corp. of Am., 257 F.3d 508 (6th Cir. 2001).

80 539 U.S. 126 (2003).

81 Oliver v. Scott, 276 F.3d 736 (5th Cir. 2002).

82 Fuentes v. Wagner, 206 F.3d 335 (3d Cir. 2000).

83 Chandler v. Crosby, 379 F.3d 1278 (11th Cir. 2004).

84 Little v. Shelby County, 384 F. Supp. 2d 1169 (W.D. Tenn. 2005).

85 668 F.2d 361 (8th Cir. 1981).

86 Kimbrough v. O'Neil, 523 F.2d 1057 (7th Cir. 1975).

87 816 F.2d 1165 (7th Cir. 1987).

88 *See, e.g.*, Ramos v. Lamm, 639 F.2d 559, 568 (10th Cir. 1980) ("a state must provide . . . reasonably adequate ventilation, sanitation, bedding, hygienic materials, and utilities (i.e., hot and cold water, light, heat, plumbing")).

89 Marsh v. Butler County, 225 F.3d 1243 (11th Cir. 2002), *on reh'g remanded*, 268 F.3d 1014 (11th Cir. 2001).

90 Delaney v. DeTella, 123 F. Supp. 2d 429 (N.D. Ill. 2000), *aff'd, remanded*, 256 F.3d 679 (7th Cir. 2001).

91 Curry v. Kerik, 163 F. Supp. 2d 232 (S.D.N.Y. 2001).

92 LeMaire v. Maass, 12 F.3d 1444, 1457 (9th Cir. 1993).

93 Housley v. Dodson, 41 F.3d 597 (10th Cir. 1994).

94 Davenport v. De Robertis, 844 F.2d 1310 (7th Cir. 1988).

95 Hutchings v. Corum, 501 F. Supp. 1276 (D. Neb. 1980).

96 Orange County v. Pierce, 526 F.3d 1190 (9th Cir. 2008).

97 *Ibid.*

98 511 U.S. 825 (1994).

99 Addressing the issue of prison reform, Winston Churchill made these remarks before the House of Commons in 1910 while he was Home Secretary.

100 Farmer v. Brennan, 511 U.S. 825 (1994).

101 Tafoya v. Salazar, 516 F.3d 912 (10th Cir. 2008).

102 Malone v. Kahle, 477 F.3d 544 (8th Cir. 2007).

103 150 F.3d 873 (8th Cir. 1998).

104 Beers-Capitol v. Whetzel, 256 F.3d 120 (3d Cir. 2001).

105 425 U.S. 238 (1976).

106 *Id.*

107 Leverette v. Bell, 247 F.3d 160 (4th Cir. 2001).

108 545 F. Supp. 728 (N.D.N.Y. 1982).

109 Finney v. Arkansas Board of Corrections, 505 F.2d 194 (8th Cir. 1974); Alberti v. Sheriff of Harris Co., Tex., 406 F. Supp. 649 (S.D. Tex. 1975).

110 Gates v. Collier, 501 F.2d 1291 (5th Cir. 1974).

111 Hart v. Hairston, 343 F.3d 762 (5th Cir. 2003); 42 U.S.C. § 1997e states: "No person reporting conditions which may constitute a violation under this Act shall be subjected to retaliation in any manner for so reporting."

112 *See* Ruiz v. Estelle, 679 F.2d 1115 (5th Cir.), *opinion amended in part and vacated in part*, 688 F.2d 266 (5th Cir. 1982), *cert. denied*, 460 U.S. 1042 (1983); Gibbs v. King, 779 F.2d 1040 (5th Cir.), *cert. denied*, 476 U.S. 1117 (1986); Andrade v. Hauck, 452 F.2d 1071 (5th Cir. 1971).

113 *See* McDonald v. Hall, 610 F.2d 16 (1st Cir. 1979).

114 *Id.*

115 Woods v. Smith, 60 F.3d 1161 (5th Cir. 1995).

116 *See* Adams v. Rice, 40 F.3d 72, 74 (4th Cir. 1994), *cert. denied*, 514 U.S. 1022 (1995).

117 928 F. 3d 520 (9th Cir. 2019).

118 *Id.*

119 Turner v. Burnside, 541 F.3d 1077 (11th Cir. 2008).

120 Kaba v. Stepp, 458 F.3d 678 (7th Cir. 2006), *reh'g denied, reh'g, en banc, denied*, 2006 U.S. App. LEXIS 26924 (7th Cir. 2006), 2008 U.S. Dist LEXIS 67035 (S.D. Ill. 2008).

121 Brookins v. Kilb, 990 F.2d 308 (7th Cir. 1993), abrogated in part by Bridges v. Gilbert, 557 F.3d 541 (7th Cir. 2009).

122 Freeman v. Tex. Dep't of Crim. Justice, 369 F.3d 854 (5th Cir. 2004).

123 Atkinson v. Taylor, 316 F.3d 257 (3d Cir. 2003).

124 Wilson v. Hofbauer, 113 Fed. Appx. 651 (6th Cir. 2004).

125 924 F.2d 1500 (9th Cir. 1991).

126 509 U.S. 25 (1993).

127 *See* Hutto v. Finney, 437 U.S. 678 (1978).

128 Weaver v. Clarke, 45 F.3d 1253 (8th Cir. 1995).

129 Collins v. Youngblood, 497 U.S. 37 (1990).

130 Weaver v. Graham, 450 U.S. 24 (1981).

131 73 F.3d 1156 (1st Cir. 1996).

132 The ex post facto clause provides: "No State shall . . . pass any . . . ex post facto law." U.S. CONST., art. I, § 10. Ex post facto laws include "every law that changes the punishment, and inflicts a greater punishment, than the law annexed to the crime, when committed." Miller v. Florida, 482 U.S. 423 (1987) (quoting *Calder v. Bull*, 3 U.S. (Dall.) 386, 390, 1 L. Ed. 648 (1798)).

133 California Department of Corrections v. Morales, 514 U.S. 499 (1995); *see also* Collins v. Youngblood, 497 U.S. 37 (1990).

134 514 U.S. 499 (1995).

135 Williams v. Lee, 33 F.3d 1010 (8th Cir. 1994).

136 For an example of ex post facto application to parole, *see* Shabazz v. Gary, 900 F. Supp. 118 (E.D. Mich. 1995).

137 Slade v. Hampton Roads Reg'l Jail, 303 F. Supp. 2d 779 (E.D. Va. 2004), *aff'd,* 407 F.3d 243 (4th Cir. 2005).

138 Schneider v. Cal. Dep't of Corr., 345 F3d 716 (9th Cir. 2003).

139 Givens v. Alabama Dep't of Corrections, 381 F.3d 1064 (11th Cir. 2004).

140 PUB. L. NO. 110–428 (2008).

Isolated Confinement—"The Hole" and Administrative Segregation

9

Chapter Outline

§ 9.1 Introduction

Prison administrators have always faced the task of maintaining order and discipline in a prison. Some means of dealing with prisoners who violate instructional rules and regulations are required. One such means is the use of punitive isolation, which is isolation from the general prison population imposed as a penalty for violating institutional rules.

> Almost every correctional institution includes a special confinement unit for those who misbehave seriously after they are incarcerated. This "prison within a prison" usually is a place of solitary confinement . . . accompanied by a reduced diet and limited access to reading materials and other diversions, and occasionally without any kind of light. Another means is administrative isolation, which is isolation from the general population for any reason other than punishment, such as protective isolation or isolation during investigation of an alleged institutional rule violation or a felony.[1]

Prior to the mid-1960s, the federal courts applied the traditional hands-off doctrine and refused to grant relief to state prisoners who challenged the use or conditions of isolated confinement. The rule of law that was applied to cases of prison policies or affairs was that these were matters of internal prison concern, beyond the power of the courts to supervise. This doctrine, with regard to federal prisons, was based on the separation of powers, because federal prisons were part of the executive branch of government. As for state prisons, the courts held that their administration was within the power reserved to the states under the Tenth Amendment to the U.S. Constitution and that any federal judicial review would interfere with prison administrators' performance of their duties. It was also held that the courts had only limited power to supervise the rules and regulations of prisons. These prisons no longer apply.

§ 9.2 Application of the Eighth Amendment

Even when a federal court is willing to review a prisoner's complaint concerning isolated confinement, a federally protected right must be involved. The right involved is created by the Eighth Amendment to the U.S. Constitution, which prohibits "cruel and unusual punishments." The Supreme Court has interpreted this clause to prohibit punishments that indicate torture, unnecessary cruelty, or something inhuman and barbarous,[2] when the punishment is disproportionate to the offense,[3] and when a punishment is unnecessarily cruel in view of the purpose for which it is used.[4]

In order for the Eighth Amendment's prohibition to apply, a punishment must be involved. In a criminal law sense, punishment is "[a]ny fine, penalty, or confinement inflicted upon a person by the authority of the law and the judgment and sentence of a court, for some crime . . . or for his omission of a duty enjoined by law."[5] As applied to correctional law, a punishment consists of four elements: (1) action by an administrative body, (2) which constitutes the imposition of a sanction, (3) for the purpose of penalizing the affected person, and (4) as the result of the commission of an offense.

There remains a significant area in which the presence of a cognizable liberty interest is not self-evident. Courts make the necessary determination by analyzing the combined import of the duration of the confinement and the conditions endured by the prisoner during that period.[6]

§ 9.2.1   – Constitutionality of the Use of Isolated Confinement

Over the years, many actions by state and federal prisoners have challenged the validity of the use of isolated confinement, claiming that the practice is per se unconstitutional; that is, unconstitutional without the need for any proof other than the fact that the prisoner is held in isolated confinement. This contention has been rejected by the federal courts.[7] The use of isolated confinement is seen as a valid means of protecting the general prison population and for preventing disobedience, disorder, or escapes. However, the conditions of isolated confinement can be disproportionate to the offense involved or used for an improper means and thus run afoul of the Eighth Amendment. Furthermore, the procedure by which isolation is enforced can be fundamentally unfair, thus violating due process of law.[8]

According to the Seventh Circuit, isolation alone is not a constitutional issue. A prisoner could not use the Civil Rights Act to contest his segregation, as a prisoner has neither liberty nor property interests in remaining in a prison's general population.[9]

Isolated confinement as a result of the exercise of constitutional rights raises a different issue. A disciplinary proceeding led to the ultimate acquittal of a prisoner on charges of stabbing a fellow prisoner. However, the charges resulted in his spending 93 days in a special housing unit, where the restrictions included loss of telephone privileges, one hour of exercise per day, and three showers per week. As a matter of law, the prisoner did not suffer atypical or significant hardship, so due process was not violated.[10]

A Fourth Circuit case held that a gay prisoner did not raise a constitutional issue when he alleged that prison officials denied him equal protection because they kept him in single occupancy. The prison officials had legitimate penological reasons for doing so, such as safety and security.[11] However, when a prisoner alleged that he suffered excessive administrative segregation as discipline without due process, he was entitled to show that his administrative segregation constituted atypical and significant hardship in relation to the ordinary incidents of prison.[12]

In a 2004 Ninth Circuit case, a prisoner was denied equal protection when, during three prison lockdowns, he was not allowed to resume prison employment until after similarly situated prisoners of other races had resumed employment. Prison officials did not place black prisoners on critical worker lists. It was clearly established that the prison officials explicitly considered race in determining threshold ineligibility for critical worker status.[13]

§ 9.2.2   — Constitutionality of the Conditions of Isolated Confinement

A federal remedy exists when the conditions of isolated confinement violate the Eighth Amendment's ban on cruel and unusual punishments. Proof of the existence of the unconstitutional condition(s) is the initial burden on the prisoner bringing an action. Failure to sufficiently establish the existence of the alleged conditions as a fact is a major basis for denying relief in complaints involving isolated confinement.[14] When the facts of the allegation are established, it is then a matter of law (as opposed to fact) as to whether the factual conditions are such that a violation of the prohibition on cruel and unusual punishments exists. At this stage, it is then a matter for the court, not a jury, to decide whether the Eighth Amendment has been violated. Each court must look at the facts as proved and determine in its judgment whether the conditions amount to the infliction of cruel and unusual punishment. Conditions that have been scrutinized include the personal hygienic conditions of the prisoner, physical conditions of the cell, exercise allowed, diet, and duration of the isolated confinement.

Where a prisoner is deprived of the means of maintaining personal hygiene, such as soap, water, towels, toilet paper, toothbrush, or clothing, the conditions become constitutionally intolerable.[15] One court has found that lack of water and a shower provided every fifth day did not constitute unhygienic conditions.[16] However, another court[17] held that the deprivation of a comb, pillow, toothbrush, and toothpaste for seven to ten days in a maximum-security cell with continuous lighting, a few roaches and mice in the cell, and no reading material, did not constitute cruel and unusual punishment because the prisoner was not denied the minimum necessities of food, water, sleep, exercise, toilet facilities, and human contact. Contrast that with *Griffin v. Smith*,[18] in which the court held that conditions that might constitute infringements of civil rights of prisoners in a special housing unit included excessive and unnecessary use of force by guards, grossly inadequate provision for exercise, denial of access to psychological specialists, unsanitary food utensils, including cigarette burns and hair on food trays, portions smaller than those provided to the general prisoner population, or loss of mail sent to the superintendent.

The physical state of the cell is another aspect of the conditions of isolated confinement. The existence of certain conditions in cells has led to varying results. Confinement of more than two men in a single cell in punitive isolation or administrative segregation is not unconstitutional per se. Courts have found that the lack of lighting or windows in the cells and lack of mattresses are not impermissible.[19] These same conditions, however, when coupled with overcrowding in the cells, unclean cells, or lack of heat, have been held to violate the Eighth Amendment.[20]

The personal hygiene of the prisoner, the physical condition of the prisoner, and the physical condition of the isolation cell have been the focal points of most judicial attention in the area of isolated confinement. However, other aspects have received judicial consideration as well. Exercise outside the cell that a prisoner is allowed during isolated confinement has been noted by several courts. Conditions have been upheld when there is an opportunity for exercise[21] even though it is for only one hour every 11 days[22] or when the allotted exercise time does not meet the requirements of the Bureau of Prisons policy.[23] It has been held that prisoners on death row may not be confined in their cells for long periods without outdoor exercise.[24] This reasoning also applies to isolated confinement. The prisoner could also be deprived of contact visits, library privileges, and radio and television, so long as nutritional and hygienic needs are met.[25]

The diet that a prisoner receives while in isolated confinement has been a factor in several cases. Where the diet is basically the same as the general prison population, no problem is presented.[26] A "reduced" diet has been approved,[27] and so has a diet of bread and water supplemented with a full meal every third day.[28] However, a bread and water diet has been termed "generally disapproved and obsolescent"[29] and has been strongly disapproved by the American Correctional Association as constituting the imposition of physical (corporal) punishment.[30] Similarly, at least one court has ruled that broadly prohibiting prisoners in isolation or segregated confinement from attending prison chapel is unconstitutional.[31]

The length of isolated confinement has been considered by several courts. A distinction exists between administrative and punitive isolation, in that the reason for isolating prisoners is either for punishment for specific actions (punitive isolation) or for more severe behavioral problems for longer periods (administrative isolation). It is a distinction of form rather than of substance, because the basic difference is the length of time. One court held that punitive isolation for a period of more than 15 days was cruel and unusual punishment,[32] but this judgment was subsequently overturned.[33] While periods of 36 days[34] and 15 days[35] have been held by some courts to be constitutionally permissible, other courts have found shorter periods, for example 48 hours, to violate a prisoner's right to be free from cruel and unusual punishment.[36] Administrative isolation lasting 12 months[37] and 187 consecutive days[38] has been upheld. Placement in disciplinary segregation for an indeterminate amount of time did not violate the prisoner's rights as long as the prisoner was given a hearing to comply with due process safeguards at the earliest reasonable time.[39]

Two hundred forty days of segregation was sufficiently long to implicate a cognizable liberty interest under the Due Process Clause if the conditions of confinement during that period were sufficiently severe. Although *Wilkinson v. Austin*[40] involved an indefinite placement of a prisoner in a more restrictive prison and disqualified the prisoner from parole consideration, the Seventh Circuit did not limit *Wilkinson's* holding as being limited to its specific facts.[41]

Confinement for five years in the maximum-security section of a prison where a prisoner is allowed out of his or her cell for one hour daily to exercise and is not permitted any outdoor exercise does not violate the Eighth Amendment's prohibition against cruel and unusual punishment. The court found that where a prisoner had participated in a riot, assaulted correctional officers, and was convicted of murdering another prisoner while in the maximum-security section of the prison, this past prison conduct justified the reclassification board's decision to keep the prisoner in maximum security.[42]

In *Hutto v. Finney*, the Supreme Court refused to overturn the district court's series of detailed remedial orders holding that punitive isolation in sections of the Arkansas penal system violated the Eighth Amendment. These orders included limits placed on the number of men that could be confined to one cell, required that each man have a bunk, discontinued the "gruel" diet, and set 30 days as the maximum isolation sentence.[43] The Court's rationale in *Hutto* was that if the state had fully complied with the district court's earlier orders, the present limits may not have been necessary. However, when a system refuses to comply with orders to remedy cruel and unusual conditions in isolation cells, a federal court is fully justified in substituting its judgment by entering a comprehensive order to ensure against the risk of inadequate compliance.

From these decisions, it is clear that a minimum standard is not yet set on the number of days or other conditions that will constitute cruel and unusual punishment in punitive isolation in every situation. The Supreme Court stated that the length of confinement was only one factor in the decision and that short durations of oppressive conditions may not rise to the level of a constitutional deprivation.

Appointed counsel must be provided to prisoners who are in administrative detention pending investigation and trial on felonies committed in prison. Counsel must be appointed prior to indictment. Solitary confinement effectively curtails a prisoner's ability to investigate evidence and interview witnesses. This is particularly meaningful, considering the transient nature of prison society. In order for the right to counsel to attach, the prisoner must ask for an attorney, establish indigence, and make a prima facie showing that the reason for his or her continued detention is the investigation of a felony. Once this is done, the prison administration must either refute the showing, appoint counsel, or return the prisoner to the general population. A decision that when these steps are not followed, there is a presumption of prejudice, was reversed by the Supreme Court.[44]

Until 1995, as a general rule, state prisoners had no liberty interest protected by the United States Constitution in continued confinement in the general prison population. However, states could create such interests by the repeated use, in the state prison regulations governing administrative segregation, of explicit mandatory language about procedures and by requirements that administrative segregation not occur absent specified substantive predicates. When such liberty interests are created, a due process hearing is required. The hearing should be an informal, nonadversarial evidentiary review that is preceded by notice to the prisoner. This notice must offer the prisoner an opportunity to submit his or her views in writing and must occur within a reasonable period after the prisoner's transfer to administrative segregation. The prison officials must then decide whether the prisoner represents a security threat, requiring confinement in administrative segregation pending completion of an investigation into misconduct charges against him or her.

In one case, the prisoner was placed in segregation pending an investigation into his role in a riot. The next day he received notice of a misconduct charge against him. Five days after his transfer, a hearing committee reviewed the evidence. The prisoner acknowledged that he had an opportunity to have his version of the events reported, but no finding of guilt was made. Criminal charges were filed but later dropped. A review committee concluded that the prisoner should remain in administrative segregation because he posed a threat to the safety of other prisoners, prison officials, and the security of the prison. Ultimately, the hearing committee, based on a second misconduct report, found the prisoner guilty of the second charge and ordered him confined in disciplinary segregation for six months, while dropping the first charge. This procedure satisfied due process.[45]

§ 9.2.3 — Purpose of Isolated Confinement

In addition to granting relief on the basis of the conditions of isolated confinement, federal courts have also found a violation of the Eighth Amendment when the punishment is imposed for an improper purpose. The courts view the proper purpose of isolated confinement to be the maintenance of order within the institution.[46] Therefore, any punishment that is not necessary to maintain order is cruel and unusual and prohibited by the Eighth Amendment.

A prisoner cannot be placed in isolated confinement because of his or her militant political ideas or his past or threatened litigation.[47] Nor can he or she be denied access to paper for use in petitioning courts or communicating with his or her attorney.[48] Also, denying food for a 50-hour period was held to go beyond what was necessary to achieve a legitimate correctional aim.[49] A trial court's order that prison officials place a defendant in solitary confinement and feed him only bread and water on the anniversary of his offense was impermissible.[50]

§ 9.2.4 — Punishment Proportional to the Offense

A further basis for granting relief is when the punishment is disproportionate to the infraction committed by the prisoner. The unsanitary conditions of a cell can make the punishment disproportionate to the offense.[51] Another example of a disproportionate punishment is when isolation was imposed for five months for failure to sign a safety sheet.[52] The unconstitutionality of disproportionate punishment also applies to other areas of correctional law. It was the basis for one court to prohibit whipping[53] and for another court to find that the entire prison system as administered in Arkansas was disproportionate punishment for any offense[54] and thus unconstitutional.

§ 9.3   Liberty Interests

In 1995, the Supreme Court in *Sandin v. Conner* severely reconfigured the analysis for determining whether a prisoner subjected to disciplinary or administrative confinement has a protected liberty interest that entitles him or her to the procedural protections afforded under the Due Process Clause.[55] In so doing, the Court rejected the analysis established by *Hewitt v. Helms* and its progeny, returning to the due process principles established in *Wolff v. McDonnell*[56] and *Meachum v. Fano*.[57] Prior to *Sandin*, analysis of whether a liberty interest was protected would require an examination of the text of prison guidelines or regulations to determine whether mandatory language that limited prison officials' discretion created an enforceable expectation that the state would produce a particular outcome with respect to the prisoner's conditions of confinement. The *Sandin* majority rejected this test because it created disincentives for states to codify prison management procedures in the interest of uniform treatment and because the approach led to the involvement of the federal courts in the day-to-day management of prisons, often squandering judicial resources with little offsetting benefit to anyone.

Insisting that protected liberty interests be of "real substance," *Sandin* limited state-created liberties to freedom from restraint which, while not exceeding the sentence in such an unexpected manner as to give rise to protection by the Due Process Clause of its own force, nonetheless imposes atypical and significant hardship on the prisoner in relation to the ordinary incidents of prison life.

Courts have difficulty applying *Sandin*. Before *Sandin*, the deprivation of any right containing some vestige or modicum of freedom within the prison that the state conferred on a prisoner was actionable. When a prisoner's status within the prison system changed, the question was not how great the change was, but whether it infringed upon a right that the state had conferred. *Sandin* shifted the focus from whether there was an entitlement to whether the entitlement related to some meaningful amount of liberty.

In a Seventh Circuit case, *Wagner v. Hanks*,[58] a state prisoner filed for federal habeas corpus, claiming to have been deprived of liberty within the meaning of the Due Process Clause of the Fourteenth Amendment by being placed in disciplinary segregation. The court recognized that, in deciding whether such a deprivation had occurred, a federal court after *Sandin* must compare conditions in disciplinary segregation with conditions in which the general population of the prison is confined or with those in which the general population of any prison in the state is confined.

The prisoner was ordered to serve one year in disciplinary segregation. Confinement in disciplinary segregation constituted a substantial incremental deprivation of his liberty. Because the prison was likely to provide facilities for and create conditions of administrative segregation and protective custody that are virtually identical to the facilities for and conditions of disciplinary segregation, this was sufficient under *Sandin* to deny the prisoner's claim. The manual of policies and procedures issued by the Indiana Department of Corrections indicated that the facilities and conditions were indeed the same in disciplinary and nondisciplinary segregation, except that prisoners in administrative segregation or protective custody were permitted "contact" visits and were entitled to make phone calls to persons other than lawyers. The denial of so limited an increment of privileges did not create a significant deprivation of liberty. However, the court hesitated to base its decision on a procedure manual that may not have been accurate or up-to-date.

The court commented that if the prison were a "country club" in which the prisoners enjoyed a great deal of freedom, spending little time in their cells or even in the prison buildings, confinement for a protracted period in what amounts to solitary confinement would work an atypical and significant deprivation of their liberty. This was not the situation in *Wagner*.

The court was bothered by the assumption that the proper comparison group was the population of the prisoner's own prison. This is not necessarily so. In the Court's view, the comparison group may be any prison population in the state or perhaps in the entire country. In that event, *Wagner* would lose unless the conditions of disciplinary segregation in his facility were substantially more restrictive than even those in the state's other Level V prisons. Under *Sandin*, the key comparison is between disciplinary segregation and nondisciplinary segregation rather than between disciplinary segregation and the general prison population.

The Seventh Circuit did not think that comparison could be limited to conditions in the same prison, unless it was the state's most secure prison. To distinguish between the different parts of the same prison and the different prisons in the same system would be arbitrary. The decision to create high-security segregation units in each prison or to concentrate them in one or a few special prisons bears no relation to any interest protected by the Constitution.

The court believed that when *Sandin* is interpreted in light of the transfer cases,[59] it is apparent that the right to litigate disciplinary confinements has become small. Prison discipline cases can, however, be actionable in the federal courts when discipline takes the form of prolonging the prisoner's incarceration or otherwise depriving him of what has been held to be liberty or property within the meaning of the Due Process Clauses.[60] But when the entire sanction is confinement in disciplinary segregation for a period that does not exceed the remaining term of the prisoner's incarceration, the court found it difficult to see how it could form the basis of a suit complaining about a deprivation of liberty after *Sandin*.

The court recognized that every state had somewhere in its prison system single-person cells in which prisoners were sometimes confined not because they misbehaved, but simply because the prison had no other space, wanted to protect some prisoners from others, wished to keep prisoners isolated from one another in order to minimize the risk of riots or other disturbances, or hoped to prevent the spread of disease.[61] Under *Sandin*, this possibility was enough to prevent any deprivation of liberty if a prisoner were transferred into segregation for a disciplinary infraction.[62]

Another issue the court considered still open was whether the comparison group could be confined to a single state. Indiana frequently swapped prisoners with other states pursuant to an interstate compact. The Seventh Circuit felt that it would make a good deal of sense to view the entire federal and state jail and prison systems as a single system in order to balance the total prisoner load, which was in excess of one million people. By this reasoning, a prisoner in Indiana could serve a portion of his sentence in another state, and that state might have even more restrictive conditions than Indiana. The logic of *Sandin* implies that the conditions of Wagner's disciplinary segregation were atypical only if no prison in the United States to which he might be transferred for nondisciplinary reasons is more restrictive.

However, *Sandin* does not mean that a prisoner can always be placed in segregated confinement without the observance of due process standards. In the Second Circuit, a prisoner received 180 days in segregation and loss of good-time but was not allowed to be present for the testimony of some witnesses or even to read transcripts of their testimony. In this case, *Sandin* did not apply.[63]

Due process is a concern only when liberty interests are at stake. Prisoners have no liberty interest in avoiding transfer to discretionary segregation—that is, segregation imposed for administrative, protective, or investigative purposes, a relatively short period of segregation.[64]

A prisoner's confinement in administrative segregation did not implicate a liberty interest. The prisoner was the subject of an internal investigation, and there was a need for his confinement during the investigation. The subsequent ten-week period of confinement before his transfer to a different facility did not transform the detention into the atypical and significant hardship contemplated in *Sandin*.[65] The prisoner's reliance on Bureau of Prison regulations is misplaced. The central teaching of *Sandin* is that a state statute or regulation conferring a right is not alone enough to trigger due process.[66] A prisoner's liberty interest in avoiding segregation is very limited or even nonexistent.[67]

§ 9.4   "Supermax" Prisons

Two constitutional issues often involved in administrative isolation are not only the conditions of confinement but also the procedures by which prisoners are either placed in or released from isolation. The Supreme Court in *Wilkinson v. Austin*[68] addressed the procedural due process issue in a case involving Ohio's most secure prison, a "supermax" prison.

Supermax prisons are maximum-security facilities with highly restrictive conditions that are designed to segregate the most dangerous prisoners from the general prison population. Their use has increased in recent years, in part as a response to the rise in prison gangs and prison violence. Almost every aspect of a prisoner's life is controlled and monitored. Incarceration in a supermax is synonymous with extreme isolation. Opportunities for visitation are rare and are conducted through glass walls. Prisoners are deprived of almost any environmental or sensory stimuli and of almost all human contact. Placement is for an indefinite period, limited only by a prisoner's sentence. Prisoners otherwise eligible for parole may also lose their eligibility while incarcerated in a supermax.

The Due Process Clause protects persons against deprivations of life, liberty, or property. Those who seek to invoke its procedural protection must establish that one of these interests is at stake. A liberty interest may arise from the Constitution itself, by reason of guarantees implicit in the word "liberty."[69] A liberty interest may also arise from an expectation or interest created by state laws or policies.[70] In the prison context, procedural due process applies to liberty interests. The first issue in *Austin* was whether assignment of a prisoner to the Ohio supermax prison involved a liberty interest.

The Constitution itself does not give rise to a liberty interest to permit a prisoner to avoid transfer to more adverse conditions of confinement.[71] However, a liberty interest in avoiding particular conditions of confinement may arise from state policies or regulations, subject to the important limitations set forth in *Sandin*.[72] The Supreme Court in *Austin* applied the *Sandin* standard and determined that assignment of a prisoner to Ohio's supermax imposed atypical and significant hardship on the prisoner in relation to the ordinary incidents of prison life. Ohio had created a liberty interest. Consequently, assignment to a supermax is protected by procedural due process.

The next issue for the Supreme Court to decide was determining what process was due a prisoner when placed in supermax. The Supreme Court applied *Mathews v. Eldridge*.[73] Under *Mathews* considerations, procedural due process involves three distinct factors: (1) the private interest that will be affected by the official action; (2) the risk of an erroneous deprivation of such interest through the procedures used, and the probable value, if any, of additional or substitute procedural safeguards; (3) the state's interest, including the function involved and the fiscal and administrative burdens that the additional or substitute procedural requirement would involve.[74]

Applying the first factor, *Austin* considered the significance of the prisoner's interest in avoiding erroneous placement at a supermax. Prisoners held in lawful confinement have their liberty curtailed by definition, so the procedural protections to which they are entitled are more limited than in cases where the right at stake is the right to be free from confinement at all.[75] The private interest at stake, while more than minimal, had to be evaluated within the context of the prison system and its attendant curtailment of liberties.

The second factor considered in *Austin* was the risk of an erroneous placement under the procedures in place and the probable value, if any, of additional or alternative procedural safeguards. The Ohio system provided that a prisoner must receive notice of the factual basis leading to consideration for supermax placement and a fair opportunity for rebuttal. These were among the most important procedural mechanisms recognized in *Austin* for purposes of avoiding erroneous deprivations.[76] Ohio required officials to provide a brief summary of the factual basis for the classification review and allowed the prisoner a rebuttal opportunity. These were safeguards against the prisoner's being mistaken for another or singled out for insufficient reasons. In addition to having the opportunity to be heard at the Classification Committee stage, Ohio also invited the prisoner to submit objections prior to the final level of review. This second opportunity further reduced the possibility of an erroneous deprivation.

In addition, although a subsequent reviewer could overturn an affirmative recommendation for supermax placement, the reverse was not true. If one reviewer declined to recommend supermax placement, the process terminated. If the recommendation was supermax placement, Ohio required that the decision maker provide a short statement of reasons. This requirement is a safeguard against arbitrary decision-making while providing the prisoner with a basis for objection before the next decision maker or in a subsequent classification review. The statement also serves as a guide for future behavior.[77]

The Ohio rules provided multiple levels of review for any decision recommending supermax placement, with power to overturn the recommendation at each level. In addition to these safeguards, Ohio further reduced the risk of erroneous placement by providing for a placement review within 30 days of a prisoner's initial assignment to supermax.

Austin addressed the third factor by looking at Ohio's interest in establishing a supermax. In the context of prison management and in the specific circumstances of *Austin*, this interest was a dominant consideration in its decision. Ohio had responsibility for imprisoning nearly 44,000 prisoners. The State's first obligation was to ensure the safety of guards and prison personnel, the public, and the prisoners themselves.[78]

Austin held that procedures by which Ohio classified prisoners for placement at its supermax facility provided prisoners with sufficient protection to comply with the due process. The Court also stressed that courts must give substantial deference to prison management decisions before mandating additional expenditures for elaborate procedural safeguards when correctional officials conclude that a prisoner has engaged in disruptive behavior.

Austin left the door open for future litigation by cautioning that if a prisoner were to demonstrate that Ohio's policies did not in practice operate in the fashion described, any cognizable injury could be the subject of an appropriate future challenge.

§ 9.5 Segregation by Race

California has an unwritten policy of racially segregating prisoners in double cells for up to 60 days each time they enter a new correctional facility. The policy is based on the rationale that it prevents violence caused by racial gangs. An African-American prisoner who had been intermittently double-celled under the policy's terms ever since his 1987 incarceration alleged that the policy violated his Fourteenth Amendment right to equal protection. On appeal to the Supreme Court, the issue was the appropriate legal standard to be used by courts in determining the constitutionality of racial segregation in prison, not racial segregation itself.

In *Johnson v. California*[79] the Supreme Court held that the strict scrutiny standard is the proper standard of review rather than the compelling state interest standard. The California policy was "immediately suspect" as an express racial classification.[80] California's argument that its policy was narrowly tailored to serve a compelling state interest was rejected. Under *Johnson* all racial classifications imposed by government must be analyzed by the courts under the strict scrutiny standard. The purpose of this higher standard is to prevent the illegitimate use of race by assuring that the state is pursuing a goal important enough to warrant such a highly suspect tool.[81]

California's claim that its policy should be exempt from the strict scrutiny standard because all prisoners in California are "equally" segregated was also rejected. This argument ignored the Supreme Court's repeated command that racial classifications receive strict scrutiny even when they may be said to burden or benefit the races equally.[82] *Johnson* stressed that the Supreme Court had never applied the *Turner*[83] standard to racial classifications. Indeed, the Supreme Court has consistently applied the *Turner* test only to rights that are "inconsistent with proper incarceration."[84]

According to *Johnson*, issues of racial discrimination are not susceptible to *Turner*'s logic because racial discrimination is not a right that should be compromised for the sake of proper prison administration. On the contrary, compliance with the Fourteenth Amendment's ban on racial discrimination not only is consistent with proper prison administration but also bolsters the legitimacy of the entire criminal justice system. Deference to the particular expertise of officials managing daily prison operations does not require a more relaxed standard in such cases. The necessities of prison security and discipline are compelling government interests justifying only the uses of race that are narrowly tailored to address those necessities. *Turner*'s standard would allow prison officials to use race-based policies even when there are race-neutral means to accomplish the same goal and even when the race-based policy does not in practice advance that goal. The *Turner* standard is too lenient a standard to ferret out invidious uses of race and cannot be used in cases involving racial issues in prison. The Supreme Court believed that a strict scrutiny standard would not make prison administrators unable to address legitimate problems of race-based violence in prisons.

As a result, the case was remanded to the lower courts. California will have the burden of demonstrating that its policy is narrowly tailored with regard to new prisoners as well as transferees, setting the stage for more litigation in this area of the law.

§ 9.6   Conclusion

Courts have found that the use of isolated confinement is a valid method of penal administration. However, federal courts will provide relief for deprivation of a prisoner's constitutional right to be free of cruel and unusual punishment during his or her stay in isolated confinement. When the conditions of the confinement become such that a prisoner is deprived of personal hygiene and the facility or his or her diet is inadequate, the Eighth Amendment is violated. In addition, punishment that is imposed for an improper purpose or is disproportionate to the offense committed can violate the Eighth Amendment.

However, the procedure used in placing a prisoner in administrative or disciplinary segregation depends on the existence of a protected liberty interest. Whether such a protected liberty interest exists remains an open question, depending upon the nature of the system for isolated confinement created under state law. Cases prior to *Sandin* that find protected liberty interests are now of questionable authority.

Notes

1 PRESIDENT'S COMMISSION ON LAW ENFORCEMENT AND ADMINISTRATION OF JUSTICE. TASK FORCE REPORT: CORRECTIONS, 50–51 (1967).
2 In re Kemmler, 136 U.S. 436 (1890); Wilkerson v. Utah, 99 U.S. 130 (1878).
3 Trop v. Dulles, 356 U.S. 86 (1958); Weems v. United States, 217 U.S. 349 (1910).
4 Robinson v. California, 370 U.S. 660 (1962) (Douglas, J., concurring opinion); Weems v. United States, 217 U.S. 349 (1910).
5 BLACK'S LAW DICTIONARY (6th ed. 1990).
6 Marion v. Columbia Correctional Institution, 559 F.3d 693 (7th Cir. 2009).
7 Sostre v. McGinnis, 442 F.2d 178 (2d Cir. 1971), *cert. denied*, 405 U.S. 978 (1972); Burns v. Swenson, 430 F.2d 771 (8th Cir. 1970); Ford v. Board of Managers of New Jersey State Prison, 407 F.2d 937 (3d Cir. 1969); Graham v. Willingham, 384 F.2d 367 (10th Cir. 1967); Krist v. Smith, 309 F. Supp. 497 (S.D. Ga. 1970), *aff'd*, 439 F.2d 146 (5th Cir. 1971); Roberts v. Barbosa, 227 F. Supp. 20 (S.D. Cal. 1964); Bauer v. Sielaff, 372 F. Supp. 1104 (E.D. Pa. 1974); Villanueva v. George, 632 F.2d 707 (8th Cir. 1980); Nadeau v. Helgemoe, 423 F. Supp. 1250 (D.N.H. 1976), modified in 561 F.2d 411 (1st Cir. 1977); Morris v. Travisono, 549 F. Supp. 291 (D.D.C. 1982), *aff'd*, 707 F.2d 28 (1st Cir. 1983) (Segregated confinement for eight years was unjustified and violates the Eighth Amendment); Gibson v. Lynch, 652 F.2d 348 (3d Cir. 1981) (There is no state-created "liberty interest" that entitles a prisoner to get out of solitary confinement and enter the general population after his or her first 30 days in prison).
8 *See* Chapter 10 for a discussion on procedures for disciplining prisoners.
9 Montgomery v. Anderson, 262 F.3d 641 (7th Cir. 2001).

10 Alvarado v. Kerrigan, 152 F. Supp. 2d 350 (S.D.N.Y. 2001).

11 Veney v. Wyche, 293 F.3d 726 (4th Cir. 2002).

12 Ramirez v. Galaza, 334 F.3d 850 (9th Cir. 2003).

13 Walker v. Gomez, 370 F.3d 969 (9th Cir. 2004).

14 Courtney v. Bishop, 409 F.2d 1185 (8th Cir.), *cert. denied*, 396 U.S. 915 (1969); Landman v. Peyton, 370 F.2d 135 (4th Cir. 1966), *cert. denied*, 388 U.S. 920 (1967).

15 Wright v. McMann, 387 F.2d 519 (2d Cir. 1967); Knuckles v. Prasse, 302 F. Supp. 1036 (E.D. Pa. 1969), *aff'd*, 435 F.2d 1255 (3d Cir. 1970); Hancock v. Avery, 301 F. Supp. 786 (M.D. Tenn. 1969); Jordan v. Fitzharris, 257 F. Supp. 674 (N.D. Cal. 1966); Kimbrough v. O'Neil, 523 F.2d 1057 (7th Cir. 1975); Brown v. State, 391 So. 2d 13 (La. Ct. App. 1980).

16 Ford v. Board of Managers of New Jersey State Prison, 407 F.2d 937 (3d Cir. 1969).

17 Bauer v. Sielaff, 372 F. Supp. 1104 (E.D. Pa. 1974).

18 493 F. Supp. 129 (W.D.N.Y. 1980).

19 Novak v. Beto, 453 F.2d 661 (5th Cir. 1971); Ford v. Board of Managers of New Jersey State Prison, 407 F.2d 937 (3d Cir. 1969); Knuckles v. Prasse, 302 F. Supp. 1036 (E.D. Pa. 1969), *aff'd*, 435 F.2d 1255 (3d Cir. 1970).

20 Anderson v. Nosser, 438 F.2d 183 (5th Cir. 1971); Wright v. McMann, 387 F.2d 519 (2d Cir. 1967); Landman v. Royster, 333 F. Supp. 621 (E.D. Va. 1971); Hancock v. Avery, 301 F. Supp. 786 (M.D. Tenn. 1969); Knuckles v. Prasse, 302 F. Supp. 1036 (E.D. Pa. 1969), *aff'd*, 435 F.2d 1255 (3d Cir. 1979); Holt v. Sarver, 300 F. Supp. 825 (E.D. Ark. 1969); Jordan v. Fitzharris, 257 F. Supp. 674 (N.D. Cal. 1966); Newson v. Sielaff, 375 F. Supp. 1189 (E.D. Pa. 1974).

21 Sostre v. McGinnis, 442 F.2d 178 (2d Cir. 1971), *cert. denied*, 405 U.S. 978 (1972); Knuckles v. Prasse, 302 F. Supp. 1036 (E.D. Pa. 1969), *aff'd*, 435 F.2d 1255 (3d Cir. 1970).

22 Lake v. Lee, 329 F. Supp. 196 (S.D. Ala. 1971).

23 Jordan v. Arnold, 408 F. Supp. 869 (M.D. Pa. 1976).

24 Sinclair v. Henderson, 331 F. Supp. 1123 (E.D. La. 1971).

25 Gibson v. Lynch, 652 F.2d 348 (3d Cir. 1981).

26 Sostre v. McGinnis, 442 F.2d 178 (2d Cir. 1971), *cert. denied*, 405 U.S. 978 (1972); Royal v. Clark, 447 F.2d 501 (5th Cir. 1971).

27 Knuckles v. Prasse, 302 F. Supp. 1036 (E.D. Pa. 1969), *aff'd*, 435 F.2d 1255 (3d Cir. 1970).

28 Novak v. Beto, 453 F.2d 661 (5th Cir. 1972); Ford v. Board of Managers of New Jersey State Prison, 407 F.2d 937 (3d Cir. 1969).

29 Landman v. Royster, 333 F. Supp. 621, 647 (E.D. Va. 1971).

30 AMERICAN CORRECTIONAL ASSOCIATION, A MANUAL OF CORRECTIONAL STANDARDS 417 (1966).

31 St. Claire v. Cuyler, 634 F.2d 109 (3d Cir. 1980).

32 Sostre v. Rockefeller, 312 F. Supp. 863 (S.D.N.Y. 1970), *aff'd, rev'd, and modified sub nom.*, Sostre v. McGinnis, 442 F.2d 178 (2d Cir. 1971), *cert. denied*, 405 U.S. 978 (1972).

33 Sostre v. McGinnis, 442 F.2d 178 (2d Cir. 1971), *cert. denied*, 405 U.S. 978 (1972).

34 Stiltner v. Rhay, 322 F.2d 314 (9th Cir. 1963), *cert. denied*, 376 U.S. 920 (1964). *See also* Bloeth v. Montanye, 514 F.2d 1192 (2d Cir. 1975).

35 Novak v. Beto, 453 F.2d 661 (5th Cir. 1971); Jackson v. Werner, 394 F. Supp. 805 (W.D. Pa. 1975).

36 O'Connor v. Keller, 510 F. Supp. 1359 (D. Md. 1981).

37 Sostre v. McGinnis, 442 F.2d 178 (2d Cir. 1971), *cert. denied*, 405 U.S. 978 (1972).

38 Knuckles v. Prasse, 302 F. Supp. 1036 (E.D. Pa. 1969), *aff'd*, 435 F.2d 1255 (3d Cir. 1970).

39 Adams v. Carlson, 376 F. Supp. 1228 (E.D. Ill. 1974).

40 545 U.S. 209 (2005).

41 Marion v. Columbia Correctional Institution, 559 F.3d 693 (7th Cir. 2009).

42 Wilkerson v. Maggio, 703 F.2d 909 (5th Cir. 1983).

43 Hutto v. Finney, 437 U.S. 678 (1978); *cf.* Rhodes v. Chapman, 452 U.S. 337 (1981).

44 United States v. Gouveia, 704 F.2d 1116 (9th Cir. 1983), *rev'd*, 467 U.S. 180 (1984).

45 Hewitt v. Helms, 459 U.S. 460 (1983).

46 River v. Fogg, 371 F. Supp. 938 (W.D.N.Y. 1974); Kelly v. Brewer, 239 N.W.2d 109 (Iowa Sup. Ct.); Daughtery v. Carlson, 372 F. Supp. 1320 (E.D. Ill. 1974); Clifton v. Robinson, 500 F. Supp. 30 (E.D. Pa. 1980).

47 Wojtczak v. Cuyler, 480 F. Supp. 1288 (E.D. Pa. 1979); Morgan v. LaVallee, 526 F.2d 221 (2d Cir. 1975).

48 Dearman v. Woods, 429 F.2d 1288 (10th Cir. 1970); McCray v. Sullivan, 399 F. Supp. 271 (S.D. Ala. 1975).

49 Dearman v. Woods, 429 F.2d 1288 (10th Cir. 1970).

50 People v. Joseph, 434 N.E.2d 453 (Ill. Ct. App. 1982).

51 Jordan v. Fitzharris, 257 F. Supp. 674, 679 (N.D. Cal. 1966).

52 Wright v. McMann, 321 F. Supp. 127 (N.D.N.Y. 1970).

53 Jackson v. Bishop, 404 F.2d 571 (8th Cir. 1968).

54 Holt v. Sarver, 309 F. Supp. 362 (E.D. Ark. 1970), *aff'd*, 442 F.2d 304 (8th Cir. 1971).

55 Sandin v. Conner, 515 U.S. 472 (1995).

56 418 U.S. 539 (1974).

57 427 U.S. 215 (1976).

58 Wagner v. Hanks, 128 F.3d 1173 (7th Cir. 1997).

59 The transfer of a prisoner from one prison to another is not actionable as a deprivation of constitutionally protected liberty even if the conditions of confinement are much more restrictive in the prison to which the prisoner is being transferred. Meachum v. Fano, 427 U.S. 215 (1976); Montanye v. Haymes, 427 U.S. 236 (1976); Olim v. Wakinekona, 461 U.S. 238 (1983). To have held otherwise would require the courts to adjudicate transfers within a prison—to determine, for example, whether the petitioner had been deprived of liberty by being transferred from a large cell to a small one. Federal judges would then be plunged into the minutiae of prison administration, much as if they were managing a hotel chain.

60 *See, e.g.,* Wolff v. McDonnell, 418 U.S. 539 (1974); Vitek v. Jones, 445 U.S. 480 (1980); Washington v. Harper, 494 U.S. 210 (1990).

61 Almost 6 percent of the nation's prison prisoners are in segregation. CRIMINAL JUSTICE INSTITUTE, INC., CORRECTIONS YEARBOOK 22 (1997). The great majority of these are not in disciplinary segregation. *See* CRIMINAL JUSTICE INSTITUTE, INC., CORRECTIONS YEARBOOK: ADULT CORRECTIONS 27 (1995). In 1995, almost 5 percent of all prison prisoners were in nondisciplinary segregation.

62 The question whether the comparison group includes other prisons did not have to be answered in Sandin and was not discussed in either the majority opinion or any of the separate opinions.

63 Miller v. Selsky, 111 F.3d 7 (2d Cir. 1997).

64 Townsend v. Fuchs, 522 F.3d 765 (7th Cir. 2008).

65 Sandin v, Connor, 515 U.S. 472 (1995).

66 Wilson v. Hogsten, 269 Fed. Appx. 193 (3d Cir. 2008).

67 Townsend v. Fuchs, 522 F.3d 765 (7th Cir. 2008).

68 545 U.S. 209 (2005).

69 For example, in Vitek v. Jones, 445 U.S. 480 (1980), there is a liberty interest in avoiding involuntary psychiatric treatment and transfer to mental institution.

70 Wolff v. McDonnell, 418 U.S. 539 (1974) found a liberty interest in avoiding withdrawal of a state-created system of good-time credits.

71 Meachum v. Fano, 427 U.S. 215. (1976). There is no liberty interest arising from the Due Process Clause itself in transferring prisoners from low- to maximum-security prison because confinement in any of the State's institutions is within the normal limits or range of custody which the conviction has authorized the State to impose.

72 Sandin v. Conner, 515 U.S. 472 (1995). Sandin involved prisoners' claims to procedural due process protection before placement in segregated confinement for 30 days, which was imposed as discipline for disruptive behavior. Sandin observed that earlier Supreme Court cases had employed a methodology for identifying state-created liberty interests that emphasized the language of a particular prison regulation instead of the nature of the

deprivation. Sandin criticized this methodology as creating a disincentive for states to promulgate procedures for prison management and as involving the federal courts in the day-to-day management of prisons. After Sandin, the jurisprudence of the Supreme Court took a new direction. Since Sandin, the touchstone of the inquiry into the existence of a protected, state-created liberty interest in avoiding restrictive conditions of confinement was not the language of regulations regarding those conditions but rather the nature of those conditions themselves in relation to the ordinary incidents of prison life. Sandin found no liberty interest protecting against a 30-day assignment to segregated confinement because it did not present a dramatic departure from the basic conditions of the prisoner's sentence. Prisoners in the general population experienced significant amounts of "lockdown time," and the degree of confinement in disciplinary segregation was not excessive. Further, the short duration of segregation did not create a major disruption in the prisoner's environment.

73 424 U.S. 319 (1976).

74 *Id.* at 335.

75 *See, e.g.*, Gerstein v. Pugh, 420 U.S. (1975); Wolff v. McDonnell, 418 U.S. 539 (1974).

76 *See* Greenholtz v. Prisoners of Neb. Penal and Correctional Complex, 442 U.S. 1 (1979); Cleveland Bd. of Ed. v. Loudermill, 470 U.S. 532 (1985); Fuentes v. Shevin, 407 U.S. 67 (1972).

77 *See* Greenholtz v. Prisoners of Neb. Penal and Correctional Complex, 442 U.S. 1 (1979), at 16.

78 Prison security, imperiled by the brutal reality of prison gangs, was an important factor in Austin. Ohio had secretly organized gangs fueled by race-based hostility committed to fear and violence as a means of disciplining their own members and their rivals. The gangs sought nothing less than to control prison life and to extend their power outside prison walls. Murder of a prisoner, a guard, or one of their family members on the outside was a common form of gang discipline and control, as well as a condition for membership in some gangs. Testifying against or otherwise informing on gang activities invited a death sentence. For prison gang members serving life sentences, some without the possibility of parole, the deterrent effects of ordinary criminal punishment was substantially diminished. The problem of scarce resources was another component of the Ohio's interest. The cost of keeping a single prisoner in one of Ohio's ordinary maximum-security prisons was $34,167 per year, and the cost to maintain each prisoner at supermax was $49,007 per year. This made it difficult to fund more effective education and vocational assistance programs to improve the lives of the prisoners.

79 543 U.S. 499 (2005).

80 *See* Shaw v. Reno, 509 U.S. 630 (1993).

81 *See* Richmond v. J. A. Croson Co., 488 U.S. 469 (1989).

82 The Supreme Court had previously applied a heightened standard of review in evaluating racial segregation in prisons in Lee v. Washington, 390 U.S. 333 (1968).

83 Turner v. Safley, 482 U.S. 78 (1987). This standard asks whether a regulation that burdens prisoners' fundamental rights is "reasonably related" to "legitimate penological interests."

84 *See* Overton v. Bazzetta, 539 U.S. 126 (2003).

Prisoner Disciplinary Proceedings 10

Chapter Outline

§ 10.1　Introduction

Discipline, order, and control are major concerns of the administrative staff of correctional institutions. These issues relate to the security of the institution, the safety of institutional staff and prisoners, and the rehabilitation of the prisoners. The body or individual generally responsible for administering discipline for the violation of institutional rules and regulations has varying names in correctional institutions, such as a rules infraction board or committee, behavior committee, summary court, or simply "court." In recent years, great emphasis has been given by the courts to the disciplinary procedures and practices of prison administrators.

§ 10.2　Due Process of Law

The phrase *due process of law* is found in both the Fifth[1] and Fourteenth[2] Amendments to the Constitution. The Fifth Amendment applies to federal action, the Fourteenth Amendment to state action. The phrase means little on its own; it depends completely on court interpretation to give it relevant meaning. The Supreme Court has indicated that there are two aspects of due process: substantive and procedural.

The substantive aspect involves the fundamental rights of the individual (such as life, liberty, and property) that are protected from government action. It is a question of whether an individual's interest can be protected by the federal courts as a constitutional right. The individual rights or interests protected by substantive due process vary, depending on whether a particular court regards the interest as "fundamental." The first eight amendments to the United States Constitution specifically enumerate the fundamental rights of citizens that are protected from federal government action, such as freedom of religion, speech, press, and right of assembly. The same fundamental rights are protected against state action by the Fourteenth Amendment. Substantive due process requires government to treat the people with "fundamental fairness."

The procedural aspect of due process deals with the procedures or means by which government action can affect the fundamental rights of the individual; it is the guarantee that only after certain fair procedures are followed can the government affect an individual's fundamental rights. The exact procedural rights guaranteed depend upon what procedural rights a particular court regards as required by "justice and liberty."[3]

A consideration of what procedures due process may require varies with the circumstances. The precise nature of the government function involved must be ascertained, as well as the private interest that has been affected by the government action.[4]

In a Third Circuit case, a planned series of disciplinary actions as retaliation for initiating a civil rights suit against prison officials violated the prisoner's rights.[5] Prison officials may not retaliate against a prisoner for exercising his or her constitutional rights. A prisoner accused prison officials of increasing his custody level, transferring him to a prison that had been documented as a place of danger, and denying him parole. Relief was denied. In retaliation cases, a prisoner must prove that he was engaged in a constitutionally protected activity and that he suffered some adverse action at the hands of the prison officials. This requirement is satisfied upon a showing that the action was sufficient to deter a person of ordinary firmness from exercising his constitutional rights. In addition, a prisoner must prove that his constitutionally protected conduct was a substantial or motivating factor in the decision to discipline him. The burden then shifts to the defendant who must prove by a preponderance of the evidence that it would have taken the same disciplinary action even in the absence of the protected activity.[6]

According to the Eighth Circuit, a correctional officer violated a prisoner's constitutional rights by writing false disciplinary reports against the prisoner in retaliation for grievances filed against him. The prisoner was transferred 250 miles from his home after he questioned the correctional officer regarding prisoners' rights to legal assistance.[7]

Prisoners were deprived of procedural due process at a disciplinary hearing in which: (1) no independent evaluation of the reliability of a confidential informant was made, (2) the hearing officer merely accepted conclusions of the investigating officer who in turn merely accepted the conclusions of the warden, and (3) the investigating officer had no direct knowledge of what the informant told the warden about a prisoner's plans for escape, who the informant was, or how he got information. The hearing officer had no evidence before him from anyone with direct contact with the informant.[8]

§ 10.3   Due Process Requirements in a Prison Disciplinary Hearing

The "due process of law" involved in prison disciplinary proceedings is the procedural aspect of the due process requirement of the Fifth and Fourteenth Amendments. In the early 1970s, the federal courts began to focus their attention on the specific procedures used in prison disciplinary proceedings. The courts have provided a forum for the protection of the right of a prisoner to procedural due process. They have sought to balance the interest of the institution in maintaining order, discipline, and control and a recognition of the need for prompt and individual treatment with the knowledge that the process can further burden a prisoner's sentence or that the disciplinary action noted on his or her institutional record may affect his or her parole eligibility.

In deciding what procedures are constitutionally required by due process at prison disciplinary hearings, federal courts have been influenced by the due process requirements of administrative law. Administrative agencies, as a branch of government whose actions directly affect individuals, must ensure that individual procedural due process rights are guaranteed. In general terms, administrative agencies are required by due process to act only after adequate notice and only after an opportunity for a fair hearing.[9] For example, in a case involving a state welfare department's procedure for terminating welfare benefits,[10] the Supreme Court found that adequate notice and an opportunity to be heard required: (1) that the affected welfare recipient receive timely and adequate notice of the proposed action, including the reasons for termination; (2) an opportunity to defend, which also meant: (a) the right to confront adverse witnesses, (b) the right to present arguments and evidence orally, and (c) the right to be represented at the hearing by retained counsel; and (3) an impartial decision-maker who must state his or her reasons and indicate the evidence relied on, if welfare is terminated.[11]

§ 10.3.1   — *Wolff v. McDonnell*

Federal courts took all or part of the requirements imposed on administrative agencies and held that due process in the prison disciplinary setting required basically the same safeguards.[12] In 1974, the Supreme Court decided *Wolff v. McDonnell*,[13] which involved a state prisoner in Nebraska who had filed a civil rights action[14] in federal court, alleging that he had been denied due process during a prison disciplinary proceeding.

Considering the nature of prison disciplinary proceedings, the Court held that the full range of procedures mandated by *Morrissey*[15] and *Scarpelli*[16] for parole revocation did not apply. The Court believed that the unique environment of a prison demanded a more flexible approach in accommodating the interests of the prisoners and the needs of the prison. Specifically, the Court held that due process in a prison disciplinary setting requires:

1. Advance written notice of the charges against the prisoner, to be given at least 24 hours before the appearance before the prison disciplinary board;

2. A written statement by the fact finders as to the evidence relied upon and reasons for the disciplinary action;

3. That the prisoner be allowed to call witnesses and present documentary evidence in his or her defense, providing there is no undue hazard to institutional safety or correctional goals;

4. Counsel substitute (either a fellow prisoner, if permitted, or staff) should be allowed when the prisoner is illiterate or when the complexity of the issues makes it unlikely that the prisoner will be able to collect and present the evidence necessary for an adequate comprehension of the case;

5. The prison disciplinary board must be impartial.

Equally important is what the Court decided was not constitutionally required:

1. The prisoner has no constitutional right to confrontation and cross-examination. Whether to permit confrontation and cross-examination is left to the discretion of the prison disciplinary board.

2. The prisoner has no constitutional right to retained or appointed counsel.

It should also be noted that *Wolff* arose in the context of discipline for "serious misconduct." The Court stated: "We do not suggest, however, that the procedures required by today's decision for the deprivation of good-time would also be required for the imposition of lesser penalties such as the loss of privileges."[17]

The decision in *Wolff* laid down constitutional guidelines but left flexibility in the conduct of disciplinary hearings. This aspect of the case has been severely criticized. One court expressed regret that the Supreme Court failed to deal more precisely with the "profound federal constitutional issues implicated in the prison system." It was noted that *Wolff* "failed to make the Constitution a living document for many human beings"[18] by not requiring additional procedural rights in the prison context.

§ 10.3.2   *— Baxter v. Palmigiano*

After the *Wolff* decision, the federal courts filled in some of the gaps, a task that *Wolff* had expressly left to the discretion of prison officials, not federal courts. For example, the Ninth Circuit held that:

*   Minimum notice and a right to respond are due a prisoner faced with even a temporary suspension of privileges;

*   A prisoner at a disciplinary hearing who is denied the privilege of confronting and cross-examining witnesses must receive written reasons or the denial will be deemed prima facie evidence of an abuse of discretion; and

*   A prisoner facing prison discipline for a violation that might also be punishable in state criminal proceedings has a right to legal counsel (not just counsel substitute) at the prison hearing.[19]

A First Circuit decision held that where a prisoner brought before a prison disciplinary committee faces possible prosecution for a violation of state law:

- He must be advised of his right to remain silent and must not be questioned further once he exercises that right;

- Such silence may not be used against him at that time or in future proceedings;

- When criminal charges are a realistic possibility, prison authorities should consider whether legal counsel (not just counsel substitute), if requested, should be permitted at the proceeding.[20]

In 1976, the Supreme Court reversed both decisions. It held in *Baxter v. Palmigiano*[21] that the procedures just listed were inconsistent with the "reasonable accommodation," reached in *Wolff v. McDonnell*, between institutional needs and objectives and the constitutional provisions of general application.

Specifically, the Court held that:

- Prisoners do not "have a right to either retained or appointed legal counsel in disciplinary hearings" (citing *Wolff*);

- An adverse inference may be drawn from a prisoner's silence at his or her disciplinary proceeding;

- Federal courts have no authority to expand the *Wolff* requirements, which leave the extent of cross-examination and confrontation of witnesses to the sound discretion of prison officials;

- The Court of Appeals acted prematurely when it required procedures such as notice and an opportunity to respond even when a prisoner is faced with a temporary suspension of privileges, as distinguished from a serious penalty.

Thus, the Supreme Court severely restricted the judicially imposed procedural requirements that had emerged in the wake of *Wolff* and added no new constitutional requirements to those set forth in *Wolff*. Thus, *Wolff* established maximum constitutional requirements and not bare minimum requirements.

§ 10.3.3　—Notice of the Hearing

A prison disciplinary proceeding in which the prisoner is not informed of the nature of the accusation against him or her or of the evidence to be used against him or her does not comply with due process requirements. Notice is required because it enables the prisoner to prepare information to explain the alleged offense or defend him or her against the accusation. It gives the prisoner information about the nature of the proceeding. The notice must adequately inform the prisoner of the offense of which he or she is accused.[22]

Wolff requires that there be a minimum of 24 hours between receipt by the prisoner of written notice of the charges and the prisoner's appearance before the prison disciplinary board. However, when a prisoner desires to expedite the hearing, he or she may waive his or her right to 24-hour notice, thereby appearing at the earliest hearing scheduled after he or she receives a conduct ticket or "write-up." The use of waivers may create legal difficulties due to the inherently coercive atmosphere of a prison. If waivers are used, it is submitted that the waiver should be in writing and signed by the prisoner under such circumstances that the prisoner is made fully aware of his or her right to the 24-hour notice and voluntarily waives it. However, the Supreme Court has said that a "knowing and intelligent" waiver is not demanded in every situation in which a person has relinquished a constitutional protection. Generally, the requirement of a "knowing and intelligent" waiver has been applied only to the rights that the Constitution guarantees to a criminal defendant in order to preserve a fair trial.[23] Wherever waivers are used, the written waiver should be witnessed. Oral waivers may also be used, but care should be taken to document the waiver, because a question of proof may arise at a later date.

Prisoners in disciplinary hearings are entitled to disclosure of the details concerning the charges against them, except when prison officials have made a specific and independent finding that: (1) retaliation against an informant will result from his or her identification; (2) disclosure of the information will identify the informant; and (3) the identity of the informant would not otherwise be known to the accused. Further, the accused must be notified that he or she has not been provided with the specific details of the incidents charged because the prison officials have determined that the information would reveal the identity of informants and present a serious risk to their safety.[24]

§ 10.3.4 — An Opportunity to Be Heard

The right to notice and an opportunity to be heard are a part of the basic concept of procedural due process of law. As such, a hearing is required in the disciplinary process. In administrative law, a hearing is an oral proceeding before a tribunal.[25] Professor Kenneth C. Davis, a leading authority in administrative law, pointed out two forms of hearings: trial and argument. The trial is a proceeding for presenting evidence, with cross-examination and rebuttal, and ends with a decision based on the record made at the proceeding. The trial is designed to resolve disputes of fact. Argument, on the other hand, is a process for the presentation of ideas, as distinguished from evidence. It is the process for resolving nonfactual issues, such as policy or discretion.

The courts have generally recognized that a hearing is fundamental to the concept of due process and thus have required a hearing in some form. It is one of the procedural safeguards to which a prisoner is entitled when action is taken against him or her.[26] As one court has said, "The right to be heard before being condemned to suffer grievous loss of any kind is a principle basic to our society."[27]

The Supreme Court in *Wolff* did not attempt to set forth comprehensive guidelines for the conduct of disciplinary hearings but only the elements that are constitutionally required. The national body of prison administrators—the American Correctional Association—recognized that a hearing is a "common . . . concept" of the disciplinary procedure.[28] The Association's manual describes the function of the hearing as "an orderly attempt to arrive at the truth and is not a formal court proceeding." The problem in defining the exact procedures required of the disciplinary hearing is that it combines two functions in the proceeding: (1) the fact-finding process and (2) the correctional process.

The fact-finding process involves a determination of the truth of the allegation that a specified institutional rule has been violated; that is, did the prisoner in fact violate the rule? This function under administrative law has traditionally been handled in a trial-type hearing. The correctional process is a policy or judgment decision by a prison administrator or board of administrators who view every action taken in terms of its correctional or rehabilitative effects on the individual involved, on the prisoners, and on the staff of the institution as a whole. The correctional process must be concerned with the best interests of the prisoner involved (as determined by the prison administrators) and not be solely geared to the facts of a particular incident.

Combining these two functions in a single proceeding caused the courts to require, prior to *Wolff*, varying and often inconsistent procedures in the hearing itself. Some courts found that certain aspects of a trial-type hearing, such as the right to call witnesses and to have counsel, were required by due process in prison disciplinary hearings. Other courts found that the same features were not required for a "fair hearing" in accordance with due process. The precise features required of the hearing depended upon the definition of a "fair" hearing as interpreted by the individual court involved.

The procedures required by *Wolff* center around the effectiveness of a prisoner's opportunity to be heard. However, a disciplinary board might be faced with a prisoner who chooses not to take advantage of that opportunity and does not speak in his or her own defense. The Supreme Court in *Baxter*[29] held that the board was permitted to draw an "adverse inference" from such silence. Thus, it would be proper for the board to consider the fact that a prisoner chose not to defend him- or herself in deciding whether he or she was guilty of the conduct charged. A prisoner may be advised, in effect: "You have the right to remain silent. However, if you choose to remain silent, your silence can and will be used against you." Care should be taken, however, to use silence to corroborate other evidence presented at the hearing. If the silence of the prisoner is the only evidence presented, a finding of guilt would be constitutional error.

In *Baxter*, the Supreme Court was very careful to point out that a disciplinary proceeding was not a criminal proceeding but a civil proceeding. Perhaps an analogy could be to a revocation of welfare benefits, even if the grounds for revocation would constitute criminal fraud.

§ 10.3.5 — Right to Counsel

In *Wolff*, the Supreme Court held that a prisoner had no constitutional right to either retained or appointed legal counsel at a disciplinary proceeding. In *Baxter* this was reiterated, even when the prisoner may be subject to outside criminal prosecution for the misconduct that is the subject of the prison proceeding.

However, *Wolff* does require a "counsel substitute" (either a fellow prisoner, if permitted, or a staff member) if the prisoner is illiterate or if the complexity of the issues makes it unlikely that the prisoner will be able to collect and present the evidence necessary for an adequate comprehension of the case.

In cases in which prisoners have complained that they were denied the right to "counsel substitute," the courts have relied on the record of the disciplinary proceeding to determine the literacy of the prisoner or whether the factual issues involved were complex.[30] The counsel substitute should be someone who is capable of offering helpful advice but does not have to be a witness or someone connected with the incident in question.[31] It is essential for prison officials to make careful inquiry, and place such inquiries in the record, in order to avoid a later legal attack based on the failure to appoint counsel substitute.

§ 10.3.6 — Witnesses; Confrontation; Cross-Examination

Wolff v. McDonnell mandates that a prisoner be allowed to call witnesses and present documentary evidence in his or her defense when there is no undue hazard to institutional safety or correctional goals. Under the *Wolff* standard, prison officials are permitted some discretion based on the "undue hazard" criterion. Care must be taken to avoid a later judicial finding of an "abuse of discretion." The disciplinary committee, or some official prior to the hearing, should review the prisoner's requests for witnesses and act on each one using the "undue hazard" standard. It is also implicit in *Wolff* that discretion may be used to avoid redundant and irrelevant testimony. Thus, when a prisoner requests 100 fellow prisoners as witnesses to an incident in a dining hall, to allow all those prisoners to appear, one by one, before the disciplinary board, could create a major security problem, as well as being unduly repetitive. Calling one or a representative number of the 100 would probably be sufficient, if it was determined that all the prisoners would be offering identical testimony. To this end, it is suggested that the charged prisoner be required to state, in a written request for witnesses prior to the hearing, what he or she expects them to say if they are called. The importance and relevance of their testimony can then be better balanced against the problems that may result if they are called as witnesses.

If the requested witness is in another institution, it has also been suggested that a written statement can be taken and that "in-person" testimony of the prisoner's witnesses is not constitutionally required. It should be recognized, however, that if written statements of a witness are used against the prisoner, the issues of confrontation and cross-examination will arise.

The decision to grant or not grant a witness request should be made in the record and should be supported by an explanation if the request is denied. The lack of such an explanation has led one court to label the refusal to call witnesses an "arbitrary" decision:[32] a label that can lead to civil liability.

Wolff left the issues of confrontation and cross-examination to the sound discretion of prison officials. By not requiring confrontation, disciplinary boards often must rely on written conduct reports as the only evidence on which to base a decision. The prisoner may, of course, deny the allegations of such reports and call witnesses or present documents to dispute them but may not directly face and question his or her accuser, except as prison officials deem wise. This exercise of discretion was reinforced by the decision in *Baxter*. It is not required that the board state reasons for denying cross-examination or confrontation. If the prisoner pleads "guilty" and thereby waives his or her rights under *Wolff*, prison officials should carefully document the factual basis for the plea and make certain that the plea was knowingly made.[33]

In the Supreme Court case *Ponte v. Real*,[34] a state prisoner was charged with violating a prison regulation as the result of a fight that occurred in the prison office. At the disciplinary board hearing, the prisoner asked that certain witnesses be called, but the board refused to call the witnesses. No explanation was given at the time or as part of the written record of the disciplinary hearing. The prisoner was found guilty and 150 days of "good-time" were forfeited. Due process does not require that the disciplinary board's reasons for denying the prisoner's witness request appear as part of the administrative record of the disciplinary hearing. However, due process does require the board, at some time, to state its reason for refusing to call witnesses, but the board may do so either by making the explanations a part of the administrative record or by later presenting evidence in court if the deprivation of a "liberty" interest, such as that afforded by good-time credits, is challenged because of the refusal to call the requested witnesses. The arguments that the burden of proving noncompliance with *Wolff v. McDonnell* is on the prisoner and that a prisoner may not challenge disciplinary procedures unless a "pattern of practice" was shown, were rejected. The Supreme Court stressed that explaining the decision at the disciplinary hearing will not immunize prison officials from later court challenges to their decision. However, as long as the reason for denying prisoner witness requests are logically related to preventing undue hazards to institutional safety or correctional goals, the explanation should satisfy due process requirements. It was also suggested that if prison security or similar paramount interests appear to require it, a court should allow, at least in the first instance, a prison official's justification for refusal to call witnesses to be presented to the court *in camera*, or outside the presence of the prisoner.

In *Walker v. Bates*, a prisoner alleged that his procedural due process rights were violated in the course of a disciplinary hearing that resulted in a decision to confine him to a Special Housing Unit. He was charged with violation of an institutional rule prohibiting the possession of contraband in the form of a weapon and violation of another institutional rule prohibiting the possession of state bedding in excess of authorized issue.[35] The procedures established by New York in disciplinary proceedings comported with the procedural due process rights in disciplinary proceedings to which prisoners are entitled under *Wolff v. McDonnell*. However, the Second Circuit held that the denial of a prisoner's right to call witnesses constituted a compensable constitutional due process violation.[36]

§ 10.3.7 — Administrative Review

Administrative review of the decision resulting from a prison disciplinary hearing is wise administrative policy, although it is not constitutionally required. A suggested procedure states that a prisoner "shall be provided and advised of a regular channel of appeal from the finding made or the penalty assessed at any disciplinary hearing."[37] The right to review of a disciplinary decision has not been interpreted as a requirement under constitutional procedural due process, but the presence of an appellate procedure has been an element encouraged by the courts.[38] However, if a statute or prison regulation provides for an appeal, the Equal Protection Clause of the Fourteenth Amendment requires that all those affected be treated alike.

The review must be restricted to the charge made and to the evidence presented. Reviewing the decision based on evidence that is not in the record is not permitted. If an appeal is granted, notice of the right to appeal must be distributed to all prisoners. Word-of-mouth notification to prisoners of their right to appeal or the procedures for such an appeal cannot be permitted. Because the Equal Protection Clause of the Fourteenth Amendment contemplates uniform treatment, failure to notify certain prisoners at the conclusion of the disciplinary procedure of their right to appeal, when other prisoners are notified, is a violation of prisoners' constitutional rights.

Administrative review by a warden or even an official of the state corrections department also provides the opportunity to set forth policy to be followed in certain situations. For example, standards can be established for the exercise of discretion in calling witnesses or allowing cross-examination. It should be noted that state statutes dealing with administrative procedures may foreclose "rulemaking" in this manner; nevertheless, the use of administrative review as a check on the arbitrary action of subordinates is a wise policy. Furthermore, judges then feel free to require prisoners to follow the administrative appeal process to its end. A system of administrative appeals may keep many cases out of the federal courts as long as the administrative review process is not a rubber stamp for arbitrary decisions made at the institutional level.

§ 10.3.8 — The Record

Wolff v. McDonnell requires that a written statement be made by the fact finders as to the evidence relied upon and reasons for the disciplinary action.

Wolff does not require that the prisoner receive a copy of the written statement, but this is essential if there is an available means of administrative appeal. No appeal procedure is meaningful if the prisoner is not made fully aware of the basis of the original decision. It is also good policy to expand the scope of the written record to include the reasons underlying any exercise of discretion concerning the disciplinary proceeding. This may include why witnesses were denied, why a prisoner's request for counsel substitute was not granted, or why a more stringent sanction than usual was imposed for a given offense. Organizing these reasons in a written record of the proceeding will help ensure that decisions are not made arbitrarily, and it can be shown that discretion was not abused. Such a record may be used not only to state the evidence relied upon (which often will be the allegations in a conduct report) but also to summarize the evidence that was rejected. Tape-recording all hearings is expensive but may prove invaluable to counter prisoner allegations of unfairness, to document prisoner literacy, or to obtain oral waivers.

§ 10.3.9 — Impartiality

Wolff v. McDonnell requires that the prison disciplinary board be impartial. This is one of the traditional aspects of a "fair hearing" and generally requires that the decision-maker not be directly involved in the incident in question or the investigation of it. This helps assure that the decision will be based strictly on the facts adduced at the hearing, and not on personal knowledge or impressions that a decision-maker brings with him or her to the hearing.[39] One court specifically held that a disciplinary committee, which included as one of its members a correctional officer involved in the incidents leading to the disciplinary hearing, was not sufficiently impartial to satisfy the Due Process Clause.[40] The court believed that the presence of the "charging party" prevented the board from rationally determining the facts.

The requirement that the decision be based strictly on facts adduced at the hearing also involves the concept of "command influence." This occurs when a warden or other official in effect dictates what the decision of the disciplinary committee should be. One court analyzed "command influence" as follows:

> It is not improper for a member of the adjustment committee to discuss with the warden the procedures which should be followed, although it would clearly be improper for the warden to tell a member of the adjustment committee what the decision of the adjustment committee should be or for them to discuss what the decision should be. Nor is it improper for the members of the adjustment committee to discuss among themselves the procedure to be followed, although it would be improper for them to decide the proper disposition of the case before the hearing.[41]

If the prison system has an appeal procedure, it is not necessary to have a different disciplinary board hear the case if the prior decision is reversed and sent back for a "new hearing." In criminal cases, the judge who pronounced sentence or determined guilt after a nonjury trial may be the judge at the new trial. Similarly, the judge who presides over a preliminary hearing is not barred from being the judge at the later hearing.

§ 10.3.10   — Prehearing Detention and Emergencies

When a prisoner has committed a physical assault, or in other cases in which his or her conduct poses an immediate threat to the security of the institution, prehearing detention may be justified, as long as a hearing complying with the requirements of *Wolff v. McDonnell* is held within a reasonable time after the detention begins. Whether to place a prisoner in prehearing detention is another area in which the discretion of prison officials comes into play. It is good administrative policy to ensure that the exercise of such discretion is not abused. Thus, standards should be developed by which a hearing officer or another official can determine what factual circumstances trigger prehearing detention under administrative guidelines. The practice of imposing prolonged detention prior to disciplinary hearings should be avoided.

One court approved a policy requiring immediate removal from a minimum-security honor farm of any prisoner charged by a formal conduct report pending a prompt hearing, even though such prisoner must spend a brief period in isolated confinement.[42] This is an example of a court balancing the requirement of *Wolff* against the practical realities of the institutional setting—the honor farm was not equipped to handle disciplinary hearings.

A few courts have also recognized the overriding concerns for security in emergency situations and have allowed greater flexibility in administering disciplinary cases than would be permissible under normal conditions.[43]

As long as the conditions of confinement do not constitute "punishment" or there is no undue delay, there would appear to be no sound reason to deny prison officials the authority to hold a prisoner in isolation for investigation prior to formal charges being made. As in prehearing detention after charges have been made, *Wolff* does not specify the maximum delay; *Wolff* requires only a minimum of 24 hours. In any event, the hearing should be held, or the prisoner returned to his or her former status, as soon as practicable.

§ 10.3.11   — Double Jeopardy

Frequently, the argument is made that it is double jeopardy for a prisoner to receive administrative punishment for conduct that is subject to a criminal prosecution. This argument was rejected in *United States v. Hedges*. "Five hundred and forty-three days of good behavior time were administratively forfeited . . . because of an attempted escape."[44] In affirming the conviction in the subsequent criminal trial, a federal court of appeals stated: "It is established . . . that administrative punishment does not render a subsequent judicial prosecution violative of the Fifth Amendment prohibition of double jeopardy."[45] The same reasoning applies to proceedings in state prisons.

However, criticism of this view is widespread. The rationale of *Hedges* was rejected in considering a disciplinary proceeding held after a prisoner was acquitted of criminal charges arising out of the same conduct in *Barrows v. Hogan*. The court said:

> The question here is not one of double jeopardy, for the [prisoner] does not allege that he has been charged twice for the same offense. The holding of a jury of twelve men and women is a final determination against the government on the question of whether [the prisoner] assaulted the officer. In view of the judicial determination that this prisoner is not guilty of the offense charged, it is impermissible for the prison administration to determine otherwise and punish the prisoner for an offense as to which he has been acquitted.[46]

Because *Baxter* carefully distinguished criminal proceedings, to which the double jeopardy clause applies, from disciplinary proceedings, which are civil in nature, the authority of prison officials to proceed independently of the criminal courts should be recognized and approved. Therefore, prison disciplinary proceedings are civil, not criminal in nature for double jeopardy purposes. Prisoners may be subjected to both criminal and prison disciplinary sanctions on the basis of the same acts.[47]

§ 10.3.12   – Evidence

The evidence relied upon in many prison disciplinary proceedings may be limited to the written conduct report of a correctional officer or other staff member. It may include the oral testimony of witnesses for both sides or documents such as letters. It is impossible to quantify the amount of evidence required to make a decision, but it is clear that the criminal trial standard of "proof beyond a reasonable doubt" does not apply to prison disciplinary proceedings. A popular standard is that borrowed from administrative law for purposes of judicial review: substantial evidence considering the record as a whole.[48] Thus, after considering the evidence on both sides of the case, if the members of the board feel that there is substantial evidence of guilt, in light of the evidence offered by the prisoner, they may validly find a prisoner guilty of the offense charged.

A conviction on a disciplinary charge cannot rest solely upon the hearsay report of an unidentified informant whose credibility is unsubstantiated.[49] In addition, although polygraph examinations are looked upon with disfavor by the courts, the results of a polygraph may be considered as evidence in a prison disciplinary proceeding. However, there must be additional evidence, in addition to the polygraph report, on which a decision is based. The polygraph may be used as corroborative evidence on the issue of guilt.

A difficult problem arises when the traditional criminal law defenses are raised. For example, an officer might come upon a fight in progress and charge the two prisoners with "fighting." At the disciplinary hearing, one prisoner might assert "self-defense." The general rule of criminal law is that one who is free from fault is privileged to use reasonable and necessary force to defend him- or herself against personal harm threatened by the unlawful act of another. The force he or she uses for this purpose must be reasonable under the circumstances. Thus, this defense would raise a number of questions, all of which should be dealt with by the disciplinary board: Which party was the aggressor? Was the prisoner who claimed self-defense free from fault? Was the force he or she used reasonable under the circumstances? Did the "defendant" become the aggressor by the use of excessive force in self-defense?

A prisoner may assert his or her ignorance of a rule of conduct. However, in response, the familiar phrase "ignorance of the law is no excuse" may be applied. This, however, applies only to offenses that would be crimes outside of the penal setting. Due process requires that prisoners be given notice of what rules of conduct govern prison life, and it further requires that those rules clearly define what conduct violates those rules. Due process is violated if a prisoner is punished for violating a rule that is so vague as to make it impossible to conform his or her conduct to the rule.[50]

§ 10.4   Liberty Interests

Before there can be federal court intervention in the management of state prison systems, there must first be a violation of a constitutional right. In the context of disciplinary proceedings, cases have arisen over the issue of a prisoner having a federally protected liberty interest that was violated by state prison officials.

In 1995, the Supreme Court completely changed the nature of protected liberty interests under the Fourteenth Amendment. In *Sandin v. Conner*,[51] a prisoner alleged that Hawaii prison officials deprived him of procedural due process when an adjustment committee refused to allow him to present witnesses during a disciplinary hearing and then sentenced him to segregation for misconduct. The district court granted the officials summary judgment, but the Court of Appeals reversed, concluding that the prisoner had a liberty interest in remaining free of disciplinary segregation and that there was a disputed question of fact whether he had received all of the process due under *Wolff v. McDonnell*.[52] The Court of Appeals based its conclusion on a prison regulation instructing the committee to find guilt when a misconduct charge was supported by substantial evidence. The court reasoned that the committee's duty to find guilt was nondiscretionary. From that regulation, it drew a negative inference that the committee could not impose segregation if it did not find substantial evidence of misconduct. This was a state-created liberty interest. Therefore, *Wolff* entitled the prisoner to call witnesses.

The Supreme Court reversed, holding that neither the Hawaii prison regulation nor the Due Process Clause itself afforded the prisoner a protected liberty interest that would entitle him to the procedural protections set forth in *Wolff*. Under *Wolff*, states in certain circumstances could create liberty interests that are protected by the Due Process Clause. However, these interests are limited to freedom from restraint that, while not exceeding the sentence in such an unexpected manner as to give rise to protection by the Due Process Clause of its own force, nonetheless imposes atypical and significant hardship on the prisoner in relation to the ordinary incidents of prison life.[53]

Sandin backed off from the methodology used in *Hewitt v. Helms*[54] and later cases, holding that these cases have impermissibly shifted the focus of the liberty interest inquiry from one based on the nature of the deprivation to one based on language of a particular regulation. Under *Hewitt*'s methodology, prison regulations, such as the one in *Sandin*, have been examined to see whether mandatory language and substantive predicates create an enforceable expectation that the state would produce a particular outcome with respect to the prisoner's confinement conditions. *Hewitt* encouraged prisoners to comb through regulations in search of mandatory language on which to base entitlements to various state-conferred privileges. Courts have, in response, drawn negative inferences from that language. *Hewitt*, it was felt, created disincentives for states to codify prison management procedures in the interest of uniform treatment in order to avoid the creation of "liberty" interests. This led to the impermissible involvement of federal courts in the day-to-day management of prisons. The Supreme Court in *Sandin* felt that the time had come to return to due process principles that were correctly established and applied in *Wolff* and *Meachum*.

The Supreme Court rejected the assertion that any state action taken for a punitive reason encroaches upon a liberty interest under the Due Process Clause, even in the absence of any state regulation.[55] In *Sandin*, the prisoner's discipline in segregated confinement did not present the type of atypical, significant deprivation in which a state might conceivably create a liberty interest. At the time of his punishment, disciplinary segregation mirrored conditions imposed upon prisoners in administrative segregation and protective custody. Moreover, the state later expunged his disciplinary record with respect to the more serious of the charges against him. Further, his confinement did not exceed similar but totally discretionary confinement in either duration or degree of restriction. The situation in *Sandin* did not present a case in which the state's action would inevitably affect the duration of his sentence, because the chance that the misconduct finding would affect his parole status was simply too attenuated to invoke the Due Process Clause's procedural guarantees.

Lower courts have been forced by *Sandin* to reconsider earlier holdings involving liberty interests. For example, in *Delaney v. Selsky*,[56] the court stated that because the due process issues raised in the case were on their way to trial when the Supreme Court decided *Sandin*, and because *Sandin* profoundly altered the standards for determining when prisoners suffer a deprivation of constitutionally protected liberty interests, a motion for reconsideration was granted.

According to *Delaney*, the Supreme Court in *Sandin* reversed the judicial trend toward expanding prisoners' constitutionally protected liberty interests. The Supreme Court instructed federal courts to focus their liberty interest inquiries on the nature of alleged deprivations rather than on negative inferences from the "shalls" that dot prison regulations designed mainly to guide the conduct of correctional officers. More specifically, *Sandin* held that where disciplinary segregation is substantially similar to the conditions imposed upon prisoners in administrative segregation and protective custody, disciplinary segregation does not present the type of atypical, significant deprivation in which a state might conceivably create a liberty interest.

The dilemma faced within the courts of the Second Circuit is typical. In the months following *Sandin*, courts had opportunities to consider its impact on the due process rights of prisoners confined to administrative or disciplinary segregation. In *Eastman v. Walker*,[57] a district court held that where a prison regulation stated that a prisoner's keeplock status "shall" be changed within 72 hours, the decision to keep a prisoner in keeplock for 96 hours instead to ensure institutional security and safety was not "atypical" and did not impose a "significant hardship" and did not violate a prisoner's liberty interest.

A similar conclusion was reached in *Carter v. Carriero*.[58] *Carter* noted that New York prison regulations allow prisoners to be placed in the segregated housing unit for disciplinary confinement, detention, administrative segregation, protective custody, keeplock confinement, and for any other reason, with the approval of the deputy commissioner for facility operations. *Carter* went on to hold that, given the similarities among segregated housing, disciplinary segregation, and administrative confinement in New York prisons, a penalty of 270 days in disciplinary segregation did not impose atypical and significant hardship on the prisoner in relation to the ordinary incidents of prison life. Therefore, no constitutionally protected liberty interest entitled the prisoner to the procedural protection that he claimed he was due.

In *Delaney*, prison officials ignored the fact that even when the conditions of disciplinary confinement mirrored the conditions imposed upon prisoners in administrative segregation and protective custody, an inappropriate duration of disciplinary confinement still raises due process concerns. The prisoner's original sentence was 168 days in disciplinary segregation after he completed the 197 days remaining on his keeplock sentence. He received this sentence after an administrative hearing whose procedural adequacy was not questioned. In *Carter*, the court held that 270 days' confinement in the segregated housing unit did not impose an atypical and significant hardship on the prisoner in relation to the ordinary incidents of prison life. The *Delaney* court was not prepared to say that, as a matter of law, 365 days' confinement in the segregated housing unit was a sufficiently typical and insignificant hardship on the prisoner relative to the ordinary incidents of life in the correctional facility, to permit the state to deprive him of procedural protections before imposing that sanction. The *Delaney* court believed that *Sandin* did not compel a different conclusion.

The court believed that the 197 days that the prisoner spent in disciplinary confinement at the correctional facility were different in degree, if not duration, from similar administrative confinement. Because of his unusual height—almost seven feet—his confinement to the segregated housing unit for one year caused "back problems." The bed in his segregated housing unit cell was too small for him and as a segregated housing unit resident, he received only one hour of recreation per day. For most of his time in segregated housing, the prisoner was forced to stand or lie in an uncomfortable and compromising position.

According to *Delaney*, *Sandin* renders both the duration and the conditions of disciplinary confinement relevant to the issue of whether the nature of a prisoner's disciplinary sanction raises a liberty interest concern.

§ 10.5 The Prisoner's Legal Remedies

A violation of rights afforded to prisoners under either state or federal law will give rise to a number of remedial actions. Although they are discussed fully in Chapter 15, it should be noted that the remedies in the federal courts are usually limited to injunctive relief, civil suit under 42 U.S.C. § 1983, and habeas corpus under 28 U.S.C. § 2241.

State courts have shown interest in the conduct of prison disciplinary proceedings. This has ranged from hearing complaints concerning conditions and practices[59] to detailed judicial review of disciplinary board findings.[60]

Whether pursued in state or federal court, one of the results of the reversal of a disciplinary board's action will probably be an order requiring the expungement of any records dealing with or relying on the disciplinary action that is found to have been invalid. One court deemed expungement appropriate to protect the prisoner "from future prejudice in obtaining parole, work assignments, and the transfer to a prison nearer his home."[61]

The invalidation of disciplinary proceedings through habeas corpus is not a prerequisite to a prisoner's § 1983 action, where a successful due process challenge to the proceedings would not necessarily result in an earlier release from incarceration. In the absence of any effect on the prisoner's term of incarceration, habeas corpus review is not available to challenge the validity of disciplinary proceedings. Section 1983 provides the prisoner's sole remedy for alleged constitutional violations.[62]

§ 10.6 Conclusion

Federal courts have indicated a willingness to inquire into all aspects of prison administration to ensure that the constitutional rights of prisoners are observed. Although the courts have traditionally been extremely hesitant to place restraints on prison authorities in matters of internal prison administration, one court noted:

> This simple hands-off attitude has been made more complex by Supreme Court cases which have held that prisoners are not stripped of their constitutional rights, including the right to due process, when the prison gate slams shut behind them. Rather, prisoners continue to enjoy the protections of the Due Process Clause subject to restrictions imposed by the practical necessities of prison life and the legitimate aims of the correctional process.[63]

In the context of "due process," it is important to note that long before the requirements of procedural due process were imposed on prison disciplinary proceedings, it was recognized that such proceedings must at least afford substantive due process,[64] in that they must be fair.

Clearly, the courts have gone beyond the era when prisoners' constitutional claims were disregarded out-of-hand by statements such as: "A convicted felon . . . has, as a consequence of his crime, not only forfeited his liberty, but all of his personal rights except those which the law in its humanity accords to him. He is for the time being the slave of the State."[65] The contemporary view in the federal courts is that if a constitutionally protected interest can be made out, and if some harm thereto can be shown that is sufficiently grievous and that cannot be justified by the exigencies of incarceration, then a proper case for relief exists.[66] However, *Baxter* makes it clear that the days of federal court tinkering with internal prison management are over. Prison disciplinarians who follow the clear teachings of *Wolff* and who initiate procedures to prevent the abuse of administrative discretion need not fear legal liability.

Sandin has severely restricted the type of hearing to which procedural due process rights apply. *Sandin* has had a profound effect on all aspects of institutional life. "Liberty" has been greatly restricted, particularly as it applies to prison discipline.

Notes

1 U.S. CONST., amend. V states in part, "no person shall . . . be deprived of life, liberty, or property, without due process of law." This amendment is a prohibition on the federal government and not the states. Barron v. Baltimore, 32 U.S. (7 Pet.) 243 (1833).
2 Palko v. Connecticut, 302 U.S. 319 (1937); Snyder v. Massachusetts, 291 U.S. 97 (1934); Hurtado v. California, 110 U.S. 516 (1884).
3 Palko v. Connecticut, 302 U.S. 319 (1937); Snyder v. Massachusetts, 291 U.S. 97 (1934); Hurtado v. California, 110 U.S. 516 (1884).
4 Cafeteria & Restaurant Workers Union v. McElroy, 367 U.S. 886 (1961).
5 Milhouse v. Carlson, 652 F.2d 371 (3d Cir. 1981).
6 McGrath v. Johnson, 155 F. Supp. 2d 294 (E.D. Pa. 2001).
7 Farver v. Schwartz, 255 F.3d 473 (8th Cir. 2001).
8 Broussard v. Johnson, 918 F. Supp. 1040 (E.D. Texas 1996), *sub. app.*, 253 F.3d 874 (5th Cir. 2001).

9 W. GELLHORN AND C. BYSE, ADMINISTRATIVE LAW 486 (3d ed. 1970).

10 Goldberg v. Kelly, 397 U.S. 254 (1970).

11 *Id.* at 267–268, 270, 271.

12 Landman v. Royster, 333 F. Supp. 621 (E.D. Va. 1971); Clutchette v. Procunier, 328 F. Supp. 767 (N.D. Cal. 1971); Clutchette v. Enomoto, 471 F. Supp. 1113 (N.D. Cal. 1979); Chavis v. Rowe, 643 F.2d 1281 (7th Cir. 1981); Wright v. Enomoto, 462 F. Supp. 397 (N.D. Cal. 1980), *summary aff'd*, 434 U.S. 1052 (1978); Powell v. Ward, 487 F. Supp. 917 (S.D.N.Y. 1980).

13 418 U.S. 539 (1974).

14 42 U.S.C. § 1983.

15 Morrissey v. Brewer, 408 U.S. 471 (1972).

16 Gagnon v. Scarpelli, 411 U.S. 778 (1973).

17 Wolff v. McDonnell, 418 U.S. at 571 (1974).

18 Taylor v. Schmidt, 380 F. Supp. 1222 (W.D. Wis. 1974).

19 Clutchette v. Procunier, 497 F.2d 809 (9th Cir. 1974), *reh'g*, 510 F.2d 613 (9th Cir. 1975) in light of *Wolff.*

20 Palmigiano v. Baxter, 510 F.2d 534 (1st Cir. 1974).

21 Baxter v. Palmigiano, 425 U.S. 308 (1976); Enomoto v. Clutchette, 425 U.S. 308 (1976).

22 Landman v. Royster, 333 F. Supp. 621 (E.D. Va. 1971); Clutchette v. Procunier, 328 F. Supp. 767 (N.D. Cal. 1971); Bundy v. Cannon, 328 F. Supp. 165 (D. Md. 1971); Carter v. McGinnis, 320 F. Supp. 1092 (W.D.N.Y. 1970); Nolan v. Scafati, 306 F. Supp. 1 (D. Mass. 1969) (dictum), *rev'd on other grounds*, 430 F.2d 548 (1st Cir. 1970); Chavis v. Rowe, 643 F.2d 1281 (7th Cir. 1981); Rinehard v. Brewer, 483 F. Supp. 165 (S.D. Iowa 1980); Flaherty v. Fogg, 421 N.Y.S.2d 736 (N.Y. App. Div. 1979).

23 Schneckloth v. Bustamonte, 412 U.S. 218 (1973).

24 Franklin v. Israel, 537 F. Supp. 1112 (W.D. Wis. 1982).

25 KENNETH C. DAVIS, ADMINISTRATIVE LAW 157 (3d ed. 1972).

26 Meola v. Fitzpatrick, 322 F. Supp. 878 (D. Mass. 1971); Tyree v. Fitzpatrick, 325 F. Supp. 554 (D. Mass. 1971); Carothers v. Follette, 314 F. Supp. 1014 (S.D.N.Y. 1970), *appeal dismissed*, 631 F.2d 725 (3d Cir. 1980); Jordan v. Arnold, 472 F. Supp. 265 (M.D. Pa. 1979); Deane v. Coughlin, 439 N.Y.S.2d 792 (N.Y. App. Div. 1981); Hayes v. Walker, 555 F.2d 625 (7th Cir. 1977).

27 Kristsky v. McGinnis, 313 F. Supp. 1247, 1250 (N.D.N.Y. 1970); *see also* Mack v. Johnson, 430 F. Supp. 1139 (E.D. Pa. 1977) ($765.00 awarded to inmate placed in punitive segregation without opportunity to present evidence at disciplinary hearing), *aff'd*, 582 F.2d 1275 (3d Cir. 1978).

28 AMERICAN CORRECTIONAL ASSOCIATION, MANUAL OF CORRECTIONAL STANDARDS 408 (1966).

29 Baxter v. Palmigiano, 425 U.S. 308 (1976).

30 Daigle v. Helgemoe, 399 F. Supp. 416 (D.N.H. 1975); Grever v. Oregon State Correctional Institution, Corrections Division, 561 P. 2d 669 (Or. App. 1977).

31 Mills v. Oliver, 367 F. Supp. 77 (E.D. Va. 1973); Clutchette v. Enomoto, 471 F. Supp. 1113 (N.D. Cal. 1979).

32 Murphy v. Wheaton, supra note 48; Devaney v. Hall, 509 F. Supp. 497 (D.C. Mass. 1981).

33 Cases deal with such diverse topics as: Smith v. Rabalais, 659 F.2d 539 (5th Cir. 1981) (In a disciplinary proceeding, it was not an abuse of discretion to refuse to provide an inmate with the identity of a confidential informant when there were possible fatal consequences to the informant and when the inmate would be given an opportunity to establish an alibi for the time, place, and date of the alleged sale of narcotics.); Kyle v. Hanberry, 677 F.2d 1386 (11th Cir. 1982) (A prison disciplinary finding based upon the affidavit of a prison chaplain, who was merely passing on the statements of a "reliable inmate source," was reversed. Minimum due process requires that the disciplinary committee undertake in good faith to establish the informant's reliability. There must be some information on the record from which a court can reasonably conclude that the committee undertook such an inquiry and, upon such inquiry, concluded that the informant was reliable. The committee should describe the nature of its

inquiry to the extent that the committee is satisfied that such disclosure would not identify an informant.); Chavis v. Rowe, 643 F.2d 1281 (7th Cir. 1981) (A disciplinary committee must disclose to an inmate any exculpatory report as well as a written statement as to the evidence relied upon and reasons for the disciplinary action taken. It must also provide him or her with a written statement as to the evidence relied upon and reasons for the disciplinary action taken against him.); Bartholomew v. Watson, 665 F.2d 915 (9th Cir. 1981) (A prison procedure that prevented an inmate from calling an inmate or staff member as a witness in a disciplinary hearing violated due process.); Langton v. Berman, 667 F.2d 231 (1st Cir. 1981) (A state prisoner in a disciplinary hearing had no right to cross-examine witnesses. His right to confront his accusers and to have full access to all evidence should be left to the discretion of state prison officials.); Ward v. Johnson, 667 F.2d 1126 (4th Cir. 1981) (An inmate was denied due process when he was not permitted to call witnesses at a disciplinary hearing. Due process was involved even though the punishment was the loss of recreational time.); Segarra v. McDade, 706 F.2d 1301 (4th Cir. 1981) (Due process is not violated by a prison official's decision to prohibit an inmate from calling witnesses at a prison disciplinary hearing concerning the loss of good-time credits. Such is not required by Wolff v. McDonnell. In this case, the request was denied when he made his request during the hearing, after earlier refusing to compile a witness list or to allow statements to be taken.)

34 471 U.S. 491 (1985).
35 Walker v. Bates, 23 F.3d 652 (2d Cir. 1994).
36 *See* also Patterson v. Coughlin, 761 F.2d 886 (2d Cir. 1985), *cert. denied*, 474 U.S. 1100 (1986).
37 AMERICAN CORRECTIONAL ASSOCIATION, MANUAL OF CORRECTIONAL STANDARDS 410 (1966).
38 Beishir v. Swenson, 331 F. Supp. 1227 (W.D. Mo. 1971); Morris v. Travisono, 310 F. Supp. 857 (D.R.I. 1970); Burns v. Swenson, 300 F. Supp. 759 (W.D. Mo. 1969); Riner v. Raines, 409 N.E.2d 575 (Ind. 1980); Scott v. DeJarnette, 470 F. Supp. 766 (E.D. Ark. 1979); Adams v. Duckworth, 412 N.E.2d 789 (Ind. 1980); Dawson v. Hearing Committee, 597 P. 2d 1353 (Wash. 1979).
39 Landman v. Royster, 333 F. Supp. 621 (E.D. Va. 1971); Langley v. Scurr, 305 N.W.2d 418 (Iowa 1981).
40 Crooks v. Warne, 516 F.2d 837 (2d Cir. 1975); *see also* Commonwealth v. Manlin, 441 A.2d 532 (Pa. Super. 1979) (Conviction of deputy warden was upheld for "official oppression" by the Superior Court).
41 Crooks v. Warne, 516 F.2d 837, 839–840 (2d Cir. 1975).
42 Bickham v. Cannon, 516 F.2d 885 (7th Cir. 1975); *see also* Deane v. Coughlin, 439 N.Y.S.2d 792 (N.Y. App. Div. 1981); Collins v. Coughlin, 442 N.Y.S.2d 191 (N.Y. App. Div. 1981); cf. United States ex rel. Smith v. Robinson, 495 F. Supp. 696 (E.D. Pa. 1980) (An inmate has a right to freedom from disciplinary sanctions until proven guilty of a rule violation. An inmate has a constitutional liberty interest in freedom from segregated confinement).
43 Morris v. Travisono, 509 F.2d 1358 (1st Cir. 1975); La Batt v. Twomey, 513 F.2d 641 (7th Cir. 1975); Aikens v. Lash, 390 F. Supp. 663 (N.D. Ind. 1975), modified in 514 F.2d 55 (7th Cir. 1975); Hayward v. Procunier, 629 F.2d 599 (9th Cir. 1981); Gray v. Levine, 455 F. Supp. 267 (D. Mo. 1978), *aff'd*, 605 F.2d 1202 (4th Cir. 1979); Clifton v. Robinson, 500 F. Supp. 30 (C.D. Pa. 1980).
44 United States v. Hedges, 458 F.2d 188, 190 (10th Cir. 1972).
45 *Id.*
46 Barrows v. Hogan, 379 F. Supp. 314 (M.D. Pa. 1974); cf. Rusher v. Arnold, 550 F.2d 896 (3d Cir. 1977).
47 Porter v. Coughlin, 421 F.3d 141 (2d Cir. 2005).
48 Universal Camera Corp. v. NLRB, 340 U.S. 474 (1951).
49 Helms v. Hewitt, 655 F.2d 487 (3d Cir. 1981), *rev'd on other grounds*, 459 U.S. 460 (1983).
50 Meyers v. Alldredge, 492 F.2d 296 (3d Cir. 1974); Sagerser v. Oregon State Penitentiary, Corrections Division, 597 P. 2d 1257 (Or. Ct. App. 1979); Haller v. Oregon State Penitentiary, Corr. Div., 570 P. 2d 983 (Or. Ct. App. 1977).

51 515 U.S. 472 (1995).

52 418 U.S. 539 (1974).

53 *See* Meachum v. Fano, 427 U.S. 215 (1976).

54 459 U.S. 460 (1983).

55 *See* Bell v. Wolfish, 441 U.S. 520 (1979) and Ingraham v. Wright, 430 U.S. 651 (1977).

56 899 F. Supp. 923 (N.D.N.Y. 1995).

57 895 F. Supp. 31 (N.D.N.Y. 1995).

58 905 F. Supp. 99 (W.D.N.Y. 1995).

59 People ex rel. Bright v. Warden, 361 N.Y.S.2d 809 (Trial term SC Bronx County, 1975); McGinnis v. Stevens, 543 P. 2d 1221 (Alaska 1975); Wilkerson v. Oregon, 544 P. 2d 198 (Or. Ct. App. 1976); Steele v. Gray, 223 N.W.2d 614 (Wis. 1974).

60 Palmer v. Oregon State Penitentiary, 545 P. 2d 141 (Or. Ct. App. 1976); Dawson v. Hearing Committee, 597 P. 2d 1353 (Wash. 1979); Sandlin v. Oregon Women's Correctional Center, Corrections Division, 559 P. 2d 1308 (Or. Ct. App. 1977); Riner v. Raines, 409 N.E.2d 575 (Ind. 1980); Reed v. Parratt, 301 N.W.2d 343 (Neb. 1981).

61 Chapman v. Kleindienst, 517 F.2d 1246 (7th Cir. 1974); Powell v. Ward, 487 F. Supp. 917 (S.D.N.Y. 1980); Hurley v. Ward, 402 N.Y.S.2d 870 (N.Y. App. Div. 1976).

62 Ramirez v. Galaza, 334 F.3d 850 (9th Cir. 2003).

63 United States ex rel. Gereau v. Henderson, 526 F.2d 889 (5th Cir. 1976).

64 Wilwording v. Swenson, 502 F.2d 844 (8th Cir. 1974).

65 Ruffin v. Commonwealth, 62 Va. (21 Gratt.) 790, 796 (1871).

66 Shimabuku v. Britton, 503 F.2d 38 (10th Cir. 1974); Haines v. Kerner, 404 U.S. 519 (1972).

Use of Force 11

Chapter Outline

§ 11.1   Introduction

As the legal custodians of large numbers of offenders, including many who are being confined for crimes of violence, prison staffs are often confronted with situations in which it is necessary to use force against a prisoner or a group of prisoners. Force, in this connection, means any physical force directed toward another, either by direct physical contact or by the use of a weapon such as tear gas, chemical spray, a baton, or a firearm.

Earlier in our jurisprudential history, all excessive force claims were analyzed under a single substantive due process standard. Quite apart from any specific provision of the Bill of Rights, application of excessive force was viewed in any context as a deprivation of substantive due process when the government official's conduct "shocked the conscience."[1]

These principles were changed in *Graham v. Connor*.[2] In *Graham*, the Supreme Court turned away from the use of the "shocks the conscience" standard applicable to all excessive force claims brought under the Civil Rights Act.[3] It ruled instead that excessive force claims must be examined under the standard applicable to the specific constitutional right allegedly violated, which in most instances will be the Fourth or Eighth Amendment (the main sources of individual protection under the Constitution against physically abusive official conduct). *Graham* arose in the context of a person's seizure by police officers. The excessive force claim was governed by Fourth Amendment objective reasonableness standards.

Graham called into question whether the substantive due process standard of the Fourteenth Amendment survived as a source of a federal right to be free from excessive force. One reading of *Graham* suggested that such protection did not survive and that the relatively unusual excessive force cases falling beyond the ambit of the Fourth and Eighth Amendments are able to be redressed only by recourse to state tort law. Other readings suggest that *Graham* leaves the law untouched in that narrow area, and in the nonseizure, nonprisoner context, the substantive due process right to be free from excessive force is alive and well.[4]

It should be noted that the Supreme Court in *Graham* took no position on the legal argument of the prison officials that the conduct of the guards was isolated, unauthorized, and against prison policy and therefore beyond the scope of "punishment" prohibited by the Eighth Amendment. This argument was not supported by the record, as the Court of Appeals left intact the lower court's determination that the violence at issue was not an isolated assault. The argument also ignored the finding that a supervisor expressly condoned the use of force.

Overall, the Supreme Court in *Graham* made clear that a distinction will be made between Eighth Amendment excessive force cases, Eighth Amendment conditions-of-confinement cases, and Eighth Amendment medical needs cases. A different standard must be applied in each type of case.

Every person, including an incarcerated felon, has the right to be free from the fear of offensive bodily contact and to be free from actual offensive bodily contact. Any person who violates either of these rights can be held liable, both civilly and criminally, unless such conduct is privileged. It has generally been recognized that prison officials are privileged to use force against prisoners in five situations: (1) self-defense, (2) defense of third persons, (3) enforcement of prison rules and regulations, (4) prevention of escape, and (5) prevention of crime.

§ 11.2   Degree of Force Permitted

The situations in which a prison official is justified in using force are relatively easy to recognize. However, the degree of force that may be used in these situations is not as clear. The courts speak of the justification of using "reasonable" force in a given situation to control the prisoner. The factual elements in each case determine whether the force used was excessive and thus not privileged.

The controlling factual elements are the degree of force used by the prisoner, the prisoner's possession or nonpossession of a deadly weapon, the reasonable perception on the part of the correctional officer that he or a third person is in danger of death or serious bodily harm, and the means of force available to the officer.

When discussing the amount of force that is legally permissible, it is helpful to distinguish deadly force and nondeadly force. *Deadly force* may be defined as force that will likely cause death or serious bodily harm. Knives and firearms are always considered instruments of deadly force. *Nondeadly* force is force that will normally cause neither death nor serious bodily harm. The use of fists, certain holds, chemical spray, and tear gas are examples of nondeadly force.

Employing certain methods of applying force cannot, in the abstract, be categorized as either the use of deadly or nondeadly force. Certain factual elements of the case, primarily the area of the body struck, must be considered. For example, a blow to the head from a baton is likely to cause death or serious bodily harm and thus must be regarded as the use of deadly force. However, a blow to the knees would probably constitute nondeadly force.

Our society places great value on human life and on the right of every person to be free from offensive physical contact by another. Consequently, the use of force by one individual against another is discouraged. For this reason, force is permissible only when all nonforce alternatives have failed.

Whenever prison officials are accused of using excessive physical force constituting "the unnecessary and wanton infliction of pain" that violates the cruel and unusual punishments clause, the core judicial inquiry used to be that set out in *Whitley v. Albers*:[5] "whether the force used was applied in a good faith effort to maintain or restore discipline, or maliciously and sadistically to cause harm." The extension of *Whitley*'s application of the "unnecessary and wanton infliction of pain" standard to all allegations of force, whether the prison disturbance is a riot or a lesser disruption, worked no innovation.

Under the *Whitley* approach, the extent of injury suffered by a prisoner is one of the factors to be considered in determining whether the use of force is wanton and unnecessary. The absence of serious injury is relevant to, but does not end the Eighth Amendment inquiry. There was no merit to the assertion that a significant injury requirement is mandated by what the Supreme Court termed, in *Wilson v. Seiter*,[6] as the "objective component" of Eighth Amendment analysis: namely, whether the alleged wrongdoing was objectively "harmful enough" to establish a constitutional violation. That component is contextual and responsive to the "contemporary standards of decency" test of *Estelle v. Gamble*.[7] In the excessive force context, such standards are always violated when prison officials maliciously and sadistically use force to cause harm, whether or not significant injury is evident. Moreover, although the Eighth Amendment does not reach *de minimis* uses of physical force, provided that such use is not of a sort repugnant to the conscience of mankind, the blows directed at the prisoner were not *de minimis*, and the extent of his injuries provided no basis for dismissal of his claim.

The Supreme Court overruled the *Whitley* approach in *Hudson v. McMillian*.[8] A prisoner testified that the minor bruises, facial swelling, loosened teeth, and cracked dental plate he suffered were the result of a beating by correctional officers. He testified that the beating took place while he was handcuffed and shackled following an argument with one of the officers and that a supervisor on duty watched the beating but merely told the officers "not to have too much fun." The district court found that the officers used force when there was no need to do so and that the supervisor expressly condoned their actions. The court ruled that they had violated the Eighth Amendment's prohibition of cruel and unusual punishments and awarded damages to the prisoner. The Court of Appeals reversed, holding, among other things, that prisoners alleging the use of excessive force in violation of the Eighth Amendment must prove "significant injury" and that the prisoner in *Hudson* could not prevail because his injuries were "minor" and required no medical attention. The United States Supreme Court reversed, holding that "the use of excessive physical force against a prisoner may constitute cruel and unusual punishment even when the inmate does not suffer serious injury."

Hudson v. McMillian clarified the standards for determining whether Eighth Amendment violations have occurred. Whenever prison officials are accused of using excessive physical force in violation of the cruel and unusual punishments clause, the core judicial inquiry is whether force was applied in a good faith effort to maintain or restore discipline or maliciously and sadistically to cause harm.

The Supreme Court used the *Hudson* holding to reverse a Fourth Circuit case in *Wilkins v. Gaddy*.[9] A North Carolina prisoner, Wilkins, filed a § 1983 suit claiming that he was assaulted by a corrections officer without any provocation when the officer slammed Wilkins onto the concrete floor and then punched, kicked, and kneed him until another officer had to physically remove him. Wilkins sustained multiple injuries including a bruised heel, lower back pain, increased blood pressure, headaches, and dizziness. The district court dismissed Wilkins's complaint because his injuries were *de minimis*, and the Fourth Circuit affirmed. In a per curium decision, the Supreme Court reversed, holding that the district court's approach was at odds with *Hudson*'s direction to decide excessive force claims based on the nature of the force rather than the extent of the injury.

With respect to pretrial detainees, it is the Due Process Clause that provides the appropriate constitutional basis for determining whether a detention official's use of deliberate force on such a detainee is excessive. According to a Fifth Circuit case,[10] neither the search and seizure clause of the Fourth Amendment nor the Cruel and Unusual Punishments Clause of the Eighth Amendment applies. Both *Bell*[11] and *Graham*[12] reason that the appropriate question under the Due Process Clause is whether the detention official applied force with the intent to punish the pretrial detainee. Guided by *Whitley*[13] and *Hudson*[14] with respect to excessive force claims in the context of prison disturbances, the court held that the question is whether force was applied in a good faith effort to maintain or restore discipline or maliciously and sadistically to cause harm. The focus of this standard is on the detention facility official's subjective intent to punish. In determining such intent, it was pointed out that the trier of fact must include such objective factors as the extent of injuries suffered, the apparent need for the application of force, the degree of force exerted, the threat reasonably perceived by the detention facility official, and the need to act quickly and decisively.

In the 2015 case *Kingsley v. Hendrickson*,[15] the Supreme Court clarified the evidentiary standard that pretrial detainees must show in an excessive force claim. Pretrial detainee Kingsley filed a complaint claiming that two jail officers used excessive force against him. At trial, the district court instructed the jury that Kingsley was required to prove that the officers "recklessly disregarded Kingsley's safety" and "acted with reckless disregard of his rights." The jury ruled in favor of the guards. On appeal, Kingsley argued that the jury instruction did not adhere to the proper standard for judging a pretrial detainee's excessive force claim, namely, objective unreasonableness. The Seventh Circuit affirmed the district court's ruling. The Supreme Court reversed, holding: "Under 42 U.S.C. § 1983, a pretrial detainee must show only that the force purposely or knowingly used against him was objectively unreasonable to prevail on an excessive force claim."

§ 11.3 Self-Defense

Every person has the right to protect him- or herself against an assault by another. Prison officials may use force against a prisoner in their own self-defense.[16] Correctional officers may use the degree of force reasonably necessary under the circumstances to protect themselves from the assault and to subdue the prisoners.[17] While prison officials are afforded broad discretion in maintaining order, they are not justified in using any amount of force when the threat of disorder has subsided.[18] The extent of such force depends upon the degree of force being used by the prisoner, the officers' reasonable perception of injury, and the means of resisting the assault. The test of reasonable force is whether the degree of force used is necessary under the facts and circumstances of the particular case[19] as illustrated by the two following cases.

In a Maryland case, a fight erupted between five prisoners and a number of correctional officers. The prisoners received numerous injuries, including severe cuts and bruises and broken bones. One of the officers was hurt so severely that he had to be hospitalized in the intensive care unit. After hearing the evidence, the court found that the prisoners were resisting prison authority and that the force used was reasonable and necessary under the circumstances.[20]

The use of excessive force by correctional officers is again illustrated in the case of *Prisoners of Attica Correctional Facility v. Rockefeller*.[21] The case arose out of the bloody rioting that occurred at the Attica (New York) Correctional Facility in September 1971. The prisoners alleged that, after the prison was retaken by force on September 13, state officials constantly subjected the prisoners to unprovoked acts of brutality, including the following:

> Injured prisoners, some on stretchers, were struck, prodded or beaten with sticks, belts, bats or other weapons. Others were forced to strip and run naked through gauntlets of guards armed with clubs which they used to strike the bodies of the prisoners as they passed. Some were dragged on the ground, some marked with an "X" on their backs, some spat upon or burned with matches, and others poked in the genitals or arms with sticks. According to the testimony of the prisoners, bloody or wounded prisoners were apparently not spared in this orgy of brutality.[22]

The Second Circuit approved of the injunction against state officials from future acts of brutality and torture and authorized the district court to station federal monitors in the institution if necessary.

Deadly force as a means of self-defense is never justified unless the prison official is in reasonable apprehension of death or serious injury and the use of deadly force is a last resort.

§ 11.4   Defense of Third Persons

Force may be used against a prisoner[23] in defense of third persons, such as another prisoner, prison staff, or visitors. The law regarding the use of force to prevent injury to third persons is similar to the rules regarding self-defense. A person is justified in using the degree of force reasonably necessary under the circumstances to protect the third party and to control the attacker. Prison officials may find themselves under a duty to provide prisoners with reasonable protection from constant threats of violence.[24] What is reasonable under the circumstances again depends upon the degree of force being used by the attacker, the person's reasonable estimate of injury to the third party, and the means available to the person to control the attacker. Deadly force may be used against the attacker only if the third party reasonably appears to be in danger of death or serious injury and the use of deadly force is the last resort.

§ 11.5   Enforcement of Prison Rules and Regulations

Courts have long recognized that penal authorities have the right and duty to prescribe rules and regulations for the internal discipline and control of prisoners. The necessary corollary to this authority is the privilege of using reasonable force to see that the rules are enforced. A distinction must be drawn between the use of force as punishment for the violation of a prison rule and the use of force as a means of ensuring that the prisoner is brought under control. For example, in the case of *Johnson v. Glick*,[25] the court stated "the management by a few guards of large numbers of prisoners, not usually the most gentle or tractable of men and women, may require and justify the use of a degree of intentional force."[26]

If a prisoner resists an officer's reasonable order, additional officers should be summoned to control the prisoner. Even when the order is based on a prison rule that is later found to be unconstitutional, guards may use reasonable force to obtain prisoner compliance.[27] It is difficult to imagine any justification for using force sufficient to kill or maim in order to compel compliance with a disciplinary rule. If the prisoner's resistance amounts to an assault upon an officer, that officer has the privilege of self-defense, and other officers have the privilege of defending third persons. The rules pertaining to self-defense and defense of third persons would then be controlling, because the situation would no longer be one of using force solely to maintain discipline.

§ 11.6   Prevention of Crime

Prison officials have the duty, sometimes imposed by statute,[28] to prevent prisoners from committing crimes within a detention facility. Therefore, these officials have the privilege of using reasonable force to prevent either a misdemeanor or a felony. However, the degree of force permissible will depend on whether the attempted crime is a misdemeanor or a felony. Generally, deadly force can be employed to prevent the commission of a felony,[29] but only after all other means reasonably available have failed.[30] Examples of common felonies committed within a prison are rioting and assault with a weapon upon another prisoner.

Deadly force is never justified to prevent the commission of a misdemeanor.[31] If, however, a prisoner physically resists nondeadly force employed by a correctional officer to prevent the commission of a misdemeanor and becomes an aggressor, the rules pertaining to self-defense apply.

§ 11.7   Prevention of Escape

Almost every state has, by statute, made escape or attempted escape by a convicted felon a felony.[32] Thus, the rules regarding use of force to prevent a felony apply to preventing an escape; that is, force, including deadly force as a last resort, may be employed. In *Henry v. Perry*,[33] a correctional officer shot an escaping prisoner. Handcuffed, the prisoner had climbed a gate beside the bus in which he was being returned to prison and was running away. Using deadly force appeared to be the only means of preventing the escape. The officer gave a verbal warning and fired warning shots in an effort to halt the escape before shooting the prisoner. Although it was acknowledged that the use of deadly force by correctional officers may be cruel and unusual punishment within the meaning of the Eighth Amendment, when the escapee has committed a crime involving the infliction of serious bodily harm, deadly force may be used if necessary to prevent escape and if, where feasible, some warning has been given.[34]

§ 11.8   The Use of Corporal Punishment to Enforce Prison Discipline

The term *corporal punishment*, as used in this book, means the infliction of physical pain upon a prisoner as a punishment for the violation of a prison rule or regulation. Such forms of conduct include but are not limited to whipping, cold showers, electrical shocking devices, and suspension from cell bars by handcuffs. The use of solitary confinement as a method for punishing violations of prison discipline is not included within the definition of corporal punishment. Many states have no statutes that specifically forbid the use of corporal punishment. Other states, however, prohibit corporal punishment in detention facilities by statute.[35]

§ 11.8.1   — Brief History of Corporal Punishment

Corporal punishment has a long history of use in prisons, as was stated in *United States v. Jones*:[36]

> From time immemorial prison officials were vested with the power and authority of imposing corporal punishment upon prisoners as a part of the discipline and restraint. . . . [F]or centuries whipping or corporal punishment has been a recognized method of discipline of convicts.

The use of corporal punishment to enforce prison discipline continued into the early parts of the twentieth century. In 1927, a North Carolina statute authorizing the whipping of convicts was upheld.[37] In 1963, in *State v. Cannon*,[38] the Delaware Supreme Court held that the use of whipping to punish certain crimes did not violate either the state or federal constitutional bans on cruel and unusual punishment. In *Talley v. Stevens*,[39] the court refused to declare whipping unconstitutional as such but held that whipping must not be excessive and must be inflicted as dispassionately as possible. A 1949 case involving handcuffing a prisoner to a cell door for 60 hours without food also discusses the use and misuse of corporal punishment.[40] Corporal punishment, including the use of electrical shocking devices, was used openly by the state of Arkansas until the 1960s. In a 1976 Minnesota case, electric shock treatments that served a legitimate purpose were not considered cruel and unusual punishment.[41]

§ 11.8.2 — Is Corporal Punishment Rational?

Advocates of corporal punishment maintain that, in order to enforce prison discipline, it is necessary to punish past offenders, hopefully deterring future rule infractions. However, the harmful effects of such treatment may well outweigh any of its supposed benefits. The possible psychological effects of inhumane punishment have been described as follows:[42]

> [M]ethods of discipline have a profound effect on the offender in regard to his mental and social attitudes both within the prison and after release. This is particularly evident in the case of first offenders, in whom permanent attitudes are often established which make for later social success or for a continued life of crime. The consequences of discipline are also grave in their effect on the mental conditions of offenders, leading them often into the so-called "prison neurosis" if unfavorable, or leading to constructive modification of personality if constructively administered.

Prison authorities have also recognized the futility of corporal punishment. The American Correctional Association has stated unequivocally that "corporal punishment should never be used under any circumstances."[43] In justifying this position, the Association commented:

> Punishments out of all proportion to the offense, employing inhumane and archaic methods and dictated by brutality coupled with ignorance, incompetence, fear and weakness, are demoralizing both to prisoners and staff. Staff punishments substantially increase the chances that the prisoners will continue to be disciplinary problems in the institution and will return to crime after release.[44]

James V. Bennett, Director of Federal Prisons from 1937 to 1964, testified during the trial of *Jackson v. Bishop* that whipping and other forms of corporal punishment were "brutal and medieval and did no real good."[45]

§ 11.8.3 — Judicial Treatment of Corporal Punishment

Until the late 1960s, cases could be found that held that corporal punishment was not cruel and unusual punishment. In *United States v. Jones*,[46] the director of a Florida convict camp was charged with deprivation of the civil rights of several prisoners, whom he allegedly assaulted and whipped. The district court, relying strongly on the proposition that the administration of state penal institutions was a matter of exclusive state jurisdiction, held that a prisoner has no constitutional right to be free from corporal punishment. The court further stated that, although Florida law prohibited the use of corporal punishment, the law was based "on principles of Christianity and humanity" and not on the United States Constitution, thereby intimating that the use of corporal punishment could be reestablished by the Florida legislature at any time.

State v. Cannon[47] involved the constitutionality of a Delaware law that prescribed whipping as a form of punishment for specified crimes. Discussing the validity of whipping in light of the state constitution's ban on cruel and unusual punishment, the court reasoned that because whipping had been permitted in the state since 1719, while other forms of punishment that had formerly been used, such as burning at the stake, had been eliminated by the state legislature, it must be presumed that whipping was not considered cruel by the people of Delaware. Any change, the court declared, must come from the state legislature. As for the Eighth Amendment to the United States Constitution, the court said that it could not find a single case as of that time in which a court had held, as a matter of federal constitutional law, that whipping violates the Eighth Amendment.

State v. Cannon was decided in 1963; in 1968, however, the United States Court of Appeals for the Eighth Circuit held, in the case of *Jackson v. Bishop*,[48] that whipping as a means of enforcing prison discipline did violate the Eighth and Fourteenth Amendments. The court stated that the prohibition against cruel and unusual punishment could not be defined exactly, but that "the applicable standards are flexible . . . and that broad and idealistic concepts of dignity, civilized standards, humanity, and decency are useful and usable."[49] Using these criteria, the court held whipping to be cruel and unusual punishment for the following reasons:

(1) We are not convinced that any rule or regulation as to the use of the strap, however seriously or sincerely conceived and drawn, will successfully prevent abuse . . . . (2) Rules in this area often seem to go unobserved . . . . (3) Regulations are easily circumvented . . . . (4) Corporal punishment is easily subject to abuse in the hands of the sadistic and unscrupulous. (5) Where power to punish is granted to persons in lower levels of administrative authority, there is an inherent and natural difficulty in enforcing the limitations of that power. (6) There can be no argument that excessive whipping or an inappropriate manner of whipping or too great

frequency of whipping or the use of studded or overlong straps all constitute cruel and unusual punishment. But if whipping were to be authorized, how does one, or any court, ascertain the point which would distinguish the permissible from that which is cruel and unusual? (7) Corporal punishment generates hate toward the keepers who punish and toward the system which permits it. It is degrading to the punisher and to the punished alike. It frustrates correctional and rehabilitative goals . . . . (8) Whipping creates other penological problems and makes adjustment to society more difficult. (9) Public opinion is obviously adverse. Counsel concede that only two states still permit the use of the strap.[50]

The reasoning of *Jackson v. Bishop* in eliminating corporal punishment has been consistently followed in judicial decisions, statutes, and administrative rulings in this country. Any attempt to revive the practice, at this time, would face serious, if not insurmountable constitutional challenges. Also significant is the fact that the opinion in *Jackson v. Bishop* was written by then-Judge Blackmun, who later became a member of the United States Supreme Court.

The Supreme Court continues to find state systems violating the most basic standards of decency. In *Hope v. Pelzer*,[51] an Alabama prisoner was twice handcuffed to a hitching post for disruptive conduct. In the first incident, during a two-hour period, the prisoner was offered drinking water and a bathroom break every 15 minutes, and his responses were recorded on an activity log. He was handcuffed above shoulder height, and when he tried moving his arms to improve circulation, the handcuffs cut into his wrists, causing pain and discomfort. In the second incident, after an altercation with a guard at his chain gang's worksite, the prisoner was subdued, handcuffed, placed in leg irons, and transported back to the prison, where he was ordered to take off his shirt, and spent seven hours in the sun handcuffed to the hitching post. During this seven-hour period, he was given one or two water breaks but no bathroom breaks, and a guard taunted him about his thirst.

According to the Court, these facts established Eighth Amendment violations. Among the unnecessary and wanton inflictions of pain constituting cruel and unusual punishment are those that are totally without penological justification. This determination is made in the prison context by ascertaining whether an official acted with deliberate indifference to the prisoner's health or safety, a state of mind that can be inferred from the fact that the risk of harm is obvious. Here, the Eighth Amendment violation was obvious. Any safety concerns had long since abated by the time the prisoner was handcuffed to the hitching post because he had already been subdued, handcuffed, placed in leg irons, and transported back to prison. He was separated from his work squad and not given the opportunity to return. Despite the clear lack of an emergency, prison officials knowingly subjected him to a substantial risk of physical harm, unnecessary pain, unnecessary exposure to the sun, prolonged thirst, and taunting, and a deprivation of bathroom breaks that created a risk of particular discomfort and humiliation.[52]

§ 11.8.4   — Alternatives to Corporal Punishment

Prison officials must have methods of punishing violations of prison rules and regulations. As previously stated, some prison administrators would like to include the use of corporal punishment among their possible methods of enforcing discipline. However, numerous other punishments may be employed, none of which involves the infliction of physical pain, and thus these punishments may be more effective both in maintaining discipline and in rehabilitating the prisoner.

§ 11.9   Conclusion

In recognizing that prisons do not house the most docile or easily governed persons, courts will allow the use of reasonable force by prison officials in five situations: self-defense, defense of third persons, enforcement of prison rules and regulations, prevention of escape, and prevention of crime. The test of reasonableness is whether the force is reasonable and necessary under the facts and circumstances of the particular case.

Unreasonable corporal punishment to enforce prison discipline is considered cruel and unusual punishment, prohibited by the Eighth Amendment. Prison officials who attempt to revive the use of corporal punishment may find themselves facing criminal and civil actions. To avoid criminal and civil liability, prison officials should refrain from corporal punishment and seek alternative methods of prisoner control.

Notes

1 Johnson v. Glick, 481 F.2d 1028, 1032–1033 (2d Cir.), *cert. denied*, 414 U.S. 1033 (1973).
2 490 U.S. 386 (1989).
3 42 U.S.C. § 1983; *see* Chapter 15.
4 *See* Bella v. Chamberlain, 24 F.3d 1251, 1257 (10th Cir. 1994) ("Without deciding the issue, we assume that excessive force claims arising outside the context of a seizure still may be analyzed under substantive due process principles."), *cert. denied*, 513 U.S. 1109 (1995); Wilson v. Northcutt, 987 F.2d 719, 722 (11th Cir. 1993) (holding, as a matter of first impression in the circuit, that a Fourteenth Amendment excessive force claim survives Graham when there is no seizure); Landol-Rivera v. Cruz Cosme, 906 F.2d 791, 796 (1st Cir. 1990) ("We assume that claims of excessive force outside the context of a seizure still may be analyzed under substantive due process principles."); Braley v. City of Pontiac, 906 F.2d 220, 225 n.5 (6th Cir. 1990) (noting that Graham "calls into question the continued existence of this 'species' of substantive due process, at least insofar as it exists apart from any specific of the Bill of Rights"); Pleasant v. Zamieski, 895 F.2d 272, 276 n.2 (6th Cir.) (despite Graham's broad phrasing, presumably substantive due process analysis is preserved for nonseizure excessive force claims), *cert. denied*, 498 U.S. 851 (1990).
5 475 U.S. 312 (1986).
6 501 U.S. 294 (1991).

7   Estelle v. Gamble, 429 U.S. 97 (1976).

8   Hudson v. McMillian, 503 U.S. 1 (1992). *See* Chapter 8, which specifically addresses conditions-of-confinement issues.

9   559 U.S. 34 (2010).

10   Valencia v. Wiggins, 981 F.2d 1440 (5th Cir. 1993).

11   Bell v. Wolfish, 441 U.S. 520 (1979).

12   Graham v. Connor, 490 U.S. 386 (1989).

13   Whitley v. Albers, 475 U.S. 312 (1986).

14   Hudson v. Palmer, 468 U.S. 517 (1984).

15   576 U.S. 389 (2015).

16   Tate v. Kassulke, 409 F. Supp. 651 (W.D. Ky. 1976).

17   Suits v. Lynch, 437 F. Supp. 38 (D. Kan. 1977).

18   Ridley v. Leavitt, 631 F.2d 358 (4th Cir. 1980); Spain v. Procunier, 600 F.2d 189 (9th Cir. 1979).

19   Jackson v. Allen, 376 F. Supp. 1393 (E.D. Ark. 1974).

20   Green v. Hawkins (Unreported, D. Md. 1977).

21   Inmates of Attica Correctional Facility v. Rockefeller, 453 F.2d 12 (2d Cir. 1971); *see also* George v. Evans, 633 F.2d 413 (5th Cir. 1980) (use of undue force by a prison guard against a prisoner is actionable as a deprivation of due process).

22   Inmates of Attica Correctional Facility v. Rockefeller, *supra* at 18–19.

23   Harrah v. Leverette, 271 S.W.2d 322 (W. Va. 1980).

24   O'Neal v. Evans, 496 F. Supp. 867 (S.D. Ga. 1980); Barnard v. State, 265 N.W.2d 620 (Iowa 1978); Woodhouse v. Virginia, 487 F.2d 889 (4th Cir. 1973); Wilson v. City of Kotzebue, 627 P. 2d 623 (Alaska 1981); Leonardo v. Moran, 611 F.2d 397 (1st Cir. 1979).

25   481 F.2d 1028 (2d Cir. 1973).

26   *Id.* at 1033.

27   Jackson v. Allen, 376 F. Supp. 1393 (E.D. Ark. 1974).

28   *See* OHIO REV. CODE § 5145.04 (Anderson 1996).

29   *See* State v. Taylor, 9 Ariz. App. 290, 451 P. 2d 648 (1969). The use of deadly force to prevent the escape of all felony suspects, whatever the circumstances, is constitutionally unreasonable. The broad common law rule has been rejected. Where a law enforcement officer has probable cause to believe that the suspect poses a threat of serious physical harm, either to the officer or to others, it is not constitutionally unreasonable to prevent an escape by the use of deadly force. If the suspect threatens the officer with a weapon or there is probable cause to believe that the suspect has committed a crime involving the infliction or threatened infliction of serious physical harm, deadly force may be used as necessary to prevent escape and, where feasible, some warning has been given. Because this case involved a fleeing burglary suspect, it is not directly applicable to prisoners going "over the wall." The law remains unclear. Tennessee v. Garner, 471 U.S. 1 (1985).

30   6 C.J.S. ARREST 13b (1937).

31   *See* State v. Jones, 211 S.C. 300, 44 S.E.2d 841 (1947).

32   *See* PA. STAT. ANN. tit. 18 § 4309 (Supp. 1972); WASH. REV. CODE Cpt. 9.31.010 (1961); MODEL PENAL CODE § 242.6 (Proposed Official Draft, 1962).

33   866 F.2d 657 (3d Cir. 1989).

34   *See* Tennessee v. Garner, 471 U.S. 1 (1985).

35   *See, e.g.,* CAL. PENAL CODE Title 16 § 673.

36   108 F. Supp. 266, 270 (S.D. Fla. 1952), *rev'd on other grounds*, 207 F.2d 785 (5th Cir. 1953).

37   State v. Revis, 193 N.C. 192, 136 S.E. 346 (1927). In 1955, however, North Carolina enacted a statute forbidding the use of corporal punishment on any prisoner. Cpt. 48, Art. 2, N.C. GEN. STAT. § 148–20 (1964).

38   55 Del. 587, 190 A.2d 514 (1963).

39   247 F. Supp. 683 (E.D. Ark. 1965).

40   State v. Carpenter, 231 N.C. 229, 56 S.E.2d 713 (1949).

41 Price v. Sheppard, 239 N.W.2d 905 (Minn. 1976).

42 J. WILSON & M. PESCOR, PROBLEMS IN PRISON PSYCHIATRY 226 (1939).

43 AMERICAN CORRECTIONAL ASSOCIATION, A MANUAL OF CORRECTIONAL STANDARDS 417 (3d ed. 1966). *See also* NATIONAL ADVISORY COMMISSION ON CRIMINAL JUSTICE STANDARDS AND GOALS, STANDARD 2.4 (1973) in Appendix.

44 *Id.*

45 Jackson v. Bishop, 268 F. Supp. 804, 813 (E.D. Ark. 1967), *aff'd*, 404 F.2d 571 (8th Cir. 1968).

46 108 F. Supp. 266 (S.D. Fla. 1952), *rev'd on other grounds*, 207 F.2d 785 (5th Cir. 1953).

47 55 Del. 587, 190 A.2d 514 (1963).

48 404 F.2d 571 (8th Cir. 1968).

49 *Id.* at 579.

50 *Id.* at 579–580.

51 536 U.S. 730 (2002).

52 Hope v. Pelzer, 536 U.S. 730 (2002).

The Death Penalty 12

Chapter Outline

§ 12.1   Introduction

The areas of prisoner complaints that have been most frequently litigated by the courts in recent years were discussed in the prior chapters. This chapter focuses on an issue that is faced less frequently by the judiciary (at least recently) but is nevertheless of importance to both prisoners and prison administrators, as well as to society as a whole: the death penalty.

§ 12.2   The Eighth Amendment and Due Process

Though the Supreme Court has never declared the death penalty itself unconstitutional, a number of cases have attacked capital punishment on constitutional grounds. Most of these cases have claimed that the death penalty violates the Eighth Amendment's prohibition against cruel and unusual punishments. The language derives from the English Bill of Rights of 1689, which states that "excessive bail ought not to be required, nor excessive fines imposed, nor cruel and unusual punishments inflicted."[1] The proscription of cruel and unusual punishments has been attributed to reaction to barbaric, torturous punishments imposed by the Stuarts[2] and to illegal punishments (such as defrocking) imposed by the King's Bench. Either way, "there is no doubt whatever that in borrowing the language and including it in the Eighth Amendment, our Founding Fathers intended to outlaw torture and other cruel punishments."[3] The clause has historically been interpreted to forbid such "punishments of torture" as disembowelment, beheading, quartering, burning at the stake, and breaking at the wheel.[4]

The Supreme Court, in its landmark 5–4 decision in *Furman v. Georgia*[5] held, in the cases under review, that the death penalty amounted to cruel and unusual punishment because it was imposed in an arbitrary manner. Only two justices held that the death penalty amounted to cruel and unusual punishment in all cases. Because each member of the Court wrote a separate opinion, the exact effect of the *Furman* decision upon the constitutionality of the death penalty as such was uncertain. The focus of the opinions holding the statute in question unconstitutional was that standard-less capital sentencing discretion, whether vested in a judge or a jury, allowed the imposition of this most irrevocable of all legal sanctions to be freakish or discriminatory.

In apparent response to the *Furman* decision, the majority of states enacted modified death penalty statutes. Some of the new statutes attempted to comply with *Furman* by complete elimination of capital sentencing discretion. These statutes specified mandatory death sentences for certain crimes. Other new statutes sought to fulfill *Furman*'s requirement of nondiscriminatory, reasoned capital sentencing by stringent specification of standards within which capital sentencing discretion must be exercised.

After careful selection of representative capital sentencing statutes, the Supreme Court decided five death penalty cases on July 2, 1976. In *Gregg v. Georgia*,[6] the Court analyzed the perennial argument that the death penalty amounts to cruel and unusual punishment in all cases. Rejecting this argument, Justice Stewart stated that the existence of capital punishment was accepted by the Framers of the Constitution and that the Supreme Court has recognized for nearly two centuries that capital punishment for the crime of murder is not invalid per se. The *Gregg* case involved a double murder during an armed robbery. The new Georgia capital sentencing statute requires a two-part trial: a guilt stage and a penalty stage. The Georgia statute provides for jury sentencing, with instructions from the judge. Jury sentencing is considered desirable in capital cases in order to maintain a link between contemporary community values and the penal system—a link without which the determination of punishment could hardly reflect the evolving standards of decency that mark the progress of a maturing society. When it is considering whether to sentence a prisoner to life imprisonment or death, a Georgia jury must consider mitigating and aggravating circumstances of the crime and the criminal. The jury's attention is directed to the specific circumstances of the crime.

Was it committed in the course of another capital felony? Was it committed for money? Was it committed upon a peace officer or judicial officer? Was it committed in a particularly heinous way or in a manner that endangered the lives of many people? In addition, the jury's attention is focused on the characteristics of the person who committed the crime: Does he have a record of prior convictions for capital offenses? Are there any special facts about this defendant that mitigate against imposing capital punishment (e.g., youth, the extent of cooperation with the police, emotional state at the time of the crime)?[7]

An automatic review of each death sentence by the Georgia Supreme Court is provided to standardize capital sentencing statewide. Such standardization is to be achieved by a comparison, on a case-by-case basis by the Georgia Supreme Court, of each new death sentence with sentences imposed on similarly situated defendants. The Georgia Supreme Court can reduce such sentences. In *Gregg*, for example, the court vacated a death sentence imposed for the armed robbery alone because the death penalty had rarely been imposed in Georgia for that offense.

Many states have implemented the Georgia procedures approved by the Supreme Court in *Gregg*: a bifurcated trial where guilt and sentence are determined at different stages, the jury's weighing of mitigating and aggravating circumstances, and automatic review or appeal.

The other four death sentence cases that the U.S. Supreme Court decided in July 1976 were *Proffitt v. Florida*,[8] *Jurek v. Texas*,[9] *Woodson v. North Carolina*,[10] and *Roberts v. Louisiana*.[11] These cases presented statutory variations on the theme of the Georgia statute, i.e., elimination of standard-less capital sentencing discretion. The Supreme Court affirmed the Florida and Texas cases and reversed the North Carolina and Louisiana cases.

The Florida capital sentencing statute approved by the Court in *Proffitt* vests capital sentencing discretion in its trial judges, who are given specific and detailed guidance to assist them in deciding whether to impose the death penalty or life imprisonment.[12] Capital cases are also two-part proceedings in Florida. Juries make advisory sentence recommendations by majority vote in the penalty stage. The trial judge must justify the imposition of the death penalty with written findings. Such written findings encourage the meaningful appellate review mandated by the statute. Trial judges are directed to weigh eight specific aggravating factors against seven justified mitigating factors to determine whether the death penalty will be imposed. This determination requires the trial judge to focus on the circumstances of the crime and the character of the convict.

In *Jurek v. Texas*,[13] a statutory scheme that is somewhat more mechanical than those upheld in *Gregg* and *Proffitt* was also upheld. Texas mandated two-part proceedings, and its juries are the actual sentencing authorities because, depending upon the jury's response to specific statutorily mandated questions, the trial judge imposes the single statutory sanction available. As Texas narrows its capital offense category, it implicitly requires its juries to find the existence of a statutory aggravating circumstance before the death penalty can be imposed. Although mitigating circumstances are not explicitly mentioned in the statute, Texas courts have construed the statute to allow juries to consider such evidence.[14] The Texas capital sentencing statute guides and focuses the jury's objective consideration of the specific circumstances of the individual offender and offense. Thus, it fulfills *Furman*'s requirement for guided discretion.

In *Woodson v. North Carolina*[15] and *Roberts v. Louisiana*,[16] the death penalty statutes of North Carolina and Louisiana were declared unconstitutional. Rather than establishing specific standards as Georgia, Florida, and Texas had, North Carolina and Louisiana tried to completely eliminate all capital sentencing discretion. To this end, they adopted mandatory capital sentencing. Historically, they were on firm ground because all the states had mandatory death sentences for specified offenses at the time of the adoption of the Eighth Amendment in 1791.

However, the Supreme Court concluded that the two crucial indicators of evolving standards of decency with respect to the imposition of punishment in our society—jury determinations and legislative enactments—conclusively point to present-day repudiation of automatic death sentences. Additionally, both the North Carolina and Louisiana statutes fall within *Furman*'s prohibition against standard-less discretion in that each merely pushes unfettered sentencing discretion into the guilt determination stage of the proceeding. The difference between the North Carolina and Louisiana statutes lies in the somewhat narrower definition of capital murder under Louisiana law.[17] In addition, Louisiana's subsequent attempt to cure the defects found in *Roberts* by narrowing the scope of mandatory capital punishment to include only cases in which the victim is a murdered police officer was similarly rejected by the Supreme Court.[18]

§ 12.2.1   – Capital Punishment Under State Constitutions

Affirmation of the constitutionality of capital punishment by the Supreme Court in *Gregg* and its related cases does not, however, resolve this issue. Other considerations must be noted. One of these considerations is the status of capital punishment under state constitutions.

In *Commonwealth v. O'Neal*,[19] the Massachusetts Supreme Judicial Court concluded that a Massachusetts statute that provided for the death penalty for a convicted rapist-murderer was unconstitutional under the Massachusetts state constitution. The major focus of this decision was that the state's imposition of capital punishment is the least compelling means available to attain its legitimate goal of public safety. This argument was specifically rejected by the Supreme Court in *Gregg v. Georgia*, but because of the vagaries of our federal system of government, it is not binding upon a state's interpretation of its own constitution. This case points out the basically minimal nature of United States Supreme Court decisions—in many areas, the minimum a state must do is mandated through the federal courts. A state is free to adopt standards higher than the federal standard if it wishes. As a result of the *O'Neal* decision, Massachusetts has ended capital punishment, regardless of the latitude that was bestowed upon all the states in the *Gregg* decision.

Another example of higher state standards is *People v. Anderson*.[20] In that case, the California Supreme Court declared its state capital punishment statute to be unconstitutional. The basis of that decision was the existence of the disjunctive "or" rather than the conjunctive "and" in the California constitution's equivalent of the federal constitution's Eighth Amendment prohibition against "cruel and unusual punishment." California's phrase reads "cruel or unusual punishment." The California Supreme Court concluded that infrequent imposition of the death penalty equals unusual punishment and struck down its use completely. The opinion noted that public acceptance of capital punishment is a relevant, but not controlling factor in any assessment of whether it is consonant with contemporary standards of decency. However, the California court readily acknowledged the distribution of political clout when it enforced the new capital punishment statute enacted in California following a statewide referendum on whether the death penalty should be used in California.[21]

§ 12.2.2   – Mitigating and Aggravating Circumstances

Since 1976, the Supreme Court has spent considerable time attempting to determine the constitutional parameters of mitigating and aggravating circumstances as utilized by the various states in the determination of whether to impose capital punishment in a particular case. In *Lockett v. Ohio*,[22] the Supreme Court held that a statute that provided too limited a range of mitigating circumstances is unconstitutional. The Court established in *Lockett* that only rarely should the sentencing authority be precluded from considering "any" mitigating factors relative to the defendant's character or the circumstances of the offense. In *Eddings v. Oklahoma*,[23] the Supreme Court vacated the death sentence of a convicted murderer by applying the rule established in *Lockett*. In *Eddings*, the Court explicitly noted that a state may not by statute preclude the sentencing authority from considering any mitigating factor. The Supreme Court continues to define "mitigating evidence."

In a capital murder case, the defendant presented as mitigating evidence his own testimony and that of his former wife, his mother, his sister, and his grandmother. He then sought to introduce testimony of two jailers and a "regular visitor" to the effect that he had "made a good adjustment" during the seven and one-half months he had spent in jail between his arrest and trial. The trial court ruled such evidence irrelevant and inadmissible, and the defendant was sentenced to death. The Supreme Court reversed and held that the trial court's exclusion of the testimony of the jailers and the visitor from the sentencing hearing denied the defendant his right to place before the sentencing jury all relevant evidence in mitigation of punishment.[24]

In another case, the trial judge instructed the advisory jury not to consider, and himself refused to consider, evidence of mitigating circumstances not specifically enumerated in the state's death penalty statute. The Supreme Court reversed and held that this procedure was inconsistent with the requirement that the sentencing authority may neither refuse to consider nor be precluded from considering any relevant mitigating evidence.[25]

While serving a life sentence without the possibility of parole for a first-degree murder conviction, a prisoner was sentenced to death for the murder of a fellow prisoner. Under Nevada statute, the death penalty was mandated in these circumstances. The Supreme Court held that under the individualized capital sentencing doctrine, it is constitutionally required that the sentencing authority consider, as a mitigating factor, any aspect of the defendant's character or record and any of the circumstances of the particular offense. Consequently, a statute that mandates the death penalty for a prisoner who is convicted of murder while serving a life sentence without possibility of parole, violates the Eighth and Fourteenth Amendments.[26]

Decisions related to aggravating factors tend to focus on the content rather than the presence or absence of statutory provisions. In *Godfrey v. Georgia*,[27] the Supreme Court held that aggravating factors may be so vague that a sentencing authority may have so much discretion as to give rise to a standard-less imposition of the death penalty, which the United States Supreme Court specifically rejected as unconstitutional in *Furman v. Georgia*.

§ 12.2.3   – The Death Penalty for Crimes Other Than Murder

In *Gregg*, the Supreme Court specifically noted that it was not deciding whether states could or could not allow death sentences in cases that do not involve murder of the victim, such as rape, kidnapping, and armed robbery. However, since 1976 the Court has begun to address this issue and has demonstrated a general reluctance to uphold the imposition of capital punishment when, although convicted of a serious crime, the defendant has not taken the life of another. By way of example, in *Coker v. Georgia*[28] the Court held that Georgia's death penalty statute was unconstitutional as applied to a defendant who, although guilty of rape, had not killed the victim. This position was modified somewhat in *Enmund v. Florida*,[29] where the Court refused to permit the death penalty to be imposed on a so-called nontriggerman in a felony-murder conviction. However, the Supreme Court carefully noted that its decision did not establish a requirement that imposition of the death penalty mandates that the defendant be the actual killer; rather, the trial court's reversible error was its refusal during sentencing to consider the defendant's lack of intent that the killings occur.

In 1987, the Supreme Court held that although two brothers neither intended to kill the victims nor inflicted the fatal wounds, the record supported a finding that they had the culpable mental state of reckless indifference to human life. Consequently, the Eighth Amendment did not prohibit the death penalty as disproportionate in the case of a defendant whose participation in a felony that results in murder is major and whose mental state is one of reckless indifference. A survey of state felony-murder laws and judicial decisions after *Enmund* indicated societal consensus that a combination of factors may justify the death penalty even without a specific "intent to kill." Reckless disregard for human life also represents a highly culpable mental state that may support a capital sentencing judgment in combination with major participation in the felony resulting in death.[30]

In a 2008 case, *Kennedy v. Louisiana*,[31] the Court effectively ruled that the death penalty can only be valid in cases that result in the death of a victim. Here, Kennedy was charged with the aggravated rape of his 8-year-old stepdaughter; he was convicted and sentenced to death under a state statute that authorized capital punishment for the rape of a child under 12. The Supreme Court held that, though child rape is an especially heinous crime, the Eighth Amendment bars the imposition of the death penalty for the rape of a child where the crime did not result in the victim's death. In reaching this decision, the Court relied in part on the "evolving standards of decency" test discussed in the next section.

§ 12.2.4   – Evolving Standards of Decency

Another consideration that should enter into any discussion of capital punishment after *Gregg* is the effect of ethical evolution. One of the primary supports for *Gregg* is the United States Supreme Court's assessment of the level of decency in the states. Several states do not authorize capital punishment under their internal laws. If these states ever become the majority, the Supreme Court may reconsider the holding of *Gregg* so as to better reflect the needs of a maturing society.

When examining claims of Eighth Amendment violations, including death penalty cases, courts employ the "evolving standards of decency" test. In the 1958 Supreme Court case *Trop v. Dulles*,[32] Chief Justice Warren stated that the Eighth Amendment's ban on cruel and unusual punishment "must draw its meaning from the evolving standards of decency that mark the progress of a maturing society." The idea is that what society considers decent and just is not static; rather, it evolves over time. As such, courts should use this evolving standard when determining whether a specific action violates the Eighth Amendment. The Supreme Court has used the evolving standards of decency test in a number of death penalty cases. Some of these cases are discussed next, and others are presented in Chapter 14.

§ 12.3 The Death Sentence — Racial Discrimination

In *McCleskey v. Kemp*,[33] a black man was convicted in Georgia of armed robbery and the murder of a white police officer. He filed a habeas corpus petition in federal court claiming that the Georgia capital sentencing process was racially discriminatory in violation of the Eighth and Fourteenth Amendments. To support his claim, he offered a statistical study of over 2,000 murder cases in Georgia in the 1970s that showed a disparity in the imposition of the death sentence in Georgia based on the murder victim's race. Specifically, the study showed that black defendants who killed white victims had the greatest likelihood of receiving the death penalty. On appeal, the Supreme Court held that the statistical study did not establish that the administration of the Georgia capital punishment system violates the Fourteenth Amendment's Equal Protection Clause. "To prevail under that Clause, petitioner must prove that the decision makers in *his* case acted with discriminatory purpose. Petitioner offered no evidence specific to his own case that would support an inference that racial considerations played a part in his sentence."[34]

In the 1986 case of *Batson v. Kentucky*[35] the Supreme Court established a three-step process for evaluating a state criminal defendant's claim that a prosecutor, in selecting a jury, had used a peremptory challenge in violation of the Equal Protection Clause. To succeed under *Batson*, three factors must exist: (1) The defendant must make a prima facie showing that the peremptory challenge was exercised on the basis of race. (2) If that showing is made, then the prosecutor must offer a race-neutral basis for striking the juror in question. (3) Then, in light of the parties' submissions, the trial court must determine whether the defendant has shown purposeful discrimination.

The *Batson* ruling was applied to death-eligible cases in the 2005 Supreme Court case *Miller-El v. Dretke*.[36] A black defendant was convicted in state court of murder and sentenced to death. The prosecution used peremptory challenges to exclude black jurors. The prosecution alleged that although 10 of 11 black venire panelists were peremptorily struck, the strikes were based on the jurors' ambivalence or opposition to the death penalty. The Supreme Court reversed. The cumulative evidence of prosecution tactics clearly raised the inference that the strikes were discriminatory and that happenstance was unlikely to produce the disparity shown by the substantial percentage of black jurors who were struck, especially where white jurors with comparable views were not challenged. The prosecutors made race-based peremptory strikes of potential jurors. The prisoner was therefore granted relief in habeas corpus.

§ 12.4 The Death Sentence — Mentally Impaired Defendants

In 2002, the Supreme Court in *Atkins v. Virginia*[37] held that executions of "mentally retarded" criminals are cruel and unusual punishments prohibited by the Eighth Amendment. The Court's rationale was that "because of their disabilities in areas of reasoning, judgment, and control of their impulses, [mentally retarded] criminals do not act with the level of moral culpability that characterizes the most serious adult criminal conduct. Moreover, their impairments can jeopardize the reliability and fairness of capital proceedings against mentally retarded defendants." The Court concluded that "no legitimate penological purpose is served by executing the intellectually disabled."

In *Hall v. Florida*,[38] Hall was on death row for a rape and murder that he committed in 1978. After the Supreme Court's ruling in *Atkins*, Hall petitioned a Florida state court to vacate his sentence, presenting evidence that he had an IQ of 71. The state court denied his motion because a Florida statute required an IQ score of 70 or below to be considered intellectually disabled (and thus ineligible for the death penalty under *Atkins*). On appeal, the U.S. Supreme Court held that Florida's threshold requirement of a 70 IQ score was unconstitutional. According to the majority in *Hall*, the Florida threshold disregarded established medical practice in two ways: (1) it takes an IQ score as final and conclusive evidence of a defendant's intellectual capacity, when experts would consider other evidence, and (2) it relies on a purportedly scientific measurement of a defendant's abilities, while refusing to recognize that measurement's inherent imprecision." "When a defendant's IQ test score falls within the test's acknowledged and inherent margin of error [roughly five points], the defendant must be able to present additional evidence of intellectual disability, including testimony regarding adaptive deficits."[39]

§ 12.5   The Death Sentence — Juries

In *Witherspoon v. Illinois*,[40] an Illinois statute allowed prosecutors to dismiss potential jurors in death-eligible murder trials "who shall . . . state that he has conscientious scruples against capital punishment, or that he is opposed to the same." Under that statute, the prosecutor in Witherspoon's murder trial dismissed nearly half of the prospective jurors who expressed qualms about the death penalty. The Supreme Court upheld the statute, holding that "[n]either on the basis of the record in this case nor as a matter of judicial notice of presently available information can it be concluded that the exclusion of jurors opposed to capital punishment results in an unrepresentative jury on the issue of guilt or substantially increases the risk of conviction."

In *Booth v. Maryland*, the jury's imposition of a death sentence after considering a presentence report that included a victim impact statement violated the Eighth Amendment. The information contained in the victim impact statement was held to be irrelevant to a capital sentencing decision, and its admission creates a constitutionally unacceptable risk that the jury may impose the death penalty in an arbitrary and capricious manner.[41] However, four years later, in *Payne v. Tennessee*,[42] *Booth* was overruled. Victim impact statements may be used.

The prosecutor's closing argument at the sentencing phase in a death penalty case included his reading to the jury at length from a religious tract the victim was carrying and commenting on the personal qualities that the prosecutor inferred from the victim's possession of the religious tract and a voter registration card. The Supreme Court held that for purposes of imposing the death penalty, the defendant's punishment must be tailored to his personal responsibility and moral guilt. The prosecutor's comments concerned the victim's personal characteristics, and allowing the jury to rely on this information could result in imposing the death sentence because of factors about which the defendant was unaware and that were irrelevant to the decision to kill. The content of the religious tract and the voter registration card could not possibly have been relevant to the "circumstances of the crime." Where there was no evidence that the defendant read either the tract or the voter card, the content of the papers the victim was carrying was purely fortuitous and could not provide any information relevant to the respondent's moral culpability, notwithstanding that the papers had been admitted in evidence for other purposes. The death penalty was set aside.[43] However, as in *Booth*, *Gathers* was overruled four years later and is no longer valid authority.

In death penalty cases, the Supreme Court in *Jones v. United States*[44] held that the Eighth Amendment does not require that a jury be instructed as to the consequences of their failure to agree. In federal cases, the Federal Death Penalty Act requires judge sentencing when the jury, after retiring for deliberations, reports itself as unable to reach a unanimous verdict. In such a case, the sentencing duty falls upon the district court.[45] The Eighth Amendment, however, does not require that a jury be instructed as to the consequences of a breakdown in the deliberative process. Such an instruction has no bearing on the jury's role in the sentencing process. Moreover, the jury system's very object is to secure unanimity, and the government has a strong interest in having the jury express the conscience of the community on the ultimate life or death question. The Supreme Court declined to invoke its supervisory power over the federal courts and require that such an instruction be given in every capital case in these circumstances.

A few years later, in *Kelly v. South Carolina*,[46] the Court held that, to ensure a jury has full information before it before deciding cases of life or death, a defendant is entitled to a jury instruction that he would be ineligible for parole under a life sentence.[47]

A death row prisoner claimed on direct appeal that a Kansas statute established an unconstitutional presumption in favor of death by directing imposition of the death penalty when aggravating and mitigating circumstances are equal. Agreeing, the Kansas Supreme Court concluded that the statute weighing equation violated the Eighth and Fourteenth Amendments and remanded the case for a new trial. The United States Supreme Court reversed[48] and remanded the case on the basis that the Kansas statute was constitutional under the doctrine of *Walton v. Arizona*.[49] *Walton* held that a state death penalty statute may give the defendant the burden of proving that mitigating circumstances outweigh aggravating circumstances. It is also consistent with the Constitution to impose the death penalty when the state has proved beyond a reasonable doubt that mitigating factors do not outweigh aggravating factors, including when the two are in equipoise.

§ 12.6   Methods of Execution

The Supreme Court has rarely addressed whether particular methods of execution employed in this country are unconstitutionally cruel. Judicial hanging was last directly addressed by the Court in 1878, in *Wilkerson v. Utah*. The Court specifically distinguished between various punishments of torture and hanging, the traditional method of execution at common law.[50]

Decisions construing the Eighth Amendment focus on whether the sentence constitutes "one of 'those modes or acts of punishment that had been considered cruel and unusual at the time that the Bill of Rights was adopted'"[51] and on whether the punishment is contrary to "the evolving standards of decency that mark the progress of a maturing society."[52]

The Ninth Circuit applied these principles in a hanging case.[53] There was no dispute that execution by hanging was acceptable when the Bill of Rights was adopted.[54] To determine whether hanging is unconstitutionally cruel and unusual, the court looked to objective factors to the maximum extent possible.[55] Among these factors are statutes passed by society's elected representatives,[56] because there is a presumption that a punishment selected by a democratically elected legislature is constitutionally valid.[57]

The court did not consider hanging to be cruel and unusual simply because it causes death or because there may be some pain associated with death. "Punishments are cruel when they involve torture or a lingering death."[58] As used in the Constitution, "cruel" implies "something inhuman and barbarous, something more than the mere extinguishment of life."[59] "The cruelty against which the Constitution protects a convicted person is cruelty inherent in the method of punishment, not the necessary suffering involved in any method employed to extinguish life humanely."[60] A prisoner is entitled to an execution free only of "the unnecessary and wanton infliction of pain."[61]

§ 12.7   Habeas Corpus

Congress has placed limits on the rights of death row prisoners to file federal habeas corpus petitions under the Antiterrorism and Effective Death Penalty Act of 1996 (AEDPA).[62] The AEDPA sets a one-year limitation period for filing a state prisoner's federal habeas corpus petition, running from the date on which the judgment became final by the conclusion of direct review or the expiration of the time for seeking such review, but stops the one-year clock while a petitioner's properly filed application for state postconviction relief is pending. However in *Day v. McDonough*,[63] the Supreme Court held that under the precedents of the Eleventh Circuit, that tolling period does not include the 90 days in which a petitioner might have sought certiorari review challenging state court denial of postconviction relief. Further, the Supreme Court held that district courts are permitted but are not obligated to consider, *sua sponte*, the timeliness of a state prisoner's habeas petition.

Facing execution in Florida, a death row prisoner brought a federal action under § 1983 to enjoin a three-drug lethal injection procedure the state likely would use to execute him. On a procedural issue, the Supreme Court held in *Hill v. McDonough*[64] that because his claim was comparable in its essentials to the § 1983 action the Supreme Court had allowed to proceed in *Nelson v. Campbell*,[65] it did not have to be brought in habeas but could proceed under § 1983. The Eleventh Circuit had construed the action as a petition for a writ of habeas corpus and dismissed the case for noncompliance with the successive petition requirements. The Supreme Court reversed on this issue.

Rhines v. Weber[66] opened the door a bit on a prisoner's use of habeas corpus to prevent executions. Although the AEDPA did not deprive district courts of the authority to issue stays of execution, it did circumscribe their discretion. Thus, any solution to the limitations problem faced by habeas petitioners in cases involving exhausted and unexhausted claims had to be consistent with the AEDPA's purposes.

Prior to the enactment of the AEDPA, issues arose with respect to a state prisoner's filing a "mixed" federal habeas corpus petition containing some claims that had been exhausted in the state courts and some that the United States Supreme Court held that federal district courts could not adjudicate.

There was a "total exhaustion" requirement, and federal courts were obligated to effectuate that requirement by dismissing a mixed petition without prejudice and allowing such a prisoner to return to a state court to present the unexhausted claims to that court in the first instance.

The AEDPA preserved the total exhaustion requirement and imposed a general one-year limitation period on filing federal habeas corpus petitions. State prisoners who came to federal court with mixed petitions ran the risk of forever losing the opportunity for any federal review of their unexhausted claims. There was a disagreement among lower federal courts as to the use of a stay-and-abeyance procedure, under which a district court, when faced with a state prisoner's mixed petition, would stay the petition to allow the prisoner to present the unexhausted claims to a state court in the first instance and to return to federal court for review of the perfected petition. This approach was rejected in *Rhines*, where it was held that a district court has discretion to stay a mixed petition to allow a petitioner to present his unexhausted claims to the state court in the first instance and then to return to federal court for review of his perfected petition. The AEDPA does not deprive district courts of the authority to issue stays that are a proper exercise of their discretion, but it does circumscribe that discretion. Any solution to this problem must be compatible with the purposes of AEDPA. Staying a federal habeas petition frustrates AEDPA's objective of encouraging finality of state court judgments by allowing a petitioner to delay the resolution of the federal proceedings. It undermines AEDPA's goal of streamlining federal habeas proceedings by decreasing a petitioner's incentive to exhaust all his claims in state court before filing his federal petition.

According to *Rhines*, stay-and-abeyance should be available only in limited circumstances. Granting a stay effectively excuses a petitioner's failure to present his claims first to the state courts. Stay-and-abeyance is only appropriate when the district court determines there was good cause for the petitioner's failure to exhaust his or her claims. Even if good cause existed, the district court would abuse its discretion if it granted a stay when the unexhausted claims are plainly meritless. Where stay-and-abeyance is appropriate, the district court's discretion is still limited by AEDPA's timeliness concerns. If a district court does not place reasonable time limits on a petitioner's actions in state court, petitioners, especially capital petitioners, could frustrate AEDPA's finality goal by dragging out indefinitely their federal habeas review. If a petitioner engages in abusive litigation tactics or intentional delay, the district court should not grant a stay at all. However, it would be an abuse of discretion for a district court to deny a stay and dismiss a mixed petition if the petitioner had good cause for his or her failure to exhaust, if the unexhausted claims were potentially meritorious, and if there was no indication that he or she engaged in intentionally dilatory litigation tactics. Such a petitioner's interest in obtaining federal review of his claims outweighs the competing interests in finality and speedy resolution of federal petitions. For the same reason, if a court determines that stay-and-abeyance is inappropriate, it should allow the petitioner to delete the unexhausted claims and proceed with the exhausted ones, if dismissing the entire petition would unreasonably impair the petitioner's right to obtain federal relief.

In a 2013 Supreme Court case, *Ryan v. Gonzales*,[67] a death row inmate sought federal habeas corpus relief. His counsel moved to stay the proceedings, claiming that Gonzales's mental incompetence prevented him from rationally communicating with or assisting counsel. The Court held that 18 U.S.C. § 3599—which provides counsel for indigent defendants—does not provide a state prisoner a right to suspension of his federal habeas proceedings when he is adjudged incompetent.

§ 12.8　Conclusion

The constitutionality of capital punishment for the crime of murder has been firmly underscored. Certain types of capital sentencing statutes are necessary to constitutionally impose the death penalty, but the death penalty is not unconstitutional per se. The cases presented in this chapter do not encompass the entirety of capital punishment jurisprudence, but they do represent the most frequently litigated issues.

In the past few decades, the Supreme Court has ruled in a number of cases regarding the death penalty, and many more are probably on the horizon. Society's changing views regarding appropriate punishments for various populations, as well as the Court's use of the "evolving standards of decency" rule in determining Eighth Amendment violations, will likely lead to at least a few significant capital punishment cases in the near future.

Notes

1　*See* Furman v. Georgia, 408 U.S. 238, 243–244 (1972) (Douglas, J., concurring).
2　*See* Furman, 408 U.S. at 253–255 (Douglas, J., concurring).
3　Furman, 408 U.S. at 319 (Marshall, J., concurring).
4　Furman, 408 U.S. at 264–265 (Brennan, J., concurring) (quoting Wilkerson v. Utah, 99 U.S. 130, 135 (1878)).
5　408 U.S. 238 (1972).
6　428 U.S. 153 (1976).
7　*Id.*
8　428 U.S. 242 (1976).
9　428 U.S. 262 (1976).
10　428 U.S. 280 (1976).
11　428 U.S. 325 (1976).
12　Proffitt v. Florida, 428 U.S. 242 (1976).
13　428 U.S. 262 (1976).
14　*Id.* at 265.
15　428 U.S. 280 (1976).
16　428 U.S. 325 (1976).
17　Roberts v. Louisiana, 428 U.S. 325 (1976).
18　Roberts v. Louisiana, 431 U.S. 633 (1977).
19　339 N.E.2d 676 (Mass. 1975).
20　6 Cal. 3d 628, 493 P. 2d 880, *cert. denied*, 406 U.S. 958 (1976).
21　*See* Gregg v. Georgia, 428 U.S. 153 (1976).

22 438 U.S. 586 (1978).

23 455 U.S. 104 (1982).

24 Skipper v. South Carolina, 476 U.S. 1 (1986).

25 Hitchcock v. Dugger, 481 U.S. 393 (1987).

26 Sumner v. Nevada, 483 U.S. 66 (1987).

27 446 U.S. 420 (1980).

28 433 U.S. 584 (1977).

29 458 U.S. 782 (1982).

30 Tison v. Arizona, 481 U.S. 137 (1987).

31 554 U.S. 407 (2008).

32 356 U.S. 86 (1958).

33 481 U.S. 279 (1987).

34 *Id.*

35 476 U.S. 79 (1986).

36 545 U.S. 231 (2005).

37 536 U.S. 304 (2002).

38 572 U.S. 701 (2014).

39 *Id.*

40 391 U.S. 510 (1968).

41 Booth v. Maryland, 482 U.S. 496 (1987), *overruled by* Payne v. Tennessee, 501 U.S. 808 (1991).

42 501 U.S. 808 (1991).

43 South Carolina v. Gathers, 490 U.S. 805 (1989), *overruled by* Payne v. Tennessee, 501 U.S. 808 (1991).

44 527 U.S. 373 (1999).

45 Pursuant to 18 U.S.C. § 3594.

46 534 U.S. 246 (2002).

47 Kelly v. South Carolina, 534 U.S. 246 (2002).

48 Kansas v. Marsh, 548 U.S. 163 (2006).

49 497 U.S. 639 (1990).

50 Wilkerson v. Utah, 99 U.S. at 135–137; *see also* In re Kemmler, 136 U.S. 436 (1890) (upholding electrocution as method of execution); Louisiana ex rel. Francis v. Resweber, 329 U.S. 459, 464 (1947) (upholding second attempt at electrocution after first attempt failed to cause death); *but see* Glass v. Louisiana, 471 U.S. 1080 (1985) (Brennan, J., dissenting).

51 Stanford v. Kentucky, 492 U.S. 361 (1989) (quoting Ford v. Wainwright, 477 U.S. 399 (1986)).

52 Trop v. Dulles, 356 U.S. 86 (1958).

53 Campbell v. Wood, 18 F.3d 662 (9th Cir. 1994).

54 *See* Wilkerson, 99 U.S. at 133–134.

55 Stanford, 492 U.S. at 369 (quoting Coker v. Georgia, 433 U.S. 584 (1977) (plurality opinion)).

56 *Id.* at 370 (citing McCleskey v. Kemp, 481 U.S. 279 (1987)).

57 Gregg, 428 U.S. at 175.

58 In re Kemmler, 136 U.S. 436 (1890).

59 *Ibid.*

60 Resweber, 329 U.S. at 464 (1947).

61 Gregg v. Georgia, 428 U.S. 153 (1976) (plurality opinion).

62 28 U.S.C.S. § 2244(d)(1)(A).

63 547 U.S. 198 (2006).

64 Hill v. McDonough, 547 U.S. 573 (2006). *See also* Evans v. Chavis, 546 U.S. 189 (2006).

65 541 U.S. 637 (2004).

66 544 U.S. 269 (2005).

67 568 U.S. 57 (2013).

Parole and Probation   13

Chapter Outline

§ 13.1 Introduction

The term *parole* means a procedure by which a duly convicted defendant who has been sentenced to a term of imprisonment is allowed to serve the last portion of his or her sentence outside the prison walls, although he or she remains under supervision. The essence of parole is release from prison before the completion of one's sentence, on the condition that the parolee abide by certain rules during the balance of the sentence. It applies only to cases in which the convicted and sentenced defendant has served part of the imposed sentence in a correctional facility. It is a conditional release from confinement, contingent upon future conduct as set forth in the terms of the parole. The parolee is subject to future confinement for the unserved portion of his or her sentence in the event that he or she violates the provisions of parole.[1]

Parole was abolished by Congress for federal crimes committed after November 1, 1987. The Comprehensive Crime Control Act of 1984[2] created a United States Sentencing Commission to establish sentencing guidelines for the federal courts and established a regime of determinate sentences. Defendants sentenced for offenses committed on or after November 1, 1987, serve determinate terms under the sentencing guidelines and are not eligible for parole consideration. Postrelease supervision, termed "supervised release," is provided as a separate part of the sentence under the jurisdiction of the court. At least 16 states have abolished parole entirely, and a handful of others have abolished parole for certain offenses.

On the other hand, *probation* is a type of sentence in which an offender is allowed to remain free in the community subject to court-sanctioned conditions and under the supervision of a probation officer. Unlike parolees, probationers are sentenced directly to a term of community supervision; they do not spend time in a prison beforehand. Like parolees, however, probationers must abide by certain conditions; if any of the conditions are violated, the offender's probation may be revoked and the offender sent to prison.

In 2018, there were approximately 4.4 million people on probation and parole in the U.S., roughly double the amount of adults incarcerated in prisons and jails.[3]

§ 13.2 Parole is Not a Right

One of the primary purposes of parole is to aid prisoners in reintegrating into society as constructive individuals as soon as they are able, without being confined for the full term of the court-imposed sentence. Another purpose is to alleviate the costs to society of keeping prisoners in prison. In some states, parole is granted automatically after prisoners serve an established minimum prison term. In others, parole is granted or withheld by the discretionary action of a parole authority that bases its decision on information about a prisoner. In essence, the parole authority makes a prediction as to whether the prisoner is ready to return to society.

In *Greenholtz v. Prisoners of the Nebraska Penal and Correctional Complex*,[4] the Supreme Court held that there is no protected liberty interest in the possibility of parole before the termination of the sentence. Because there is no entitlement, due process hearings are not required by the state's parole system. States are not constitutionally required to establish a parole system; it is instead a discretionary decision of the state to determine when a prisoner is ready for release. The Court explained that the reason for not requiring due process standards is simply that a decision for the granting of parole is not the equivalent of a guilt determination, as in a criminal proceeding or in the revocation of parole.

In *Connecticut Board of Pardons v. Dumschat*,[5] a prisoner applied for commutation of his life sentence. His application was rejected without any explanation being given. Relying upon *Greenholtz*, the Supreme Court held that a prisoner has no constitutionally inherent right to commutation of a life sentence. The prisoner has nothing more than an expectation, as, for example, the expectation that he will not be transferred to another prison within the system. It is not a constitutional right but a unilateral hope. It was pointed out that the Connecticut statute at issue referred to the mere existence of a power to commute. There was no limit on what procedure was to be followed, what evidence could be considered, or what criteria were to be applied, all in contrast to the statute in *Greenholtz*, which created a right to parole under state law. However, this does not mean that the prisoner has no constitutional rights in the procedure used in granting or denying parole.

Statutes usually control the time at which specific groups of prisoners will become eligible for parole, if at all. The right to be considered at a parole hearing and the timing of the parole hearing are frequently within the sole discretion of the parole authority. However, in *Grasso v. Norton*,[6] the court held that a federal prisoner who is sentenced under a statute that permits parole eligibility consideration at any time is entitled to "effective and meaningful" parole consideration at or before the one-third point of the maximum sentence. This was required even though the prisoner was given an initial parole hearing when entering the prison. "Meaningful" consideration for parole was satisfied by a "file review" and did not require a personal interview.

Similarly, the paroling authority is given wide discretion in determining how the interview or hearing with the prisoner will be conducted. *Menechino v. Oswald*[7] summarized the rights of the prisoner at a parole hearing. The petitioner alleged that due process rights had been violated at his parole hearing. He claimed that the Constitution required that he be given: (1) notice;

(2) a fair hearing with right to counsel, cross-examination, and presentation of witnesses; and (3) specification of the reasons used by the parole authority in its determination. The court denied that the prisoner had any due process rights at his parole hearing. It asserted that many of the essential conditions necessary for the application of due process standards are absent in the context of a parole hearing.

First, the proceeding is nonadversarial in nature. Both parties (the parole authority and the prisoner) have the same concern—rehabilitation. Second, the primary function of the hearing is not fact-finding. On the contrary, the parole authority is making a determination based upon numerous tangible and intangible factors. Third, the prisoner has no present private interest to be protected, as is required before the Due Process Clause is applicable.

The wide discretion given to the paroling authority is limited, however. Written reasons for the denial of parole must be given to the prisoner. In *United States ex rel. Johnson v. Chairman, New York State Board of Parole*,[8] the court stated that the Due Process Clause of the Fourteenth Amendment requires the parole board to provide a written statement of reasons to the prisoner when parole is denied. This conclusion is consistent with *Menechino*, which held only that a prisoner was not entitled to a specification of charges, counsel, and cross-examination.

The purpose of requiring written reasons for the denial of parole is to provide the courts with a record upon which to determine whether the actions of the Parole Board have been "arbitrary and capricious"—a standard of judicial review of administrative acts. The reason for denial that has been attacked most often is "release at this time would depreciate the seriousness of the offense." Although many courts still recognize the broad discretion vested in the paroling authority,[9] courts have held that something more than a general reason for the denial of parole is required.[10] Denial of parole based in general language and not specifically addressed to the prisoner's personal situation may amount to no reason at all and does not protect the prisoner from arbitrary and capricious action by the parole board.

The Parole Commission and Reorganization Act, applicable to federal prisoners, was repealed as of 1992 by the Sentencing Reform Act of 1994[11] which, among other things, created the United States Sentencing Commission[12] as an independent body in the Judicial Branch, with power to promulgate Sentencing Guidelines establishing a range of determinate sentences for all categories of federal offenses and defendants according to specific and detailed factors. The Sentencing Reform Act was held to be constitutional in *Mistretta v. United States*.[13] However, the binding nature of the sentencing guidelines were declared unconstitutional in *United States v. Booker*,[14] leaving sentencing essentially to the informed discretion of the trial judge.

In discussing limitations on the discretion of the parole authority to grant or refuse release, we should note that the preceding cases are exceptional. The prevailing view is that the discretion of the parole authority in release hearings is broad.

In *California Department of Corrections v. Morales*,[15] a prisoner was sentenced to 15 years to life for the 1980 murder of his wife and became eligible for parole in 1990. As required by California law, the Board of Prison Terms held a hearing in 1989, at which time it found the prisoner unsuitable for parole for numerous reasons, including the fact that he had committed his crime while on parole for an earlier murder. The prisoner would have been entitled to subsequent suitability hearings annually under the law in place when he murdered his wife. The law was amended in 1981, however, to allow the Board to defer subsequent hearings for up to three years for a prisoner convicted of more than one offense involving the taking of a life, if the Board finds that it is not reasonable to expect that parole would be granted at a hearing during the intervening years and states the bases for the finding. Pursuant to this amendment, the Board scheduled the prisoner's next hearing for 1992. The prisoner then filed a federal habeas corpus petition, asserting that as applied to him, the 1981 amendment constituted an ex post facto law barred by the U.S. Constitution. The Supreme Court held that the amendment's application to prisoners who committed their crimes before it was enacted did not violate the ex post facto clause. The amendment did not increase the "punishment" attached to the prisoner's crime. It left untouched his indeterminate sentence and the substantive formula for securing any reductions to the sentencing range. By introducing the possibility that the Board would not have to hold another parole hearing in the year or two after the initial hearing, the amendment simply altered the method to be followed in fixing a parole release date under identical substantive standards.[16]

The argument that the clause would forbid any legislative change that has any conceivable risk of affecting a prisoner's punishment was rejected. In contrast, the Supreme Court has long held that the question of what legislative adjustments are of sufficient moment to transgress the constitutional prohibition must be a matter of degree and has declined to articulate a single "formula" for making this determination. The Supreme Court believed that there was no need to do so here, either, because the amendment creates only the most speculative and attenuated possibility of increasing the measure of punishment for covered crimes, and such conjectural effects are insufficient under any threshold that might be established under the clause. The amendment applies only to those who have taken more than one life, a class of prisoners for whom the likelihood of release on parole is quite remote. In addition, the amendment affects only the timing of subsequent hearings and does so only when the Board makes specific findings in the first hearing. Moreover, the Board has the authority to tailor the frequency of subsequent hearings. The prisoner offered no support for his speculation that prisoners might experience an unanticipated change that is sufficiently monumental to alter their suitability for parole or that such prisoners might be precluded from receiving a subsequent expedited hearing. Nor was there a reason to think that postponing an expedited hearing would extend any prisoner's actual confinement period. Because a parole release date often comes at least several years after a suitability finding, the Board could consider when a prisoner became "suitable" for parole in setting the actual release date.

The information used during the grant of parole may also raise constitutional issues. In *Johnson v. Texas Department of Criminal Justice*,[17] prisoners sued the Parole Board of Texas to prohibit them from using furlough history, writ-writing activities, and the Board's receipt of protest letters when making parole determinations. Relief was denied with respect to a consideration of a prisoner's furlough history when making parole determinations. However, with respect to the writ-writing activities, the district court noted that historically there has been a bias against prisoners considered to be writ-writers by the employees of the Texas Department of Corrections (TDC), and it determined that there should be a Board rule that prohibits the consideration of a prisoner's legal activities when the Board determines that prisoner's candidacy for parole. To do anything less would restrict, at least as a practical matter, a prisoner's access to the courts. The state and its officers may not abridge or impair the petitioner's right to apply to a federal court for a writ of habeas corpus. Whether a writ of habeas corpus addressed to a federal court is properly drawn and what allegations it must contain are questions for that court alone to determine. Given prisoners' constitutional right of access to the courts, any consideration of writ-writing as a factor in the parole decision is a deprivation of due process and also violates the Equal Protection Clause.[18] Any distinction made between prisoners who seek access to the courts and those who do not violates the Equal Protection Clause. Further, prison officials may not retaliate against or harass a prisoner for exercising the right of access to the courts.[19]

With respect to the Board's receipt of protest letters when making parole determinations, the Board sends out notification to persons entitled to receive notice under Texas law. Many of the recipients then send protests to the Board in varying forms: some are simply form letters indicating opposition to release, some express opinions that the prisoner has not done enough time for the crime, others contain newspaper clippings or first-person narratives describing the original crime. Other letters come from victims and their families describing the effects that the crime has had upon them, while others include information about the prisoner, such as his criminal history, unadjudicated offenses, and family circumstances. Motives for sending letters vary widely from a concern for the safety of the general public, personal dislike of a prisoner, local political considerations, and a desire to obtain an advantage over a prisoner.

In 1995, the Texas Code of Criminal Procedure was amended to allow for victims or their representative to present oral statements to board members. The parole panel is obligated to allow one person to appear before the board members to present a statement of that person's views about the offense, the defendant, and the effect of the offense on the victim.[20] The court recognized that Texas law does not create a liberty interest in release on parole. Thus, having no constitutionally protected right, a prisoner cannot state "a claim for either civil rights or habeas relief by his allegation that he was denied due process when seeking parole because he has no constitutionally protected expectancy of release."[21] A prisoner may, however, assert an equal protection claim in a civil rights suit.[22]

The evidence showed that prisoners who received protest letters of any kind are treated differently from those who do not. According to the court, a prisoner's potential for receiving protest letters is unpredictable; this fact, coupled with the unpredictability of the contents of those letters, leads to disparate results among prisoners eligible and being reviewed for parole. A system has been created that is extremely arbitrary and capricious and violates the equal protection rights of the plaintiff and the plaintiff class, no matter how small the number of parole candidates adversely affected by protest letters.

Consequently, the Court determined that the statutory scheme under which the Board can accept statements, whether written or oral, and then prevent knowledge of said statements' existence and prohibit disclosure of their contents and of the writer's or speaker's identity violates the equal protection rights of prisoners because the Board, as a rule, denies parole to prisoners who have received protest statements. The Board's sole function is to determine whether a prisoner should be released on parole; its function is not to effectively retry the case by accepting "testimony" that was inadmissible at trial on evidentiary grounds (or would have been inadmissible had introduction been attempted) or was excluded as part of trial strategy or by entering findings that the actual jury did not find at the prisoner's trial. Evidentiary determinations are made in the trial court. The Board was ordered not to consider unadjudicated offenses or offenses extraneous to the conviction for which the prisoner is currently incarcerated, as the Board must be bound by the conviction that the prisoner received and must apply the statutory requirements regarding the time to be served on parole for that conviction, without adding ad hoc information that results in additional time being served.

Executive clemency consideration is not the same as parole consideration. After a murder conviction and death sentence were affirmed on direct appeal, the Ohio Adult Parole Authority commenced a clemency investigation in accordance with state law. The prisoner was informed that he could have his voluntary interview with Authority members on a particular date and that his clemency hearing would be held one week later. The prisoner filed a civil rights action, alleging that Ohio's clemency process violated his Fourteenth Amendment due process right and his Fifth Amendment right to remain silent.

Noting that *Connecticut Board of Pardons v. Dumschat*[23] had decisively rejected the argument that federal law created any liberty interest in clemency, the Sixth Circuit held that the prisoner failed to establish a life or liberty interest protected by due process. The court also held, however, that the prisoner's "original" pretrial life and liberty interests were protected by a "second strand" of due process analysis, although the amount of process due could be minimal because clemency, while an "integral part" of the adjudicatory system, was far removed from trial. The court remanded the case for the lower court to decide what that process should be. Finally, the Sixth Circuit concluded that Ohio's voluntary interview procedure presented the prisoner with a "Hobson's choice" between asserting his Fifth Amendment privilege against self-incrimination and participating in Ohio's clemency review process, thereby raising the specter of an unconstitutional condition on further appeal. The Supreme Court reversed in *Ohio Adult Parole Authority v. Woodard*.[24]

On the Fifth Amendment issue, the Supreme Court unanimously held that giving a prisoner the option of voluntarily participating in an interview as part of the clemency process did not violate any Fifth Amendment rights. Even on assumptions most favorable to the prisoner's claim—i.e., that nothing in the clemency procedure granted applicants immunity for what they might say or makes the interview in any way confidential, and that the Authority would draw adverse inferences from a refusal to answer questions—the testimony at a voluntary interview was not "compelled." A prisoner merely faces a choice similar to those made by a criminal defendant in the course of criminal proceedings, as for example, when a defendant chooses to testify in his or her own defense. He or she abandons the privilege against self-incrimination when the prosecution seeks to cross-examine him or her and may be impeached by proof of prior convictions. In these situations, the undoubted pressures to testify that are generated by the strength of the case do not constitute "compulsion" for Fifth Amendment purposes. Similarly, at the clemency hearing, a prisoner has the choice of providing information to the Authority—at the risk of damaging his or her case for clemency or for postconviction relief—or of remaining silent. The pressure to speak did not make the interview "compelled."

On the clemency issue, the Court was split. Four members of the Court[25] concluded that a prisoner does not establish a violation of the Due Process Clause in clemency proceedings where the procedures in question do no more than confirm that such decisions are committed, as is the nation's tradition, to the executive's authority. Pardon and commutation decisions are rarely, if ever, appropriate subjects for judicial review. The argument that there was a continuing life interest in clemency that is broader in scope than the "original" life interest adjudicated at trial and sentencing was barred by *Dumschat*. The process that the prisoner sought would be inconsistent with the heart of executive clemency, which is to grant clemency as a matter of grace, thus allowing the executive to consider a wide range of factors not comprehended by earlier judicial proceedings and sentencing determinations. Although the prisoner maintained a residual life interest, e.g., in not being summarily executed by prison guards, he could not use that interest to challenge the clemency determination by requiring the procedural protections he sought. The four Justices also rejected any claim that clemency procedures are entitled to due process protection.

Four justices[26] in *Woodard* concluded that because a prisoner under a death sentence has a continuing interest in his or her life, the issue in *Woodard* was what process was constitutionally necessary to protect that interest, recognizing that due process demands are reduced once society has validly convicted an individual of a crime. According to these four justices, some minimal procedural safeguards apply to clemency proceedings. Judicial intervention might, for example, be warranted in the face of a scheme whereby a state official flipped a coin to determine whether to grant clemency, or in a case in which the state arbitrarily denied a prisoner any access to its clemency process.

The ninth member of the Court[27] concurred in part and dissented in part, which emphasized the difficulty in analyzing recent Supreme Court cases for their precedential value. Justice Stevens believed that when a parole board conducts a hearing to determine whether the state shall actually execute one of its death row prisoners—in other words, whether the state shall deprive that person of life—it has an obligation to comply with the due process cause of the Fourteenth Amendment. He specifically dissented from Chief Justice Rehnquist's view that a clemency proceeding could never violate the Due Process Clause. Under the Rehnquist view, according to Justice Stevens, even procedures infected by bribery, personal or political animosity, or the deliberate fabrication of false evidence would be constitutionally acceptable.

Justice Stevens joined in the part of the Court's opinion that concluded that giving a prisoner the option of voluntarily participating in an interview as part of the clemency process did not violate his or her Fifth Amendment rights but thought that this case should be remanded to the district court for a determination of whether Ohio's procedures met the minimum requirements of due process. It thus remains unclear to what extent due process applies to clemency proceedings, if at all.

§ 13.3   Parole Revocation

Three theories have been advanced in the past to justify the unlimited discretion of a parole authority in revoking the parole once it is granted: the privilege theory, the contract theory, and the continuing custody theory. The present judicial treatment of parole revocation modifies these theories by subjecting parole authorities to the requirements of due process in revoking parole.

§ 13.3.1   — The Privilege Theory

Most frequently argued is the privilege theory. This theory holds that parole is an act of grace by the state. Because release on parole is granted to the prisoner as a matter of privilege, no right attaches to it even after it is given. The release may be given, conditioned, or terminated, according to the theory, at the whim of the granting authority.

There are weaknesses to the use of this particular theory of parole. The system of parole has been an integral part of the American criminal justice process. Prison administrators use it as a rehabilitative tool as well as a stimulus for good behavior of prisoners. Furthermore, it is relied upon by the prisoners and is frequently the reason prisoners behave properly while incarcerated. To allow parole authorities unlimited control over the parolee would appear, in that light, to be unwise and unjust. Further, courts have expressed their displeasure with the whole concept of "privilege" as opposed to "right." The Supreme Court, in cases concerning students, welfare recipients, and security clearances, has reviewed the privilege theory and has rejected it as improper in these cases. The "privilege" theory of parole was repudiated, however, by the United States Supreme Court in *Morrissey v. Brewer*.[28]

§ 13.3.2   – The Contract Theory

A second theory used as a reason for allowing unreviewable revocation of parole is the contract theory. It is argued that release by the parole authority is contingent upon the parolee's acceptance of the conditions of such release. The acceptance constitutes a contractual obligation on the part of the prisoner to live up to the conditions specified. If the conditions are violated, there is a "breach of contract" that justifies revocation. An obvious difficulty in the contract theory is that the parolee has no bargaining power in determining the terms of the contract. Furthermore, any "consent" to the terms of his or her contractual release is coerced by virtue of the fact that no alternative means of obtaining release is available.

§ 13.3.3   – The Continuing Custody Theory

A third theory used in conjunction with parole is that of "continuing custody." It is argued that because parolees remain in the custody of the granting authority, they are still subject to the same restrictions they were prior to their release on parole. However, the avowed purpose of the parole system is rehabilitation. A prisoner is released so that he or she may readjust to the conditions of society, under supervision. It cannot be denied that his or her situation is substantially distinct from that of a prisoner. This theory contends that attempting to apply the standards used in dealing with a prisoner to a parolee is inherently irrational.

§ 13.3.4   – The Due Process Theory

The present approach to parole revocation modifies—if not rejects—these three theories. This approach recognizes that one of the chief goals of the correctional system is to impress upon those within the system the belief that the criminal justice process operates fairly for the protection of all society. It is recognized that the arbitrary operation of the parole system can only result in the parolees' loss of respect for a system that claims to encourage responsible action in accordance with established law. Furthermore, it is acknowledged that the interests of the people are best served by proper treatment of the parolee in order to prevent recidivism.

If revocation is accomplished through an arbitrary procedure, respect for society will be further diminished. Finally, although it cannot be asserted that the parolee maintains the same rights as a free person, it is recognized that basic constitutionally protected rights apply to the parolee. Consequently, the requirements of due process should apply to parole revocation.

§ 13.4   Parole Revocation Proceedings

In *Morrissey v. Brewer*,[29] the United States Supreme Court held that due process applies to parole revocation proceedings. Prior to *Morrissey*, the leading case dealing with revocation proceeding rights was *Mempa v. Rhay*.[30] However, *Mempa v. Rhay* dealt with probation revocation. In *Mempa*, two defendants had each been convicted of felonies and had been placed on probation. Both had violated the conditions of their probation and consequently were given the maximum sentence at a revocation hearing. The petitioners had not been represented by counsel at these proceedings, nor were they offered court-appointed counsel. The Supreme Court held that the "right to counsel is not a right confined to representation during the trial on the merits."[31] On the contrary, "appointment of counsel for an indigent is required at every stage of a criminal proceeding where substantial rights of an accused may be affected."[32] For this reason, the Court found that the failure to provide representation at the probation revocation hearing was reversible error.

As noted, the decision rendered in *Mempa* specifically dealt with probation rather than parole. Furthermore, it was limited to the right to counsel rather than to the full panoply of procedural due process rights. In *Morrissey*, the Supreme Court distinguished parole from probation. Unlike probation, parole only arises at the end of a criminal prosecution, including the imposition of sentence. Further, in parole, supervision is not directed by the courts but by an administrative agency. Most significantly, parole revocation deprives an individual not of the absolute liberty to which every citizen is entitled, but only of the conditional liberty that depends on compliance with special parole restrictions.

Nevertheless, the requirements of due process apply to parole revocations. The Supreme Court completely rejected the theory that constitutional rights turn upon whether the government benefit is characterized as a "right" or a "privilege." Rather, the crucial issue is the extent to which the individual will be condemned to suffer "grievous loss."

In *Morrissey*, the Supreme Court held that revocation of parole was a "grievous loss" to the parolee.

> The liberty of a parolee enables him to do a wide range of things open to persons who have never been convicted of any crime. The parolee has been released from prison based on an evaluation that he shows reasonable promise of being able to return to society and function as a responsible, self-reliant person. Subject to the conditions of his parole, he can be gainfully

employed and is free to be with family and friends and to form the other enduring attachments of normal life. Though the state properly subjects him to many restrictions not applicable to other citizens, his conditions are very different from that of confinement in a prison. He may have been on parole for a number of years and may be living a relatively normal life at the time he is faced with revocation. The parolee has relied on at least an implicit promise that parole will be revoked only if he fails to live up to the parole conditions. In many cases, the parolee faces lengthy incarceration if his parole is revoked.

We see, therefore, that the liberty of a parolee, although indeterminate, includes many of the core values of unqualified liberty and its termination inflicts a "grievous loss" on the parolee and often on others. It is hardly useful any longer to try to deal with this problem in terms of whether the parolee's liberty is a "right" or a "privilege." By whatever name, the liberty is valuable and must be seen as within the protection of the Fourteenth Amendment. Its termination calls for some orderly process, however informal.[33]

The remaining issue is the extent of the "orderly process." The Supreme Court in *Morrissey* recognized that, given the previous criminal conviction and the proper imposition of parole conditions, the state has an interest in being able to return the parolee to imprisonment without the burden of a new criminal trial on the merits if, in fact, the parolee has failed to live up to the conditions of his or her parole. However, the summary treatment that may be necessary in controlling a large group of potentially disruptive prisoners in actual custody, as well as the argument that revocation is so totally a discretionary matter that some form of hearing would be administratively intolerable, was rejected.

The parolee is not the only one who has a stake in his conditional liberty. Society has a stake in whatever may be the chance of restoring him or her to normal and useful life within the law. Society thus has an interest in not having parole revoked because of erroneous information or because of an erroneous evaluation of the need to revoke parole, given the breach of parole conditions. And society has a further interest in treating the parolee with basic fairness: Fair treatment in parole revocations will enhance the chance of rehabilitation by avoiding reactions to arbitrariness.[34]

Therefore, what the Supreme Court believed was needed was an informal hearing structured to assure that the findings of a parole violation would be based on verified facts and that the exercise of discretion would be based on accurate knowledge of the parolee's behavior. The *Morrissey* Court outlined six due process procedures that must be followed before parole may be revoked (see § 13.4.3).

§ 13.4.1 — Arrest and Preliminary Hearing

The first step in the parole revocation process is the arrest of the parolee. This can occur either by arrest on new criminal charges or at the direction of a parole officer for a breach of the terms of parole. There is usually a substantial period between arrest and the eventual determination by the parole authority that parole should be revoked. Further, the parolee is often arrested at a place far distant from the prison to which he or she may be returned prior to the formal action of the parole authority.

Given these circumstances, the Supreme Court held in *Morrissey v. Brewer* that:

> [D]ue process would seem to require that some minimal inquiry be conducted at or reasonably near the place of the alleged parole violation or arrest and as promptly as convenient after arrest while information is fresh and sources are available.[35]

The inquiry required is in the nature of a "preliminary hearing," in which it must be determined that there is probable cause or reasonable grounds to believe that the arrested parolee has committed acts that would constitute a violation of the conditions of parole. Therefore, *Morrissey* deals with both the "place" and the "promptness" of the initial inquiry. Of these two, the promptness issue has triggered considerable litigation. In addition, questions have arisen as to what proceedings may serve as a "substitute" for the *Morrissey* preliminary hearing. "Promptness" has been determined by statute in some jurisdictions.[36] Other parole authorities have had "promptness" defined for them by the courts.[37]

Nevertheless, the entire revocation process should ideally be completed within two months because *Morrissey* stated that this was not an unreasonable period.

Another problem that has arisen concerning the timing of both the preliminary and the final *Morrissey* revocation hearing occurs when a parolee is held in a different jurisdiction for criminal acts committed while on parole and the paroling authority has issued a detainer against the parolee. The issue is whether the issuance of the detainer triggers the requirement for a "prompt" revocation hearing. *Moody v. Daggett*[38] solved the dilemma by holding that there is no requirement for an immediate hearing in this circumstance. The loss of liberty stems from the new conviction, and thus the detainer has no immediate effect. Parole authorities may therefore hold the warrant for either execution or dismissal at the completion of the term of the new sentence. It is at that time that the *Morrissey* standard applies.[39]

Some courts have determined that preliminary hearings on new criminal charges may serve as the *Morrissey* preliminary hearing.[40] The parolee must, however, receive prior notification that the criminal hearing will serve as a substitute. Other situations have been held sufficient to substitute for the *Morrissey* preliminary hearing. Foremost among these is when the parolee is convicted of a new crime. In *United States v. Tucker*,[41] the court stated that when a probationer was incarcerated pursuant to a final conviction at the time of the attempted probation revocation, there was no requirement that there be a preliminary as well as a final probation revocation hearing. This has been held to apply even though the conviction is under appeal. However, if the conviction is reversed, logic would suggest that a prompt hearing be held at that time.

Where a parole board has relied on criminal proceedings as a substitute for the *Morrissey* preliminary hearing, and the parolee was acquitted of the charge, at least one court[42] has held that the parole board was "collaterally estopped" from revoking parole based on the same set of facts. The court held that such a revocation violated the doctrine of collateral estoppel as contained in the double jeopardy clause of the Fifth Amendment.[43] The court rejected the state's argument that the lesser burden of proof (preponderance of evidence) at the revocation hearing permitted the parole board to revoke parole based on the same facts presented at the criminal trial, in which the burden of proof was "beyond a reasonable doubt."

In contrast, *In re Coughlin*[44] held that a court, at a probation revocation hearing, or the Adult Authority, at a parole revocation hearing, may properly consider evidence indicating that a probationer or parolee has committed another criminal offense during the period of his or her probation or parole, despite the fact that he or she was acquitted of the criminal charge at trial.[45] Further, in *Standlee v. Rhay*,[46] the court of appeals held that the doctrine of collateral estoppel did not prohibit the parole board from finding the parolee guilty of a parole violation even after the accused had been acquitted in a criminal trial on the same charges. Parole revocation proceedings require a lower standard of proof than criminal adjudicatory proceedings. This may result in the revocation of parole even though the accused is found not guilty of the charges at the trial level.

The split in opinion centers on the different burden of proof requirements for a criminal trial and a revocation proceeding and on the nature of the proceeding itself. It has been stated that proof beyond a reasonable doubt of the violation of a condition of probation is not required by statute or the Constitution in a revocation proceeding.[47] In spite of this recognized difference in the burden of proof, some courts have imposed the criminal acquittal as a final decision for the parole board. This appears to be too broad, because a technical violation of parole that occurred in the same factual setting as the criminal charge would be precluded from consideration by the parole board in the revocation hearing. In addition, the Supreme Court suggested in *Baxter v. Palmigiano*[48] that a prison disciplinary hearing was not a criminal proceeding but a civil proceeding and authorized a prison court to hold a disciplinary hearing while state criminal charges were pending, both of which involved the same facts. Although the law is not clear, it can be argued that the revocation of parole is not a criminal proceeding, that the civil standards for burden of proof (preponderance of the evidence) should apply at the revocation hearing, and that the doctrine of double jeopardy should not apply.

At the preliminary hearing, the parolee must be given notice that the hearing will take place and that its purpose is to determine whether there is probable cause to believe that he has committed a parole violation. The parole conditions alleged to have been violated must be stated in the notice. At the hearing, the parolee has the right to appear and to speak in his or her own behalf. Further, he or she may bring letters, documents, or witnesses who are able to give relevant information to the hearing officer. If the parolee asks to question in his or her presence persons who have given adverse information upon which the revocation is to be based, the request must be granted, unless the hearing officer determines that the adverse witness or informant would risk harm if his or her identity were disclosed.

Finally, the hearing officer must make a summary of the proceedings, including the responses of the parolee, the substance of the documents or evidence given in support of revocation, and the parolee's position. Based upon such information, the hearing officer must then determine whether there is probable cause to hold the parolee for the parole authority's final decision on revocation. Thereafter, the parolee may lawfully be continued in detention and returned to prison pending the final decision of the parole authority.

§ 13.4.2 — The Revocation Hearing

The *Morrissey* holding requires that the parolee be given the opportunity for a hearing, if he or she so desires, prior to the final decision or revocation by the parole authority. The revocation hearing must lead to a final evaluation of any contested relevant facts and must consider whether the facts, as determined, warrant parole revocation.

Minimum due process at the parole revocation hearing now requires that the parolee be given an opportunity to be heard and to show, if he or she is able, that he or she did not violate the conditions of the parole, or, if he or she did, the mitigating circumstances that might suggest that the violation does not warrant revocation.

§ 13.4.3 — Procedural Due Process at the Revocation Hearing

The *Morrissey* Court held that, to conform to the requirements of due process, the following procedure must be followed in a parole revocation hearing:

1. There must be written notice of the claimed violations of parole.

2. The evidence against the parolee must be disclosed to him or her.

3. The parolee must be given the opportunity to be heard in person and to present witnesses and documentary evidence.

4. The parolee has the right to confront and cross-examine adverse witnesses, unless the parole authority specifically finds good cause for not allowing confrontation, such as a risk of harm to the informant if his or her identity were disclosed.

5. The hearing body, such as a traditional parole board, must be neutral and detached but need not be judicial officers or lawyers.

6. The parole authority must compose a written statement as to the evidence it relied on and the reasons for revoking the parole.[49]

There was no intent by the Supreme Court to equate the revocation hearing to a formal criminal prosecution. Further, a process flexible enough to consider material that would be inadmissible in an adversary criminal trial, such as letters and affidavits, was sanctioned. Also, the power of the parole authorities over the proceedings was authorized to assure that the delaying tactics and other abuses often present in traditional criminal trials do not occur. In any case, a parolee cannot use the revocation hearing to relitigate issues decided against him or her in other forums, such as when the revocation is based on conviction of another crime.

§ 13.4.4 — The Revocation Hearing — Right to Counsel

In *Morrissey*, the Supreme Court stated: "We do not reach or decide the question whether the parolee is entitled to the assistance of retained counsel or to appointed counsel if he is indigent."[50] The Supreme Court answered that question in *Gagnon v. Scarpelli*.[51]

In *Scarpelli*, the Court dealt with the question of whether a previously sentenced probationer was entitled to be represented by state-appointed counsel at a probation revocation hearing. As to parole revocation, the Court relied heavily on *Morrissey v. Brewer*, and stated that it could not perceive any relevant difference between the revocation of parole and the revocation of probation.

The court recognized that, despite the informal nature of the proceedings and the absence of technical rules of procedure or evidence, an unskilled or uneducated probationer or parolee might have difficulty presenting his or her version of a disputed set of facts without the aid of a lawyer. This was recognized to be particularly true in cases in which the proceedings required the examining or cross-examining of witnesses or the offering or dissecting of complex documentary evidence. However, the Court did not mandate that counsel be appointed for every parolee in every case but held that "the need for counsel must be made on a case-by-case basis in the exercise of a sound discretion by the state authority charged with responsibility for administering the probation and parole system."[52]

The Court set no firm guidelines as to when counsel must be provided but said that the state should do so where the indigent probationer or parolee may have difficulty presenting his or her version of disputed facts or, if the violation is not disputed, there are substantial reasons in justification or mitigation that make revocation inappropriate. The Court did hold that "in every case in which a request for counsel at a preliminary or final hearing is refused, the grounds for refusal should be stated succinctly in the record."[53]

Courts dealing with the issue of counsel at revocation proceedings have not found *Scarpelli* helpful. The Supreme Court of Indiana, in *Russell v. Douthitt*,[54] stated that the suggestion that appointment of counsel be made on a case-by-case basis serves to "delude and only becloud the issue and create uncertainty as to what the law is."[55] The court finally threw up its hands and held:

> In our opinion, "on a case-by-case basis" means that those involved in parole revocation can take no other course than to appoint counsel in all cases and to have a full-blown trial for every alleged charge of parole violation.[56]

§ 13.4.5   — The Revocation Hearing — Right to Appointed Counsel

Related to the issue of the right to counsel is the right to appointed counsel for the parolee if he or she cannot afford to hire one with private funds. It is arguable that counsel must be provided in all cases in which retained counsel is permitted. In other words, if the state permits counsel to participate at parole revocation hearings for those who can afford it, it should provide counsel at state expense for those who cannot afford representation.

The majority of cases still find that the question of whether a revocation proceeding involving a particular parolee is one that requires counsel is to be determined in the first instance by the paroling authority. The decision is to be made on a case-by-case basis in the exercise of sound discretion and on the guidelines set forth in *Scarpelli*.[57] In contrast, when a revocation proceeding amounts to a resentencing, appointment of counsel for an indigent person is required under *Mempa v. Rhay* and not under the discretionary standards of *Scarpelli*.[58]

When the facts show that counsel is required, it has been held that lack of authority or funds by a state parole commission to appoint counsel is not a legally sufficient reason for refusing to appoint counsel for a parolee.[59] Some states have provided for counsel under the guidelines of *Scarpelli* by regulation or statute. The right to counsel at the preliminary hearing in New York is the same test as *Scarpelli*, a case-by-case approach, but the New York rule on final revocation proceedings guarantees the right to counsel.[60] In Indiana, the Supreme Court has declared that counsel is required in all cases.[61]

Scarpelli states that access to counsel is a presumptive right only, but *Preston v. Piggman*[62] held that the burden is on the paroling authority to overcome that presumption. A silent record containing no reasons for denying counsel or not providing counsel would open the possibility for a reversal of the proceedings. It would appear that the presumptive right to counsel could be overcome when the parolee is made aware of the charges against him or her, and the record shows that he or she understands the nature of the proceedings and is capable of adequately expressing him- or herself and explaining the circumstances. Under *Scarpelli*, it is also clear that the presumptive right to counsel applies to both preliminary and final revocation hearings.

§ 13.4.6 — Evidence at the Revocation Hearing

Morrissey provides that at the preliminary hearing, "a parolee may appear and speak in his own behalf; he may bring letters, documents, or individuals who can give relevant information to the hearing officer." The court pointed out that the hearing officer should state the reasons for his or her decision and the evidence upon which he or she relied. Because the preliminary hearing is not a final determination, there is no requirement of "formal findings of fact and conclusions of law" at that stage.

As to the final hearing, *Morrissey* states that the inquiry involved is a narrow one. "The process should be flexible enough to consider evidence including letters, affidavits, and other material that would not be admissible in an adversary criminal trial."[63]

In *Scarpelli*, the court makes a distinction between a criminal trial and the revocation hearing.

> In a criminal trial, the State is represented by a prosecutor; formal rules of evidence are in force; a defendant enjoys a number of procedural rights which may be lost if not timely raised; and, in a jury trial, a defendant must make a presentation understandable to untrained jurors. In short, a criminal trial under our system is an adversary proceeding with its own unique characteristics. In a revocation hearing, on the other hand, the State is represented not by a prosecutor, but by a parole officer . . .; formal procedures and rules of evidence are not employed; and the members of the hearing body are familiar with the problems and practice of probation or parole.[64]

The references in *Morrissey* and *Scarpelli* to a revocation hearing as a proceeding not subject to the formal rules of evidence applicable to a criminal trial have raised the question of whether hearsay evidence will be permitted in evidence at the revocation hearing. In simple terms, hearsay is a statement made by someone outside of the hearing, offered at the hearing to prove the truth of the statement. Hearsay may be a statement, conduct, or a writing. The main objection to hearsay is that the person who made the original statement is not available at the hearing to be questioned or cross-examined. Therefore, hearsay evidence cannot be tested for its truthfulness. However, the courts have recognized that hearsay can be admitted under circumstances that assure truthfulness. There are, therefore, many exceptions to the hearsay rule.[65] Although courts have permitted hearsay to be considered at revocation hearings,[66] there is judicial reluctance to accept hearsay at revocation hearings[67] as the sole basis of the final decision.

The United States Supreme Court in *Pennsylvania Board of Probation and Parole v. Scott* held in a 5–4 decision that the federal exclusionary rule does not bar the introduction of evidence seized in violation of parolees' Fourth Amendment rights at parole revocation hearings.[68] The State's use of such evidence did not violate the Constitution.

In *Scott*, an offender was released on parole on the condition that he could not own or possess any weapons. Suspecting a violation, parole officers entered his home and found firearms, a bow, and arrows. After a hearing, the parolee was recommitted to prison, even though the parole officers obtained the evidence against him from an alleged unlawful search under the Fourth Amendment. The Supreme Court ruled that it would not apply the exclusionary rule even though the search violated the Fourth Amendment. Taking a restricted view toward the exclusionary rule, the Court held that a violation of the Fourth Amendment is "fully accomplished" by the illegal search or seizure and no exclusion of evidence can cure the invasion of rights a person has already suffered. The exclusionary rule is a judicially created means of deterring illegal searches and seizures. There is no provision in the Constitution prohibiting the introduction of illegally seized evidence in all proceedings or against all persons but applies only in contexts in which its remedial objectives are thought to be most efficiently served. The rule is prudential rather than constitutionally mandated. It applies only when its deterrence benefits outweigh the substantial social costs inherent in precluding consideration of reliable, probative evidence. Consequently, the Supreme Court has repeatedly declined to extend the exclusionary rule to proceedings other than criminal trials.

The Court commented that the social costs of allowing convicted criminals who violate their parole to remain at large are particularly high and are compounded by the fact that parolees (particularly those who have already committed parole violations) are more likely to commit future crimes than are average citizens. Application of the exclusionary rule would be incompatible with the traditionally flexible, nonadversarial, administrative procedures of parole revocation in that it would require extensive litigation to determine whether particular evidence must be excluded. The exclusionary rule would provide only minimal deterrence benefits in this context. Its application in criminal trials already provides significant deterrence of unconstitutional searches. The Supreme Court has never suggested that the exclusionary rule must apply in every circumstance in which it might provide marginal deterrence. Such a piecemeal approach would add an additional layer of collateral litigation regarding an officer's knowledge of the parolee's status. In any event, any additional deterrence would be minimal, whether the person conducting the search was a police officer or a parole officer.

§ 13.4.7   — Rescission of Parole

"Rescission" of parole raises the question of the due process rights of a prisoner who has been given a "future parole date" but subsequently has that date changed or withdrawn. There would appear to be three alternatives. (1) Consider the "loss" as a revocation and apply the standards of *Morrissey* and *Scarpelli*. (2) Equate the "loss" to a prison disciplinary finding and apply the standards of *Wolff v. McDonnell*.[69] (3) Treat the "loss" as a denial of parole and apply the same standards as those applicable to parole hearings in general.

At one time, the grant of parole could be summarily rescinded without notice or a hearing prior to final physical release, unless a statute or regulation provided otherwise. The courts, however, have recognized that although the loss of liberty is more grievous to a parolee out on the street, taking away a future parole date clearly seems to be a grievous loss subject to some minimal due process protections.[70]

In *Jackson v. Wise*,[71] the court compared the rescission of parole to a prison hearing subject to the requirements of *Wolff v. McDonnell* and determined that the following were the minimum due process requirements for rescission:

1. Advance written notice of the charge;

2. Written statement by fact finders of the evidence relied on and the reasons for their decision;

3. Right of prisoner to be present;

4. Right of prisoner to present witnesses and documentary evidence on his behalf, if so doing would not be unduly hazardous to institutional safety or correctional goals;

5. The right, if the prisoner is found to be illiterate or otherwise incompetent to protect his own interests, to have an attorney-substitute; and

6. Adjudication of the charges by a panel sufficiently impartial to satisfy due process requirements. Other decisions have also found that minimum due process must accompany the rescission of parole.[72]

However, in *Williams v. United States Board of Parole*,[73] the court required the full procedural requirements of *Morrissey* and *Scarpelli*. There are also decisions that follow the earlier view that a future date of parole may be rescinded summarily without notice or a hearing, until the time that the prisoner has been physically released from custody of the institution.[74] Also, where a prisoner had escaped and was not returned until after his parole release date, a state court held that he was not entitled to a full-scale hearing.[75]

Beginning in 1983, the Florida legislature enacted a series of statutes authorizing the award of early release credits to prisoners when the state prison population exceeded predetermined levels. In 1986, a prisoner received a 22-year prison sentence on a charge of attempted murder. In 1992, he was released, based on the determination that he had accumulated five different types of early release credits totaling 5,668 days, including 1,860 days of "provisional credits" awarded as a result of prison overcrowding. Shortly thereafter, the state attorney general issued an opinion interpreting a 1992 statute as having retroactively canceled all provisional credits awarded to prisoners convicted of murder and attempted murder. The prisoner was therefore rearrested and returned to custody. He filed a habeas corpus petition alleging that the retroactive cancellation of provisional credits violated the ex post facto clause of the United States Constitution. The United States Supreme Court held that the 1992 statute canceling provisional release credits violated the ex post facto clause.[76]

To fall within the ex post facto prohibition, a law must be retrospective and disadvantage the offender affected by, among other things, increasing the punishment for the crime. The operation of the 1992 statute was clearly retrospective, and it obviously disadvantaged the prisoner by increasing his punishment.

The Supreme Court also rejected an argument that the prisoner was not entitled to relief because his provisional overcrowding credits were awarded pursuant to statutes enacted after the date of his offense rather than pursuant to the 1983 statute. Although the overcrowding statute in effect at the time of his crime was slightly modified in subsequent years, its basic elements remained the same, and the changes did not affect his core ex post facto claim.

§ 13.5   Probation

Probation is a fundamentally different concept from parole, though in practice they are often indistinguishable. In general, probation is controlled by the court either at the time of sentencing or postsentencing while the court still has jurisdiction over the offender. Revocation of probation is controlled by the court, whereas revocation of parole is controlled by an administrative agency that is part of the executive branch of government. As indicated by the preceding cases, most procedural safeguards that apply to parole revocation also apply to probation revocation.

In federal practice, probation is controlled by statute under the Sentencing Guidelines. The guidelines have caused the federal judiciary much difficulty in their interpretation and application. One example is *United States v. Granderson*.[77] A mail carrier was sentenced to five years' probation and a fine. However, after he tested positive for cocaine, the court resentenced him under 18 U.S.C. § 3565(a), which provides that if a person serving a sentence of probation possesses illegal drugs, the court shall revoke the sentence of probation and sentence the defendant to not less than one-third of the original sentence. Accepting the government's reading of the statute, a district court concluded that the phrase "original sentence" referred to the term of probation actually imposed (60 months) rather than the zero to six-month imprisonment range authorized by the Sentencing Guidelines.

The Supreme Court held that the minimum revocation sentence under § 3565(a)'s drug possession proviso is one-third the maximum of the originally applicable guidelines range of imprisonment and that the maximum revocation sentence is the guidelines' maximum. The proviso mandates imprisonment, not renewed probation, as the required type of punishment. The contrast in §§ 3565(a) (1) and (2) between "continuing" and "revoking" probation as the alternative punishments for a defendant who violates a probation condition suggests that a revocation sentence must be a sentence of imprisonment, not a continuation of probation. Moreover, the court believed that it would be absurd to punish drug-possessing probationers by revoking their probation and imposing a new term of probation no longer than the original. The "original sentence" that sets the duration of the revocation sentence is the applicable Guidelines sentence of imprisonment, not the revoked term of probation.

§ 13.6 Probation and Parole Conditions

One of the more difficult issues regarding the legal status of probationers and parolees is what rights the individual has while supervised in the community. The conditions attached to the issuance of probation and parole—referred to hereafter as community supervision—frequently conflict with the retained constitutional rights of the offender.

The "contract" rationale is frequently used as a justification for revocation of community supervision after a violation of a particular condition. The acceptance of certain conditions of supervision is said to prevent the offender from later claiming that one of the conditions imposed was invalid. This contract theory may be discredited, however, because the consent is coerced. However, most challenges to the legality of conditions continue to be dismissed by the courts by virtue of the contract theory.

It would appear that the only conditions that courts are likely to invalidate are those that require illegal, immoral, or impossible actions by the offender. For example, if the pathological nature of one's alcoholism made it impossible to abstain from alcohol completely, a condition requiring complete abstention from alcohol would be invalidated as unreasonable.[78] Another condition that would usually be invalidated as unreasonable, even though possible of performance, is a condition of banishment.[79] A number of cases have addressed various conditions of probation and parole:

- Requiring participation in psychological counseling as a condition of probation does not violate privacy rights.[80]

- Due process is violated by the automatic revocation of probation because of an indigent probationer's failure to meet a condition of probation requiring him or her to pay a fine or make restitution. Absent findings that the probationer willfully refused to make bona fide efforts to pay or that alternate forms of punishment, other than imprisonment, are inadequate to meet the state's interests in punishment and deterrence, imprisonment violates the Fourteenth Amendment.[81]

- A California statute requires every prisoner eligible for release on state parole to agree in writing to be subject to search or seizure by a parole officer or other peace officer with or without a search warrant and with or without cause. This policy was approved in *Samson v. California*.[82] The

Fourth Amendment does not prohibit a police officer from conducting a random, suspicionless search of a parolee.

- Banning a probationer on supervised release conditions who was convicted of sexually preying on minors from gaining access to the Internet is constitutional.[83]

- A supervised release condition that required a convicted mail thief to spend eight hours standing outside a post office wearing a signboard stating, "I stole mail. This is my punishment." did not equate to an Eighth Amendment violation.[84]

- A convicted sex offender violated a condition of probation mandating that he have "no contact" with minors under the age of 16 when he attended a weekly gathering of antique car aficionados at which a number of children were present.[85]

- An allegation that conditioning eligibility for parole on signing an agreement to take allegedly inappropriate medication was not frivolous under 28 U.S.C.S. § 1915A. The prisoner had a liberty interest in avoiding an unwanted administration of antipsychotic drugs.[86]

- Probation was properly revoked for leaving the jurisdiction without permission.[87]

§ 13.6.1 　－Free Speech and Conditions

It is more difficult to predict the validity of conditions that limit the probationers and parolees in areas in which free individuals enjoy broad constitutional rights. These rights, particularly First Amendment freedoms, are respected above other personal rights and thus the courts generally subject conditions that diminish these freedoms to more intensive review. For example, *Hyland v. Procunier*[88] held that a condition requiring a parolee to secure permission before making any public speech is invalid. Such a condition would have "an unwarranted chilling effect on the exercise by plaintiff of his undisputed rights."[89]

A similar decision was handed down in *Sobell v. Reed*,[90] in which a parolee was denied the right to give an antiwar speech. The court found that this denial of First Amendment freedoms was beyond the parole authority. Such freedoms may be restricted only "upon a showing that such prevention or withholding of permission is necessary to safeguard against specific, concretely described and highly likely dangers of misconduct by plaintiff himself."[91]

In re Mannino[92] upheld a condition that prohibited speaking at and participating in public demonstrations because the probationer's offense (kicking a police officer) had occurred during the heat of such events. The reason for the condition was the explosive temperament of the defendant. However, a ban on writing and distributing written materials was held invalid because of a lack of relation to the underlying offense.

Similarly, a condition of probation that stipulated that the defendant not communicate with any of his children, except through the State Department of Welfare, and not have any of his children live with him until they reached 18 years of age, did not violate due process. The defendant had been convicted of aggravated crimes against nature, directed at his children.[93]

In *Commonwealth v. Power*,[94] a woman was placed on probation for 20 years with a special condition that she not profit from the sale of her story to the news media. The woman was placed on probation for her second conviction of armed robbery, an offense punishable by life imprisonment. The probationer argued that the special condition quoted amounted to a prior restraint on content-based speech in violation of her First Amendment rights. This argument was rejected, although it was agreed that because the condition placed a financial disincentive on the probationer based on the content of her speech, it did implicate her First Amendment rights.[95] The condition in this case allowed the probationer to speak on any subject, including her crimes. The condition merely prohibited the defendant from profiting financially from speech about her crime or her experience as a fugitive. According to the court, the purpose of the special condition was to deter convicted persons from seeking to profit directly or indirectly from criminality.[96]

Statements given by a probationer in compliance with a condition of probation requiring him or her to answer "promptly and truthfully" all reasonable questions posed by the probation officer were compelled in violation of his or her Fifth Amendment privilege against self-incrimination and are inadmissible at his or her trial on a new charge.[97]

§ 13.6.2 — Search as a Condition

A difficult question is presented when a probationer's or parolee's Fourth Amendment rights are involved. The Fourth Amendment protects citizens from unreasonable interference with their privacy by the government and generally requires that a warrant be obtained before a government official may undertake a search or seizure. However, there are exceptions. The Fourth Amendment prohibits only unreasonable searches. When a person is arrested, a search incident to that arrest may lawfully be made. A search may also be undertaken when reasonable cause exists to believe that the law has been or is being broken and a search warrant cannot be obtained without unreasonable delay. Even without a warrant, a search may be made if a person waives Fourth Amendment protection by consenting to the search. All other searches have been held unconstitutional. The argument is made, of course, that probationers and parolees, as a condition of community supervision, consent to searches by authorities.

In searches of parolees and probationers, the courts have focused on the "reasonableness" of the search and on the admissibility of any evidence found while conducting the search in later criminal or revocation proceedings. A probation or parole officer's searches and seizures are subject to a less stringent standard than the probable cause required for searches of ordinary citizens. In other words, probationers and parolees are not entitled to the full protection of the Fourth Amendment.

§ 13.6.2.1   — Searches of Probationers

The major Supreme Court case regarding searches of probationers is *Griffin v. Wisconsin*.[98] This case involved the search of a probationer's home by a probation officer. Wisconsin law places probationers in the legal custody of the State Department of Health and Social Services and renders them subject to conditions set by the rules and regulations established by the department. One such regulation permitted any probation officer to search a probationer's home without a warrant, as long as his supervisor approved and as long as there were "reasonable grounds" to believe contraband was present. In determining whether "reasonable grounds" existed, an officer was required to consider a variety of factors, including information provided by an informant, the reliability and specificity of that information, the informant's reliability, the officer's experience with the probationer, and the need to verify compliance with the rules of probation and with the law. Another Wisconsin regulation forbade a probationer to possess a firearm without a probation officer's advance approval.

Upon information received from a police detective that there were or might be guns in a probationer's apartment, probation officers searched the apartment and found a handgun. The probationer was tried and convicted of the felony of possession of a firearm by a convicted felon. The trial court denied his motion to suppress the evidence seized during the search. It concluded that no warrant was necessary and that the search was reasonable.

The Supreme Court held that the warrantless search of the probationer's residence was "reasonable" within the meaning of the Fourth Amendment because it was conducted pursuant to a regulation that is itself a reasonable response to the "special needs" of a probation system. The Court recognized that supervision of probationers was a "special need" of the state that justified departures from the usual warrant and probable cause requirements of the Fourth Amendment. Supervision was necessary to ensure that probation restrictions were in fact observed, that the probation served as a genuine rehabilitation period, and that the community was not harmed by the probationer being at large.

In this case, the search regulation was valid because the "special needs" of Wisconsin's probation system made the warrant requirement impracticable and justified replacement of the probable cause standard with the regulation's "reasonable grounds" standard. It was reasonable to dispense with the warrant requirement here, because such a requirement would interfere to an appreciable degree with the probation system by setting up a magistrate rather than the probation officer as the determiner of how closely the probationer must be supervised. It would also make it more difficult for probation officials to respond quickly to evidence of misconduct. It would reduce the deterrent effect that the possibility of expeditious searches would otherwise create. Moreover, unlike a police officer who conducts an ordinary search, a probation officer is required to have the probationer's welfare particularly in mind.

It was believed by the Court that a probable cause requirement would unduly disrupt the probation system by reducing the deterrent effect of the supervisory arrangement and by lessening the range of information the probation officer could consider in deciding whether to search. A probation agency must be able to act based upon a lesser degree of certainty in order to intervene before the probationer damages him- or herself or society. It must be able to proceed on the basis of its entire experience with the probationer and to assess probabilities in the light of its knowledge of his or her life, character, and circumstances. Thus, the Supreme Court held that it was reasonable to permit information provided by a police officer, whether or not on the basis of first-hand knowledge, to support a probationary search. All that was required was that the information provided indicate, as it did here, the likelihood of facts justifying the search.

The conclusion that the regulation in question was constitutional made it unnecessary to consider whether any search of a probationer's home is lawful when there are "reasonable grounds" to believe contraband is present. The Supreme Court deferred this issue to another day.

A similar Supreme Court case is *United States v. Knights.*[99] A California court's order sentencing a defendant to probation for a drug offense included the condition that he submit to search at any time, with or without a search or arrest warrant or reasonable cause, by any probation or law enforcement officer. The Supreme Court held that the warrantless search of a probationer, supported by reasonable suspicion and authorized by a probation condition, satisfied the Fourth Amendment. Here, the sentencing judge reasonably concluded that the search condition would further the two primary goals of probation— rehabilitation and protecting society from future criminal violations. The probationer was unambiguously informed of the search condition. Thus, the probationer's reasonable expectation of privacy was significantly diminished.

The Court in *Knights* recognized that the very assumption of probation is that the probationer is more likely than others to violate the law. The state's interest in apprehending criminal law violators, thereby protecting potential victims, may justifiably focus on probationers in a way that it does not focus on the ordinary citizen. On balance, no more than r easonable suspicion was required to search a probationer's house. The degree of individualized suspicion required is a determination that a sufficiently high probability of criminal conduct makes the intrusion on the individual's privacy interest reasonable. Although the Fourth Amendment ordinarily requires probable cause, a lesser degree satisfies the Constitution when the balance of governmental and private interests makes such a standard reasonable. The same circumstances that lead to the conclusion that reasonable suspicion is constitutionally sufficient also render a warrant requirement unnecessary.

§ 13.6.2.2   — Searches of Parolees

According to the Supreme Court's opinion in *Samson v. California*,[100] it appears that parolees enjoy even fewer Fourth Amendment protections than do probationers. A California statute requires every prisoner eligible for release on parole to agree in writing to be subject to search or seizure by a parole officer or other peace officer, with or without a search warrant and with or without cause. Based solely on an offender's parolee status, an officer searched him and found methamphetamine. On appeal to the Supreme Court, *Samson v. California*[101] held that the Fourth Amendment does not prohibit a police officer from conducting a suspicionless search of a parolee who signed a search condition.

The Court examined the issue under the "totality of the circumstances" doctrine to determine whether a search is reasonable under the Fourth Amendment.[102] Reasonableness is determined by assessing, on the one hand, the degree to which the search intrudes upon an individual's privacy and, on the other, the degree to which it is needed for the promotion of legitimate governmental interests.

In *Knights*, previously discussed, involving the search of a probationer, the Court found reasonable the warrantless search of a probationer's apartment based on reasonable suspicion and a probation condition authorized by California law. Parolees have fewer expectations of privacy than probationers because parole is more akin to imprisonment than probation is. The essence of parole is release from prison before the completion of sentence on the condition that the prisoner abide by certain rules during the balance of the sentence.[103]

A prisoner electing to complete his sentence out of physical custody remains in the state's legal custody for the remainder of his term and must comply with the terms and conditions of his parole. The extent and reach of those conditions demonstrate that parolees have severely diminished privacy expectations by virtue of their status alone. In addition, the state law's parole search condition was clearly expressed to the parolee, who signed a document submitting to the condition and thus was unambiguously aware of it. The parolee did not have any expectation of privacy that society would recognize as legitimate. Further, the state's interests were substantial. A state has an "overwhelming interest" in supervising parolees because they are more likely to commit future criminal offenses.[104]

The Court also held that a state's interests in reducing recidivism, thereby promoting reintegration and positive citizenship among probationers and parolees, warranted privacy intrusions that would not otherwise be tolerated under the Fourth Amendment. It was noted that California had a 60–70 percent recidivism rate. This demonstrates that most parolees are ill prepared to handle the pressures of reintegration and require intense supervision. Given California's number of parolees and its high recidivism rate, an individualized suspicion requirement would undermine its ability to effectively supervise parolees and protect the public from criminal acts by reoffenders. Further, the fact that some states and the federal government require a level of individualized suspicion before searching a parolee was of little relevance to the Supreme Court in determining whether California's system was drawn to meet the state's needs and is reasonable, taking into account a parolee's substantially diminished expectation of privacy.

§ 13.7 Conclusion

The decisions of *Morrissey v. Brewer* and *Gagnon v. Scarpelli* have defined the center limits of procedural due process with respect to probation and parole revocation. The administrative decisions of granting, rescinding, revoking, and continuing parole will always be subject to judicial attack by those who are adversely affected. Disenchantment with the parole process has led to movements to abolish indeterminate sentencing, upon which parole is based. Whether the proponents of determinate or indeterminate sentencing ultimately win, the majority of jurisdictions in the foreseeable future will be faced with complying with procedural due process requirements necessary for a "fundamentally fair" community supervision system.

The federal system of parole was abolished in 1992 and was replaced by the United States Sentencing Commission. Although the new scheme was held to be constitutional in *Mistretta* but nonbinding on federal district court sentencing decisions in *Booker*, the relationship between sentencing and release decisions continues to develop.

In addition, the Supreme Court has addressed numerous topics pertinent to those on probation or parole. For example, in *Griffin*, *Knights*, *Samson*, and *Scott*, the Court has severely curtailed the Fourth Amendment protections of offenders on community supervision, holding that the state has a "special needs" interest in ensuring probationers and parolees are abiding by their conditions.

Notes

1 Nibert v. Carroll Trucking Co., 82 S.E.2d 445 (W. Va. 1954); Richmond v. Commonwealth, 402 A.2d 1134 (Pa. Commw. 1979).

2 PUB. L. NO. 98–473.

3 Laura M. Maruschak & Todd D. Minton, BUREAU OF JUSTICE STATISTICS, CORRECTIONAL POPULATIONS IN THE UNITED STATES, 2017–2018 (2020), http://bjs.gov/content/pub/pdf/cpus1718.pdf.

4 442 U.S. 1 (1979); Board of Pardons v. Alleni, 482 U.S. 369 (1987) (A Montana statute provided that a prisoner eligible for parole "shall" be released when there is a reasonable probability that no detriment will result to him or the community and specified that parole

shall be ordered for the best interests of society and when the State Board of Pardons believes that the prisoner is able and willing to assume the obligations of a law-abiding citizen. This statute created the same liberty interest that was protected in Greenholtz).

5   452 U.S. 458 (1981).

6   520 F.2d 27 (2d Cir. 1975); Didousis v. New York State Board of Parole, 391 N.Y.S.2d 222 (1977).

7   430 F.2d 403 (2d Cir. 1970).

8   363 F. Supp. 416 (W.D.N.Y. 1973), *aff'd*, 500 F.2d 925 (2d Cir. 1974), *vacated as moot*, Regan v. Johnson, 419 U.S. 1015 (1974).

9   Wiley v. United States Board of Parole, 380 F. Supp. 1194 (M.D. Pa. 1974); Roach v. Board of Pardons and Paroles, Arkansas, 503 F.2d 1367 (8th Cir. 1974); Calabro v. United States Board of Parole, 525 F.2d 660 (5th Cir. 1975); Zannino v. Arnold, 531 F.2d 687 (3d Cir. 1976); Lott v. Dalsheim, 474 F. Supp. 897 (N.Y. 1979); Campbell v. Montana State Board of Pardons, 470 F. Supp. 1301 (D. Mont. 1979).

10   Soloway v. Weger, 389 F. Supp. 409 (M.D. Pa. 1974); Candarini v. United States Attorney General, 369 F. Supp. 1132 (E.D.N.Y. 1974); Craft v. United States Attorney General, 379 F. Supp. 538 (M.D. Pa. 1974); cf. Young v. Duckworth, 394 N.E.2d 123 (Ind. 1979); Bowles v. Tenant, 613 F.2d 776 (9th Cir. 1980).

11   28 U.S.C. §§ 991, 994, and 995(a)(1) (1998).

12   18 U.S.C. § 3551 *et seq.* (1982 ed., Supp. IV), and 28 U.S.C. §§ 991–998 (1982 ed., Supp. IV).

13   488 U.S. 361 (1989).

14   543 U.S. 220 (2005).

15   514 U.S. 499 (1995).

16   *See* Lindsey v. Washington, 301 U.S. 397 (1937); Miller v. Florida, 482 U.S. 423 (1987); and Weaver v. Graham, 450 U.S. 24 (1981).

17   910 F. Supp. 1208 (W.D. Tex. 1995).

18   City of Cleburne, Texas v. Cleburne Living Center, Inc., 473 U.S. 432 (1985) (equal protection requires that similarly situated persons be treated alike).

19   Woods v. Smith, 60 F.3d 1161 (5th Cir. 1995).

20   Tex. Crim. Proc. Code Ann. Art. 42.18, § 8(f)(2) (as amended by Act of May 29, 1995, 74th Leg., R.S., ch. 253, § 1, 1995 Tex. Sess. Law Serv. 2179 (Vernon)).

21   Hilliard v. Board of Pardons and Paroles, 759 F.2d 1190 (5th Cir. 1985).

22   *Hilliard*, 759 F.2d at 1193.

23   452 U.S. 458 (1981).

24   Ohio Adult Parole Authority v. Woodard, 523 U.S. 272 (1998).

25   Justices Rehnquist, Scalia, Kennedy, and Thomas.

26   Justices O'Connor, Souter, Ginsburg, and Breyer.

27   Justice Stevens.

28   408 U.S. 471 (1972).

29   408 U.S. 471 (1972).

30   398 U.S. 128 (1967).

31   *Id.* at 133.

32   *Id.* at 134.

33   Morrissey v. Brewer, 408 U.S. 471 (1972).

34   *Id.* at 484.

35   408 U.S. 471 at 485. *But see* Moody v. Daggett, 429 U.S. 78 (1976).

36   Michigan, M.S.A. § 28.2310 (1).

37   Thompson v. McEvoy, 337 N.Y.S.2d 83 (1972); State v. Sylvester, 401 So. 2d 1123 (Fla. Dist. Ct. App. 1981); Commonwealth v. Boykin, 411 A.2d 1244 (Pa. Super. 1979).

38   429 U.S. 78 (1976).

39   Reese v. United States Board of Parole, 530 F.2d 231 (9th Cir. 1976); Gaddy v. Michael, 519 F.2d 699 (4th Cir. 1975); Small v. Britton, 500 F.2d 299 (10th Cir. 1974); Moody v. Daggett,

429 U.S. 78 (1976).

40 Inmates' Councilmatic Voice v. Rogers, 541 F.2d 633 (6th Cir. 1976); In re Law, 513 P. 2d 621 (Cal. Sup. Ct. 1973); Battle v. Commonwealth, Pennsylvania Board of Probation and Parole, 403 A.2d 1063 (Pa. Commw. Ct. 1979); Commonwealth v. Del Conte, 419 A.2d 780 (Pa. Super. 1980).

41 524 F.2d 77 (5th Cir. 1975).

42 Standlee v. Rhay, 403 F. Supp. 1247 (E.D. Wash. 1975).

43 *See also* Barrows v. Hogan, 379 F. Supp. 314 (M.D. Pa. 1974); People v. Grayson, 319 N.E.2d 43 (Ill. 1974), *cert. denied*, 421 U.S. 994 (1975); cf. People ex rel. Murray v. New York State Board of Parole, 417 N.Y.S.2d 286 (N.Y. App. Div. 1979) and People ex rel. Froats v. Hammock, 443 N.Y.S.2d 500 (N.Y. App. Div. 1981).

44 545 P. 2d 249 (Cal. 1976).

45 United States ex rel. Carrasquillo v. Thomas, 527 F. Supp. 1105 (S.D.N.Y. 1981), *aff'd*, 677 F.2d 225 (2d Cir. 1982). (The fact that an indictment was dismissed with prejudice did not preclude a parole revocation proceeding resting upon the same allegations as those contained in the indictment); *see also* In re Dunham, 545 P. 2d 255 (Cal. 1976); Standlee v. Smith, 518 P. 2d 721 (Wash. 1974).

46 557 F.2d 1303 (9th Cir. 1977).

47 State v. Rasler, 532 P. 2d 1077 (Kan. Sup. Ct. 1975); People ex rel. Walker v. Hammock, 435 N.Y.S.2d 410 (N.Y. App. Div. 1981); Avery v. State, 616 P. 2d 872 (Alaska 1980).

48 425 U.S. 308 (1976).

49 Atkins v. Marshall, 533 F. Supp. 1324 (S.D. Ohio 1982) (A parolee's rights at a revocation hearing were violated when there was a disparity in the notice of reasons for revocation and the parole board's asserted grounds for revocation); Morishita v. Morris, 702 F.2d 207 (10th Cir. 1983) (Written findings in a probation revocation hearing are constitutionally required only when the record is such that a reviewing court is unable to determine the reasons for revocation. Failure to make written findings does not violate a probationer's due process rights when the revocation is based upon a single ground).

50 Morrissey v. Brewer, 408 U.S. at 389.

51 411 U.S. 778 (1973).

52 *Id.* at 790.

53 *Id.* at 791.

54 304 N.E.2d 793 (Ind. 1973).

55 *Id.* at 794.

56 *Id.*

57 Cottle v. Wainwright, 493 F.2d 397 (5th Cir. 1974).

58 United States v. Ross, 503 F.2d 940 (5th Cir. 1974).

59 Rhodes v. Wainwright, 378 F. Supp. 329 (M.D. Fla. 1974).

60 People ex rel. Donohoe v. Montanye, 318 N.E.2d 781 (N.Y. 1974).

61 *Supra* at nn. 61 and 62; cf. Passaro v. Commonwealth, Pennsylvania Board of Probation and Parole, 424 A.2d 561 (Pa. Commw. 1981) (The Board has no duty or responsibility to appoint counsel for an indigent appearing before it); Gates v. DeLorenzo, 544 F.2d 82 (2d Cir. 1976), *cert. denied*, 430 U.S. 941 (1977) (Due process does not require the participation of counsel in parole release hearings).

62 496 F.2d 270 (6th Cir. 1974).

63 Morrissey v. Brewer, 408 U.S. at 489.

64 Gagnon v. Scarpelli, 411 U.S. 778 at 789.

65 FED. R. EVID. Appendix II, Rules 803 and 804.

66 Commonwealth v. Kates, 305 A.2d 701 (Pa. 1973); Ward v. Parole Board, 192 N.W.2d 537 (Mich. Ct. App. 1971); Zizzo v. United States, 470 F.2d 105 (7th Cir. 1972); United States v. Miller, 514 F.2d 41 (9th Cir. 1975); State v. Marrapese, 409 A.2d 544 (R.I. 1979); cf. In re Diane B., 29 Cr. L. 2040 (D.C. Super. Ct. 1981) (Hearsay evidence may not be used in the D.C. court to revoke a juvenile's probation).

67 State v. Miller, 42 Ohio St. 2d 102 (1975); Birzon v. King, 469 F.2d 1241 (2d Cir. 1972); People v. Lewis, 329 N.E.2d 390 (Ill. App. Ct. 1975); People ex rel. Wallace v. State, 417 N.Y.S.2d 531 (N.Y. App. Div. 1979); Anaya v. State, 606 P. 2d 156 (Nev. 1980).

68 Pennsylvania Board of Probation and Parole v. Scott, 524 U.S. 357 (1998).

69 418 U.S. 539, 71 Ohio Op. 2d 336 (1974).

70 Lepre v. Butler, 394 F. Supp. 185 (E.D. Pa. 1975).

71 390 F. Supp. 19 (C.D. Cal. 1974).

72 *Id.* at 21. *See also* Karger v. Sigler, 384 F. Supp. 10 (D. Mass. 1974); Batchelder v. Kenton, 383 F. Supp. 299 (C.D. Cal. 1974).

73 383 F. Supp. 402 (D. Conn. 1974).

74 Sexton v. Wise, 494 F.2d 1176 (5th Cir. 1974); McIntosh v. Woodward, 514 F.2d 95 (5th Cir. 1975); State ex rel. Van Curen v. Ohio Adult Parole Authority, 45 Ohio St. 2d 298 (1976); Van Curen v. Jago, 454 U.S. 14 (1981) (When a state does not make parole a "right," the rescission of parole without a hearing violates no constitutional rights of the prisoner).

75 Temple v. Smith, 548 P. 2d 1274 (Utah Sup. Ct. 1976).

76 Lynce v. Mathis, 519 U.S. 433, 117 S. Ct. 891 (1997).

77 511 U.S. 39 (1994).

78 Sweeney v. United States, 353 F.2d 10 (7th Cir. 1965); *see also* cf. State v. Cooper (N.C. Ct. App. 1981), 29 Cr. L. 2125 (A credit card defendant's condition of probation that he be forbidden to drive a car between midnight and 5:30 A.M. was held to be reasonably related to his offense and therefore valid).

79 Bird v. State, 190 A.2d 804 (Md. Ct. App. 1963); But cf. State v. Morgan 28 Cr. L. 2260 (La. Sup. Ct. 1980) (A probation condition that required a woman convicted of attempted prostitution to stay out of the French Quarter was valid).

80 United States v. Stine, 675 F.2d 69 (3d Cir. 1982).

81 Bearden v. Georgia, 461 U.S. 660 (1983).

82 547 U.S.843 (2006).

83 United States v. Johnson, 446 F.3d 272 (2d Cir. 2006).

84 Gementera v. United States, 379 F.3d 596 (9th Cir. 2005).

85 Commonwealth v. Kendrick, No. SJC-09514 (Mass. 2006).

86 Bundy v. Stommel, 168 Fed. Appx. 870 (10th Cir. 2006).

87 *Id.*

88 311 F. Supp. 749 (N.D. Cal. 1970).

89 *Id.* at 750; *see also* Barton v. Malley, 626 F.2d 151 (10th Cir. 1980).

90 327 F. Supp. 1294 (S.D.N.Y. 1971).

91 *Id.* at 1306.

92 92 Cal. Rptr. 880 (Cal. Ct. App. 1971).

93 State v. Credeur, 328 So. 2d 59 (La. 1976).

94 420 Mass. 410 (1995).

95 Simon & Schuster, Inc. v. New York Crime Victims Board, 502 U.S. 105 (1991).

96 *See also* United States v. Terrigno, 838 F.2d 371 (9th Cir. 1988).

97 United States v. Saechao, 418 F.3d 1073 (9th Cir. 2005).

98 438 U.S. 868 (1987).

99 534 U.S. 112 (2001).

100 547 U.S. 843 (2006).

101 547 U.S.843 (2006).

102 United States v. Knights, 534 U.S. 112 (2001).

103 Morrissey v. Brewer, 408 U.S. 471 (1972).

104 Pennsylvania Bd. of Probation and Parole v. Scott, 524 U.S. 357 (1998).

Juvenile and Youthful Offenders 14

Chapter Outline

§ 14.1 Introduction

Prior to the nineteenth century, juveniles who came into contact with the criminal justice system were treated the same as adults. Juveniles had the same rights and expectations as adults, and they received the same punishments—including both corporal and capital punishments.[1] There was no separate juvenile justice system or juvenile court, and convicted juveniles were housed in the same correctional facilities as adults. For the purposes of the criminal justice system, juveniles were simply "little adults." This began to change, however, in the early 1800s. During this time, "children began to be viewed as persons at a unique stage of human development instead of smaller versions of adults with equal cognitive and moral capacities."[2] Adolescence became recognized as a distinctive stage of life characterized by physical, intellectual, social, emotional, and moral maturation.

The first juvenile court was created in Cook County (Chicago), Illinois, in 1899. The purpose of the early courts was to rehabilitate and educate delinquent and wayward youth. They were based on the *parens patriae* philosophy in which the court can assume responsibility over delinquent or unruly youth. It is then up to the court to take action that is in the best interest of the juvenile. Depending on the specific circumstances for each youth, this action may include—among others—probation, removing neglected or abused youths from their home and placing them in a safe setting, or placing delinquent youth in a secure confinement facility (i.e., the juvenile equivalent of an adult prison or jail).

All of the constitutional rights discussed in Chapters 2 through 11 also apply to juveniles who are confined in a correctional institution. For example, in *Nelson v. Heyne*,[3] the Indiana Boys School routinely used corporal punishment (i.e., paddling) to control youth in the facility. The Seventh Circuit held that this violated the juveniles' Eighth Amendment protection against cruel and unusual punishment, stating that "the infliction of a severe punishment by the State cannot comport with human dignity when it is nothing more than the pointless infliction of suffering."

Further, due to their status as juveniles, some courts have granted incarcerated juveniles constitutional protections above those granted to adult inmates. In *N.G. v. Connecticut*,[4] for example, the Second Circuit held that strip searches conducted on female juveniles after their transfer from one detention facility to another were unlawful. As discussed in Chapter 3, these searches would not be constitutional violations were they conducted on adult offenders.

The balance of this chapter focuses on Supreme Court cases directly related to juvenile offenders. It includes cases governing juvenile court proceedings, the death penalty for juveniles, and sentences of life without parole.

§ 14.2   Juvenile Court Proceedings

Early juvenile court hearings involving allegedly delinquent youth were considered to be civil proceedings, as opposed to criminal proceedings, due to the court's reliance on the *parens patriae* philosophy and the assertion that youths in the juvenile court were not being punished (and thus did not require a criminal proceeding). Instead, the court process was likened to civil proceedings in which the goal was to make decisions that were in the best interest of all parties involved, particularly the juvenile. However, because these hearings were not considered criminal in nature, youths who came in front of the juvenile court were not guaranteed any of the constitutional protections that adult defendants received, such as the right to counsel, the right against self-incrimination, or the right to notice of the charge(s) against them.

In the early twentieth century, due to the potential ethical violations and judicial misconduct inherent in adjudication hearings where juveniles have no constitutional rights, many advocates argued that youth should share the same rights afforded to adults in court proceedings.[5] It was not until 1966, however, that the U.S. Supreme Court began to apply constitutional safeguards to juvenile court proceedings.

The Court's first foray into constitutional rights in the juvenile court process was the 1966 case *Kent v. U.S.*[6] At 16 years old, Kent was arrested for burglary, robbery, and rape. His case was waived to criminal court without a hearing. On appeal, the issue before the Supreme Court was whether juveniles have any due process rights in situations where their case is transferred, or waived, from juvenile court to criminal court. Because the transfer decision is a "critically important stage" in the judicial process, the Court ruled that juveniles must be provided four safeguards before transfer: (1) a transfer hearing, (2) the right to counsel at the hearing, (3) access to the records used by the juvenile court when making the transfer decision, and (4) a written statement of the reasons for the judge's decision. Though this case applied only to transfer hearings, it is significant because it is the first case in which the Supreme Court provided oversight into the juvenile court process.

Arguably the most significant Supreme Court case regarding juvenile court procedure was *In re Gault.*[7] Gault was 15 years old when he was arrested for making lewd phone calls. His court hearing was held the next day, and the petition filed against him did not include an actual charge; it simply stated he was a "delinquent minor." Without representation by an attorney, Gault was ultimately committed to a training school (i.e., a juvenile prison) until his twenty-first birthday, or a total of six years. The maximum sentence for an adult convicted of the same crime would have been a $50 fine or a maximum of two months in jail.

Gault filed a habeas corpus petition, claiming denial of various due process protections. The Arizona Supreme Court denied the petition. On appeal, the U.S. Supreme Court held that Gault had been denied due process because the court hearing did not meet the minimum requirements for fair treatment under the Constitution: "When proceedings may result in incarceration in an institution of confinement, it would be extraordinary if our Constitution did not require the procedural regularity and exercise of care implied in the phrase *due process*."[8] The *Gault* ruling required that juveniles be provided with four due process rights during delinquency hearings when there is a possibility of placement in a secure facility: (1) the right to counsel, (2) the right to confront and cross-examine witnesses, (3) the right against self-incrimination, and (4) the right to notice of the hearing and the charges.

In the case *In re Winship*,[9] the Court was faced with the issue of whether the Due Process Clause of the Fourteenth Amendment requires "proof beyond a reasonable doubt" in adjudication hearings. Before *Winship*, prosecutors in most states only had to prove their case against juveniles by a "preponderance of the evidence," a lesser standard than that required in adult court proceedings. In *Winship*, the Court ruled: "Proof beyond a reasonable doubt, which is required by the Due Process Clause in criminal trials, is among the essentials of due process and fair treatment required during the adjudicatory stage when a juvenile is charged with an act that would constitute a crime if committed by an adult."[10]

In *Breed v. Jones*,[11] the Court had to determine whether the Fifth Amendment's protection against double jeopardy (i.e., being tried twice for the same offense) applied to juveniles. At age 17, Jones was arrested for robbery. He was adjudicated delinquent in juvenile court but was determined to be unamenable "to the care, treatment and training program available through the facilities of the juvenile court."[12] As such, Jones was transferred to criminal court, where he was again tried for the same offense and found guilty.

On appeal, the Supreme Court ruled that being tried in both juvenile and criminal court for the same offense constituted double jeopardy: "[Jones] was subjected to the burden of two trials for the same offense; he was twice put to the task of marshaling his resources against those of the State, twice subjected to the 'heavy personal strain' that such an experience represents."[13] The result of this case is that whichever court—juvenile or criminal—hears the facts of the case must also issue the sanction if the youth is found guilty.

In a 1984 case, *Schall v. Martin*,[14] the New York Family Court Act authorized pretrial detention of a juvenile delinquent if there was a serious risk that the juvenile may commit another crime if released prior to his or her next court hearing. A group of juveniles who had been detained under the act filed a habeas corpus petition claiming that the New York law violated the Due Process Clause of the Fourteenth Amendment. The federal district court struck down the statute, and the Second Circuit affirmed. The Supreme Court reversed, holding that pretrial detention of a juvenile defendant does not violate the Due Process Clause: "Preventative detention under the statute serves the legitimate state objective, held in common with every

State, of protecting both the juvenile and society from the hazards of pretrial crime. That objective is compatible with the 'fundamental fairness' demanded by the Due Process Clause in juvenile proceedings."[15]

Finally, there is one constitutional right that has not been extended to juvenile court proceedings. In *McKeiver v. Pennsylvania*,[16] the Supreme Court ruled that although prior cases had given juveniles many of the same rights enjoyed by adult defendants, the Constitution does not require jury trials in the juvenile court. The Court argued that "in our legal system, the jury is not a necessary component of accurate fact finding. . . . The imposition of the jury trial on the juvenile court system would not strengthen greatly, if at all, the fact finding function, and would, contrarily, provide an attrition of the juvenile court's assumed ability to function in a unique manner."[17]

§ 14.3   Juvenile Sentences

One of the primary legal issues in juvenile justice jurisprudence over the past few decades has been whether certain sentences are appropriate for juvenile delinquents due to their diminished culpability. More specifically, courts have had to determine whether capital punishment and life without parole (LWOP) sentences are permissible under the Eighth Amendment's ban on cruel and unusual punishment. Prior to the Supreme Court's decision in *Roper v. Simmons*, juveniles who committed capital murder could receive the death penalty or LWOP, the same as adults. Indeed, since the founding of the United States, approximately 365 executions have occurred in which the offender was either a juvenile at the time of execution or at the time the crime was committed.[18] However, only 22 of these executions occurred between 1976 (when the death penalty was reinstated after a short moratorium) and 2005 (when *Roper* was decided).

§ 14.3.1   – The Death Penalty

The issue of capital punishment for juvenile offenders has had a back-and-forth history in the courts. In the 1988 case *Thompson v. Oklahoma*,[19] 15-year-old Thompson participated in the brutal murder of his former brother-in-law. The juvenile court judge waived jurisdiction; Thompson was then tried as an adult, convicted, and sentenced to death. An Oklahoma appellate court affirmed the conviction and sentence. The U.S. Supreme Court granted certiorari to determine "whether the execution of [the death sentence] would violate the constitutional prohibition against the infliction of 'cruel and unusual punishments.'"[20]

A 5–4 Court vacated Thompson's sentence, holding that the Eighth Amendment prohibits the execution of a person who was under 16 years of age at the time of his or her offense. In making their decision, the majority relied on the "evolving standards of decency" standard.[21] They argued that multiple state statutes, professional organizations, and other nations had expressly condemned capital punishment for those under the age of 16 at the time of their offense, thus supporting the view that it would "offend civilized standards of decency" to do so. The Court concluded:

> The juvenile's reduced culpability, and the fact that the application of the death penalty to this class of offenders does not measurably contribute to the essential purposes underlying the penalty, also support the conclusion that the imposition of the penalty on persons under the age of 16 constitutes unconstitutional punishment.

The Court in *Thompson* left unanswered the question of whether a juvenile who was 16 or 17 at the time of his or her offense can receive the death penalty. However, that question was answered less than one year later in *Stanford v. Kentucky*.[22] The procedural facts in *Stanford* were very similar to those in *Thompson*, except that Stanford was 17 years old when he committed murder.

In a 5–3 plurality opinion, the *Stanford* Court upheld the death sentence for those who commit capital crimes at 16 or 17 years old. Relying on the same "evolving standards of decency" test, the Court stated:

> The primary and most reliable evidence of national consensus—the pattern of federal and state laws—fails to meet [Stanford's] heavy burden of proving a settled consensus against the execution of 16- and 17-year-old offenders. Of the 37 States that permit capital punishment, 15 decline to impose it on 16-year-olds and 12 on 17-year-olds. This does not establish the degree of national agreement this Court has previously thought sufficient to label a punishment cruel and unusual.[23]

Though the use of capital punishment for those who committed murder as a juvenile decreased throughout the twentieth century, it was officially abolished in 2005 with the Court's decision in *Roper v. Simmons*.[24] With five new justices on the Court who were not there in 1989, *Roper* overruled the Court's decision in *Stanford*.

At 17 years old, Simmons committed a capital murder and was sentenced to death. After the Court's decision in *Atkins v. Virginia*,[25] which prohibited the execution of a mentally retarded person, Simmons filed a habeas corpus petition arguing that the *Atkins'* reasoning established that the Constitution prohibits the execution of a juvenile who was under 18 when he committed the crime. The Missouri Supreme Court agreed and changed Simmons's sentence to life imprisonment without the possibility of parole, holding that a national consensus had developed since *Stanford* against the execution of juvenile 17-year-old offenders.

On appeal, the U.S. Supreme Court affirmed the Missouri Supreme Court's decision. The Court argued that there was now a national and international consensus that executing juveniles had become a rarity: "The objective indicia of consensus in this case—the rejection of the juvenile death penalty in the majority of states; the infrequency of its use even where it remains on the books; and the consistency in the trend toward abolition of the practice—provide sufficient evidence that today our society views juveniles as categorically less culpable than the average criminal."[26] The Court also stated that three differences between juveniles and adults demonstrate that the former cannot be classified among the worst offenders and thus be deserving of the death penalty: (1) Scientific research has shown that juveniles have a lack of maturity and an underdeveloped sense of responsibility; (2) juveniles are more susceptible to outside influences; and (3) a juvenile's character is not as well formed as that of an adult. Based on these arguments, the Court ruled that offenders who commit a capital offense under the age of 18 cannot be executed for their crimes.

§ 14.3.2   — Life Without Parole

Though *Roper* prohibited capital punishment for crimes committed by juveniles, many states at the time still sentenced juveniles to life without parole (LWOP)—the second most severe penalty permitted by law—for both homicide and nonhomicide offenses. Supreme Court cases in 2010 and 2012 limited the use of LWOP for juvenile offenders, though they did not completely prohibit the sanction.

In *Graham v. Florida*,[27] 17-year-old Graham was already on felony probation when he was arrested for robbery and possession of a firearm. He was sentenced to life in prison. Because Florida had abolished its parole system, the life sentence left Graham with no possibility of release. He thus challenged his sentence claiming that, due to his age, it constituted cruel and unusual punishment. A Florida appellate court affirmed the sentence, and then the Supreme Court granted certiorari.

In making their decision, the Supreme Court again relied on the "evolving standards of decency" criteria and ruled that the Eighth Amendment prohibits juvenile offenders from being sentenced to LWOP for a nonhomicide offense. The Court argued that, in practice, there is a national consensus against the use of LWOP for juvenile nonhomicide offenders: "Nationwide, there are only 129 juvenile offenders serving life without parole sentences for nonhomicide crimes. Because 77 of those offenders are serving sentences imposed in Florida and the other 52 are imprisoned in just 10 States and in the federal system, it appears that only 12 jurisdictions nationwide in fact impose life without parole sentences on juvenile nonhomicide offenders."[28] It should be noted that *Graham* only barred LWOP for juvenile nonhomicide offenses; the Court left to the states to determine whether to use LWOP for juveniles who commit murder.

Two years later, in *Miller v. Alabama*,[29] the Court addressed an Alabama statute that required all juveniles convicted of homicide—without exception—to receive a sentence of life without parole. On appeal, the Supreme Court held that the Eighth Amendment forbids a sentencing statute that mandates

LWOP for juvenile homicide offenders. In their opinion, the Court relied on the reduced culpability of juvenile offenders:

> Their lack of maturity and underdeveloped sense of responsibility lead to recklessness, impulsivity, and heedless risk-taking. They are more vulnerable . . . to negative influences and outside pressures, including from their family and peers; they have limited control over their own environment and lack the ability to extricate themselves from horrific, crime-producing settings. And because a child's character is not as well formed as an adult's, his traits are less fixed and his actions are less likely to be evidence of irretrievable depravity. *Roper* and *Graham* emphasized that the distinctive attributes of youth diminish the penological justifications for imposing the harshest sentences on juvenile offenders, even when they commit terrible crimes.[30]

It is important to note, however, that the *Graham* and *Miller* rulings do not prevent juvenile offenders from spending the rest of their lives in prison. Instead, these offenders must simply be given the opportunity for parole at some point; if the paroling authority determines that the offender is still a threat to society, it may deny parole and the offender will remain incarcerated.

§ 14.4   Conclusion

The constitutional rights discussed in the previous chapters also apply to juvenile offenders. Indeed, some states have granted incarcerated juveniles constitutional protections above those granted to adult inmates, due primarily to their age and reduced culpability. This chapter focused on three areas of case law that directly impact juvenile offenders. First, since the 1960s, the Supreme Court has afforded juveniles interacting with the juvenile court all of the constitutional protections adult defendants enjoy, except the right to a jury trial. Second, the constitutionality of the death penalty for juvenile offenders was settled after the Court's decision in *Roper*. It is now the "law of the land" that juveniles under the age of 18 who commit capital offenses cannot be executed for their crimes. Finally, *Graham* and *Miller* limited states' use of life imprisonment without parole sentences for juvenile offenders to only those who commit murder. Even then, the offender must be given the opportunity for release at some point.

Notes

1 ANN H. CROWE, JURISDICTIONAL TECHNICAL ASSISTANCE PACKAGE FOR JUVENILE CORRECTIONS (2000).

2 *Id.* at 26.

3 491 F. 2d 352 (7th Cir. 1974).

4 382 F. 3d 225 (2nd Cir. 2004).

5 CRAIG HEMMENS ET AL. 2 SIGNIFICANT CASES IN JUVENILE JUSTICE (2013).

6 383 U.S. 541 (1966).

7 387 U.S. 1 (1967).

8 *Id.*

9 397 U.S. 358 (1970).

10 *Id.*

11 421 U.S. 519 (1975).

12 *Id.* at 523.

13 *Id.* at 533.

14 467 U.S. 253 (1984).

15 *Id.*

16 403 U.S. 528 (1971).

17 *Id.* at 547.

18 AMY LINN, HISTORY OF DEATH PENALTY FOR JUVENILE OFFENDERS. JUVENILE JUSTICE INFORMATION EXCHANGE (2016).

19 487 U.S. 815 (1988).

20 *Id.* at 818.

21 Trop v. Dulles, 356 U.S. 86 (1958). *See* Chapter 12.

22 492 U.S. 361 (1989).

23 *Id.* at 362.

24 543 U.S. 551 (2005).

25 536 U.S. 304 (2002).

26 *Id.* at 567.

27 560 U.S. 48 (2010).

28 *Id.* at 64.

29 567 U.S. 460 (2012).

30 *Id.* at 461.

Legal Remedies Available to Prisoners   15

Chapter Outline

§ 15.1   Introduction

The preceding chapters have described various constitutional rights that offenders retain while they are incarcerated or on probation or parole. This chapter will set forth, in general terms, the judicial remedies that exist to vindicate past violations and to prevent future deprivations of those rights. Several frequently encountered obstacles to prisoner suits will also be discussed.

It is important to note that this chapter will discuss only judicial remedies. Not included is a discussion of possible "administrative remedies"—that is, methods and procedures that have been established within the correctional system itself to investigate, punish, and prevent deprivations of prisoner rights.[1]

The need for states to establish comprehensive administrative remedies for prisoner complaints is of critical importance. The Prison Litigation Reform Act[2] makes it imperative for a prison system to have a comprehensive grievance procedure to implement the protections offered through the exhaustion of remedies doctrine. This is the most effective way to resolve prisoner complaints within the prison environment and avoid costly litigation.

§ 15.2   The Old View or the Hands-Off Doctrine

Courts have traditionally abstained from hearing suits brought by prisoners against their keepers. This practice became so prevalent that it acquired its own name—the hands-off doctrine. Some courts have explained the doctrine in terms of a lack of subject matter jurisdiction over prisoner claims.[3] Courts rely on three separate reasons to support the doctrine:[4] (1) separation of powers (administration of prisons is an executive function), (2) lack of judicial expertise in penology, and (3) fear that judicial intervention will subvert prison discipline.

The hands-off doctrine has subsided in importance and has probably been sent to the dustbin of history. One extremely important step in the doctrine's decline was *Cooper v. Pate*,[5] in which the United States Supreme Court expressly held that a state prisoner could bring suit against his or her keepers under the 1970 Civil Rights Act, 42 U.S.C. § 1983. Any remnant left of the hands-off doctrine in federal courts today can probably best be described as a reluctance on the part of the judiciary to interfere in prison administration, but a reluctance that it will quickly shed upon allegations of denials of important constitutional or statutory rights.[6] The increasing number of prisoner suits being heard in federal courts tends to indicate that many courts today will liberally construe prisoner complaints as alleging denials of important federal rights.[7]

However, it is important to note that the flood of prisoner suits that has ended up in federal courts has created great concern for the federal judiciary system. As stated by then-Chief Justice Burger of the U.S. Supreme Court in 1976:

> Fully a sixth of the 117,000 cases of the civil docket of federal courts (19,000) are petitions from prisoners, most of which could be handled effectively and fairly within the prison systems. . . . Federal judges should not be dealing with prisoner complaints which, although important to a prisoner, are so minor that any well-run institution should be able to resolve them fairly without resorting to federal judges.[8]

This would indicate that the courts may not be willing to liberally construe prisoner complaints unless it appears that there have been denials of important federally protected rights. One result was the adoption of the Prison Litigation Reform Act, which stresses the importance of the mandated exhaustion of administrative remedies doctrine.

§ 15.3   Jurisdiction of Federal Courts

The subject matter jurisdiction of federal courts is limited to cases arising under the Constitution or laws of the United States.[9] Thus, before a federal court can render a valid decision in a case, the plaintiff must show that he or she is being denied a right secured to him or her by either the Constitution or a specific federal statute.

Representative statutes include:

1. The various civil rights statutes;

2. The Prison Litigation Reform Act;

3. The Americans with Disabilities Act;

4. The Religious Land Use and Institutionalized Persons Act;

5. The Federal Tort Claims Act; and

6. The *Bivens* doctrine.

If the prisoner-plaintiff's allegations do not constitute a violation of a federal right, the case must be dismissed if it is instituted in a federal court.[10] Because the judicial power of federal courts is defined and limited by the Constitution, federal courts are commonly referred to as courts of limited jurisdiction. If there is no federal jurisdiction to redress a wrong, relief must then be sought in state court, if at all.

When given a choice, prisoners and litigators prefer to take their claims to federal court. There are many reasons for this.

1. Procedure and the law are relatively standard throughout the United States, unlike the wide differences among the 50 states.

2. Federal judges have life tenure and are not subject to local political pressure as are many state judges.

3. Federal juries are drawn from throughout the district rather than on a county-by-county basis.

4. There is a "feeling" that better justice is obtained in federal court than in state court.

5. The backlog of cases is generally shorter in federal court.

§ 15.4   Jurisdiction of State Courts

In contrast to federal courts, state courts are courts of general jurisdiction. That is, there is a presumption that they have jurisdiction over a particular controversy unless a contrary showing is made. The subject matter jurisdiction of state courts is much broader than that of federal courts. In addition to being the exclusive means of judicially enforcing rights created by the state's constitution, statutes, and common law, a state court also has concurrent jurisdiction with the federal courts to decide cases based entirely on a federal claim,[11] provided that Congress has not given the federal judiciary exclusive jurisdiction in the matter. Therefore, a prisoner who alleges a violation of his or her federal constitutional rights may have a choice of forums in which he or she may bring the action, that is, either state or federal court.

Traditional common remedies, such as breach of contract, torts based on negligence, and intentional wrongdoing constitute the bulk of civil litigation in state courts. However, state law may prevent a claimant from any recovery in its state courts. California law is an example of similar laws in many states. In a California case, parole authorities were sued in state court based on the fact that a parolee had committed a murder while on parole.[12] Under California law, both the legislature and the courts have squarely rejected public liability for harm resulting from the failure to properly supervise a parolee. Parole authorities are immunized by § 845.8 of the California Government Code, which provides in relevant part:

Neither a public entity or [sic] public employee is liable for: (a) Any injury resulting from determining whether to parole or release a prisoner or from determining the terms and conditions of his parole or release or from determining whether to revoke his parole or release. (b) Any injury caused by:

(1) An escaping or escaped prisoner;

(2) An escaping or escaped arrested person; or

(3) A person resisting arrest.

In addition, § 846 of the Government Code states: "Neither a public entity nor a public employee is liable for injury caused by the failure to make an arrest or by the failure to retain an arrested person in custody."

In *Brenneman v. State of California*,[13] it was alleged that a child had been molested and murdered by a parolee. The appellate court dismissed the lawsuit, despite allegations of negligent supervision of the parolee and breach of a mandatory duty to conduct a reassessment of his risks and needs, stating that the allegations fit squarely under Government Code § 845.8, subdivision (a).

It was also argued that there was a deprivation of due process rights[14] by the release on parole, and the parole officer's failure to make mandatory home visits and to follow other mandatory provisions of California's parole procedures manual. These failings, however, were held to be insufficient to remove this case from the general rule that members of the public have no constitutional right to recover damages from state employees who fail to protect them from harm inflicted by third parties.[15]

Such immunity from suit in state court has, of course, no effect on a remedy in federal court.

§ 15.5   Barriers to Prisoner Lawsuits — Doctrine of Sovereign Immunity

A prisoner attempting to sue his or her keepers faces several serious obstacles, one of which is the doctrine of sovereign immunity. According to this doctrine, a private citizen may not sue a government unit or its agent without its consent. Various reasons advanced in support of the doctrine are: the idea that "the King can do no wrong," that public funds should not be dissipated to compensate private injuries, and that governmental officials need to be free from the threat of suit in order to function most effectively for the common good.

§ 15.5.1   — The Eleventh Amendment

For state liability, this principle of immunity is restated in the Eleventh Amendment to the United States Constitution, which provides:

> The Judicial power of the United States shall not be construed to extend to any suit in law or equity, commenced or prosecuted against one of the United States by Citizens of another State, or by Citizens or Subjects of any Foreign State.[16]

As a general proposition, the Eleventh Amendment prohibits a federal court from hearing a suit by private parties seeking to impose a liability that must be paid from state treasury funds, unless the state has consented to such a suit or immunity is waived by a federal statute. Regardless of the type of relief sought, states and their state agencies and departments are protected by the Eleventh Amendment from suit in federal court.[17] Further, absent consent by a state, the Eleventh Amendment prohibits federal court suits for monetary relief against state officers in their official capacity.[18] A state's Eleventh Amendment immunity extends to suits brought pursuant to the Civil Rights Act (42 U.S.C. § 1983).

Neither states nor governmental entities that are considered arms of the state for Eleventh Amendment purposes, nor state officials sued in their official capacity for money damages, are "persons" within the meaning of the Civil Rights Act. Although state officials literally are persons, a suit against a state official in his or her official capacity is not a suit against the official but rather a suit against the official's office. As such, it is no different from a suit against the state itself, and the Eleventh Amendment is applicable.

Immunity from suit is a fundamental aspect of the sovereignty that the states enjoyed before the ratification of the Constitution and that they retain today. The phrase *Eleventh Amendment immunity* is a convenient shorthand, but something of a misnomer, because the sovereign immunity of the states neither derives from nor is limited by the terms of the Eleventh Amendment. Historical sovereignty is the source of immunity from suit. Only states and arms of the state possess immunity from suits otherwise authorized by federal law.[19]

Sovereign immunity does not extend to counties even when they exercise a slice of state power. As a county may claim immunity neither based upon its identity as a county nor under an expansive arm-of-the-state test, it is subject to suit unless it was acting as an arm of the state, as delineated by precedents of the Supreme Court. However, county probation departments in California are considered arms of the state and are protected by the Eleventh Amendment.[20] California courts have held that the operation of a jail by a municipality or a county is a governmental function and that therefore a prisoner may not sue the political subdivision for injuries received while he or she is incarcerated.[21]

Municipalities, unlike states, do not enjoy a constitutionally protected immunity from suit as they are not arms of the state.[22]

§ 15.5.2   – State Sovereign Immunity

In a state where sovereign immunity is recognized, the state prison system is immune from a private suit for damages.[23] However, many states have either totally or partially repealed the doctrine of sovereign immunity by judicial decision or by constitutional or statutory amendment.[24] Thus, the defense of sovereign immunity in a prisoner's suit depends on the law in each state.

A prisoner whose rights are violated has, in theory, a choice of suing for damages in either a state court or under some federal statutory system, such as the Civil Rights Act. Such prisoners face two problems: First, the state may invoke sovereign immunity under its internal state constitutional system. In such situations, the doors to state courts are barred to the prisoner. Second, under circumstances when federal statutory or constitutional rights are violated, federal courts may be available under such statutes as the Civil Rights Act, but the prisoner may not be able to recover against the state itself due to the Eleventh Amendment.

Even in states that retain the doctrine of sovereign immunity, a prisoner who has been denied his or her constitutional rights may obtain an injunction against the allegedly wrongful conduct of an official in his or her individual capacity in order to prevent a future wrong. Violation of a court order against individuals results in a contempt citation, either civil or criminal.

In *Alabama v. Pugh*,[25] the Supreme Court dismissed an injunction sought by prisoners of the Alabama prison system against the state and the Alabama Board of Corrections because the Eleventh Amendment prohibits federal courts from entertaining suits against states and their agencies without its consent. The case, which alleged that conditions of the Alabama prisons constituted cruel and unusual punishment, had to proceed against the individual officials responsible for the administration of the prisons, instead of the state government itself. Even though it is a legal fiction, the courts treat such a suit as being against the defendant personally and not against the state. Therefore the defense of sovereign immunity is not available. The courts reason that a government official acting unconstitutionally is not acting as an agent of the government.[26]

Although states cannot be held monetarily liable in Civil Rights Act cases, state government officials can be held liable in their official or individual capacity under federal law. The liability of government officials in monetary damage suits presents a confusing picture. Unlike state officials, federal employees on practically every level are given immunity from suit, even if they act maliciously.[27] The rationale of these decisions is that federal officers must be free from fear of monetary liability for their acts in order to accomplish their public duties. However, this doctrine has been diminished by the *Bivens*[28] case, where federal agents were held to be monetarily liable for their actions on the same basis that a state official would be liable under § 1983.

In many states, government employees can be sued as individuals for committing intentional wrongs. Thus, in *Gullatte v. Potts*,[29] a state classification officer could be sued for the death of a prisoner where the officer could reasonably have expected his action to result in harm to the prisoner. The court stated that the action involved in this case was precisely the sort of abuse of governmental power that is necessary to raise an ordinary tort by a government agent to the stature of a constitutional violation. In states adhering to sovereign immunity, the liability of officers for negligence will often depend upon the discretionary or nondiscretionary nature of their acts, as will be more fully discussed later in this chapter.[30]

It is clear that the defense of sovereign immunity will often deny relief to innocent citizens injured by government officers. On the other hand, it is also clear that immunity for such officers will encourage them to work vigorously for the public good without fear of nuisance lawsuits. One possible solution to this paradox is suggested by Professor Kenneth C. Davis, a leading authority on administrative law in America.

According to Professor Davis, what the law of tort liability of public officers and employees needs most is an expansion of tort liability of government units. If the particular government unit is liable for the tort, so that the loss will be properly allocated, then the courts will be relieved of the need to choose between leaving a deserving plaintiff without a remedy and imposing liability upon the individual officer or employee, who is usually either ill equipped to bear the loss or is performing the type of function that can be properly performed only if the officer is free from the need to consider his or her own pocketbook. The public interest in fearless administration usually should come first, so that officers are immune from liability even when the plaintiff asserts that the officers have acted maliciously. When this is so, the only proper way to compensate deserving plaintiffs is to impose liability on the government unit. In this view, when the public receives the benefit of a program, the public should pay for the torts that may be expected, in order to carry out the program. The only satisfactory solution of many problems regarding liability of officers and employees is to compensate the plaintiff but to hold the officer or employee immune.[31]

§ 15.6   Suits Against State and Federal Prison Officials

Lawsuits are filed against the governmental entity involved, state or federal, and against those specific individuals responsible for the injury or wrong. Due to historical sovereign immunity issues, courts have attempted to avoid its application through legal fictions. One such fiction is the distinction between a public official being sued in his official capacity, in which the "real" defendant is a government unit, and a public official being sued for his or her individual conduct.

§ 15.6.1   – Official Capacity Suits

Official capacity suits, as long as the governmental entity receives notice and an opportunity to respond, is in all respects other than the name, a suit against the entity. It is not a suit against the official personally, because the real party in interest is the governmental entity.

A plaintiff seeking to recover on a judgment in an official capacity suit must look to the governmental entity itself. To establish liability, it must be shown that the official, acting under color of law, caused the deprivation of a federal right. More is required in an official capacity suit. It must be shown that the governmental entity was a "moving force" behind the deprivations. In an official capacity suit, the entity's "policy or custom" must have played a part in the violation of federal law.

The only immunities that can be claimed in an official capacity action are forms of sovereign immunity that the entity may possess, such as the Eleventh Amendment. This is no longer true with respect to suits against local governments, because local governments are not instruments of the state and thus are not immune from lawsuits under federal statutes.[32] There is no longer any need to bring official capacity suits against officials of local government, because local government may be sued directly for damages and injunctive or declaratory relief. Absent waiver, however, under the Eleventh Amendment, a state cannot be sued directly in its own name, regardless of the relief sought.

Neither a state nor state officials acting in their official capacities are "persons" within meaning of the Civil Rights Act. This is supported by the statute's language, congressional purpose, and legislative history. In common usage, the term *person* does not include a state. This usage is particularly applicable where it is claimed that Congress has subjected the states to liability to which they had not been subject before. Reading § 1983 to include states would be a decidedly awkward way of expressing such a congressional intent. The statute's language also falls short of satisfying the ordinary rule of statutory construction that Congress must make its intention to alter the constitutional balance between the states and the federal government unmistakably clear in a statute's language. Moreover, the doctrine of sovereign immunity was one of the well established common law immunities and defenses that Congress did not intend to override in enacting §1983.

It should be noted that the Supreme Court in *Monell v. Department of Social Services*[33] held that a municipality is a person under § 1983 because states are protected by the Eleventh Amendment, while municipalities are not. A lawsuit against state officials in their official capacities is not a suit against the officials but rather is a suit against the officials' offices and, thus, is no different from a suit against the state itself. Such a lawsuit cannot be predicated on § 1983.[34]

§ 15.6.2   – Personal Capacity Suits

Personal capacity suits seek to impose personal liability upon a government official for actions taken under color of state law for violating rights protected by the Constitution or a federal statute. An award of damages against an official in his or her personal capacity can be enforced only against the official's personal assets and not the assets of a governmental entity. As to defenses of liability, an official in a personal capacity suit may, depending on his or her position, be able to assert personal immunity defenses, such as objectively reasonable reliance on existing law. The immunity defenses are discussed next.

§ 15.7　Federal Remedies — Civil Suits Against Federal Prison Officials

A federal prisoner who claims that he suffered injuries as a result of negligent conduct by federal prison officials should theoretically be able to sue for damages. However, the doctrine of sovereign immunity[35] precluded such suits until Congress, in 1946, passed the Federal Tort Claims Act (FTCA), in which the federal government consented to be sued in certain situations. In 1963, the Supreme Court held that federal prisoners could maintain an action under the FTCA.[36]

Claims arising from certain specific fact situations are expressly excepted from the Act.[37] Excluded are: "Any claim arising out of assault, battery, false imprisonment, false arrest, malicious prosecution, abuse of process, libel, slander, misrepresentation, deceit, or interference with contract rights."[38] Also excluded from coverage under the FTCA are claims by prisoners for damage to their personal property.[39]

However, subject to the immunity doctrine,[40] federal officers are now liable for "constitutional torts" to the same extent as state officials under 42 U.S.C. § 1983.[41] In addition, under the *Bivens*[42] doctrine, federal agents are held monetarily liable for their actions on the same basis that a state official would be liable under § 1983.

§ 15.8　Federal Remedies — Civil Suits Against State Officials

The federal remedy most frequently used today by state prisoners is § 1983 of the Civil Rights Act, which provides:

> Every person who, under color of any statute, ordinance, regulation, custom, or usage, of any State or Territory, subjects, or causes to be subjected, any citizen of the United States or other person within the jurisdiction thereof to the deprivation of any rights, privileges, or immunities secured by the Constitution and laws, shall be liable to the party injured in an action at law, suit in equity, or other proper proceeding for redress.[43]

In 1964, the Supreme Court held that state prisoners can bring suit against their keepers under the Civil Rights Act.[44] In 1973, it further held that a § 1983 action was a proper remedy for a state prisoner to make a constitutional challenge to the conditions of his prison life, but not to the fact or length of his custody.[45] If the fact or length of custody is challenged, habeas corpus must be used.

To be liable under § 1983, a defendant must act under "color of law." Not every injury is a "federal case." For example, if an administrator at a state university unjustly prevents a peaceful protest rally, § 1983 is available.

However, if the same conduct occurs at a private college, the administrator did not act under "color of law." As there is no "state action," § 1983 is not available.

Questions often arise as to whether private parties who contract with state agencies act under "color of law" in dealing with prisoners. A private physician was under contract with North Carolina to provide orthopedic services at a state prison hospital on a part-time basis.[46] He treated a prisoner for a leg injury sustained in prison. The prisoner was barred by state law from employing or electing to see a physician of his own choosing. The doctor's conduct in treating the prisoner was fairly attributable to the state. The state has an obligation, under the Eighth Amendment and state law, to provide adequate medical care to those whom it has incarcerated. The state had delegated that function to physicians and deferred to their professional judgment. This result was not altered by the fact that the doctor was paid by contract and was not on the state payroll, nor by the fact that he was not required to work exclusively for the prison. It was the physician's function within the state system, not the precise terms of his employment, that was determinative.[47] The physician was acting "under color of law."

In addition to acting "under color of law" the liability of a defendant in a civil rights case must be personal. In civil rights litigation, there is no basis for *respondeat superior* liability,[48] where an employer is strictly liable for the actions of their employees. The employer–employee basis for liability does not apply in these federal lawsuits, as it would under the common law. To be liable under the federal Civil Rights Act, the action of a defendant must have directly caused the injury. Mere negligence is not enough.[49] For example, a sheriff was accused of condoning a deputy's use of excessive force against a county detention center detainee, who was not resisting, by failing to immediately terminate the deputy. As the failure to terminate occurred after the fact, the sheriff's failure to terminate the employee was not a cause of the deputy's conduct. Therefore, there was no basis for holding the sheriff individually liable under § 1983.[50]

Constitutional rights are not involved when a state official's negligent act causes an unintended loss of or injury to life, liberty, or property. The Constitution is intended to protect individuals from the abuse of power by government officials. Far from an abuse of power, lack of due care, such as from negligence, suggests no more than a failure to measure up to the conduct of a reasonable person. To hold that injury caused by such conduct is a deprivation within the meaning of the Constitution would trivialize the centuries-old principle of due process of law.[51]

The Constitution does not purport to supplant traditional tort law in laying down rules of conduct to regulate liability for injuries that attend living together in society. While the Due Process Clause speaks to some facets of the relationship between jailers and prisoners, its protections are not triggered by lack of due care by the jailers. Jailers may owe a special duty of care under state tort law to those in their custody, but the Due Process Clause does not embrace such a broad tort law concept.[52]

§ 15.8.1　 — State Remedies — Civil Suits

Prison officials have the duty, often imposed by statute,[53] to provide their prisoners with the basic necessities of life, such as clothing, food, shelter, and medical care. Failure to provide these items will render the official liable to the prisoner in a civil action. Thus, prison officials have been held liable in state courts for failing to provide needed medical services,[54] food,[55] and other necessities such as bedding, clothing, and sanitary conditions.[56]

In addition to their duties to provide the necessities of life, prison officials have a general duty to use reasonable care to prevent injuries to their prisoners. Failure to exercise such care is negligence, and a prison official will be liable in damages for the injuries caused by his or her negligence. Thus, a complaint stating that the superintendent of a camp for delinquent juveniles used one of his charges to fight a forest fire, without warning the youth of the danger, was held to state a cause of action for the boy's wrongful death.[57]

A prison official who intentionally injures a prisoner will be liable to him or her in a tort action for damages. Assault and battery are the most common intentional tort situations in a prison environment. A prisoner, like any other person, has the right to be free from offensive bodily contact that is intentionally inflicted upon him.[58]

These principles do not apply, however, to states that have granted their public officials sovereign immunity under their own statutes.

§ 15.9　 Federal Remedies Against Municipalities and Local Governments

Although cities and local governments are not protected by the Eleventh Amendment and sovereign immunity, they may only be held accountable in Civil Rights Act cases if the deprivation was the result of a "custom or policy." Local governments cannot be held liable solely on the basis of the acts of their officers and agents. As a general rule, local governments are not responsible for the unauthorized and unlawful acts of their officers, even though done under color of law.

For a local government to be liable for damages, it must appear that its officers were expressly authorized to do the acts or that the acts were done legitimately pursuant to a general authority to act for the local government on the subject to which they related, or that, in either case, the Act was adopted and ratified by the governmental entity. The word "policy" generally implies a course of action consciously chosen from among various alternatives.

In *Monell v. Department of Social Services*,[59] the Supreme Court required that it must be the "official policy" of a city to be liable for the acts of its agents. *Monell* intended to distinguish acts of the municipality from acts of the municipality's employees. As a result, municipal liability is limited to actions for which the municipality is actually responsible. *Monell* held that recovery from a municipality is limited to acts that are, properly speaking, "of the municipality"—that is, acts that the municipality has officially sanctioned or ordered. Municipal liability may be imposed for a single decision by municipal policymakers under appropriate circumstances. If the decision to adopt a particular course of action is directed by those who establish government policy, the municipality is equally responsible whether that action is to be taken only once or repeatedly.[60] Further, when there is a basis for § 1983 liability against a municipality, the city is not entitled to a defense of "good faith," as is an individual.[61]

For the purposes of liability under *Monell*, official policy may be created by custom, by training, or by a policymaker.

§ 15.9.1 — Custom

When officers act according to an accepted custom, the government agency may be liable for damages. However, custom is difficult to prove. In *Gregory v. Shelby County*,[62] a custom, for purposes of liability, was not established where one prisoner was beaten to death by another. Two cell doors were left open by a jail officer, allowing one prisoner to attack the other. The official policy of the county was that no two cell doors were to be open simultaneously. Although two doors were sometimes left open and disregard of the policy was tolerated, this was insufficient to create a custom and liability of the county.

§ 15.9.2 — Training

The Supreme Court held in *Pembaur v. City of Cincinnati*,[63] that a municipality may, in certain circumstances, be held liable under § 1983 for constitutional violations resulting from its failure to train its employees. The contention that § 1983 liability can be imposed only when the municipal policy in question is itself unconstitutional was rejected. There are circumstances in which a "failure to train" allegation can be the basis for liability.

Inadequacy of training may serve as the basis for § 1983 liability only when the failure to train in a relevant respect amounts to deliberate indifference to the constitutional rights of persons with whom the officials come into contact. This "deliberate indifference" standard is consistent with the rule of *Monell*— that a city is not liable under § 1983 unless a municipal "policy" or "custom" is the moving force behind the constitutional violation. Only when a failure to train reflects a "deliberate" or "conscious" choice by the municipality can the failure be properly thought of as an actionable city "policy." *Monell* cannot be satisfied by a mere allegation that a training program represents a policy for which the city is responsible. Rather, the focus must be on whether the program is adequate to the tasks the particular employees must perform, and if it is not, on whether such inadequate training can justifiably be said to represent "city policy." Moreover, the identified deficiency in the training program must be closely related to the ultimate injury. A Civil Rights Act plaintiff must still prove that the deficiency in training actually caused the constitutional violation. To adopt lesser standards of fault and causation would open municipalities to unprecedented liability under § 1983, would result in *de facto respondeat superior* liability, a result rejected in *Monell*, and would engage federal courts in an endless exercise of second-guessing municipal employee training programs. This would implicate serious questions of federalism.[64]

In *Barney v. Pulsipher*,[65] a county was held liable where a sheriff, as policymaker, made a conscious decision not to train reserve deputy sheriffs. The need to train reserve deputies was obvious. The failure to train constitutes deliberate indifference to the constitutional rights of citizens. The failure to train was the moving force behind severe injuries inflicted on an arrestee who was hurt by a reserve deputy when he used force because the arrestee got out of a car too slowly.

On the other hand, women who were sexually assaulted by a jailer while they were detained in a jail failed to establish liability on the grounds that the county failed to train jailers or to properly screen jailers before hiring them. The county did not act with deliberate indifference, as the sheriff and commissioners were unaware of any previous incidents involving a sexual assault of prisoners by a jailer. The jailer had completed a state certification training program and correctional officer course, and the jailer's background did not indicate that he was highly likely to sexually assault female prisoners.[66]

§ 15.9.3 — Policymaker

Counties create conceptual problems. Are they local governments or arms of the state? Alabama sheriffs, when executing their law enforcement duties, represent the state of Alabama, not their counties. Although the sheriff in *McMillian v. Monroe County Alabama*,[67] had final policymaking authority in the area of law enforcement, there was a disagreement in the lower court about whether Alabama sheriffs were policymakers for the state or for the county when acting in their law enforcement capacity. In deciding this dispute, the question was not whether Alabama sheriffs act as county or state officials in all of their official actions but whom they represented in a particular area or on a particular issue. The answer depended on the definition of the official's functions under relevant state law. In other words, Alabama procedural law governed the outcome of the case.

The Supreme Court determined that under Alabama law, the state's constitutional provisions concerning sheriffs, the historical development of those provisions, and the interpretation given them by the state supreme court strongly supported the proposition that sheriffs represent the state when acting in their law enforcement capacity. The Supreme Court reasoned that the nation's federal system allows the states wide authority to establish their state and local governments. The Court stressed that local variations can be tolerated under the federal system.

Reaffirming its earlier decisions in *Monell*[68] and *Pembaur*,[69] the Supreme Court held in *Board of the County Commissioners of Bryan County, Oklahoma v. Brown*,[70] that a municipality may not be held liable under § 1983 solely because it employs a person who caused an injury. To recover damages, a plaintiff must identify a municipal "policy" or "custom" that caused the injury. A "policy" giving rise to liability cannot be established merely by identifying a policymaker's conduct that is properly attributable to the municipality. A successful plaintiff must also demonstrate that, through its deliberate conduct, the municipality was the "moving force" behind the injury. A plaintiff must show that the municipal action was taken with the requisite degree of culpability and must demonstrate a direct causal link between the municipal action and the deprivation of federal rights.

A claim that a policymaker's single, facially lawful hiring decision triggers municipal liability presents difficult problems of proof. In *Pembaur*, the Supreme Court held that a § 1983 cause of action based on a single decision attributable to a municipality will exist only where the municipality had acted and that the plaintiff who had suffered a deprivation of federal rights also proved fault and causation. Claims not involving an allegation that the municipal action had itself violated federal law or directed or authorized the deprivation of federal rights require application of rigorous culpability and causation standards in order to ensure that the municipality is not held liable solely for its employees' actions.[71]

Predicting the consequences of a single hiring decision, even one based on an inadequate assessment of a record, will impose liability only where adequate scrutiny of the applicant's background would lead a reasonable policymaker to conclude that the plainly obvious consequence of the decision to hire the applicant would be the deprivation of a third party's federally protected right. An official's failure to adequately scrutinize an applicant's background does not constitute "deliberate indifference."

Pembaur further commented that even assuming that proof of a single instance of inadequate screening could trigger municipal liability, the sheriff's failure to scrutinize the deputy's record did not constitute "deliberate indifference" to any federally protected right to be free from the use of excessive force. To establish the link between the sheriff's action and the injury, a plaintiff must prove that from a full review of the deputy's record, the sheriff should have concluded that the deputy's use of excessive force would be a plainly obvious consequence of his decision to hire the deputy.

Under ordinary principles of tort law, there is no liability for failure to take action unless there is a legal duty to act. A claim against a prison officer for failing to protect an attacked prisoner who later died from injuries inflicted by other prisoners was denied. The officer did not callously, deliberately, or recklessly disregard the prisoner's safety. The prisoners were not engaged in any argument that was visible to the officer. The officer's failure to properly inspect the barracks at lights-out time demonstrated negligence at most. The officer did not know something was wrong between the prisoners until the fight was over and the attacked prisoner was beaten.[72] Further, no policy or custom was involved.

§ 15.10   Settlement Agreements and Procedural Issues

Settlement agreements to preclude future litigation may be enforced in certain situations. In *Town of Newbury v. Rumery*,[73] an agreement was negotiated whereby the prosecutor would dismiss the charges against the defendant if he would agree to release any claims that he might have against the town, its officials, or the victim for any harm caused by his arrest. The agreement was enforced when, ten months later, he filed an action under § 1983 alleging that the town and its officers had violated his constitutional rights by arresting him, defaming him, and imprisoning him falsely. The suit was dismissed on the basis of the assertion by the defendants of the release-dismissal agreement as an affirmative defense. The Supreme Court held that such agreements are not invalid per se. The question of whether the policies underlying § 1983 may in some circumstances render a waiver of the right to sue unenforceable is one of federal law, to be resolved by reference to traditional common law principles. The relevant principle is that a promise is unenforceable if the interest in its enforcement is outweighed in the circumstances by a public policy harmed by enforcement of the agreement.

Courts make every effort to summarily dismiss prisoner civil rights actions before protracted pretrial discovery and trial. One court of appeals attempted to accomplish this aim by adopting a "clear and convincing" evidence requirement to deal with civil rights suits against prison officials who allegedly violate a prisoner's constitutional rights. The usual standard of proof in civil cases is the lesser "preponderance of the evidence" standard. The court reasoned that because an official's state of mind was easy to allege and difficult to disprove, insubstantial claims turning on improper intent may be less amenable to summary disposition than other types of claims against government officials. The Supreme Court reversed,[74] holding that changing the burden of proof for an entire category of claims would stray far from the traditional limits on judicial authority. Nothing in § 1983 or any other federal statute or the Federal Rules of Civil Procedure provide any support for imposing a clear and convincing burden of proof. The lower court's unprecedented change lacked any common law authority and altered the cause of action in a way that undermined § 1983's very purpose—to provide a remedy for the violation of federal rights.

To the extent that the lower court was concerned with preventing excessive discovery, such questions are most frequently and effectively resolved by the rule-making or legislative process, not by the judicial process. In the Supreme Court's view, the lower court's indirect effort to regulate discovery employed a blunt instrument with a high cost that also imposed a heightened standard of proof at trial upon plaintiffs with *bona fide* constitutional claims.

In order to prevent threats and harassment of prison officials and to address these issues, in 1998 Congress passed a statute limiting a prisoner's access to information relating to prison employees.[75] The Act provides that in any civil rights action brought against a federal, state, or local jail, prison, or correctional facility, or any of their employees or former employees, that arises out of a prisoner's incarceration, the financial records of any employee cannot be disclosed without the written consent of the employee or pursuant to a court order, unless a verdict of liability has been entered against the employee. Also not subject to disclosure without the written consent of the employee or pursuant to a court order is the home address, home phone number, Social Security number, identity of family members, personal tax returns, and personal banking information of the employee, as well as any other records or information of a similar nature relating to that person.

Congress has further fashioned special rules to discourage prisoners' insubstantial suits enacting the Prison Litigation Reform Act.[76] The Act draws no distinction between constitutional claims that require proof of an improper motive and those that do not.

§ 15.10.1 — Civil Rights Act — Exhaustion of Remedies

Before passage of the Prison Reform Litigation Act in 1996, total exhaustion of state remedies in Civil Rights Act cases was not required.[77] The Supreme Court confused the question by stressing that futility or unavailability of state remedies in a particular case will not require a prisoner to perform the act of processing his claim through state agencies. Thus, a state prisoner complaining of poor living conditions at the Missouri State Penitentiary did not need to exhaust state judicial or administrative remedies.[78] As the great bulk of prisoner complaints under the Civil Rights Act deal with past deprivations of constitutional rights, no exhaustion was required.[79] However, the exhaustion doctrine was radically changed by the Prison Litigation Reform Act (PLRA).[80]

In two Supreme Court decisions,[81] the court held that one of the most important provisions of the PLRA is that prisoners, jailed individuals, and certain juveniles confined in correctional or detention facilities must exhaust any available administrative remedies before filing a federal lawsuit. This applies even when a prisoner seeks only money damages but the administrative process has no provision for recovery of money damages.

§ 15.10.2 — Standing

"Standing" is a judicial requirement that litigants have a personal stake in the outcome. American courts will not give advisory opinions. Lack of standing may be asserted as a defense in prison litigation. In *Leeke v. Timmerman*,[82] a lower court decision awarding $3,000 in compensatory damages, $1,000 in punitive damages, and attorney's fees, against the legal advisor to the South Carolina Department of Corrections and the Director of the Department of Corrections, was reversed. The allegation was that the defendants had attempted to prevent criminal charges from being filed by a prisoner against correctional officers after an alleged beating within the prison by intervening with the local prosecutor. The Supreme Court held that a private citizen (in this case the prisoner) had no standing in federal court to challenge the discretion of a prosecutor in his determination that criminal charges should or should not be filed. Because a complaining witness has the right to try to persuade a prosecutor to file charges, potential targets also have the right to try to persuade a prosecutor to not file charges.

§ 15.10.3   — Statute of Limitations

Statutes of limitations prevent the litigation of "stale" claims. Section 1983 does not specify the appropriate statute of limitations for civil rights actions. Federal rather than state law governs the characterization of a § 1983 claim for statute of limitations purposes. However, the length of the limitations period and related questions of tolling and application are to be governed by state law.[83] For example, in Ohio, the two-year statute of limitations[84] governs actions brought under § 1983.[85] A § 1983 claim is to be treated as a personal injury action for statute of limitations purposes.[86]

A state "notice of claim" statute has the same effect as an abbreviated statute of limitations. These are unconstitutional when applied to Civil Rights Act cases when litigated in a state court. Application of "notice of claims" statutes to state court § 1983 actions cannot be approved as a matter of equitable federalism. Just as federal courts are constitutionally obligated to apply state law to state claims, the supremacy clause of the Constitution imposes on state courts a constitutional duty to proceed in such a manner that all the substantial rights of the parties under controlling federal law are protected. A state law that predictably alters the outcome of § 1983 claims depending solely on whether they are brought in state or federal court within the state is obviously inconsistent with the federal interest in intrastate uniformity.[87]

It should be noted that under the continuing tort theory, when wrongful conduct in violation of § 1983 has occurred over a period of time, the violation is considered a continuing wrong.[88] The continuing wrong doctrine has been applied by the courts as an equitable remedy to ameliorate the harsh effects that may occur when a date must otherwise be arbitrarily selected to test whether a statute of limitations has expired. Under the continuing wrong doctrine, a cause of action for a continuous tort accrues and the limitations period begins when the wrongful conduct ceases.[89]

§ 15.11   Monetary Damages

A plaintiff who brings an action under the Civil Rights Act is entitled to an award of monetary damages in order to redress deprivations of his or her constitutional rights. There are three distinct classes of damages that a prisoner might recover from prison officials who have violated his or her constitutional rights: (1) actual damages to compensate the prisoner for out-of-pocket expenses and mental suffering; (2) nominal damages to vindicate the prisoner's rights, if no actual damages were sustained; and (3) punitive damages, if the wrongful act was done intentionally and maliciously.[90]

In *Sostre v. McGinnis*,[91] the court upheld an award of $9,300 in compensatory damages against a prison warden and the state commissioner of corrections. The damages were based upon the rate of $25 per day for the 372 days that the plaintiff spent in isolated confinement in deplorable conditions.[92] However, the court reversed an additional award of $3,720 in punitive damages because it found no malice on the part of the defendants.

In *Cruz v. Beto*,[93] the following formula was used by the court in determining monetary damages to the prisoners:

1. $1.00 to each prisoner-plaintiff for each day the segregation policy was imposed upon him . . .;

2. $25.00 to each prisoner-plaintiff for being deprived of PIP (merit) points while segregated;

3. $250.00 to each prisoner-plaintiff who was classified as medically unfit and who should not have been required, but was required, to perform field labor while segregated;

4. $250.00 to each prisoner-plaintiff who was prohibited from continuing college-level or secondary-level education while segregated. In addition, the court found that the attorney involved in the *Cruz* case was entitled to damages of $1,000.00 for "embarrassment, humiliation, and improper deprivation . . . of the right to practice law through representation of . . . prisoners."

Damages based on the abstract "value" or "importance" of constitutional rights are not a permissible element of compensatory damages in § 1983 cases. The basic purpose of a damage award in a § 1983 case is to compensate for injuries that are caused by the deprivation of constitutional rights. Damages measured by a jury's perception of the abstract "importance" of a constitutional right are not necessary to vindicate the constitutional rights that § 1983 protects and moreover are an unwieldy tool for ensuring compliance with the Constitution. Because such damages are wholly divorced from any compensatory purpose, they cannot be justified as presumed damages, which are a substitute for ordinary compensatory damages, not a supplement for an award that fully compensates the alleged injury.[94]

Punitive damages may be recovered in Civil Rights Act cases for reckless or callously indifferent deprivations of federal statutory or constitutional rights, as well as for deprivations motivated by actual malicious intent. Punitive damages may be recovered for reckless or callous indifference to federally protected rights even when the standard of liability for compensatory damages is also one of recklessness.

A prisoner in a Missouri reformatory for youthful first offenders was awarded $25,000 in compensatory damages and $5,000 in punitive damages. Smith, the correctional officer, placed the prisoner in administrative segregation in a cell with another prisoner. Smith later placed a third prisoner in the cell. The cellmates harassed, beat, and sexually assaulted the prisoner-plaintiff. Evidence at trial showed that the prisoner-plaintiff had placed himself in protective custody because of prior incidents of violence against him by other prisoners. The third prisoner that Smith placed in the cell had been placed in administrative segregation for fighting. Smith made no effort to find out whether another cell was available. In fact, there was another cell in the same dormitory with only one occupant. Further, only a few weeks earlier, another prisoner had been beaten to death in the same dormitory during the same shift, while Smith was on duty. It was held that Smith knew or should have known that an assault against the prisoner-plaintiff was likely under the circumstances.[95]

§ 15.12   Attorney's Fees

An item of monetary expense that a defendant prison official may be required to pay if he is violating constitutional rights is the cost of attorney's fees to the prisoner-plaintiff. The Supreme Court in *Alyeska Pipeline Service Co. v. Wilderness Society*[96] reaffirmed the general rule that, absent a statute or enforceable contract, litigants must pay their own attorney's fees. The Court pointed out, however, that there are recognized exceptions to this general rule. One exception is that a court may assess attorneys' fees for the willful disobedience of a court order, or when the losing party has acted in bad faith, vexatiously, wantonly, or for oppressive reasons. In response to the *Alyeska* decision in 1976, Congress passed a statute that grants attorney's fees in various civil rights actions, including suits against prison officials.[97] Attorney's fees may be granted to the "prevailing party."

An example of court-awarded attorney's fees is *Gates v. Collier*.[98] The court stated that under the Civil Rights Attorney's Fees Award Act,[99] the court may order that fees be paid out of the state treasury and, to effectuate this, may join the state auditor and treasurer as defendants. The court also held that interest may be awarded on attorney's fees but not on out-of-pocket costs, which are reimbursed under the Act. *Hutto v. Finney*[100] also held that the award of attorney's fees to be paid out of Department of Correction funds is adequately supported by the court's finding that state officials acted in bad faith and did not violate the Eleventh Amendment. The court further held that the statute[101] supports the court's award of additional attorney's fees to offset the cost of appeal.[102] Attorney's fees under 42 U.S.C. § 1988 may be awarded to the appropriate prevailing party in any § 1983 action, even though the action was brought in state court rather than federal court.[103]

A favorable judicial statement of law in the course of litigation that results in a judgment against the plaintiff in civil rights cases is insufficient to render a plaintiff a "prevailing party" and justify an award of attorney fees. Even if the prisoner's nonmonetary claims were not rendered moot by his release from prison, and it could be said that those claims were kept alive by his interest in expunging his misconduct conviction from his prison record, his counsel never took the steps necessary to have a declaratory judgment or expungement order properly entered. The argument that the initial holding of the district court was a "vindication of rights"—that is, at least the equivalent of declaratory relief—ignored the fact that a judicial decree is not the end of the judicial process but rather is the means of prompting some action (or cessation of action) by the defendant. In this case, the prisoner obtained nothing from the state. Moreover, equating statements of law (even legal holdings en route to a final judgment for the defendant) with declaratory judgments has the practical effect of depriving a defendant of any valid defenses that a court might take into account in deciding whether to enter a declaratory judgment. Furthermore, the same considerations that influence courts to issue declaratory judgments may not enter into the decision of whether to include statements of law in opinions. However, if they do, the court's decision is not appealable in the same manner as is its entry of a declaratory judgment.[104]

A prevailing party must be one who has succeeded on any significant claim involving some of the relief sought, either during litigation or at the conclusion of the litigation. A plaintiff has crossed the threshold to a fee award of some kind if he or she satisfies the "significant issue–some benefit" standard. Under that standard, at a minimum, the plaintiff must be able to point to a resolution of the dispute that materially alters the parties' legal relationship in a manner that Congress sought to promote in the fee statute. When the plaintiff's success on a legal claim can be characterized as purely technical or *de minimis*, a district court would be justified in concluding that it is so insignificant as to be insufficient to support designating the prisoner as a prevailing party. However, when the parties' relationship has been materially changed, the degree of the plaintiff's overall success goes to the reasonableness of the award under *Hensley*, not to the availability of the fee award.[105]

The extent of a plaintiff's success is a crucial factor in determining the proper amount of such fees. The time spent on unsuccessful claims that are completely distinct from successful claims is excluded in determining a reasonable fee. However, the fee should not be reduced simply because the court did not adopt each of several related claims. A plaintiff who achieves only limited success with a group of related claims should be awarded only the amount that is reasonably related to the results obtained. Plaintiffs may be considered prevailing parties for attorney's fee purposes if they succeed on any significant issue in litigation that achieves some of the benefit the parties sought in bringing the suit.

The starting point for the calculation of fees is the number of hours reasonably expended on the litigation, multiplied by a reasonable hourly rate. The fee may then be adjusted up or down, depending upon the results obtained. The burden is on the fee applicant to establish entitlement to an award and to document the appropriate hours expended and hourly rates. For appellate review, if a district court has articulated a fair explanation for its fee award in a given case, the court of appeals should not reverse or remand the judgment unless the award is so low as to provide clearly inadequate compensation to the attorneys in the case or so high as to constitute a windfall. However, in *Hensley v. Eckerhart*, the decision of the district court was reversed because the opinion did not properly consider the relationship between the extent of success and the amount of the fee award. The fee award against Missouri hospital officials at the forensic unit of a Missouri state hospital was in excess of $133,000.[106]

An issue arises when a plaintiff recovers only monetary damages. Fees in excess of the amount of damages recovered are not necessarily unreasonable. Although the amount of damages recovered is relevant to the amount of attorney's fees to be awarded under § 1988, it is only one of many factors that a court should consider in calculating an award of attorney's fees.

A civil rights action for damages is not merely a private tort suit benefiting only the individual plaintiffs whose rights were violated. Unlike most private tort litigants, a civil rights plaintiff seeks to vindicate important civil and constitutional rights that cannot be valued solely in monetary terms. Because damage awards do not fully reflect the public benefit advanced by civil rights litigation, Congress did not intend for fees in civil rights cases, unlike most private law cases, to depend on obtaining substantial monetary relief, but instead recognized that reasonable attorney's fees under § 1988 are not conditioned upon, and need not be proportionate to, an award of money damages. Consequently, a rule limiting attorney's fees in civil rights cases to a proportion of the damages awarded would seriously undermine Congress's purpose in enacting § 1988. Congress enacted § 1988 specifically because it found that the private market for legal services failed to provide many victims of civil rights violations with effective access to the judicial process. A rule of proportionality would make it difficult, if not impossible for individuals with meritorious civil rights claims but relatively small potential damages to obtain redress from the courts and would be totally inconsistent with Congress's purpose of ensuring sufficiently vigorous enforcement of civil rights. In order to ensure that lawyers would be willing to represent persons with legitimate civil rights grievances, Congress determined that it would be necessary to compensate lawyers for all time reasonably expended on a case.[107]

A distinction must be made between a public official being sued in his or her official capacity when the "real" defendant is a governmental unit, and when the public official is sued for his or her individual conduct. In official capacity suits, as long as the government entity receives notice and an opportunity to respond, the suit is, in all respects other than the name, a suit against the entity. When a state becomes involved in a § 1983 action either because the state was a proper party defendant or because state officials were sued in their official capacity, attorney's fees may be awarded from the state under § 1988. Only in an official capacity action is a plaintiff who wins entitled to seek relief, both on the merits and for attorney's fees, from the government entity.[108]

It is important to note that lawsuits filed under statutory provisions other than § 1983 may limit the amount of attorney's fees recoverable in prisoners' rights lawsuits.[109] The attorney fees discussed in this section are fees authorized in Civil Rights Act cases and not provisions found for the payment of attorney fees under other federal statutes.

§ 15.13 Injunctive Relief

In addition to monetary damages, the Civil Rights Act authorizes equitable remedies, such as injunctions. An injunction is a judicial order that requires the person to whom it is directed to do a particular thing or to refrain from doing it. Injunctive relief is extremely useful in prison litigation, because the successful prisoner-plaintiff will usually remain in custody and thus will wish to prevent future deprivations of his or her constitutional rights.

A trend in prison litigation is a judicial examination of the totality of internal conditions at specific detention facilities. In a number of cases, federal courts have declared such conditions to be so intolerable as to amount to the imposition of cruel and unusual punishment.[110] Although some courts in such cases have allowed the prison administrators to submit plans to the court for rectification of the facility's deficiencies,[111] several courts have judicially detailed the changes that must be made,[112] and other courts have offered the state legislature the opportunity to solve the problem before intervening.[113] In *Jones v. Wittenberg*,[114] several months after declaring that the totality of conditions within an Ohio county jail made incarceration there cruel and unusual punishment,[115] the federal court issued a lengthy relief decree mandating many specific changes.[116] This remedial relief covered all aspects of operating the institution, from the required wattage of light bulbs to work-release programs, and in effect made the federal judge the jailer for Lucas County, Ohio.

The substandard conditions that exist in many American detention facilities and the courts' awareness that needed changes are not being initiated by prison administrators or legislators have and will continue to result in judicial orders specifying the required changes to bring the facilities up to constitutional standards. The complaint that money is not available to make the required changes is not an acceptable excuse for maintaining unconstitutional confinement conditions.[117]

§ 15.14   The Immunity Defenses

A prison official who is sued for violating prisoners' constitutional rights may assert the defense that he or she is protected by immunity. Immunity may be *absolute* or *qualified*. The immunity defenses generally arise during the pleading stage of a lawsuit and often result in the lawsuit being dismissed prior to beginning expensive discovery and depositions. The federal courts have long struggled with finding a balance between protecting prison officials who act in good faith and granting relief to prisoners whose constitutional rights are violated.

§ 15.14.1   − Sovereign Immunity

It is evident that if sovereign immunity could be asserted by state officials as a defense to a lawsuit based on the Civil Rights Act, the statute would be stripped of its vitality, as it literally applies to all persons acting under state law. Thus it is not surprising to find that the Civil Rights Act has been successfully used against prison wardens[118] and prison guards.[119]

There are no reported cases in which money damages have been recovered from a state's chief executive under the Civil Rights Act. However, the Supreme Court has stated that Congress did not intend "to abolish wholesale all common-law immunities"[120] when it passed the Civil Rights Act. Thus, the Court has approved the immunity of state legislators[121] and state judges.[122] In 1909, the Supreme Court had an opportunity to give state governors absolute immunity, but it refused to do so, apparently satisfied with giving governors a qualified immunity when they act in good faith.[123]

In *Scheuer v. Rhodes*,[124] the Supreme Court stated: "[T]he Eleventh Amendment provides no shield for a state official confronted by a claim he had deprived another of a federal right under the color of state law."[125] The Court cited the case of *Ex parte Young*,[126] stating that a state official acting under state law in a manner that violates the federal Constitution is "stripped of his official or representative character and is subjected in his person to the consequences of his individual conduct."[127]

United States v. Georgia[128] involved the issue of whether states could use the defense of sovereign immunity against lawsuits filed by prisoners under Title II of the Americans with Disabilities Act of 1990 (ADA).[129] In *Georgia*, the Supreme Court held that the ADA was an unequivocal expression of Congress's intent to abrogate state sovereign immunity in ADA cases. In this case, the prisoner's claims for money damages against the state under Title II of the ADA were based on conduct that independently violated the Fourteenth and Eighth Amendment's guarantee against cruel and unusual punishment. As Title II of the ADA created a private cause of action for damages against the states for conduct that actually violated the Fourteenth Amendment, Title II of the ADA validly abrogated state sovereign immunity. This means that Congress has the authority to abolish state protections under the Eleventh Amendment if it so desires.

§ 15.14.2 — Executive Immunity — Absolute Immunity

The idea that government officials are immune from personal liability follows the same rationale that created the doctrine of sovereign immunity. The general proposition that has supported this immunity has been that the public has an interest in public officials making decisions and taking action to enforce the laws for the protection of the public, without worrying about facing numerous lawsuits for their actions. This immunity has been the product of constitutional and legislative provisions as well as judicial determination, as previously pointed out.

Whenever the issue of official immunity is discussed, a distinction must be made between absolute immunity and qualified immunity. Absolute immunity means just that. If the doctrine applies, it is not possible to maintain a civil action for personal damages against the individual, no matter how extensive the injuries or malicious the intent. If such injury occurs, the remedy is injunctive relief, impeachment, or criminal prosecution. The class of persons protected by absolute immunity is basically limited to judges,[130] prosecutors,[131] and legislators.[132] However, executive officials exercising discretion are entitled to the qualified immunity specified in *Scheuer v. Rhodes*,[133] subject to situations in which the official is performing judicial acts, such as an agency attorney. In those cases, the official is entitled to absolute immunity because it is deemed essential for the conduct of the public business. However, even though there may be no absolute immunity, the government official may still use the defense of qualified immunity.

The director of prisoner disciplinary programs, as a judge, has absolute immunity for his actions on administrative appeals arising out of determinations of disciplinary hearings held in New York State prisons. He performs a quasi-judicial role as a professional civilian hearing officer.[134]

A lawsuit against a state official in his or her official capacity is not a suit against the official but rather a suit against the official's office and was no different from a lawsuit against state itself. Even though § 1983 provides a forum to remedy many deprivations of civil liberties, it does not provide a forum for litigants who seek a remedy against the state for alleged deprivations of civil liberties. The Eleventh Amendment bars such suits unless the state waives its immunity or unless Congress exercises its power to override that immunity. Neither the state nor its officials acting in their official capacities are "persons" under § 1983.[135]

Defendants who perform quasi-judicial functions and/or whose actions are functionally comparable to those of judges and prosecutors are entitled to absolute immunity in § 1983 suits against them in their individual capacities. However, this principle does not apply to official-capacity claims. The only immunities that can be claimed in official-capacity actions are forms of sovereign immunity that the underlying governmental entity may possess, such as the Eleventh Amendment.[136]

§ 15.14.3   — Qualified Immunity

In many cases in which lawsuits are filed by prisoners against prison officials, the outcome depends on whether the official is granted immunity for his actions. This issue constitutes the bulk of prison litigation.

Whether an official has qualified immunity will depend on the functions and responsibilities of the official claiming the immunity, as well as the purposes behind the Civil Rights Act. Section 1983 includes "misuse of power, possessed by virtue of state law and made possible only because the wrongdoer is clothed with the authority of state law."

The Court in *Scheuer* stated:

> In varying scope, a qualified immunity is available to officers of the executive branch of government, the violation being dependent upon the scope of discretion and responsibilities of the office and all the circumstances as they reasonably appeared at the time of the action on which liability is sought to be based. It is the existence of reasonable grounds for the belief formed at the time and in light of all the circumstances, coupled with good-faith belief, that affords a basis for qualified immunity of executive officers for acts performed in the course of official conduct.[137]

The definition of "good faith" came in *Wood v. Strickland*.[138] The Supreme Court established a two-pronged test based on "subjective" and "objective" good-faith determinations. The Court held:

> Therefore, in the specific context of school discipline, we hold that a school board member is not immune from liability for damages under § 1983 if he knew or reasonably should have known that the action he took within his sphere of official responsibility would violate the constitutional rights of the student affected, or if he took the action with the malicious intention to cause a deprivation of constitutional rights or other injury to the student. That is not to say that school board members are "charged with predicting the future course of constitutional law." A compensatory award will be appropriate with such disregard of the student's clearly established constitutional rights that his action cannot reasonably be characterized as being in good faith.[139]

Under the *Wood* test, the official involved must act sincerely and with a belief that he or she is doing right. However, an act violating a constitutional right cannot be justified by ignorance or disregard of settled law. In other words, an executive official is held to a standard of conduct based not only on permissible intentions but also on knowledge of the basic, unquestioned constitutional rights of the individuals for whom the official is responsible.

Wood was a 5–4 decision. The dissenting justices argued, in effect, that it is unsound to hold public officials liable for actions taken, without malice, that violated "unquestioned constitutional rights," when the Supreme Court itself cannot determine unanimously what those rights are. Justice Powell, writing for the dissent, stated:

> The Court states the standard of required knowledge in two cryptic phrases: "settled, indisputable law" and "unquestioned constitutional rights." Presumably these are intended to mean the same thing, although the meaning of neither phrase is likely to be self-evident to constitutional law scholars—much less the average school board member. One need only look to the decisions of this Court—to our reversals, our recognition of evolving concepts, and our five–four splits—to recognize the hazard of even informed prophecy as to what are "unquestioned constitutional rights."[140]

The dilemma facing public officials is highlighted by *O'Connor v. Donaldson*.[141] In *O'Connor*, a mental patient sued the superintendent of the mental institution for depriving him of his liberty. The judge and jury agreed, and the mental patient recovered a judgment of $38,500 against the superintendent personally. The superintendent argued on appeal that he was merely acting pursuant to an Alabama statute and that he could not reasonably have been expected to know that the state law, as he understood it, was constitutionally invalid. The Court of Appeals was not sympathetic and affirmed the money judgment. On appeal to the Supreme Court, the case was reversed and remanded to the lower courts for reconsideration in light of *Wood v. Strickland*.

The subsequent decision on remand found "bad faith" along more traditional lines. The court found that the state officials had maintained a defense stratagem of delay for delay's sake, as well as an unconscionable—and continued—denial of facts that were well documented and known to all parties interested in the subject. An award of $52,000 was made.[142]

In *Procunier v. Navarette*,[143] the *Wood* standard was applied to prison officials. The court ruled that, as prison officials, they were not absolutely immune from liability in a § 1983 damage suit and could rely only on qualified immunity as described in *Scheuer* and *Wood*. Using the first standard put forth in *Wood*, the court stated:

> [T]he immunity defense would be unavailing to [the prison officials] if the constitutional right allegedly infringed by them was clearly established at the time of their challenged conduct, if they knew or should have known of that right, and if they knew or *should have known* that their conduct violated the constitutional norm. [Emphasis added.]

Another case applying the *Wood* standard to prison officials is *Cruz v. Beto*,[144] in which the former Director of the Texas Department of Corrections was held liable in the amount of approximately $10,000 for violating a prisoner's rights. The violations that were actionable for money damages included: (1) wrongful segregation, humiliation, denial of access to the courts and to the attorney of the prisoner's choice, and improper censorship of mail between attorney and client; (2) denial of access to educational materials with a corresponding interference in prisoners' efforts to rehabilitate themselves; (3) wrongful deprivation of the opportunity to earn Point Incentive Program merit points solely because of prisoner's choice of counsel; and (4) imposition of excessive demands of physical labor upon prisoners who were duly categorized by corrections officials as medically unfit to perform such tasks.

Cruz is an example of facts alleged by prison officials to justify their decisions and actions that were not proved in court. The court took note that the witnesses who were to testify regarding the danger to security failed to appear, that no complaints were ever made to the Texas Bar Association about the conduct of the attorney, nor were any criminal charges ever filed. Prison officials must realize that naked allegations are not a sufficient defense. The burden of proving justification for interfering with fundamental constitutional rights is on the prison officials—and this must be proved in court.

Taking a new direction, the doctrine of qualified immunity was substantially changed in *Harlow v. Fitzgerald*.[145] In *Harlow*, the Supreme Court thought that too many cases were going to the jury or leading to overly extensive pretrial discovery. The Supreme Court also thought that more cases should be disposed of at the pleading stage on summary judgment. The Court stated:

> [B]are allegations of malice should not suffice to subject government officials either to the costs of trial or to the burdens of broad-reaching discovery. . . . [G]overnment officials performing discretionary functions generally are shielded from liability for civil damages insofar as their conduct does not violate clearly established statutory or constitutional rights of which a reasonable person would have known. . . . On summary judgment, the judge appropriately may determine, not only the currently applicable law, but whether that law was clearly established at the time the action occurred. If the law at that time was not clearly established, an official could not reasonably be expected to anticipate subsequent legal developments, nor could he fairly be said to 'know' that the law forbade conduct not previously identified as unlawful. Until this threshold immunity question is resolved, discovery should not be allowed. If the law was clearly established, the immunity defense ordinarily should fail, since a reasonably competent public official should know the law governing his conduct. Nevertheless, if the official pleading the defense claims extraordinary circumstances and can prove that he neither knew nor should have known the relevant legal standard, the defense should be sustained.

Bad faith will remove an immunity defense. Examples of bad faith include *Williams v. Treen*[146] and *Bennett v. Williams*.[147] In *Williams v. Treen*, where state prison officials violated clearly established state law, their belief in the lawfulness of their actions was per se unreasonable. They were not entitled to claim immunity based upon the defense of good faith. In other words, a good faith immunity from liability in a civil rights action cannot be asserted by officials whose actions clearly violate established state law. In this case, applicable state fire, safety, and health regulations were violated. State officials are charged with knowledge of their state's own explicit and clearly established regulations.

In *Bennett v. Williams*—in light of a determination that living conditions in Alabama prisons constituted cruel and unusual punishment in violation of the Eighth Amendment in a prior § 1983 case—prison officials were precluded from invoking qualified immunity. The prior litigation put them on notice of the continuing violations of the prisoner's constitutional rights. Also, a jury instruction suggesting that the state could not be required to pay any part of the judgment against the officials and employees was prejudicial to the prisoner that reversal of the favorable judgment for the prison officials was reversed.

The defense of qualified immunity is available as long as the official's actions do not violate clearly established statutory or constitutional rights of which a reasonable person would have known. This standard permits an official to carry out his or her duties free from concern for his or her personal liability. On the other hand, he or she may on occasion have to consider whether a proposed course of action can be squared with the Constitution and laws of the United States. Where an official could be expected to know that his or her conduct would violate statutory or constitutional rights, he or she should hesitate. The essential issue—and problem—of the qualified immunity defense is timing. If the best that a public official-defendant can expect is a favorable jury instruction at the termination of a case, the defense is really unsatisfactory. What is needed is a summary procedure early in the proceedings that will avoid long and costly pretrial discovery proceedings and the trial itself.

According to the Supreme Court,[148] a qualified immunity defense must be considered in proper sequence. A ruling should be made early in the proceedings so that the cost and expenses of trial are avoided where the defense is dispositive. Such immunity is an entitlement not to stand trial, not a defense from liability. The initial inquiry is whether a constitutional right would have been violated on the facts alleged, for if no right would have been violated, there is no need for further inquiry into immunity. However, if a violation could be made out on a favorable view of the parties' submissions, the next step is to determine whether the right was clearly established. This inquiry must be undertaken in light of the case's specific context, not as a broad general proposition. The relevant, dispositive inquiry is whether it would be clear to a reasonable officer that the conduct was unlawful in the situation he confronted.

The scope of qualified immunity was narrowed in *Hope v. Pelzer*.[149] Under the *Hope* doctrine, defendants in civil rights cases may be shielded from liability for their constitutionally impermissible conduct if their actions did not violate clearly established statutory or constitutional rights of which a reasonable person would have known. Courts commit error in requiring that the facts of previous cases and a prisoner's case be "materially similar." Qualified immunity operates to ensure that before they are subjected to suit, officers are on notice that their conduct is unlawful. Officers sued in a civil rights action have the same fair notice right as do defendants charged under the criminal statutes,[150] which makes it a crime for a state official to act willfully and under color of state law to deprive a person of constitutional rights. Officials can be on notice that their conduct violates established law even in novel fact situations. The Supreme Court expressly rejected a requirement that previous cases be "fundamentally similar." Accordingly, the salient question a court must ask is whether the state of the law gave prison officials fair warning that a prisoner's alleged treatment was unconstitutional.

The same analysis for § 1983 lawsuits applies to *Bivens* suits against federal officials.[151] A court evaluating a qualified immunity claim must first determine whether the plaintiff has alleged the deprivation of a constitutional right and, if so, proceed to determine whether that right was clearly established at the time of the violation. "Clearly established" for qualified immunity purposes means that the contours of the right must be sufficiently clear that a reasonable official would understand that what he is doing violates that right. His very action need not previously have been held unlawful, but in the light of preexisting law its unlawfulness must be apparent. When the state of the law is at best undeveloped at the relevant time, and the officers cannot have been expected to predict the future course of constitutional law, qualified immunity applies.

§ 15.14.3.1   — Qualified Immunity Granted

The following cases are examples of Civil Rights Act cases in which the defendant officials were granted immunity:

- Youth detention center employees were entitled to qualified immunity for a sexual assault on a minor while he was in the custody of the Center. A four-hour delay in medical attention did not amount to deliberate indifference to serious medical needs where the youth told no one of the assault, the blood stain on his underwear was reasonably assumed to be evidence of gastrointestinal problems for which he was already being treated, emergency treatment was not required, and there was no medical evidence indicating that the four-hour delay before he was taken to hospital worsened his medical condition.[152]

- Prison officials were entitled to qualified immunity in a prisoner's claim that officials violated the prisoner's right to privacy of medical information regarding his HIV-positive status. The law was not clearly established that the officials' conduct in not keeping the prisoner's medical condition confidential violated the prisoner's constitutional rights.[153]

- Qualified immunity protected jail personnel sued by a prisoner who was catheterized against his will. The procedure was ordered by a prison doctor for diagnostic purposes after a scuffle with a guard. It would not have been either apparent or sufficiently clear to a reasonable official at that time that the forcible catheterizing of a prisoner for medical purposes only would constitute an unreasonable search under the Fourth Amendment.[154]

- An eight-day lockdown and search of two prison blocks did not result in liability where the search followed a rash of assaults and stabbings. The search resulted in the recovery of 88 weapons. Even if any of various inconveniences caused to the prisoners during the lockdown rose to the level of an Eighth Amendment violation, no reasonable prison official would have believed his actions violated the law at the time of the lockdown.[155]

- County officials were entitled to qualified immunity arising out of the two–and-one-half-year administrative segregation of a detainee after he was suspected of killing another prisoner. Any reasonable person in the officials' position would have believed that holding the detainee in segregation did not violate any of his rights but that it promoted the safety of other prisoners and promoted the detainee's safety.[156]

- Jail officials, who held objectively reasonable beliefs that they were not violating a Muslim prisoner's constitutional rights by offering him pork-free diet and not the vegetarian diet he had requested, were entitled to qualified immunity.[157]

- The right to possess a crystal as part of a prisoner's practice of Odinism was not clearly established by any law at the time he was denied the crystal. The prison officials were entitled to qualified immunity.[158]

- Prisoners claimed that officials, along with other state actors, committed an unconstitutional taking by failing to pay interest on funds deposited in the prison prisoner trust accounts. At the time they made their decisions, the officials reasonably could have believed that the failure to account for any interest accrued to individual prisoner accounts from prisoner trust accounts did not violate any clearly established constitutional right.[159]

- A prison guard, who assigned a prisoner a cellmate who later sexually assaulted him, did not deliberately disregard the prisoner's safety. The prisoner denied "having any problem" with his cellmate at the time of assignment. The fact that the prisoner told the guard in earlier private conversations that he feared for his life from this cellmate did not make the guard's actions unreasonable. The question was not what the guard should have believed but rather whether he knew or deliberately disregarded the fact that his actions subjected the prisoner to a substantial risk of serious harm.[160]

- There was fecal contamination of blankets and clothing used to sop up sewage. Improper laundering caused blankets and clothes to continue to smell of sewage even after laundering. When the prisoners rerinsed the clothes, the resulting rinse water was brown. However, there was no deliberate indifference by prison officials because prison officials were not aware of the problems prior to the filing of a complaint.[161]

- In a detainee suicide case, a caseworker was entitled to qualified immunity because there was no clearly established precedent that would have alerted reasonable people in her position that her conduct was unlawful.[162]

- A correctional officer whose actions did not violate any of a prisoner's clearly established rights of which a reasonable person in a correctional officer's position would have known is entitled to qualified immunity.[163]

§ 15.14.3.2   — Qualified Immunity Denied

The following cases are examples of Civil Rights Act cases in which the defendant officials were denied immunity:

- A prison guard's unprovoked and unjustified act of throwing a prisoner across a hallway and into a wall, which allegedly caused bruising, soreness, and emotional damage, was found to violate the prisoner's then-existing constitutional rights.[164] The Court held that such action could reasonably be understood by a guard to violate the prisoner's then-existing constitutional rights and thus a qualified immunity defense would be unavailable to the guard.

- A Tennessee prison regulation created a constitutionally protected liberty interest in visitation. The officials' threats to remove visitation rights in retaliation for visitors' refusal to submit to strip and body cavity searches in the absence of probable cause was contrary to the prison regulation, and therefore the officials were not entitled to qualified immunity.[165]

- A prison guard is not entitled to qualified immunity in a civil rights action based on an Eighth Amendment violation resulting from three blows to a prisoner's face by the guard. The guard knew his actions were unlawful. He acted with a wanton state of mind, and the law of the circuit made it clear that contemporary standards of decency are always violated when a prison guard wantonly applies force to a prisoner to cause harm, regardless of whether significant injury results.[166]

- A unit manager was aware that a prisoner's cellmate regularly assaulted vulnerable white prisoners and that a known homosexual forced other prisoners to have sex with him. The manager disregarded the risk by not transferring the prisoner or segregating him from his cellmate. This constituted deliberate indifference, and the manager had no qualified immunity.[167]

- A warden's knowledge that feminine-appearing male prisoners are vulnerable to attacks from other prisoners was sufficient to raise a triable issue of fact as to whether the warden was deliberately indifferent to the safety of a transgendered prisoner who was severely beaten by a fellow prisoner while in protective custody. That the warden knew the prisoner's attacker posed a danger to others provided another basis for denying the warden's qualified immunity.[168]

- A prison guard was accused of attempted rape of a preoperative male-to-female transsexual prisoner. His conduct was clearly prohibited at the time of the attack, whether the assault was same-sex or opposite-sex.[169]

- Correctional officers took no actions to prevent an assault by fellow prisoners, even though the officers knew of the fellow prisoners' intent to cause serious physical injury to the prisoner. There was deliberate indifference to the prisoner's safety from other prisoners, which resulted in significant physical injury.[170]

- A state employee was not entitled to qualified immunity based on rape and sexual abuse by the employee who acted as a supervisor in a prison work program. The employee acted as the functional equivalent of a prison guard by virtue of penological responsibility delegated to a state agency. The unlawfulness of the employee's conduct was clearly established in light of preexisting law.[171]

- Officials were not entitled to qualified immunity as to claims of lack of notice and nondisclosure of evidence at a disciplinary hearing. The notice given the prisoner was clearly inadequate, and the officials did not show why the substance of an informant's disclosures could not have been provided.[172]

- A prisoner was incarcerated under conditions posing a substantial risk of harm of contracting AIDS. Two prison officials were aware that another prisoner was infected with AIDS. The warden had read and responded to grievances filed by the prisoner. The warden knew that the other prisoner had AIDS, knew that the prisoner had threatened to infect other prisoners through assault and failed to reasonably respond to the risk in violation of the prison's own policy.[173]

- While a prisoner was in custody, a urologist indicated that his symptoms required urgent urologic assessment of biopsy and definitive treatment. A biopsy never occurred while he was in custody. He did not receive treatment until he was released, but by then the cancer had metastasized and he died one year later. Immunity was denied.[174]

- A prison official was not entitled to qualified immunity when he ordered a prisoner to continue operating prison work equipment that the official had been warned, and had reason to believe, was unnecessarily dangerous. Even if the prisoner had voluntarily obtained his work, the supervisor was not free to visit cruel and unusual punishments on him in violation of the Eighth Amendment once the prisoner was employed. The supervisor would have understood that compelling the prisoner to use defective and dangerous prison work equipment violates the Eighth Amendment.[175]

- A prisoner on death row died of wounds sustained in a beating. The prison had a reputation for abusing prisoners. The warden was warned repeatedly by the former warden that certain guards were dangerous and should be restricted in their work but the warden did not heed the warnings and instead promoted one of those guards to captain. The prisoner did not resist a cell extraction, and while lying in a fetal position was stomped on, punched, and tasered. The warden discontinued a policy requiring cell extractions to be videotaped conveying a message that abuse would be tolerated. The warden ignored many grievances and letters stating that guards were abusive and that certain prisoners were in danger. The right to be free from cruel and unusual punishment was violated and such right was clearly established at the time he was beaten. As such, the warden was not entitled to qualified immunity.[176]

- A correctional officer was not entitled to qualified immunity where the amount of pepper spray used while extracting a prisoner from his cell constituted excessive force. The lack of efforts to temper the effects of pepper spray provided an inference that officer wantonly inflicted pain upon the prisoner.[177]

- After earlier assaults of female prisoners by male detention officers, the sheriff was aware of prison conditions that were substantially likely to result in sexual assaults of female prisoners. The sheriff was under a duty not only to take reasonable measures to remedy the circumstances that directly led to sexual assaults but to cure his own lack of attention and unresponsiveness to prisoner complaints and other indicators of serious problems with his detention staff.[178]

- Prison officials were denied qualified immunity because they should have known that forcing a prisoner to choose between religious observance and adequate nutrition imposed a substantial burden on his right to free exercise of religion.[179]

§ 15.14.4 — Effect of Sovereign Immunity on State Litigation

A prisoner seeking to recover damages in state court against prison officials for neglect, negligence, or intentional injury will often be faced with the defense of sovereign immunity. The courts have generally split on the question of liability, depending upon whether the officials' actions are labeled ministerial or discretionary. A ministerial duty is one that is absolute and certain. It is a duty that involves no freedom of choice on the part of the official. Several states have held that the duty of prison officials to provide their prisoners with necessities is ministerial, and so the official is liable to the prisoners for failure to fulfill that duty.[180] Other states, however, interpret the officials' duties as "discretionary." That is, the official has a certain freedom of choice in providing necessities to the prisoners. Officials are thus free from liability for their acts, and they should not be discouraged by fear of lawsuits from freely exercising this discretion.[181] However, if the discretion is grossly abused, the result is liability.

Appeals are taken from final decisions of the district courts. However, there is a small class of judgments that are not complete and final but are immediately appealable and are called *interlocutory appeals*. States and state entities that claim to be "arms of the state" may take an interlocutory appeal from a district court order that denies a claim of Eleventh Amendment immunity from a lawsuit in federal court under three circumstances. First, denials of Eleventh Amendment immunity claims purport to be conclusive determinations that states and their entities have no right not to be sued in federal court. Second, a motion to dismiss on Eleventh Amendment grounds involves a claim to a fundamental constitutional protection whose resolution generally will have no bearing on the merits of the underlying action. Third, the value to the states of their constitutional immunity—like the benefits conferred by qualified immunity to individual officials[182]—is for the most part lost as litigation proceeds past motion practice, such that the denial order will be effectively unreviewable on appeal from a final judgment. The claim that the Eleventh Amendment does not confer immunity from suit but is merely a defense to liability misunderstands the role of the Amendment in the American system of federalism and is rejected.[183]

§ 15.15　Private Prisons

Some states hire private firms to run jails and prisons. However, according to the Supreme Court, prison guards employed by private firms are not entitled to qualified immunity from suit by prisoners charging a § 1983 violation.[184] While government-employed prison guards may have enjoyed an immunity defense arising out of their status as public employees at common law,[185] correctional functions have never been exclusively public. In the nineteenth century, both private entities and government carried on prison management activities. The Court found no conclusive evidence of a historical tradition of immunity for private parties carrying out these functions.

Further, the governmental immunity doctrine's purposes do not warrant immunity for private prison guards. The mere performance of a governmental function does not support any immunity for a private person, especially one who performs a job without government supervision or direction. There are significant differences between private and public persons with respect to immunity. First, the most important special government immunity-producing concern—protecting the public from unwarranted timidity on the part of public officials—is less likely to be present when a private company subject to competitive market pressures operates a prison. A firm whose guards are too aggressive will face damages that raise costs, thereby threatening its replacement by another contractor, but a firm whose guards are too timid will face replacement by firms with safer and more effective job records.

Marketplace pressures were present in *Richardson v. McKnight*.[186] The private firm was systematically organized. It performed independently, was statutorily obligated to carry insurance, and had to renew its first contract after three years. The private firm was provided with incentives to avoid overly timid job performance. Consequently, private employees differ from government employees. Government employees act within a system that is responsible through elected officials to the voters, often characterized by civil service rules providing employee security but limiting the government departments' flexibility to reward or punish individual employees.

Second, privatization helps to meet the immunity-related need to ensure that talented candidates are not deterred from entering public service by the threat of damage suits. Comprehensive insurance coverage that is available to private companies increases the likelihood of employee indemnification and thereby reduces the employment-discouraging fear of unwarranted liability. A private firm is also freed from many civil service restraints. Unlike a government department, a private firm may offset increased employee liability risk with higher pay or extra benefits. Third, while lawsuits may distract private employees from their duties, the risk of distraction alone cannot be sufficient grounds for immunity.

A private corporation was under contract with the Federal Bureau of Prisons to operate a Community Correctional Center, a facility that housed federal prisoners. A federal prisoner afflicted with a heart condition that limited his ability to climb stairs was assigned to a bedroom on the fifth floor. The Center instituted a policy requiring prisoners residing below the sixth floor to use the stairs rather than the elevator. The prisoner was exempted from this policy. But when a Center employee forbade the prisoner to use the elevator to reach his bedroom, he climbed the stairs, suffered a heart attack, and fell. A district court treated the complaint as raising claims under *Bivens v. Six Unknown Fed. Narcotics Agents*.[187] In *Bivens*, the Supreme Court recognized for the first time an implied private action for damages against federal officers alleged to have violated a citizen's constitutional rights. In *Correctional Services Corp. v. Malesko*,[188] the Supreme Court held that the *Bivens* holding may not be extended to confer a right of action for damages against private entities acting under color of federal law.

The Supreme Court's authority to create a new constitutional tort, not expressly authorized by statute, is anchored in its general jurisdiction to decide all cases arising under federal law. The Supreme Court first exercised this authority in *Bivens*. From a discussion of that and subsequent cases, it was clear that the prisoner's claim was fundamentally different from anything the Supreme Court had previously recognized. In 50 years of *Bivens* jurisprudence, the Supreme Court has extended its holding only twice, to provide an otherwise nonexistent cause of action against individual officers alleged to have acted unconstitutionally and to provide a cause of action for a plaintiff who lacked any alternative remedy for harms caused by an individual officer's unconstitutional conduct. Where such circumstances are not present, the Supreme Court has consistently rejected invitations to extend *Bivens*. The purpose of *Bivens* is to deter individual federal officers, not the agency, from committing constitutional violations. In *Malesko*, liability under federal law was denied, leaving the prisoner to a state remedy.

§ 15.16   Federal Remedies — Declaratory Judgments

In the Anglo-American judicial system, court action is normally based upon past actions between two or more adverse parties. However, many situations arise in which two or more parties are uncertain of their legal relationship and desire a judicial determination of their respective rights and responsibilities prior to committing an act that might result in legal liability. In order to provide such a remedy, Congress passed the Declaratory Judgment Act, which provides in part:

> In a case of actual controversy within its jurisdiction . . . any court of the United States, upon the filing of an appropriate pleading, may declare the rights and other legal relations of any interested party seeking such declaration.[189]

The law further authorizes federal courts to grant "necessary or proper relief based on a declaratory judgment."[190] This power to grant relief beyond the declaratory judgment is discretionary with the court. Thus, a court that is wary of interfering with the management of a prison, but that has found a certain rule or regulation or course of conduct by the prison officials to be unconstitutional, may partially avoid interference by issuing a judgment declaring the alleged practice to be unconstitutional but allowing the administrators to submit to the court plans for remedying the problem.

Thus, a federal district court,[191] after examining the totality of conditions at Arkansas's two state prison farms, declared incarceration there to be cruel and unusual punishment. The burden of eliminating these constitutional defects, however, was placed upon the state prison administration, whose progress (or lack of progress) would be monitored by the court through submission of reports by the defendants.

§ 15.16.1   — State Remedies — Declaratory Judgments

Many states[192] have enacted declaratory judgment acts similar in scope to the federal act. Although a state declaratory judgment action would be an excellent method of testing the legality of conditions of confinement in state institutions, this state remedy has been almost completely ignored by prisoners and prison officials in the past.

§ 15.17   Federal Remedies – Habeas Corpus

Almost all lawsuits by prisoners in the federal courts are petitions for habeas corpus[193] or under the Civil Rights Act. Petitions for habeas corpus concern the validity of confinement or issues affecting the duration of confinement. Damages and injunctive relief affecting the conditions of confinement, on the other hand, are within the purview of the Civil Rights Act. Courts continue to wrestle with cases that concern both issues—with a prisoner seeking relief unavailable in habeas corpus, such as damages or injunctive relief, but when the prisoner also seeks the invalidity of either an underlying conviction or of a particular ground by which the prisoner is denied release prior to serving his maximum term of confinement. In 1994, *Heck v. Humphrey*[194] held that where success in a prisoner's § 1983 damages action would implicitly question the validity of his conviction or duration of his sentence, the prisoner must first obtain a favorable termination of his available state remedies or use federal habeas corpus. The 1997 case of *Edwards v. Balisok*[195] applied *Heck* where a prisoner in a § 1983 case sought both damages and equitable relief resulting from a procedural defect in the prison's administrative process involving the prisoner's good-time credits. *Edwards* denied § 1983 relief. As a result, federal petitions for habeas corpus may be granted only after the prisoner has exhausted all other avenues of relief, whereas Civil Rights Act suits face a lower threshold. Further, habeas corpus petitions must satisfy the heightened standards of the Antiterrorism and Effective Death Penalty Act.[196]

Only certain kinds of alleged sentencing errors may be raised in a collateral proceeding in habeas corpus.[197] These are: (1) A sentence violates the Constitution or the laws of the United States; (2) the district court was without jurisdiction to impose the sentence; (3) the sentence is greater than the statutory maximum; and (4) the sentence is otherwise subject to collateral attack.[198] The Supreme Court has narrowly confined the scope and availability of collateral attack for claims that do not allege constitutional or jurisdictional errors.[199] Such claims are properly brought in habeas corpus only if the claimed error is a fundamental defect that inherently results in a complete miscarriage of justice or an omission inconsistent with the rudimentary demands of fair procedure. The error must present exceptional circumstances where the need for the remedy afforded by the writ of habeas corpus is apparent.[200]

Traditionally, the writ of habeas corpus has been used to contest the legality of confinement itself.[201] However, in a 1944 case, a federal appellate court expanded the scope of federal habeas corpus to include suits that contest the conditions of confinement and not merely the legality of the confinement itself.[202] The court reasoned that:

> A prisoner is entitled to the writ of habeas corpus when, though lawfully in custody, he is deprived of some right to which he is lawfully entitled even in his confinement, the deprivation of which serves to make his imprisonment more burdensome than the law allows or curtails his liberty to a greater extent than the law permits.[203]

The 1963 ruling of the Supreme Court in *Jones v. Cunningham*[204] that expressly approved the expanded use of habeas corpus is now seriously questioned. Although the doctrine remains valid, over the years there have been serious setbacks regarding federal relief for prisoners in habeas corpus.

Using federal habeas corpus to rectify an allegedly unconstitutional condition of incarceration presents a serious procedural problem to state prisoners. The habeas corpus statute requires them to exhaust state judicial and administrative remedies before they apply for the writ in federal court.[205] In *Preiser v. Rodriguez*,[206] the Supreme Court held that federal habeas corpus must be used by a prisoner in a state institution to obtain release by challenging the fact or duration of his physical imprisonment and that he could not avoid the "exhaustion of state remedies" doctrine by using the Civil Rights Act. Thus, even though § 1983 on its face gives a remedy for every deprivation of federal rights by state law, the writ of habeas corpus is the exclusive federal remedy for state prisoners who, on the grounds that they were unconstitutionally deprived of good-time credits under prison disciplinary rules, challenge the fact or duration of their confinement and seek immediate release.

Wolff v. McDonnell[207] considered whether *Preiser* applied to a § 1983 action involving the validity of the procedures for denying good-time credits. The Court held that although *Preiser* prevented the restoration of good-time credits under § 1983, damage claims were properly before the Court. Consequently, the district court was held to have jurisdiction under the Civil Rights Act to determine the validity of the procedures employed for imposing punishment, including loss of good-time credits, for flagrant or serious misconduct. However, exhaustion of state remedies will not be required if resort to them would obviously be futile.[208] An example of a futile state remedy that would not have to be pursued by the prisoner is a prior adverse decision by the state's highest court on the identical federal question that the prisoner seeks to raise.[209]

Since the Supreme Court's 1977 decision in *Wainwright v. Sykes*,[210] there has been a trend to cut back on the availability of federal habeas corpus review afforded to state prisoners. In *Wainwright*, the Court held that a petitioner's procedural default on a constitutional claim in state court bars federal habeas corpus review of that claim unless he or she can demonstrate cause for the default and actual prejudice. The Supreme Court stated in *Caldwell v. Mississippi*[211] that the state court must actually have relied on the procedural bar as an independent basis for its disposition of the case. Further, the ambiguities associated with reliance on state grounds is to be resolved by application of the *Michigan v. Long*[212] standard. In *Long*, the Court adopted a presumption in favor of federal court review when a state court decision fairly appears to rest primarily on federal law or appears to be interwoven with the federal law, and when the adequacy and independence of any possible state law ground are not clear from the face of the opinion. The presumption is based on the assumption that when the state court's judgment contains no plain statement to the effect that federal cases are being used solely as persuasive authority, and when state law is interwoven with federal law, it can be accepted as the most reasonable explanation that the state court decided the case the way it did because it believed that federal law required it to do so.

In *Harris v. Reed*,[213] the Supreme Court extended *Long*'s "plain statement" rule to federal habeas corpus review. In that case, it declared that a judgment appearing to rest primarily on federal law is conclusively presumed to so rest, unless the state court makes a plain statement to the contrary. The Court reasoned that because, as *Sykes* made clear, the adequate and independent state ground doctrine applies to federal habeas corpus and because federal courts on habeas corpus review commonly face the same problem of ambiguity that was resolved by *Long*, the "plain statement" rule is to be adopted for federal habeas corpus cases. A procedural default will not bar consideration of a federal claim on habeas corpus review unless the last state court rendering a judgment in the case clearly and expressly stated that its judgment rested on a state procedural bar.

In *Coleman v. Thompson*,[214] the petitioner sought federal relief when state habeas corpus relief was denied. The state appellate court refused to consider certain issues on appeal because the time for filing had passed. He petitioned to the state supreme court, which denied relief. The petitioner then sought federal habeas corpus on the same claims. The Fourth Circuit upheld the state judgment because it was based on an adequate and independent state ground—the procedural default—and the petitioner failed to show "cause" to excuse default.[215] On appeal to the Supreme Court, the petitioner relied on *Harris*, arguing that because the state supreme court's order did not "clearly and expressly" state that it was based on adequate and independent state law, the state's judgment should be presumed to be based on federal law and thus federal review of his claims would be appropriate. The majority of the Supreme Court rejected this broad application of *Harris* and held that one predicate to the application of the *Harris* presumption is that the state holding must be fairly susceptible to being read as resting primarily on federal law.

In *Preiser v. Rodriguez*,[216] the Supreme Court delineated what constitutes a habeas corpus action as opposed to a § 1983 claim. The prisoner's label cannot control. The essence of habeas corpus is an attack by a person in custody upon the legality of that custody. If a prisoner is not challenging the validity of his or her conviction or the length of his or her detention, such as loss of good-time credits, then a writ of habeas corpus is not the proper remedy. It is the substance of the relief sought that counts. Where a petitioner seeks a writ of habeas corpus and fails to attack the validity of his or her sentence or the length of his or her state custody, the district court lacks the power or subject matter jurisdiction to issue a writ. There are fundamental differences between a civil rights action under § 1983, in which a prisoner might seek money damages or injunctive relief from unlawful treatment, and an action for habeas corpus. Under a petition for a writ of habeas corpus, a petitioner must exhaust his or her state judicial remedies,[217] whereas under a § 1983 action, exhaustion was not required[218] until enactment of the Prison Litigation Reform Act in 1995. Furthermore, a state court judgment is not binding on the petitioner in a habeas corpus action, whereas the doctrines of issue and claim preclusion[219] apply to the issues in a § 1983 case that had been fully litigated in the state court.[220]

§ 15.17.1 — State Remedies — Habeas Corpus

The availability of state habeas corpus proceedings to contest conditions of state confinement depends on the wording of the state statute and the judicial interpretation of it. For example, Ohio's habeas corpus statute has a section that provides:

> If it appears that a person alleged to be restrained of his liberty is in the custody of an officer under process issued by a court or magistrate, or by virtue of the judgment or order of a court of record, and that the court or magistrate had jurisdiction to issue the process, render the judgment, or make the order, the writ of habeas corpus shall not be allowed.[221]

Thus, habeas corpus relief is not available in Ohio courts unless the court ordering confinement lacked jurisdiction.[222] In other words, Ohio limits habeas corpus to cases that would result in release from confinement for the petitioner if he were successful in his action.[223] Thus, state habeas corpus is not a proper method of contesting conditions of confinement in Ohio.

Other states, however, have extended the scope of habeas corpus to include cases of alleged unlawful treatment of a prisoner lawfully in custody[224] and follow the federal analogy.

§ 15.18 Federal Remedies — Contempt

Contempt of court has been defined as "disobedience to the court, by acting in opposition to the authority, justice, and dignity thereof."[225] Because they are responsible for executing sentences imposed by the courts, prison officials are regarded as officers of the courts. Moreover, a state official who is holding a prisoner sentenced by a federal court has been held to be an official of the sentencing federal court, in relation to his treatment of the federal prisoner.[226] In *In re Birdsong*,[227] a federal judge held a county jailer in contempt for mistreating a federal prisoner who was being detained in the local jail.

§ 15.18.1 — State Remedies — Contempt

Prison officials are officers of the sentencing court and can be held in contempt by such a court for mistreating a prisoner sentenced to the institution by the court. At least two states have sanctioned the use of contempt to punish mistreatment of prisoners. In *Howard v. State*,[228] the Arizona Supreme Court upheld a contempt citation against the superintendent of an adult prison who allegedly mistreated prisoners. However, the same court dismissed a contempt proceeding against the director of a boys' training school,[229] expressly overruling any holding of the *Howard* case that might lead to an opposite result. Another case seemed to reaffirm the *Howard* decision as it pertained to adult correctional officials. *Dutton v. Eytnan*[230] held that state habeas corpus is not a valid method of contesting the conditions of confinement. However, the court cited the *Howard* case with approval of contempt as a possible remedy in such a situation.

The Supreme Court of Rhode Island has also held that contempt is a proper method of punishing abuse of prisoners.[231]

§ 15.19　Conclusion

A prisoner has a wide variety of remedies to rectify past denials of constitutional rights and to ensure future respect of these rights by prison administrators. The prisoner often has the choice of going to either federal or state courts. However, many obstacles in the past, most notably the hands-off doctrine, blocked judicial redress of constitutional deprivations. With the decline, if not elimination of this doctrine in recent years, courts are hearing and deciding an increasing number of prisoner complaints.

The judicial concern for penal reform has probably abated, and judicial intervention in prison administration will probably decrease as time goes on. Federal and state correctional officials have initiated necessary administrative reforms in many of the areas of constitutional concern.

With the "exhaustion of remedies" doctrine at play in both habeas corpus and Civil Rights Act cases involving prisoners, there are many procedural traps that prisoners must avoid when suing their keepers. The doors to the courtroom are becoming smaller and smaller.

Prison officials have become increasingly aware of the potential for liability when conducting the operations and forming the policies for the prison system. Supreme Court decisions make it clear that prison officials are expected to know the constitutional rights of prisoners, and this places the burden on prison officials to keep themselves apprised of the current state of the law. Ignorance is not a defense when confronted with a lawsuit for monetary damages.

Notes

1　*See* Chapter 1.
2　*See* Chapter 16.
3　Garcia v. Steele, 193 F.2d 276 (8th Cir. 1951).
4　Ronald L. Goldfarb & Linda R. Singer,*Redressing Prisoners' Grievances*, 39 Geo. Wash. L. Rev. 175, 181 (1970).

5   378 U.S. 546 (1964).

6   Johnson v. Avery, 393 U.S. 483 (1969); Wright v. McMann, 387 F.2d 519 (2d Cir. 1967).

7   For an exhaustive study of judicial treatment of prisoner suits, *see* Ronald L. Goldfarb & Linda R. Singer, *Redressing Prisoners' Grievances*, 39 Geo. Wash. L. Rev. 175 (1976).

8   62 American Bar Association Journal 189 (Feb. 1976).

9   U.S. Const., art. III, § 2.

10   United States ex rel. Atterbury v. Ragen, 237 F.2d 953 (7th Cir. 1956).

11   Claflin v. Houseman, 93 U.S. 130 (1976).

12   Fleming v. California, 34 Cal. App. 4th 1378 (1995).

13   208 Cal. App. 3d 812 (1989).

14   42 U.S.C. § 1983.

15   DeShaney v. Winnebago County Dept. of Soc. Servs., 489 U.S. 189 (1989) (no liability for failure of social workers to remove child from custody of abusive father).

16   U.S. Const., amend. XI.

17   *See* Pennhurst State Sch. & Hosp. v. Halderman, 465 U.S. 89 100 (1984).

18   *See* Kentucky v. Graham, 473 U.S. 159 (1985).

19   Northern Ins. Co. v. Chatham County, 547 U.S. 189, 126 S. Ct. 1689 (2006).

20   *See* Clark v. Tarrant County, Texas, 798 F.2d 736, 745 (5th Cir. 1986) (holding that the county probation department, as part of a state probation program administered by the judicial districts, was an arm of the state within the meaning of the Eleventh Amendment, and entitled to Eleventh Amendment immunity from appellant's § 1983 claims); Lovelace v. Dekalb Cent. Probation, 144 Fed. Appx. 793 (11th Cir. 2005) (unpublished) (district court correctly concluded that plaintiff's § 1983 claims against a county probation department were barred by the Eleventh Amendment); Beckdett v. Vega, ___ F. Supp. 2d ___, 2006 U.S. Dist. LEXIS 28204 (2006).

21   Grove v. County of San Joaquin, 156 Cal. App. 2d 808, 320 P. 2d 161 (1958); Bruce v. Riddle, 631 F.2d 272 (4th Cir. 1980); cf. Meyer v. City of Oakland, 166 Cal. Rptr. 79 (Cal. App. 1980) (The City of Oakland was held liable in the amount of $35,000 for an assault on a prisoner by fellow prisoners. The court, while recognizing the doctrine of sovereign immunity, did not apply it to the facts of this case. The court held that a detainee in a drunk tank is not a "prisoner" for purposes of this statute).

22   Monell v. New York City Dept. of Social Services, 436 US 658 (1978).

23   Moody v. State's Prison, 128 N.C. 12, 38 S.E. 131 (1901); Pharr v. Garibaldi, 252 N.C. 803, 115 S.E.2d 18 (1960); Staley v. Commonwealth, 380 A.2d 515 (Pa. Commw. 1977); McKnight v. Civiletti, 497 F. Supp. 657 (E.D. Pa. 1980); City of Newport v. Fact Concerts, 453 U.S. 247 (1981).

24   Van Alstyne, *Governmental Tort Liability: A Decade of Change*, U. Ill. L. R. 919 (1966).

25   438 U.S. 781 (1978).

26   Ex parte Young, 209 U.S. 123 (1908).

27   Barr v. Matteo, 360 U.S. 564 (1959) (acting director of Office of Rent Stabilization); Norton v. McShane, 332 F.2d 855 (5th Cir. 1964) (Deputy United States Marshal); Eide v. Timberlake, 497 F. Supp. 1272 (D. Kan. 1980); cf. Procunier v. Navarette, 434 U.S. 555 (1978).

28   Bivens v. Six Unknown Fed. Narcotics Agents, 403 U.S. 388 (1971) (grants equivalent relief against federal officials as 42 U.S.C. § 1983 grants against state officials).

29   654 F.2d 1007 (5th Cir. 1981); Bogard v. Cook, 586 F.2d 399 (5th Cir. 1978); Fitchette v. Collins, 402 F. Supp. 147 (D. Md. 1975); *see also* Carder v. Steiner, 170 A.2d 220 (1961).

30   *See* Chapter 16.

31   Kenneth C. Davis, Administrative Law § 26.07 (1959).

32   Monell v. New York City Dept. of Social Services, 436 U.S. 658 (1978).

33   438 U.S. 658 (1978).

34   Will v. Michigan Department of State Police, 491 U.S. 58 (1989).

35   *See* Chapter 16.

36   United States v. Muniz, 374 U.S. 150 (1963).

37   *See* Chapter 16.

38   28 U.S.C. § 2680 (h) (1964).

39   Haywood v. Drown, 556 U.S. 729, 129 S. Ct. 2108 (2009).

40   *See* Chapter 16.

41   Bivens v. Six Unknown Fed. Narcotics Agents, 403 U.S. 388 (1971); Butz v. Economou, 438 U.S. 478 (1978). A plaintiff may maintain a Bivens action, with trial by jury, even though he or she also has a remedy under the Federal Tort Claims Act. Further, when a defendant's unconstitutional act leads to death, federal common law permits survival of the *Bivens* claim, even though state law would not permit survival. Carlson v. Green, 446 U.S. 14 (1980).

42   Bivens v. Six Unknown Fed. Narcotics Agents, 403 U.S. 388 (1971).

43   42 U.S.C. § 1983 (1970).

44   Cooper v. Pate, 378 U.S. 546 (1964). Even though the state is exempt from damages under a 42 U.S.C. § 1983 action, cities do not have a similar immunity. In Monell v. Department of Social Services, 436 U.S. 658 (1978), the Supreme Court held that cities are not immune from civil rights suits. Under this holding, municipalities can now be directly liable for their constitutional deprivations as long as the violation stems from official policy and not simply from the actions of an employee or agent. In the latter instance, a complaining party would have to seek relief from the individual official and not the city itself. Monell left open the issue of whether a municipality could cloak itself with the good faith immunity defense available to its public officers. This issue was decided in the negative in Owen v. City of Independence, 445 U.S. 622 (1980). Municipalities are not subject to immunity from liability in § 1983 actions, even though the unconstitutional conduct was undertaken in good faith.

45   Preiser v. Rodriguez, 411 U.S. 475 (1973).

46   West v. Atkins, 487 U.S. 42 (1988).

47   *Id.*

48   City of Los Angeles v. Heller, 475 U.S. 796 (1986).

49   Estelle v. Gamble, 429 U.S. 97 (1976); Stewart v. Love, 696 F.2d 43 (6th Cir. 1982) (A prisoner was assaulted by another prisoner. Because the conduct of the prison officials did not constitute gross negligence or deliberate indifference to the prisoner's risk of injury, there was no violation of the Eighth Amendment. In the context of prison cases involving assaults on prisoners by prisoners, mere negligence on the part of prison officials is insufficient to give rise to liability.)

50   Morris v. Crawford County, 173 F. Supp. 2d 870 (W.D. Ark. 2001).

51   Parratt v. Taylor was overruled in Estelle v. Gamble to the extent that it stated otherwise.

52   Daniels v. Williams, 474 U.S. 327 (1985).

53   *See, e.g.*, MASS. GEN. LAWS ANN. 16, 28, 34 (1958) (county detention facilities); N.Y. CORRECTIONAL LAWS 137 (Supp. 1971) (state penal institutions).

54   Farmer v. State, 224 Miss. 96, 79 So. 2d 528 (1955); State ex rel. Morris v. National Surety Co., 162 Tenn. 547, 39 S.W.2d 581 (1931); State ex rel. Williams v. Davis, 219 S.E.2d 198 (N.C. 1975).

55   Smith v. Slack, 125 W. Va. 812, 26 S.E.2d 387 (1943); Richardson v. Capwell, 63 Utah 616, 176 P. 205 (1918).

56   Clark v. Kelly, 101 W. Va. 650, 133 S.E. 365 (1926); Roberts v. Williams, 456 F.2d 819 (5th Cir. 1972).

57   Collenburg v. County of Los Angeles, 150 Cal. App. 2d 795, 310 P. 2d 989 (1957) (sovereign immunity protects the county but not the individual official).

58   Fernelius v. Pierce, 22 Cal. 2d 226, 138 P. 2d 12 (1943); Farmer v. Rutherford, 136 Kan. 298, 15 P. 2d 474 (1932); Bowman v. Hayward, 1 Utah 2d 131, 262 P. 2d 957 (1953).

59   436 U.S. 658 (1978).

60   Pembaur v. City of Cincinnati, 475 U.S. 469 (1986).

61 Brandon v. Holt, 469 U.S. 464 (1984).

62 220 F.3d 433 (6th Cir. 2000).

63 475 U.S. 469 (1986).

64 City of Canton v. Harris, 489 U.S. 378 (1989); *see also* Oklahoma City v. Tuttle, 471 U.S. 808 (1985).

65 142 F.3d. 1229 (10th Cir. 1998).

66 Barney v. Pulsipher, 143 F.3d 1299 (10th Cir. 1998).

67 520 U.S. 781 (1997).

68 Monell v. Department of Social Services, 436 U.S. 658 (1978).

69 Pembaur v. City of Cincinnati, 475 U.S. 469 (1986).

70 520 U.S. 397 (1997).

71 In City of Canton v. Harris, 489 U.S. 378 (1989), the Court held that a plaintiff seeking to establish municipal liability on the theory that a facially lawful municipal action—in that case, an allegedly inadequate training program that led an employee to violate a plaintiff's rights—must demonstrate that the municipal action was not simply negligent but was taken with "deliberate indifference" as to its known or obvious consequences.

72 Tucker v. Evans, 276 F.3d 999 (8th Cir. 2002).

73 480 U.S. 386 (1986).

74 Crawford-El v. Britton, 523 U.S. 574 (1998).

75 Act Oct. 21, 1998, P.L. 105–277, Div. A, § 101(b) [Title I, § 127], 112 STAT. 2681–74. The text of the statute is in Appendix II.

76 *See* Chapter 16.

77 McNeese v. Board of Educ., 373 U.S. 668 (1963); Monroe v. Pape, 365 U.S. 167 (1961); Steffel v. Thompson, 415 U.S. 452 (1974); Preiser v. Rodriguez, 411 U.S. 475 (1973); Huffman v. Pursue, Ltd., 420 U.S. 592 (1975).

78 Wilwording v. Swenson, 404 U.S. 249 (1971); *see also* United States v. Mogavero, 521 F.2d 625 (4th Cir. 1975). *See also* Dickerson v. Warden, Marquette Prison, 298 N.W.2d 841 (Mich. Ct. App. 1980).

79 *See, e.g.*, Sostre v. McGinnis, 442 F.2d 178 (2d Cir. 1971), *cert. denied*, 405 U.S. 978 (1972); Clutchette v. Procunier, 328 F. Supp. 767 (N.D. Cal. 1971).

80 *See* Chapter 16.

81 Booth v. Churner, 532 U.S. 731 (2001); Porter v. Nussle, 534 U.S. 516 (2002).

82 Leeke v. Timmerman, 454 U.S. 83 (1981).

83 Wilson v. Garcia, 471 U.S. 261 (1985).

84 OHIO REV. CODE ANN. § 2305.10.

85 LRL Properties v. Portage Metro Housing Auth., 55 F.3d 1097, 1105 (6th Cir. 1995).

86 Meadows v. Whetsel, 227 Fed. Appx. 769 (10th Cir. 2007).

87 Felder v. Casey, 487 U.S. 131 (1988).

88 *See* United Airlines, Inc. v. Evans, 431 U.S. 553 (1977).

89 *See* Pope v. Bond, 641 F. Supp. 489 (D.D.C. 1986).

90 Wilson v. Prasse, 325 F. Supp. 9 (W.D. Pa. 1971).

91 442 F.2d 178 (2d Cir. 1971), *rev'g in part*, 312 F. Supp. 863 (S.D.N.Y. 1971), *cert. denied*, 405 U.S. 978 (1972).

92 The district court expressly held that the conditions of confinement, such as lack of exercise, restricted diet, sensory deprivation, and deprivation of intellectual stimulation, constituted cruel and unusual punishment, and based its award of compensatory damages on this finding. Sostre v. Rockefeller, 312 F. Supp. 863, 885 (S.D. N.Y. 1970). However, the appellate court overruled this finding, stating that the conditions of segregated confinement did not amount to cruel and unusual punishment. Sostre v. McGinnis, 442 F.2d 178, 190–194 (2d Cir. 1971), *cert. denied*, 405 U.S. 978 (1972). Nevertheless, the appellate court based its affirmation of the compensatory damages upon "the conditions . . . of segregation." *Id.* at 205, n. 52. Thus, exactly what the plaintiff was being compensated for is somewhat unclear, but because the appellate court held that the prison officials placed Sostre in segregated confinement for

invalid reasons, it may be presumed that damages were upheld merely because Sostre had been placed in isolation.

 93 Cruz v. Beto, 453 F. Supp. 905 (S.D. Texas 1976), *aff'd*, 603 F.2d 1178 (5th Cir. 1979).
 94 Memphis Community School District v. Stachura, 477 U.S. 299 (1986).
 95 Smith v. Wade, 461 U.S. 302 (1983).
 96 421 U.S. 240 (1975).
 97 42 U.S.C. § 1988 (1976).
 98 616 F.2d 1268 (5th Cir. 1980).
 99 42 U.S.C. § 1988.
100 437 U.S. 678 (1978).
101 42 U.S.C. § 1988.
102 *Id.* at 689.
103 Maine v. Thiboutot, 448 U.S. 1 (1980).
104 Hewitt v. Helms, 482 U.S. 755 (1987).
105 Texas State Teachers Association v. Garland, 489 U.S. 782 (1989).
106 Hensley v. Eckerhart, 457 U.S. 496 (1983).
107 City of Riverside v. Rivera, 477 U.S. 561 (1986).
108 Kentucky v. Graham, 473 U.S. 159 (1985).
109 *See* Chapter 16.
110 Jones v. Wittenberg, 328 F. Supp. 93 (N.D. Ohio 1971), *aff'd sub nom.*, Jones v. Metzger, 456 F.2d 854 (6th Cir. 1972); Hamilton v. Schriro, 338 F. Supp. 1016 (E.D. La. 1970); Holt v. Sarver, 309 F. Supp. 362 (E.D. Ark. 1970), *aff'd*, 442 F.2d 304 (8th Cir. 1971); Felciano v. Barcelo, 497 F. Supp. 14 (D.P.R. 1979); Ramos v. Lamm, 520 F. Supp. 1059 (D. Colo. 1981).
111 *See, e.g.*, Holt v. Sarver, 309 F. Supp. 362 (E.D. Ark. 1970), *aff'd*, 442 F.2d 304 (8th Cir. 1971).
112 Costello v. Wainwright, 397 F. Supp. 20 (M.D. Fla. 1975); Gates v. Collier, 390 F. Supp. 482 (N.D. Miss. 1975); James v. Wallace, 406 F. Supp. 318 (M.D. Ala. 1976).
113 McCray v. Sullivan, 399 F. Supp. 271 (S.D. Ala. 1975).
114 323 F. Supp. 93 (N.D. Ohio 1971), *aff'd sub nom.*, Jones v. Metzger, 456 F.2d 854 (6th Cir. 1972); Jones v. Wittenberg, 509 F. Supp. 653 (N.D. Ohio 1980) (In the federal supervision of the Lucas County Jail, the court held that the sheriff had complied with most of the rules adopted by the state court but had not complied with others).
115 The declaratory judgment opinion, which sets forth in detail the deplorable conditions of the jail, can be found in Jones v. Wittenberg, 323 F. Supp. 93 (N.D. Ohio 1971).
116 The relief decree in Jones v. Wittenberg is set out in 330 F. Supp. 707 (N.D. Ohio 1971).
117 Alberti v. Sheriff of Harris Co. Tex., 406 F. Supp. 649 (S.D. Tex. 1975); Costello v. Wainwright, 525 F.2d 1239 (5th Cir. 1976); Miller v. Carson, 401 F. Supp. 835 (M.D. Fla. 1975); Gates v. Collier, 501 F.2d 1291 (5th Cir. 1974); Smith v. Sullivan, 553 F.2d 373 (5th Cir. 1977); Mitchell v. Untreiner, 421 F. Supp. 886 (N.D. Fla. 1976); Martinez-Rodriguez v. Jiminez, 409 F. Supp. 582 (D.P.R. 1976).
118 Sostre v. McGinnis, 442 F.2d 178 (2d Cir. 1971), *cert. denied*, 405 U.S. 978 (1972); Withers v. Levine, 615 F.2d 158 (4th Cir. 1980); Estelle v. Gamble, 429 U.S. 97 (1976).
119 Wiltsie v. California Department of Corrections, 406 F.2d 515 (9th Cir. 1968). *See also* Meredith v. Arizona, 523 F.2d 481 (9th Cir. 1975); Harris v. Chancellor, 537 F.2d 204 (5th Cir. 1976); Collins v. Cundy, 603 F.2d 824 (10th Cir. 1979).
120 Pierson v. Ray, 386 U.S. 547, 554 (1967).
121 Tenney v. Brandhove, 341 U.S. 367 (1951).
122 Pierson v. Ray, 386 U.S. 547 (1967); Briscoe v. LaHue, 460 U.S. 325 (1983) (Even though a testifying police officer allegedly committed perjury at a criminal trial, he is immune from a suit for damages under the Civil Rights Act [42 U.S.C. 1983] brought by the former defendant. The common law provides absolute immunity from subsequent damages liability for all persons, governmental or private, who are integral parts of the judicial process.)

123 Moyer v. Peabody, 212 U.S. 78 (1909) (state governor not liable for ordering arrest of plaintiff when governor acted in good faith belief that such arrest was necessary to prevent insurrection).

124 416 U.S. 232 (1974).

125 Scheuer v. Rhodes, 416 U.S. at 237; Ex parte Young, 209 U.S. 123 (1908).

126 209 U.S. 123 (1908).

127 *Id.* at 159–160.

128 546 U.S. 151, 126 S. Ct. 877 (2006). *See also* Tennessee v. Lane, 541 U.S. 509 (2004).

129 42 U.S.C.S. § 12131 *et seq.*

130 Pierson v. Ray, 386 U.S. 547, 554 (1967).

131 Burns v. Reed, 500 U.S. 478 (1981); *see* Hoffman v. Harris, No. 92–6161 (6th Cir. 1994), *cert. denied*, 511 U.S. 1060 (1994) (social workers who file legal actions). The public policy embodied in the doctrine of absolute immunity is not one that the courts have invented recently. According to Bradley v. Fisher, 80 U.S. (13 Wall.) 335, 20 L. Ed. 646, the doctrine of absolute immunity for persons performing a judicial function has roots stretching far back into the common law. *See* Pierson v. Ray, 386 U.S. 547, 553–554 (1967); *see* Burns v. Reed, 111 S. Ct. at 1941, quoting the observation of Lord Mansfield in King v. Skinner, Lofft 55, 56, 98 A.E.R. 529, 530 (K.B. 1772), that "neither party, witness, counsel, jury, or judge can be put to answer, civilly or criminally, for words spoken in office." The Burns Court went on to note that "this immunity extended to 'any hearing before a tribunal which performed a judicial function.' W. Prosser, Law of Torts § 94, pp. 826–827 (1941). The same sort of absolute immunity that applies to judges in the performance of judicial acts applies as well to prosecutors in the performance of their official functions. Yaselli v. Goff, 275 U.S. 503 (1927), *aff'g*, 12 F.2d 396 (2d Cir. 1926); Imbler v. Pachtman, 424 U.S. 409 (1976). *See* Butz v. Economou, 438 U.S. 478 (1978), for a full exposition of the development of the modern absolute immunity doctrine as applied to judges and prosecutors. *See* Watts v. Burkhart, 978 F.2d 269 (6th Cir. 1992); in *Salyer v. Patrick*, 874 F.2d 374, 378 (6th Cir. 1989), the Sixth Circuit held that "due to their quasi-prosecutorial function in the initiation of child abuse proceedings," social workers are absolutely immune from liability for filing juvenile abuse petitions. However, *see* Antoine v. Byers & Anderson, Inc., 508 U.S. 429 (1993) (denying court reporter absolute immunity in large part because official court reporters did not begin appearing in state courts until the late nineteenth century).

132 Tenney v. Brandhove, 341 U.S. 367 (1951).

133 416 U.S. 232 (1974).

134 Gaston v. Coughlin, 861 F. Supp. 199 (W.D.N.Y. 1994), *remanded*, 249 F.3d 156 (2d Cir. 2001).

135 Campos-Martinez v. Superintendence of Capitol of Commonwealth of P.R., 502 F. Supp. 2d 210 (C.C. P.R. 2007).

136 VanHorn v. Oelschlager, 502 F.3d 775 (8th Cir. 2007).

137 416 U.S. 232, 247 (1974).

138 420 U.S. 308 (1975).

139 *Id.* at 322.

140 *Id.* at 329.

141 422 U.S. 563 (1975).

142 Gates v. Collier, 70 F.R.D. 341 (N.D. Miss. 1976).

143 434 U.S. 555 (1978).

144 405 U.S. 319 (1972).

145 457 U.S. 800 (1982).

146 671 F.2d 892 (5th Cir. 1982).

147 689 F.2d 1370 (11th Cir. 1983).

148 Saucier v. Katz, 533 U.S. 194 (2001).

149 536 U.S. 730 (2002).

150 18 U.S.C. § 242.

151 Wilson v. Lane, 526 U.S. 603 (1999).
152 Hill v. Dekalb Regional Youth Detention Ctr., 40 F.3d 1176 (11th Cir. 1994), *criticized in* United States v. Lopez-Lukis, 102 F.3d 1164 (11th Cir. 1997), and Lancaster v. Monroe County, 116 F.3d 1419 (11th Cir. 1997).
153 Doe v. Delie, 257 F.3d 309 (3d Cir. 2001).
154 Sauleberry v. Maricopa County, 151 F. Supp. 2d 1109 (D.C. Ariz. 2001).
155 Waring v. Meachum, 175 F. Supp. 2d 230 (D.C. Conn. 2001).
156 Love v. Cook County, 82 F. Supp. 2d 911 (N.D. Ill. 2000), *dismissed in part*, 156 F. Supp. 2d 749 (N.D. Ill. 2001).
157 Kind v. Frank, 329 F.3d 979 (8th Cir. 2003).
158 Smith v. Haley, 401 F. Supp. 2d 1240 (M.D. Ala 2005).
159 Schneider v. California Dep't of Corr., 345 F.3d 716 (9th Cir. 2003).
160 Riccardo v. Rausch, 375 F.3d 521 (7th Cir. 2004).
161 Shannon v. Graves, 257 F.3d 1164 (10th Cir. 2001).
162 Perez v. Oakland County, 466 F.3d 416 (6th Cir. 2007).
163 Pettus v. McGinnis, 533 F. Supp. 2d 337 (W.D.N.Y. 2008).
164 Maxie v. Felix, 939 F.2d 699 (9th Cir. 1991), *cert. denied*, 502 U.S. 1093 (1992).
165 Long v. Norris, 929 F.2d 1111 (6th Cir.), *cert. denied*, 502 U.S. 863 (1991).
166 Romaine v. Rawson, 140 F. Supp. 2d 204 (N.D.N.Y. 2001).
167 Brown v. Scott, 329 F. Supp. 2d 905 (E.D. Mich. 2004).
168 Greene v. Bowles, 361 F.3d 290 (6th Cir. 2004).
169 Schwenk v. Hartford, 204 F3d 1187 (9th Cir. 2000).
170 Odom v. S.C. Dep't of Corr., 349 F3d 765 (4th Cir. 2003).
171 Smith v. Cochran, 339 F.3d 1205 (10th Cir. 2003).
172 Sira v. Morton, 380 F.3d 57 (2d Cir. 2004).
173 Nei v. Dooley, 372 F.3d 1003 (8th Cir. 2004).
174 Castaneda v. United States, 546 F.3d 682 (9th Cir. 2008).
175 Morgan v. Morgensen, 465 F.3d 1041 (9th Cir. 2006).
176 Valdes v. Crosby, 450 F.3d 1231 (11th Cir. 2006).
177 Iko v. Shreve, 535 F.3d 225 (4th Cir. 2008).
178 Tafoya v. Salazar, 516 F.3d 912 (10th Cir. 2008).
179 Agrawal v. Briley, 2006 U.S. Dist. LEXIS 88697 (N.D. Ill. 2006).
180 Kusah v. McCorkle, 100 Wash. 318, 170 P. 1023 (1918); Smith v. Slack, 125 W. Va. 812, 26 S.E.2d 387 (1943).
181 Bush v. Babb, 23 Ill. App. 2d 285, 162 N.E.2d 594 (1959); St. Louis ex rel. Forest v. Nickolas, 374 S.W.2d 547 (Mo. Ct. App. 1964); Rose v. Toledo, 1 Ohio C.C.R. (N.S.) 321, 14 Ohio C. Dec. 540 (1903).
182 *See* Mitchell v. Forsyth, 472 U.S. 511 (1985).
183 Puerto Rico Aqueduct and Sewer Authority v. Metcalf & Eddy, Inc., 506 U.S. 139 (1993).
184 Richardson v. McKnight, 521 U.S. 399 (1997).
185 *See* Procunier v. Navarette, 434 U.S. 555 (1978).
186 521 U.S. 399 (1997).
187 403 U.S. 388 (1971).
188 534 U.S. 61 (2001).
189 28 U.S.C. § 2201 (1970).
190 28 U.S.C. § 2202 (1970).
191 Holt v. Sarver, 309 F. Supp. 362 (E.D. Ark. 1970), *aff'd*, 442 F.2d 304 (8th Cir. 1971).
192 *See, e.g.*, N.Y. Civil. Prac. Law and Rules 3001 (McKinney 1963); Ohio Rev. Code Ann. § 2721.02 (Anderson 1998).
193 28 U.S.C. § 2254.
194 512 U.S. 477(1994).
195 520 U.S. 641 (1997).
196 Pub. L. No. 104–132, 110 Stat. 1214 (1996).

197 *See* Oscar Diaz-Cruz v. United States, 1996 U.S. App. LEXIS 3526 (1st Cir. 1996).

198 *See* 28 U.S.C. § 2255; Knight v. United States, 37 F.3d 769, 772 (1st Cir. 1994).

199 *Knight*, 37 F.3d at 772.

200 *Id.*; Hill v. United States, 368 U.S. 424 (1962).

201 28 U.S.C. § 2254 (1970) authorizes federal courts to hear applications for writs of habeas corpus from persons who allege that their detention by the state violates a federal right.

202 Coffin v. Reichard, 143 F.2d 443 (6th Cir. 1944).

203 *Id.* at 445.

204 Jones v. Cunningham, 371 U.S. 236 (1963).

205 28 U.S.C. § 2254(b) (1970).

206 411 U.S. 475 (1973).

207 418 U.S. 539 (1974).

208 Patton v. North Carolina, 381 F.2d 636 (4th Cir. 1967), *cert. denied*, 390 U.S. 905 (1968).

209 *See, e.g.*, Davis v. Sigler, 415 F.2d 1159 (8th Cir. 1969).

210 433 U.S. 72 (1977).

211 472 U.S. 320, 327 (1985).

212 463 U.S. 1032 (1983).

213 489 U.S. 255 (1989).

214 501 U.S. 722 (1991).

215 Coleman v. Thompson, 895 F.2d 139 (4th Cir. 1990).

216 411 U.S. 475 (1973).

217 *See* 28 U.S.C. § 2254(b); Heck v. Humphrey, 512 U.S. 477 (1994).

218 Wilwording v. Swenson, 404 U.S. 249 (1971).

219 As well as 28 U.S.C. § 1738.

220 *See* Migra v. Warren City Sch. Dist. Bd. of Educ., 465 U.S. 75 (1984); Kruger v. Erickson, 77 F.3d 1071 (8th Cir. 1996).

221 Ohio Rev. Code Ann. § 2725.05 (1976).

222 In re Edsall, 26 Ohio St. 2d 145 (1971).

223 Ball v. Maxwell, 177 Ohio St. 39 (1964).

224 See In re Riddle, 57 Cal. 2d 848, 372 P. 2d 304, 22 Cal. Rptr. 472 (1962). *See generally* 155 A.L.R. 145 (1945).

225 17 C.J.S. Contempt § 2 (1963).

226 Randolph v. Donaldson, 13 U.S. (9 Cranch) 76 (1815).

227 39 F. 599 (S.D. Ga. 1889); *see also* United States v. Shipp, 203 U.S. 563 (1906); McCall v. Swain, 510 F.2d 167 (D.C. Cir. 1975).

228 28 Ariz. 433, 237 P. 203 (1925).

229 Ridgway v. Superior Court, 74 Ariz. 117, 245 P. 2d 268 (1952).

230 95 Ariz. 95, 387 P. 2d 799 (1963).

231 State v. Brant, 99 R.I. 583, 209 A.2d 455 (1965).

Selected Federal Statutes Affecting Prisoners 16

Chapter Outline

§ 16.1 Introduction

In addition to the constitutional rights discussed in the previous chapters, a number of federal statutes affect prisons, inmates, and persons on probation or parole. The federal statutes discussed in this chapter are the Prison Litigation Reform Act, the Federal Tort Claims Act, the Americans with Disabilities Act, and the Prison Rape Elimination Act. Two other federal laws, the Religious Freedom Restoration Act and the Religious Land Use and Institutional Persons Act, were discussed in Chapter 2.

§ 16.2 The Prison Litigation Reform Act

Since the 1970s, there has been a virtual explosion of lawsuits in the federal courts by prisoners challenging the conditions of their confinement or otherwise alleging violations of their constitutional rights. During the 1960s, prisoners filed only a few hundred such suits in the federal courts. In 1993, the number rose to more than 33,000 and in 1994 to more than 39,000. These cases absorbed more than 15 percent of the federal caseload and an inordinate amount of judicial time and energy. Judicial orders involved issues ranging from the temperature of food to whether a prisoner's hair could be cut only by a licensed barber. Lawsuits alleged constitutional violations for a prisoner receiving Converse shoes rather than Reebok shoes and claims that prison guards got a prisoner's pinochle cards wet after the prisoner had intentionally flooded his own cell. It has been estimated that more than 70 percent of such lawsuits were without merit and indeed frivolous. In the Ninth Circuit, the figure was more than 99 percent.[1]

As many of these lawsuits were filed by prisoners who were indigent, the costs of litigation were in effect paid by the taxpayers. There was no meaningful disincentive to filing lawsuit after lawsuit. If a prisoner were lucky, filing a lawsuit might gain him or her a trip to a federal court and a day out of the routine life of a prison. Perjury or filing false documents was not a disincentive, and it is not uncommon for prisoners to tailor the facts of their complaint to those of a reported federal court decision granting relief in another case.

Public opinion strongly supported reform. Whether true or not, stories were reported that prisons were nothing less than country clubs, where the prisoners enjoyed a standard of living surpassing many citizens in free society, with luxuries such as cable TV, catered food, and exercise facilities. Federal judicial orders required medical facilities in prisons that sometimes surpassed the facilities available to law-abiding citizens.[2]

The Prison Litigation Reform Act[3] (PLRA) was passed in 1995 to address the large number of prisoner complaints filed in federal court. One of its provisions requires an early judicial screening of prisoner complaints. The Act also requires prisoners to exhaust available prison grievance procedures before filing suit.[4] However, The Supreme Court held in *Jones v. Bock*[5] that the burden of proof is on prison officials to show that available administrative remedies have been exhausted. A prisoner is not required to plead exhaustion in his complaint.[6]

When courts of appeal review decisions of a district court under the PLRA, there are two standards of review that may be applied. The "review *de novo*" standard applies to issues of dismissals for failure to state a claim. The "abuse of discretion" standard applies to review on the grounds of frivolousness.[7]

One important limitation of the PLRA is that it applies only to those who are incarcerated. A former jail prisoner no longer incarcerated at the time he filed a lawsuit against jail officials is not a "prisoner" for purposes of 42 U.S.C.S. § 1997e(h). The Prison Litigation Reform Act's exhaustion requirement did not apply to his complaint.[8] However, a prisoner who was locked up in a halfway house 16 to 24 hours a day and could leave only for limited purposes was a "prisoner" under the PLRA because his confinement was due to a criminal violation, as a component of Texas's overall scheme of imprisoning and reforming felons and reintegrating them into society. His halfway house confinement could only be for the amount of time remaining on his criminal sentence. He was on mandatory supervision while he was serving the remainder of his sentence.[9]

§ 16.2.1 — Congressional Legislation

Prior to the enactment of the PLRA, it was relatively easy for prisoners to file federal lawsuits alleging violations of constitutional rights. However, in 1994 Congress enacted a statute that restricted the federal courts in cases involving overcrowding of prisons.[10] When such cases were before the federal judiciary, the statute required a prisoner to show that the crowding resulted in cruel and unusual punishment against him or her in violation of the Eighth Amendment.[11] Relief under the statute for this violation could extend no further than was necessary to remove those conditions.[12] The statute also prohibited the imposition of population caps unless the overcrowding was inflicting cruel and unusual punishment on identified prisoners in violation of the Eighth Amendment.[13] One restriction on this provision, however, was to permit judicial intervention to award equitable relief for cruel and unusual conditions other than overcrowding. In other words, the restrictions on the federal judiciary in the statute were limited to cases involving overcrowding.[14]

No federal statute required any particular judicial screening of prisoner lawsuits. However, prisoners without funds were subject to a special statute[15] dealing with proceedings *in forma pauperis*. Under this statute, indigent prisoners could file a lawsuit without paying the filing fee and other costs normally incurred by litigants. The only requirement was the filing of an affidavit showing indigence. However, the statute did authorize the federal courts to dismiss a case if the allegations of poverty were untrue or if satisfied that the action was frivolous or malicious.[16]

These relaxed standards changed upon the enactment of the Prison Litigation Reform Act. The emphasis and purpose of the new legislation were to limit the ability of prisoners to complain about their conditions of confinement and to limit the jurisdiction of the federal courts to issue orders relieving conditions of confinement that allegedly violated the constitutional rights of the prisoners. The Act was also intended to give the states more authority to manage their prison systems and to prevent federal judges from micro-managing state and local prison systems. Congress, in effect, was concerned about the number of prisoners' lawsuits clogging up the federal courts at great expense.

The reason that Congress enacted the PLRA—which precluded the bringing of any action with respect to prison conditions under 42 U.S.C. § 1983 or any other federal law until available administrative remedies were exhausted—was to reduce the quantity and improve the quality of prisoner suits. In the Act, Congress intended to give corrections officials time and opportunity to address complaints internally before allowing initiation of a federal lawsuit.[17] The PLRA does not define "prison conditions," and applies to all prisoner suits seeking redress for prison circumstances or occurrences, whether suits involved general circumstances or particular episodes, and whether the lawsuit alleges excessive force or some other wrong.[18]

Due to the great expenses and abuses of special masters appointed by district courts to operate prisons under the supervision of a district court, the PLRA places a number of restrictions on the appointment, compensation, and powers of special masters in prison conditions cases. Special masters are forbidden from engaging in any *ex parte* communications with the parties, or with one party without the presence of the other.

§ 16.2.2   – Limiting Frivolous Lawsuits

A number of provisions in the PLRA limit the filing of frivolous lawsuits by prisoners. First, prisoners who cannot afford to pay the full filing fee when bringing a civil action or appeal usually must still pay an initial partial filing fee. The prisoner must then generally make incremental payments each month thereafter until the balance of the filing fee has been paid.

Second, under the "three-strikes" provision, prisoners who have had civil suits or appeals dismissed on three or more occasions because they were frivolous, malicious, or failed to state a claim for which relief can be granted must, in most cases, pay the full filing fee up front when bringing a lawsuit or appeal in a civil case. Only if a prisoner is unable to pay the full fee and is facing an imminent threat of serious physical injury can the prisoner with three strikes bring a complaint or appeal *in forma pauperis*.

Third, the PLRA mandates a physical injury requirement. Prisoners cannot seek monetary damages for mental or emotional injuries sustained while they were in custody unless they also suffered a physical injury.

Fourth, federal courts must screen prisoners' civil complaints and dismiss any claims that are frivolous or malicious, fail to state a claim upon which relief can be granted, or seek damages from a defendant with immunity from damages liability. The PLRA authorizes a dismissal on these grounds by the court itself. A motion by the defendant is not necessary.

Fifth, a federal prisoner whom a court finds has brought a claim for malicious reasons or to harass prison officials can lose good-time credits, thereby extending the length of his or her incarceration. Courts can also revoke credits earned by a federal prisoner who testifies falsely or otherwise knowingly presents false evidence to the court.

Sixth, the PLRA limits the amount of the attorney's fees that the court can award to prevailing prisoners.[19] The fee restrictions include a requirement that the fees be proportionately related to the relief awarded by the court. For example, if a prisoner receives an award of damages, a portion of the judgment, not to exceed 25 percent, must be paid toward the attorney's fees awarded against the defendant. If the fee award does not exceed 150 percent of the judgment, the defendant must pay the balance of the fee award. There is also a limitation on the hourly rate that can be used when calculating the fee award. The Act directs that the hourly rate not exceed 150 percent of the hourly rate under the Criminal Justice Act.

Seventh, and one of the most important provisions of the PLRA, prisoners, jail prisoners, and certain juveniles confined in correctional or detention facilities must exhaust any available administrative remedies before filing a lawsuit in federal court. The exhaustion requirement applies even when a prisoner seeks only money damages and the administrative process has no provision for recovery of money damages.[20]

Courts have ruled that the PLRA is constitutional. It neither nullifies the Eighth Amendment by leaving violations without a remedy nor violates the Equal Protection Clause. The statute is rationally related to the stated purpose of Congress to limit frivolous lawsuits.[21]

§ 16.2.3 — Judicial Discretion Is Restricted

A 1994 statute titled "Appropriate Remedies with Respect to Prison Conditions"[22] was amended in three significant ways by the PLRA. First, new requirements for prospective judicial relief are required in all civil actions concerning conditions of confinement in prisons. In any civil action concerning the conditions of confinement of a prisoner, a federal court cannot grant or approve any prospective relief unless it finds that such relief is narrowly drawn, extends no further than necessary to correct the violation of a federal right, and is the least intrusive means necessary to correct the violation of any federal right.[23] Prospective relief includes all relief other than compensatory monetary damages, including preliminary injunctive relief.[24]

Second, the availability of prisoner release orders as a remedial option is limited. No release order may be entered unless the federal court has already ordered less intrusive relief, the relief ordered has failed to remedy the deprivation of the federal right sought to be remedied, and the prison officials have had a reasonable period in which to comply with the earlier relief.[25] Further, only a three-judge panel is authorized to enter a release order and then only after the panel has found by clear and convincing evidence that overcrowding is the primary cause of the violation of a federal right and that no other remedy would remedy the violation of the federal right.[26]

Third, previously granted prospective judicial relief is automatically stayed and potentially terminated, pending a hearing. The termination provision provides that in any prison conditions case, prospective relief is terminable upon the motion of any party or intervener two years after the date the court granted or approved the prospective relief, one year after the date the court has entered an order denying termination of prospective relief under the Act or, in the case of an order issued on or before the date of enactment of the Act, two years after such date of enactment.[27]

Either the prison authorities or an intervener is entitled to the immediate termination of prospective relief if the federal court approved or granted the relief without a finding that it met the initial three requirements for relief listed previously. The relief may be continued, however, if the federal court makes written findings that the prospective relief remains necessary to correct a current or ongoing violation of a federal right, extends no further than necessary to correct the violation of the federal right, and that the prospective relief is narrowly drawn and the least intrusive means of correcting the violation.[28] Finally, while the motion for termination is pending, the prospective relief must be stayed automatically on the thirtieth day after the motion was filed.[29]

§ 16.2.4   — Meritless Litigation

The PLRA discourages the filing of meritless lawsuits by prisoners. First, prisoners have trust fund accounts in their place of incarceration. They are required to file a trust fund account statement when they seek to file a claim or appeal as an indigent. Further, prisoners must make at least partial payment of the filing fees and costs in all civil suits and appeals.[30] If a prisoner cannot pay the full amount at the time of filing, the prisoner's account will be attached each month until the fee is paid.[31] There are provisions, however, that permit a truly indigent prisoner to file his or her claim or appeal without financial burden.[32]

Second, federal courts may summarily dismiss such a case at any time if they find that the complaint fails to state a claim upon which relief may be granted.[33] This added disincentive also requires a prisoner to pay the entire filing fee even when a federal court dismisses the case. Third, there is a three-strikes provision that bars indigent prisoners from filing new lawsuits when they have previously filed frivolous or meritless claims, unless there is an immediate threat of physical harm.[34] Fourth, attorneys for prisoners in many cases are prevented from or limited in receiving compensation from the defendant as part of court costs.

§ 16.2.5   – Screening of Cases

Under the PLRA, a federal court is required to screen a complaint in any civil action in which a prisoner seeks redress from a governmental entity or from an officer or employee of a governmental entity before they are docketed, if feasible, or, in any event, as soon as practicable after docketing.[35]

Under this procedure, a federal court is required to identify cognizable claims or dismiss the complaint, or any portion of the complaint, if the complaint is frivolous, malicious, or fails to state a claim upon which relief can be granted or seeks monetary relief from a defendant who is immune from such relief.[36]

This provision applies to any incarcerated or detained person, adult or juvenile, who files a civil suit in federal court, and applies to both indigent and nonindigent prisoners.[37]

§ 16.2.6   – Proceedings In Forma Pauperis: Three Strikes and You're Out

The PLRA is intended to limit prisoners' lawsuits arising out of a prison environment. Consequently, the Second Circuit held that the fee requirements of the PLRA do not apply to writs directed at judges conducting criminal trials.[38] A lawsuit was dismissed under the three-strikes rule prohibiting prisoners from bringing a civil action *in forma pauperis* where the prisoner had previously filed three meritless suits and was not in imminent danger of any serious physical injury.[39]

However, the three-strikes rule does not apply to habeas corpus petitions,[40] which are different from traditional civil actions. The application of the three-strikes rule would be contrary to a long tradition of ready access of prisoners to federal habeas corpus. Further, the nearly contemporaneous enactment of the Antiterrorism and Effective Death Penalty Act,[41] which contains separate procedures for addressing abuses of the habeas corpus process, strongly suggested that Congress did not intend the PLRA to apply to habeas corpus petitions.[42]

Routine dismissals for failure to exhaust administrative remedies do not count as a strike. A dismissal for failure to exhaust is not listed in the statute.[43] However, a district court is not limited in its discretion in nonroutine cases, where evidence of frivolousness or malice existed beyond the mere fact that exhaustion had not been obtained.[44]

§ 16.2.7   — Exhaustion of Remedies

The PLRA requires a prisoner to exhaust "such administrative remedies as are available" before suing over prison conditions. For example, a prisoner claimed that correctional officers violated his Eighth Amendment right to be free from cruel and unusual punishment by assaulting him, using excessive force against him, and denying him medical attention to treat ensuing injuries. He sought various forms of injunctive relief and money damages. At the time, Pennsylvania provided an administrative grievance and appeals system that addressed the prisoner's complaints but had no provision for recovery of money damages. Before resorting to federal court, the prisoner filed an administrative grievance but did not seek administrative review after the prison authority denied relief. In the lower federal courts, the lawsuit was dismissed because the prisoner failed to exhaust his administrative remedies under Pennsylvania law. The Supreme Court in *Booth v. Churner*[45] affirmed and held that a prisoner seeking only money damages must complete any prison administrative process capable of addressing his or her complaint and providing some form of relief, even if the process does not make specific provision for monetary relief.

Resolving a conflict in the lower courts concerning the exhaustion requirement of the PLRA,[46] the Supreme Court held in *Woodford v. Ngo*[47] that the PLRA requires a prisoner to exhaust any and all available administrative remedies, including the administrative review process, before challenging prison conditions in federal court. These include deadlines under the administrative process. According to the Supreme Court, proper exhaustion serves the PLRA's goals. It gives prisoners an effective incentive to make full use of the prison grievance process while providing prison officials with a fair opportunity to correct their own errors. It reduces the quantity of prisoner suits and improves the quality of the suits that are filed because proper exhaustion often results in creation of an administrative record that is helpful to the court. The benefits of exhaustion can only be realized if the prison grievance system is given a fair opportunity to consider the grievance. This cannot happen unless the prisoner complies with the system's critical procedural rules. Looking to both administrative law and habeas corpus law, where exhaustion of remedies is an integral part of doctrine, the Supreme Court commented that no statute or case purports to require exhaustion while at the same time allowing a party to deliberately bypass the administrative process by flouting the agency's procedural rules. Further, the prisoner's interpretation would allow a prisoner to deliberately bypass administrative review with no risk of sanction.

The PLRA is designed to reduce the quantity and improve the quality of prisoner suits and to give correctional officials an opportunity to address complaints internally before allowing the initiation of a federal case. In some instances, corrective action taken in response to a prisoner's grievance might improve prison administration and satisfy the prisoner, thereby obviating the need for litigation. In other instances, the internal review might filter out some frivolous claims. And for cases ultimately brought to court, an administrative record clarifying the controversy's contours could facilitate adjudication.[48]

In exhaustion cases, the burden of proof to show the failure to exhaust is on the prison officials.[49] Further, the exhaustion doctrine applies to both § 1983 and *Bivens* actions.[50]

§ 16.2.8   — Timeliness

In the federal system, regulations[51] require both informal and formal grievances to be made within 20 days of any alleged deliberate indifference to medical claims. A federal prisoner's grievance outside the 20-day period is untimely. Therefore, dismissal of his Eighth Amendment medical treatment claim against prison doctors was affirmed for failure to exhaust.[52] However, a prisoner's grievance was considered timely filed for exhaustion purposes because he alleged that prison officials were deliberately indifferent to his medical conditions, which caused him chronic pain. Chronic pain constitutes a "continuing violation."[53]

§ 16.2.9   — Multiple Claims

Prisoner lawsuits often claim multiple violations of the Constitution, including the First Amendment and due process, as well as the Eighth Amendment. A prisoner's compliance with the PLRA exhaustion requirement as to some but not all claims does not warrant dismissal of the entire action.[54] If the complaint contains both good and bad claims, the court must proceed with the good and leave the bad.[55]

The only grievance that a prisoner submitted concerned facts of one claim but contained multiple issues. The prisoner's grievance was a complaint about being punished in various ways for conduct that he had never been informed of or charged with. Under these circumstances, requiring the prisoner to grieve each of alleged components of his punishment separately would have prevented him from fairly presenting his claim in its entirety. The prisoner's grievance was proper, and he exhausted his administrative remedies.[56]

A prisoner was placed in administrative segregation for several years and later in a Special Housing Unit because prison officials determined that he was affiliated with a prison gang and posed a threat to prison safety. A prisoner lawsuit that contained both exhausted and unexhausted claims could go forward on the exhausted claims. The text and structure of the PLRA demonstrates that Congress intended no special dismissal rules for § 1983 prisoner suits in addition to those spelled out in the PLRA.[57]

§ 16.2.10 — De Minimis Injuries

As previously mentioned, the PLRA mandates a physical injury requirement. Prisoners cannot seek monetary damages for mental or emotional injuries sustained while they were in custody unless they also suffered a physical injury. Furthermore, *de minimis* injuries are not "injuries" under the PLRA. For example, the Eleventh Circuit ruled that the mere bruising from the application of restraints resulting in welts was only a *de minimis* injury[58] and therefore not subject to monetary damages. Similarly, a demonstrated failure to protect a prisoner against threats and assaults upon him as a "snitch" resulted in no physical injury, even those he suffered were cuts and bruises lasting no longer than two or three days. Such injuries are *de minimis* and not an actual physical injury required to sustain a claim.[59]

§ 16.2.11 — Attorney Fees

Under the traditional American system, attorney fees are paid by the parties and are not regarded as part of a damage award. Unless a statute or policy dictates otherwise, attorney fees are not recoverable or regarded as court costs. They are the responsibility of the person who hired the attorney. Court costs are usually paid by the losing party. In the United States, many plaintiffs are represented by lawyers on a contingent fee basis. This means that if the plaintiff wins, a percentage of the damages recovered will be paid to the attorney out of the award. Usually, this is one-third. If the plaintiff loses, the attorney gets nothing. However, defendants must pay their own attorney fees.

In order to deter prisoner suits under the Civil Rights Act, the PLRA imposes a cap on attorney's fees recoverable by prisoner litigants. The cap does not violate equal protection.[60] Of course, nothing in the Act or in law prevents a prisoner from paying his attorney from private funds. The statutory cap of a defendant's liability for attorneys' fees at 150 percent of the judgment applies to awards of nominal damages.[61] Thus, an attorney's fee cap was properly applied to a $1.00 nominal damages award, resulting in a maximum attorney's fee under the PLRA of $1.50.[62]

On the effective date of the PLRA, the prevailing market rate for attorney's fees was $150 per hour. However, the PLRA limits the size of fees that may be awarded to attorneys who litigate prisoner lawsuits. In Michigan, those fees were capped at a maximum hourly rate of $112.50. The Supreme Court held that the PLRA limits attorney's fees for postjudgment monitoring services performed after the PLRA's effective date but does not limit fees for monitoring performed before that date.

A class action brought by female state prisoners who claimed that prison conditions violated their Eighth Amendment rights was settled by a consent decree. A district court granted the prisoners' motion for attorney's fees and costs incurred through the date that the settlement agreements were approved and made final. Also approved were fees and expenses incurred in litigating the fees issue and monitoring and enforcing the decree during two-year period following the entry of the final judgment, along with interest.[63] The prisoners were prevailing parties[64] because the court incorporated the terms of the agreements into its final judgment and explicitly retained jurisdiction to enforce them. Even though the matter was resolved by a consent decree, the court could award fees under the PLRA attorney's fees provision,[65] in the context of the PLRA's prospective-relief provision.[66] The court awarded fees for the time spent on unsuccessful claims only to the extent that work on those claims contributed to the final consent decree. It reduced fees sought for time spent on various matters that were not compensable. The attorneys were entitled to the maximum rate of 150 percent of the Judicial Conference's rate of $113, or $169.50 per hour.[67]

It is important to note that the PLRA's[68] cap on awards of attorney fees does not apply to the successful litigation of Americans with Disability Act claims.[69]

§ 16.2.12   – Remedies in Prison Conditions Cases

Prisoners brought a class action, and the district court issued an injunction to remedy violations of the Eighth Amendment regarding conditions of confinement. Congress subsequently enacted the Prison Litigation Reform Act, which sets a standard for the entry and termination of prospective relief in civil actions challenging prison conditions. Specifically, the Act provides that a defendant or intervener may move to terminate prospective relief under an existing injunction that does not meet that standard. A court may not terminate such relief if it makes certain findings, and a motion to terminate such relief shall operate as a stay of that relief beginning 30 days after the motion is filed and ending when the court rules on the motion. The Supreme Court held in *Miller v. French*[70] that Congress clearly intended to make operation of the PLRA's automatic stay provision mandatory, precluding courts from exercising their equitable power to enjoin the stay. Under the Act, a stay is automatic once a state defendant has filed an appropriate motion, and the command that it shall operate as a stay during the specified period indicates that it is mandatory throughout that period. The PLRA provides for an appeal from an order preventing the automatic stay's operation, not from the denial of a motion to enjoin a stay. While construing the PLRA to remove courts' equitable discretion raises constitutional questions, the canon of constitutional doubt permits the Supreme Court to avoid such questions only where the saving construction is not plainly contrary to Congress's intent.

However, as the PLRA places limitations on the federal district courts, they do not easily relinquish their jurisdiction or power. The federal district courts have a tendency to protect their "turf" from congressional efforts to restrict their jurisdiction or authority. For example, a Michigan district court held that the PLRA's restrictions on its authority was an unconstitutional encroachment by Congress into a court's final order.[71] The district court also held that the automatic stay provision of the PLRA, which allows the stay of any prospective relief that has been approved or granted beginning 30 days after a motion for termination of relief has been filed, violated the vested right doctrine grounded in the Due Process Clause of the Fifth Amendment by removing prisoners' vested rights in a consent decree, which was a final judgment, without granting due process.[72] As a result, a consent decree reforming a state prison would not be disturbed by the district court because, in its opinion, the statute violated the separation of powers by retroactively instructing federal courts to reopen final judgments.[73] As could be expected, the Sixth Circuit reversed and remanded the case.[74] The Court of Appeals construed the automatic stay provision to permit the courts to exercise their inherent equitable powers and thus did not give rise to an unconstitutional incursion by Congress into the powers reserved for the judiciary.

Significant to the Sixth Circuit's ruling was that, while on appeal, Congress amended the Act's automatic stay provision.[75] Prior to the amendments, the automatic stay provision instituted an automatic stay of all prospective relief on the thirtieth day after the filing of a motion to terminate such relief. The amended provision additionally permits a court to "postpone the effective date of an automatic stay . . . for not more than 60 days for good cause."[76] "Good cause" does not include matters concerning the general congestion of a court's calendar.

Although the amended provision enabled a court to extend for good cause the effective date of an automatic stay by 60 days, it still provided that a court-enforced consent decree would automatically be stayed if the court failed to make the findings required by the PLRA within the prescribed period. Congress also added a subsection providing for interlocutory appeal of "any order staying, suspending, delaying, or barring the operation of the automatic stay," other than an order postponing the stay for up to 60 days.[77] Because the PLRA as amended implicitly recognizes the lower courts' discretionary power to suspend an automatic stay in accordance with principles of equity, Congress did not intend to bar the courts from issuing orders suspending operation of the automatic stay.

The Sixth Circuit's interpretation of the amended statute and its accompanying legislative history indicated a failure of Congress to reveal any clear congressional intent to displace the equitable powers of the federal courts. Consequently, the Sixth Circuit construed the PLRA's automatic stay provision as preserving the courts' inherent power to suspend the automatic stay in accordance with general equitable principles. Given this construction, the amended automatic stay provision of the Act was held to be constitutional.

Examples of other district courts that have attempted to avoid the requirements of the PLRA include:

- An Arizona district court held that a consent decree involving prison conditions would not be terminated. According to this district court, the legislative history clearly illustrated a congressional intent to set aside judgments made by "liberal federal judges" based on populist sentiment that courts were mollycoddling prisoners. According to this court, this is precisely the type of legislation that is inimical to separation of powers and is unconstitutional.[78]

- One district court avoided the constitutional issue by deciding that for purposes of a motion to terminate consent decrees governing certain conditions in city jails, decrees were not "final judgments." As a result, the PLRA did not violate the principle that the separation of powers doctrine prevents Congress from requiring courts to reopen final judgments. Rather, consent decrees were "executory judgments" that had prospective effects and over which the court retained supervisory jurisdiction.[79]

- The PLRA did not apply to a district court's order reinstating nine institutions that had been partially released from the court's supervision under a consent decree governing state prisons, because the court had yet to fashion prospective relief. Thus, the PLRA's provisions had not yet been triggered.[80]

- Another means by which courts have circumvented the PLRA is to label overcrowding as "failure to protect," which focused not on overcrowding but on the manner of assignment of new prisoners to cells.[81]

- A district court properly considered an individual's attendance at two state drug and alcohol treatment programs designed to rehabilitate drug-addicted criminals to be "confinement" for purposes of the PLRA. Individuals enter the programs only after admitting a probation violation. The complainant was required to enter and live at the facility and to abide by its restrictive rules.[82]

§ 16.3   The Federal Tort Claims Act

The Federal Tort Claims Act (FTCA), passed by Congress in 1946, permits a federal prisoner to bring an action against the United States for injuries caused by the tortious acts of its employees. To the extent that the claim is subject to FTCA jurisdiction, sovereign immunity is waived.[83] However, federal prisoners are not restricted to the FTCA in redressing constitutional violations by prison authorities. Remedies can also be pursued under the *Bivens* doctrine.[84] Federal prison officials do not have absolute immunity from *Bivens* actions under the FTCA. The FTCA is not an equally effective remedy as a *Bivens* claim. FTCA damages remain recoverable only against the United States and not against individuals, and punitive damages are unavailable under the FTCA. A jury trial cannot be demanded, and the FTCA remedy depends on the law of the place where the act or omission occurred.

However, there are several important exclusions under the FTCA. The intentional torts of government officials, for example, are excluded from the Act. Further excluded are federal prisoners' claims for damage to their property.[85]

Ali v. Federal Bureau of Prisons[86] further limited the Federal Tort Claims Act involving prisoner claims against the United States under the Act. Excluded from relief under the FTCA are claims for the unlawful detention of property by federal correctional officers. Sovereign immunity applies in such cases. Congress intended to preserve immunity for claims arising from the detention of property, and relief under the FTCA is not available to prisoners.

In *Payton v. United States*,[87] the federal government was not liable for the allegedly negligent parole of a dangerously psychotic prisoner who later killed a woman. The actual decision to grant or deny parole is within the complete discretion of the parole board and therefore falls under the "discretionary function" exemption of the Federal Tort Claims Act. However, the Bureau of Prisons may be held liable for its failure to supply the parole board with records that would show a prisoner to be dangerously psychotic and a menace to society when that prisoner, after being paroled, kills a woman. Further, the law places an affirmative nondiscretionary mandate upon the federal government to examine prisoners who may be insane. Any negligence on the part of the federal government for failure to examine a prisoner and later report their findings to the Attorney General or his designee is actionable.

Similar provisions apply in the various states. In many instances, state sovereign immunity is waived in certain types of cases, and those seeking damages are referred to a special Court of Claims.

§ 16.3.1   — Interaction of the FTCA with Other Statutes: Exhaustion

Exhaustion of remedies under the FTCA does not eliminate the exhaustion requirement for claims based on other federal statutes. Although a prisoner had properly exhausted his claim under the FTCA, the prisoner did not exhaust either his First or Eighth Amendment claims. He failed to follow proper procedure in presenting his complaints and also presented them prematurely, so the claims were dismissed.[88]

§ 16.4   The Americans with Disabilities Act

The Americans with Disabilities Act[89] became law in 1990. The ADA is a comprehensive statute that prohibits, under certain circumstances, discrimination based on disability. The ADA applies to all federal, state, and local governmental agencies. Disability is defined as a physical or mental impairment that substantially limits a major life activity such as hearing, seeing, speaking, moving, breathing, self-care, or learning.

The ADA has had a rocky road in the courts. Part of Title I was held to be unconstitutional[90] insofar as it allowed states to be sued by private citizens for money damages. This violated the Eleventh Amendment.

Title II prohibits disability discrimination by all public entities at the local and state levels, including county jails and state prisons. They must comply with all Title II regulations issued by the U.S. Department of Justice. These regulations cover access to all programs and services offered by jails and prisons. Access includes physical access described in the ADA Standards for Accessible Design and programmatic access that might be obstructed by discriminatory policies or procedures of the entity.

The ADA allows private plaintiffs to receive only injunctive relief (a court order requiring the public accommodation to remedy violations of the accessibility regulations) and attorneys' fees and does not provide monetary rewards to private plaintiffs who sue noncompliant entities.

Toward the end of the 1997–1998 Term of the Supreme Court, two important cases were decided that have had a profound effect on the management of prisons. In *Pennsylvania Department of Corrections v. Yeskey*,[91] an offender was sentenced to 18 to 36 months in a Pennsylvania correctional facility but was recommended for placement in a motivational boot camp for first-time offenders, the successful completion of which would have led to his parole in just six months. He was refused admission because of his medical history of hypertension. He then sued the Pennsylvania Department of Corrections and several officials, alleging that the exclusion violated the Americans with Disabilities Act of 1990 (ADA), Title II of which prohibits a "public entity" from discriminating against a "qualified individual with a disability" on account of that disability.[92] The Supreme Court unanimously held that state prisons fall squarely within Title II's statutory definition of "public entity," which includes "any . . . instrumentality of a State . . . or local government."[93] The attempt to derive an intent not to cover prisons from the statutory references to the "benefits" of programs, and to "qualified individual" was rejected. The second case, *Bragdon v. Abbott*, made it clear that HIV was a covered disability under the ADA.[94]

Many ADA issues were addressed in an Orange County, California, jail case, including its impact on older jails and prisons.[95] With respect to structural issues, where reasonable alternative methods achieve compliance with the ADA, any structural changes to existing facilities need not be made. With regard to small level changes, avoiding structural modification in favor of another reasonable method of achieving compliance was reasonable. However, a vague assertion that some accommodations might be costly cannot be construed as a legitimate basis for failing to comply with the ADA, whether through structural modifications or other reasonable methods.

Detainees in the jail complex argued that, by virtue of being housed exclusively in the Men's and Women's Central Jails, they were denied access to a variety of programs, activities, and services for which they would otherwise be eligible. The jail had a policy of segregating disabled detainees rather than allowing them to reside, recreate, and consume meals in integrated settings and regardless of where they were housed. When viewed in its entirety, each service program, or activity was operated so that the service, program, or activity, was readily accessible to and usable by individuals with disabilities.[96]

Nondisabled detainees housed in the jail complex retained at least the possibility of access to the programs offered while disabled detainees—solely by virtue of their status as disabled—had no possibility of access to the superior services offered outside of the Central Jail Complex. The ADA does not require perfect parity among programs offered by various facilities that are operated by the same umbrella institution. But a prisoner cannot be categorically excluded from a beneficial prison program based on his or her disability alone.

Applicable ADA regulations contemplate a reassignment of services to accessible buildings as a permissible means of accommodation.[97] Therefore it was not necessary to make alternate jail complex facilities physically or structurally ADA compliant. The county could redistribute some programs available at those two facilities. When viewed in their entirety, the jail's programs were readily accessible to and usable by individuals with disabilities.[98] However, the jail could not shunt the disabled detainees into facilities where there is no possibility of access to those programs.[99]

While a jail need not make all of its existing facilities accessible to individuals with or without disabilities, it is expected to provide "program access."[100] Any type of educational, vocational, rehabilitative, or recreational program, service, or activity offered to nondisabled detainees should, when viewed in its entirety, be similarly available to disabled detainees who, with or without reasonable accommodations, meet the essential eligibility requirements to participate. Whether this "program access" standard may reasonably be met or whether any restriction on access is reasonably related to a legitimate government objective is necessarily fact-specific.

§ 16.4.1 — 2010 Revised Regulations

In 2010, the Department of Justice published revised regulations for Titles II and III of the ADA. Some of the new standards, in particular § 35.152, directly addressed prisons and jails.[101] Section (b), "Discrimination prohibited," of the revised § 35.152, "Jails, detention and correctional facilities, and community correctional facilities," states:

(1) Public entities shall ensure that qualified inmates or detainees with disabilities shall not, because a facility is inaccessible to or unusable by individuals with disabilities, be excluded from participation in, or be denied the benefits of, the services, programs, or activities of a public entity, or be subjected to discrimination by any public entity.

(2) Public entities shall ensure that inmates or detainees with disabilities are housed in the most integrated setting appropriate to the needs of the

individuals. Unless it is appropriate to make an exception, a public entity—

(i) Shall not place inmates or detainees with disabilities in inappropriate security classifications because no accessible cells or beds are available;

(ii) Shall not place inmates or detainees with disabilities in designated medical areas unless they are actually receiving medical care or treatment;

(iii) Shall not place inmates or detainees with disabilities in facilities that do not offer the same programs as the facilities where they would otherwise be housed; and

(iv) Shall not deprive inmates or detainees with disabilities of visitation with family members by placing them in distant facilities where they would not otherwise be housed.

(3) Public entities shall implement reasonable policies, including physical modifications to additional cells in accordance with the 2010 Standards, so as to ensure that each inmate with a disability is housed in a cell with the accessible elements necessary to afford the inmate access to safe, appropriate housing.

§ 16.4.2　− Attorney Fees Under the ADA

The attorneys' fees provision of Title III creates an incentive for lawyers to specialize and engage in ADA litigation. However, disabled prisoners may not obtain any financial reward from attorneys' fees unless they act as their own attorneys. There is a benefit to "private attorneys general" who identify and compel the correction of illegal conditions as they may increase the number of public accommodations accessible to persons with disabilities.

To encourage ADA litigation, the PLRA's cap on awards of attorney's fees[102] does not apply to the successful litigation of ADA claims.[103]

§ 16.4.3　− Exhaustion Under the ADA

Prisoners bringing claims under the Americans with Disabilities Act are required to exhaust those claims through available administrative remedies before filing suit.[104]

§ 16.5　The Prison Rape Elimination Act

Congress passed the Prison Rape Elimination Act (PREA)[105] in 2003. The stated purposes of the Act were to:

(1) establish a zero-tolerance standard for the incidence of prison rape in prisons in the United States;

(2) make the prevention of prison rape a top priority in each prison system;

(3) develop and implement national standards for the detection, prevention, reduction, and punishment of prison rape;

(4) increase the available data and information on the incidence of prison rape, consequently improving the management and administration of correctional facilities;

(5) standardize the definitions used for collecting data on the incidence of prison rape;

(6) increase the accountability of prison officials who fail to detect, prevent, reduce, and punish prison rape;

(7) protect the Eighth Amendment rights of Federal, State, and local prisoners;

(8) increase the efficiency and effectiveness of Federal expenditures through grant programs such as those dealing with health care; mental health care; disease prevention; crime prevention, investigation, and prosecution; prison construction, maintenance, and operation; race relations; poverty; unemployment; and homelessness; and

(9) reduce the costs that prison rape imposes on interstate commerce.[106]

Under PREA, the Bureau of Justice Statistics is required to perform annual statistical reviews and analysis of the incidence and effects of prison rape and sexual assault, including identification of the common characteristics of both victims and perpetrators, as well as prisons with a high incidence of rape and sexual assault.[107] In addition, the Act created the National Prison Rape Elimination Commission, whose duties include conducting a "comprehensive legal and factual study of the penological, physical, mental, medical, social, and economic impacts of prison rape in the United States"[108] and drafting standards for eliminating prison rape. Those standards were submitted to the Department of Justice, who published the final PREA standards in the *Federal Register* in June 2012. Governors of each state are required to submit a yearly certification that all correctional facilities in their state comply with the PREA standards. States that fail to meet these standards risk losing 5 percent of their federal grant money.

§ 16.6 Conclusion

The 1995 Prison Litigation Reform Act was intended to have a substantial impact in limiting prisoner litigation and in curtailing the interference of federal judges in state and local correctional systems. The PLRA has been successful in this regard and prison administrators once again have the authority to run their institutions without fear of burdensome federal court intervention. Only time will tell how effective it will be in curtailing the propensities of federal district judges to exercise their power to remedy what they perceive as gross violations of constitutional rights by correctional administrators. Many issues are left unresolved, and there are disagreements among the Circuits as to the application and interpretation of the PLRA.

Prison litigation is extremely confusing as the law is no longer determined solely by the Constitution and judicial interpretation. Congress repeatedly has enacted piecemeal legislation that addresses some of the issues but has created in the process a patchwork of statutes and has caused difficulty in their interpretation and application. One thing is certain. Prison litigation will tax the best of the minds for the foreseeable future.

Other federal statutes that have had a significant impact on correctional operations are the Americans with Disabilities Act and the Prison Rape Elimination Act. The 2010 revisions to Titles II and III of the ADA outlined specific requirements that all levels of government must adhere to regarding the accessibility of public facilities. PREA addressed a significant problem in many correctional facilities: rape and sexual assault. The national standards to prevent, detect, and respond to prison rape were released in 2012. Only time will tell how successful these standards will be.

Notes

1 *See* the comments of various senators at 141 Cong. Rec. S14413 (Sept. 27, 1995).
2 The medical facilities and conditions at the maximum-security state prison in Lucasville, Ohio, far exceed that of Vinton County with a population of more than 15,000.
3 PUB. L. No. 104–134.
4 42 U.S.C. § 1997e(a).
5 549 U.S. 199 (2007).
6 Peoples v. Choppler, 261 Fed. Appx. 858 (6th Cir. 2008). For a 2004 review of the PLRA presented to the Second Circuit by The Legal Aid Society, Prisoners' Rights Project.
7 Moore v. Bennette, 517 F.3d 717 (4th Cir. 2008).
8 Cofield v. Bowser, 247 Fed. Appx. 413 (4th Cir. 2007); 294 Fed. Appx. 49 (4th Cir. 2008).
9 Jackson v. Johnson, 475 F.3d 261 (5th Cir. 2007).
10 18 U.S.C. § 3626 (1998).
11 18 U.S.C. § 3626(a)(1) (1998).
12 18 U.S.C. § 3626(a)(2) (1998).
13 18 U.S.C. § 3626(b)(1) (1998).
14 18 U.S.C. § 3626(b)(2) (1998).
15 15 U.S.C. § 1915.
16 28 U.S.C. § 1915(d) (1998).
17 *See* Booth v. Churner, 532 U.S. 731 (2001), and Porter v. Nussle, 534 U.S. 516 (2002). *See* the full PLRA in Appendix II.
18 *Ibid.*
19 42 U.S.C. § 1988.

20 *See* Booth v. Churner, 532 U.S. 731 (2001); Porter v. Nussle, 534 U.S. 516 (2002).
21 Zehner v. Trigg, 133 F.3d 459 (7th Cir. 1997).
22 18 U.S.C. § 3626.
23 18 U.S.C. § 3626(a)(1)(A) (1998).
24 18 U.S.C. § 3626(g)(7); 18 U.S.C. § 3626(a)(2) (1998).
25 18 U.S.C. § 3626(a)(3)(A)(i) (1998).
26 18 U.S.C. § 3626(a)(3)(B), (E) (1998).
27 18 U.S.C. § 3626(b)(1) (1998).
28 18 U.S.C. § 3626(b)(3) (1998).
29 18 U.S.C. § 3626(e)(2) (1998).
30 28 U.S.C. § 1915(a)(2); (b)(1) (1998).
31 28 U.S.C. § 1915(b)(2) (1998).
32 28 U.S.C. § 1915(b)(4) (1998).
33 28 U.S.C. § 1915(e)(2(b)(ii) (1998).
34 28 U.S.C. § 1915(g) (1998).
35 42 U.S.C. § 1915A(a) (1998).
36 42 U.S.C. § 1915A(b) (1998).
37 42 U.S.C. § 1915A(c) (1998).
38 In re Nagy, 89 F.3d 115 (2d Cir. 1996).
39 Higgins v. Carpenter, 258 F.3d 797 (8th Cir. 2001).
40 28 U.S.C. § 2254.
41 28 U.S.C. § 2254(d).
42 Smith v. Angelone, 111 F.3d 1126 (4th Cir. 1997); Carson v. Johnson, 112 F.3d 818 (5th Cir. 1997); United States v. Simmonds, 111 F.3d 737 (10th Cir. 1997); Anderson v. Singletary, 111 F.3d 801 (11th Cir. 1997); United States v. Levi, 111 F.3d 955 (D.C. Cir. 1997).
43 § 1915(g).
44 Green v. Young, 454 F.3d 405 (4th Cir. 2006).
45 Booth v. Churner, 532 U.S. 731 (2001).
46 42 U.S.C. § 1997e(a).
47 548 U.S. 81 (2006).
48 Porter v. Nussle, 534 U.S. 516 (2002); Woodford v. Ngo, 548 U.S. 81 (2006).
49 Jones v. Bock, 549 U.S. 199 (2007).
50 O'Brien v. Seay, 263 Fed. Appx. 5 (11th. Cir. 2008).
51 28 C.F.R. § 542.14(a).
52 Davis v. United States, 272 Fed. Appx. 863 (11th Cir. 2008).
53 Ellis v. Vadlamudi, 568 F. Supp. 2d 778 (E.D. Mich. 2008).
54 Jones v. Bock, 649 U.S. 199 (2007).
55 Jones v. Bock, 549 U.S. 199 (2007); Fisher v. Primstaller 2007 Fed. Appx. 73N (6th Cir. 2007).
56 Moore v. Bennette, 517 F.3d 717 (4th Cir. 2008).
57 Lira v. Herrera, 427 F.3d 1164 (9th Cir. 2005).
58 Dixon v. Toole, 2007 U.S. App. LEXIS 8135 (11th Cir. 2007).
59 Luong v. Hatt, 979 F. Supp. 481 (N.D. Texas 1997), *criticized in* Pierce v. County of Orange, 519 F.3d 985 (9th Cir. 2008); 526 F.3d 1190 (9th Cir. 2008).
60 Sallier v. Scott, 151 F. Supp. 2d 836 (E.D. Mich. 2001), *subsequent app.*, 343 F.3d 868 (6th Cir. 2003).
61 Boivin v. Black, 225 F.3d 36 (1st Cir. 2000).
62 Foulk v. Charrier, 262 F.3d 687 (8th Cir. 2001); *criticized in* Steele v. Fed. Bureau of Prisons, 355 F.3d 1204 (10th Cir. 2003).
63 Calculated pursuant to 28 U.S.C.S. § 1961.
64 Within the meaning of 42 U.S.C.S. § 1988(b).
65 42 U.S.C.S. § 1997e(d).
66 18 U.S.C.S. § 3626.

67   Pursuant to the PLRA and 18 U.S.C.S. § 3006A; 18 U.S.C.S. § 3006A(d)(1); 42 U.S.C.S. § 1997e(d)(3).

68   §1997e(d)(3).

69   Armstrong v. Davis, 318 F.3d 965 (9th Cir. 2003).

70   Miller v. French, 530 U.S. 327 (2000).

71   Hadix v. Johnson, 933 F. Supp. 1360 (E.D. Mich. 1966), *rev'd in*, Hadix v. Johnson, 144 F.3d 925 (6th Cir. 1998).

72   *Ibid.*, *motion gr. sub nom.*, Knop v. Johnson, 1996 U.S. Dist. LEXIS 16719 (W.D. Mich. 1996). *See also* Glover v. Johnson, 957 F. Supp. 110 (E.D. Mich. 1997).

73   Hadix v. Johnson, 947 F. Supp. 1100 (E.D. Mich. 1996), *request gr.*, 947 F. Supp. 1113 (E.D. Mich. 1996), *rev'd in*, Hadix v. Johnson, 144 F.3d 925 (6th Cir. 1998).

74   Hadix v. Johnson, 144 F.3d 925 (6th Cir. 1998).

75   PUB. L. No. 105–119, § 123, 111 STAT. 2440, 2470 (1997).

76   § 123(a)(3)(c), 111 STAT. at 2470, *amending*, 18 U.S.C. § 3626(e) (1998).

77   § 123(a)(4), 111 STAT. at 2470, *amending*, 18 U.S.C. § 3626(e) (1998).

78   Taylor v. Arizona, 972 F. Supp. 1239 (D. Ariz. 1997), *aff'd sub nom.*, Taylor v. United States, 143 F.3d 1178 (9th Cir. 1998).

79   Benjamin v. Jacobson, 935 F. Supp. 332 (S.D.N.Y. 1996).

80   Williams v. Edwards, 87 F.3d 126 (5th Cir. 1996).

81   Jensen v. Clarke, 94 F.3d 1191 (8th Cir. 1996).

82   Witzke v. Femal, 376 F.3d 744 (7th Cir. 2004).

83   28 U.S.C.S. §§ 1346(b), 2671–2680.

84   Bivens v. Six Unknown Fed. Narcotics Agents, 403 U.S. 388 (1971).

85   28 U.S.C.S. §§ 1346(b), 2671–2680.

86   552 U.S. 214 (2008).

87   679 F.2d 475 (5th Cir. 1982).

88   Robinson-Bey v. Feketee, 219 Fed. Appx. 738 (10th. Cir. 2007).

89   42 U.S.C.S. §§ 12101 *et seq.*

90   Board of Trustees of the University of Alabama v. Garrett, 531 U.S. 356 (2001).

91   524 U.S. 206 (1998).

92   42 U.S.C. § 12132 (1998).

93   42 U.S.C. § 12131(1)(B) (1998).

94   Bragdon v. Abbott, 524 U.S. 624 (1998). *See also* Onishea v. Hopper, 126 F.3d 1323 (11th Cir. 1997), which held that a district court must consider claims of HIV-positive prisoners that their segregation from virtually all prison programs violated the 1973 Rehabilitation Act. The decision of the Eleventh Circuit was vacated and a rehearing ordered *en banc*, 113 F.3d 1377 (11th Cir. 1998).

95   Orange County v. Pierce, 526 F.3d 1190 (9th Cir. 2008).

96   Required by 28 C.F.R. § 35.150(a).

97   28 C.F.R. § 35.150(b)(1).

98   28 C.F.R. § 35.150(a).

99   Orange County v. Pierce, 526 F.3d 1190 (9th Cir. 2008).

100   28 C.F.R. Pt. 35, App. A.

101   28 C.F.R. Pt. 35.

102   §1997e(d)(3).

103   Armstrong v. Davis, 318 F.3d 965 (9th Cir. 2003).

104   O'Guinn v. Lovelock Corr. Ctr., 502 F.3d 1056 (9th Cir. 2007).

105   PUB. L. No. 108–79 (2003).

106   34 U.S.C. §30302 (2003).

107   34 U.S.C. §30303 (2003).

108   34 U.S.C. §30306 (2003).

Part II:
Supreme Court Decisions
Relating to Part I

Note: Only the case syllabi are presented here. To view the full opinion for a particular case, including any applicable dissenting and/or concurring opinions, the authors recommend searching for the case using Oyez (www.oyez.org) or the U.S. Supreme Court Reporter (www.supremecourt.gov/opinions/obtainopinions.aspx).

Part II: Table of Cases

Cases Relating to Chapter 2

Religion in Prison

CRUZ
V.
BETO

405 U.S. 319; 92 S. CT. 1079; 31 L. ED. 2D 263 (1972)

ON PETITION FOR WRIT OF CERTIO-
RARI TO THE UNITED STATES COURT
OF APPEALS FOR THE FIFTH CIRCUIT

No. 71–5552   Decided March 20, 1972

Petitioner prisoner, an alleged Buddhist, complained that he was not allowed to use the prison chapel, that he was prohibited from writing to his religious advisor, and that he was placed in solitary confinement for sharing his religious material with other prisoners. The Federal District Court denied relief without a hearing or findings, holding the complaint to be in an area that should be left "to the sound discretion of prison administration." The Court of Appeals affirmed.

Held: On the basis of the allegations, Texas has discriminated against petitioner by denying him a reasonable opportunity to pursue his Buddhist faith comparable to that offered other prisoners adhering to conventional religious precepts, and the cause is remanded for a hearing and appropriate findings.

Certiorari granted; 445 F.2d 801, vacated
and remanded.
PER CURIAM.

O'LONE
V.
ESTATE OF SHABAZZ

482 U.S. 342; 107 S. CT. 2400; 96 L. ED. 2D 282 (1987)

CERTIORARI TO THE UNITED STATES
COURT OF APPEALS FOR THE THIRD
CIRCUIT

No. 85–1722   Argued March 24, 1987—
Decided June 9, 1987

Respondents, prison inmates and members of the Islamic faith, brought suit under 42 U.S.C. § 1983 contending that two policies adopted by New Jersey prison officials prevented them from attending Jumu'ah, a Muslim congregational service held on Friday afternoons, and thereby violated their rights under the Free Exercise Clause of the First Amendment. The first such policy, Standard 853, required inmates in respondents' custody classifications to work outside the buildings in which they were housed and in which Jumu'ah was held, while the second, a policy memorandum, prohibited inmates assigned to outside work from returning to those buildings during the day. The Federal District Court concluded that no constitutional violation had occurred, but the Court of Appeals vacated and remanded, ruling that the prison policies could be sustained only if the State showed that the challenged regulations were intended to and did serve the penological goal of security, and that no reasonable method existed by which prisoners' religious rights could be accommodated without creating bona fide security problems. The court also held that the expert testimony of prison officials should be given due weight on, but is not dispositive of, the accommodation issue.

Held:

1. The Court of Appeals erred in placing the burden on prison officials to disprove the availability of alternative methods of accommodating prisoners' religious rights. That approach fails to reflect the respect and deference the Constitution allows for the judgment of prison administrators.

2. The District Court's findings establish that the policies challenged here are reasonably related to legitimate penological interests, and therefore do not offend the Free Exercise Clause. Both policies have a rational connection to the legitimate governmental interests in institutional order and security invoked to justify them, as is demonstrated by findings that Standard 853 was a response to critical overcrowding and was designed to ease tension and drain on the facilities during that part of the day when the inmates were outside, and that the policy memorandum was necessary since returns from outside work details generated congestion and delays at the main gate, a high-risk area, and since the need to decide return requests placed pressure on guards supervising outside work details. Rehabilitative concerns also support the policy memorandum, in light of testimony indicating that corrections officials sought thereby to simulate working conditions and responsibilities in society. Although the policies at issue may prevent some Muslim prisoners from attending Jumu'ah, their reasonableness is supported by the fact that they do not deprive respondents of all forms of religious exercise, but instead allow participation in a number of Muslim religious ceremonies. Furthermore, there are no obvious, easy alternatives to the policies, since both of respondents' suggested

accommodations would, in the judgment of prison officials, have adverse effects on the prison institution. Placing all Muslim inmates in inside work details would be inconsistent with the legitimate concerns underlying Standard 853, while providing weekend labor for Muslims would require extra supervision that would be a drain on scarce human resources. Both proposed accommodations would also threaten prison security by fostering "affinity groups" likely to challenge institutional authority, while any special arrangements for one group would create a perception of favoritism on the part of other inmates.

3. Even where claims are made under the First Amendment, this Court will not substitute its judgment on difficult and sensitive matters of institutional administration for the determinations of those charged with the formidable task of running a prison.

782 F.2d 416, reversed.

REHNQUIST, C.J., delivered the opinion of the Court, in which WHITE, POWELL, O'CONNOR, and SCALIA, JJ., joined. BRENNAN, J., filed a dissenting opinion, in which MARSHALL, BLACKMUN, and STEVENS, JJ., joined.

CUTTER
V.
WILKINSON

544 U.S. 709; 125 S. CT. 2113; 161 L. ED. 2D 1020 (2005)

CERTIORARI TO THE UNITED STATES COURT OF APPEALS FOR THE SIXTH CIRCUIT

No 03–9877   Argued March 21, 2005— Decided May 31, 2005

Section 3 of the Religious Land Use and Institutionalized Persons Act of 2000 (RLUIPA), 42 U. S. C. §2000cc—1(a)(1)—(2), provides in part: "No government shall impose a substantial burden on the religious exercise of a person residing in or confined to an institution," unless the burden furthers "a compelling governmental interest," and does so by "the least restrictive means." Petitioners, current and former inmates of Ohio state institutions, allege, *inter alia*, that respondent prison officials violated §3 by failing to accommodate petitioners' exercise of their "nonmainstream" religions in a variety of ways. Respondents moved to dismiss that claim, arguing, among other things, that §3, on its face, improperly advances religion in violation of the First Amendment's Establishment Clause. Rejecting that argument, the District Court stated that RLUIPA permits safety and security—undisputedly compelling state interests—to outweigh an inmate's claim to a religious accommodation. On the thin record before it, the court could not find that enforcement of RLUIPA, inevitably, would compromise prison security. Reversing on interlocutory appeal, the Sixth Circuit held that §3 impermissibly advances religion by giving greater protection to religious rights than to other constitutionally protected rights, and suggested that affording religious prisoners superior rights might encourage prisoners to become religious.

Held: Section 3 of RLUIPA, on its face, qualifies as a permissible accommodation that is not barred by the Establishment Clause.

(a) Foremost, §3 is compatible with the Establishment Clause because it alleviates exceptional government-created burdens on private religious exercise. See, *e.g., Board of Ed. of Kiryas Joel Village School Dist.* v. *Grumet,* 512 U. S. 687, 705. Furthermore, the Act on its face does not founder on shoals the Court's prior decisions have identified: Properly applying RLUIPA, courts must take adequate account of the burdens a requested accommodation may impose on nonbeneficiaries, see *Estate of Thornton* v. *Caldor, Inc.,* 472 U. S. 703; and they must be satisfied that the Act's prescriptions are and will be administered neutrally among different faiths, see *Kiryas Joel,* 512 U. S. 687. "[T]he 'exercise of religion' often involves not only belief and profession but the performance of . . . physical acts [such as] assembling with others for a worship service [or] participating in sacra-

mental use of bread and wine. . . ." *Employment Div., Dept. of Human Resources of Ore.* v. *Smith,* 494 U. S. 872, 877. Section 3 covers state-run institutions—mental hospitals, prisons, and the like—in which the government exerts a degree of control unparalleled in civilian society and severely disabling to private religious exercise. 42 U. S. C. §2000cc—1(a); §1997. RLUIPA thus protects institutionalized persons who are unable freely to attend to their religious needs and are therefore dependent on the government's permission and accommodation for exercise of their religion. But the Act does not elevate accommodation of religious observances over an institution's need to maintain order and safety. An accommodation must be measured so that it does not override other significant interests. See *Caldor,* 472 U. S., at 709–710. There is no reason to believe that RLUIPA would not be applied in an appropriately balanced way, with particular sensitivity to security concerns. While the Act adopts a "compelling interest" standard, §2000cc—1(a), "[c]ontext matters" in the application of that standard, see *Grutter* v. *Bollinger,* 539 U. S. 306, 327. Lawmakers supporting RLUIPA were mindful of the urgency of discipline, order, safety, and security in penal institutions and anticipated that courts would apply the Act's standard with due deference to prison administrators' experience and expertise. Finally, RLUIPA does not differentiate among bona fide faiths. It confers no privileged status on any particular religious sect. Cf. *Kiryas Joel,* 512 U. S., at 706.

(b) The Sixth Circuit misread this Court's precedents to require invalidation of RLUIPA as impermissibly advancing religion by giving greater protection to religious rights than to other constitutionally protected rights. *Corporation of Presiding Bishop of the Church of Jesus Christ of Latter-Day Saints* v. *Amos,* 483 U. S. 327, counsels otherwise. There, in upholding against an Establishment Clause challenge a provision exempting religious organizations from the prohibition against religion-based employment discrimination in Title VII of the Civil Rights Act of 1964, the Court held that religious accommodations need not "come packaged with benefits to secular entities." *Id.,* at 338. Were the

Court of Appeals' view correct, all manner of religious accommodations would fall. For example, Ohio could not, as it now does, accommodate traditionally recognized religions by providing chaplains and allowing worship services. In upholding §3, the Court emphasizes that respondents have raised a facial challenge and have not contended that applying RLUIPA would produce unconstitutional results in any specific case. There is no reason to anticipate that abusive prisoner litigation will overburden state and local institutions. However, should inmate requests for religious accommodations become excessive, impose unjustified burdens on other institutionalized persons, or jeopardize an institution's effective functioning, the facility would be free to resist the imposition. In that event, adjudication in as-applied challenges would be in order.

349 F. 3d 257, reversed and remanded.
GINSBURG, J., delivered the opinion for a unanimous Court. THOMAS, J., filed a concurring opinion.

HOLT, AKA MUHAMMAD V.
HOBBS, DIRECTOR, ARKANSAS DEPARTMENT OF CORRECTION,

ET AL. 574 U.S. 352; 135 S. CT. 853; 190 L. ED. 2D 747 (2015)

CERTIORARI TO THE UNITED STATES COURT OF APPEALS FOR THE EIGHTH CIRCUIT

No. 13–6827.   Argued October 7, 2014—Decided January 20, 2015

Section 3 of the Religious Land Use and Institutionalized Persons Act of 2000 (RLUIPA) provides that "[n]o government shall impose a substantial burden on the religious exercise" of an institutionalized person unless the government demonstrates that the burden "is the least restrictive means of furthering [a] compelling governmental interest." 42 U. S. C. §2000cc—1(a).

Petitioner is an Arkansas inmate and devout Muslim who wishes to grow a ½-inch beard in accordance with his religious beliefs. Respondent Arkansas Department of Correction (Department) prohibits its prisoners from growing beards, with the single exception that inmates with diagnosed skin conditions may grow ¼-inch beards. Petitioner sought an exemption on religious grounds and, although he believes that his faith requires him not to trim his beard at all, he proposed a compromise under which he would be allowed to maintain a ½-inch beard. Prison officials denied his request, and petitioner sued in Federal District Court. At an evidentiary hearing before a Magistrate Judge, Department witnesses testified that beards compromised prison safety because they could be used to hide contraband and because an inmate could quickly shave his beard to disguise his identity. The Magistrate Judge recommended dismissing petitioner's complaint, emphasizing that prison officials are entitled to deference on security matters and that the prison permitted petitioner to exercise his religion in other ways. The District Court adopted the recommendation in full, and the Eighth Circuit affirmed, holding that the Department had satisfied its burden of showing that the grooming policy was the least restrictive means of furthering its compelling security interests, and reiterating that courts should defer to prison officials on matters of security.

Held: The Department's grooming policy violates RLUIPA insofar as it prevents petitioner from growing a ½-inch beard in accordance with his religious beliefs.

(a) Under RLUIPA, the challenging party bears the initial burden of proving that his religious exercise is grounded in a sincerely held religious belief, see *Burwell* v. *Hobby Lobby Stores, Inc.*, 573 U. S. ___, ___, n. 28, and that the government's action substantially burdens his religious exercise. Here, petitioner's sincerity is not in dispute, and he easily satisfies the second obligation. The Department's policy forces him to choose between "engag[ing] in conduct that seriously violates [his] religious belie[f]," *id.*, at ___, or contravening the grooming policy and risking disciplinary action. In reaching the opposite conclusion, the District Court misunderstood the analysis that RLUIPA demands. First, the District Court erred by concluding that the grooming policy did not substantially burden petitioner's religious exercise because he could practice his religion in other ways. Second, the District Court erroneously suggested that the burden on petitioner's religious exercise was slight because petitioner testified that his religion would "credit" him for attempting to follow his religious beliefs, even if that attempt proved unsuccessful. RLUIPA, however, applies to religious exercise regardless of whether it is "compelled." §2000cc—5(7)(A). Finally, the District Court improperly relied on petitioner's testimony that not all Muslims believe that men must grow beards. Even if petitioner's belief were idiosyncratic, RLUIPA's guarantees are "not limited to beliefs which are shared by all of the members of a religious sect." *Thomas* v. *Review Bd. of Indiana Employment Security Div.*, 450 U. S. 707–716.

(b) Once the challenging party satisfies his burden, the burden shifts to the government to show that substantially burdening the religious exercise of the "particular claimant" is "the least restrictive means of furthering [a] compelling governmental interest." *Hobby Lobby, supra*, at ___; §2000cc—1(a). The Department fails to show that enforcing its beard prohibition against petitioner furthers its compelling interests in preventing prisoners from hiding contraband and disguising their identities.

(i) While the Department has a compelling interest in regulating contraband, its argument that this interest is compromised by allowing an inmate to grow a ½-inch beard is unavailing, especially given the difficulty of hiding contraband in such a short beard and the lack of a corresponding policy regulating the length of hair on the head. RLUIPA does not permit the unquestioning deference required to accept the Department's assessment. See *Gonzales* v. *O Centro Espírita*

Beneficente União do Vegetal, 546 U. S. 418. Even if the Department could show that denying petitioner a ½-inch beard furthers its interest in rooting out contraband, it would still have to show that its policy is the least restrictive means of furthering that interest, a standard that is "exceptionally demanding" and requires the government to "sho[w] that it lacks other means of achieving its desired goal without imposing a substantial burden on the exercise of religion by the objecting part[y]." *Hobby Lobby, supra*, at ___. Here, the Department fails to establish that its security concerns cannot be satisfied by simply searching a ½-inch beard.

(ii) Even if the Department's grooming policy furthers its compelling interest in prisoner identification, its policy still violates RLUIPA as applied in the present circumstances. As petitioner argues, requiring inmates to be photographed both with and without beards and then periodically thereafter is a less restrictive means of solving the Department's identification concerns. The Department fails to show why its prison system is so different from the many institutions that allow facial hair that the dual-photo method cannot be employed at its institutions. It also fails to show why the security risk presented by a prisoner shaving a ½-inch beard is so different from the risk of a prisoner shaving a mustache, head hair, or ¼-inch beard.

(c) In addition to the Department's failure to prove that petitioner's proposed alternatives would not sufficiently serve its security interests, the Department also fails to adequately explain the substantial underinclusiveness of its policy, since it permits ¼-inch beards for prisoners with medical conditions and more than ½ inch of hair on the head. Its failure to pursue its proffered objectives with regard to such "analogous nonreligious conduct" suggests that its interests "could be achieved by narrower ordinances that burdened religion to a far lesser degree." *Church of Lukumi Babalu Aye, Inc.* v. *Hialeah*, 508 U. S. 520. Nor does the Department explain why the vast majority of States and the Federal Government can permit inmates to grow ½-inch beards, either for any reason or for religious reasons, but it cannot. Such evidence requires a prison, at a minimum, to offer persuasive reasons why it believes it must take a different course. See *Procunier* v. *Martinez*, 416 U. S. 396, n. 14.

509 Fed. Appx. 561, reversed and remanded.

ALITO, J., delivered the opinion for a unanimous Court. GINSBURG, J., filed a concurring opinion, in which SOTOMAYOR, J., joined. SOTOMAYOR, J., filed a concurring opinion.

Cases Relating to Chapter 3

Searches, Seizures, and Privacy

BELL
V.
WOLFISH

441 U.S. 520; 99 S. CT. 1861; 60 L. ED. 2D 447 (1979)

CERTIORARI TO THE UNITED STATES COURT OF APPEALS FOR THE SECOND CIRCUIT

No. 77–1829   Argued January 16, 1979— Decided May 14, 1979

Respondent inmates brought this class action in Federal District Court challenging the constitutionality of numerous conditions of confinement and practices in the Metropolitan Correctional Center (MCC), a federally operated short-term custodial facility in New York City designed primarily to house pretrial detainees. The District Court, on various constitutional grounds, enjoined, *inter alia*, the practice of housing, primarily for sleeping purposes, two inmates in individual rooms originally intended for single occupancy ("double-bunking"); enforcement of the so-called "publisher only" rule prohibiting inmates from receiving hard-cover books that are not mailed directly from publishers, book clubs, or bookstores; the prohibition against inmates' receipt of packages of food and personal items from outside the institution; the practice of body cavity searches of inmates following contact visits with persons from outside the institution; and the requirement that pretrial detainees remain outside their rooms during routine inspections by MCC officials.

The Court of Appeals affirmed these rulings, holding with respect to the "double-bunking" practice that the MCC had failed to make a showing of "compelling necessity" sufficient to justify such practice.

Held:

1. The "double-bunking" practice does not deprive pretrial detainees of their liberty without due process of law in contravention of the Fifth Amendment.

    (a) There is no source in the Constitution for the Court of Appeals' "compelling necessity" standard. Neither the presumption of innocence, the Due Process Clause of the Fifth Amendment, nor a pretrial detainee's right to be free from punishment provides any basis for such standard.

    (b) In evaluating the constitutionality of conditions or restrictions of pretrial detention that implicate only the protection against deprivation of liberty without due process of law, the proper inquiry is whether those conditions or restrictions amount to punishment of the detainee. Absent a showing of an expressed intent to punish, if a particular condition or restriction is reasonably related to a legitimate nonpunitive governmental objective, it does not, without more, amount to "punishment," but, conversely, if a condition or restriction is arbitrary or purposeless, a court may permissibly infer that the purpose of the governmental action is punishment that may not constitutionally be inflicted upon detainees *qua* detainees. In addition to ensuring the detainees' presence at trial, the effective management of the detention facility once the individual is confined is a valid objective that may justify imposition of conditions and restrictions of pretrial detention and dispel any inference that such conditions and restrictions are intended as punishment.

(c) Judged by the above analysis and on the record, "double-bunking" as practiced at the MCC did not, as a matter of law, amount to punishment, and hence did not violate respondents' rights under the Due Process Clause of the Fifth Amendment. While "double-bunking" may have taxed some of the equipment or particular facilities in certain of the common areas in the MCC, this does not mean that the conditions at the MCC failed to meet the standards required by the Constitution, particularly where it appears that nearly all pretrial detainees are released within 60 days.

2. Nor do the "publisher only" rule, body cavity searches, the prohibition against the receipt of packages, or the room search rule violate any constitutional guarantees.

(a) Simply because prison inmates retain certain constitutional rights does not mean that these rights are not subject to restrictions and limitations. There must be a "mutual accommodation between institutional needs and objectives and the provisions of the Constitution that are of general application," Wolff v. McDonnell, 418 U. S. 539, 418 U. S. 556, and this principle applies equally to pretrial detainees and convicted prisoners. Maintaining institutional security and preserving internal order and discipline are essential goals that may require limitation or retraction of the retained constitutional rights of both convicted prisoners and pretrial detainees. Since problems that arise in the day-to-day operation of a corrections facility are not susceptible of easy solutions, prison administrators should be accorded wide-ranging deference in the adoption and execution of policies and practices that, in their judgment, are needed to preserve internal order and discipline and to maintain institutional security.

(b) The "publisher only" rule does not violate the First Amendment rights of MCC inmates but is a rational response by prison officials to the obvious security problem of preventing the smuggling of contraband in books sent from outside. Moreover, such rule operates in a neutral fashion, without regard to the content of the expression, there are alternative means of obtaining reading material, and the rule's impact on pretrial detainees is limited to a maximum period of approximately 60 days.

(c) The restriction against the receipt of packages from outside the facility does not deprive pretrial detainees of their property without due process of law in contravention of the Fifth Amendment, especially in view of the obvious fact that such packages are handy devices for the smuggling of contraband.

(d) Assuming that a pretrial detainee retains a diminished expectation of privacy after commitment to a custodial facility, the room search rule does not violate the Fourth Amendment, but simply facilitates the safe and effective performance of the searches, and thus does not render the searches "unreasonable" within the meaning of that Amendment.

(e) Similarly, assuming that pretrial detainees retain some Fourth Amendment rights upon commitment to a corrections facility, the body cavity searches do not violate that Amendment. Balancing the significant and legitimate security interests of the institution against the inmates' privacy interests, such searches can be conducted on less than probable, cause and are not unreasonable.

(f) None of the security restrictions and practices described above constitute "punishment" in violation of the rights of pretrial detainees under the Due Process Clause of the Fifth Amendment. These restrictions and practices were reasonable responses by MCC officials to legitimate security concerns, and, in any event, were of only limited duration so far as the pretrial detainees were concerned.

573 F.2d 118, reversed and remanded.
REHNQUIST, J., delivered the opinion of the Court, in which BURGER, C.J., and STEWART, WHITE, and BLACKMUN, JJ., joined. POWELL, J., filed an opinion concurring in part and dissenting in part. MARSHALL, J., filed a dissenting opinion. STEVENS, J., filed a dissenting opinion, in which BRENNAN, J., joined.

ILLINOIS
V.
LAFAYETTE

462 U.S. 640; 103 S. CT. 2605; 77 L. ED. 2D 65 (1983)

CERTIORARI TO THE APPELLATE COURT OF ILLINOIS, THIRD DISTRICT

No. 81–1859   Argued April 20, 1983—Decided June 20, 1983

After respondent was arrested for disturbing the peace, he was taken to the police station. There, without obtaining a warrant and in the process of booking him and inventorying his possessions, the police removed the contents of a shoulder bag respondent had been carrying, and found amphetamine pills. Respondent was subsequently charged with violating the Illinois Controlled Substances Act, and, at a pretrial hearing, the trial court ordered suppression of the pills. The Illinois Appellate Court affirmed, holding that the shoulder bag search did not constitute a valid search incident to a lawful arrest or a valid inventory search of respondent's belongings.
Held: The search of respondent's shoulder bag was a valid inventory search.

(a) Consistent with the Fourth Amendment, it is reasonable for police to search the personal effects of a person under lawful arrest as part of the routine administrative procedure at a police station incident to booking and jailing the suspect. The justification for such searches does not rest on probable cause, and hence the absence of a warrant is immaterial to the reasonableness of the search. Here, every consideration of orderly police administration—protection of a suspect's property, deterrence of false claims of theft against the police, security, and identification of the suspect—benefiting both the police and the public points toward the appropriateness of the examination of respondent's shoulder bag.

(b) The fact that the protection of the public and of respondent's property might have been achieved by less intrusive means does not, in itself, render the search unreasonable. Even if some less intrusive means existed, it would be unreasonable to expect police officers in the everyday course of business to make fine and subtle distinctions in deciding which containers or items may be searched, and which must be sealed without examination as a unit.

99 Ill. App. 3d 830, 425 N.E.2d 1383, reversed and remanded.
BURGER, C.J., delivered the opinion of the Court, in which WHITE, BLACKMUN, POWELL, REHNQUIST, STEVENS, and O'CONNOR, JJ., joined. MARSHALL, J., filed an opinion concurring in the judgment, in which BRENNAN, J., joined.

HUDSON
V.
PALMER

468 U.S. 517; 104 S. CT. 3194; 82 L. ED. 2D 393 (1984)

CERTIORARI TO THE UNITED STATES COURT OF APPEALS FOR THE FOURTH CIRCUIT

No. 82–1630   Argued December 7, 1983—Decided July 3, 1984

Respondent, an inmate at a Virginia penal institution, filed an action in Federal District Court under 42 U.S.C. § 1983 against petitioner, an officer at the institution, alleging that petitioner had conducted an unreasonable "shakedown" search of respondent's prison locker and cell and had brought a false charge, under prison disciplinary procedures, of destroying state property against respondent solely to harass him; and that, in violation of respondent's Fourteenth Amendment right not to be deprived of property without due process of law, petitioner had intentionally destroyed certain of respondent's noncontraband personal property during the search. The District Court granted summary judgment for petitioner, and the Court of Appeals affirmed with regard to the District Court's holding that respondent was not deprived of his property without due process. The Court of Appeals concluded that the decision in *Parratt v. Taylor*, 451 U. S. 527—holding that a negligent deprivation of a prison inmate's property by state officials does not violate the Due Process Clause of the Fourteenth Amendment if an adequate postdeprivation state remedy exists—should extend also to intentional deprivations of property. However, the Court of Appeals reversed and remanded with regard to respondent's claim that the "shakedown" search was unreasonable. The court held that a prisoner has a "limited privacy right" in his cell entitling him to protection against searches conducted solely to harass or to humiliate, and that a remand was necessary to determine the purpose of the search here.

Held:

1. A prisoner has no reasonable expectation of privacy in his prison cell entitling him to the protection of the Fourth Amendment against unreasonable searches. While prisoners enjoy many protections of the Constitution that are not fundamentally inconsistent with imprisonment itself or incompatible with the objectives of incarceration, imprisonment carries with it the circumscription or loss of many rights as being necessary to accommodate the institutional needs and objectives of prison facilities, particularly internal security and safety. It would be impossible to accomplish the prison objectives of

preventing the introduction of weapons, drugs, and other contraband into the premises if inmates retained a right of privacy in their cells. The unpredictability that attends random searches of cells renders such searches perhaps the most effective weapon of the prison administrator in the fight against the proliferation of weapons, drugs, and other contraband. A requirement that random searches be conducted pursuant to an established plan would seriously undermine the effectiveness of this weapon.

2. There is no merit to respondent's contention that the destruction of his personal property constituted an unreasonable seizure of that property violative of the Fourth Amendment. Assuming that the Fourth Amendment protects against the destruction of property, in addition to its mere seizure, the same reasons that lead to the conclusion that the Amendment's proscription against unreasonable searches is inapplicable in a prison cell apply with controlling force to seizures. Prison officials must be free to seize from cells any articles which, in their view, disserve legitimate institutional interests.

3. Even if petitioner intentionally destroyed respondent's personal property during the challenged "shakedown" search, the destruction did not violate the Due Process Clause of the Fourteenth Amendment, since respondent had adequate postdeprivation remedies under Virginia law for any loss suffered. The decision in *Parratt v. Taylor, supra*, as to negligent deprivation by a state employee of a prisoner's property—as well as its rationale that, when deprivations of property are effected through random and unauthorized conduct of a state employee, predeprivation procedures are "impracticable," since the state cannot know when such deprivations will occur—also applies to intentional deprivations of property. Both the District Court and, at least implicitly, the Court of Appeals held that several common law remedies were available to respondent under Virginia law, and would provide adequate compensation for his property loss, and there is no reason to question that determina-

tion. The fact that respondent might not be able to recover under state law remedies the full amount which he might receive in a § 1983 action is not determinative of the adequacy of the state remedies. As to respondent's contention that relief under state law was uncertain because a state employee might be entitled to sovereign immunity, the courts below held that respondent's claim would not be barred by sovereign immunity, since, under Virginia law, a state employee may be held liable for his intentional torts.

697 F.2d 1220, affirmed in part and reversed in part.
BURGER, C.J., delivered the opinion of the Court, in which WHITE, POWELL, REHNQUIST, and O'CONNOR, JJ., joined, and in Part II-B of which BRENNAN, MARSHALL, BLACKMUN, and STEVENS, JJ., also joined. O'CONNOR, J., filed a concurring opinion. STEVENS, J., filed an opinion concurring in part and dissenting in part, in which BRENNAN, MARSHALL, and BLACKMUN, JJ., joined.

FLORENCE
V.
BOARD OF CHOSEN FREEHOLDERS OF COUNTY OF BURLINGTON

566 U.S. 318; 132 S. CT. 1510; 182 L. ED. 2D 566 (2012)

CERTIORARI TO THE UNITED STATES COURT OF APPEALS FOR THE THIRD CIRCUIT

No. 10–945   Argued October 12, 2011—Decided April 2, 2012

Petitioner was arrested during a traffic stop by a New Jersey state trooper who checked a statewide computer database and found a bench warrant issued for petitioner's arrest after he failed to appear at a hearing to enforce a fine. He was initially detained in the Burlington County Detention Center and later in the Essex County Correctional Facility, but was released once it was determined that the fine had been paid. At the first jail, petitioner, like every incoming detainee, had to shower with a delousing agent and was checked for scars, marks, gang tattoos, and contraband as he disrobed. Petitioner claims that he also had to open his mouth, lift his tongue, hold out his arms, turn around, and lift his genitals. At the second jail, petitioner, like other arriving detainees, had to remove his clothing while an officer looked for body markings, wounds, and contraband; had an officer look at his ears, nose, mouth, hair, scalp, fingers, hands, armpits, and other body openings; had a mandatory shower; and had his clothes examined. Petitioner claims that he was also required to lift his genitals, turn around, and cough while squatting. He filed a 42 U. S. C. §1983 action in the Federal District Court against the government entities that ran the jails and other defendants, alleging Fourth and Fourteenth Amendment violations, and arguing that persons arrested for minor offenses cannot be subjected to invasive searches unless prison officials have reason to suspect concealment of weapons, drugs, or other contraband. The court granted him summary judgment, ruling that "strip-searching" nonindictable offenders without reasonable suspicion violates the Fourth Amendment. The Third Circuit reversed.
Held: The judgment is affirmed.

621 F. 3d 296, affirmed.

Justice Kennedy delivered the opinion of the Court, except as to Part IV, concluding that the search procedures at the county jails struck a reasonable balance between inmate privacy and the needs of the institutions, and thus the Fourth and Fourteenth Amendments do not require adoption of the framework and rules petitioner pro- poses.

(a) Maintaining safety and order at detention centers requires the expertise of correctional officials, who must have substantial discretion to devise reasonable solutions to problems. A regulation impinging on an inmate's constitutional rights must be upheld "if it is reasonably related to legitimate penological interests." Turner v. Safley, 482 U. S. 78. This Court, in Bell v. Wolfish, 441 U. S. 520, upheld a rule requiring pretrial detainees in federal correctional facilities "to expose their body cavities for visual inspection as a part of a strip search conducted after every contact visit with a person from outside the institution[s]," deferring to the judgment of correctional officials that the inspections served not only to discover but also to deter the smuggling of weapons, drugs, and other prohibited items. In Block v. Rutherford, 468 U. S. 576 −587, the Court upheld a general ban on contact visits in a county jail, noting the smuggling threat posed by such visits and the difficulty of carving out exceptions for certain detainees. The Court, in Hudson v. Palmer, 468 U. S. 517 −523, also recognized that deterring the possession of contraband depends in part on the ability to conduct searches without predictable exceptions when it upheld the constitutionality of random searches of inmate lockers and cells even without suspicion that an inmate is concealing a prohibited item. These cases establish that correctional officials must be permitted to devise reasonable search policies to detect and deter the possession of contraband in their facilities, and that "in the absence of substantial evidence in the record to indicate that the officials have exaggerated their response to these considerations courts should ordinarily defer to their expert judgment in such matters," Block, supra, at 584–585.

Persons arrested for minor offenses may be among the detainees to be processed at jails. See Atwater v. Lago Vista, 532 U. S. 318.

(b)   The question here is whether undoubted security imperatives involved in jail supervision override the assertion that some detainees must be exempt from the invasive search procedures at issue absent reasonable suspicion of a concealed weapon or other contraband. Correctional officials have a significant interest in conducting a thorough search as a standard

part of the intake process. The admission of new inmates creates risks for staff, the existing detainee population, and the new detainees themselves. Officials therefore must screen for contagious infections and for wounds or injuries requiring immediate medical attention. It may be difficult to identify and treat medical problems until detainees remove their clothes for a visual inspection. Jails and prisons also face potential gang violence, giving them reasonable justification for a visual inspection of detainees for signs of gang affiliation as part of the intake process. Additionally, correctional officials have to detect weapons, drugs, alcohol, and other prohibited items new detainees may possess. Drugs can make inmates aggressive toward officers or each other, and drug trading can lead to violent confrontations. Contraband has value in a jail's culture and underground economy, and competition for scarce goods can lead to violence, extortion, and disorder.

(c)   Petitioner's proposal—that new detainees not arrested for serious crimes or for offenses involving weapons or drugs be exempt from invasive searches unless they give officers a particular reason to suspect them of hiding contraband— is unworkable. The seriousness of an offense is a poor predictor of who has contraband, and it would be difficult to determine whether individual detainees fall within the proposed exemption. Even persons arrested for a minor offense may be coerced by others into concealing contraband. Exempting people arrested for minor offenses from a standard search protocol thus may put them at greater risk and result in more contraband being brought into the detention facility.

It also may be difficult to classify inmates by their current and prior offenses before the intake search. Jail officials know little at the outset about an arrestee, who may be carrying a false ID or lie about his identity. The officers conducting an initial search often do not have access to criminal history records. And those records can be inaccurate or incomplete. Even with accurate information, officers would encounter serious implementation difficulties.

They would be required to determine quickly whether any underlying offenses were serious enough to authorize the more invasive search protocol. Other possible classifications based on characteristics of individual detainees also might prove to be unworkable or even give rise to charges of discriminatory application. To avoid liability, officers might be inclined not to conduct a thorough search in any close case, thus creating unnecessary risk for the entire jail population. While the restrictions petitioner suggests would limit the intrusion on the privacy of some detainees, it would be at the risk of increased danger to everyone in the facility, including the less serious offenders. The Fourth and Fourteenth Amendments do not require adoption of the proposed framework.

KENNEDY, J., delivered the opinion of the Court, except as to Part IV. ROBERTS, C. J., and SCALIA and ALITO, JJ., joined that opinion in full, and THOMAS, J., joined as to all but Part IV. ROBERTS, C. J., and ALITO, J., filed concurring opinions. BREYER, J., filed a dissenting opinion, in which GINSBURG, SOTOMAYOR, and KAGAN, JJ., joined.

Cases Relating to Chapter 4

Rights to Visitation and Association

PELL
V.
PROCUNIER

417 U.S. 817; 94 S. CT. 2800; 41 L. ED. 2D 495 (1974)

APPEAL FROM THE UNITED STATES DISTRICT COURT FOR THE NORTHERN DISTRICT OF CALIFORNIA

No. 73–918   Argued April 11, 1974— Decided June 24, 1974

Four California prison inmates and three professional journalists brought this suit in the District Court challenging the constitutionality of a regulation, § 415.071, of the California Department of Corrections Manual, which provides that "[p]ress and other media interviews with specific individual inmates will not be permitted." That provision was promulgated following a violent prison episode that the correction authorities attributed at least in part to the former policy of free face-to-face prisoner-press interviews, which had resulted in a relatively small number of inmates gaining disproportionate notoriety and influence among their fellow inmates. The District Court granted the inmate appellees' motion for summary judgment, holding that § 415.071, insofar as it prohibited inmates from having face-to-face communication with journalists unconstitutionally infringed the inmates' First and Fourteenth Amendment freedoms. The court granted a motion to dismiss with respect to the claims of the media appellants, holding that their rights were not infringed, in view of

their otherwise available rights to enter state institutions and interview inmates at random and the even broader access afforded prisoners by the court's ruling with respect to the inmate appellees. The prison officials (in No. 73–754) and the journalists (in No. 73–918) have appealed.

Held:

1. In light of the alternative channels of communication that are open to the inmate appellees, § 415.071 does not constitute a violation of their rights of free speech.

    (a) A prison inmate retains those First Amendment rights that are not inconsistent with his status as prisoner or with the legitimate penological objectives of the corrections system, and here the restrictions on inmates' free speech rights must be balanced against the State's legitimate interest in confining prisoners to deter crime, to protect society by quarantining criminal offenders for a period during which rehabilitative procedures can be applied, and to maintain the internal security of penal institutions.

    (b) Alternative means of communication remain open to the inmates; they can correspond by mail with persons (including media representatives), *Procunier v. Martinez*, 416 U. S. 396; they have rights of visitation with family, clergy, attorneys, and friends of prior acquaintance; and they have unrestricted opportunity to communicate with the press or public through their prison visitors.

2. The rights of the media appellants under the First and Fourteenth Amendments are not infringed by § 415.071, which does not deny the press access to information available to the general public. Newsmen, under California policy, are free to visit both maximum security and minimum security sections of California penal institutions and to speak with inmates whom they may encounter, and (unlike members of the general public) are also free to interview inmates selected at random. "[T]he First Amendment does not guarantee the press a constitutional right of special access to information not available to the public generally." *Branzburg v. Hayes*, 408 U. S. 665, 408 U. S. 684.

364 F. Supp. 196, vacated and remanded. STEWART, J., delivered the opinion of the Court, in which BURGER, C.J., and WHITE, BLACKMUN, and REHNQUIST, JJ., joined and in Part I of which POWELL, J., joined. POWELL, J., filed an opinion concurring in part and dissenting in part. DOUGLAS, J., filed a dissenting opinion, in which BRENNAN and MARSHALL, JJ., joined.

SAXBE
V.
WASHINGTON POST CO.

417 U.S. 843; 94 S. CT. 2811; 41 L. ED. 2D 514 (1974)

CERTIORARI TO THE UNITED STATES COURT OF APPEALS FOR THE DISTRICT OF COLUMBIA CIRCUIT

No. 73–1265   Argued 17, 1974—Decided June 24, 1974

The Policy Statement of the Federal Bureau of Prisons prohibiting personal interviews between newsmen and individually designated inmates of federal medium security and maximum security prisons does not abridge the freedom of the press that the First Amendment guarantees, *Pell v. Procunier, ante* p. 417 U. S. 817, since it "does not deny the press access to sources of information available to members of the general public," but is merely a particularized application of the general rule that nobody may enter the prison and designate an inmate whom he would like to visit unless the prospective visitor is a lawyer, clergyman, relative, or friend of that inmate.

161 U.S. App. D.C. 75, 494 F.2d 994, reversed and remanded.

STEWART, J., delivered the opinion of the Court, in which BURGER, C.J., and WHITE, BLACKMUN, and REHNQUIST, JJ., joined. DOUGLAS, J., filed a dissenting opinion. POWELL, J., filed a dissenting opinion, in which BRENNAN and MARSHALL, JJ., joined.

JONES
V.
NORTH CAROLINA PRISONERS' LABOR UNION INC.

433 U.S. 119; 97 S. CT. 2532; 53 L. ED. 2D 629 (1977)

APPEAL FROM THE UNITED STATES DISTRICT COURT FOR THE EASTERN DISTRICT OF NORTH CAROLINA

No. 75–1874   Argued April 19, 1977—Decided June 23, 1977

Appellee prisoners' labor union brought this action under 42 U.S.C. § 1983, claiming that its First Amendment and equal protection rights were violated by regulations promulgated by the North Carolina Department of Correction that prohibited prisoners from soliciting other inmates to join the Union and barred Union meetings and bulk mailings concerning the Union from outside sources. A three-judge District Court, which noted that appellants had "permitted" inmates to join the Union, granted substantial injunctive relief, having concluded that prohibiting inmate-to-inmate solicitation "border[ed] on the irrational," and that, since bulk mailings to and meetings with inmates by the Jaycees, Alcoholics Anonymous, and, in one institution, the Boy Scouts (hereafter collectively "service organizations") had been permitted, appellants, absent a showing of detriment to penological objectives, "may not pick and choose depending on [their] approval or disapproval of the message or purpose of the group."

Held:

1. The challenged regulations do not violate the First Amendment as made applicable to the States by the Fourteenth.

    (a) The fact of confinement and the needs of the penal institution impose limitations on constitutional rights, including those derived from the First Amendment, *Pell v. Procunier*, 417 U. S. 817, 417 U. S. 822, perhaps the most obvious of which is associational rights that the First Amendment protects outside of prison walls.

    (b) The District Court overstated what appellants' concession as to true membership entailed—appellants permitted membership in the Union (which involved no dues or obligations) because of the reasonable assumption that the individual could believe what he chose to believe, but appellants never acquiesced in, or permitted, group activity by the Union, and the ban on inmate solicitation and group meetings was rationally related to the reasonable objectives of prison administration.

    (c) First Amendment speech rights are barely implicated here, mail rights themselves not being involved, but only the cost savings through bulk mailings.

    (d) The prohibition on inmate-to-inmate solicitation does not unduly abridge inmates' free speech rights. If the prison officials are otherwise entitled to control organized union activity within the confines of a prison, the solicitation ban is not impermissible under the First Amendment, for such a prohibition is both reasonable and necessary. *Pell v. Procunier, supra* at 417 U. S. 822.

    (e) First Amendment associational rights are also not unduly abridged here. Appellants' conclusion that the presence of a prisoners' union would be detrimental to prison order and security has not been conclusively shown to be wrong, and the regulations drafted were no broader than necessary to meet the perceived threat of group meetings and organizational activity to such order and security.

2. Appellants' prohibition against the receipt by and distribution to the inmates of bulk mail from the Union as well as the prohibition of Union meetings among inmates whereas the service organizations were given bulk mailing and meeting rights, does not violate the Equal Protection Clause. The prison does not constitute a "public forum," and appellants demonstrated a rational basis for distinguishing between the Union (which occupied an adversary role and espoused a purpose illegal under North Carolina law) and the service organizations (which performed rehabilitation services).

409 F. Supp. 937, reversed.

REHNQUIST, J., delivered the opinion of the Court, in which BURGER, C.J., and STEWART, WHITE, BLACKMUN, and POWELL, JJ., joined. BURGER, C.J., filed a concurring opinion. STEVENS, J., filed an opinion concurring in part and dissenting in part. MARSHALL, J., filed a dissenting opinion, in which BRENNAN, J., joined.

BLOCK
V.
RUTHERFORD

468 U.S. 576; 104 S. CT. 3227; 82 L. ED. 2D 438 (1984)

CERTIORARI TO THE UNITED STATES COURT OF APPEALS FOR THE NINTH CIRCUIT

No. 83–317   Argued March 28, 1984—Decided July 3, 1984

Respondents, pretrial detainees at the Los Angeles County Central Jail, brought a class action in Federal District Court against the County Sheriff and other officials, challenging, on due process grounds, the jail's policy of denying pretrial detainees contact visits with their spouses, relatives, children, and friends, and the jail's practice of conducting random, irregular "shakedown" searches of cells while the detainees were away at meals, recreation, or other activities. The District Court sustained the challenges, and ordered that low risk detainees incarcerated for more than a month be allowed contact visits, and that all detainees be allowed to watch searches of their cells if they are in the area when the searches are conducted. The Court of Appeals affirmed.

Held:

1. Where it is alleged that a pretrial detainee has been deprived of liberty without due process, the dispositive inquiry is whether the challenged practice or policy constitutes punishment or is reasonably related to a legitimate governmental objective. *Bell v. Wolfish*, 441 U. S. 520. In considering whether a specific practice or policy is "reasonably related" to security interests, courts should play a very limited role, since such considerations are peculiarly within the province and professional expertise of corrections officials. *Id.* at 441 U. S. 540–541, n. 23.

2. Here, the Central Jail's blanket prohibition on contact visits is an entirely reasonable, nonpunitive response to legitimate security concerns, consistent with the Fourteenth Amendment. Contact visits invite a host of security problems. They open a detention facility to the introduction of drugs, weapons, and other contraband. Moreover, to expose to others those detainees who, as is often the case, are awaiting trial for serious, violent offenses or have prior convictions carries with it the risks that the safety of innocent individuals will be jeopardized. Totally disallowing contact visits is not excessive in relation to the security and other interests at stake. There are many justifications for denying contact visits entirely, rather than attempting the difficult task of establish-

ing a program of limited visits such as that imposed here. Nothing in the Constitution requires that detainees be allowed contact visits; responsible, experienced administrators have determined, in their sound discretion, that such visits will jeopardize the security of the facility and other persons.

3. The Central Jail's practice of conducting random, irregular "shakedown" searches of cells in the absence of the cell occupants is also a reasonable response by the jail officials to legitimate security concerns. *Bell v. Wolfish, supra.* This is also a matter lodged in the sound discretion of those officials.

710 F.2d 572, reversed.
BURGER, C.J., delivered the opinion of the Court, in which WHITE, POWELL, REHNQUIST, and O'CONNOR, JJ., joined. BLACKMUN, J., filed an opinion concurring in the judgment. MARSHALL, J., filed a dissenting opinion, in which BRENNAN and STEVENS, JJ., joined.

KENTUCKY DEPARTMENT OF CORRECTIONS
V.
THOMPSON

490 U.S. 454; 109 S. CT. 1904; 104 L. ED. 2D 506 (1989)

CERTIORARI TO THE UNITED STATES COURT OF APPEALS FOR THE SIXTH CIRCUIT

No. 87–1815   Argued January 18, 1989— Decided May 15, 1989

Following the District Court's issuance of a consent decree settling a class action brought by Kentucky penal inmates under 42 U.S.C. § 1983, the Commonwealth promulgated "Corrections Policies and Procedures," which, *inter alia*, contain a nonexhaustive list of prison visitors who "may be excluded," including those who "would constitute a clear and probable danger to the institution's security or interfere with [its] orderly operation." The Kentucky State Reformatory at La Grange subsequently issued its own "Procedures Memorandum," which, in addition to including language virtually identical to that of the state regulations, sets forth procedures under which a visitor "may" be refused admittance and have his or her visitation privileges suspended by reformatory officials. After the reformatory refused to admit several visitors and denied them future visits without providing them a hearing, the representatives of an inmate class filed a motion with the District Court, claiming, among other things, that the suspensions violated the Due Process Clause of the Fourteenth Amendment. The court agreed, and directed that minimal due process procedures be developed. The Court of Appeals affirmed and remanded, concluding, *inter alia*, that the language of the relevant prison policies created a liberty interest protected by the Due Process Clause.

Held: The Kentucky regulations do not give state inmates a liberty interest in receiving visitors that is entitled to the protections of the Due Process Clause.

(a) In order to create a protected liberty interest in the prison context, state regulations must use "explicitly mandatory language," in connection with the establishment of "specific substantive predicates" to limit official discretion, and thereby require that a particular outcome be reached upon a finding that the relevant criteria have been met. *Hewitt v. Helms,* 459 U. S. 460, 459 U. S. 472.

(b) Although the regulations at issue do provide certain "substantive predicates" to guide prison decisionmakers in determining whether to allow visitation, the regulations lack the requisite relevant mandatory language, since visitors "may," but need not, be excluded whether they fall within or without one of the listed categories of excludable visitors. Thus, the regulations are not worded in such a way that an inmate could reasonably form an objective expectation that a visit would necessarily be allowed absent the occurrence of one of the listed conditions or reasonably expect to enforce the regulations against prison officials should

that visit not be allowed.

833 F.2d 614, reversed.

BLACKMUN, J., delivered the opinion of the Court, in which REHNQUIST, C.J., and WHITE, O'CONNOR, SCALIA, and KENNEDY, JJ., joined. KENNEDY, J., filed a concurring opinion. MARSHALL, J., filed a dissenting opinion, in which BRENNAN and STEVENS, JJ., joined.

OVERTON
V.
BAZZETTA

539 U.S. 126; 123 S. CT. 2161; 156 L. ED. 2D 162 (2003)

CERTIORARI TO THE UNITED STATES COURT OF APPEALS FOR THE SIXTH CIRCUIT

No. 02–94   Argued March 26, 2003— Decided June 16, 2003

Responding to concerns about prison security problems caused by the increasing number of visitors to Michigan's prisons and about substance abuse among inmates, the Michigan Department of Corrections (MDOC) promulgated new regulations limiting prison visitation. An inmate may be visited by qualified clergy and attorneys on business and by persons placed on an approved list, which may include an unlimited number of immediate family members and 10 others; minor children are not permitted to visit unless they are the children, stepchildren, grandchildren, or siblings of the inmate; if the inmate's parental rights are terminated, the child may not visit; a child visitor must be accompanied by a family member of the child or inmate or the child's legal guardian; former prisoners are not permitted to visit except that a former prisoner who is an immediate family member of an inmate may visit if the warden approves. Prisoners who commit two substance-abuse violations may receive only clergy and attorneys, but may apply for reinstatement of visitation privileges after two years. Respondents-prisoners, their friends, and family members-filed a 42 U. S. C. § 1983 action, alleging that the regulations as they pertain to noncontact visits violate the First, Eighth, and Fourteenth Amendments. The District Court agreed, and the Sixth Circuit affirmed.

Held:

1. The fact that the regulations bear a rational relation to legitimate penological interests suffices to sustain them regardless of whether respondents have a constitutional right of association that has survived incarceration. This Court accords substantial deference to the professional judgment of prison administrators, who bear a significant responsibility for defining a corrections system's legitimate goals and determining the most appropriate means to accomplish them. The regulations satisfy each of four factors used to decide whether a prison regulation affecting a constitutional right that survives incarceration withstands constitutional challenge. See *Turner* v. *Safley,* 482 U. S. 78, 89–91. First, the regulations bear a rational relationship to a legitimate penological interest. The restrictions on children's visitation are related to MDOC's valid interests in maintaining internal security and protecting child visitors from exposure to sexual or other misconduct or from accidental injury. They promote internal security, perhaps the most legitimate penological goal, by reducing the total number of visitors and by limiting disruption caused by children. It is also reasonable to ensure that the visiting child is accompanied and supervised by adults charged with protecting the child's best interests. Prohibiting visitation by former inmates bears a self-evident connection to the State's interest in maintaining prison security and preventing future crime. Restricting visitation for inmates with two substance-abuse violations serves the legitimate goal of

deterring drug and alcohol use within prison. Second, respondents have alternative means of exercising their asserted right of association with those prohibited from visiting. They can send messages through those who are permitted to visit, and can communicate by letter and telephone. Visitation alternatives need not be ideal; they need only be available. Third, accommodating the associational right would have a considerable impact on guards, other inmates, the allocation of prison resources, and the safety of visitors by causing a significant reallocation of the prison system's financial resources and by impairing corrections officers' ability to protect all those inside a prison's walls. Finally, respondents have suggested no alternatives that fully accommodate the asserted right while not imposing more than a *de minimis* cost to the valid penological goals. Pp. 131–136.

2. The visitation restriction for inmates with two substance-abuse violations is not a cruel and unusual confinement condition violating the Eighth Amendment. Withdrawing visitation privileges for a limited period in order to effect prison discipline is not a dramatic departure from accepted standards for confinement conditions. Nor does the regulation create inhumane prison conditions, deprive inmates of basic necessities or fail to protect their health or safety, or involve the infliction of pain or injury or deliberate indifference to their risk.

286 F.3d 311, reversed.
KENNEDY, J., delivered the opinion of the Court, in which REHNQUIST, C. J., and STEVENS, O'CONNOR, SOUTER, GINSBURG, and BREYER, JJ., joined. STEVENS, J., filed a concurring opinion, in which SOUTER, GINSBURG, and BREYER, JJ., joined. THOMAS, J., filed an opinion concurring in the judgment, in which SCALIA, J., joined.

Cases Relating to Chapter 5

Rights to Use of Mail, Internet, and Telephone

PROCUNIER
V.
MARTINEZ

416 U.S. 396; 94 S. CT. 1800; 40 L. ED. 2D 224 (1974)

APPEAL FROM THE UNITED STATES DISTRICT COURT FOR THE NORTHERN DISTRICT OF CALIFORNIA

No. 72–1465   Argued December 3, 1973— Decided April 29, 1974

Appellees, prison inmates, brought this class action challenging prisoner mail censorship regulations issued by the Director of the California Department of Corrections and the ban against the use of law students and legal paraprofessionals to conduct attorney-client interviews with inmates. The mail censorship regulations, *inter alia*, proscribed inmate correspondence that "unduly complain[ed]," "magnif[ied] grievances," "express[ed] inflammatory political, racial, religious or other views or beliefs," or contained matter deemed "defamatory" or "otherwise inappropriate." The District Court held these regulations unconstitutional under the First Amendment, void for vagueness, and violative of the Fourteenth Amendment's guarantee of procedural due process, and it enjoined their continued enforcement. The court required that an inmate be notified of the rejection of correspondence, and that the author of the correspondence be allowed to protest the decision and secure review by a prison official other than the original censor. The District Court also held that the ban against the use of law students and legal paraprofessionals to conduct attorney-client interviews with inmates abridged the right of access to the courts and enjoined its continued enforcement. Appellants contend that the District Court should have abstained from deciding the constitutionality of the mail censorship regulations.

Held:

1. The District Court did not err in refusing to abstain from deciding the constitutionality of the mail censorship regulations.

2. The censorship of direct personal correspondence involves incidental restrictions on the right to free speech of both prisoners and their correspondents, and is justified if the following criteria are met: (1) it must further one or more of the important and substantial governmental interests of security, order, and the rehabilitation of inmates, and (2) it must be no greater than is necessary to further the legitimate governmental interest involved.

3. Under this standard, the invalidation of the mail censorship regulations by the District Court was correct.

4. The decision to censor or withhold delivery of a particular letter must be accompanied by minimum procedural safeguards against arbitrariness or error, and the requirements specified by the District Court were not unduly burdensome.

5. The ban against attorney-client interviews conducted by law students or legal para-professionals, which was not limited to prospective interviewers who posed some colorable threat to security or to those inmates thought to be especially dangerous and which created an arbitrary distinction between law students employed by attorneys and those associated with law school programs (against whom the ban did not operate), constituted an unjustifiable restriction on the inmates' right of access to the courts. *Johnson v. Avery*, 393 U.S. 483.

354 F. Supp. 1092, affirmed.
POWELL, J., delivered the opinion of the Court, in which BURGER, C.J., and BRENNAN, STEWART, WHITE, MARSHALL, BLACKMUN, and REHNQUIST, JJ., joined. MARSHALL, J., filed a concurring opinion, in which BRENNAN, J., joined and in Part II of which DOUGLAS, J., joined. DOUGLAS, J., filed an opinion concurring in the judgment.

WOLFF
V.
MCDONNELL

418 U.S. 539; 94 S. CT. 2963; 41 L. ED. 2D 935 (1974)

CERTIORARI TO THE UNITED STATES COURT OF APPEALS FOR THE EIGHTH CIRCUIT

No. 73–679. Argued April 22, 1974— Decided June 26, 1974

Respondent, on behalf of himself and other inmates at a Nebraska prison, filed a complaint for damages and injunctive relief under 42 U.S.C. § 1983, in which he alleged that disciplinary proceedings at the prison violated due process; that the inmate legal assistance program did not meet constitutional standards; and that the regulations governing inmates' mail were unconstitutionally restrictive. After

an evidentiary hearing, the District Court granted partial relief. Though rejecting respondent's procedural due process claim, the court held that the prison's policy of inspecting all attorney-prisoner mail was improper, but that restrictions on inmate legal assistance were not constitutionally defective. The Court of Appeals reversed with respect to the due process claim, holding that the procedural requirements outlined in the intervening decisions in *Morrissey v. Brewer*, 408 U.S. 471, and *Gagnon v. Scarpelli*, 411 U.S. 778, should be generally followed in prison disciplinary hearings, but leaving the specific requirements (including the circumstances in which counsel might be required) to be determined by the District Court on remand. The Court of Appeals further held that *Preiser v. Rodriguez*, 411 U.S. 475, forbade restoration of good-time credits in a 1983 suit, but ordered expunged from prison records misconduct determinations reached in proceedings that had not comported with due process. The court generally affirmed the District Court's judgment respecting correspondence with attorneys, but added some additional prescriptions and ordered further proceedings to determine whether the State was meeting its burden under *Johnson v. Avery*, 393 U.S. 483, to provide legal assistance to prisoners, a duty the court found to extend to civil rights cases as well as habeas corpus proceedings. Under Nebraska's disciplinary scheme, forfeiture or withholding of good time credits or confinement in a disciplinary cell is provided for serious misconduct and deprivation of privileges for less serious misconduct. To establish misconduct, (1) a preliminary conference is held with the chief corrections supervisor and the charging party, where the prisoner is orally informed of the charge and preliminarily discusses the merits; (2) a conduct report is prepared and a hearing held before the prison's disciplinary body, the Adjustment Committee (composed of three prison officials), where (3) the inmate can ask questions of the charging party.

Held:

1. Though the Court of Appeals correctly held that restoration of good time credits under § 1983 is foreclosed under *Preiser, supra*, damages and declaratory and other

relief for improper revocation of good time credits are cognizable under that provision.

2. A prisoner is not wholly stripped of constitutional protections, and though prison disciplinary proceedings do not implicate the full panoply of rights due a defendant in a criminal prosecution, such proceedings must be governed by a mutual accommodation between institutional needs and generally applicable constitutional requirements.

3. Since prisoners in Nebraska can only lose good time credits if they are guilty of serious misconduct, the procedure for determining whether such misconduct has occurred must observe certain minimal due process requirements (though not the full range of procedures mandated in *Morrissey, supra,* and *Scarpelli, supra,* for parole and probation revocation hearings) consonant with the unique institutional environment and therefore involving a more flexible approach reasonably accommodating the interests of the inmates and the needs of the institution.

   (a) Advance written notice of charges must be given to the disciplinary action inmate, no less than 24 hours before his appearance before the Adjustment Committee.

   (b) There must be "a written statement by the factfinders as to the evidence relied on and reasons for [the disciplinary action]." *Morrissey v. Brewer, supra,* at 408 U. S. 489.

   (c) The inmate should be allowed to call witnesses and present documentary evidence in his defense if permitting him to do so will not jeopardize institutional safety or correctional goals.

   (d) The inmate has no constitutional right to confrontation and cross-examination in prison disciplinary proceedings, such procedures in the current environment, where prison disruption remains a serious concern, being discretionary with the prison officials.

   (e) Inmates have no right to retained or appointed counsel in such proceed-

ings, although counsel substitutes should be provided in certain cases.

   (f) On the record here, it cannot be concluded that the Adjustment Committee is not sufficiently impartial to satisfy due process requirements.

4. The Court of Appeals erred in holding that the due process requirements in prison disciplinary proceedings were to be applied retroactively by requiring the expunging of prison records of improper misconduct determinations. *Morrissey, supra,* at 408 U. S. 490.

5. The State may constitutionally require that mail from an attorney to a prisoner be identified as such, and that his name and address appear on the communication; and—as a protection against contraband—that the authorities may open such mail in the inmate's presence. A lawyer desiring to correspond with a prisoner may also be required first to identify himself and his client to the prison officials to ensure that letters marked "privileged" are actually from members of the bar. Other restrictions on the attorney-prisoner mail procedure required by the courts below are disapproved.

6. The District Court, as the Court of Appeals suggested, is to assess the adequacy of the legal assistance available for preparation of civil rights actions, applying the standard of *Johnson v. Avery, supra,* at 373 U. S. 490, that "unless and until the State provides some reasonable alternative to assist inmates in the preparation of petitions for post-conviction relief," inmates could not be barred from furnishing assistance to each other.

483 F.2d 1059, affirmed in part, reversed in part, and remanded.

WHITE, J., delivered the opinion of the Court, in which BURGER, C.J., and STEWART, BLACKMUN, POWELL, and REHNQUIST, JJ., joined. MARSHALL, J., filed an opinion concurring in part and dissenting in part, in which BRENNAN, J., joined. DOUGLAS, J., filed an opinion dissenting in part and concurring in the result in part.

TURNER
V.
SAFLEY

482 U.S. 78; 107 S. CT. 2254; 96 L. ED. 2D 64 (1987)

CERTIORARI TO THE UNITED STATES COURT OF APPEALS FOR THE EIGHTH CIRCUIT

No. 85–1384   Argued January 13, 1987— Decided June 1, 1987

Respondent inmates brought a class action challenging two regulations promulgated by the Missouri Division of Corrections. The first permits correspondence between immediate family members who are inmates at different institutions within the Division's jurisdiction, and between inmates "concerning legal matters," but allows other inmate correspondence only if each inmate's classification/treatment team deems it in the best interests of the parties. The second regulation permits an inmate to marry only with the prison superintendent's permission, which can be given only when there are "compelling reasons" to do so. Testimony indicated that generally only a pregnancy or the birth of an illegitimate child would be considered "compelling." The Federal District Court found both regulations unconstitutional, and the Court of Appeals affirmed.

Held:

1. The lower courts erred in ruling that *Procunier v. Martinez*, 416 U. S. 396, and its progeny require the application of a strict scrutiny standard of review for resolving respondents' constitutional complaints. Rather, those cases indicate that a lesser standard is appropriate whereby inquiry is made into whether a prison regulation that impinges on inmates' constitutional rights is "reasonably related" to legitimate penological interests. In determining reasonableness, relevant factors include (a) whether there is a "valid, rational connection" between the regulation and a legitimate and neutral governmental interest put forward to justify it, which connection cannot be so remote as to render the regulation arbitrary or irrational; (b) whether there are alternative means of exercising the asserted constitutional right that remain open to inmates, which alternatives, if they exist, will require a measure of judicial deference to the corrections officials' expertise; (c) whether and the extent to which accommodation of the asserted right will have an impact on prison staff, on inmates' liberty, and on the allocation of limited prison resources, which impact, if substantial, will require particular deference to corrections officials; and (d) whether the regulation represents an "exaggerated response" to prison concerns, the existence of a ready alternative that fully accommodates the prisoner's rights at *de minimis* costs to valid penological interests being evidence of unreasonableness.

2. The Missouri inmate correspondence regulation is, on the record here, reasonable and facially valid. The regulation is logically related to the legitimate security concerns of prison officials, who testified that mail between prisons can be used to communicate escape plans, to arrange violent acts, and to foster prison gang activity. Moreover, the regulation does not deprive prisoners of all means of expression, but simply bars communication with a limited class of people— other inmates—with whom authorities have particular cause to be concerned. The regulation is entitled to deference on the basis of the significant impact of prison correspondence on the liberty and safety of other prisoners and prison personnel, in light of officials' testimony that such correspondence facilitates the development of informal organizations that threaten safety and security at penal institutions. Nor is there an obvious, easy alternative to the regulation, since monitoring inmate correspondence clearly would impose more than a *de minimis* cost in terms of the burden on staff resources required to conduct item-by-item censorship, and would create an appreciable risk of missing dangerous communications. The regulation is con-

tent-neutral, and does not unconstitutionally abridge the First Amendment rights
of prison inmates.

3. The constitutional right of prisoners to
marry is impermissibly burdened by the
Missouri marriage regulation.

(a) Prisoners have a constitutionally protected right to marry under *Zablocki
v. Redhail*, 434 U. S. 374. Although
such a marriage is subject to substantial restrictions as a result of incarceration, sufficient important attributes
of marriage remain to form a constitutionally protected relationship.
Butler v. Wilson, 415 U.S. 953, distinguished.

(b) The regulation is facially invalid
under the reasonable relationship
test. Although prison officials may
regulate the time and circumstances
under which a marriage takes place,
and may require prior approval by
the warden, the almost complete
ban on marriages here is not, on the
record, reasonably related to legitimate penological objectives. The
contention that the regulation serves
security concerns by preventing
"love triangles" that may lead to violent inmate confrontations is without
merit, since inmate rivalries are likely
to develop with or without a formal
marriage ceremony. Moreover, the
regulation's broad prohibition is not
justified by the security of fellow
inmates and prison staff, who are not
affected where the inmate makes the
private decision to marry a civilian.
Rather, the regulation represents an
exaggerated response to the claimed
security objectives, since allowing
marriages unless the warden finds a
threat to security, order, or the public
safety represents an obvious, easy
alternative that would accommodate
the right to marry while imposing a
de minimis burden. Nor is the regulation reasonably related to the articulated rehabilitation goal of fostering
self-reliance by female prisoners. In
requiring refusal of permission to
marry to all inmates absent a com-

pelling reason, the regulation sweeps
much more broadly than is necessary, in light of officials' testimony
that male inmates' marriages had
generally caused them no problems,
and that they had no objections to
prisoners marrying civilians.

777 F.2d 1307, affirmed in part, reversed
in part, and remanded.

O'CONNOR, J., delivered the opinion of
the Court, in which REHNQUIST, C.J.,
and WHITE, POWELL, and SCALIA,
JJ., joined, and in Part III-B of which
BRENNAN, MARSHALL, BLACK-
MUN, and STEVENS, JJ., joined.
STEVENS, J., filed an opinion concur-
ring in part and dissenting in part, in
which BRENNAN, MARSHALL, and
BLACKMUN, JJ., joined.

THORNBURGH
V.
ABBOTT

490 U.S. 401; 109 S. CT. 1874; 104 L. ED. 2D 459 (1989)

CERTIORARI TO THE UNITED STATES
COURT OF APPEALS FOR THE DISTRICT
OF COLUMBIA CIRCUIT

No. 87–1344   Argued November 8, 1988—
Decided May 15, 1989

Federal Bureau of Prisons regulations generally permit prisoners to receive publications
from the "outside," but authorize wardens,
pursuant to specified criteria, to reject an
incoming publication if it is found "to be detrimental to the security, good order, or discipline of the institution or if it might facilitate
criminal activity." Wardens may not reject a
publication "solely because its content is religious, philosophical, political, social[,] sexual,
or . . . unpopular or repugnant," or establish
an excluded list of publications, but must
review each issue of a subscription separately.
Respondents, a class of inmates and certain
publishers, filed suit in the District Court,
claiming that the regulations, both on their

face and as applied to 46 specifically excluded publications, violated their First Amendment rights under the standard set forth in *Procunier v. Martinez*, 416 U. S. 396. The District Court refrained from adopting the *Martinez* standard in favor of an approach more deferential to the judgment of prison authorities, and upheld the regulations without addressing the propriety of the 46 exclusions. The Court of Appeals, however, utilized the *Martinez* standard, found the regulations wanting, and remanded the case for an individualized determination on the constitutionality of the 46 exclusions.

Held:

1. Regulations such as those at issue that affect the sending of publications to prisoners must be analyzed under the standard set forth in *Turner v. Safley*, 482 U. S. 78, 482 U. S. 89, and are therefore "valid if [they are] reasonably related to legitimate penological interests." Prison officials are due considerable deference in regulating the delicate balance between prison order and security and the legitimate demands of "outsiders" who seek to enter the prison environment. The less deferential standard of *Martinez*— whereby prison regulations authorizing mail censorship must be "generally necessary" to protect one or more legitimate governmental interests—is limited to regulations concerning outgoing personal correspondence from prisoners, regulations which are not centrally concerned with the maintenance of prison order and security. Moreover, *Martinez* is overruled to the extent that it might support the drawing of a categorical distinction between incoming correspondence from prisoners (to which *Turner* applied its reasonableness standard) and incoming correspondence from nonprisoners.

2. The regulations at issue are facially valid under the *Turner* standard. Their underlying objective of protecting prison security is undoubtedly legitimate, and is neutral with regard to the content of the expression regulated. Also, the broad discretion the regulations accord wardens is rationally related to security interests. Furthermore, alternative means of expression

remain open to the inmates, since the regulations permit a broad range of publications to be sent, received, and read, even though specific publications are prohibited. Moreover, respondents have established no alternative to the regulations that would accommodate prisoners' constitutional rights at a *de minimis* cost to valid penological interests.

3. The case is remanded for an examination of the validity of the regulations as applied to any of the 46 publications introduced at trial as to which there remains a live controversy.

263 U.S. App. D.C. 186, 824 F.2d 1166, vacated and remanded.

BLACKMUN, J., delivered the opinion of the Court, in which REHNQUIST, C.J., and WHITE, O'CONNOR, SCALIA, and KENNEDY, JJ., joined. STEVENS, J., filed an opinion concurring in part and dissenting in part, in which BRENNAN and MARSHALL, JJ., joined.

BEARD, SECRETARY, PENNSYLVANIA DEPARTMENT OF CORRECTIONS V. BANKS

548 U.S. 521, 126 S. CT. 2572; 165 L. ED. 2D 697 (2006)

CERTIORARI TO THE UNITED STATES COURT OF APPEALS FOR THE THIRD CIRCUIT

No. 04–1739　　Argued March 27, 2006— Decided June 28, 2006

Pennsylvania houses its 40 most dangerous and recalcitrant inmates in a Long Term Segregation Unit (LTSU). Inmates begin in level 2, which has the most severe restrictions, but may graduate to the less restrictive level 1. Plaintiff-respondent Banks, a level 2 inmate, filed this federal-court action against defendant-petitioner, the Secretary of the Department of Corrections, alleging that a level 2 policy (Policy) forbidding inmates any access to newspapers, magazines, and photographs violates the First Amendment. During discovery, Banks deposed Deputy Prison Superintendent Dickson and the parties introduced prison policy manuals and related documents into the record. The Secretary then filed a summary judgment motion, along with a statement of undisputed facts and the deposition. Rather than filing an opposition to the motion, Banks filed a cross-motion for summary judgment, relying on the undisputed facts, including those in the deposition. Based on this record, the District Court granted the Secretary's motion and denied Banks'. Reversing the Secretary's summary judgment award, the Third Circuit held that the prison regulation could not be supported as a matter of law.

Held: The judgment is reversed, and the case is remanded.

399 F. 3d 134, reversed and remanded.

JUSTICE BREYER, joined by THE CHIEF JUSTICE, JUSTICE KENNEDY, and JUSTICE SOUTER, concluded that, based on the record before this Court, prison officials have set forth adequate legal support for the Policy, and Banks has failed to show specific facts that could warrant a determination in his favor.

(a) *Turner* v. *Safley*, 482 U. S. 78, and *Overton* v. *Bazzetta*, 539 U. S. 126, contain the basic substantive legal standards covering this case. While imprisonment does not automatically deprive a prisoner of constitutional protections, *Turner*, 482 U. S., at 93, the Constitution sometimes permits greater restriction of such rights in a prison than it would allow elsewhere, *id.*, at 84–85. As *Overton, supra,* at 132, pointed out, courts also owe "substantial deference to the professional judgment of prison administrators." Under *Turner*, restrictive prison regulations are permissible if they are "reasonably related to legitimate penological interests." 482 U. S., at 89. Because this case is here on the Secretary's summary judgment motion, the Court examines the record to determine whether he has demonstrated "the absence of a genuine issue of material fact" and his entitlement to judgment as

a matter of law. See, *e.g.,* Fed. Rule Civ. Proc. 56. If he has, the Court determines whether Banks has "by affidavits or as otherwise provided" in Rule 56, "set forth specific facts showing . . . a genuine issue for trial," Rule 56(e). Inferences about disputed facts must be drawn in Banks' favor, but deference must be accorded prison authorities' views with respect to matters of professional judgment.

(b) The Secretary rested his motion primarily on the undisputed facts statement and Dickson's affidavit. The first of his justifications for the Policy—the need to motivate better behavior on the part of particularly difficult prisoners—sufficiently satisfies *Turner*'s requirements. The statement and affidavit set forth a "'valid, rational connection'" between the Policy and "'legitimate penological interests,'" 482 U. S., at 89, 95. Dickson noted that prison authorities are limited in what they can and cannot deny or give a level 2 inmate, who has already been deprived of most privileges, and that the officials believe that the specified items are legitimate as incentives for inmate growth. The undisputed facts statement added that the Policy encourages progress and discourages backsliding by level 1 inmates. These statements point to evidence that the regulations serve the function identified. The articulated connections between newspapers and magazines, the deprivation of virtually the last privilege left to an inmate, and a significant incentive to improve behavior, are logical ones. Thus, this factor supports the Policy's "reasonableness." The second, third, and fourth *Turner* factors—whether there are "alternative means of exercising the right that remain open to prison inmates," *id.*, at 90; the "impact" that accommodating "the asserted constitutional right [will] have on guards and other inmates, and on the allocation of prison resources," *ibid.*; and whether there are "ready alternatives" for furthering the governmental interest, *ibid.*—add little to the first factor's logical rationale here. That two of these three factors seem to favor the Policy therefore does not help the Secretary. The real task in this case is not balancing the *Turner* factors but determining whether the Secretary's summary judgment material shows not just a logical relation but a *reasonable* relation. Given the deference courts must show to prison officials' professional judgment, the material presented here is sufficient. *Overton* provides significant support for this conclusion. In both cases, the deprivations (family visits in *Overton* and access to newspapers, magazines, and photographs here) have an important constitutional dimension; prison officials have imposed the deprivation only upon those with serious prison-behavior problems; and those officials, relying on their professional judgment, reached an experience-based conclusion that the policies help to further legitimate prison objectives. Unless there is more, the Secretary's supporting material brings the Policy within *Turner*'s scope.

(c)   Although summary judgment rules gave Banks an opportunity to respond to these materials, he did not do so in the manner the rules provide. Instead, he filed a cross-motion for summary judgment, arguing that the Policy fell of its own weight. Neither the cases he cites nor the statistics he notes support his argument. In reaching a contrary conclusion, the Third Circuit placed too high an evidentiary burden on the Secretary and offered too little deference to the prison officials' judgment. Such deference does not make it impossible for those attacking prison policies to succeed. A prisoner may be able to marshal substantial evidence, for example through depositions, that a policy is not reasonable or that there is a genuine issue of material fact for trial. And, as *Overton* noted, if faced with a *de facto* permanent ban involving a severe restric-

tion, this Court might reach a different conclusion.

JUSTICE THOMAS, joined by JUSTICE SCALIA, concluded that, using the framework set forth in Justice Thomas' concurrence in *Overton* v. *Bazzetta,* 539 U. S. 126, 138, Pennsylvania's prison regulations are permissible. That framework provides the least perilous approach for resolving challenges to prison regulations and is the approach most faithful to the Constitution. "Sentencing a criminal to a term of imprisonment may . . . carry with it the implied delegation to prison officials to discipline and otherwise supervise the criminal while he is incarcerated." *Id.,* at 140, n. A term of imprisonment in Pennsylvania includes such an implied delegation. Inmates are subject to Department of Corrections rules and disciplinary rulings, and the challenged regulations fall with the Department's discretion. This conclusion is supported by the plurality's *Turner* v. *Safley,* 482 U. S. 78, analysis. The "history of incarceration as punishment [also] supports the view that the sentenc[e] . . . terminated" respondent's unfettered right to magazines, newspapers, and photographs. *Overton,* 539 U. S., at 142. While Pennsylvania "is free to alter its definition of incarceration to include the retention" of unfettered access to such materials, it appears that the Commonwealth instead sentenced respondent against the backdrop of its traditional conception of imprisonment, which affords no such privileges. *Id.,* at 144–145.

BREYER, J., announced the judgment of the Court and delivered an opinion, in which ROBERTS, C. J., and KENNEDY and SOUTER, JJ., joined. THOMAS, J., filed an opinion concurring in the judgment, in which SCALIA, J., joined. STEVENS, J., filed a dissenting opinion, in which GINSBURG, J., joined. GINSBURG, J., filed a dissenting opinion. ALITO, J., took no part in the consideration or decision of the case.

Cases Relating to Chapter 6

Rights to Rehabilitation Programs and Medical Care

MILLS
V.
ROGERS

457 U.S. 291; 102 S. CT. 2442; 73 L. ED. 2D 16 (1982)

CERTIORARI TO THE UNITED STATES COURT OF APPEALS FOR THE FIRST CIRCUIT

No. 80–1417   Argued January 13, 1982— Decided June 18, 1982

Respondents, present or former mental patients at a Massachusetts state hospital, instituted a class action against petitioner officials and staff of the hospital in Federal District Court, alleging that forcible administration of antipsychotic drugs to patients violated rights protected by the Federal Constitution. The court held that mental patients enjoy constitutionally protected liberty and privacy interests in deciding for themselves whether to submit to drug therapy; that, under state law, an involuntary commitment provides no basis for an inference of legal "incompetency" to make such decision; and that, without consent either by the patient or the guardian of a patient who has been adjudicated incompetent, the patient's liberty interests may be overridden only in an emergency. The Court of Appeals affirmed in part and reversed in part. It agreed with the District Court's first two holdings above, but reached different conclusions as to the circumstances under which state interests might override the patient's liberty interests. The Court

of Appeals reserved to the District Court, on remand, the task of developing mechanisms to ensure adequate procedural protection of the patient's interests. This Court granted certiorari to determine whether an involuntarily committed mental patient has a constitutional right to refuse treatment with antipsychotic drugs. Shortly thereafter, the Massachusetts Supreme Judicial Court ruled on the rights— under both Massachusetts common law and the Federal Constitution—of a nonintitutionalized incompetent mental patient as to involuntary treatment with antipsychotic drugs.

Held: The Court of Appeals' judgment is vacated, and the case is remanded for that court's consideration, in the first instance, of whether the correct disposition of this case is affected by the Massachusetts Supreme Judicial Court's intervening decision.

(a) Assuming (as the parties agree) that the Constitution recognizes a liberty interest in avoiding the unwanted administration of antipsychotic drugs, a substantive issue remains as to the definition of that protected constitutional interest, as well as identification of the conditions under which competing state interests might outweigh it. There is also a procedural issue concerning the minimum procedures required by the Constitution for determining that an individual's liberty interest actually is outweighed in a particular instance. As a practical matter, both issues are intertwined with questions of state law, which may create liberty interests and procedural protections broader than those protected by the Federal Constitution. If so, the minimal requirements of the Federal Constitution would not be controlling, and would not need to be identified in order to determine the legal rights and duties of persons within the State.

(b) While the record is unclear as to respondents' position in the District Court concerning the effect of state law on their asserted federal rights, in their brief in this Court, they clearly assert state law arguments as alternative grounds for affirming both the "substantive" and "procedural" decisions of the Court of Appeals. In applying the policy of avoiding unnecessary decisions of constitutional issues, it is not clear which, if any, constitutional issues now must be decided to resolve the controversy between the parties. Because of its greater familiarity both with the record and with Massachusetts law, the Court of Appeals is better situated than this Court to determine how the intervening state court decision may have changed the law of Massachusetts and how any changes may affect this case.

634 F.2d 650, vacated and remanded.

POWELL, J., delivered the opinion for a unanimous Court.

YOUNGBERG
V.
ROMEO

457 U.S. 307; 102 S. CT. 2452; 73 L. ED. 2D 28 (1982)

CERTIORARI TO THE UNITED STATES COURT OF APPEALS FOR THE THIRD CIRCUIT

No. 80–1429   Argued January 11, 1982— Decided June 18, 1982

Respondent, who is mentally retarded, was involuntarily committed to a Pennsylvania state institution. Subsequently, after becoming concerned about injuries which respondent had suffered at the institution, his mother filed an action as his next friend in Federal District Court for damages under 42 U.S.C. § 1983 against peti-

tioner institution officials. She claimed that respondent had constitutional rights to safe conditions of confinement, freedom from bodily restraint, and training or "habilitation" and that petitioners knew, or should have known, about his injuries, but failed to take appropriate preventive procedures, thus violating his rights under the Eighth and Fourteenth Amendments. In the ensuing jury trial, the District Court instructed the jury on the assumption that the Eighth Amendment was the proper standard of liability, and a verdict was returned for petitioners, on which judgment was entered. The Court of Appeals reversed and remanded for a new trial, holding that the Fourteenth, rather than the Eighth, Amendment provided the proper constitutional basis for the asserted rights.

Held: Respondent has constitutionally protected liberty interests under the Due Process Clause of the Fourteenth Amendment to reasonably safe conditions of confinement, freedom from unreasonable bodily restraints, and such minimally adequate training as reasonably may be required by these interests. Whether respondent's constitutional rights have been violated must be determined by balancing these liberty interests against the relevant state interests. The proper standard for determining whether the State has adequately protected such rights is whether professional judgment, in fact, was exercised. And in determining what is "reasonable," courts must show deference to the judgment exercised by a qualified professional, whose decision is presumptively valid.

644 F.2d 147, vacated and remanded.

POWELL, J., delivered the opinion of the Court, in which BRENNAN, WHITE, MARSHALL, BLACKMUN, REHNQUIST, STEVENS, and O'CONNOR, JJ., joined. BLACKMUN, J., filed a concurring opinion, in which BRENNAN and O'CONNOR, JJ., joined. BURGER, C.J., filed an opinion concurring in the judgment.

TURNER
V.
SAFLEY

482 U.S. 78; 107 S. CT. 2254; 96 L. ED. 2D 64 (1987)

CERTIORARI TO THE UNITED STATES
COURT OF APPEALS FOR THE EIGHTH
CIRCUIT

No. 85–1384   Argued January 13, 1987—
Decided June 1, 1987

Respondent inmates brought a class action
challenging two regulations promulgated by
the Missouri Division of Corrections. The first
permits correspondence between immediate
family members who are inmates at different
institutions within the Division's jurisdiction,
and between inmates "concerning legal matters," but allows other inmate correspondence
only if each inmate's classification/treatment
team deems it in the best interests of the parties. The second regulation permits an inmate
to marry only with the prison superintendent's
permission, which can be given only when
there are "compelling reasons" to do so. Testimony indicated that generally only a pregnancy
or the birth of an illegitimate child would be
considered "compelling." The Federal District
Court found both regulations unconstitutional,
and the Court of Appeals affirmed.

Held:

1. The lower courts erred in ruling that *Pro-
    cunier v. Martinez*, 416 U. S. 396, and its
    progeny require the application of a strict
    scrutiny standard of review for resolving
    respondents' constitutional complaints.
    Rather, those cases indicate that a lesser
    standard is appropriate whereby inquiry
    is made into whether a prison regulation
    that impinges on inmates' constitutional
    rights is "reasonably related" to legiti-
    mate penological interests. In determining
    reasonableness, relevant factors include
    (a) whether there is a "valid, rational
    connection" between the regulation and
    a legitimate and neutral governmental
    interest put forward to justify it, which
    connection cannot be so remote as to ren-
    der the regulation arbitrary or irrational;
    (b) whether there are alternative means
    of exercising the asserted constitutional
    right that remain open to inmates, which
    alternatives, if they exist, will require a
    measure of judicial deference to the cor-
    rections officials' expertise; (c) whether

and the extent to which accommodation
of the asserted right will have an impact
on prison staff, on inmates' liberty, and on
the allocation of limited prison resources,
which impact, if substantial, will require
particular deference to corrections officials; and (d) whether the regulation
represents an "exaggerated response" to
prison concerns, the existence of a ready
alternative that fully accommodates the
prisoner's rights at *de minimis* costs to
valid penological interests being evidence
of unreasonableness.

2. The Missouri inmate correspondence
    regulation is, on the record here, reason-
    able and facially valid. The regulation is
    logically related to the legitimate secu-
    rity concerns of prison officials, who
    testified that mail between prisons can
    be used to communicate escape plans, to
    arrange violent acts, and to foster prison
    gang activity. Moreover, the regulation
    does not deprive prisoners of all means of
    expression, but simply bars communica-
    tion with a limited class of people—other
    inmates—with whom authorities have
    particular cause to be concerned. The
    regulation is entitled to deference on the
    basis of the significant impact of prison
    correspondence on the liberty and safety
    of other prisoners and prison personnel, in
    light of officials' testimony that such cor-
    respondence facilitates the development
    of informal organizations that threaten
    safety and security at penal institutions.
    Nor is there an obvious, easy alternative
    to the regulation, since monitoring inmate
    correspondence clearly would impose
    more than a *de minimis* cost in terms of
    the burden on staff resources required
    to conduct item-by-item censorship,
    and would create an appreciable risk of
    missing dangerous communications. The
    regulation is content-neutral, and does
    not unconstitutionally abridge the First
    Amendment rights of prison inmates.

3. The constitutional right of prisoners to
    marry is impermissibly burdened by the
    Missouri marriage regulation.

    (a) Prisoners have a constitutionally
        protected right to marry under
        Zablocki v. Redhail, 434 U. S. 374.
        Although such a marriage is subject

to substantial restrictions as a result of incarceration, sufficient important attributes of marriage remain to form a constitutionally protected relationship. *Butler v. Wilson*, 415 U.S. 953, distinguished.

(b) The regulation is facially invalid under the reasonable relationship test. Although prison officials may regulate the time and circumstances under which a marriage takes place, and may require prior approval by the warden, the almost complete ban on marriages here is not, on the record, reasonably related to legitimate penological objectives. The contention that the regulation serves security concerns by preventing "love triangles" that may lead to violent inmate confrontations is without merit, since inmate rivalries are likely to develop with or without a formal marriage ceremony. Moreover, the regulation's broad prohibition is not justified by the security of fellow inmates and prison staff, who are not affected where the inmate makes the private decision to marry a civilian. Rather, the regulation represents an exaggerated response to the claimed security objectives, since allowing marriages unless the warden finds a threat to security, order, or the public safety represents an obvious, easy alternative that would accommodate the right to marry while imposing a *de minimis* burden. Nor is the regulation reasonably related to the articulated rehabilitation goal of fostering self-reliance by female prisoners. In requiring refusal of permission to marry to all inmates absent a compelling reason, the regulation sweeps much more broadly than is necessary, in light of officials' testimony that male inmates' marriages had generally caused them no problems, and that they had no objections to prisoners marrying civilians.

777 F.2d 1307, affirmed in part, reversed in part, and remanded.

O'CONNOR, J., delivered the opinion of the Court, in which REHNQUIST, C.J., and WHITE, POWELL, and SCALIA, JJ., joined, and in Part III-B of which BRENNAN, MARSHALL, BLACK-MUN, and STEVENS, JJ., joined. STEVENS, J., filed an opinion concurring in part and dissenting in part, in which BRENNAN, MARSHALL, and BLACKMUN, JJ., joined.

ESTELLE
V.
GAMBLE

429 U.S. 97; 97 S. CT. 285; 50 L. ED. 2D 251 (1976)

CERTIORARI TO THE UNITED STATES COURT OF APPEALS FOR THE FIFTH CIRCUIT

No. 75–929   Argued October 5, 1976—Decided November 30, 1976

Respondent state inmate brought this civil rights action under 42 U.S.C. § 1983 against petitioners, the state corrections department medical director (Gray) and two correctional officials, claiming that he was subjected to cruel and unusual punishment in violation of the Eighth Amendment for inadequate treatment of a back injury assertedly sustained while he was engaged in prison work. The District Court dismissed the complaint for failure to state a claim upon which relief could be granted. The Court of Appeals held that the alleged insufficiency of the medical treatment required reinstatement of the complaint.

Held: Deliberate indifference by prison personnel to a prisoner's serious illness or injury constitutes cruel and unusual punishment contravening the Eighth Amendment. Here, however, respondent's claims against Gray do not suggest such indifference, the allegations revealing that Gray and other medical personnel saw respondent on 17 occasions during a 3-month span and treated his injury and other problems. The failure to perform an X-ray or to use additional diagnostic techniques does not constitute cruel and unusual punishment, but is, at most, medical malpractice cognizable in the state courts. The question whether respondent has stated a constitutional claim against the other petitioners, the Director of the Department of Corrections and the warden of the prison, was not separately evaluated by the Court of Appeals, and should be considered on remand.

516 F.2d 937, reversed and remanded.
MARSHALL, J., delivered the opinion of the Court, in which BURGER, C.J., and BRENNAN, STEWART, WHITE, POWELL, and REHNQUIST, JJ., joined. BLACKMUN, J., concurred in the judgment. STEVENS, J., filed a dissenting opinion.

HELLING
V.
MCKINNEY

509 U.S. 25; 113 S. CT. 2475; 125 L. ED. 2D 22 (1993)

CERTIORARI TO THE UNITED STATES COURT OF APPEALS FOR THE NINTH CIRCUIT

No. 91–1958   Argued January 13, 1993— Decided June 18, 1993

Respondent McKinney, a Nevada state prisoner, filed suit against petitioner prison officials, claiming that his involuntary exposure to environmental tobacco smoke (ETS) from his cellmate's and other inmates' cigarettes posed an unreasonable risk to his health, thus subjecting him to cruel and unusual punishment in violation of the Eighth Amendment. A federal magistrate granted petitioners' motion for a directed verdict, but the Court of Appeals reversed in part, holding that McKinney should have been permitted to prove that his ETS exposure was sufficient to constitute an unreasonable danger to his future health. It reaffirmed its decision after this Court remanded for further consideration in light of *Wilson* v. *Seiter,* 501 U.S. 294, in which the Court held that Eighth Amendment claims arising from confinement conditions not formally imposed as a sentence for a crime require proof of a

subjective component, and that where the claim alleges inhumane confinement conditions or failure to attend to a prisoner's medical needs, the standard for that state of mind is the "deliberate indifference" standard of *Estelle* v. *Gamble,* 429 U.S. 97. The Court of Appeals held that *Seiter*'s subjective component did not vitiate that court's determination that it would be cruel and unusual punishment to house a prisoner in an environment exposing him to ETS levels that pose an unreasonable risk of harming his health-the objective component of McKinney's claim.

Held:

1. It was not improper for the Court of Appeals to decide the question whether McKinney's claim could be based on possible future effects of ETS. From its examination of the record, the court was apparently of the view that the claimed entitlement to a smoke-free environment subsumed the claim that ETS exposure could endanger one's future, not just current, health.

2. By alleging that petitioners have, with deliberate indifference, exposed him to ETS levels that pose an unreasonable risk to his future health, McKinney has stated an Eighth Amendment claim on which relief could be granted. An injunction cannot be denied to inmates who plainly prove an unsafe, life-threatening condition on the ground that nothing yet has happened to them. See *Hutto* v. *Finney,* 437 U.S. 678, 682. Thus, petitioners' central thesis that only deliberate indifference to inmates' current serious health problems is actionable is rejected. Since the Court cannot at this juncture rule that McKinney cannot possibly prove an Eighth Amendment violation based on ETS exposure, it also would be premature to base a reversal on the Federal Government's argument that the harm from ETS exposure is speculative, with no risk sufficiently grave to implicate a serious medical need, and that the exposure is not contrary to current standards of decency. On remand, the District Court must give McKinney the opportunity to prove his allegations, which will require that he

establish both the subjective and objective elements necessary to prove an Eighth Amendment violation. With respect to the objective factor, he may have difficulty showing that he is being exposed to unreasonably high ETS levels, since he has been moved to a new prison and no longer has a cellmate who smokes, and since a new state prison policy restricts smoking to certain areas and makes reasonable efforts to respect nonsmokers' wishes with regard to double bunking. He must also show that the risk of which he complains is not one that today's society chooses to tolerate. The subjective factor, deliberate indifference, should be deter-

mined in light of the prison authorities' current attitudes and conduct, which, as evidenced by the new smoking policy, may have changed considerably since the Court of Appeals' judgment. The inquiry into this factor also would be an appropriate vehicle to consider arguments regarding the realities of prison administration.

959 F.2d 853, affirmed and remanded.
WHITE, J., delivered the opinion of the Court, in which REHNQUIST, C. J., and BLACKMUN, STEVENS, O'CONNOR, KENNEDY, and SOUTER, JJ., joined. THOMAS, J., filed a dissenting opinion, in which SCALIA, J.

Cases Relating to Chapter 7

Prisoner Legal Services

JOHNSON
V.
AVERY

393 U.S. 483; 89 S. CT. 747; 21 L. ED. 2D 718 (1969)

CERTIORARI TO THE UNITED STATES COURT OF APPEALS FOR THE SIXTH CIRCUIT

No. 40   Argued November 14, 1968— Decided February 24, 1969

Petitioner, a Tennessee prisoner, was disciplined for violating a prison regulation which prohibited inmates from assisting other prisoners in preparing writs. The District Court held the regulation void because it had the effect of barring illiterate prisoners from access to federal habeas corpus and conflicted with 28 U.S.C. § 2242. The Court of Appeals reversed, finding that the State's interest in preserving prison discipline and limiting the practice of law to attorneys justified any burden the regulation might place on access to federal habeas corpus.

Held: In the absence of some provision by the State of Tennessee for a reasonable alternative to assist illiterate or poorly educated inmates in preparing petitions for post-conviction relief, the State may not validly enforce a regulation which absolutely bars inmates from furnishing such assistance to other prisoners.

382 F.2d 353, reversed and remanded.

MR. JUSTICE FORTAS delivered the opinion of the Court.

BOUNDS
V.
SMITH

430 U.S. 817; 97 S. CT. 1491; 52 L. ED. 2D 72 (1977)

CERTIORARI TO THE UNITED STATES COURT OF APPEALS FOR THE FOURTH CIRCUIT

No. 75–915   Argued November 1, 1976— Decided April 27, 1977

The fundamental constitutional right of access to the courts held to require prison authorities to assist inmates in the preparation and filing of meaningful legal papers by providing prisoners with adequate law libraries or adequate assistance from persons trained in the law. *Younger v. Gilmore*, 404 U. S. 15.

538 F.2d 541, affirmed.

MARSHALL, J., delivered the opinion of the Court, in which BRENNAN, WHITE, BLACKMUN, POWELL, and STEVENS, JJ., joined. POWELL, J., filed a concurring opinion. BURGER, C.J., filed a dissenting opinion. STEWART, J., and REHNQUIST, J., filed dissenting opinions, in which BURGER, C.J., joined.

MURRAY
V.
GIARRATANO

492 U.S. 1; 109 S. CT. 2765; 106 L. ED. 2D 1 (1989)

CERTIORARI TO THE UNITED STATES COURT OF APPEALS FOR THE FOURTH CIRCUIT

No. 88–411   Argued March 22, 1989—Decided June 23, 1989

Respondents, a class of indigent Virginia death row inmates who do not have counsel to pursue postconviction proceedings, brought a suit under 42 U.S.C. § 1983 in the District Court against various state officials, alleging that the Constitution required that they be provided with counsel at the State's expense for the purpose of pursuing collateral proceedings related to their convictions and sentences. The District Court concluded that respondents should receive greater assistance than that outlined in *Bounds v. Smith*, 430 U. S. 817—which held that a prisoner's "right of access" to the courts required a State to furnish access to adequate law libraries or other legal aid so the prisoners might' prepare petitions for judicial relief—since death row inmates have a limited amount of time to prepare petitions, since their cases are unusually complex, and since the shadow of impending execution interferes with their ability to do legal work. It found that Virginia's efforts—access to a law library or lawbooks, the availability of "unit attorneys," and appointment of counsel after a petition is filed—did not afford prisoners meaningful access to the courts because they did not guarantee the prisoners continuous assistance of counsel. Thus, it ordered Virginia to develop a program for the appointment of counsel, upon request, to indigent death row inmates wishing to pursue habeas corpus in state court, but, in light of *Ross v. Moffitt*, 417 U. S. 600, not in federal court. The Court of Appeals affirmed. It viewed the lower court's special "considerations" relating to death row inmates as findings of fact which were not clearly erroneous. It reasoned that the case was not controlled by *Pennsylvania v. Fin-*

ley, 481 U. S. 551—which held that neither the Due Process Clause of the Fourteenth Amendment nor the equal protection guarantee of "meaningful access" required the State to appoint counsel for indigent prisoners seeking postconviction relief—since *Finley* was not a "meaningful access" case, since it did not address the rule enunciated in *Bounds*, and since it did not involve the death penalty.

Held: The judgment is reversed, and the case is remanded.

847 F.2d 1118, reversed and remanded.

THE CHIEF JUSTICE, joined by JUSTICE WHITE, JUSTICE O'CONNOR, and JUSTICE SCALIA, concluded that neither the Eighth Amendment nor the Due Process Clause requires States to appoint counsel for indigent death row inmates seeking state postconviction relief.

(a) This Court's decisions require the conclusion that the rule of *Pennsylvania v. Finley* should apply no differently in capital cases than in noncapital cases. *See, e.g., Smith v. Murray*, 477 U. S. 527. State collateral proceedings are not constitutionally required as an adjunct to the state criminal proceeding, and serve a different and more limited purpose than either the trial or appeal. Eighth Amendment safeguards imposed at the trial stage—where the court and jury hear testimony, receive evidence, and decide the question of guilt and punishment—are sufficient to assure the reliability of the process by which the death penalty is imposed.

(b) There is no inconsistency whatever between the holdings in *Bounds* and *Finley*. The right of access at issue in *Bounds* rests on a constitutional theory considered in *Finley*. Extending *Bounds* would partially overrule the subsequently decided *Finley* and would' reject a categorical rule—the usual tack taken in right to counsel cases—for the adoption of a case-by-case determination based on "factual" findings, which, under a "clearly erroneous" standard, could result in different constitutional rules being applied in different States.

JUSTICE KENNEDY, joined by JUS-TICE O'CONNOR, concluded that Virginia's scheme for securing representation for indigent death row inmates does not violate the Constitution. Although Virginia's procedures are not as far-reaching and effective as those available in other States, no Virginia death row inmates have been unable to obtain counsel to represent them in postconviction proceedings, and Virginia's prison system is staffed by institutional lawyers to assist inmates in such matters. *Bounds'* meaningful access requirement can be satisfied in various ways, and state legislatures and prison administrators must be given "wide discretion" to select appropriate solutions from a range of complex options.

REHNQUIST, C.J., announced the judgment of the Court and delivered an opinion, in which WHITE, O'CONNOR, and SCA-LIA, JJ., joined. O'CONNOR, J., filed a concurring opinion. KENNEDY, J., filed an opinion concurring in the judgment, in which O'CONNOR, J., joined. STEVENS, J., filed a dissenting opinion, in which BRENNAN, MARSHALL, and BLACKMUN, JJ., joined.

LEWIS, DIRECTOR, ARIZONA DEPARTMENT OF CORRECTIONS, ET AL. V. CASEY ET AL.

518 U.S. 343; 116 S. CT. 2174; 135 L. ED. 2D 606 (1996)

CERTIORARI TO THE UNITED STATES COURT OF APPEALS FOR THE NINTH CIRCUIT

No. 94–1511   Argued November 29, 1995—Decided June 24, 1996

Respondents, who are inmates of various prisons operated by the Arizona Department of Corrections (ADOC), brought a class action against petitioners, ADOC officials, alleging that petitioners were furnishing them with inadequate legal research facilities and thereby depriving them of their right of access to the courts, in violation of *Bounds* v. *Smith, 430* U. S. 817. The District Court found petitioners to be in violation of *Bounds* and issued an injunction mandating detailed, systemwide changes in ADOC's prison law libraries and in its legal assistance programs. The Ninth Circuit affirmed both the finding of a *Bounds* violation and the injunction's major terms.

Held: The success of respondents' systemic challenge was dependent on their ability to show widespread actual injury, and the District Court's failure to identify anything more than isolated instances of actual injury renders its finding of a systemic *Bounds* violation invalid.

(a) *Bounds* did not create an abstract, free-standing right to a law library or legal assistance; rather, the right that *Bounds* acknowledged was the right of *access to the courts. E. g.,* 430 U. S., at 817, 821, 828. Thus, to establish a *Bounds* violation, the "actual injury" that an inmate must demonstrate is that the alleged shortcomings in the prison library or legal assistance program have hindered, or are presently hindering, his efforts to pursue a nonfrivolous legal claim. This requirement derives ultimately from the doctrine of standing. Although *Bounds* made no mention of an actual injury requirement, it can hardly be thought to have eliminated that constitutional prerequisite.

(b) Statements in *Bounds* suggesting that prison authorities must also enable the prisoner to *discover* grievances, and to *litigate effectively* once in court, have no antecedent in this Court's *pre-Bounds* cases, and are now disclaimed. Moreover, *Bounds* does not guarantee inmates the wherewithal to file any and every type of legal claim, but requires only that they be provided with the tools to attack their sentences, directly or collaterally, and to challenge the conditions of their confinement.

(c) The District Court identified only two instances of actual injury:

It found that ADOC's failures with respect to illiterate prisoners had resulted in the dismissal with prejudice of inmate Bartholic's lawsuit and the inability of inmate Harris to file a legal action.

(d) These findings as to injury do not support the systemwide injunction ordered by the District Court. The remedy must be limited to the inadequacy that produced the injury in fact that the plaintiff has established; that this is a class action changes nothing, for even named plaintiffs in a class action must show that they personally have been injured, see, *e. g., Simon* v. *Eastern Ky. Welfare Rights Organization,* 426 U. S. 26, 40. Only one named plaintiff, Bartholic, was found to have suffered actual injury-as a result of ADOC's failure to provide the special services he would have needed, in light of his particular disability (illiteracy), to avoid dismissal of his case. Eliminated from the proper scope of the injunction, therefore, are provisions directed at special services or facilities required by non-English speakers, by prisoners in lockdown, and by the inmate population at large. Furthermore, the inadequacy that caused actual injury to illiterate inmates Bartholic and Harris was not sufficiently widespread to justify systemwide relief. There is no finding, and no evidence discernible from the record, that in ADOC prisons other than those occupied by Bartholic and Harris illiterate inmates cannot obtain the minimal help necessary to file legal claims.

(e) There are further reasons why the order here cannot stand. In concluding that ADOC's restrictions on lockdown inmates were unjustified, the District Court failed to accord the judgment of prison authorities the substantial deference required by cases such as *Turner* v. *Safley,* 482 U. S. 78, 89. The court also failed to leave with prison officials the primary responsibility for devising a remedy. Compare *Preiser* v. *Rodriguez,* 411 U. S. 475, 492. The result of this improper procedure was an inordinately intrusive order.

43 F.3d 1261, reversed and remanded.

SCALIA, J., delivered the opinion of the Court, in which REHNQUIST, C. J., and O'CONNOR, KENNEDY, and THOMAS, JJ., joined, and in Parts I and III of which SOUTER, GINS-BURG, and BREYER, JJ., joined. THOMAS, J., filed a concurring opinion. SOUTER, J., filed an opinion concurring in part, dissenting in part, and concurring in the judgment, in which GINSBURG and BREYER, JJ., joined. STEVENS, J., filed a dissenting opinion.

SHAW
V.
MURPHY

532 U.S. 223; 121 S. CT. 1475; 149 L. ED. 2D 420 (2001)

CERTIORARI TO THE UNITED STATES COURT OF APPEALS FOR THE NINTH CIRCUIT

No. 99–1613   Argued January 16, 2001—Decided April 18, 2001

While respondent Murphy was incarcerated in state prison, he learned that a fellow inmate had been charged with assaulting a correctional officer. Murphy decided to assist the inmate with his defense and sent him a letter, which was intercepted in accordance with prison policy. Based on the letter's content, the prison sanctioned Murphy for violating prison rules prohibiting insolence and interfering with due process hearings. Murphy then sought declaratory and injunctive relief under 42 U. S. C. § 1983, alleging that the disciplinary action violated, *inter alia,* his First Amendment rights, including the right to provide legal assistance to other inmates. In granting petitioners summary judgment, the District Court applied the decision in *Turner* v. *Safley, 482* U. S. 78, 89-that a prison regulation impinging on inmates' constitutional rights is valid if it is reasonably related to legitimate penological interests-and found a valid, rational connection between the inmate correspondence policy and the objectives of prison order, security, and inmate rehabilitation. The Ninth Circuit reversed, finding that inmates have a First Amendment right to give legal assistance to other inmates and that this right affected the *Turner* analysis.

Held:

1. Inmates do not possess a special First Amendment right to provide legal assistance to fellow inmates that enhances the protections otherwise available under *Turner.* Prisoners' constitutional rights are more limited in scope than the constitutional rights held by individuals in society at large. For instance, some First Amendment rights are simply inconsistent with the corrections system's "legitimate penological objectives," *Pell v. Procunier*, 417 U. S. 817,822, and thus this Court has sustained restrictions on, *e. g.*, inmate-to-inmate written correspondence, *Turner, supra,* at 93. Moreover, because courts are ill equipped to deal with the complex and intractable problems of prisons, *Procunier v. Martinez*, 416 U. S. 396, 404–405, this Court has generally deferred to prison officials' judgment in upholding such regulations against constitutional challenge. *Turner* reflects this understanding, setting a unitary, deferential standard for reviewing prisoners' claims that does not permit an increase in the constitutional protection whenever a prisoner's communication includes legal advice. To increase the constitutional protection based upon a communication's content first requires an assessment of that content's value. But the *Turner* test simply does not accommodate valuations of content. On the contrary, it concerns only the relationship between the asserted penological interests and the prison regulation. Moreover, prison officials are to remain the primary arbiters of the problems that arise in prison management. 482 U. S., at 89. Seeking to avoid unnecessarily perpetuating federal courts' involvement in prison administration affairs, the Court rejects an alteration of the *Turner* analysis that would entail additional federal-court oversight. Even if this Court were to consider giving special protection to particular kinds of speech based on content, it would not do so for speech that includes legal advice. Augmenting First Amendment protection for such advice would undermine prison officials' ability to address the complex and intractable problems of prison administration. *Id.,* at 84. The legal text could be an excuse for making clearly inappropriate comments, which may circulate among prisoners despite prison measures to screen individual inmates or officers from the remarks.

2. To prevail on remand on the question whether the prison regulations, as applied to Murphy, are reasonably related to legitimate penological interests, he must overcome the presumption that the prison officials acted within their broad discretion.

195 F.3d 1121, reversed and remanded.

THOMAS, J., delivered the opinion for a unanimous Court. GINSBURG, J., filed a concurring opinion.

Cases Relating to Chapter 8

Additional Constitutional Issues

MEACHUM
V.
FANO

427 U.S. 215; 96 S. CT. 2532; 49 L. ED. 2D 451 (1976)

CERTIORARI TO THE UNITED STATES COURT OF APPEALS FOR THE FIRST CIRCUIT

No. 75–252   Argued April 21, 1976— Decided June 25, 1976

The Due Process Clause of the Fourteenth Amendment *held* not to entitle a duly convicted state prisoner to a factfinding hearing when he is transferred to a prison the conditions of which are substantially less favorable to him, absent a state law or practice conditioning such transfers on proof of serious misconduct or the occurrence of other specified events. Such a transfer does not infringe or implicate a "liberty" interest of the prisoner within the meaning of the Due Process Clause.

(a) Given a valid conviction, the criminal defendant has been constitutionally deprived of his liberty to the extent that the State may confine him and subject him to the rules of its prison system so long as the conditions of confinement do not otherwise violate the Constitution.

(b) The Due Process Clause does not, in and of itself, protect a duly convicted prisoner against transfer from one institution to another, and that life in one prison is much more disagreeable than in another does not, in itself, signify that a Fourteenth Amendment liberty interest is implicated when a prisoner is transferred to the institution with the more severe rules.

(c) To hold that any substantial deprivation imposed by prison authorities triggers the procedural protections of the Due Process Clause would subject to judicial review a wide spectrum of discretionary actions that traditionally have been the business of prison administrators, rather than of the federal courts. *Wolff v. McDonnell*, 418 U. S. 539, distinguished.

(d) Whatever expectation the prisoner may have in remaining at a particular prison so long as he behaves himself, it is too ephemeral and insubstantial to trigger procedural due process protections as long as prison officials have discretion to transfer him for any reason whatsoever, or for no reason at all.

520 F.2d 374, reversed.

WHITE, J., delivered the opinion of the Court, in which BURGER, C.J., and STEWART, BLACKMUN, POWELL, and REHNQUIST, JJ., joined. STEVENS, J., filed a dissenting opinion, in which BRENNAN and MARSHALL, JJ., joined.

MONTANYE
V.
HAYMES

427 U.S. 236; 96 S. CT. 2543; 49 L. ED. 2D 466 (1976)

CERTIORARI TO THE UNITED STATES COURT OF APPEALS FOR THE SECOND CIRCUIT

No. 74–520   Argued April 21, 1976— Decided June 25, 1976

The Due Process Clause of the Fourteenth Amendment *held* not to require a hearing in connection with the transfer of a state prisoner to another institution in the State whether or not such transfer resulted from the prisoner's misbehavior or was disciplinary or punitive, where, under state law, the prisoner had no right to remain at any particular prison and no justifiable expectation that he would not be transferred unless found guilty of misconduct, and the transfer of prisoners is not conditional upon or limited to the occurrence of misconduct. *Meachum v. Fano, ante* p. 427 U. S. 215.

505 F.2d 977, reversed and remanded.
   WHITE, J., delivered the opinion of the Court, in which BURGER, C.J., and STEWART, BLACKMUN, POWELL, and REHNQUIST, JJ., joined. STEVENS, J., filed a dissenting opinion in which BRENNAN and MARSHALL, JJ., joined.

VITEK
V.
JONES

445 U.S. 480; 100 S. CT. 1254; 63 L. ED. 2D 552 (1980)

APPEAL FROM THE UNITED STATES DISTRICT COURT FOR THE DISTRICT OF NEBRASKA

No. 78–1155   Argued December 3, 1979— Decided March 25, 1980

Appellee, a convicted felon, was transferred from state prison to a mental hospital pursuant to a Nebraska statute (§ 83–180(1)) which provides that, if a designated physician or psychologist finds that a prisoner "suffers from a mental disease or defect" that "cannot be given proper treatment" in prison, the Director of Correctional Services may transfer the prisoner to a mental hospital. In an action challenging the constitutionality of § 83–180(1) on procedural due process grounds, the District Court declared the statute unconstitutional as applied to appellee, holding that transferring him to the mental hospital without adequate notice and opportunity for a hearing deprived him of liberty without due process of law contrary to the Fourteenth Amendment, and that such transfers must be accompanied by adequate notice, an adversary hearing before an independent decisionmaker, a written statement by the factfinder of the evidence relied on and the reasons for the decision, and the availability of appointed counsel for indigent prisoners. The court permanently enjoined the State from transferring appellee (who meanwhile had been transferred back to prison) to the mental hospital without following the prescribed procedures. Subsequently, appellee was paroled on condition that he accept mental treatment, but he violated that parole and was returned to prison. Relying on appellee's history of mental illness and the State's representation that he was a serious threat to his own and others' safety, the District Court held that the parole and revocation thereof did not render the case moot, because appellee was still subject to being transferred to the mental hospital.
   Held: The judgment is affirmed as modified.

Affirmed as modified.

   MR. JUSTICE WHITE delivered the opinion of the Court with respect to Parts I, II, III, IV-A, and V, concluding that:

1.   The District Court properly found that the case is not moot. The reality of the controversy between appellee and the State has not been lessened by the cancellation of his parole and his return to prison, where he is protected from further transfer by the District Court's judgment and injunc-

tion. Under these circumstances, it is not "absolutely clear," absent the injunction, that the State's alleged wrongful behavior could not reasonably be expected to recur.

2. The involuntary transfer of appellee to a mental hospital implicates a liberty interest that is protected by the Due Process Clause of the Fourteenth Amendment.

    (a) The District Court properly identified a liberty interest rooted in § 83–180(1), under which a prisoner could reasonably expect that he would not be transferred to a mental hospital without a finding that he was suffering from a mental illness for which he could not secure adequate treatment in prison. The State's reliance on the opinion of a designated physician or psychologist for determining whether the conditions warranting transfer exist neither removes the prisoner's interest from due process protection nor answers the question of what process is due under the Constitution.

    (b) The District Court was also correct in holding that, independently of § 83–180(1), the transfer of a prisoner from a prison to a mental hospital must be accompanied by appropriate procedural protections. Involuntary commitment to a mental hospital is not within the range of conditions of confinement to which a prison sentence subjects an individual. While a conviction and sentence extinguish an individual's right to freedom from confinement for the term of his sentence, they do not authorize the State to classify him as mentally ill and to subject him to involuntary psychiatric treatment without affording him additional due process protections. Here, the stigmatizing consequences of a transfer to a mental hospital for involuntary psychiatric treatment, coupled with the subjection of the prisoner to mandatory behavior modification as a treatment for mental illness, constitute the kind of deprivations of liberty that requires procedural protections.

3. The District Court properly identified and weighed the relevant factors in arriving at its judgment.

    (a) Although the State's interest in segregating and treating mentally ill patients is strong, the prisoner's interest in not being arbitrarily classified as mentally ill and subjected to unwelcome treatment is also powerful, and the risk of error in making the determinations required by § 83–180(1) is substantial enough to warrant appropriate procedural safeguards against error.

    (b) The medical nature of the inquiry as to whether or not to transfer a prisoner to a mental hospital does not justify dispensing with due process requirements.

    (c) Because prisoners facing involuntary transfer to a mental hospital are threatened with immediate deprivation of liberty interests, and because of the risk of mistaken transfer, the District Court properly determined that certain procedural protections, including notice and an adversary hearing, were appropriate in the circumstances present in this case.

MR. JUSTICE WHITE, joined by MR. JUSTICE BRENNAN, MR. JUSTICE MARSHALL, and MR. JUSTICE STEVENS, concluded in Part IV-B that it is appropriate that counsel be provided to indigent prisoners whom the State seeks to treat as mentally ill. Such a prisoner has an even greater need for legal assistance than does a prisoner who is illiterate and uneducated, because he is more likely to be unable to understand or exercise his rights.

MR. JUSTICE POWELL concluded that, although the State is free to appoint a licensed attorney to represent a prisoner who is threatened with involuntary transfer to a mental hospital, it is not constitutionally required to do so, and that due process will be satisfied so long as such a prisoner is provided qualified and independent assistance.

WHITE, J., announced the Court's judgment and delivered the opinion of the Court with respect to Parts I, II, III, IV-A, and V, in which BRENNAN, MARSHALL, POWELL, and STEVENS, JJ., joined, and an opinion with respect to Part IV-B, in which BRENNAN, MARSHALL, and STEVENS, JJ., joined. POWELL, J., filed an opinion concurring in part. STEWART, J., filed a dissenting opinion, in which BURGER, C.J., and REHNQUIST, J., joined. BLACKMUN, J., filed a dissenting opinion.

CUYLER
V.
ADAMS

449 U.S. 433; 101 S. CT. 703; 66 L. ED. 2D 641 (1981)

CERTIORARI TO THE UNITED STATES COURT OF APPEALS FOR THE THIRD CIRCUIT

No. 78–1841   Argued October 7, 1980—Decided January 21, 2981

While respondent was serving a sentence in a Pennsylvania correctional institution, the Camden County, N.J., prosecutor's office lodged a detainer against him and sought custody pursuant to Art. IV of the Interstate Agreement on Detainers (Detainer Agreement) in order to try him in New Jersey on criminal charges. Article IV, which provides the procedure whereby the receiving State may initiate the prisoner's transfer, states in paragraph (d) that nothing in the Article shall be construed to deprive the prisoner "of any right which he may have to contest the legality of his delivery as provided in paragraph (a) hereof," but that such delivery may not be opposed on the ground that the sending State's executive authority has not affirmatively consented to or ordered the delivery. Respondent filed an action in the Federal District Court for the Eastern District of Pennsylvania under 42 U.S.C. §§ 1981 and 1983, alleging that petitioners had violated the Due Process and Equal Protection Clauses by failing to grant him the pretransfer hearing that would have been available had his transfer been sought under the Uniform Criminal Extradition Act (Extradition Act), and that petitioners had violated the Due Process Clause by failing to inform him of his right under Art. IV (a) of the Detainer Agreement to petition Pennsylvania's Governor to disapprove New Jersey's request for custody. The District Court dismissed respondent's complaint. The Court of Appeals vacated the District Court judgment and remanded the case, finding it unnecessary to reach respondent's constitutional claims and holding as a matter of statutory construction under federal law that respondent had a right under Art. IV (d) of the Detainer Agreement to the procedural safeguards, including a pretransfer hearing, prescribed by the Extradition Act.

Held:

1. The Detainer Agreement is a congressionally sanctioned interstate compact the interpretation of which presents a question of federal law. An interstate agreement does not fall within the scope of the Federal Constitution's Compact Clause, and will not be invalidated for lack of congressional consent, where the agreement is not "directed to the formation of any combination tending to the increase of political power in the States, which may encroach upon or interfere with the just supremacy of the United States." But where Congress has authorized the States to enter into a cooperative agreement and the subject matter of that agreement is an appropriate subject for congressional legislation, Congress' consent transforms the States' agreement into federal law under the Compact Clause, and construction of that agreement presents a federal question. Here, Congress gave its consent to the Detainer Agreement in advance by enacting the Crime Control Consent Act of 1934. That Act was intended to be a grant of consent under the Compact Clause, and the subject matter of the Act is an appropriate subject for congressional legislation.

2. As a matter of statutory construction, a prisoner incarcerated in a jurisdiction that has adopted the Extradition Act is entitled to the procedural protections of that Act, including the right to a pretransfer hearing, before being transferred to another jurisdiction pursuant to Art. IV of the

Detainer Agreement. Both the language and legislative history of the Detainer Agreement support the interpretation that, whereas a prisoner initiating the transfer procedure under Art. III waives rights which the sending State affords persons being extradited, including rights provided under the Extradition Act, a prisoner's extradition rights are preserved when the receiving State seeks the prisoner's involuntary transfer under Art. IV of the Detainer Agreement. The phrase "as provided in paragraph (a) hereof," contained in Art. IV (d), modifies "delivery," not "right," and thus Art. IV (d) preserves all the prisoner's extradition rights under state or other law except his right, otherwise available under the Extradition Act, to oppose his transfer on the ground that the sending State's Governor had not explicitly approved the custody request. Moreover, the remedial purpose of the Detainer Agreement in protecting prisoners against whom detainers are outstanding supports an interpretation that gives prisoners the right to a judicial hearing in which they can bring a limited challenge to the receiving State's custody request.

592 F.2d 720, affirmed.

BRENNAN, J., delivered the opinion of the Court, in which WHITE, MARSHALL, BLACKMUN, POWELL, and STEVENS, JJ., joined. REHNQUIST, J., filed a dissenting opinion, in which BURGER, C.J., and STEWART, J., joined.

HOWE
V.
SMITH

452 U.S. 473; 101 S. CT. 2468; 69 L. ED. 2D 171 (1981)

CERTIORARI TO THE UNITED STATES COURT OF APPEALS FOR THE SECOND CIRCUIT

No. 80–5392   Argued April 28, 1981—Decided June 17, 1981

Title 18 U.S.C. § 5003(a) authorizes the Attorney General to contract with a state "for the custody, care, subsistence, education, treatment, and training of persons convicted of criminal offenses in the courts of such State," when the Director of the United States Bureau of Prisons certifies that proper and adequate federal "treatment facilities and personnel are available." Petitioner was convicted in a Vermont state court of first-degree murder arising out of the rape and strangulation of an elderly woman. Since Vermont had previously closed its only maximum security prison, petitioner was assigned to a state prison having the capacity for short-term, but not long-term, incarceration of inmates with high security needs, and it was recommended, because of the nature of his offense, that he be transferred to a federal prison. A hearing was held before the Vermont Department of Corrections at which it was determined that petitioner was a high security risk, and, ultimately, under a contract between Vermont and the United States, petitioner was transferred to the federal prison system pursuant to § 5003(a). Subsequently, petitioner filed an action in Federal District Court, challenging his transfer on the ground that the federal officials lacked statutory authority to accept custody. He claimed that § 5003(a) requires federal authorities to make an individual determination that each state prisoner transferred to the federal system needs a particular specialized treatment program available in that system, and that no such determination had been made in his case. The District Court denied petitioner's request for relief, and the Court of Appeals affirmed.

Held: Section 5003(a) authorizes a transfer of a state prisoner to the federal system such as occurred in this case.

(a) Section 5003(a)'s plain language authorizes contracts not simply for treatment, but also for custody, care, subsistence, education, and training of state prisoners in federal facilities. The requirement for certification by the Director of the Bureau of Prisons is simply a housekeeping measure designed to ensure that the federal system has the capacity to absorb the state prisoners. Nothing in § 5003(a)'s language restricts or limits the use of federal prison facilities to those state prisoners who are in need of some particular treatment.

(b) Section 5003's legislative history reveals that it was enacted to deal with the simple and practical problem of permitting states to transfer their prisoners to federal custody in the same way that the Federal Government had, for some time, been placing prisoners in state custody pursuant to 18 U.S.C. § 4002. And nothing in the legislative history makes this case one of the "rare and exceptional cases" requiring a departure from the statute's plain language.

(c) The contemporaneous and uniform construction of § 5003(a) by the Bureau of Prisons, the agency that proposed its enactment and is charged with its administration, has been that the statute authorizes contracts based on a broad range of purposes, including such a transfer as is shown by the record in this case. In the absence of any evidence of congressional objection, the agency's interpretation must be given great weight.

625 F.2d 454, affirmed.

BURGER, C.J., delivered the opinion of the Court, in which BRENNAN, WHITE, MARSHALL, BLACKMUN, POWELL, and REHNQUIST, JJ., joined. STEVENS, J., filed an opinion concurring in the judgment. STEWART, J., filed a dissenting statement.

OLIM
V.
WAKINEKONA

461 U.S. 238; 103 S. CT. 1741; 75 L. ED. 2D 813 (1983)

CERTIORARI TO THE UNITED STATES COURT OF APPEALS FOR THE NINTH CIRCUIT

No. 81–1581   Argued January 19, 1983— Decided April 26, 1983

Petitioner members of a prison "Program Committee," after investigating a breakdown in discipline and the failure of certain programs within the maximum control unit of the Hawaii State Prison outside Honolulu, singled out respondent and another inmate as troublemakers. After a hearing—respondent having been notified thereof and having retained counsel to represent him—the same Committee recommended that respondent's classification as a maximum security risk be continued and that he be transferred to a prison on the mainland. Petitioner administrator of the Hawaii prison accepted the Committee's recommendation, and respondent was transferred to a California state prison. Respondent then filed suit against petitioners in Federal District Court, alleging that he had been denied procedural due process because the Committee that recommended his transfer consisted of the same persons who had initiated the hearing, contrary to a Hawaii prison regulation, and because the Committee was biased against him. The District Court dismissed the complaint, holding that the Hawaii regulations governing prison transfers did not create a substantive liberty interest protected by the Due Process Clause of the Fourteenth Amendment. The Court of Appeals reversed.

Held:

1. An interstate prison transfer does not deprive an inmate of any liberty interest protected by the Due Process Clause in and of itself. Just as an inmate has no justifiable expectation that he will be incarcerated in any particular prison within a State so as to implicate the Due Process Clause directly when an intrastate prison transfer is made, *Meachum v. Fano*, 427 U. S. 215; *Montanye v. Haymes*, 427 U. S. 236, he has no justifiable expectation that he will be incarcerated in any particular State. Statutes and interstate agreements recognize that, from time to time, it is necessary to transfer inmates to prisons in other States. Confinement in another State is within the normal limits or range of custody which the conviction has authorized the transferring State to impose. Even when, as here, the transfer involves long distances and an ocean crossing, the confinement remains within constitutional limits.

2. Nor do Hawaii's prison regulations create a constitutionally protected liberty

interest. Although a State creates a protected liberty interest by placing substantive limitations on official discretion, Hawaii's prison regulations place no substantive limitations on the prison administrator's discretion to transfer an inmate. For that matter, the regulations prescribe no substantive standards to guide the Program Committee whose task is to advise the administrator. Thus, no significance attaches to the fact that the prison regulations require a particular kind of hearing before the administrator can exercise his unfettered discretion.

664 F.2d 708, reversed.

BLACKMUN, J., delivered the opinion of the Court, in which BURGER, C.J., and WHITE, POWELL, REHNQUIST, and O'CONNOR, JJ., joined. MARSHALL, J., filed a dissenting opinion, in which BRENNAN, J., joined, and in Part I of which STEVENS, J., joined.

WILSON
V.
SEITER

501 U.S. 294; 111 S. CT. 2321; 115 L. ED. 2D 271 (1991)

CERTIORARI TO THE UNITED STATES COURT OF APPEALS FOR THE SIXTH CIRCUIT

No. 89–7376   Argued January 7, 1991—Decided June 17, 1991

Petitioner Wilson, an Ohio prison inmate, filed suit under 42 U.S.C. § 1983 against respondents, state prison officials, alleging that certain conditions of his confinement constituted cruel and unusual punishment in violation of the Eighth and Fourteenth Amendments. His affidavits described the challenged conditions and charged that the authorities, after notification, had failed to take remedial action. The District Court granted summary judgment for respondents, and the Court of Appeals affirmed on the ground, *inter alia*,

that the affidavits failed to establish the requisite culpable state of mind on the part of respondents.

Held:

1. A prisoner claiming that the conditions of his confinement violate the Eighth Amendment must show a culpable state of mind on the part of prison officials. *See, e.g., Whitley v. Albers*, 475 U. S. 312, 475 U. S. 319. *Rhodes v. Chapman*, 452 U. S. 337, distinguished. An intent requirement is implicit in that Amendment's ban on cruel and unusual punishment. Wilson's suggested distinction between "short-term" or "one-time" prison conditions (in which a state of mind requirement would apply) and "continuing" or "systemic" conditions (where official state of mind would be irrelevant) is rejected.

2. The "deliberate indifference" standard applied in *Estelle v. Gamble*, 429 U. S. 97, 429 U. S. 106, to claims involving medical care applies generally to prisoner challenges to conditions of confinement. There is no merit to respondents' contention that that standard should be applied only in cases involving personal, physical injury, and that a malice standard is appropriate in cases challenging conditions. As *Whitley* teaches, the "wantonness" of conduct depends not on its effect on the prisoner, but on the constraints facing the official.

3. The Court of Appeals erred in failing to consider Wilson's claims under the "deliberate indifference" standard and applying instead a standard of "behavior marked by persistent malicious cruelty." It is possible that the error was harmless, since the court said that Wilson's affidavits established "[a]t best ... negligence." Conceivably, however, the court would have reached a different disposition under the correct standard, and so the case is remanded for reconsideration on that basis.

893 F.2d 861 (CA6 1990), vacated and remanded.

SCALIA, J., delivered the opinion of the Court, in which REHNQUIST, C.J., and O'CONNOR, KENNEDY, and

SOUTER, JJ., joined. WHITE, J., filed an opinion concurring in the judgment, in which MARSHALL, BLACKMUN, and STEVENS, JJ., joined.

FARMER
V.
BRENNAN

511 U.S. 825; 114 S. CT. 1970; 128 L. ED. 2D 811 (1994)

CERTIORARI TO THE UNITED STATES COURT OF APPEALS FOR THE SEVENTH CIRCUIT

No. 92–7274   Argued January 12, 1994— Decided June 6, 1994

Petitioner, a preoperative transsexual who projects feminine characteristics, has been incarcerated with other males in the federal prison system, sometimes in the general prison population but more often in segregation. Petitioner claims to have been beaten and raped by another inmate after being transferred by respondent federal prison officials from a correctional institute to a penitentiary-typically a higher security facility with more troublesome prisoners-and placed in its general population. Filing an action under *Bivens v. Six Unknown Fed. Narcotics Agents*, 403 U. S. 388, petitioner sought damages and an injunction barring future confinement in any penitentiary, and alleged that respondents had acted with "deliberate indifference" to petitioner's safety in violation of the Eighth Amendment because they knew that the penitentiary had a violent environment and a history of inmate assaults and that petitioner would be particularly vulnerable to sexual attack. The District Court granted summary judgment to respondents, denying petitioner's motion under Federal Rule of Civil Procedure 56(f) to delay its ruling until respondents complied with a discovery request. It concluded that failure to prevent inmate assaults violates the Eighth Amendment only if prison officials were "reckless in a criminal sense," i. e., had "actual knowledge" of a potential danger, and that respondents lacked such knowledge because petitioner

never expressed any safety concerns to them. The Court of Appeals affirmed.

Held:

1. A prison official may be held liable under the Eighth Amendment for acting with "deliberate indifference" to inmate health or safety only if he knows that inmates face a substantial risk of serious harm and disregards that risk by failing to take reasonable measures to abate it.

   (a) Prison officials have a duty under the Eighth Amendment to provide humane conditions of confinement. They must ensure that inmates receive adequate food, clothing, shelter, and medical care, and must protect prisoners from violence at the hands of other prisoners. However, a constitutional violation occurs only where the deprivation alleged is, objectively, "sufficiently serious," *Wilson v. Seiter*, 501 U.S. 294, 298, and the official has acted with "deliberate indifference" to inmate health or safety.

   (b) Deliberate indifference entails something more than negligence, but is satisfied by something less than acts or omissions for the very purpose of causing harm or with knowledge that harm will result. Thus, it is the equivalent of acting recklessly. However, this does not establish the level of culpability deliberate indifference entails, for the term recklessness is not self-defining, and can take subjective or objective forms.

   (c) Subjective recklessness, as used in the criminal law, is the appropriate test for "deliberate indifference." Permitting a finding of recklessness only when a person has disregarded a risk of harm of which he was aware is a familiar and workable standard that is consistent with the Cruel and Unusual Punishments Clause as interpreted in this Court's cases. The Eighth Amendment outlaws cruel and unusual "punishments," not "conditions," and the failure to alleviate a significant risk that an official should have perceived but did not, while no cause for commendation, cannot be condemned as the infliction of punishment under the Court's cases. Petitioner's invitation to adopt a purely objective test for determining liability-whether the risk is known or should have been known-is rejected. This Court's cases "mandate inquiry into a prison official's state of mind," *id.,* at 299, and it is no accident that the Court has repeatedly said that the Eighth Amendment has a "subjective component."

(d) The subjective test does not permit liability to be premised on obviousness or constructive notice. Canton v. Harris, 489 U. S. 378, distinguished. However, this does not mean that prison officials will be free to ignore obvious dangers to inmates. Whether an official had the requisite knowledge is a question of fact subject to demonstration in the usual ways, and a factfinder may conclude that the official knew of a substantial risk from the very fact that it was obvious. Nor may an official escape liability by showing that he knew of the risk but did not think that the complainant was especially likely to be assaulted by the prisoner who committed the act. It does not matter whether the risk came from a particular source or whether a prisoner faced the risk for reasons personal to him or because all prisoners in his situation faced the risk. But prison officials may not be held liable if they prove that they were unaware of even an obvious risk or if they responded reasonably to a known risk, even if the harm ultimately was not averted.

(e) Use of a subjective test will not foreclose prospective injunctive relief, nor require a prisoner to suffer physical injury before obtaining prospective relief. The subjective test adopted today is consistent with the principle that "[o]ne does not have to await the consummation of threatened injury to obtain preventive relief." Pennsylvania v. West Virginia, 262 U. S. 553. In a suit for prospective relief, the subjective factor, deliberate indifference, "should be determined in light of the prison authorities' current attitudes and conduct," Helling v. McKinney, 509 U. S. 25, 36: their attitudes and conduct at the time suit is brought and persisting thereafter. In making the requisite showing of subjective culpability, the prisoner may rely on developments that postdate the pleadings and pretrial motions, as prison officials may rely on such developments to show that the prisoner is not entitled to an injunction. A court that finds the Eighth Amendment's objective and subjective requirements satisfied may grant appropriate injunctive relief, though it should approach issuance of injunctions with the usual caution. A court need not ignore a prisoner's failure to take advantage of adequate prison procedures to resolve inmate grievances, and may compel a prisoner to pursue them.

2. On remand, the District Court must reconsider its denial of petitioner's Rule 56(f) discovery motion and apply the Eighth Amendment principles explained herein. The court may have erred in placing decisive weight on petitioner's failure to notify respondents of a danger, and such error may have affected the court's ruling on the discovery motion, so that additional evidence may be available to petitioner. Neither of two of respondents' contentions-that some of the officials had no knowledge about the confinement conditions and thus were alleged to be liable only for the transfer, and that there is no present threat that petitioner will be placed in a penitentiary-is so clearly correct as to justify affirmance.

Vacated and remanded.

SOUTER, J., delivered the opinion of the Court, in which REHNQUIST, C. J., and BLACKMUN, STEVENS, O'CONNOR, SCALIA, KENNEDY, and GINSBURG, JJ., joined. BLACK-MUN, J., and STEVENS, J. filed concurring opinions. THOMAS, J., filed an opinion concurring in the judgment.

KANSAS
V.
HENDRICKS

521 U.S. 346; 117 S. CT. 2072; 138 L. ED. 2D 501 (1997)

CERTIORARI TO THE SUPREME COURT OF KANSAS

No. 95–1649   Argued December 10, 1996—Decided June 23, 1997

Kansas' Sexually Violent Predator Act establishes procedures for the civil commitment of persons who, due to a "mental abnormality" or a "personality disorder," are likely to engage in "predatory acts of sexual violence." Kansas filed a petition under the Act in state court to commit respondent (and cross-petitioner) Hendricks, who had a long history of sexually molesting children and was scheduled for release from prison. The court reserved ruling on Hendricks' challenge to the Act's constitutionality, but granted his request for a jury trial. After Hendricks testified that he agreed with the state physician's diagnosis that he suffers from pedophilia and is not cured and that he continues to harbor sexual desires for children that he cannot control when he gets "stressed out," the jury determined that he was a sexually violent predator. Finding that pedophilia qualifies as a mental abnormality under the Act, the court ordered him committed. On appeal, the State Supreme Court invalidated the Act on the ground that the pre commitment condition of a "mental abnormality" did not satisfy what it perceived to be the "substantive" due process requirement that involuntary civil commitment must be predicated on a "mental illness" finding. It did not address Hendricks' *ex post facto* and double jeopardy claims.

Held:

1. The Act's definition of "mental abnormality" satisfies "substantive" due process

requirements. An individual's constitutionally protected liberty interest in avoiding physical restraint may be overridden even in the civil context. *Jacobson v. Massachusetts,* 197 U. S. 11, 26. This Court has consistently upheld involuntary commitment statutes that detain people who are unable to control their behavior and thereby pose a danger to the public health and safety, provided the confinement takes place pursuant to proper procedures and evidentiary standards. *Foucha v. Louisiana,* 504 U. S. 71, 80. The Act unambiguously requires a pre commitment finding of dangerousness either to one's self or to others, and links that finding to a determination that the person suffers from a "mental abnormality" or "personality disorder." Generally, this Court has sustained a commitment statute if it couples proof of dangerousness with proof of some additional factor, such as a "mental illness" or "mental abnormality," see, *e. g., Heller* v. *Doe,* 509 U. S. 312, 314–315, for these additional requirements serve to limit confinement to those who suffer from a volitional impairment rendering them dangerous beyond their control. The Act sets forth comparable criteria with its pre commitment requirement of "mental abnormality" or "personality disorder." Contrary to Hendricks' argument, this Court has never required States to adopt any particular nomenclature in drafting civil commitment statutes and leaves to the States the task of defining terms of a medical nature that have legal significance. Cf. *Jones* v. *United States,* 463 U. S. 354, 365, n. 13. The legislature is therefore not required to use the specific term "mental illness" and is free to adopt any similar term.

2. The Act does not violate the Constitution's double jeopardy prohibition or its ban on *ex post facto* lawmaking.

   (a) The Act does not establish criminal proceedings, and involuntary confinement under it is not punishment. The categorization of a particular proceeding as civil or criminal is a question of statutory construction. *Allen* v. *Illinois,* 478 U. S. 364, 368.

Nothing on the face of the Act suggests that the Kansas Legislature sought to create anything other than a civil commitment scheme. That manifest intent will be rejected only if Hendricks provides the clearest proof that the scheme is so punitive in purpose or effect as to negate Kansas' intention to deem it civil. *United States* v. *Ward,* 448 U. S. 242, 248–249. He has failed to satisfy this heavy burden. Commitment under the Act does not implicate either of the two primary objectives of criminal punishment: retribution or deterrence. Its purpose is not retributive: It does not affix culpability for prior criminal conduct, but uses such conduct solely for evidentiary purposes; it does not make criminal conviction a prerequisite for commitment; and it lacks a scienter requirement, an important element in distinguishing criminal and civil statutes. Nor can the Act be said to act as a deterrent, since persons with a mental abnormality or personality disorder are unlikely to be deterred by the threat of confinement. The conditions surrounding confinement-essentially the same as conditions for any civilly committed patient-do not suggest a punitive purpose. Although the commitment scheme here involves an affirmative restraint, such restraint of the dangerously mentally ill has been historically regarded as a legitimate nonpunitive objective. Cf. *United States* v. *Salerno,* 481 U. S. 739, 747. The confinement's potentially indefinite duration is linked, not to any punitive objective, but to the purpose of holding a person until his mental abnormality no longer causes him to be a threat to others. He is thus permitted immediate release upon a showing that he is no longer dangerous, and the longest he can be detained pursuant to a single judicial proceeding is one year. The State's use of procedural safeguards applicable in criminal trials does not itself turn the proceedings into criminal prosecutions. *Allen, supra,* at 372. Finally, the Act is not necessarily punitive if it fails to offer treatment where treatment for a condition is not possible, or if treatment, though possible, is merely an ancillary, rather than an overriding, state concern. The conclusion that the Act is nonpunitive removes an essential prerequisite for both Hendricks' double jeopardy and *ex post facto* claims.

(b) Hendricks' confinement does not amount to a second prosecution and punishment for the offense for which he was convicted. Because the Act is civil in nature, its commitment proceedings do not constitute a second prosecution. Cf. *Jones, supra.* As this commitment is not tantamount to punishment, the detention does not violate the Double Jeopardy Clause, even though it follows a prison term. *Baxstrom* v. *Herold,* 383 U. S. 107. Hendricks' argument that, even if the Act survives the "multiple punishments" test, it fails the "same elements" test of *Blockburger* v. *United States,* 284 U. S. 299, is rejected, since that test does not apply outside of the successive prosecution context.

(c) Hendricks' *ex post facto* claim is similarly flawed. The *Ex Post Facto* Clause pertains exclusively to penal statutes. *California Dept. of Corrections* v. *Morales,* 514 U. S. 499, 505. Since the Act is not punishment, its application does not raise *ex post facto* concerns. Moreover, the Act clearly does not have retroactive effect. It does not criminalize conduct legal before its enactment or deprive Hendricks of any defense that was available to him at the time of his crimes.

259 Kan. 246, 912 P. 2d 129, reversed.

THOMAS, J., delivered the opinion of the Court, in which REHNQUIST, C. J., and O'CONNOR, SCALIA, and KENNEDY, JJ., joined. KENNEDY, J., filed a concurring opinion. BREYER,

J., filed a dissenting opinion, in which STEVENS and SOUTER, JJ., joined, and in which GINSBURG, J., joined as to Parts II and III.

BROWN
V.
PLATA

563 U.S. 493; 131 S. CT. 1910; 179 L. ED. 2D 969 (2011)

APPEAL FROM THE UNITED STATES DISTRICT COURTS FOR THE EASTERN AND NORTHERN DISTRICTS OF CALIFORNIA

No. 09–1233   Argued November 30, 2010—Decided May 23, 2011

California's prisons are designed to house a population just under 80,000, but at the time of the decision under review the population was almost double that. The resulting conditions are the subject of two federal class actions. In *Coleman* v. *Brown,* filed in 1990, the District Court found that prisoners with serious mental illness do not receive minimal, adequate care. A Special Master appointed to oversee remedial efforts reported 12 years later that the state of mental health care in California's prisons was deteriorating due to increased overcrowding. In *Plata* v. *Brown*, filed in 2001, the State conceded that deficiencies in prison medical care violated prisoners' Eighth Amendment rights and stipulated to a remedial injunction. But when the State had not complied with the injunction by 2005, the court appointed a Receiver to oversee remedial efforts. Three years later, the Receiver described continuing deficiencies caused by overcrowding. Believing that a remedy for unconstitutional medical and mental health care could not be achieved without reducing overcrowding, the *Coleman* and *Plata* plaintiffs moved their respective District Courts to convene a three-judge court empowered by the Prison Litigation Reform Act of 1995 (PLRA) to order reductions in the prison population. The judges in both actions granted the request, and the cases were consolidated before a single three-judge court. After hearing testimony and making extensive

findings of fact, the court ordered California to reduce its prison population to 137.5% of design capacity within two years. Finding that the prison population would have to be reduced if capacity could not be increased through new construction, the court ordered the State to formulate a compliance plan and submit it for court approval.

Held:

1. The court-mandated population limit is necessary to remedy the violation of prisoners' constitutional rights and is authorized by the PLRA.

    (a) If a prison deprives prisoners of basic sustenance, including adequate medical care, the courts have a responsibility to remedy the resulting Eighth Amendment violation. See *Hutto* v. *Finney,* 437 U. S. 678, 687, n. 9. They must consider a range of options, including the appointment of special masters or receivers, the possibility of consent decrees, and orders limiting a prison's population. Under the PLRA, only a three-judge court may limit a prison population. 18 U.S.C. §3626(a)(3). Before convening such a court, a district court must have entered an order for less intrusive relief that failed to remedy the constitutional violation and must have given the defendant a reasonable time to comply with its prior orders. §3626(a)(3)(A). Once convened, the three-judge court must find by clear and convincing evidence that "crowding is the primary cause of the violation" and "no other relief will remedy [the] violation," §3626(a)(3)(E); and that the relief is "narrowly drawn, extends no further than necessary . . ., and is the least intrusive means necessary to correct the violation," §3626(a)(1)(A). The court must give "substantial weight to any adverse impact on public safety or the operation of a criminal justice system caused by the relief." *Ibid.* Its legal determinations are reviewed *de novo*, but its factual findings are reviewed for clear error.

(b) The *Coleman* and *Plata* courts acted reasonably in convening a three-judge court.

    (1) The merits of the decision to convene are properly before this Court, which has exercised its 28 U. S. C. §1253 jurisdiction to determine the authority of a court below, including whether a three-judge court was properly constituted. *Gonzalez* v. *Automatic Employees Credit Union*, 419 U. S. 90, 95, n. 12.

    (2) Section 3626(a)(3)(A)(i)'s previous order requirement was satisfied in *Coleman* by the Special Master's 1995 appointment and in *Plata* by the 2002 approval of a consent decree and stipulated injunction. Both orders were intended to remedy constitutional violations and were given ample time to succeed—12 years in *Coleman*, and 5 years in *Plata*. Contrary to the State's claim, §3626(a)(3)(A)(ii)'s reasonable time requirement did not require the District Courts to give more time for subsequent remedial efforts to succeed. Such a reading would in effect require courts to impose a moratorium on new remedial orders before issuing a population limit, which would delay an eventual remedy, prolong the courts' involvement, and serve neither the State nor the prisoners. The *Coleman* and *Plata* courts had a solid basis to doubt that additional efforts to build new facilities and hire new staff would achieve a remedy, given the ongoing deficiencies recently reported by both the Special Master and the Receiver.

(c) The three-judge court did not err in finding that "crowding [was] the primary cause of the violation," §3626(a)(3)(E)(i).

    (1) The trial record documents the severe impact of burgeoning demand on the provision of care. The evidence showed that there were high vacancy rates for medical and mental health staff, *e.g.*, 20% for surgeons and 54.1% for psychiatrists; that these numbers understated the severity of the crisis because the State has not budgeted sufficient staff to meet demand; and that even if vacant positions could be filled, there would be insufficient space for the additional staff. Such a shortfall contributes to significant delays in treating mentally ill prisoners, who are housed in administrative segregation for extended periods while awaiting transfer to scarce mental health treatment beds. There are also backlogs of up to 700 prisoners waiting to see a doctor for physical care. Crowding creates unsafe and unsanitary conditions that hamper effective delivery of medical and mental health care. It also promotes unrest and violence and can cause prisoners with latent mental illnesses to worsen and develop overt symptoms. Increased violence requires increased reliance on lockdowns to keep order, and lockdowns further impede the effective delivery of care. Overcrowding's effects are particularly acute in prison reception centers, which process 140,000 new or returning prisoners annually, and which house some prisoners for their entire incarceration period. Numerous experts testified that crowding is the primary cause of the constitutional violations.

    (2) Contrary to the State's claim, the three-judge court properly admitted, cited, and considered evidence of current prison conditions as relevant to the

issues before it. Expert witnesses based their conclusions on recent observations of prison conditions; the court admitted recent reports on prison conditions by the Receiver and Special Master; and both parties presented testimony related to current conditions. The court's orders cutting off discovery a few months before trial and excluding evidence not pertinent to the issue whether a population limit is appropriate under the PLRA were within the court's sound discretion. Orderly trial management may require discovery deadlines and a clean distinction between litigation of the merits and the remedy. The State points to no significant evidence that it was unable to present and that would have changed the outcome here.

(3) It was permissible for the three-judge court to conclude that overcrowding was the "primary," but not the only, cause of the violations, and that reducing crowding would not entirely cure the violations. This understanding of the primary cause requirement is consistent with the PLRA. Had Congress intended to require that crowding be the only cause, the PLRA would have said so.

(d) The evidence supports the three-judge court's finding that "no other relief [would] remedy the violation," §3626(a)(3)(E)(ii). The State's claim that out-of-state transfers provide a less restrictive alternative to a population limit must fail because requiring transfers is a population limit under the PLRA. Even if they could be regarded as a less restrictive alternative, the three-judge court found no evidence of plans for transfers in numbers sufficient to relieve overcrowding. The court also found no realistic possibility

that California could build itself out of this crisis, particularly given the State's ongoing fiscal problems. Further, it rejected additional hiring as a realistic alternative, since the prison system was chronically understaffed and would have insufficient space were adequate personnel retained. The court also did not err when it concluded that, absent a population reduction, the Receiver's and Special Master's continued efforts would not achieve a remedy. Their reports are persuasive evidence that, with no reduction, any remedy might prove unattainable and would at the very least require vast expenditures by the State. The State asserts that these measures would succeed if combined, but a long history of failed remedial orders, together with substantial evidence of overcrowding's deleterious effects on the provision of care, compels a different conclusion here.

(e) The prospective relief ordered here was narrowly drawn, extended no further than necessary to correct the violation, and was the least intrusive means necessary to correct the violation.

(1) The population limit does not fail narrow tailoring simply because prisoners beyond the plaintiff class will have to be released through parole or sentencing reform in order to meet the required reduction. While narrow tailoring requires a "fit" between the [remedy's] ends and the means chosen to accomplish those ends," *Board of Trustees of State Univ. of N. Y. v. Fox*, 492 U. S. 469, 480, a narrow and otherwise proper remedy for a constitutional violation is not invalid simply because it will have collateral effects. Nor does the PLRA require that result. The order gives the State flexibility to determine who should be released, and the State could move the three-

judge court to modify its terms. The order also is not overbroad because it encompasses the entire prison system, rather than separately assessing each institution's need for a population limit. The *Coleman* court found a systemwide violation, and the State stipulated to systemwide relief in *Plata*. Assuming no constitutional violation results, some facilities may retain populations in excess of the 137.5% limit provided others fall sufficiently below it so the system as a whole remains in compliance with the order. This will afford the State flexibility to accommodate differences between institutions. The order may shape or control the State's authority in the realm of prison administration, but it leaves much to the State's discretion. The order's limited scope is necessary to remedy a constitutional violation. The State may move the three-judge court to modify its order, but it has proposed no realistic alternative remedy at this time.

(2) The three-judge court gave "substantial weight" to any potential adverse impact on public safety from its order. The PLRA's "substantial weight" requirement does not require the court to certify that its order has no possible adverse impact on the public. Here, statistical evidence showed that prison populations had been lowered without adversely affecting public safety in some California counties, several States, and Canada. The court found that various available methods of reducing overcrowding—good time credits and diverting low-risk offenders to community programs—would have little or no impact on public safety, and its order took account of such concerns by giving the State

substantial flexibility to select among the means of reducing overcrowding. The State complains that the court approved the State's population reduction plan without considering whether its specific measures would substantially threaten public safety. But the court left state officials the choice of how best to comply and was not required to second-guess their exercise of discretion. Developments during the pendency of this appeal, when the State has begun to reduce the prison population, support the conclusion that a reduction can be accomplished without an undue negative effect on public safety.

2. The three-judge court's order, subject to the State's right to seek its modification in appropriate circumstances, must be affirmed.

(a) To comply with the PLRA, a court must set a population limit at the highest level consistent with an efficacious remedy, and it must order the population reduction to be achieved in the shortest period of time reasonably consistent with public safety.

(b) The three-judge court's conclusion that the prison population should be capped at 137.5% of design capacity was not clearly erroneous. The court concluded that the evidence supported a limit between the 130% limit supported by expert testimony and the Federal Bureau of Prisons and the 145% limit recommended by the State Corrections Independent Review Panel. The PLRA's narrow tailoring requirement is satisfied so long as such equitable, remedial judgments are made with the objective of releasing the fewest possible prisoners consistent with an efficacious remedy.

(c) The three-judge court did not err in providing a 2-year deadline for relief, especially in light of the State's failure to contest the issue at trial. The State has not asked this Court to extend the deadline, but the three-judge court has the authority, and responsibility, to amend its order as warranted by the exercise of sound discretion. Proper respect for the State and for its governmental processes require that court to exercise its jurisdiction to accord the State considerable latitude to find mechanisms and make plans that will promptly and effectively correct the violations consistent with public safety. The court may, *e.g.*, grant a motion to extend the deadline if the State meets appropriate preconditions designed to ensure that the plan will be implemented without undue delay. Such observations reflect the fact that the existing order, like all ongoing equitable relief, must remain open to appropriate modification, and are not intended to cast doubt on the validity of the order's basic premise.

Affirmed.

Kennedy, J., delivered the opinion of the Court, in which Ginsburg, Breyer, Sotomayor, and Kagan, JJ., joined. Scalia, J., filed a dissenting opinion, in which Thomas, J., joined. Alito, J., filed a dissenting opinion, in which Roberts, C. J., joined.

Cases Relating to Chapter 9

Isolated Confinement — "The Hole" and Administrative Segregation

RHODES

V.

CHAPMAN

452 U.S. 337; 101 S. CT. 2392; 69 L. ED. 2D 59 (1981)

CERTIORARI TO THE UNITED STATES COURT OF APPEALS FOR THE SIXTH CIRCUIT

No. 80.332   Argued March 2, 1981— Decided June 15, 1981

Respondents, who were housed in the same cell in an Ohio maximum security prison, brought a class action in Federal District Court under 42 U.S.C. § 1983 against petitioner state officials, alleging that "double celling" violated the Constitution and seeking injunctive relief. Despite its generally favorable findings of fact, the District Court concluded that the double celling was cruel and unusual punishment in violation of the Eighth Amendment, as made applicable to the States through the Fourteenth Amendment. This conclusion was based on five considerations: (1) inmates at the prison were serving long-terms of imprisonment; (2) the prison housed 38% more inmates than its "design capacity"; (3) the recommendation of several studies that each inmate have at least 555 square feet of living quarters, as opposed to the 63 square feet shared by the double celled inmates; (4) the suggestion that double celled inmates spend most of their time in their cells with their cellmates; and (5) the fact that double celling at the prison was not a temporary condition. The Court of Appeals affirmed.

Held: The double celling in question is not cruel and unusual punishment prohibited by the Eighth and Fourteenth Amendments.

(a) Conditions of confinement, as constituting the punishment at issue, must not involve the wanton and unnecessary infliction of pain, nor may they be grossly disproportionate to the severity of the crime warranting imprisonment. But conditions that cannot be said to be cruel and unusual under contemporary standards are not unconstitutional. To the extent such conditions are restrictive and even harsh, they are part of the penalty that criminals pay for their offenses against society.

(b) In view of the District Court's findings of fact, virtually every one of which tends to *refute* respondents' claim, its conclusion that double celling at the prison constituted cruel and unusual punishment is insupportable.

(c) The five considerations on which the District Court relied are insufficient to support its constitutional conclusion. Such considerations properly are weighed by the legislature and prison administration, rather than by a court. They fall far short, in themselves, of proving cruel and unusual punishment, absent evidence that double celling under the circumstances either inflicts unnecessary or wanton pain or is grossly disproportionate to the severity of the crime warranting imprisonment.

(d) In discharging their oversight responsibility to determine whether prison conditions amount to cruel and unusual punishment,

445

courts cannot assume that state legislatures and prison officials are insensitive to the requirements of the Constitution or to the sociological problems of how best to achieve the goals of the penal function in the criminal justice system.

624 F.2d 1099, reversed.

POWELL, J., delivered the opinion for the Court, in which BURGER, C.J., and STEWART, WHITE, and REHNQUIST, JJ., joined. BRENNAN, J., filed an opinion concurring in the judgment, in which BLACKMUN and STEVENS, JJ., joined. BLACKMUN, J., filed an opinion concurring in the judgment. MARSHALL, J., filed a dissenting opinion.

BOAG
V.
MACDOUGALL

454 U.S. 364; 102 S. CT. 700; 70 L. ED. 2D 551 (1982)

ON PETITION FOR WRIT OF CERTIORARI TO THE UNITED STATES COURT OF APPEALS FOR THE NINTH CIRCUIT

No. 80–6845   Decided January 11, 1982

Petitioner state prisoner filed a crudely written *pro se* complaint in Federal District Court alleging wrongful solitary confinement in a certain prison facility. The District Court dismissed the complaint on the ground of mootness because petitioner in the meantime had been transferred to another facility. The Court of Appeals affirmed, but on the ground that the action was frivolous because it did not state a claim upon which relief could be granted.

Held: The Court of Appeals' ground for dismissing the complaint was erroneous as a matter of law. Federal courts must construe inartful pleading liberally in *pro se* actions, *Haines v. Kerner*, 404 U. S. 519, and, so construed, the complaint here states a cause of action.

Certiorari granted; 642 F.2d 455, reversed and remanded.
PER CURIAM.

HEWITT
V.
HELMS

459 U.S. 460; 103 S. CT. 864; 74 L. ED. 2D 675 (1983)

CERTIORARI TO THE UNITED STATES COURT OF APPEALS FOR THE THIRD CIRCUIT

No. 81–638   Argued November 8, 1982— Decided February 22, 1983

Following a riot in the Pennsylvania State Prison where he was an inmate, respondent was removed from his cell and the general prison population and confined to administrative segregation within the prison pending an investigation into his role in the riot. The next day, respondent received notice of a misconduct charge against him. Five days after his transfer to administrative segregation, a Hearing Committee reviewed the evidence against respondent, and he acknowledged in writing that he had an opportunity to have his version of the events reported, but no finding of guilt was made. Subsequently, criminal charges based on the riot were filed against respondent, but were later dropped. In the meantime, a Review Committee concluded that respondent should remain in administrative segregation as posing a threat to the safety of other inmates and prison officials and to the security of the prison. Ultimately, the Hearing Committee, based on a second misconduct report and after hearing testimony from a prison guard and respondent, found respondent guilty of the second misconduct charge and ordered him confined to disciplinary segregation for six months, while dropping the earlier misconduct charge. Respondent sued in Federal District Court, claiming that petitioner prison officials' actions in confining him to administrative segregation violated his rights under the Due Process Clause of the Fourteenth Amendment. The District Court granted petitioners' motion for summary judgment. The Court of Appeals reversed, holding that, on the facts, respondent had a protected liberty interest in continuing to reside in the general prison population, which interest was created by the Pennsylvania regulations governing the administration of state prisons; that respondent could not be deprived of this interest without a hearing in compliance with the requirements of *Wolff v. McDonnell*, 418 U. S. 539; and that, since the court was uncertain whether the Hearing Committee's initial proceeding satisfied such requirements, the case would be remanded to the District Court for a hearing regarding the character of that proceeding.

Held:

1. Prison officials have broad administrative and discretionary authority over the institutions they manage, and lawfully incarcerated persons retain only a narrow range of protected liberty interests. Administrative segregation is the sort of confinement that inmates should reasonably anticipate receiving at some point in their incarceration, and does not involve an interest independently protected by the Due Process Clause. But in light of the Pennsylvania statutes and regulations setting forth the procedures for confining an inmate to administrative segregation, respondent did acquire a protected liberty interest in remaining in the general prison population.

2. The process afforded respondent satisfied the minimum requirements of the Due Process Clause.

   (a) In view of the wide-ranging deference accorded prison administrators in adopting and executing policies and practices needed to preserve order and discipline and to maintain security, petitioners were obligated to engage only in an informal, nonadversary review of the information supporting respondent's administrative confinement.

   (b) Under *Mathews v. Eldrige*, 424 U. S. 319, the private interests at stake in a governmental decision, the governmental interests involved, and the value of procedural requirements are considered in determining what process is due under the Fourteenth Amendment. Here, respondent's private interest was not of great consequence, but the governmental interests in the safety of the prison guards and other inmates and in isolating respondent pending investiga-

tion of the charges against him were of great importance. Neither of the grounds for confining respondent to administrative segregation involved decisions or judgments that would have been materially assisted by a detailed adversary proceeding.

   (c) An informal, nonadversary evidentiary review is sufficient both for the decision that an inmate represents a security threat and the decision to confine him to administrative segregation pending completion of an investigation into misconduct charges against him. In either situation, an inmate must merely receive notice of the charges against him and an opportunity to present his views to the prison official charged with deciding whether to transfer him to administrative segregation. Measured against these standards, respondent received all the process that was due after being confined to administrative segregation.

655 F.2d 487, reversed.

REHNQUIST, J., delivered the opinion of the Court, in which BURGER, C.J., and WHITE, POWELL, and O'CONNOR, JJ., joined. BLACKMUN, J., filed an opinion concurring in part and dissenting in part. STEVENS, J., filed a dissenting opinion, in which BRENNAN and MARSHALL, JJ., joined, and in Parts II and III of which BLACKMUN, J., joined.

WILKINSON
V.
AUSTIN

545 U.S. 209; 125 S. CT. 2384; 162 L. ED. 2D 174 (2005)

CERTIORARI TO THE UNITED STATES COURT OF APPEALS FOR THE SIXTH CIRCUIT

No. 04–495   Argued March 30, 2005—Decided June 13, 2005

"Supermax" prisons are maximum security facilities with highly restrictive conditions, designed to segregate the most dangerous prisoners from the general prison population. Their use has increased in recent years, in part as a response to the rise in prison gangs and prison violence. Ohio opened its only Supermax facility, the Ohio State Penitentiary (OSP), after a riot in one of its maximum security prisons. In the OSP almost every aspect of an inmate's life is controlled and monitored. Incarceration there is synonymous with extreme isolation. Opportunities for visitation are rare and are always conducted through glass walls. Inmates are deprived of almost any environmental or sensory stimuli and of almost all human contact. Placement at OSP is for an indefinite period, limited only by an inmate's sentence. Inmates otherwise eligible for parole lose their eligibility while incarcerated at OSP.

When OSP first became operational, no official policy governing placement there was in effect, and the procedures used to assign inmates to the facility were inconsistent and undefined, resulting in haphazard and erroneous placements. In an effort to establish guidelines for the selection and classification of OSP inmates, Ohio issued its Policy 111–07. Relevant here are two versions of the policy: the "Old Policy" and the "New Policy." Because assignment problems persisted after the Old Policy took effect, Ohio promulgated the New Policy to provide more guidance regarding the factors to be considered in placement decisions and to afford inmates more procedural protection against erroneous placement. Under the New Policy, a prison official conducts a classification review either (1) upon entry into the prison system if the inmate was convicted of certain offenses, e.g., organized crime, or (2) during the incarceration if the inmate engages in specified conduct, e.g., leads a prison gang. The New Policy also provides for a three-tier review process after a recommendation that an inmate be placed in OSP. Among other things, the inmate must receive notice of the factual basis leading to consideration for OSP placement and a fair opportunity for rebuttal at a hearing, although he may not call witnesses. In addition, the inmate is invited to submit objections prior to the final level of review. Although a subsequent reviewer may overturn an affirmative recommendation for OSP place-

ment at any level, the reverse is not true; if one reviewer declines to recommend OSP placement, the process terminates. Ohio also provides for a placement review within 30 days of an inmate's initial assignment to OSP, and annual review thereafter.

A class of current and former OSP inmates filed this suit for equitable relief under 42 U. S. C. §1983, alleging, inter alia, that the Old Policy, which was then in effect, violated the Fourteenth Amendment's Due Process Clause. On the eve of trial, Ohio promulgated its New Policy and represented that it contained the procedures to be followed in the future. After extensive evidence was presented, the District Court made findings and conclusions and issued a detailed remedial order. First, relying on San-din v. Conner, 515 U. S. 472, the court found that inmates have a liberty interest in avoiding assignment to OSP. Second, it found Ohio had denied the inmates due process by failing to afford many of them notice and an adequate opportunity to be heard before transfer; failing to give them sufficient notice of the grounds for their retention at OSP; and failing to give them sufficient opportunity to understand the reasoning and evidence used to retain them at OSP. Third, it held that, although the New Policy provided more procedural safeguards than the Old Policy, it was nonetheless inadequate to meet procedural due process requirements. The court therefore ordered modifications to the New Policy, including substantive modifications narrowing the grounds that Ohio could consider in recommending assignment to OSP, and various specific procedural modifications. The Sixth Circuit affirmed the District Court's conclusion that the inmates had a liberty interest in avoiding OSP placement and upheld the lower court's procedural modifications in their entirety, but set aside the far-reaching substantive modifications on the ground they exceeded the District Court's authority.

Held: The procedures by which Ohio's New Policy classifies prisoners for placement at its Supermax facility provide prisoners with sufficient protection to comply with the Due Process Clause.

(a) Inmates have a constitutionally protected liberty interest in avoiding assignment at OSP. Such an interest may arise from state policies or regulations, subject to the important limitations set forth in *Sandin*, which requires a determination whether OSP assignment "imposes atypical and significant hardship on the inmate in relation to the ordinary incidents of prison life." 515 U. S., at 483. The Court is satisfied that assignment to OSP imposes such a hardship compared to any plausible baseline from which to measure the Ohio prison system. For an inmate placed in OSP, almost all human contact is prohibited, even to the point that conversation is not permitted from cell to cell; his cell's light may be dimmed, but is on for 24 hours; and he may exercise only one hour per day in a small indoor room. Save perhaps for the especially severe limitations on all human contact, these conditions likely would apply to most solitary confinement facilities, but here there are two added components. First is the duration. Unlike the 30-day placement in segregated confinement at issue in *Sandin*, placement at OSP is indefinite and, after an initial 30-day review, is reviewed just annually. Second is that placement disqualifies an otherwise eligible inmate for parole consideration. Taken together these conditions impose an atypical and significant hardship within the correctional context.

(b) The New Policy's procedures are sufficient to satisfy due process. Evaluating the sufficiency of particular prison procedures requires consideration of three distinct factors: (1) the private interest that will be affected by the official action; (2) the risk of an erroneous deprivation of such interest through the procedures used, and the probable value, if any, of additional or substitute procedural safeguards; and (3) the government's interest, including the function involved and the fiscal and administrative burdens that additional or substitute procedural requirement would entail. *Mathews* v. *Eldridge*, 424 U. S. 319, 335. Applying those factors demonstrates that Ohio's New Policy provides a sufficient level of process. First, the inmate's interest in avoiding erroneous placement at OSP, while more than minimal, must nonetheless be evaluated within the context of the prison system and its attendant curtailment of liberties. The liberty of prisoners in lawful confinement is curtailed by definition, so their procedural protections are more limited than in cases where the right at stake is the right to be free from all confinement. Second, the risk of an erroneous placement is minimized by the New Policy's requirements. Ohio provides multiple levels of review for any decision recommending OSP placement, with power to overturn the recommendation at each level. In addition, Ohio reduces the risk of erroneous placement by providing for a placement review within 30 days of an inmate's initial assignment to OSP. Notice of the factual basis for a decision and a fair opportunity for rebuttal are among the most important procedural mechanisms for purposes of avoiding erroneous deprivations. See, *e.g., Greenholtz* v. *Inmates of Neb. Penal and Correctional Complex*, 442 U. S. 1, 15. Third, in the context of prison management and the specific circumstances of this case, Ohio's interest is a dominant consideration. Ohio's first obligation must be to ensure the safety of guards and prison personnel, the public, and the prisoners themselves. See *Hewitt* v. *Helms*, 459 U. S. 460, 473. Prison security, imperiled by the brutal reality of prison gangs, provides the backdrop of the State's interest. Another component of Ohio's interest is the problem of scarce resources. The high cost of maintaining an inmate at OSP would make it difficult to fund more effective education and vocational assistance programs to improve prisoners' lives. Courts must give substantial deference to prison management decisions before mandating additional expenditures for elaborate procedural safeguards when correctional officials conclude that a prisoner has engaged in disruptive behavior. Were Ohio required to provide other attributes of an adversary hearing before ordering transfer to OSP, both the State's immediate objective of controlling the prisoner and its greater objective of controlling the prison could be defeated. Where, as here, the inquiry draws more on the experience of prison administrators, and where the State's interest implicates the safety of other inmates and prison personnel, the informal, nonadversary procedures set forth in *Greenholtz* and *Hewitt* provide the appropriate model. If an inmate were to demonstrate that the New Policy did not in practice operate in the fashion described, any cognizable injury could be the subject of an appropriate future challenge. In light of the foregoing, the procedural modifications ordered by the District Court and affirmed by the Sixth Circuit were in error.

372 F. 3d 346, affirmed in part, reversed in part, and remanded.
KENNEDY, J., delivered the opinion for a unanimous Court.

JOHNSON
V.
CALIFORNIA

543 U.S. 499; 126 S. CT. 1141; 160 L. ED. 2D 949 (2005)

CERTIORARI TO THE UNITED STATES COURT OF APPEALS FOR THE NINTH CIRCUIT

No. 03–636   Argued November 2, 2004—Decided February 23, 2005

The California Department of Corrections' (CDC) unwritten policy of racially segregating prisoners in double cells for up to 60 days each time they enter a new correctional facility is based on the asserted rationale that it prevents violence caused by racial gangs. Petitioner Johnson, an African-American inmate who has been intermittently double-celled under the policy's terms ever since his 1987 incarceration, filed this suit alleging that the policy violates his Fourteenth Amendment right to equal protection. The District Court ultimately granted defendant former CDC officials' summary judgment on grounds that they were entitled to qualified immunity. The Ninth Circuit affirmed, holding that the policy's constitutionality should be reviewed under the deferential standard articulated in *Turner* v. *Safley*,

482 U. S. 78, not under strict scrutiny, and that the policy survived *Turner* scrutiny.

Held: Strict scrutiny is the proper standard of review for an equal protection challenge to the CDC's policy.

(a) Because the CDC's policy is "immediately suspect" as an express racial classification, *Shaw* v. *Reno*, 509 U. S. 630, 642, the Ninth Circuit erred in failing to apply strict scrutiny and thereby to require the CDC to demonstrate that the policy is narrowly tailored to serve a compelling state interest, see *Adarand Constructors, Inc.* v. *Peña*, 515 U. S. 200, 227. "[A]ll racial classifications [imposed by government] . . . must be analyzed . . . under strict scrutiny," *ibid.*, in order to "'smoke out' illegitimate uses of race by assuring that [government] is pursuing a goal important enough to warrant [such] a highly suspect tool," *Richmond* v. *J. A. Croson Co.*, 488 U. S. 469, 493. The CDC's claim that its policy should be exempt from this categorical rule because it is "neutral"—*i.e.*, because all prisoners are "equally" segregated—ignores this Court's repeated command that "racial classifications receive close scrutiny even when they may be said to burden or benefit the races equally," *Shaw, supra*, at 651. Indeed, the Court rejected the notion that separate can ever be equal—or "neutral"—50 years ago in *Brown* v. *Board of Education*, 347 U. S. 483, and refuses to resurrect it today. The Court has previously applied a heightened standard of review in evaluating racial segregation in prisons. *Lee* v. *Washington*, 390 U. S. 333. The need for strict scrutiny is no less important here. By perpetuating the notion that race matters most, racial segregation of inmates "may exacerbate the very patterns of [violence that it is] said to counteract." *Shaw, supra*, at 648. Virtually all other States and the Federal Government manage their prison systems without reliance on racial segregation. In fact, the United States argues that it is possible to address prison security concerns through individualized consideration without using racial segregation, unless it is warranted as a necessary and temporary response to a serious threat of race-related violence. As to transferees, in particular, whom the CDC has already evaluated at least once, it is not clear why more individualized determinations are not possible.

(b) The Court declines the CDC's invitation to make an exception to the categorical strict scrutiny rule and instead to apply *Turner*'s deferential review standard on the ground that the CDC's policy applies only in the prison context. The Court has never applied the *Turner* standard—which asks whether a regulation that burdens prisoners' fundamental rights is "reasonably related" to "legitimate penological interests," 482 U. S., at 89—to racial classifications. *Turner* itself did not involve such a classification, and it cast no doubt on *Lee*. That is unsurprising, as the Court has applied the *Turner* test *only* to rights that are "inconsistent with proper incarceration." *Overton* v. *Bazzetta*, 539 U. S. 126, 131. The right not to be discriminated against based on one's race is not susceptible to *Turner*'s logic because it is not a right that need necessarily be compromised for the sake of proper prison administration. On the contrary, compliance with the Fourteenth Amendment's ban on racial discrimination is not only consistent with proper prison administration, but also bolsters the legitimacy of the entire criminal justice system. Cf. *Batson* v. *Kentucky*, 476 U. S. 79, 99. Deference to the particular expertise of officials managing daily prison operations does not require a more relaxed standard here. The Court did not relax the standard of review for racial classifications in prison in *Lee*, and it refuses to do so today. Rather, it explicitly

reaffirms that the "necessities of prison security and discipline," *Lee*, *supra*, at 334, are a compelling government interest justifying only those uses of race that are narrowly tailored to address those necessities, see, *e.g.*, *Grutter v. Bollinger*, 539 U. S. 306, 353. Because *Turner*'s standard would allow prison officials to use race-based policies even when there are race-neutral means to accomplish the same goal, and even when the race-based policy does not in practice advance that goal, it is too lenient a standard to ferret out invidious uses of race. Contrary to the CDC's protest, strict scrutiny will not render prison administrators unable to address legitimate problems of race-based violence in prisons. On remand, the CDC will have the burden of demonstrating that its policy is narrowly tailored with regard to new inmates as well as transferees. Pp. 9–15.

(c) The Court does not decide whether the CDC's policy violates equal protection, but leaves it to the Ninth Circuit, or the District Court, to apply strict scrutiny in the first instance. See, *e.g.*, *Consolidated Rail Corporation* v. *Gottshall*, 512 U. S. 532, 557–558.

321 F. 3d 791, reversed and remanded.

O'CONNOR, J., delivered the opinion of the Court, in which KENNEDY, SOUTER, GINSBURG, and BREYER, JJ., joined. GINSBURG, J., filed a concurring opinion, in which SOUTER and BREYER, JJ., joined. STEVENS, J., filed a dissenting opinion. THOMAS, J., filed a dissenting opinion, in which SCALIA, J., joined. REHNQUIST, C. J., took no part in the decision of the case.

Cases Relating to Chapter 10

Prisoner Disciplinary Proceedings

BAXTER
V.
PALMIGIANO

425 U.S. 308; 96 S. CT. 1551; 47 L. ED. 2D 810 (1976)

CERTIORARI TO THE UNITED STATES COURT OF APPEALS FOR THE FIRST CIRCUIT

No. 74–1187 Argued December 15, 1975—Decided April 20, 1976

Respondent state prison inmates in No. 74–1194 filed an action for declaratory and injunctive relief alleging that procedures used in prison disciplinary proceedings violated their rights to due process and equal protection of the laws under the Fourteenth Amendment. The District Court granted relief, and the Court of Appeals affirmed, holding that minimum notice and a right to respond are due an inmate faced even with a temporary suspension of privileges, that an inmate at a disciplinary hearing who is denied the privilege of confronting and cross-examining witnesses must receive written reasons or the denial will be deemed *prima facie* evidence of abuse of discretion, and that an inmate facing prison discipline for a violation that might also be punishable in state criminal proceedings has a right to counsel (not just counsel substitute) at the prison hearing. Respondent state prison inmate in No. 74–1187, upon being charged with inciting a prison disturbance, was summoned before prison authorities and informed that he might be prosecuted for a violation of state law, that he should consult an attorney

(although the attorney would not be permitted to be present during the disciplinary hearing), and that he had a right to remain silent during the hearing, but that, if he did so, his silence would be held against him. On the basis of the hearing, at which respondent remained silent, he was placed in "punitive segregation" for 30 days. He then filed an action for damages and injunctive relief, claiming that the disciplinary hearing violated the Due Process Clause of the Fourteenth Amendment. The District Court denied relief, but the Court of Appeals reversed, holding that an inmate at a prison disciplinary proceeding must be advised of his right to remain silent, that he must not be questioned further once he exercises that right, that such silence may not be used against him at that time or in future proceedings, and that, where criminal charges are a realistic possibility, prison authorities should consider whether defense counsel, if requested, should be permitted at the proceeding.

Held: The procedures required by the respective Courts of Appeals are either inconsistent with the "reasonable accommodation" reached in *Wolff v. McDonnell*, 418 U. S. 539, between institutional needs and objectives and the constitutional provisions of general application, or are premature on the basis of the case records.

(a) Prison inmates do not "have a right to either retained or appointed counsel in disciplinary hearings." *Wolff, supra*, at 418 U. S. 570.

(b) Permitting an adverse inference to be drawn from an inmate's silence at his disciplinary proceedings is not, on its face, an invalid practice, and there is no basis

453

in the record for invalidating it as applied to respondent in No. 74–1187.

(c) Mandating that inmates should have the privilege of confrontation and cross-examination of witnesses at prison disciplinary proceedings, except where prison officials can justify their denial of such privilege on grounds that would satisfy a court of law, effectively preempts the area that *Wolff, supra*, left to the sound discretion of prison officials, and there is no evidence of abuse of such discretion by the prison officials in No. 74–1194.

(d) Where there was no evidence that any of the respondents in No. 74–1194 were subject to the "lesser penalty" of loss of privileges, but rather it appeared that all were charged with "serious misconduct," the Court of Appeals acted prematurely to the extent it required procedures such as notice and an opportunity to respond even when an inmate is faced with a temporary suspension of privileges.

No. 74–1187, 510 F.2d 534; No. 74–1194, 510 F.2d 613, reversed.

WHITE, J., delivered the opinion of the Court, in which BURGER, C.J., and STEWART, BLACKMUN, POWELL, and REHNQUIST, JJ., joined, and in Part V of which BRENNAN and MARSHALL, JJ., joined. BRENNAN, J., filed an opinion concurring in part and dissenting in part, in which MARSHALL, J., joined. STEVENS, J., took no part in the consideration or decision of the cases.

WOLFF
V.
MCDONNELL

418 U.S. 539; 94 S. CT. 2963; 41 L. ED. 2D 935 (1974)

CERTIORARI TO THE UNITED STATES COURT OF APPEALS FOR THE EIGHTH CIRCUIT

No. 73–679   Argued April 22, 1974— Decided June 26, 1974

Respondent, on behalf of himself and other inmates at a Nebraska prison, filed a complaint for damages and injunctive relief under 42 U.S.C. § 1983, in which he alleged that disciplinary proceedings at the prison violated due process; that the inmate legal assistance program did not meet constitutional standards; and that the regulations governing inmates' mail wcrc unconstitutionally restrictive. After an evidentiary hearing, the District Court granted partial relief. Though rejecting respondent's procedural due process claim, the court held that the prison's policy of inspecting all attorney-prisoner mail was improper, but that restrictions on inmate legal assistance were not constitutionally defective. The Court of Appeals reversed with respect to the due process claim, holding that the procedural requirements outlined in the intervening decisions in *Morrissey v. Brewer*, 408 U. S. 471, and *Gagnon v. Scarpelli*, 411 U. S. 778, should be generally followed in prison disciplinary hearings, but leaving the specific requirements (including the circumstances in which counsel might be required) to be determined by the District Court on remand. The Court of Appeals further held that *Preiser v. Rodriguez*, 411 U. S. 475, forbade restoration of good time credits in a 1983 suit, but ordered expunged from prison records misconduct determinations reached in proceedings that had not comported with due process. The court generally affirmed the District Court's judgment respecting correspondence with attorneys, but added some additional prescriptions and ordered further proceedings to determine whether the State was meeting its burden under *Johnson v. Avery*, 393 U. S. 483, to provide legal assistance to prisoners, a duty the court found to extend to civil rights cases as well as habeas corpus proceedings. Under Nebraska's disciplinary scheme, forfeiture or withholding of good time credits or confinement in a disciplinary cell is provided for serious misconduct and deprivation of privileges for less serious misconduct. To establish misconduct, (1) a preliminary conference is held with the chief corrections supervisor and the charging party, where the prisoner is orally informed of the charge and preliminarily discusses the merits; (2) a conduct report is prepared and a hearing held before the prison's disciplinary body, the Adjustment Committee (composed of three prison officials), where (3) the inmate can ask questions of the charging party.

Held:

1. Though the Court of Appeals correctly held that restoration of good time credits under § 1983 is foreclosed under *Preiser, supra*, damages and declaratory and other relief for improper revocation of good time credits are cognizable under that provision.
2. A prisoner is not wholly stripped of constitutional protections, and though prison disciplinary proceedings do not implicate the full panoply of rights due a defendant in a criminal prosecution, such proceedings must be governed by a mutual accommodation between institutional needs and generally applicable constitutional requirements.
3. Since prisoners in Nebraska can only lose good time credits if they are guilty of serious misconduct, the procedure for determining whether such misconduct has occurred must observe certain minimal due process requirements (though not the full range of procedures mandated in *Morrissey, supra*, and *Scarpelli, supra*, for parole and probation revocation hearings) consonant with the unique institutional environment and therefore involving a more flexible approach reasonably accommodating the interests of the inmates and the needs of the institution.

    (a) Advance written notice of charges must be given to the disciplinary action inmate, no less than 24 hours before his appearance before the Adjustment Committee.
    (b) There must be "a written statement by the factfinders as to the evidence relied on and reasons for [the disciplinary action]." *Morrissey v. Brewer, supra*, at 408 U. S. 489.
    (c) The inmate should be allowed to call witnesses and present documentary evidence in his defense if permitting him to do so will not jeopardize institutional safety or correctional goals.
    (d) The inmate has no constitutional right to confrontation and cross-ex-

amination in prison disciplinary proceedings, such procedures in the current environment, where prison disruption remains a serious concern, being discretionary with the prison officials.
    (e) Inmates have no right to retained or appointed counsel in such proceedings, although counsel substitutes should be provided in certain cases.
    (f) On the record here, it cannot be concluded that the Adjustment Committee is not sufficiently impartial to satisfy due process requirements.

4. The Court of Appeals erred in holding that the due process requirements in prison disciplinary proceedings were to be applied retroactively by requiring the expunging of prison records of improper misconduct determinations. *Morrissey, supra*, at 408 U. S. 490.
5. The State may constitutionally require that mail from an attorney to a prisoner be identified as such, and that his name and address appear on the communication; and—as a protection against contraband—that the authorities may open such mail in the inmate's presence. A lawyer desiring to correspond with a prisoner may also be required first to identify himself and his client to the prison officials to ensure that letters marked "privileged" are actually from members of the bar. Other restrictions on the attorney-prisoner mail procedure required by the courts below are disapproved.
6. The District Court, as the Court of Appeals suggested, is to assess the adequacy of the legal assistance available for preparation of civil rights actions, applying the standard of *Johnson v. Avery, supra*, at 373 U. S. 490, that "unless and until the State provides some reasonable alternative to assist inmates in the preparation of petitions for post-conviction relief," inmates could not be barred from furnishing assistance to each other.

483 F.2d 1059, affirmed in part, reversed in part, and remanded.

WHITE, J., delivered the opinion of the Court, in which BURGER, C.J., and

STEWART, BLACKMUN, POWELL, and REHNQUIST, JJ., joined. MARSHALL, J., filed an opinion concurring in part and dissenting in part, in which BRENNAN, J., joined. DOUGLAS, J., filed an opinion dissenting in part and concurring in the result in part.

SANDIN
V.
CONNER

515 U.S. 472; 115 S. CT. 2293; 132 L. ED. 2D 418 (1995)

CERTIORARI TO THE UNITED STATES COURT OF APPEALS FOR THE NINTH CIRCUIT

No. 93–1911   Argued February 28, 1995— Decided June 19, 1995

In this suit, respondent Conner alleged that petitioner and other Hawaii prison officials deprived him of procedural due process when an adjustment committee refused to allow him to present witnesses during a disciplinary hearing and then sentenced him to segregation for misconduct. The District Court granted the officials summary judgment, but the Court of Appeals reversed, concluding that Conner had a liberty interest in remaining free of disciplinary segregation and that there was a disputed question of fact whether he had received all of the process due under *Wolff v. McDonnell,* 418 U. S. 539. The court based its conclusion on a prison regulation instructing the committee to find guilt when a misconduct charge is supported by substantial evidence, reasoning that the committee's duty to find guilt was nondiscretionary. From that regulation, it drew a negative inference that the committee may not impose segregation if it does not find substantial evidence of misconduct, that this is a state-created liberty interest, and that therefore *Wolff* entitled Conner to call witnesses.

Held: Neither the Hawaii prison regulation nor the Due Process Clause itself affords Conner a protected liberty interest that would entitle him to the procedural protections set forth in *Wolff.*

(a) Under *Wolff,* States may in certain circumstances create liberty interests that are protected by the Due Process Clause. But these interests will generally be limited to freedom from restraint which, while not exceeding the sentence in such an unexpected manner as to give rise to protection by the Due Process Clause of its own force, nonetheless imposes atypical and significant hardship on the inmate in relation to the ordinary incidents of prison life. See also *Meachum v. Fano, 427* U. S. 215. The methodology used in *Hewitt* v. *Helms,* 459 U. S. 460, and later cases has impermissibly shifted the focus of the liberty interest inquiry from one based on the nature of the deprivation to one based on language of a particular regulation. Under *Hewitt's* methodology, prison regulations, such the one in this case, have been examined to see whether mandatory language and substantive predicates create an enforceable expectation that the State would produce a particular outcome with respect to the prisoner's confinement conditions. This shift in focus has encouraged prisoners to comb regulations in search of mandatory language on which to base entitlements to various state conferred privileges. Courts have, in response, drawn negative inferences from that language. *Hewitt* creates disincentives for States to codify prison management procedures in the interest of uniform treatment in order to avoid the creation of "liberty" interests, and it has led to the involvement of federal courts in the day-to-day management of prisons. The time has come to return to those due process principles that were correctly established and applied in *Wolff* and *Meachum.*

(b) Conner asserts, incorrectly, that any state action taken for a punitive reason encroaches upon a liberty interest under the Due Process Clause even in the absence of any state regulation. *Bell* v. *Wolfish, 441* U. S. 520 (1979), and *Ingraham* v. *Wright,* 430 U. S. 651 (1977), distinguished.

(c) Conner's discipline in segregated confinement did not present the type of atypical, significant deprivation in which a

State might conceivably create a liberty interest. At the time of his punishment, disciplinary segregation mirrored those conditions imposed upon inmates in administrative segregation and protective custody. Moreover, the State later expunged his disciplinary record, with respect to the more serious of the charges against him. And, his confinement did not exceed similar, but totally discretionary confinement in either duration or degree of restriction. Conner's situation also does not present a case where the State's action will inevitably affect the duration of his sentence, since the chance that the misconduct finding will affect his parole status is simply too attenuated to invoke the Due Process Clause's procedural guarantees.

15 F.3d 1463, reversed.

REHNQUIST, C. J., delivered the opinion of the Court, in which O'CONNOR, SCALIA, KENNEDY, and THOMAS, JJ., joined. GINSBURG, J., filed a dissenting opinion, in which STEVENS, J. BREYER, J., filed a dissenting opinion, in which SOUTER, J., joined.

Cases Relating to Chapter 11

Use of Force

WHITLEY
V.
ALBERS

475 U.S. 312; 106 S. CT. 1078; 89 L. ED. 2D 251 (1986)

CERTIORARI TO THE UNITED STATES COURT OF APPEALS FOR THE NINTH CIRCUIT

No. 84–1077   Argued December 10, 1985— Decided March 4, 1986

During the course of a riot at the Oregon State Penitentiary, a prison officer was taken hostage and placed in a cell on the upper tier of a two-tier cellblock. In an attempt to free the hostage, prison officials worked out a plan that called for the prisoner security manager to enter the cellblock unarmed, followed by prison officers armed with shotguns. The security manager ordered one of the officers to fire a warning shot and to shoot low at any inmates climbing the stairs to the upper tier, since he would be climbing the stairs to free the hostage. One of the officers, after firing a warning shot, shot respondent in the left knee when he started up the stairs. Respondent subsequently brought an action in Federal District Court against petitioner prison officials pursuant to 42 U.S.C. § 1983, alleging, *inter alia*, that they had deprived him of his rights under the Eighth and Fourteenth Amendments. At the conclusion of the trial, the District Court directed a verdict for petitioners. The Court of Appeals reversed and remanded for a new trial on respondent's Eighth Amendment claim.

Held:

1. The shooting of respondent did not violate his Eighth Amendment right to be free from cruel and unusual punishments.

    (a) It is obduracy and wantonness, not inadvertence or error in good faith, that characterize the conduct prohibited by the Cruel and Unusual Punishments Clause, whether that conduct occurs in connection with establishing conditions of confinement, supplying medical needs, or restoring control over a tumultuous cellblock. The infliction of pain in the course of a prison security measure, therefore, does not amount to cruel and unusual punishment simply because it may appear in retrospect that the degree of force authorized or applied for security purposes was unreasonable, and hence unnecessary in the strict sense. The general requirement that an Eighth Amendment claimant establish the unnecessary and wanton infliction of pain should also be applied with due regard for differences in the kind of conduct involved. Thus, where a prison security measure is undertaken to resolve a disturbance, such as occurred in this case, that poses significant risks to the safety of inmates and prison staff, the question whether the measure taken inflicted unnecessary and wanton pain and suffering ultimately turns on whether force was applied in a good faith effort to maintain or restore dis-

459

cipline or maliciously and sadistically for the purpose of causing harm.

(b) Viewing the evidence in the light most favorable to respondent, as must be done in reviewing the decision reversing the trial court's directed verdict for petitioners, it does not appear that the evidence supports a reliable inference of wantonness in the infliction of pain under the above standard. Evidence arguably showing that the prison officials erred in judgment when they decided on a plan that employed potentially deadly force falls far short of a showing that there was no plausible basis for their belief that this degree of force was necessary. In particular, the order to shoot, qualified by an instruction to shoot low, falls short of commanding the infliction of pain in a wanton and unnecessary fashion. Nor was the failure to provide for a verbal warning, in addition to a warning shot, so insupportable as to be wanton, since any inmate running up the stairs after the prison security manager could reasonably be thought to pose a threat to the rescue attempt. And the failure to take into account the possibility that respondent might climb the stairs in an effort to return to his cell does not rise to the level of an Eighth Amendment violation. Assuming that the prison officer shot at respondent, rather than at the inmates as a group, does not establish that the officer shot respondent knowing that it was unnecessary to do so. Under all these circumstances, the shooting was part and parcel of a good faith effort to restore prison security.

2. In this case, the Due Process Clause of the Fourteenth Amendment cannot serve as an alternative basis for affirmance, independently of the Eighth Amendment. In the prison security context, the Due Process Clause affords respondent no greater protection than does the Cruel and Unusual Punishments Clause.

743 F.2d 1372, reversed.

O'CONNOR, J., delivered the opinion of the Court, in which BURGER, C.J., and WHITE, POWELL, and REHNQUIST, JJ., joined. MARSHALL, J., filed a dissenting opinion, in which BRENNAN and BLACKMUN, JJ., joined, and in all but n. 2 of which STEVENS, J., joined.

HUDSON
V.
MCMILLIAN

503 U.S. 1; 112 S. CT. 995; 117 L. ED. 2D 156 (1992)

CERTIORARI TO THE UNITED STATES COURT OF APPEALS FOR THE FIFTH CIRCUIT

No. 90–6531   Argued November 13, 1991— Decided February 25, 1992

Petitioner Hudson, a Louisiana prison inmate, testified that minor bruises, facial swelling, loosened teeth, and a cracked dental plate he had suffered resulted from a beating by respondent prison guards McMillian and Woods while he was handcuffed and shackled following an argument with McMillian, and that respondent Mezo, a supervisor on duty, watched the beating but merely told the officers "not to have too much fun." The Magistrate trying Hudson's District Court suit under 42 U. S. C. § 1983 found that the officers used force when there was no need to do so and that Mezo expressly condoned their actions, ruled that respondents had violated the Eighth Amendment's prohibition on cruel and unusual punishments, and awarded Hudson damages. The Court of Appeals reversed, holding, *inter alia,* that inmates alleging use of excessive force in violation of the Amendment must prove "significant injury" and that Hudson could not prevail because his injuries were "minor" and required no medical attention.

Held: The use of excessive physical force against a prisoner may constitute cruel and unusual punishment even though the inmate does not suffer serious injury.

(a) Whenever prison officials stand accused of using excessive physical force constituting "the unnecessary and wanton infliction of pain" violative of the Cruel and Unusual Punishments Clause, the core judicial inquiry is that set out in *Whitley* v. *Albers,* 475 U. S. 312, 320–321: whether force was applied in a good-faith effort to maintain or restore discipline, or maliciously and sadistically to cause harm. Extending *Whitley's* application of the "unnecessary and wanton infliction of pain" standard to all allegations of force, whether the prison disturbance is a riot or a lesser disruption, works no innovation. See, *e. g., Johnson* v. *Glick,* 481 F.2d 1028, cert. denied, 414 U. S. 1033.

(b) Since, under the *Whitley* approach, the extent of injury suffered by an inmate is one of the factors to be considered in determining whether the use of force is wanton and unnecessary, 475 U. S., at 321, the absence of serious injury is relevant to, but does not end, the Eighth Amendment inquiry. There is no merit to respondents' assertion that a significant injury requirement is mandated by what this Court termed, in *Wilson* v. *Seiter,* 501 U. S. 294, 298, the "objective component" of Eighth Amendment analysis: whether the alleged wrongdoing is objectively "harmful enough" to establish a constitutional violation, *id.,* at 303. That component is contextual and responsive to "contemporary standards of decency." *Estelle* v. *Gamble,* 429 U. S. 97, 103. In the excessive force context, such standards always are violated when prison officials maliciously and sadistically use force to cause harm, see *Whitley,* 475 U. S., at 327, whether or not significant injury is evident. Moreover, although the Amendment does not reach *de minimis* uses of physical force, provided that such use is not of a sort repugnant to the conscience of mankind, *ibid.,* the blows directed at Hudson are not *de minimis,* and the extent of his injuries thus provides no basis for dismissal of his § 1983 claim.

(c) The dissent's theory that *Wilson* requires an inmate who alleges excessive force to show significant injury *in addition to* the unnecessary and wanton infliction of pain misapplies *Wilson* and ignores the body of this Court's Eighth Amendment jurisprudence. *Wilson* did not involve an allegation of excessive force and, with respect to the "objective component" of an Eighth Amendment claim, suggested no departure from *Estelle* and its progeny. The dissent's argument that excessive force claims and conditions-of-confinement claims are no different in kind is likewise unfounded. To deny the difference between punching a prisoner in the face and serving him unappetizing food is to ignore the concepts of dignity, civilized standards, humanity, and decency that animate the Eighth Amendment. See *Estelle, supra,* at 102.

(d) This Court takes no position on respondents' legal argument that their conduct was isolated, unauthorized, and against prison policy and therefore beyond the scope of "punishment" prohibited by the Eighth Amendment. That argument is inapposite on the record, since the Court of Appeals left intact the Magistrate's determination that the violence at issue was not an isolated assault, and ignores the Magistrate's finding that supervisor Mezo expressly condoned the use of force. Moreover, to the extent that respondents rely on the unauthorized nature of their acts, they make a claim not addressed by the Court of Appeals, not presented by the question on which this Court granted certiorari, and, accordingly, not before this Court.

929 F.2d 1014, reversed.

O'CONNOR, J., delivered the opinion of the Court, in which REHNQUIST, C. J., and WHITE, KENNEDY, and SOUTER, JJ., joined, and in which STEVENS, J., joined as to Parts I, II-A, II-B, and II-C. STEVENS, J., filed an opinion concurring in part and concurring in the judgment. BLACKMUN, J., filed an opinion concurring in the judgment. THOMAS, J., filed a dissenting opinion, in which SCALIA, J., joined.

HOPE
V.
PELZER

536 U.S. 730; 122 S. CT. 2508; 153 L. ED. 2D 666 (2002)

CERTIORARI TO THE UNITED STATES COURT OF APPEALS FOR THE ELEV-ENTH CIRCUIT

No. 01–309 Argued April 17, 2002—Decided June 27, 2002

In 1995, petitioner Hope, then an Alabama prison inmate, was twice handcuffed to a hitching post for disruptive conduct. During a 2-hour period in May, he was offered drinking water and a bathroom break every 15 minutes, and his responses were recorded on an activity log. He was handcuffed above shoulder height, and when he tried moving his arms to improve circulation, the handcuffs cut into his wrists, causing pain and discomfort. After an altercation with a guard at his chain gang's work site in June, Hope was subdued, hand-cuffed, placed in leg irons, and transported back to the prison, where he was ordered to take off his shirt, thus exposing himself to the sun, and spent seven hours on the hitching post. While there, he was given one or two water breaks but no bathroom breaks, and a guard taunted him about his thirst. Hope filed a 42 U. S. C. § 1983 suit against three guards. Without deciding whether placing Hope on the hitching post as punishment violated the Eighth Amendment, the Magistrate Judge found that the guards were entitled to qual-ified immunity. The District Court entered summary judgment for respondents, and the Eleventh Circuit affirmed. The latter court answered the constitutional question, find-ing that the hitching post's use for punitive purposes violated the Eighth Amendment. In finding the guards nevertheless entitled to qualified immunity, it concluded that Hope could not show, as required by Circuit prece-dent, that the federal law by which the guards' conduct should be evaluated was established by cases that were "materially similar" to the facts in his own case.

Held: The defense of qualified immunity was precluded at the summary judgment phase.

(a) Hope's allegations, if true, establish an Eighth Amendment violation. Among the "'unnecessary and wanton' inflictions of pain [constituting cruel and unusual pun-ishment forbidden by the Amendment] are those that are 'totally without penologi-cal justification.'" *Rhodes* v. *Chapman,* 452 U. S. 337, 346. This determination is made in the context of prison condi-tions by ascertaining whether an official acted with "deliberate indifference" to the inmates' health or safety, *Hudson* v. *McMillian,* 503 U. S. 1, 8, a state of mind that can be inferred from the fact that the risk of harm is obvious, *Farmer* v. *Brennan,* 511 U.S. 825. The Eighth Amendment violation here is obvious on the facts alleged. Any safety concerns had long since abated by the time Hope was handcuffed to the hitching post, because he had already been subdued, handcuffed, placed in leg irons, and transported back to prison. He was separated from his work squad and not given the opportunity to return. Despite the clear lack of emer-gency, respondents knowingly subjected him to a substantial risk of physical harm, unnecessary pain, unnecessary exposure to the sun, prolonged thirst and taunting, and a deprivation of bathroom breaks that created a risk of particular discomfort and humiliation.

(b) Respondents may nevertheless be shielded from liability for their consti-tutionally impermissible conduct if their actions did not violate "clearly established statutory or constitutional rights of which a reasonable person would have known." *Harlow* v. *Fitzgerald,* 457 U.S. 800, 818. In its assessment, the Eleventh Circuit erred in requiring that the facts of previ-ous cases and Hope's case be "materially similar." Qualified immunity operates to ensure that before they are subjected to suit, officers are on notice that their con-duct is unlawful. Officers sued in a § 1983 civil action have the same fair notice right as do defendants charged under 18 U. S. C. § 242, which makes it a crime for a state official to act willfully and under color of law to deprive a person of con-stitutional rights. This Court's opinion in *United States* v. *Lanier,* 520 U. S. 259, a

§ 242 case, makes clear that officials can be on notice that their conduct violates established law even in novel factual situations. Indeed, the Court expressly rejected a requirement that previous cases be "fundamentally similar." Accordingly, the salient question that the Eleventh Circuit should have asked is whether the state of the law in 1995 gave respondents fair warning that Hope's alleged treatment was unconstitutional.

(c) A reasonable officer would have known that using a hitching post as Hope alleged was unlawful. The obvious cruelty inherent in the practice should have provided respondents with some notice that their conduct was unconstitutional. In addition, binding Circuit precedent should have given them notice. *Gates* v. *Collier,* 501 F.2d 1291, found several forms of corporal punishment impermissible, including handcuffing inmates to fences or cells for long periods, and *Ort* v. *White, 813* F. 2d 318, 324, warned that "physical abuse directed at [a] prisoner *after* he terminate[s] his resistance to authority would constitute an actionable eighth amendment violation." Relevant to the question whether *Ort* provided fair notice is a subsequent Alabama Department of Corrections (ADOC) regulation specifying procedures for using a hitching post, which included allowing an inmate to rejoin his squad when he tells an officer that he is ready to work. If regularly observed, that provision would have made Hope's case less like the kind of punishment *Ort* described as impermissible. But conduct showing that the provision was a sham, or that respondents could ignore it with impunity, provides equally strong support for the conclusion that they were fully aware of their wrongful conduct. The conclusion here is also buttressed by the fact that the Justice Department specifically advised the ADOC of the constitutional infirmity of its practices before the incidents in this case took place.

240 F.3d 975, reversed.

STEVENS, J., delivered the opinion of the Court, in which O'CONNOR, KENNEDY, SOUTER, GINSBURG, and BREYER, JJ., joined. THOMAS, J., filed a dissenting opinion, in which REHNQUIST, C. J., and SCALIA, J., joined.

KINGSLEY
V.
HENDRICKSON

576 U.S. 389; 135 S. CT. 2466; 192 L. ED. 2D 416 (2015)

CERTIORARI TO THE UNITED STATES COURT OF APPEALS FOR THE SEVENTH CIRCUIT

No. 14–6368   Argued April 27, 2015—Decided June 22, 2015

While petitioner Kingsley was awaiting trial in county jail, officers forcibly removed him from his cell when he refused to comply with their instructions. Kingsley filed a complaint in Federal District Court claiming, as relevant here, that two of the officers used excessive force against him in violation of the Fourteenth Amendment's Due Process Clause. At the trial's conclusion, the District Court instructed the jury that Kingsley was required to prove, *inter alia,* that the officers "recklessly disregarded [Kingsley's] safety" and "acted with reckless disregard of [his] rights." The jury found in the officers' favor. On appeal, Kingsley argued that the jury instruction did not adhere to the proper standard for judging a pretrial detainee's excessive force claim, namely, objective unreasonableness. The Seventh Circuit disagreed, holding that the law required a subjective inquiry into the officers' state of mind, *i.e.,* whether the officers actually intended to violate, or recklessly disregarded, Kingsley's rights.

Held:

1. Under 42 U. S. C. §1983, a pretrial detainee must show only that the force purposely or knowingly used against him was objectively unreasonable to prevail on an excessive force claim.

   (a) This determination must be made from the perspective of a reasonable officer on the scene, including what the officer knew at the time, see *Graham* v. *Connor,* 490 U. S. 386, and must account for the "legitimate interests [stemming from the government's] need to manage the facility in which the individual is detained," appropriately deferring to "policies and practices that in th[e] judgment" of jail officials "are needed to preserve internal order and discipline and to maintain institutional security," *Bell* v. *Wolfish,* 441 U. S. 520, 540, 547.

(b) Several considerations lead to this conclusion. An objective standard is consistent with precedent. In *Bell,* for instance, this Court held that a pretrial detainee could prevail on a claim that his due process rights were violated by providing only objective evidence that the challenged governmental action was not rationally related to a legitimate governmental objective or that it was excessive in relation to that purpose. 441 U. S., at 541–543. Cf. *Block* v. *Rutherford,* 468 U. S. 576–586. Experience also suggests that an objective standard is workable. It is consistent with the pattern jury instructions used in several Circuits, and many facilities train officers to interact with detainees as if the officers' conduct is subject to objective reasonableness. Finally, the use of an objective standard adequately protects an officer who acts in good faith, *e.g.,* by acknowledging that judging the reasonableness of the force used from the perspective and with the knowledge of the defendant officer is an appropriate part of the analysis.

(c) None of the cases respondents point to provides significant support for a subjective standard. *Whitley* v. *Albers,* 475 U. S. 312, and *Hudson* v. *McMillian,* 503 U. S. 1, lack relevance in this context because they involved claims brought by convicted prisoners under the Eighth Amendment's Cruel and Unusual Punishment Clause, not claims brought by pretrial detainees under the Fourteenth Amendment's Due Process Clause. And in *County of Sacramento* v. *Lewis,* 523 U.S. 833, a statement indicating the need to show "purpose to cause harm," *id.,* at 854, for due process liability refers not to whether the force intentionally used was excessive, but whether the defendant intended to commit the acts in question, *id.,* at 854, and n. 13. Finally, in *Johnson* v. *Glick,* 481 F. 2d 1028 (CA2), a malicious-and-sadistic-purpose-to-cause-harm factor was not suggested as a *necessary* condition for liability, but as a factor, among others, that might help show that the use of force was excessive.

2. Applying the proper standard, the jury instruction was erroneous. Taken together, the features of that instruction suggested that the jury should weigh respondents' subjective reasons for using force and subjective views about the excessiveness of that force. Respondents' claim that, irrespective of this Court's holding, any error in the instruction was harmless is left to the Seventh Circuit to resolve on remand.

744 F. 3d 443, vacated and remanded.

Breyer, J., delivered the opinion of the Court, in which Kennedy, Ginsburg, Sotomayor, and Kagan, JJ., joined. Scalia, J., filed a dissenting opinion, in which Roberts, C. J., and Thomas, J., joined. Alito, J., filed a dissenting opinion.

Cases Relating to Chapter 12

The Death Penalty

WITHERSPOON
V.
ILLINOIS

391 U.S. 510; 88 S. CT. 1770; 20 L. ED. 2D 776 (1968)

CERTIORARI TO THE SUPREME COURT OF ILLINOIS

No. 1015   Argued April 24, 1968—Decided June 3, 1968

Petitioner was adjudged guilty of murder and the jury fixed his penalty at death. An Illinois statute provided for challenges for cause in murder trials "of any juror who shall, on being examined, state that he has conscientious scruples against capital punishment, or that he is opposed to the same." At petitioner's trial, the prosecution, under that statute, eliminated nearly half the venire of prospective jurors by challenging all who expressed qualms about the death penalty. Most of the veniremen thus challenged for cause were excluded with no effort to find out whether their scruples would invariably compel them to vote against capital punishment. The Illinois Supreme Court denied post-conviction relief.

Held:

1. Neither on the basis of the record in this case nor as a matter of judicial notice of presently available information can it be concluded that the exclusion of jurors opposed to capital punishment results in an unrepresentative jury on the issue of guilt or substantially increases the risk of conviction.

2. Although it has not been shown that this jury was biased with respect to guilt, it is self-evident that, in its distinct role as arbiter of the punishment to be imposed, this jury fell woefully short of that impartiality to which a defendant is entitled under the Sixth and Fourteenth Amendments.

3. A man who opposes the death penalty, no less than one who favors it, can make the discretionary choice of punishment entrusted to him by the State, and can thus obey the oath he takes as a juror; but in a nation where so many have come to oppose capital punishment, a jury from which all such people have been excluded cannot perform the task demanded of it—that of expressing the conscience of the community on the ultimate question of life or death.

4. Just as a State may not entrust the determination of whether a man is innocent or guilty to a tribunal organized to convict, so it may not entrust the determination of whether a man should live or die to a tribunal organized to return a verdict of death, and no sentence of death can be carried out, regardless of when it was imposed, if the *voir dire* testimony indicates that the jury that imposed or recommended that sentence was chosen by excluding veniremen for cause simply because they voiced general objections to capital punishment or expressed conscientious or religious scruples against its infliction.

36 Ill. 2d 471, 224 N.E.2d 259, reversed.

MR. JUSTICE STEWART delivered the opinion of the Court.

GREGG
V.
GEORGIA

428 U.S. 153; 96 S. CT. 2909; 49 L. ED. 2D 859 (1976)

CERTIORARI TO THE SUPREME COURT OF GEORGIA

No. 74–6257 Argued March 31, 1976—Decided July 2, 1976

Petitioner was charged with committing armed robbery and murder on the basis of evidence that he had killed and robbed two men. At the trial stage of Georgia's bifurcated procedure, the jury found petitioner guilty of two counts of armed robbery and two counts of murder. At the penalty stage, the judge instructed the jury that it could recommend either a death sentence or a life prison sentence on each count; that it was free to consider mitigating or aggravating circumstances, if any, as presented by the parties; and that it would not be authorized to consider imposing the death sentence unless it first found beyond a reasonable doubt (1) that the murder was committed while the offender was engaged in the commission of other capital felonies, *viz.*, the armed robberies of the victims; (2) that he committed the murder for the purpose of receiving the victims' money and automobile; or (3) that the murder was "outrageously and wantonly vile, horrible and inhuman" in that it "involved the depravity of [the] mind of the defendant." The jury found the first and second of these aggravating circumstances, and returned a sentence of death. The Georgia Supreme Court affirmed the convictions. After reviewing the trial transcript and record and comparing the evidence and sentence in similar cases, the court upheld the death sentences for the murders, concluding that they had not resulted from prejudice or any other arbitrary factor, and were not excessive or disproportionate to the penalty applied in similar cases, but vacated the armed robbery sentences on the ground, *inter alia*, that the death penalty had rarely been imposed in Georgia for that offense. Petitioner challenges imposition of the death sentence under the Georgia statute as "cruel and unusual" punishment under the Eighth and Fourteenth Amend-

ments. That statute, as amended following *Furman v. Georgia*, 408 U. S. 238 (where this Court held to be violative of those Amendments death sentences imposed under statutes that left juries with untrammeled discretion to impose or withhold the death penalty), retains the death penalty for murder and five other crimes. Guilt or innocence is determined in the first stage of a bifurcated trial, and, if the trial is by jury, the trial judge must charge lesser included offenses when supported by any view of the evidence. Upon a guilty verdict or plea, a presentence hearing is held where the judge or jury hears additional extenuating or mitigating evidence and evidence in aggravation of punishment if made known to the defendant before trial. At least one of 10 specified aggravating circumstances must be found to exist beyond a reasonable doubt and designated in writing before a death sentence can be imposed. In jury cases, the trial judge is bound by the recommended sentence. In its review of a death sentence (which is automatic), the State Supreme Court must consider whether the sentence was influenced by passion, prejudice, or any other arbitrary factor; whether the evidence supports the finding of a statutory aggravating circumstance; and whether the death sentence "is excessive or disproportionate to the penalty imposed in similar cases, considering both the crime and the defendant." If the court affirms the death sentence, it must include in its decision reference to similar cases that it has considered.

Held: The judgment is affirmed.

233 Ga. 117, 210 S.E.2d 659, affirmed.

MR. JUSTICE STEWART, MR. JUSTICE POWELL, and MR. JUSTICE STEVENS concluded that:

1. The punishment of death for the crime of murder does not, under all circumstances, violate the Eighth and Fourteenth Amendments.

    (a) The Eighth Amendment, which has been interpreted in a flexible and dynamic manner to accord with evolving standards of decency, forbids the use of punishment that is "excessive" either because it involves the unnecessary and wanton infliction of pain or because it is grossly disproportionate to the severity of the crime.

(b) Though a legislature may not impose excessive punishment, it is not required to select the least severe penalty possible, and a heavy burden rests upon those attacking its judgment.

(c) The existence of capital punishment was accepted by the Framers of the Constitution, and, for nearly two centuries, this Court has recognized that capital punishment for the crime of murder is not invalid *per se*.

(d) Legislative measures adopted by the people's chosen representatives weigh heavily in ascertaining contemporary standards of decency; and the argument that such standards require that the Eighth Amendment be construed as prohibiting the death penalty has been undercut by the fact that, in the four years since *Furman, supra*, was decided, Congress and at least 35 States have enacted new statutes providing for the death penalty.

(e) Retribution and the possibility of deterrence of capital crimes by prospective offenders are not impermissible considerations for a legislature to weigh in determining whether the death penalty should be imposed, and it cannot be said that Georgia's legislative judgment that such a penalty is necessary in some cases is clearly wrong.

(f) Capital punishment for the crime of murder cannot be viewed as invariably disproportionate to the severity of that crime.

2. The concerns expressed in *Furman* that the death penalty not be imposed arbitrarily or capriciously can be met by a carefully drafted statute that ensures that the sentencing authority is given adequate information and guidance, concerns best met by a system that provides for a bifurcated proceeding at which the sentencing authority is apprised of the information relevant to the imposition of sentence and provided with standards to guide its use of that information.

3. The Georgia statutory system under which petitioner was sentenced to death is constitutional. The new procedures, on their face, satisfy the concerns of *Furman*, since, before the death penalty can be imposed, there must be specific jury findings as to the circumstances of the crime or the character of the defendant, and the State Supreme Court thereafter reviews the comparability of each death sentence with the sentences imposed on similarly situated defendants to ensure that the sentence of death in a particular case is not disproportionate. Petitioner's contentions that the changes in Georgia's sentencing procedures have not removed the elements of arbitrariness and capriciousness condemned by *Furman* are without merit.

(a) The opportunities under the Georgia scheme for affording an individual defendant mercy—whether through the prosecutor's unfettered authority to select those whom he wishes to prosecute for capital offenses and to plea bargain with them; the jury's option to convict a defendant of a lesser included offense; or the fact that the Governor or pardoning authority may commute a death sentence—do not render the Georgia statute unconstitutional.

(b) Petitioner's arguments that certain statutory aggravating circumstances are too broad or vague lack merit, since they need not be given overly broad constructions or have been already narrowed by judicial construction. One such provision was held impermissibly vague by the Georgia Supreme Court. Petitioner's argument that the sentencing procedure allows for arbitrary grants of mercy reflects a misinterpretation of *Furman*, and ignores the reviewing authority of the Georgia Supreme Court to determine whether each death sentence is proportional to other sentences imposed for similar crimes. Petitioner also urges that the scope of the evidence and argument that can be considered at the presentence hearing is too wide, but it is desirable for a jury to have as much information as possible when it makes the sentencing decision.

(c) The Georgia sentencing scheme also provides for automatic sentence review by the Georgia Supreme Court to safeguard against prejudicial or arbitrary factors. In this very case, the court vacated petitioner's death sentence for armed robbery as an excessive penalty.

MR. JUSTICE WHITE, joined by THE CHIEF JUSTICE and MR. JUSTICE REHNQUIST, concluded that:

1. Georgia's new statutory scheme, enacted to overcome the constitutional deficiencies found in *Furman v. Georgia*, 408 U. S. 238, to exist under the old system, not only guides the jury in its exercise of discretion as to whether or not it will impose the death penalty for first-degree murder, but also gives the Georgia Supreme Court the power and imposes the obligation to decide whether in fact the death penalty was being administered for any given class of crime in a discriminatory, standardless, or rare fashion. If that court properly performs the task assigned to it under the Georgia statutes, death sentences imposed for discriminatory reasons or wantonly or freakishly for any given category of crime will be set aside. Petitioner has wholly failed to establish that the Georgia Supreme Court failed properly to perform its task in the instant case, or that it is incapable of performing its task adequately in all cases. Thus, the death penalty may be carried out under the Georgia legislative scheme consistently with the *Furman* decision.

2. Petitioner's argument that the prosecutor's decisions in plea bargaining or in declining to charge capital murder are standardless, and will result in the wanton or freakish imposition of the death penalty condemned in *Furman*, is without merit, for the assumption cannot be made that prosecutors will be motivated in their charging decisions by factors other than the strength of their case and the

likelihood that a jury would impose the death penalty if it convicts; the standards by which prosecutors decide whether to charge a capital felony will be the same as those by which the jury will decide the questions of guilt and sentence.

3. Petitioner's argument that the death penalty, however imposed and for whatever crime, is cruel and unusual punishment is untenable for the reasons stated in MR. JUSTICE WHITE's dissent in *Roberts v. Louisiana, post* at 428 U. S. 350–356.

MR. JUSTICE BLACKMUN concurred in the judgment. *See Furman v. Georgia*, 408 U.S. at 408 U. S. 405–414 (BLACKMUN, J., dissenting), and *id.* at 408 U. S. 375 (BURGER, C.J., dissenting); *id.* at 408 U.S. 414 (POWELL, J., dissenting); *id.* at 408 U. S. 465 (REHNQUIST, J., dissenting).

Judgment of the Court, and opinion of STEWART, POWELL, and STEVENS, JJ., announced by STEWART, J., BURGER, C.J., and REHNQUIST, J., filed a statement concurring in the judgment. WHITE, J., filed an opinion concurring in the judgment, in which BURGER, C.J., and REHNQUIST, J., joined. BLACKMUN, J., filed a statement concurring in the judgment. BRENNAN, J., and MARSHALL, J., filed dissenting opinions.

MCCLESKEY
V.
KEMP

481 U.S. 279; 107 S. CT. 1756; 95 L. ED. 2D 262 (1987)

CERTIORARI TO THE UNITED STATES COURT OF APPEALS FOR THE ELEVENTH CIRCUIT

No. 84–6811   Argued October 15, 1986—Decided April 22, 1987

In 1978, petitioner, a black man, was convicted in a Georgia trial court of armed robbery and murder, arising from the killing of a white police officer during the robbery of a store. Pursuant to Georgia statutes, the jury at the penalty hearing considered the mitigating and aggravating circumstances of petitioner's conduct, and recommended the death penalty on the murder charge. The trial court followed the recommendation, and the Georgia Supreme Court affirmed. After unsuccessfully seeking postconviction relief in state courts, petitioner sought habeas corpus relief in Federal District Court. His petition included a claim that the Georgia capital sentencing process was administered in a racially discriminatory manner in violation of the Eighth and Fourteenth Amendments. In support of the claim, petitioner proffered a statistical study (the Baldus study) that purports to show a disparity in the imposition of the death sentence in Georgia based on the murder victim's race and, to a lesser extent, the defendant's race. The study is based on over 2,000 murder cases that occurred in Georgia during the 1970's, and involves data relating to the victim's race, the defendant's race, and the various combinations of such persons' races. The study indicates that black defendants who killed white victims have the greatest likelihood of receiving the death penalty. Rejecting petitioner's constitutional claims, the court denied his petition insofar as it was based on the Baldus study, and the Court of Appeals affirmed the District Court's decision on this issue. It assumed the validity of the Baldus study, but found the statistics insufficient to demonstrate unconstitutional discrimination in the Fourteenth Amendment context or to show irrationality, arbitrariness, and capriciousness under Eighth Amendment analysis.

Held:

1. The Baldus study does not establish that the administration of the Georgia capital punishment system violates the Equal Protection Clause.

    (a) To prevail under that Clause, petitioner must prove that the decisionmakers in *his* case acted with discriminatory purpose. Petitioner offered no evidence specific to his own case that would support an inference that racial considerations played a part in his sentence, and the Baldus study is insufficient to support an inference that any of the decisionmakers in his case acted with discriminatory purpose.

This Court has accepted statistics as proof of intent to discriminate in the context of a State's selection of the jury venire, and in the context of statutory violations under Title VII of the Civil Rights Act of 1964. However, the nature of the capital sentencing decision and the relationship of the statistics to that decision are fundamentally different from the corresponding elements in the venire selection or Title VII cases. Petitioner's statistical proffer must be viewed in the context of his challenge to decisions at the heart of the State's criminal justice system. Because discretion is essential to the criminal justice process, exceptionally clear proof is required before this Court will infer that the discretion has been abused.

    (b) There is no merit to petitioner's argument that the Baldus study proves that the State has violated the Equal Protection Clause by adopting the capital punishment statute and allowing it to remain in force despite its allegedly discriminatory application. For this claim to prevail, petitioner would have to prove that the Georgia Legislature enacted or maintained the death penalty statute *because* of an anticipated racially discriminatory effect. There is no evidence that the legislature either enacted the statute to further a racially discriminatory purpose or maintained the statute because of the racially disproportionate impact suggested by the Baldus study.

2. Petitioner's argument that the Baldus study demonstrates that the Georgia capital sentencing system violates the Eighth Amendment's prohibition of cruel and unusual punishment must be analyzed in the light of this Court's prior decisions under that Amendment. Decisions since *Furman v. Georgia*, 408 U. S. 238, have identified a constitutionally permissible range of discretion in imposing the death penalty. First, there is a required threshold below which the death penalty cannot be imposed, and the State must

establish rational criteria that narrow the decisionmaker's judgment as to whether the circumstances of a particular defendant's case meet the threshold. Second, States cannot limit the sentencer's consideration of any relevant circumstance that could cause it to decline to impose the death penalty. In this respect, the State cannot channel the sentencer's discretion, but must allow it to consider any relevant information offered by the defendant.

3. The Baldus study does not demonstrate that the Georgia capital sentencing system violates the Eighth Amendment.

(a) Petitioner cannot successfully argue that the sentence in his case is disproportionate to the sentences in other murder cases. On the one hand, he cannot base a constitutional claim on an argument that his case differs from other cases in which defendants *did* receive the death penalty. The Georgia Supreme Court found that his death sentence was not disproportionate to other death sentences imposed in the State. On the other hand, absent a showing that the Georgia capital punishment system operates in an arbitrary and capricious manner, petitioner cannot prove a constitutional violation by demonstrating that other defendants who may be similarly situated did *not* receive the death penalty. The opportunities for discretionary leniency under state law do not render the capital sentences imposed arbitrary and capricious. Because petitioner's sentence was imposed under Georgia sentencing procedures that focus discretion "on the particularized nature of the crime and the particularized characteristics of the individual defendant," it may be presumed that his death sentence was not "wantonly and freakishly" imposed, and thus that the sentence is not disproportionate within any recognized meaning under the Eighth Amendment. *Gregg v. Georgia*, 428 U. S. 153, 428 U. S. 206, 428 U. S. 207.

(b) There is no merit to the contention that the Baldus study shows that Georgia's capital punishment system is arbitrary and capricious in *application*. The statistics do not *prove* that race enters into any capital sentencing decisions or that race was a factor in petitioner's case. The likelihood of racial prejudice allegedly shown by the study does not constitute the constitutional measure of an unacceptable risk of racial prejudice. The inherent lack of predictability of jury decisions does not justify their condemnation. On the contrary, it is the jury's function to make the difficult and uniquely human judgments that defy codification and that build discretion, equity, and flexibility into the legal system.

(c) At most, the Baldus study indicates a discrepancy that appears to correlate with race, but this discrepancy does not constitute a major systemic defect. Any mode for determining guilt or punishment has its weaknesses and the potential for misuse. Despite such imperfections, constitutional guarantees are met when the mode for determining guilt or punishment has been surrounded with safeguards to make it as fair as possible.

4. Petitioner's claim, taken to its logical conclusion, throws into serious question the principles that underlie the entire criminal justice system. His claim easily could be extended to apply to other types of penalties and to claims based on unexplained discrepancies correlating to membership in other minority groups and even to gender. The Constitution does not require that a State eliminate any demonstrable disparity that correlates with a potentially irrelevant factor in order to operate a criminal justice system that includes capital punishment. Petitioner's arguments are best presented to the legislative bodies, not the courts.

753 F.2d 877, affirmed.

POWELL, J., delivered the opinion of the Court, in which REHNQUIST, C.J., and WHITE, O'CONNOR, and SCALIA, JJ., joined. BRENNAN, J., filed a dissenting opinion in which MARSHALL, J., joined, and in all but Part I of which BLACKMUN and STEVENS, JJ., joined. BLACK-MUN, J., filed a dissenting opinion in which MARSHALL and STEVENS, JJ., joined, and in all but Part IV-B of which BRENNAN, J., joined. STE-VENS, J., filed a dissenting opinion in which BLACKMUN, J., joined.

ATKINS
V.
VIRGINIA

536 U.S. 304; 122 S. CT. 2242; 153 L. ED. 2D 335 (2002)

CERTIORARI TO THE SUPREME COURT OF VIRGINIA

No. 00–8452   Argued February 20, 2002—Decided June 20, 2002

Petitioner Atkins was convicted of capital murder and related crimes by a Virginia jury and sentenced to death. Affirming, the Virginia Supreme Court relied on *Penry v. Lynaugh*, 492 U. S. 302, in rejecting Atkins' contention that he could not be sentenced to death because he is mentally retarded.

Held: Executions of mentally retarded criminals are "cruel and unusual punishments" prohibited by the Eighth Amendment.

(a) A punishment is "excessive," and there-fore prohibited by the Amendment, if it is not graduated and proportioned to the offense. *E. g., Weems v. United States*, 217 U. S. 349, 367. An excessiveness claim is judged by currently prevailing standards of decency. *Trop v. Dulles*, 356 U. S. 86, 100–101. Proportionality review under such evolving standards should be informed by objective factors to the max-imum possible extent, see, *e. g., Har-melin v. Michigan*, 501 U. S. 957, 1000, the clearest and most reliable of which is the legislation enacted by the country's legislatures, *Penry*, 492 U. S., at 331. In addition to objective evidence, the Con-stitution contemplates that this Court will bring its own judgment to bear by asking whether there is reason to agree or dis-agree with the judgment reached by the citizenry and its legislators,

(b) Much has changed since *Penry's* con-clusion that the two state statutes then existing that prohibited such executions, even when added to the 14 States that had rejected capital punishment completely, did not provide sufficient evidence of a consensus. 492 U. S., at 334. Subse-quently, a significant number of States have concluded that death is not a suit-able punishment for a mentally retarded criminal, and similar bills have passed at least one house in other States. It is not so much the number of these States that is significant, but the consistency of the direction of change. Given that anticrime legislation is far more popular than legislation protecting violent crimi-nals, the large number of States prohib-iting the execution of mentally retarded persons (and the complete absence of legislation reinstating such executions) provides powerful evidence that today society views mentally retarded offend-ers as categorically less culpable than the average criminal. The evidence carries even greater force when it is noted that the legislatures addressing the issue have voted overwhelmingly in favor of the pro-hibition. Moreover, even in States allow-ing the execution of mentally retarded offenders, the practice is uncommon.

(c) An independent evaluation of the issue reveals no reason for the Court to dis-agree with the legislative consensus. Clinical definitions of mental retarda-tion require not only subaverage intel-lectual functioning, but also significant limitations in adaptive skills. Mentally retarded persons frequently know the difference between right and wrong and are competent to stand trial, but, by definition, they have diminished capaci-ties to understand and process informa-tion, to communicate, to abstract from mistakes and learn from experience, to engage in logical reasoning, to control impulses, and to understand others' reac-tions. Their deficiencies do not warrant an exemption from criminal sanctions, but diminish their personal culpability. In light of these deficiencies, the Court's death penalty jurisprudence provides two reasons to agree with the legislative consensus. First, there is a serious question whether either justification underpinning the death penalty-retribution and deterrence of capital crimes-applies to mentally retarded offenders. As to retribution, the severity of the appropriate punishment necessarily depends on the offender's culpability. If the culpability of the average murderer is insufficient to justify imposition of death, see *Godfrey v. Georgia*, 446 U. S. 420, 433, the lesser culpability of the mentally retarded offender surely does not merit that form of retribution. As to deterrence, the same cognitive and behavioral impairments that make mentally retarded defendants less morally culpable also make it less likely that they can process the information of the possibility of execution as a penalty and, as a result, control their conduct based upon that information. Nor will exempting the mentally retarded from execution lessen the death penalty's deterrent effect with respect to offenders who are not mentally retarded. Second, mentally retarded defendants in the aggregate face a special risk of wrongful execution because of the possibility that they will unwittingly confess to crimes they did not commit, their lesser ability to give their counsel meaningful assistance, and the facts that they are typically poor witnesses and that their demeanor may create an unwarranted impression of lack of remorse for their crimes.

260 Va. 375, 534 S. E. 2d 312, reversed and remanded.

STEVENS, J., delivered the opinion of the Court, in which O'CONNOR, KENNEDY, SOUTER, GINSBURG, and BREYER, JJ., joined. REHNQUIST, C. J., filed a dissenting opinion, in which SCALIA and THOMAS, JJ., joined, *post*, p. 321. SCALIA, J., filed a dissenting opinion, in which REHNQUIST, C. J., and THOMAS, J., joined.

KENNEDY
V.
LOUISIANA

554 U.S. 407; 128 S. CT. 2641; 171 L. ED. 2D 525 (2008)

CERTIORARI TO THE SUPREME COURT OF LOUISIANA

No. 07–343   Argued April 16, 2008— Decided June 25, 2008

Louisiana charged petitioner with the aggravated rape of his then-8-year-old stepdaughter. He was convicted and sentenced to death under a state statute authorizing capital punishment for the rape of a child under 12. The State Supreme Court affirmed, rejecting petitioner's reliance on *Coker* v. *Georgia*, 433 U. S. 584, which barred the use of the death penalty as punishment for the rape of an adult woman but left open the question which, if any, other nonhomicide crimes can be punished by death consistent with the Eighth Amendment. Reasoning that children are a class in need of special protection, the state court held child rape to be unique in terms of the harm it inflicts upon the victim and society and concluded that, short of first-degree murder, there is no crime more deserving of death. The court acknowledged that petitioner would be the first person executed since the state law was amended to authorize the death penalty for child rape in 1995, and that Louisiana is in the minority of jurisdictions authorizing death for that crime. However, emphasizing that four more States had capitalized child rape since 1995 and at least eight others had authorized death for other nonhomicide crimes, as well as that, under *Roper* v. *Simmons*, 543 U. S. 551, and *Atkins* v. *Virginia*, 536 U. S. 304, it is the direction of change rather than the numerical count that is significant, the court held petitioner's death sentence to be constitutional.

Held: The Eighth Amendment bars Louisiana from imposing the death penalty for the rape of a child where the crime did not result, and was not intended to result, in the victim's death.

1.   The Amendment's Cruel and Unusual Punishment Clause "draw[s] its meaning

from the evolving standards of decency that mark the progress of a maturing society." *Trop v. Dulles*, 356 U.S. 86, 101. The standard for extreme cruelty "itself remains the same, but its applicability must change as the basic mores of society change." *Furman v. Georgia*, 408 U.S. 238, 382. Under the precept of justice that punishment is to be graduated and proportioned to the crime, informed by evolving standards, capital punishment must "be limited to those offenders who commit 'a narrow category of the most serious crimes' and whose extreme culpability makes them 'the most deserving of execution.'" *Roper, supra*, at 568. Applying this principle, the Court held in *Roper* and *Atkins* that the execution of juveniles and mentally retarded persons violates the Eighth Amendment because the offender has a diminished personal responsibility for the crime. The Court also has found the death penalty disproportionate to the crime itself where the crime did not result, or was not intended to result, in the victim's death. See, *e.g., Coker, supra; Enmund v. Florida*, 458 U.S. 782. In making its determination, the Court is guided by "objective indicia of society's standards, as expressed in legislative enactments and state practice with respect to executions." *Roper, supra*, at 563. Consensus is not dispositive, however. Whether the death penalty is disproportionate to the crime also depends on the standards elaborated by controlling precedents and on the Court's own understanding and interpretation of the Eighth Amendment's text, history, meaning, and purpose.

2.   A review of the authorities informed by contemporary norms, including the history of the death penalty for this and other nonhomicide crimes, current state statutes and new enactments, and the number of executions since 1964, demonstrates a national consensus against capital punishment for the crime of child rape.

(a)   The Court follows the approach of cases in which objective indicia of consensus demonstrated an opinion against the death penalty for juve-

niles, see *Roper, supra*, mentally retarded offenders, see *Atkins, supra*, and vicarious felony murderers, see *Enmund, supra*. Thirty-seven jurisdictions—36 States plus the Federal Government—currently impose capital punishment, but only six States authorize it for child rape. In 45 jurisdictions, by contrast, petitioner could not be executed for child rape of any kind. That number surpasses the 30 States in *Atkins* and *Roper* and the 42 in *Enmund* that prohibited the death penalty under the circumstances those cases considered.

(b)   Respondent's argument that *Coker*'s general discussion contrasting murder and rape, 433 U. S., at 598, has been interpreted too expansively, leading some States to conclude that *Coker* applies to child rape when in fact it does not, is unsound. *Coker*'s holding was narrower than some of its language read in isolation indicates. The *Coker* plurality framed the question as whether, "with respect to rape of an adult woman," the death penalty is disproportionate punishment, *id.*, at 592, and it repeated the phrase "adult woman" or "adult female" eight times in discussing the crime or the victim. The distinction between adult and child rape was not merely rhetorical; it was central to *Coker*'s reasoning, including its analysis of legislative consensus. See, *e.g., id.*, at 595–596. There is little evidence to support respondent's contention that state legislatures have understood *Coker* to state a broad rule that covers minor victims, and state courts have uniformly concluded that *Coker* did not address that crime. Accordingly, the small number of States that have enacted the death penalty for child rape is relevant to determining whether there is a consensus against capital punishment for the rape of a child.

(c)   A consistent direction of change in support of the death penalty for child rape might counterbalance an otherwise weak demonstration of consensus, see, *e.g.*, *Atkins,* 536 U. S., at 315, but no showing of consistent change has been made here. That five States may have had pending legislation authorizing death for child rape is not dispositive because it is not this Court's practice, nor is it sound, to find contemporary norms based on legislation proposed but not yet enacted. Indeed, since the parties submitted their briefs, the legislation in at least two of the five States has failed. Further, evidence that, in the last 13 years, six new death penalty statutes have been enacted, three in the last two years, is not as significant as the data in *Atkins*, where 18 States between 1986 and 2001 had enacted legislation prohibiting the execution of mentally retarded persons. See *id.*, at 314–315. Respondent argues that this case is like *Roper* because, there, only five States had shifted their positions between 1989 and 2005, one less State than here. See 543 U. S., at 565. But the *Roper* Court emphasized that the slow pace of abolition was counterbalanced by the total number of States that had recognized the impropriety of executing juvenile offenders. See *id.,* at 566–567. Here, the fact that only six States have made child rape a capital offense is not an indication of a trend or change in direction comparable to the one in *Roper.* The evidence bears a closer resemblance to that in *Enmund*, where the Court found a national consensus against death for vicarious felony murder despite eight jurisdictions having authorized it. See 458 U. S., at 789, 792.

(d) Execution statistics also confirm that there is a social consensus against the death penalty for child rape. Nine States have permitted capital punishment for adult or child rape for some length of time between the Court's 1972 *Furman* decision and today; yet no individual has been executed for the rape of an adult or child since 1964, and no execution for any other nonhomicide offense has been conducted since 1963. Louisiana is the only State since 1964 that has sentenced an individual to death for child rape, and petitioner and another man so sentenced are the only individuals now on death row in the United States for nonhomicide offenses.

3. Informed by its own precedents and its understanding of the Constitution and the rights it secures, the Court concludes, in its independent judgment, that the death penalty is not a proportional punishment for the crime of child rape.

(a) The Court's own judgment should be brought to bear on the death penalty's acceptability under the Eighth Amendment. See, *e.g.*, *Coker, supra,* at 597. Rape's permanent and devastating impact on a child suggests moral grounds for questioning a rule barring capital punishment simply because the crime did not result in the victim's death, but it does not follow that death is a proportionate penalty for child rape. The constitutional prohibition against excessive or cruel and unusual punishments mandates that punishment "be exercised within the limits of civilized standards." *Trop,* 356 U. S., at 99–100. Evolving standards of decency counsel the Court to be most hesitant before allowing extension of the death penalty, especially where no life was taken in the commission of the crime. See, *e.g., Coker,* 433 U. S., at 597–598; *Enmund*, 458 U. S., at 797. Consistent with those evolving standards and the teachings of its precedents, the Court concludes that there is a distinction between intentional first-degree murder on the one hand and nonhomicide crimes against individuals, even including child rape, on the other. The latter crimes may be devastating in their harm, as here, but "in terms of moral depravity and of the injury to the person and to the public," they cannot compare to murder in their "severity and irrevocability," *id,* at 598. The Court finds significant the substantial number of executions that would be allowed for child rape under respondent's approach. Although narrowing aggravators might be used to ensure the death penalty's restrained application in this context, as they are in the context of capital murder, all such standards have the potential to result in some inconsistency of application. The Court, for example, has acknowledged that the requirement of general rules to ensure consistency of treatment, see, *e.g., Godfrey* v. *Georgia*, 446 U. S. 420, and the insistence that capital sentencing be individualized, see, *e.g., Woodson* v. *North Carolina*, 428 U. S. 280, have resulted in tension and imprecision. This approach might be sound with respect to capital murder but it should not be introduced into the justice system where death has not occurred. The Court has spent more than 32 years developing a foundational jurisprudence for capital murder to guide the States and juries in imposing the death penalty. Beginning the same process for crimes for which no one has been executed in more than 40 years would require experimentation in an area where a failed experiment would result in the execution of individuals undeserving of death.

(b) The Court's decision is consistent with the justifications offered for the death penalty, retribution and deterrence, see, *e.g., Gregg* v. *Georgia,* 428 U. S. 153, 183. Among the factors for determining whether retribution is served, the Court must look to whether the death penalty balances the wrong to the victim in nonhomicide cases. Cf. *Roper, supra,* at 571. It is not at all evident that the child rape victim's hurt is lessened when the law permits the perpetrator's death, given that capital cases require a long-term commitment by those testifying for the prosecution. Society's desire to inflict death for child rape by enlisting the child victim to assist it over the course of years in asking for capital punishment forces a moral choice on the child, who is not of mature age to make that choice. There are also relevant systemic concerns in prosecuting child rape, including the documented problem of unreliable, induced, and even imagined child testimony, which creates a "special risk of wrongful execution" in some cases. Cf. *Atkins, supra,* at 321. As to deterrence, the evidence suggests that the death penalty may not result in more effective enforcement, but may add to the risk of nonreporting of child rape out of fear of negative consequences for the perpetrator, especially if he is a family member. And, by in effect making the punishment for child rape and murder equivalent, a State may remove a strong incentive for the rapist not to kill his victim.

4. The concern that the Court's holding will effectively block further development of a consensus favoring the death penalty for child rape overlooks the principle that the Eighth Amendment is defined by "the evolving standards of decency that mark the progress of a maturing society," *Trop,* 356 U. S., at 101. Confirmed by the Court's repeated, consistent rulings, this principle requires that resort to capital punishment be restrained, limited in its instances of application, and reserved for the worst of crimes, those that, in the case of crimes against individuals, take the victim's life.

957 So. 2d 757, reversed and remanded.
KENNEDY, J., delivered the opinion of the Court, in which STEVENS, SOUTER, GINSBURG, and BREYER, JJ., joined. ALITO, J., filed a dissenting opinion, in which ROBERTS, C. J., and SCALIA and THOMAS, JJ., joined.

RYAN, DIRECTOR, ARIZONA DEPARTMENT OF CORRECTIONS
V.
VALENCIA GONZALES

568 U.S. 57; 133 S. CT. 696; 184 L. ED. 2D 528 (2013)

CERTIORARI TO THE UNITED STATES COURT OF APPEALS FOR THE NINTH CIRCUIT

No. 10–930 Argued October 9, 2012—Decided January 8, 2013

Respondent Valencia Gonzales, a death row inmate in Arizona, sought federal habeas relief. His counsel moved to stay the proceedings, contending that Gonzales' mental incompetence prevented him from rationally communicating with or assisting counsel, and that Gonzales was thus entitled to a stay because, under the Ninth Circuit's Rohan decision, what is now 18 U. S. C. §3599(a)(2) requires a stay when a petitioner is adjudged incompetent. The District Court denied a stay, finding that the claims before it were record based or resolvable as a matter of law and thus would not benefit from Gonzales' input. Gonzales thereafter sought a writ of mandamus in the Ninth Circuit. Applying Rohan and its recent decision in Nash—which gave habeas petitioners a right to competence even on record-based appeals—the court granted the writ, concluding that §3599 gave Gonzales the right to a stay pending a competency determination.

Respondent Sean Carter, a death row inmate in Ohio, initiated federal habeas proceedings but eventually moved for a competency determination and stay of the proceedings. The District Court granted the motion and found Carter incompetent to assist counsel. Applying the Ninth Circuit's Rohan test, it determined that Carter's assistance was required to develop four of his exhausted claims. It thus dismissed his habeas petition without prejudice and prospectively tolled the statute of limitations. On appeal, the Sixth Circuit, relying in part on Rees v. Peyton, 384 U. S. 312 (Rees I), located a statutory right to competence in 18 U. S. C. §4241, and found that a court could employ that provision whenever a capital habeas petitioner seeks to forgo his petition. It thus ordered that Carter's petition be stayed indefinitely with respect to any claims requiring his assistance.

Held:

1. Section 3599 does not provide a state prisoner a right to suspension of his federal habeas proceedings when he is adjudged incompetent.

   (a) The assertion of such a right lacks any basis in the provision's text. Section 3599 guarantees federal habeas petitioners on death row the right to federally funded counsel, §3599(a)(2), and sets out various requirements that appointed counsel must meet, §§3599(b)—(e), but it does not direct district courts to stay proceedings when petitioners are found incompetent. The assertion is also difficult to square with the Court's constitutional precedents. If the Sixth Amendment right carried with it an implied right to competence, the right to competence at trial would flow from that Amendment, not from the right to due process, see Cooper v. Oklahoma, 517 U. S. 348. But while the benefits flowing from the right to counsel at trial could be affected if an incompetent defendant is unable to communicate with his attorney, this Court has never said that the right to competence derives from the right to counsel. And the Court will not assume or infer that Congress intended to depart from such precedent and locate a right to competence in federal habeas proceedings within the right to counsel. See Merck & Co. v. Reynolds, 559 U. S. ___, ___.

   (b) The Ninth Circuit identified its rule in Rohan, concluding there that a petitioner's mental incompetency could "eviscerate the statutory right to counsel" in federal habeas proceedings. But given the backward-looking, record-based nature of §2254 proceedings, counsel can generally provide effective representation to a habeas petitioner regardless of the petitioner's competence. Rees I, supra, Rees v. Peyton, 386 U. S. 989, and Rees v. Superintendent of the Va. State Penitentiary, 516 U. S 802, which involved an incompetent death row inmate's attempt to withdraw his certiorari petition, offer no support for federal habeas petitioners seeking to stay district court proceedings or for the Ninth Circuit's opinions in Rohan, Nash, or this case. The Ninth Circuit's interpretation is also not supported by McFarland v. Scott, 512 U. S. 849, in which this Court held that a district court could stay an execution after a capital prisoner had invoked his right to counsel but before he had filed his habeas petition. In contrast, Gonzales is seeking to stay the District Court's proceedings, and he sought a stay more than six years after initiating his habeas petition, certainly ample time for his attorney to research and present the claims.

2. Section 4241 also does not provide a statutory right to competence during federal habeas proceedings. The Sixth Circuit based its conclusion largely on a misreading of Rees I, which did not recognize such a right. Moreover, §4241 does not even apply to habeas proceedings. By its terms, it applies only to trial proceedings prior to sentencing and "at any time after the commencement of probation or supervised release." Federal habeas proceedings, however, commence after sentencing, and federal habeas petitioners are incarcerated, not on probation. Furthermore, §4241, like the rest of Title 18 generally, applies exclusively to federal defendants, not to state prisoners like Carter. Finally, §4241(a) authorizes a district court to grant a motion for a competency determination if there is reasonable cause to believe that the defendant's mental incompetence renders him "unable to understand ... the proceedings against him or to assist properly in his defense," while a §2254 habeas proceeding is a civil action against a state-prison warden, in which the petitioner collaterally attacks his conviction in an earlier state trial.

3. For purposes of resolving these cases, it

is sufficient to address the outer limits of the district court's discretion to issue stays; it is unnecessary to determine the precise contours of that discretion. In Gonzales' case, the District Court did not abuse its discretion in denying a stay after finding that Gonzales' claims were all record based or resolvable as a matter of law, regardless of his competence. Review of a petitioner's record-based claims subject to §2254(d) is limited to the record before the state court that heard the case on the merits. Any evidence that Gonzales might have would be inadmissible. In Carter's case, three of his claims do not warrant a stay because they were adjudicated on the merits in state postconviction proceedings and thus subject to review under §2254(d). Thus, extrarecord evidence that he might have concerning these claims would be inadmissible. It is unclear from the record whether he exhausted his fourth claim. If it was exhausted, it too would be record based. But even if it was both unexhausted and not procedurally defaulted, an indefinite stay would be inappropriate, since such a stay would permit petitioners to "frustrate [the Antiterrorism and Effective Death Penalty Act of 1996's] goal of finality by dragging out indefinitely their federal habeas review." Rhines v. Weber, 544 U. S. 269–278.

623 F. 3d 1242, No. 10–930, reversed; 644 F. 3d 329, No. 11–218, reversed and remanded.

THOMAS, J., delivered the opinion for a unanimous Court.

HALL
V.
FLORIDA

572 U.S. 701; 134 S. CT. 1986; 188 L. ED. 2D 1007 (2014)

CERTIORARI TO THE SUPREME COURT OF FLORIDA

No. 12–10882 Argued March 3, 2014—Decided May 27, 2014

After this Court held that the Eighth and Fourteenth Amendments forbid the execution of persons with intellectual disability, see Atkins v. Virginia, 536 U. S. 304, Hall asked a Florida state court to vacate his sentence, presenting evidence that included an IQ test score of 71. The court denied his motion, determining that a Florida statute mandated that he show an IQ score of 70 or below before being permitted to present any additional intellectual disability evidence. The State Supreme Court rejected Hall's appeal, finding the State's 70-point threshold constitutional.

Held: The State's threshold requirement, as interpreted by the Florida Supreme Court, is unconstitutional.

(a) The Eighth Amendment, which "reaffirms the duty of the government to respect the dignity of all persons," Roper v. Simmons, 543 U. S. 551, prohibits the execution of persons with intellectual disability. No legitimate penological purpose is served by executing the intellectually disabled. Atkins, 563 U. S., at 317, 320. Prohibiting such executions also protects the integrity of the trial process for individuals who face "a special risk of wrongful execution" because they are more likely to give false confessions, are often poor witnesses, and are less able to give meaningful assistance to their counsel. Id., at 320–321. In determining whether Florida's intellectual disability definition implements these principles and Atkins' holding, it is proper to consider the psychiatric and professional studies that elaborate on the purpose and meaning of IQ scores and how the scores relate to Atkins, and to consider how the several States have implemented Atkins.

(b) Florida's rule disregards established medical practice. On its face, Florida's statute could be consistent with the views of the medical community discussed in Atkins and with the conclusions reached here. It defines intellectual disability as the existence of concurrent deficits in intellectual and adaptive functioning, long the defining characteristic of intellectual disability. See Atkins, supra, at 308. And nothing in the statute precludes Florida from considering an IQ test's standard error of measurement

(SEM), a statistical fact reflecting the test's inherent imprecision and acknowledging that an individual score is best understood as a range, e.g., five points on either side of the recorded score. As interpreted by the Florida Supreme Court, however, Florida's rule disregards established medical practice in two interrelated ways: It takes an IQ score as final and conclusive evidence of a defendant's intellectual capacity, when experts would consider other evidence; and it relies on a purportedly scientific measurement of a defendant's abilities, while refusing to recognize that measurement's inherent imprecision. While professionals have long agreed that IQ test scores should be read as a range, Florida uses the test score as a fixed number, thus barring further consideration of other relevant evidence, e.g., deficits in adaptive functioning, including evidence of past performance, environment, and upbringing.

(c) The rejection of a strict 70-point cutoff in the vast majority of States and a "consistency in the trend," Roper, supra, at 567, toward recognizing the SEM provide strong evidence of consensus that society does not regard this strict cutoff as proper or humane. At most, nine States mandate a strict IQ score cutoff at 70. Thus, in 41 States, an individual in Hall's position would not be deemed automatically eligible for the death penalty. The direction of change has been consistent. Since Atkins, many States have passed legislation to comply with the constitutional requirement that persons with intellectual disability not be executed. Two of those States appear to set a strict cutoff at 70, but at least 11 others have either abolished the death penalty or passed legislation allowing defendants to present additional intellectual disability evidence when their IQ score is above 70. Every state legislature, save one, to have considered the issue after Atkins and whose law has been interpreted by its courts has taken a position contrary to Florida's.

(d) Atkins acknowledges the inherent error in IQ testing and provides substantial guidance on the definition of intellectual disability. The States play a critical role in advancing the protections of Atkins and providing this Court with an understanding of how intellectual disability should be measured and assessed, but Atkins did not give them unfettered discretion to define the full scope of the constitutional protection. Clinical definitions for intellectual disability which, by their express terms, rejected a strict IQ test score cutoff at 70, and which have long included the SEM, were a fundamental premise of Atkins. See 536 U. S., at 309, nn. 3, 5. A fleeting mention of Florida in a citation listing States that had outlawed the execution of the intellectually disabled, id., at 315, did not signal the Atkins Court's approval of the State's current understanding of its law, which had not yet been interpreted by the Florida Supreme Court to require a strict 70-point cutoff.

(e) When a defendant's IQ test score falls within the test's acknowledged and inherent margin of error, the defendant must be able to present additional evidence of intellectual disability, including testimony regarding adaptive deficits. This legal determination of intellectual disability is distinct from a medical diagnosis but is informed by the medical community's diagnostic framework, which is of particular help here, where no alternative intellectual disability definition is presented, and where this Court and the States have placed substantial reliance on the medical profession's expertise. Pp. 19–22.

109 So. 3d 704, reversed and remanded.

Kennedy, J., delivered the opinion of the Court, in which Ginsburg, Breyer, Sotomayor, and Kagan, JJ., joined. Alito, J., filed a dissenting opinion, in which Roberts, C. J., and Scalia and Thomas, JJ., joined.

Cases Relating to Chapter 13

Parole and Probation

MORRISSEY
V.
BREWER

408 U.S. 471; 92 S. CT. 2593; 33 L. ED. 2D 484 (1972)

CERTIORARI TO THE UNITED STATES COURT OF APPEALS FOR THE EIGHTH CIRCUIT

No. 71–5103   Argued April 11, 1972— Decided June 29, 1972

Petitioners in these habeas corpus proceedings claimed that their paroles were revoked without a hearing and that they were thereby deprived of due process. The Court of Appeals, in affirming the District Court's denial of relief, reasoned that, under controlling authorities, parole is only "a correctional device authorizing service of sentence outside a penitentiary," and concluded that a parolee, who is still "in custody," is not entitled to a full adversary hearing such as would be mandated in a criminal proceeding.

Held:

1. Though parole revocation does not call for the full panoply of rights due a defendant in a criminal proceeding, a parolee's liberty involves significant values within the protection of the Due Process Clause of the Fourteenth Amendment, and termination of that liberty requires an informal hearing to give assurance that the finding of a parole violation is based on verified facts to support the revocation.

2. Due process requires a reasonably prompt informal inquiry conducted by an impartial hearing officer near the place of the alleged parole violation or arrest to determine if there is reasonable ground to believe that the arrested parolee has violated a parole condition. The parolee should receive prior notice of the inquiry, its purpose, and the alleged violations. The parolee may present relevant information and (absent security considerations) question adverse informants. The hearing officer shall digest the evidence on probable cause and state the reasons for holding the parolee for the parole board's decision.

3. At the revocation hearing, which must be conducted reasonably soon after the parolee's arrest, minimum due process requirements are: (a) written notice of the claimed violations of parole; (b) disclosure to the parolee of evidence against him; (c) opportunity to be heard in person and to present witnesses and documentary evidence; (d) the right to confront and cross-examine adverse witnesses (unless the hearing officer specifically finds good cause for not allowing confrontation); (e) a "neutral and detached" hearing body such as a traditional parole board, members of which need not be judicial officers or lawyers; and (f) a written statement by the factfinders as to the evidence relied on and reasons for revoking parole.

443 F.2d 942, reversed and remanded.

BURGER, C.J., delivered the opinion of the Court, in which STEWART, WHITE, BLACKMUN, POWELL

481

and REHNQUIST, JJ., joined. BREN-
NAN, J., filed an opinion concurring in
the result, in which MARSHALL, J.,
joined. DOUGLAS, J., filed an opinion
dissenting in part.

GAGNON
V.
SCARPELLI

411 U.S. 778; 93 S. CT. 1756; 36 L. ED. 2D 656 (1973)

CERTIORARI TO THE UNITED STATES
COURT OF APPEALS FOR THE SEVENTH
CIRCUIT

No. 71–1225   Argued January 9, 1973—
Decided May 14, 1973

Respondent, a felony probationer, was
arrested after committing a burglary. He admitted involvement in the crime, but later claimed
that the admission was made under duress,
and was false. The probation of respondent,
who was not represented by an attorney, was
revoked without a hearing. After filing a habeas
corpus petition, he was paroled. The District
Court concluded that revocation of probation
without hearing and counsel was a denial of
due process. The Court of Appeals affirmed.

Held:

1. Due process mandates preliminary and
    final revocation hearings in the case of a
    probationer under the same conditions as
    are specified in *Morrissey v. Brewer*, 408
    U. S. 471, in the case of a parolee.
2. The body conducting the hearings should
    decide in each individual case whether
    due process requires that an indigent
    probationer or parolee be represented by
    counsel. Though the State is not consti-
    tutionally obliged to provide counsel in
    all cases, it should do so where the indi-
    gent probationer or parolee may have
    difficulty in presenting his version of
    disputed facts without the examination
    or cross-examination of witnesses or the
    presentation of complicated documentary

evidence. Presumptively, counsel should
be provided where, after being informed
of his right, the probationer or parolee
requests counsel, based on a timely and
colorable claim that he has not committed
the alleged violation or, if the violation is
a matter of public record or uncontested,
there are substantial reasons in justification or mitigation that make revocation
inappropriate.

3. In every case where a request for counsel
    is refused, the grounds for refusal should
    be stated succinctly in the record.

454 F.2d 416, affirmed in part, reversed in
part, and remanded.
POWELL, J., delivered the opinion of
the Court, in which BURGER, C.J.,
and BRENNAN, STEWART, WHITE,
MARSHALL, BLACKMUN, and
REHNQUIST, JJ., joined. DOUGLAS,
J., filed a statement dissenting in part.

GREENHOLTZ
V.
INMATES OF THE NEBRASKA
PENAL AND CORRECTION
COMPLEX

442 U.S. 1; 99 S. CT. 2100; 60 L. ED. 2D 668 (1979)

CERTIORARI TO THE UNITED STATES
COURT OF APPEALS FOR THE EIGHTH
CIRCUIT

No. 78–201   Argued January 17, 1979—
Decided May 29, 1979

Under Nebraska statutes, a prison inmate
becomes eligible for discretionary parole
when his minimum term, less good-time
credits, has been served. Hearings are conducted in two stages to determine whether
to grant or deny parole: initial review hearings and final parole hearings. Initial review
hearings must be held at least once a year for
every inmate. At the first stage, the Board of
Parole examines the inmate's preconfinement
and postconfinement record, and holds an
informal hearing; the Board interviews the

inmate and considers any letters or statements presented in support of a claim for release. If the Board determines that the inmate is not yet a good risk for release, it denies parole, stating why release was deferred. If the Board determines that the inmate is a likely candidate for release, a final hearing is scheduled, at which the inmate may present evidence, call witnesses, and be represented by counsel. A written statement of the reasons is given if parole is denied. One section of the statutes (§ 83–1,114(1)) provides that the Board "shall" order an inmate's release unless it concludes that his release should be deferred for at least one of four specified reasons. Respondent inmates, who had been denied parole, brought a class action in Federal District Court, which upheld their claim that the Board's procedures denied them procedural due process. The Court of Appeals, agreeing, held that the inmates had the same kind of constitutionally protected "conditional liberty" interest as was recognized in *Morrissey v. Brewer*, 408 U. S. 471, also found a statutorily defined, protectible interest in § 83–1, 114(1), and required, *inter alia*, that a formal hearing be held for every inmate eligible for parole and that every adverse parole decision include a statement of the evidence relied upon by the Board.

Held:

1. A reasonable entitlement to due process is not created merely because a State provides for the possibility of parole, such possibility providing no more than a mere hope that the benefit will be obtained. Parole revocation, for which certain due process standards must be met, *Morrissey v. Brewer, supra,* entails deprivation of a liberty one has, and is a decision involving initially a wholly retrospective factual question as to whether the parolee violated his parole. Parole release involves denial of a liberty desired by inmates, and that decision depends on an amalgam of elements, some factual, but many purely subjective evaluations by the Board.

2. While the language and structure of § 83–1,114(1) provides a mechanism for parole that is entitled to some constitutional protection, the Nebraska procedure

provides all the process due with respect to the discretionary parole decision.

(a) The formal hearing required by the Court of Appeals would provide, at best, a negligible decrease in the risk of error. Since the Board of Parole's decision at its initial review hearing is one that must be made largely on the basis of the inmate's file, this procedure adequately safeguards against serious risks of error, and thus satisfies due process.

(b) Nothing in due process concepts requires the Board to specify the particular "evidence" in the inmate's file or at his interview on which it rests its discretionary determination to deny release. The Nebraska procedure affords an opportunity to be heard, and, when parole is denied, it informs the inmate in what respects he falls short of qualifying for parole; this affords all the process that is due in these circumstances, nothing more being required by the Constitution.

576 F.2d 1274, reversed and remanded.
BURGER, C.J., delivered the opinion of the Court, in which STEWART, WHITE, BLACKMUN, and REHNQUIST, JJ., joined. POWELL, J., filed an opinion concurring in part and dissenting in part. MARSHALL, J., filed an opinion dissenting in part, in which BRENNAN and STEVENS, JJ., joined.

JAGO
V.
VAN CUREN

454 U.S. 14; 102 S. CT. 31; 70 L. ED. 2D 13 (1981)

ON PETITION FOR WRIT OF CERTIORARI TO THE UNITED STATES COURT OF APPEALS FOR THE SIXTH CIRCUIT

No. 81942   Decided November 9, 1981

Held: The Due Process Clause of the Fourteenth Amendment was not violated by the

Ohio Adult Parole Authority's rescission, without a hearing, of its decision to grant respondent early parole. The rescission, which occurred before respondent was released, resulted from the Authority's having learned that respondent had made false statements in an interview conducted before the decision to grant parole and in his proposed parole plan. After conceding that Ohio law created no protected "liberty" interest in early parole, the Court of Appeals erred in concluding that a liberty interest arose from the "mutually explicit understandings" of the parties, and that the rescission without a hearing thus violated due process. The "mutually explicit understandings" language of *Perry v. Sindermann*, 408 U. S. 593, relied on by the Court of Appeals, relates to the Fourteenth Amendment's protection of "property" interests, rather than "liberty" interests such as that asserted by respondent. *Cf. Connecticut Board of Pardons v. Dumschat*, 452 U. S. 458.

Certiorari granted; 641 F.2d 411, reversed. PER CURIAM.

MARTINEZ
V.
CALIFORNIA

444 U.S. 277; 100 S. CT. 553; 62 L. ED. 2D 481 (1980)

APPEAL FROM THE COURT OF APPEAL OF CALIFORNIA, FOURTH APPELLATE DISTRICT

No. 78–1268   Argued November 5, 1979— Decided January 15, 1980

Appellants' decedent, a 15-year-old girl, was murdered by a parolee five months after he was released from prison despite his history as a sex offender. Appellants brought an action in a California court under state law and 42 U.S.C. § 1983, claiming that appellee state officials, by their action in releasing the parolee, subjected the decedent to a deprivation of her life without due process of law, and were therefore liable in damages for the harm caused by the parolee. The trial court sustained a demurrer to the complaint. The Califor-

nia Court of Appeal affirmed, holding that a California statute granting public employees absolute immunity from liability for any injury resulting from parole release determinations provided appellees with a complete defense to appellants' state law claims, and that appellees enjoyed quasi-judicial immunity from liability under 42 U.S.C. § 1983.

Held:

1. The California immunity statute is not unconstitutional when applied to defeat a tort claim arising under state law.

    (a) The statute, which merely provides a defense to potential state tort law liability, did not deprive appellants' decedent of her life without due process of law because it condoned a parole decision that led indirectly to her death. A legislative decision that has an incremental impact on the probability that death will result in any given situation cannot be characterized as state action depriving a person of life just because it may set in motion a chain of events that ultimately leads to the random death of an innocent bystander.

    (b) Even if the statute can be characterized as a deprivation of property, the State's interest in fashioning its own rules of tort law is paramount to any discernible federal interest, except perhaps an interest in protecting the individual citizen from wholly arbitrary or irrational state action. The statute is not irrational, because the California Legislature could reasonably conclude that judicial review of parole decisions "would inevitably inhibit the exercise of discretion," and that this inhibiting effect could impair the State's ability to implement a parole program designed to promote rehabilitation of inmates, as well as security within prisons by holding out a promise of potential rewards.

2. Appellants did not allege a claim for relief under federal law.

    (a) The Fourteenth Amendment protected appellants' decedent only from deprivation by the State of life without due process of law, and although the decision to release the parolee from prison was action by the State, the parolee's action five months later cannot be fairly characterized as state action.

(b) Regardless of whether, as a matter of state tort law, the parole board either had a "duty" to avoid harm to the parolee's victim or proximately caused her death, appellees did not "deprive" appellants' decedent of life within the meaning of the Fourteenth Amendment.

(c) Under the particular circumstances where the parolee was in no sense an agent of the parole board, and the board was not aware that appellants' decedent, as distinguished from the public at large, faced any special danger, appellants' decedent's death was too remote consequence of appellees' action to hold them responsible under § 1983.

85 Cal. App. 3d 430, 149 Cal. Rptr. 519, affirmed.

STEVENS, J., delivered the opinion for a unanimous Court.

GRIFFIN
V.
WISCONSIN

483 U.S. 868; 107 S. CT. 3164; 97 L. ED. 2D 709 (1987)

CERTIORARI TO THE SUPREME COURT OF WISCONSIN

No. 86–5324   Argued April 20, 1987— Decided June 26, 1987

Wisconsin law places probationers in the legal custody of the State Department of Health and Social Services and renders them "subject to . . . conditions set by the . . . rules and regulations established by the department." One such regulation permits any probation officer to search a probationer's home

without a warrant as long as his supervisor approves and as long as there are "reasonable grounds" to believe the presence of contraband. In determining whether "reasonable grounds" exist, an officer must consider a variety of factors, including information provided by an informant, the reliability and specificity of that information, the informant's reliability, the officer's experience with the probationer, and the need to verify compliance with the rules of probation and with the law. Another regulation forbids a probationer to possess a firearm without a probation officer's advance approval. Upon information received from a police detective that there were or might be guns in petitioner probationer's apartment, probation officers searched the apartment and found a handgun. Petitioner was tried and convicted of the felony of possession of a firearm by a convicted felon, the state trial court having denied his motion to suppress the evidence seized during the search after concluding that no warrant was necessary and that the search was reasonable. The State Court of Appeals and the State Supreme Court affirmed.

Held:

1. The warrantless search of petitioner's residence was "reasonable" within the meaning of the Fourth Amendment because it was conducted pursuant to a regulation that is itself a reasonable response to the "special needs" of a probation system.

(a) Supervision of probationers is a "special need" of the State that may justify departures from the usual warrant and probable cause requirements. Supervision is necessary to ensure that probation restrictions are in fact observed, that the probation serves as a genuine rehabilitation period, and that the community is not harmed by the probationer's being at large.

(b) The search regulation is valid because the "special needs" of Wisconsin's probation system make the warrant requirement impracticable and justify replacement of the probable cause standard with the regulation's "reasonable grounds" standard. It is reasonable to dispense with the warrant requirement here, since such a requirement would interfere to an appreciable degree with the probation system by setting up a magistrate, rather than the probation officer, as the determiner of how closely the probationer must be supervised, by making it more difficult for probation officials to respond quickly to evidence of misconduct, and by reducing the deterrent effect that the possibility of expeditious searches would otherwise create. Moreover, unlike the police officer who conducts the ordinary search, the probation officer is required to have the probationer's welfare particularly in mind. A probable cause requirement would unduly disrupt the probation system by reducing the deterrent effect of the supervisory arrangement and by lessening the range of information the probation officer could consider in deciding whether to search. The probation agency must be able to act based upon a lesser degree of certainty in order to intervene before the probationer damages himself or society, and must be able to proceed on the basis of its entire experience with the probationer and to assess probabilities in the light of its knowledge of his life, character, and circumstances. Thus, it is reasonable to permit information provided by a police officer, whether or not on the basis of firsthand knowledge, to support a probationary search. All that is required is that the information provided indicates, as it did here, the likelihood of facts justifying the search.

2. The conclusion that the regulation in question was constitutional makes it unnecessary to consider whether any search of a probationer's home is lawful when there are "reasonable grounds" to believe contraband is present.

131Wis.2d 41, 388 N.W.2d 535, affirmed. SCALIA, J., delivered the opinion of the Court, in which REHNQUIST, C.J.,

and WHITE, POWELL, and O'CONNOR, JJ., joined. BLACKMUN, J., filed a dissenting opinion, in which MARSHALL, J., joined, in Parts I-B and I-C of which BRENNAN, J., joined, and in Part I-C of which STEVENS, J., joined. STEVENS, J., filed a dissenting opinion, in which MARSHALL, J., joined.

UNITED STATES
V.
KNIGHTS

534 U.S. 112; 122 S. CT. 587; 151 L. ED. 2D 497 (2001)

CERTIORARI TO THE UNITED STATES COURT OF APPEALS FOR THE NINTH CIRCUIT

No. 00–1260   Argued November 6, 2001— Decided December 10, 2001

A California court's order sentencing respondent Knights to probation for a drug offense included the condition that Knights submit to search at anytime, with or without a search or arrest warrant or reasonable cause, by any probation or law enforcement officer. Subsequently, a sheriff's detective, with reasonable suspicion, searched Knights' apartment. Based in part on items recovered, a federal grand jury indicted Knights for conspiracy to commit arson, for possession of an unregistered destructive device, and for being a felon in possession of ammunition. In granting Knights' motion to suppress, the District Court held that, although the detective had "reasonable suspicion" to believe that Knights was involved with incendiary materials, the search was for "investigatory" rather than "probationary" purposes. The Ninth Circuit affirmed.

Held: The warrantless search of Knights, supported by reasonable suspicion and authorized by a probation condition, satisfied the Fourth Amendment. As nothing in Knights' probation condition limits searches to those with a "probationary" purpose, the question here is whether the Fourth Amendment imposes such a limitation. Knights argues that a warrantless search of a probationer satisfies the Fourth Amendment only if it is just like the search at issue in Griffin v. Wisconsin, 483 U. S. 868, i.e., a "special needs" search conducted by a probation officer monitoring whether the probationer is complying with probation restrictions. This dubious logic-that an opinion upholding the constitutionality of a particular search implicitly holds unconstitutional any search that is not like it-runs contrary to Griffin's express statement that its "special needs" holding made it "unnecessary to consider whether" warrantless searches of probationers were otherwise reasonable under the Fourth Amendment. Id., at 878, 880. And this Court need not decide whether Knights' acceptance of the search condition constituted consent to a complete waiver of his Fourth Amendment rights in the sense of Schneckloth v. Bustamonte, 412 U. S. 218, because the search here was reasonable under the Court's general Fourth Amendment "totality of the circumstances" approach, Ohio v. Robinette, 519 U. S. 33, 39, with the search condition being a salient circumstance. The Fourth Amendment's touchstone is reasonableness, and a search's reasonableness is determined by assessing, on the one hand, the degree to which it intrudes upon an individual's privacy and, on the other, the degree to which it is needed to promote legitimate governmental interests. Wyoming v. Houghton, 526 U. S. 295, 300. Knights' status as a probationer subject to a search condition informs both sides of that balance. The sentencing judge reasonably concluded that the search condition would further the two primary goals of probation-rehabilitation and protecting society from future criminal violations. Knights was unambiguously informed of the search condition. Thus, Knights' reasonable expectation of privacy was significantly diminished. In assessing the governmental interest, it must be remembered that the very assumption of probation is that the probationer is more likely than others to violate the law. Griffin, supra, at 880. The State's interest in apprehending criminal law violators, thereby protecting potential victims, may justifiably focus on probationers in a way that it does not on the ordinary citizen. On balance, no more than reasonable suspicion was required to search this probationer's house. The degree of individualized suspicion

required is a determination that a sufficiently high probability of criminal conduct makes the intrusion on the individual's privacy interest reasonable. Although the Fourth Amendment ordinarily requires probable cause, a lesser degree satisfies the Constitution when the balance of governmental and private interests makes such a standard reasonable. See, e. g., Terry v. Ohio, 392 U. S. 1. The same circumstances that lead to the conclusion that reasonable suspicion is constitutionally sufficient also render a warrant requirement unnecessary. See Illinois v. McArthur, 531 U. S. 326, 330. Because the Court's holding rests on ordinary Fourth Amendment analysis that considers all the circumstances of a search, there is no basis for examining official purpose.

219 F.3d 1138, reversed and remanded.
REHNQUIST, C. J., delivered the opinion for a unanimous Court. SOUTER, J., filed a concurring opinion.

SAMSON
V.
CALIFORNIA

547 U.S. 843, 126 S. CT. 2193; 153 L. ED. 2D 250 (2006)

CERTIORARI TO THE COURT OF APPEAL OF CALIFORNIA, FIRST APPELLATE DISTRICT

No. 04–9728   Argued February 22, 2006—
Decided June 19, 2006

Pursuant to a California statute—which requires every prisoner eligible for release on state parole to "agree in writing to be subject to search or seizure by a parole officer or other peace officer . . ., with or without a search warrant and with or without cause"—and based solely on petitioner's parolee status, an officer searched petitioner and found methamphetamine. The trial court denied his motions to suppress that evidence, and he was convicted of possession. Affirming, the State Court of Appeal held that suspicionless searches of parolees are lawful under California law and that the search in this case was reasonable under the Fourth Amendment because it was not arbitrary, capricious, or harassing.

Held: The Fourth Amendment does not prohibit a police officer from conducting a suspicionless search of a parolee.

(a) The "totality of the circumstances" must be examined to determine whether a search is reasonable under the Fourth Amendment. *United States* v. *Knights,* 534 U. S. 112, 118. Reasonableness "is determined by assessing, on the one hand, the degree to which [the search] intrudes upon an individual's privacy and, on the other, the degree to which it is needed for the promotion of legitimate governmental interests." *Id.,* at 118–119. Applying this approach in *Knights,* the Court found reasonable the warrantless search of a probationer's apartment based on reasonable suspicion and a probation condition authorized by California law. In evaluating the degree of intrusion into Knights' privacy, the Court found his probationary status "salient," *id.,* at 118, observing that probation is on a continuum of possible punishments and that probationers "do not enjoy 'the absolute liberty'" of other citizens, *id.,* at 119. It also found probation searches necessary to promote legitimate governmental interests of integrating probationers back into the community, combating recidivism, and protecting potential victims. Balancing those interests, the intrusion was reasonable. However, because the search was predicated on both the probation search condition and reasonable suspicion, the Court did not address the reasonableness of a search solely predicated upon the probation condition.

(b) Parolees, who are on the "continuum" of state-imposed punishments, have fewer expectations of privacy than probationers, because parole is more akin to imprisonment than probation is. "The essence of parole is release from prison, before the completion of sentence, on the condition that the prisoner abides by certain rules during the balance of the sentence." *Morrissey* v. *Brewer,* 408 U. S. 471, 477. California's system is consistent with these observations. An inmate electing to complete his sentence out of physical custody remains in the Department of Corrections' legal custody for the remainder of his term and must comply with the terms and conditions of his parole. The extent and reach of those conditions demonstrate that parolees have severely diminished privacy expectations by virtue of their status alone. Additionally, as in *Knights,* the state law's parole search condition was clearly expressed to petitioner, who signed an order submitting to the condition and thus was unambiguously aware of it. Examining the totality of the circumstances, petitioner did not have an expectation of privacy that society would recognize as legitimate. The State's interests, by contrast, are substantial. A State has an "overwhelming interest" in supervising parolees because they "are more likely to commit future criminal offenses." *Pennsylvania Bd. of Probation and Parole* v. *Scott,* 524 U. S. 357, 365. Similarly, a State's interests in reducing recidivism, thereby promoting reintegration and positive citizenship among probationers and parolees, warrant privacy intrusions that would not otherwise be tolerated under the Fourth Amendment. The Amendment does not render States powerless to address these concerns effectively. California's 60-to70-percent recidivism rate demonstrates that most parolees are ill prepared to handle the pressures of reintegration and require intense supervision. The State Legislature has concluded that, given the State's number of parolees and its high recidivism rate, an individualized suspicion requirement would undermine the State's ability to effectively supervise parolees and protect the public from criminal acts by reoffenders. Contrary to petitioner's argument, the fact that some States and the Federal Government require a level of individualized suspicion before searching a parolee is of little relevance in determining whether California's system is drawn to meet the State's needs and is reasonable, taking into account a parolee's substantially diminished expectation of privacy. Nor is there merit to the argument that California's law grants discretion without procedural safeguards. The concern that the system gives officers unbridled discretion to conduct searches, thereby inflicting dignitary harms that arouse strong resentment in parolees and undermine their ability to reintegrate into society, is belied by the State's prohibition on arbitrary, capricious, or harassing searches. And petitioner's concern that the law frustrates reintegration efforts by permitting intrusions into the privacy interests of third persons is unavailing because that concern would arise under a suspicion-based system as well.

Affirmed.

THOMAS, J., delivered the opinion of the Court, in which ROBERTS, C. J., and SCALIA, KENNEDY, GINSBURG, and ALITO, JJ., joined. STEVENS, J., filed a dissenting opinion, in which SOUTER and BREYER, JJ., joined.

Cases Relating to Chapter 14

Juvenile and Youthful Offenders

IN RE GAULT

387 U.S. 1; 87 S. CT. 1428; 18 L. ED. 2D 527 (1967)

APPEAL FROM THE SUPREME COURT OF ARIZONA

No. 116   Argued December 6, 1966— Decided May 15, 1967

Appellants' 15-year-old son, Gerald Gault, was taken into custody as the result of a complaint that he had made lewd telephone calls. After hearings before a juvenile court judge, Gerald was ordered committed to the State Industrial School as a juvenile delinquent until he should reach majority. Appellants brought a habeas corpus action in the state courts to challenge the constitutionality of the Arizona Juvenile Code and the procedure actually used in Gerald's case, on the ground of denial of various procedural due process rights. The State Supreme Court affirmed dismissal of the writ. Agreeing that the constitutional guarantee of due process applies to proceedings in which juveniles are charged as delinquents, the court held that the Arizona Juvenile Code impliedly includes the requirements of due process in delinquency proceedings, and that such due process requirements were not offended by the procedure leading to Gerald's commitment.

Held:

1. *Kent v. United States*, 383 U. S. 541, 383 U. S. 562 (1966), held "that the [waiver] hearing must measure up to the essen-

tials of due process and fair treatment." This view is reiterated, here in connection with a juvenile court adjudication of "delinquency," as a requirement which is part of the Due Process Clause of the Fourteenth Amendment of our Constitution. The holding in this case relates only to the adjudicatory stage of the juvenile process, where commitment to a state institution may follow. When proceedings may result in incarceration in an institution of confinement, "it would be extraordinary if our Constitution did not require the procedural regularity and exercise of care implied in the phrase *due process.*'"

2. Due process requires, in such proceedings, that adequate written notice be afforded the child and his parents or guardian. Such notice must inform them "of the specific issues that they must meet," and must be given "at the earliest practicable time, and, in any event, sufficiently in advance of the hearing to permit preparation." Notice here was neither timely nor adequately specific, nor was there waiver of the right to constitutionally adequate notice.

3. In such proceedings, the child and his parents must be advised of their right to be represented by counsel and, if they are unable to afford counsel, that counsel will be appointed to represent the child. Mrs. Gault's statement at the habeas corpus hearing that she had known she could employ counsel, is not "an *intentional relinquishment or abandonment' of a fully known right.*"

4. The constitutional privilege against self-incrimination is applicable in such proceedings:

> "an admission by the juvenile may [not] be used against him in the absence of clear and unequivocal evidence that the admission was made with knowledge that he was not obliged to speak, and would not be penalized for remaining silent."
>
> "[T]he availability of the privilege does not turn upon the type of proceeding in which its protection is invoked, but upon the nature of the statement or admission and the exposure which it invites.... [J]uvenile proceedings to determine 'delinquency,' which may lead to commitment to a state institution, must be regarded as 'criminal' for purposes of the privilege against self-incrimination."
>
> Furthermore, experience has shown that "admissions and confessions by juveniles require special caution" as to their reliability and voluntariness, and "[i]t would indeed be surprising if the privilege against self-incrimination were available to hardened criminals, but not to children."
>
> "[S]pecial problems may arise with respect to waiver of the privilege by or on behalf of children, and ... there may well be some differences in technique—but not in principle— depending upon the age of the child and the presence and competence of parents.... If counsel was not present for some permissible reason when an admission was obtained, the greatest care must be taken to assure that the admission was voluntary...."

Gerald's admissions did not measure up to these standards, and could not properly be used as a basis for the judgment against him.

5. Absent a valid confession, a juvenile in such proceedings must be afforded the rights of confrontation and sworn testimony of witnesses available for cross-examination.

6. Other questions raised by appellants, including the absence of provision for appellate review of a delinquency adju-

dication, and a transcript of the proceedings, are not ruled upon.

99 Ariz. 181, 407 P. 2d 760, reversed and remanded.

MR. JUSTICE FORTAS delivered the opinion of the Court.

MCKEIVER
V.
PENNSYLVANIA

403 U.S. 528; 91 S. CT. 1976; 29 L. ED. 2D 647 (1971)

APPEAL FROM THE SUPREME COURT OF PENNSYLVANIA

No. 322   Argued December 10, 1970— December June 21, 1971

The requests of appellants in No. 322 for a jury trial were denied, and they were adjudged juvenile delinquents under Pennsylvania law. The State Supreme Court, while recognizing the applicability to juveniles of certain due process procedural safeguards, held that there is no constitutional right to a jury trial in juvenile court. Appellants argue for a right to a jury trial because they were tried in proceedings "substantially similar to a criminal trial," and note that the press is generally present at the trial, and that members of the public also enter the courtroom. Petitioners in No. 128 were adjudged juvenile delinquents in North Carolina, where their jury trial requests were denied, and in proceedings where the general public was excluded.

Held: A trial by jury is not constitutionally required in the adjudicative phase of a state juvenile court delinquency proceeding.

No. 322, 438 Pa. 339, 265 A.2d 350, and No. 128, 275 N.C. 517, 169 S.E.2d 879, affirmed.

MR. JUSTICE BLACKMUN joined by THE CHIEF JUSTICE, MR. JUSTICE STEWART, and MR. JUSTICE WHITE, concluded that:

1. The applicable due process standard in juvenile proceedings is fundamental fair-

ness, as developed by *In re Gault*, 387 U. S. 1, and *In re Winship*, 397 U. S. 358, which emphasized factfinding procedures, but, in our legal system, the jury is not a necessary component of accurate factfinding.

2. Despite disappointments, failures, and shortcomings in the juvenile court procedure, a jury trial is not constitutionally required in a juvenile court's adjudicative stage.

(a) The Court has not heretofore ruled that all rights constitutionally assured to an adult accused are to be imposed in a juvenile proceeding.

(b) Compelling a jury trial might remake the proceeding into a fully adversary process, and effectively end the idealistic prospect of an intimate, informal protective proceeding.

(c) Imposing a jury trial on the juvenile court system would not remedy the system's defects, and would not greatly strengthen the factfinding function.

(d) The States should be free to experiment to achieve the high promise of the juvenile court concept, and they may install a jury system; or a juvenile court judge may use an advisory jury in a particular case.

(e) Many States, by statute or judicial decision, deny a juvenile a right to jury trial, and the great majority that have faced that issue since *Gault, supra,* and *Duncan v. Louisiana*, 391 U. S. 145, have concluded that the considerations involved in those cases do not compel trial by jury in juvenile court.

(f) Jury trial would entail delay, formality, and clamor of the adversary system, and possibly a public trial.

(g) Equating the adjudicative phase of the juvenile proceeding with a criminal trial ignores the aspects of fairness, concern, sympathy, and paternal attention inherent in the juvenile court system.

MR. JUSTICE BRENNAN concluded that:

Due process in juvenile delinquency proceedings, which are not "criminal prosecutions," does not require the States to provide jury trials on demand so long as some other aspect of the process adequately protects the interests that Sixth Amendment jury trials are intended to serve. In the juvenile context, those interests may be adequately protected by allowing accused individuals to bring the community's attention to bear upon their trials. Since Pennsylvania has no statutory bar to public juvenile trials, and since no claim is made that members of the public were excluded over appellants' objections, the judgment in No. 322 should be affirmed.

MR. JUSTICE HARLAN concurred in the judgments in these cases on the ground that criminal jury trials are not constitutionally required of the States, either by the Sixth Amendment or by due process.

BLACKMUN, J., announced the Court's judgments and delivered an opinion in which BURGER, C.J., and STEWART and WHITE, JJ., joined. WHITE, J., filed a concurring opinion. BRENNAN, J., filed an opinion concurring in the judgment in No. 322 and dissenting in No. 128. HARLAN, J., filed an opinion concurring in the judgments. DOUGLAS, J., filed a dissenting opinion, in which BLACK and MARSHALL, JJ., joined.

BREED
V.
JONES

421 U.S. 519; 95 S. CT. 1779; 44 L. ED. 2D 346 (1975)

CERTIORARI TO THE UNITED STATES COURT OF APPEALS FOR THE NINTH CIRCUIT

No. 73–1995   Argued February 25–26, 1975—Decided May 27, 1975

The prosecution of respondent as an adult in California Superior Court, after an adjudicatory finding in Juvenile Court that he had violated a criminal statute and a subsequent finding that he was unfit for treatment as a juvenile, violated the Double Jeopardy Clause of the Fifth Amendment, as applied to the States through the Fourteenth Amendment.

(a) Respondent was put in jeopardy at the Juvenile Court adjudicatory hearing, whose object was to determine whether he had committed acts that violated a criminal law and whose potential consequences included both the stigma inherent in that determination and the deprivation of liberty for many years. Jeopardy attached when the Juvenile Court, as the trier of the facts, began to hear evidence.

(b) Contrary to petitioner's contention, respondent's trial in Superior Court for the same offense as that for which he had been tried in Juvenile Court, violated the policies of the Double Jeopardy Clause, even if respondent "never faced the risk of more than one punishment," since the Clause "is written in terms of potential or risk of trial and conviction, not punishment." *Price v. Georgia*, 398 U. S. 323, 398 U. S. 329. Respondent was subjected to the burden of two trials for the same offense; he was twice put to the task of marshaling his resources against those of the State, twice subjected to the "heavy personal strain" that such an experience represents.

(c) If there is to be an exception to the constitutional protection against a second trial in the context of the juvenile court system, it must be justified by interests of society, reflected in that unique institution, or of juveniles themselves, of sufficient substance to render tolerable the costs and burdens that the exception will entail in individual cases.

(d) Giving respondent the constitutional protection against multiple trials in this context will not, as petitioner claims, diminish the flexibility and informality of juvenile court proceedings to the extent that those qualities relate uniquely to the goals of the juvenile court system. A requirement that transfer hearings be held prior to adjudicatory hearings does not alter the nature of the latter proceedings. More significantly, such a requirement need not affect the quality of decisionmaking at transfer hearings themselves. The burdens petitioner envisions would not pose a significant problem for the administration of the juvenile court system, and, quite apart from that consideration, transfer hearings prior to adjudication will aid the objectives of that system.

497 F.2d 1160, vacated and remanded. BURGER, C.J., delivered the opinion for a unanimous Court.

SCHALL
V.
MARTIN

467 U.S. 253; 104 S. CT. 2403; 81 L. ED. 2D 207 (1984)

APPEAL FROM THE UNITED STATES COURT OF APPEALS FOR THE SECOND CIRCUIT

No. 82–1248   Argued January 17, 1984— Decided June 4, 1984

Section 320.5(3)(b) of the New York Family Court Act authorizes pretrial detention of an accused juvenile delinquent based on a finding that there is a "serious risk" that the juvenile "may before the return date commit an act which if committed by an adult would constitute a crime." Appellees, juveniles who had been detained under § 320.5(3)(b), brought a habeas corpus class action in Federal District Court, seeking a declaratory judgment that § 320.5(3)(b) violates, *inter alia*, the Due Process Clause of the Fourteenth Amendment. The District Court struck down the statute as permitting detention without due process and ordered the release of all class members. The Court of Appeals affirmed, holding that, since the vast majority of juveniles detained under the statute either have their cases dismissed before an adjudication of delinquency or are released after adjudication, the statute is administered, not for preventive purposes, but to impose punishment for unadjudicated criminal acts, and that therefore the statute is unconstitutional as to all juveniles.

Held: Section 320.5(3)(b) is not invalid under the Due Process Clause of the Fourteenth Amendment.

(a) Preventive detention under the statute serves the legitimate state objective, held in common with every State, of protecting both the juvenile and society from the hazards of pretrial crime. That objective is compatible with the "fundamental fairness" demanded by the Due Process Clause in juvenile proceedings, and the terms and condition of confinement under § 320.5(3)(b) are compatible with that objective. Pretrial detention need not be considered punishment merely because a juvenile is subsequently discharged subject to conditions or put on probation. And even when a case is terminated prior to factfinding, it does not follow that the decision to detain the juvenile pursuant to § 320.5(3)(b) amounts to a due process violation.

(b) The procedural safeguards afforded by the Family Court Act to juveniles detained under § 320.5(3)(b) prior to factfinding provide sufficient protection against erroneous and unnecessary deprivations of liberty. Notice, a hearing, and a statement of facts and reasons are given to the juvenile prior to any detention, and a formal probable cause hearing is then held within a short time thereafter, if the factfinding hearing is not itself scheduled within three days. There is no merit to the argument that the risk of erroneous and unnecessary detention is too high despite these procedures because the standard for detention is fatally vague. From a legal point of view, there is nothing inherently unattainable about a prediction of future criminal conduct. Such a prediction is an experienced one based on a host of variables that cannot be readily codified. Moreover, the post-detention procedures—habeas corpus review, appeals, and motions for reconsideration—provide a sufficient mechanism for correcting on a case-by-case basis any erroneous detention.

689 F.2d 365, reversed.

REHNQUIST, J., delivered the opinion of the Court, in which BURGER, C.J.,

and WHITE, BLACKMUN, POWELL, and O'CONNOR, JJ., joined. MARSHALL, J., filed a dissenting opinion, in which BRENNAN and STEVENS, JJ., joined.

ROPER
V.
SIMMONS

543 U.S. 551; 125 S. CT. 1183; 161 L. ED. 2D 1 (2005)

CERTIORARI TO THE SUPREME COURT OF MISSOURI

No. 03–633   Argued October 13, 2004—Decided March 1, 2005

At age 17, respondent Simmons planned and committed a capital murder. After he had turned 18, he was sentenced to death. His direct appeal and subsequent petitions for state and federal postconviction relief were rejected. This Court then held, in *Atkins* v. *Virginia*, 536 U. S. 304, that the Eighth Amendment, applicable to the States through the Fourteenth Amendment, prohibits the execution of a mentally retarded person. Simmons filed a new petition for state postconviction relief, arguing that *Atkins'* reasoning established that the Constitution prohibits the execution of a juvenile who was under 18 when he committed his crime. The Missouri Supreme Court agreed and set aside Simmons' death sentence in favor of life imprisonment without eligibility for release. It held that, although *Stanford* v. *Kentucky*, 492 U. S. 361, rejected the proposition that the Constitution bars capital punishment for juvenile offenders younger than 18, a national consensus has developed against the execution of those offenders since *Stanford*.

Held: The Eighth and Fourteenth Amendments forbid imposition of the death penalty on offenders who were under the age of 18 when their crimes were committed.

(a) The Eighth Amendment's prohibition against "cruel and unusual punishments" must be interpreted according to its text, by considering history, tradition, and precedent, and with due regard for its purpose and function in the constitutional design. To implement this framework this Court has established the propriety and affirmed the necessity of referring to "the evolving standards of decency that mark the progress of a maturing society" to determine which punishments are so disproportionate as to be "cruel and unusual." *Trop v. Dulles*, 356 U. S. 86, 100–101. In 1988, in *Thompson* v. *Oklahoma*, 487 U. S. 815, 818–838, a plurality determined that national standards of decency did not permit the execution of any offender under age 16 at the time of the crime. The next year, in *Stanford*, a 5-to-4 Court referred to contemporary standards of decency, but concluded the Eighth and Fourteenth Amendments did not proscribe the execution of offenders over 15 but under 18 because 22 of 37 death penalty States permitted that penalty for 16-year-old offenders, and 25 permitted it for 17-year-olds, thereby indicating there was no national consensus. 492 U. S., at 370–371. A plurality also "emphatically reject[ed]" the suggestion that the Court should bring its own judgment to bear on the acceptability of the juvenile death penalty. *Id.*, at 377–378. That same day the Court held, in *Penry* v. *Lynaugh*, 492 U. S. 302, 334, that the Eighth Amendment did not mandate a categorical exemption from the death penalty for mentally retarded persons because only two States had enacted laws banning such executions. Three Terms ago in *Atkins,* however, the Court held that standards of decency had evolved since *Penry* and now demonstrated that the execution of the mentally retarded is cruel and unusual punishment. The *Atkins* Court noted that objective indicia of society's standards, as expressed in pertinent legislative enactments and state practice, demonstrated that such executions had become so truly unusual that it was fair to say that a national consensus has developed against them. 536 U. S., at 314–315. The Court also returned to the rule, established in decisions predating *Stanford*, that the Constitution contemplates that the Court's own judgment be brought to bear on the question of the acceptability of the

death penalty. *Id.*, at 312. After observing that mental retardation diminishes personal culpability even if the offender can distinguish right from wrong, *id.*, at 318, and that mentally retarded offenders' impairments make it less defensible to impose the death penalty as retribution for past crimes or as a real deterrent to future crimes, *id.*, at 319–320, the Court ruled that the death penalty constitutes an excessive sanction for the entire category of mentally retarded offenders, and that the Eighth Amendment places a substantive restriction on the State's power to take such an offender's life, *id.*, at 321. Just as the *Atkins* Court reconsidered the issue decided in *Penry*, the Court now reconsiders the issue decided in *Stanford*.

(b) Both objective indicia of consensus, as expressed in particular by the enactments of legislatures that have addressed the question, and the Court's own determination in the exercise of its independent judgment, demonstrate that the death penalty is a disproportionate punishment for juveniles.

(1) As in *Atkins*, the objective indicia of national consensus here—the rejection of the juvenile death penalty in the majority of States; the infrequency of its use even where it remains on the books; and the consistency in the trend toward abolition of the practice—provide sufficient evidence that today society views juveniles, in the words *Atkins* used respecting the mentally retarded, as "categorically less culpable than the average criminal," 536 U. S., at 316. The evidence of such consensus is similar, and in some respects parallel, to the evidence in *Atkins:* 30 States prohibit the juvenile death penalty, including 12 that have rejected it altogether and 18 that maintain it but, by express provision or judicial interpretation, exclude juveniles from its reach. Moreover, even in the 20 States without a formal prohibition, the execution of juveniles is infrequent. Although, by contrast to *Atkins*, the rate of change in reducing the incidence of the juvenile death penalty, or in taking specific steps to abolish it, has been less dramatic, the difference between this case and *Atkins*

in that respect is counterbalanced by the consistent direction of the change toward abolition. Indeed, the slower pace here may be explained by the simple fact that the impropriety of executing juveniles between 16 and 18 years old gained wide recognition earlier than the impropriety of executing the mentally retarded.

(2) Rejection of the imposition of the death penalty on juvenile offenders under 18 is required by the Eighth Amendment. Capital punishment must be limited to those offenders who commit "a narrow category of the most serious crimes" and whose extreme culpability makes them "the most deserving of execution." *Atkins*, 536 U. S. at 319. Three general differences between juveniles under 18 and adults demonstrate that juvenile offenders cannot with reliability be classified among the worst offenders. Juveniles' susceptibility to immature and irresponsible behavior means "their irresponsible conduct is not as morally reprehensible as that of an adult." *Thompson* v. *Oklahoma*, 487 U. S. 815, 835. Their own vulnerability and comparative lack of control over their immediate surroundings mean juveniles have a greater claim than adults to be forgiven for failing to escape negative influences in their whole environment. See *Stanford, supra*, at 395. The reality that juveniles still struggle to define their identity means it is less supportable to conclude that even a heinous crime committed by a juvenile is evidence of irretrievably depraved character. The *Thompson* plurality recognized the import of these characteristics with respect to juveniles under 16. 487 U. S., at 833–838. The same reasoning applies to all juvenile offenders under 18. Once juveniles' diminished culpability is recognized, it is evident that neither of the two penological justifications for the death penalty—retribution and deterrence of capital crimes by prospective offenders, *e.g., Atkins*, 536 U. S., at 319—provides adequate justification for imposing that penalty on juveniles. Although the Court cannot deny or overlook the brutal crimes too many juvenile offenders have committed, it disagrees with petitioner's contention that, given the Court's own insistence on individualized consideration in capital sentencing, it is arbitrary and unnecessary to adopt a categorical rule barring imposition of the death penalty on an offender under 18. An unacceptable likelihood exists that the brutality or cold-blooded nature of any particular crime would overpower mitigating arguments based on youth as a matter of course, even where the juvenile offender's objective immaturity, vulnerability, and lack of true depravity should require a sentence less severe than death. When a juvenile commits a heinous crime, the State can exact forfeiture of some of the most basic liberties, but the State cannot extinguish his life and his potential to attain a mature understanding of his own humanity. While drawing the line at 18 is subject to the objections always raised against categorical rules, that is the point where society draws the line for many purposes between childhood and adulthood and the age at which the line for death eligibility ought to rest. *Stanford* should be deemed no longer controlling on this issue.

(c) The overwhelming weight of international opinion against the juvenile death penalty is not controlling here, but provides respected and significant confirmation for the Court's determination that the penalty is disproportionate punishment for offenders under 18. See, *e.g., Thompson, supra*, at 830–831, and n. 31. The United States is the only country in the world that continues to give official sanction to the juvenile penalty. It does not lessen fidelity to the Constitution or pride in its origins to acknowledge that the express affirmation of certain fundamental rights by other nations and peoples underscores the centrality of those same rights within our own heritage of freedom.

112 S. W. 3d 397, affirmed.

KENNEDY, J., delivered the opinion of the Court, in which STEVENS, SOUTER, GINSBURG, and BREYER, JJ., joined. STEVENS, J., filed a concurring opinion, in which GINSBURG, J., joined. O'CONNOR, J., filed a dissenting opinion. SCALIA,

J., filed a dissenting opinion, in which REHNQUIST, C. J., and THOMAS, J., joined.

GRAHAM
V.
FLORIDA

560 U.S. 48; 130 S. CT. 2011; 176 L. ED. 2D 825 (2010)

CERTIORARI TO THE DISTRICT COURT OF APPEAL OF FLORIDA, 1ST DISTRICT

No. 08–7412   Argued November 9, 2009— Decided May 17, 2010

Petitioner Graham was 16 when he committed armed burglary and another crime. Under a plea agreement, the Florida trial court sentenced Graham to probation and withheld adjudication of guilt. Subsequently, the trial court found that Graham had violated the terms of his probation by committing additional crimes. The trial court adjudicated Graham guilty of the earlier charges, revoked his probation, and sentenced him to life in prison for the burglary. Because Florida has abolished its parole system, the life sentence left Graham no possibility of release except executive clemency. He challenged his sentence under the Eighth Amendment's Cruel and Unusual Punishments Clause, but the State First District Court of Appeal affirmed.

Held: The Clause does not permit a juvenile offender to be sentenced to life in prison without parole for a nonhomicide crime.

(a) Embodied in the cruel and unusual punishments ban is the "precept ... that punishment for crime should be graduated and proportioned to [the] offense." *Weems v. United States*, 217 U. S. 349, 367. The Court's cases implementing the proportionality standard fall within two general classifications. In cases of the first type, the Court has considered all the circumstances to determine whether the length of a term-of-years sentence is unconstitutionally excessive for a par-

ticular defendant's crime. The second classification comprises cases in which the Court has applied certain categorical rules against the death penalty. In a subset of such cases considering the nature of the offense, the Court has concluded that capital punishment is impermissible for nonhomicide crimes against individuals. *E.g.*, *Kennedy* v. *Louisiana*, 554 U. S. ___, ___. In a second subset, cases turning on the offender's characteristics, the Court has prohibited death for defendants who committed their crimes before age 18, *Roper* v. *Simmons*, 543 U. S. 551, or whose intellectual functioning is in a low range, *Atkins* v. *Virginia*, 536 U. S. 304. In cases involving categorical rules, the Court first considers "objective indicia of society's standards, as expressed in legislative enactments and state practice" to determine whether there is a national consensus against the sentencing practice at issue. *Roper, supra*, at 563. Next, looking to "the standards elaborated by controlling precedents and by the Court's own understanding and interpretation of the Eighth Amendment's text, history, meaning, and purpose," *Kennedy, supra*, at ___, the Court determines in the exercise of its own independent judgment whether the punishment in question violates the Constitution, *Roper, supra*, at 564. Because this case implicates a particular type of sentence as it applies to an entire class of offenders who have committed a range of crimes, the appropriate analysis is the categorical approach used in *Atkins, Roper,* and *Kennedy.*

(b) Application of the foregoing approach convinces the Court that the sentencing practice at issue is unconstitutional.

(1) Six jurisdictions do not allow life without parole sentences for any juvenile offenders. Seven jurisdictions permit life without parole for juvenile offenders, but only for homicide crimes. Thirty-seven States, the District of Columbia, and the Federal Government permit sentences of life without parole for a juvenile nonhomicide offender in some circumstances. The State relies on these data to argue that no national consensus against the sentencing practice in question exists. An

examination of actual sentencing practices in those jurisdictions that permit life without parole for juvenile nonhomicide offenders, however, discloses a consensus against the sentence. Nationwide, there are only 129 juvenile offenders serving life without parole sentences for nonhomicide crimes. Because 77 of those offenders are serving sentences imposed in Florida and the other 52 are imprisoned in just 10 States and in the federal system, it appears that only 12 jurisdictions nationwide in fact impose life without parole sentences on juvenile nonhomicide offenders, while 26 States and the District of Columbia do not impose them despite apparent statutory authorization. Given that the statistics reflect nearly all juvenile nonhomicide offenders who have received a life without parole sentence stretching back many years, moreover, it is clear how rare these sentences are, even within the States that do sometimes impose them. While more common in terms of absolute numbers than the sentencing practices in, *e.g.*, *Atkins* and *Enmund* v. *Florida*, 458 U. S. 782, the type of sentence at issue is actually as rare as those other sentencing practices when viewed in proportion to the opportunities for its imposition. The fact that many jurisdictions do not expressly prohibit the sentencing practice at issue is not dispositive because it does not necessarily follow that the legislatures in those jurisdictions have deliberately concluded that such sentences would be appropriate. See *Thompson* v. *Oklahoma*, 487 U. S. 815, 826, n. 24, 850.

(2) The inadequacy of penological theory to justify life without parole sentences for juvenile nonhomicide offenders, the limited culpability of such offenders, and the severity of these sentences all lead the Court to conclude that the sentencing practice at issue is cruel and unusual. No recent data provide reason to reconsider *Roper*'s holding that because juveniles have lessened culpability they are less deserving of the most serious forms of punishment. 543 U. S., at 551. Moreover, defendants who do not kill, intend to kill, or foresee that life will be taken are cat-

egorically less deserving of such punishments than are murderers. *E.g., Kennedy, supra.* Serious nonhomicide crimes "may be devastating in their harm ... but 'in terms of moral depravity and of the injury to the person and to the public,' ... they cannot be compared to murder in their 'severity and irrevocability.'" *Id.*, at ___. Thus, when compared to an adult murderer, a juvenile offender who did not kill or intend to kill has a twice diminished moral culpability. Age and the nature of the crime each bear on the analysis. As for the punishment, life without parole is "the second most severe penalty permitted by law," *Harmelin* v. *Michigan*, 501 U. S. 957, 1001, and is especially harsh for a juvenile offender, who will on average serve more years and a greater percentage of his life in prison than an adult offender, see, *e.g.*, *Roper, supra*, at 572. And none of the legitimate goals of penal sanctions—retribution, deterrence, incapacitation, and rehabilitation, see *Ewing* v. *California*, 538 U. S. 11, 25—is adequate to justify life without parole for juvenile nonhomicide offenders, see, *e.g., Roper*, 543 U. S., at 571, 573. Because age "18 is the point where society draws the line for many purposes between childhood and adulthood," it is the age below which a defendant may not be sentenced to life without parole for a nonhomicide crime. *Id.*, at 574. A State is not required to guarantee eventual freedom to such an offender, but must impose a sentence that provides some meaningful opportunity for release based on demonstrated maturity and rehabilitation. It is for the State, in the first instance, to explore the means and mechanisms for compliance.

(3) A categorical rule is necessary, given the inadequacy of two alternative approaches to address the relevant constitutional concerns. First, although Florida and other States have made substantial efforts to enact comprehensive rules governing the treatment of youthful offenders, such laws allow the imposition of the type of sentence at issue based only on a discretionary, subjective judgment by a judge or jury that the juvenile offender is irredeemably depraved, and are therefore

insufficient to prevent the possibility that the offender will receive such a sentence despite a lack of moral culpability. Second, a case-by-case approach requiring that the particular offender's age be weighed against the seriousness of the crime as part of a gross disproportionality inquiry would not allow courts to distinguish with sufficient accuracy the few juvenile offenders having sufficient psychological maturity and depravity to merit a life without parole sentence from the many that have the capacity for change. Cf. *Roper, supra*, at 572–573. Nor does such an approach take account of special difficulties encountered by counsel in juvenile representation, given juveniles' impulsiveness, difficulty thinking in terms of long-term benefits, and reluctance to trust adults. A categorical rule avoids the risk that, as a result of these difficulties, a court or jury will erroneously conclude that a particular juvenile is sufficiently culpable to deserve life without parole for a nonhomicide. It also gives the juvenile offender a chance to demonstrate maturity and reform.

(4) Additional support for the Court's conclusion lies in the fact that the sentencing practice at issue has been rejected the world over: The United States is the only Nation that imposes this type of sentence. While the judgments of other nations and the international community are not dispositive as to the meaning of the Eighth Amendment, the Court has looked abroad to support its independent conclusion that a particular punishment is cruel and unusual. See, *e.g., Roper, supra*, at 575–578.

982 So. 2d 43, reversed and remanded.

KENNEDY, J., delivered the opinion of the Court, in which STEVENS, GINSBURG, BREYER, and SOTOMAYOR, JJ., joined. STEVENS, J., filed a concurring opinion, in which GINSBURG and SOTOMAYOR, JJ., joined. ROBERTS, C. J., filed an opinion concurring in the judgment. THOMAS, J., filed a dissenting opinion, in which SCALIA, J., joined, and in which ALITO, J., joined as to Parts I and III. ALITO, J., filed a dissenting opinion.

MILLER
V.
ALABAMA

567 U.S. 460; 132 S. CT. 2455; 183 L. ED. 2D 407 (2012)

CERTIORARI TO THE COURT OF CRIMINAL APPEALS OF ALABAMA

No. 10–9646   Argued March 20, 2012—Decided June 25, 2012

In each of these cases, a 14-year-old was convicted of murder and sentenced to a mandatory term of life imprisonment without the possibility of parole. In No. 10–9647, petitioner Jackson accompanied two other boys to a video store to commit a robbery; on the way to the store, he learned that one of the boys was carrying a shotgun. Jackson stayed outside the store for most of the robbery, but after he entered, one of his co-conspirators shot and killed the store clerk. Arkansas charged Jackson as an adult with capital felony murder and aggravated robbery, and a jury convicted him of both crimes. The trial court imposed a statutorily mandated sentence of life imprisonment without the possibility of parole. Jackson filed a state habeas petition, arguing that a mandatory life-without-parole term for a 14-year-old violates the Eighth Amendment. Disagreeing, the court granted the State's motion to dismiss. The Arkansas Supreme Court affirmed.

In No. 10–9646, petitioner Miller, along with a friend, beat Miller's neighbor and set fire to his trailer after an evening of drinking and drug use. The neighbor died. Miller was initially charged as a juvenile, but his case was removed to adult court, where he was charged with murder in the course of arson. A jury found Miller guilty, and the trial court imposed a statutorily mandated punishment of life without parole. The Alabama Court of Criminal Appeals affirmed, holding that Miller's sentence was not overly harsh when compared to his crime, and that its mandatory nature was permissible under the Eighth Amendment.

Held: The Eighth Amendment forbids a sentencing scheme that mandates life in prison without possibility of parole for juvenile homicide offenders.

(a) The Eighth Amendment's prohibition of cruel and unusual punishment "guarantees individuals the right not to be subjected to excessive sanctions." Roper v. Simmons, 543 U. S. 551. That right "flows from the basic 'precept of justice that punishment for crime should be graduated and proportioned'" to both the offender and the offense.

Two strands of precedent reflecting the concern with proportionate punishment come together here. The first has adopted categorical bans on sentencing practices based on mismatches between the culpabil[ity of a class of offenders and the severity of a penalty. See, e.g., Kennedy v. Louisiana, 554 U. S. 407. Several cases in this group have specially focused on juvenile offenders, because of their lesser culpability. Thus, Roper v. Simmons held that the Eighth Amendment bars capital punishment for children, and Graham v. Florida, 560 U. S. ___, concluded that the Amendment prohibits a sentence of life without the possibility of parole for a juvenile convicted of a nonhomicide offense. Graham further likened life without parole for juveniles to the death penalty, thereby evoking a second line of cases. In those decisions, this Court has required sentencing authorities to consider the characteristics of a defendant and the details of his offense before sentencing him to death. See, e.g., Woodson v. North Carolina, 428 U. S. 280 (plurality opinion). Here, the confluence of these two lines of precedent leads to the conclusion that mandatory life without parole for juveniles violates the Eighth Amendment.

As to the first set of cases: Roper and Graham establish that children are constitutionally different from adults for sentencing purposes. Their "'lack of maturity'" and "'underdeveloped sense of responsibility'" lead to recklessness, impulsivity, and heedless risk-taking. Roper, 543 U. S., at 569. They "are more vulnerable . . . to negative influences and outside pressures," including from their family and peers; they have limited "contro[l] over their own environment" and lack the ability to extricate themselves from horrific, crime-producing settings. Ibid. And because a child's character is not as "well formed" as an adult's, his traits are "less fixed" and his actions are less likely to be "evidence of irretrievabl[e] deprav[ity]."

Id., at 570. Roper and Graham emphasized that the distinctive attributes of youth diminish the penological justifications for imposing the harshest sentences on juvenile offenders, even when they commit terrible crimes.

While Graham's flat ban on life without parole was for nonhomicide crimes, nothing that Graham said about children is crime-specific. Thus, its reasoning implicates any life-without-parole sentence for a juvenile, even as its categorical bar relates only to nonhomicide offenses. Most fundamentally, Graham insists that youth matters in determining the appropriateness of a lifetime of incarceration without the possibility of parole. The mandatory penalty schemes at issue here, however, prevent the sentencer from considering youth and from assessing whether the law's harshest term of imprisonment proportionately punishes a juvenile offender. This contravenes Graham's (and also Roper's) foundational principle: that imposition of a State's most severe penalties on juvenile offenders cannot proceed as though they were not children.

Graham also likened life-without-parole sentences for juveniles to the death penalty. That decision recognized that life-without-parole sentences "share some characteristics with death sentences that are shared by no other sentences." 560 U. S., at ___. And it treated life without parole for juveniles like this Court's cases treat the death penalty, imposing a categorical bar on its imposition for nonhomicide offenses. By likening life-without-parole sentences for juveniles to the death penalty, Graham makes relevant this Court's cases demanding individualized sentencing in capital cases. In particular, those cases have emphasized that sentencers must be able to consider the mitigating qualities of youth. In light of Graham's reasoning, these decisions also show the flaws of imposing mandatory life-without-parole sentences on juvenile homicide offenders.

(b) The counterarguments of Alabama and Arkansas are unpersuasive.

(1) The States first contend that Harmelin v. Michigan, 501 U. S. 957, forecloses a holding that mandatory life-without-parole sentences for juveniles violate the Eighth Amendment. Harmelin declined to extend the individualized sentencing

requirement to noncapital cases "because of the qualitative difference between death and all other penalties." Id., at 1006 (Kennedy, J., concurring in part and concurring in judgment). But Harmelin had nothing to do with children, and did not purport to apply to juvenile offenders. Indeed, since Harmelin, this Court has held on multiple occasions that sentencing practices that are permissible for adults may not be so for children. See Roper, 543 U. S. 551; Graham, 560 U.S. ___.

The States next contend that mandatory life-without-parole terms for juveniles cannot be unconstitutional because 29 jurisdictions impose them on at least some children convicted of murder. In considering categorical bars to the death penalty and life without parole, this Court asks as part of the analysis whether legislative enactments and actual sentencing practices show a national consensus against a sentence for a particular class of offenders. But where, as here, this Court does not categorically bar a penalty, but instead requires only that a sentencer follow a certain process, this Court has not scrutinized or relied on legislative enactments in the same way. See, e.g., Sumner v. Schuman, 483 U. S. 66.

In any event, the "objective indicia of society's standards," Graham, 560 U. S., at ___, that the States offer do not distinguish these cases from others holding that a sentencing practice violates the Eighth Amendment. Fewer States impose mandatory life-without-parole sentences on juvenile homicide offenders than authorized the penalty (life-without-parole for nonhomicide offenders) that this Court invalidated in Graham. And as Graham and Thompson v. Oklahoma, 487 U. S. 815, explain, simply counting legislative enactments can present a distorted view. In those cases, as here, the relevant penalty applied to juveniles based on two separate provisions: One allowed the transfer of certain juvenile offenders to adult court, while another set out penalties for any and all individuals tried there. In those circumstances, this Court reasoned, it was impossible to say whether a legislature had endorsed a given penalty for children (or would do so if presented with the choice). The same is true here.

(2) The States next argue that courts and prosecutors sufficiently consider a juvenile defendant's age, as well as his background and the circumstances of his crime, when deciding whether to try him as an adult. But this argument ignores that many States use mandatory transfer systems. In addition, some lodge the decision in the hands of the prosecutors, rather than courts. And even where judges have transfer-stage discretion, it has limited utility, because the decisionmaker typically will have only partial information about the child or the circumstances of his offense. Finally, because of the limited sentencing options in some juvenile courts, the transfer decision may present a choice between a light sentence as a juvenile and standard sentencing as an adult. It cannot substitute for discretion at posttrial sentencing.

No. 10–9646, 63 So. 3d 676, and No. 10–9647, 2011 Ark. 49, ___ S. W. 3d ___, reversed and remanded.

KAGAN, J., delivered the opinion of the Court, in which KENNEDY, GINSBURG, BREYER, and SOTOMAYOR, JJ., joined. BREYER, J., filed a concurring opinion, in which SOTOMAYOR, J., joined. ROBERTS, C. J., filed a dissenting opinion, in which SCALIA, THOMAS, and ALITO, JJ., joined. THOMAS, J., filed a dissenting opinion, in which SCALIA, J., joined. ALITO, J., filed a dissenting opinion, in which SCALIA, J., joined.

Cases Relating to Chapter 15

Legal Remedies Available to Prisoners

DANIELS
V.
WILLIAMS

474 U.S. 327; 106 S. CT. 662; 88 L. ED. 2D 662 (1986)

CERTIORARI TO THE UNITED STATES COURT OF APPEALS FOR THE FOURTH CIRCUIT

No. 84–5872   Argued November 6, 1985— Decided January 21, 1986

Petitioner brought an action in Federal District Court under 42 U.S.C. § 1983, seeking to recover damages for injuries allegedly sustained when, while an inmate in a Richmond, Virginia, jail, he slipped on a pillow negligently left on a stairway by respondent sheriff's deputy. Petitioner contends that such negligence deprived him of his "liberty" interest in freedom from bodily injury "without due process of law" within the meaning of the Due Process Clause of the Fourteenth Amendment. The District Court granted respondent's motion for summary judgment, and the Court of Appeals affirmed.

Held: The Due Process Clause is not implicated by a state official's negligent act causing unintended loss of or injury to life, liberty, or property.

(a) The Due Process Clause was intended to secure an individual from an abuse of power by government officials. Far from an abuse of power, lack of due care, such as respondent's alleged negligence here, suggests no more than a failure to measure up to the conduct of a reasonable person. To hold that injury caused by such conduct is a deprivation within the meaning of the Due Process Clause would trivialize the centuries-old principle of due process of law. *Parratt v. Taylor*, 451 U. S. 527, overruled to the extent that it states otherwise.

(b) The Constitution does not purport to supplant traditional tort law in laying down rules of conduct to regulate liability for injuries that attend living together in society. While the Due Process Clause speaks to some facets of the relationship between jailers and inmates, its protections are not triggered by lack of due care by the jailers. Jailers may owe a special duty of care under state tort law to those in their custody, but the Due Process Clause does not embrace such a tort law concept.

748 F.2d 229, affirmed.

REHNQUIST, J., delivered the opinion of the Court, in which BURGER, C.J., and BRENNAN, WHITE, POWELL, and O'CONNOR, JJ., joined. MARSHALL, J., concurred in the result. BLACKMUN, J., and STEVENS, J., filed opinions concurring in the judgment.

CARLSON
V.
GREEN

446 U.S. 14; 100 S. CT. 1468; 64 L. ED. 2D 15 (1980)

CERTIORARI TO THE UNITED STATES COURT OF APPEALS FOR THE SEVENTH CIRCUIT

No. 78–1261   Argued January 7, 1980— Decided April 22, 1980

Respondent brought suit in Federal District Court in Indiana on behalf of her deceased son's estate, alleging that her son, while a prisoner in a federal prison in Indiana, suffered personal injuries from which he died because petitioner prison officials violated, *inter alia*, his Eighth Amendment rights by failing to give him proper medical attention. Asserting jurisdiction under 28 U.S.C. § 1331(a), respondent claimed compensatory and punitive damages. The District Court held that the allegations pleaded a violation of the Eighth Amendment's proscription against cruel and unusual punishment, thus giving rise to a cause of action for damages under *Bivens v. Six Unknown Fed. Narcotics Agents*, 403 U. S. 388, under which it was established that victims of a constitutional violation by a federal official have a right to recover damages against the official in federal court despite the absence of any statute conferring such a right. But the court dismissed the complaint on the ground that, although the decedent could have maintained the action if he had survived, the damages remedy, as a matter of federal law, was limited to that provided by Indiana's survivorship and wrongful death laws, which the court construed as making the damages available to the decedent's estate insufficient to meet § 1331(a)'s $10,000 jurisdictional amount requirement. While otherwise agreeing with the District Court, the Court of Appeals held that the latter requirement was satisfied because, whenever a state survivorship statute would abate a *Bivens*-type action, the federal common law allows survival of the action.

Held:

1. A *Bivens* remedy is available to respondent even though the allegations could

also support a suit against the United States under the Federal Tort Claims Act (FTCA).

(a) Neither of the situations in which a cause of action under *Bivens* may be defeated are present here. First, the case involves no special factors counseling hesitation in the absence of affirmative action by Congress, petitioners not enjoying such independent status in our constitutional scheme as to suggest that judicially created remedies against them might be inappropriate. Second, there is no explicit congressional declaration that persons injured by federal officers' violations of the Eighth Amendment may not recover damages from the officers, but must be remitted to another remedy, equally effective in Congress' view. There is nothing in the FTCA or its legislative history to show that Congress meant to preempt a *Bivens* remedy or to create an equally effective remedy for constitutional violations. Rather, in the absence of a contrary expression from Congress, the FTCA's provision creating a cause of action against the United States for intentional torts committed by federal law enforcement officers, contemplates that victims of the kind of intentional wrongdoing alleged in the complaint in this case shall have an action under the FTCA against the United States as well as a *Bivens* action against the individual officials alleged to have infringed their constitutional rights.

(b) The following factors also support the conclusion that Congress did not intend to limit respondent to an FTCA action: (i) the *Bivens* remedy, being recoverable against individuals, is a more effective deterrent than the FTCA remedy against the United States; (ii) punitive damages may be awarded in a *Bivens* suit, but are statutorily prohibited in an FTCA suit; (iii) a plaintiff cannot opt for a jury trial in an FTCA action, as he may in a *Bivens* suit; and (iv) an action under the FTCA exists only if the State in which the alleged misconduct occurred would permit a cause of action for that misconduct to go forward.

2. Since *Bivens* actions are a creation of federal law, the question whether respondent's action survived her son's death is a question of federal law. Only a uniform federal rule of survivorship will suffice to redress the constitutional deprivation here alleged and to protect against repetition of such conduct. *Robertson v. Wegmann*, 436 U. S. 584 distinguished.

581 F.2d 669, affirmed.
BRENNAN, J., delivered the opinion of the Court, in which WHITE, MARSHALL, BLACKMUN, and STEVENS, JJ., joined. POWELL, J., filed an opinion concurring in the judgment, in which STEWART, J., joined. BURGER, C.J., and REHNQUIST, J., filed dissenting opinions.

SMITH
V.
WADE

461 U.S. 30; 103 S. CT. 1625; 75 L. ED. 2D 632 (1983)

CERTIORARI TO THE UNITED STATES COURT OF APPEALS FOR THE EIGHTH CIRCUIT

No. 81–1196   Argued November 10, 1982—Decided April 20, 1983

Respondent, while an inmate in a Missouri reformatory for youthful first offenders, was harassed, beaten, and sexually assaulted by his cellmates. He brought suit under 42 U.S.C. § 1983 in Federal District Court against petitioner, a guard at the reformatory, and others, alleging that his Eighth Amendment rights had been violated. Because of petitioner's qualified immunity, as a prison guard, from § 1983 liability, the trial judge instructed the jury that respondent could recover only if petitioner was guilty of "gross negligence" or "egregious

failure to protect" respondent. The judge also charged the jury that it could award punitive damages in addition to actual damages if petitioner's conduct was shown to be "a reckless or callous disregard of, or indifference to, the rights or safety of others." The District Court entered judgment on a verdict finding petitioner liable and awarding both compensatory and punitive damages. The Court of Appeals affirmed.

Held:

1. Punitive damages are available in a proper case under § 1983. While there is little in the legislative history of § 1 of the Civil Rights Act of 1871 (from which § 1983 is derived) concerning the damages recoverable for the tort liability created by the statute, the availability of punitive damages was accepted as settled law by nearly all state and federal courts at the time of enactment. Moreover, this Court has rested decisions on related issues on the premise that punitive damages are available under § 1983.

2. A jury may be permitted to assess punitive damages in a § 1983 action when the defendant's conduct involves reckless or callous indifference to the plaintiff's federally protected rights, as well as when it is motivated by evil motive or intent. The common law, both in 1871 and now, allows recovery of punitive damages in tort cases not only for actual malicious intent, but also for reckless indifference to the rights of others. Neither the policies nor the purposes of § 1983 require a departure from the common law rule. Petitioner's contention that an actual intent standard is preferable to a recklessness standard because it is less vague, and would more readily serve the purpose of deterrence of future egregious conduct, is unpersuasive. *Cf. Gertz v. Robert Welch, Inc.*, 418 U. S. 323.

3. The threshold standard for allowing punitive damages for reckless or callous indifference applies even in a case, such as here, where the underlying standard of liability for compensatory damages is also one of recklessness. There is no merit to petitioner's contention that actual

malicious intent should be the standard for punitive damages because the deterrent purposes of such damages would be served only if the threshold for those damages is higher in every case than the underlying standard for liability in the first instance. The common law rule is otherwise, and there is no reason to depart from the common law rule in the context of § 1983.

663 F.2d 778, affirmed.

BRENNAN, J., delivered the opinion of the Court, in which WHITE, MARSHALL, BLACKMUN, and STEVENS, JJ., joined. REHNQUIST, J., filed a dissenting opinion, in which BURGER, C.J., and POWELL, J., joined. O'CONNOR, J., filed a dissenting opinion.

CORRECTIONAL SERVICES CORPORATION
V.
MALESKO

534 U.S. 61; 122 S. CT. 515; 151 L. ED. 2D 456 (2001)

CERTIORARI TO THE UNITED STATES COURT OF APPEALS FOR THE SECOND CIRCUIT

No. 00–860   Argued October 1, 2001— Decided November 27, 2001

Petitioner Correctional Services Corporation (CSC), under contract with the federal Bureau of Prisons (BOP), operates Le Marquis Community Correctional Center (Le Marquis), a facility that houses federal inmates. After respondent, a federal inmate afflicted with a heart condition limiting his ability to climb stairs, was assigned to a bedroom on Le Marquis' fifth floor, CSC instituted a policy requiring inmates residing below the sixth floor to use the stairs rather than the elevator. Respondent was exempted from this policy. But when a CSC employee forbade respondent to use the elevator to reach his bedroom, he climbed the stairs, suffered a heart attack, and fell.

Subsequently, respondent filed this damages action against CSC and individual defendants, alleging, inter alia, that they were negligent in refusing him the use of the elevator. The District Court treated the complaint as raising claims under Bivens v. Six Unknown Fed. Narcotics Agents, 403 U. S. 388, in which this Court recognized for the first time an implied private action for damages against federal officers alleged to have violated a citizen's constitutional rights. In dismissing the suit, the District Court relied on FDIC v. Meyer, 510 U. S. 471, reasoning, inter alia, that a Bivens action may only be maintained against an individual, not a corporate entity. The Second Circuit reversed in pertinent part and remanded, remarking, with respect to CSC, that Meyer expressly declined to expand the category of defendants against whom Bivens-type actions may be brought to include not only federal agents, but also federal agencies. But the court reasoned that such private entities should be held liable under Bivens to accomplish the important Bivens goal of providing a remedy for constitutional violations.

Held: Bivens' limited holding may not be extended to confer a right of action for damages against private entities acting under color of federal law. The Court's authority to imply a new constitutional tort, not expressly authorized by statute, is anchored in its general jurisdiction to decide all cases arising under federal law. The Court first exercised this authority in Bivens. From a discussion of that and subsequent cases, it is clear that respondent's claim is fundamentally different from anything the Court has heretofore recognized. In 30 years of Bivens jurisprudence, the Court has extended its holding only twice, to provide an otherwise nonexistent cause of action against individual officers alleged to have acted unconstitutionally, e. g., Carlson v. Green, 446 U. S. 14, and to provide a cause of action for a plaintiff who lacked any alternative remedy for harms caused by an individual officer's unconstitutional conduct, e. g., Davis v. Passman, 442 U. S. 228, 245. Where such circumstances are not present, the Court has consistently rejected invitations to extend Bivens, often for reasons that foreclose its extension here. See, e. g., Bush v. Lucas, 462 U. S. 367. Bivens' purpose is to deter individual federal officers, not the agency, from committing constitutional violations. Meyer made clear, inter alia, that the threat of suit against an individual's employer was not the kind of deterrence contemplated by Bivens. 510 U. S., at 485. This case is, in every meaningful sense, the same. For if a corporate defendant is available for suit, claimants will focus their collection efforts on it, and not the individual directly responsible for the alleged injury. On Meyer's logic, inferring a constitutional tort remedy against a private entity like CSC is therefore foreclosed. Respondent's claim that requiring private corporations acting under color of federal law to pay for the constitutional harms they commit is the best way to discourage future harms has no relevance to Bivens, which is concerned solely with deterring individual officers' unconstitutional acts. There is no reason here to consider extending Bivens beyond its core premise. To begin with, no federal prisoners enjoy respondent's contemplated remedy. If such a prisoner in a BOP facility alleges a constitutional deprivation, his only remedy lies against the offending individual officer. Whether it makes sense to impose asymmetrical liability costs on private prison facilities alone is a question for Congress to decide. Nor is this a situation in which claimants in respondent's shoes lack effective remedies. It was conceded at oral argument that alternative remedies are at least as great, and in many respects greater, than anything that could be had under Bivens. For example, federal prisoners in private facilities enjoy a parallel tort remedy that is unavailable to prisoners housed in government facilities. Inmates in respondent's position also have full access to remedial mechanisms established by the BOP, including suits in federal court for injunctive relief-long recognized as the proper means for preventing entities from acting unconstitutionally-and grievances filed through the BOP's Administrative Remedy Program.

229 F.3d 374, reversed.

REHNQUIST, C. J., delivered the opinion of the Court, in which O'CONNOR, SCALIA, KENNEDY, and THOMAS, JJ., joined. SCALIA, J., filed a concurring opinion, in which THOMAS, J., joined. STEVENS, J., filed a dissenting

opinion, in which SOUTER, GINSBURG, and BREYER, JJ., joined.

HOPE
V.
PELZER

536 U.S. 730; 122 S. CT. 2508; 153 L. ED. 2D 666 (2002)

CERTIORARI TO THE UNITED STATES COURT OF APPEALS FOR THE ELEVENTH CIRCUIT

No. 01–309   Argued April 17, 2002—Decided June 27, 2002

In 1995, petitioner Hope, then an Alabama prison inmate, was twice handcuffed to a hitching post for disruptive conduct. During a 2-hour period in May, he was offered drinking water and a bathroom break every 15 minutes, and his responses were recorded on an activity log. He was handcuffed above shoulder height, and when he tried moving his arms to improve circulation, the handcuffs cut into his wrists, causing pain and discomfort. After an altercation with a guard at his chain gang's work site in June, Hope was subdued, handcuffed, placed in leg irons, and transported back to the prison, where he was ordered to take off his shirt, thus exposing himself to the sun, and spent seven hours on the hitching post. While there, he was given one or two water breaks but no bathroom breaks, and a guard taunted him about his thirst. Hope filed a 42 U. S. C. § 1983 suit against three guards. Without deciding whether placing Hope on the hitching post as punishment violated the Eighth Amendment, the Magistrate Judge found that the guards were entitled to qualified immunity. The District Court entered summary judgment for respondents, and the Eleventh Circuit affirmed. The latter court answered the constitutional question, finding that the hitching post's use for punitive purposes violated the Eighth Amendment. In finding the guards nevertheless entitled to qualified immunity, it concluded that Hope could not show, as required by Circuit precedent, that the federal law by which the guards' conduct should be evaluated was established by cases that were "materially similar" to the facts in his own case.

Held: The defense of qualified immunity was precluded at the summary judgment phase.

(a) Hope's allegations, if true, establish an Eighth Amendment violation. Among the "'unnecessary and wanton' inflictions of pain [constituting cruel and unusual punishment forbidden by the Amendment] are those that are 'totally without penological justification.'" *Rhodes* v. *Chapman,* 452 U. S. 337, 346. This determination is made in the context of prison conditions by ascertaining whether an official acted with "deliberate indifference" to the inmates' health or safety, *Hudson* v. *McMillian,* 503 U. S. 1, 8, a state of mind that can be inferred from the fact that the risk of harm is obvious, *Farmer* v. *Brennan,* 511 U. S. 825. The Eighth Amendment violation here is obvious on the facts alleged. Any safety concerns had long since abated by the time Hope was handcuffed to the hitching post, because he had already been subdued, handcuffed, placed in leg irons, and transported back to prison. He was separated from his work squad and not given the opportunity to return. Despite the clear lack of emergency, respondents knowingly subjected him to a substantial risk of physical harm, unnecessary pain, unnecessary exposure to the sun, prolonged thirst and taunting, and a deprivation of bathroom breaks that created a risk of particular discomfort and humiliation.

(b) Respondents may nevertheless be shielded from liability for their constitutionally impermissible conduct if their actions did not violate "clearly established statutory or constitutional rights of which a reasonable person would have known." *Harlow* v. *Fitzgerald,* 457 U.S. 800, 818. In its assessment, the Eleventh Circuit erred in requiring that the facts of previous cases and Hope's case be "materially similar." Qualified immunity operates to ensure that before they are subjected to suit, officers are on notice that their conduct is unlawful. Officers sued in a § 1983 civil action have the same fair notice right as do defendants charged under 18 U. S. C. § 242, which makes it a crime for a state official to act willfully and under color of law to deprive a person of constitutional rights. This Court's opinion in *United States* v. *Lanier,* 520 U. S. 259, a § 242 case, makes clear that officials can be on notice that their conduct violates established law even in novel factual situations. Indeed, the Court expressly rejected a requirement that previous cases be "fundamentally similar." Accordingly, the salient question that the Eleventh Circuit should have asked is whether the state of the law in 1995 gave respondents fair warning that Hope's alleged treatment was unconstitutional.

(c) A reasonable officer would have known that using a hitching post as Hope alleged was unlawful. The obvious cruelty inherent in the practice should have provided respondents with some notice that their conduct was unconstitutional. In addition, binding Circuit precedent should have given them notice. *Gates* v. *Collier,* 501 F.2d 1291, found several forms of corporal punishment impermissible, including handcuffing inmates to fences or cells for long periods, and *Ort* v. *White, 813* F. 2d 318, 324, warned that "physical abuse directed at [a] prisoner *after* he terminate[s] his resistance to authority would constitute an actionable eighth amendment violation." Relevant to the question whether *Ort* provided fair notice is a subsequent Alabama Department of Corrections (ADOC) regulation specifying procedures for using a hitching post, which included allowing an inmate to rejoin his squad when he tells an officer that he is ready to work. If regularly observed, that provision would have made Hope's case less like the kind of punishment *Ort* described as impermissible. But conduct showing that the provision was a sham, or that respondents could ignore it with impunity, provides equally strong support for the conclusion that they were fully aware of their wrongful conduct. The conclusion here is also buttressed by the fact that the Justice Department specifically advised the ADOC of the constitutional infirmity of its practices before the incidents in this case took place.

240 F.3d 975, reversed.

STEVENS, J., delivered the opinion of the Court, in which O'CONNOR, KENNEDY, SOUTER, GINSBURG, and BREYER, JJ., joined. THOMAS, J., filed a dissenting opinion, in which REHNQUIST, C. J., and SCALIA, J., joined.

UNITED STATES
V.
GEORGIA

546 U.S. 151, 126 S. CT. 877; 163 L. ED. 2D 650 (2006)

ON WRITS OF CERTIORARI TO THE UNITED STATES COURT OF APPEALS FOR THE ELEVENTH CIRCUIT

No. 04–1203 Argued November 9, 2005—Decided January 10, 2006

Goodman, petitioner in No. 04–1236, is a paraplegic who sued respondent state defendants and others, challenging the conditions of his confinement in a Georgia prison under, *inter alia*, 42 U. S. C. §1983 and Title II of the Americans with Disability Act of 1990. As relevant here, the Federal District Court dismissed the §1983 claims because Goodman's allegations were vague, and granted respondents summary judgment on the Title II money damages claims because they were barred by state sovereign immunity. The United States, petitioner in No. 04–1203, intervened on appeal. The Eleventh Circuit affirmed the District Court's judgment as to the Title II claims, but reversed the §1983 ruling, finding that Goodman had alleged facts sufficient to support a limited number of Eighth Amendment claims against state agents and should be permitted to amend his complaint. This

Court granted certiorari to decide the validity of Title II's abrogation of state sovereign immunity.

Held: Insofar as Title II creates a private cause of action for damages against States for conduct that *actually* violates the Fourteenth Amendment, Title II validly abrogates state sovereign immunity.

(a) Because this Court assumes that the Eleventh Circuit correctly held that Goodman had alleged actual Eighth Amendment violations for purposes of §1983, and because respondents do not dispute Goodman's claim that this same conduct violated Title II, Goodman's Title II money damages claims were evidently based, at least in part, on conduct that independently violated §1 of the Fourteenth Amendment. No one doubts that §5 grants Congress the power to enforce the Fourteenth Amendment's provisions by creating private remedies against the States for actual violations of those provisions. This includes the power to abrogate state sovereign immunity by authorizing private suits for damages against the States. Thus, the Eleventh Circuit erred in dismissing those of Goodman's claims based on conduct that violated the Fourteenth Amendment.

(b) Once Goodman's complaint is amended, the lower courts will be best situated to determine in the first instance, on a claim-by-claim basis, (1) which aspects of the State's alleged conduct violated Title II; (2) to what extent such misconduct also violated the Fourteenth Amendment; and (3) insofar as such conduct violated Title II but did not violate the Fourteenth Amendment, whether Congress's purported abrogation of sovereign immunity in such contexts is nevertheless valid.

120 Fed. Appx. 785, reversed and remanded.

SCALIA, J., delivered the opinion for a unanimous Court. STEVENS, J., filed a concurring opinion, in which GINSBURG, J., joined.

Together with No. 04–1236, *Goodman* v. *Georgia et al.*, also on certiorari to the same court.

HAYWOOD
V.
DROWN 556

U.S. 729; 129 S. CT. 2108; 173 L. ED. 2D 920 (2009)

CERTIORARI TO THE COURT OF APPEALS OF NEW YORK

No. 07–10374   Argued December 3, 2008—Decided May 26, 2009

Believing that damages suits filed by prisoners against state correction officers were largely frivolous and vexatious, New York passed Correction Law §24, which divested state courts of general jurisdiction of their jurisdiction over such suits, including those filed under 42 U. S. C. §1983, and replaced those claims with the State's preferred alternative. Thereunder, a prisoner will have his claim against a correction officer dismissed for want of jurisdiction and will be left to pursue a damages claim against the State in the Court of Claims, a court of limited jurisdiction in which the prisoner will not be entitled to attorney's fees, punitive damages, or injunctive relief. Petitioner filed two §1983 damages actions against correction employees in state court. Finding that it lacked jurisdiction under Correction Law §24, the trial court dismissed the actions. Affirming, the State Court of Appeals rejected petitioner's claim that the state statute's jurisdictional limitation violated the Supremacy Clause. It reasoned that because that law treats state and federal damages actions against correction officers equally—*i.e.*, neither can be brought in New York courts—it was a neutral rule of judicial administration and thus a valid excuse for the State's refusal to entertain the federal cause of action.

Held: Correction Law §24, as applied to §1983 claims, violates the Supremacy Clause.

(a) Federal and state law "together form one system of jurisprudence, which consti-

tutes the law of the land for the State; and the courts of the two jurisdictions are … courts of the same country, having jurisdiction partly different and partly concurrent." *Claflin* v. *Houseman*, 93 U.S. 130, 136–137. Both state and federal courts have jurisdiction over §1983 suits. So strong is the presumption of concurrency that it is defeated only when Congress expressly ousts state courts of jurisdiction, see *e.g., id.,* at 136; or "[w]hen a state court refuses jurisdiction because of a neutral state rule regarding the administration of the courts," *Howlett* v. *Rose*, 496 U. S. 356, 372. As to whether a state law qualifies as such a neutral rule, States retain substantial leeway to establish the contours of their judicial systems, but lack authority to nullify a federal right or cause of action they believe is inconsistent with their local policies. Whatever its merits, New York's policy of shielding correction officers from liability when sued for damages arising out of conduct performed in the scope of their employment is contrary to Congress' judgment that *all* persons who violate federal rights while acting under color of state law shall be held liable for damages. "A State may not … relieve congestion in its courts by declaring a whole category of federal claims to be frivolous." *Id.*, at 380.

(b) The New York Court of Appeals' holding was based on the misunderstanding that Correction Law §24's equal treatment of federal and state claims would guarantee that the statute would pass constitutional muster. Although the absence of discrimination is essential to this Court's finding a state law neutral, nondiscrimination alone is not sufficient to guarantee that a state law will be deemed neutral. In addition to this misplaced reliance on equality, respondents mistakenly treat this case as implicating the "great latitude [States enjoy] to establish the structure and jurisdiction of their own courts." *Howlett*, 496 U. S., at 372. However, this Court need not decide whether Congress can compel a State to offer a forum, otherwise unavailable under state law, to hear §1983 suits, because New York has courts of general jurisdiction that routinely sit to hear analogous §1983 actions.

9 N. Y. 3d 481, 881 N. E. 2d 180, reversed and remanded.

STEVENS, J., delivered the opinion of the Court, in which KENNEDY, SOUTER, GINSBURG, and BREYER, JJ., joined. THOMAS, J., filed a dissenting opinion, in which ROBERTS, C. J., and SCALIA and ALITO, JJ., joined as to Part III.

Cases Relating to Chapter 16

Selected Federal Statutes Affecting Prisoners

PENNSYLVANIA
V.
YESKEY

524 U.S. 206, 118 S. CT. 1952, 141 L. ED. 2D 215 (1998)

CERTIORARI TO THE UNITED STATES COURT OF APPEALS FOR THE THIRD CIRCUIT

No. 97–634   Argued April 28, 1998—Decided June 15, 1998

Respondent Yeskey was sentenced to 18 to 36 months in a Pennsylvania correctional facility, but was recommended for placement in a Motivational Boot Camp for first-time offenders, the successful completion of which would have led to his parole in just six months. When he was refused admission because of his medical history of hypertension, he sued petitioners, Pennsylvania's Department of Corrections and several officials, alleging that the exclusion violated the Americans with Disabilities Act of 1990 (ADA), Title II of which prohibits a "public entity" from discriminating against a "qualified individual with a disability" on account of that disability, 42 U. S. C. § 12132. The District Court dismissed for failure to state a claim, holding the ADA inapplicable to state prison inmates, but the Third Circuit reversed. *Held:* State prisons fall squarely within Title II's statutory definition of "public entity," which includes "any . . . instrumentality of a State . . . or local government." § 12131(1)(B). Unlike the situation that obtained in *Gregory* v. *Ashcroft,*

501 U. S. 452, there is no ambiguous exception that renders the coverage uncertain. For that reason the plain-statement requirement articulated in *Gregory,* if applicable to federal intrusion upon the administration of state prisons, has been met. Petitioners' attempts to derive an intent not to cover prisons from the statutory references to the "benefits" of programs and to "qualified individual" are rejected; some prison programs, such as this one, have benefits and are restricted to qualified inmates. The statute's lack of ambiguity also requires rejection of petitioners' appeal to the doctrine of constitutional doubt. The Court does not address the issue whether applying the ADA to state prisons is a constitutional exercise of Congress's power under either the Commerce Clause or the Fourteenth Amendment because it was addressed by neither of the lower courts.

118 F.3d 168, affirmed.
SCALIA, J., delivered the opinion for a unanimous Court.

BOOTH
V.
CHURNER

532 U.S. 731; 121 S. CT. 1819; 149 L. ED. 2D 958 (2001)

CERTIORARI TO THE UNITED STATES COURT OF APPEALS FOR THE THIRD CIRCUIT

No. 99–1964   Argued March 20, 2001—Decided May 29, 2001

The Prison Litigation Reform Act of 1995 amended 42 U. S. C. § 1997e(a), which now requires a prisoner to exhaust "such administrative remedies as are available" before suing over prison conditions. Petitioner Booth was a Pennsylvania state prison inmate when he began this 42 U.S.C. § 1983 action in Federal District Court, claiming that respondent corrections officers violated his Eighth Amendment right to be free from cruel and unusual punishment by assaulting him, using excessive force against him, and denying him medical attention to treat ensuing injuries. He sought various forms of injunctive relief and money damages. At the time, Pennsylvania provided an administrative grievance and appeals system, which addressed Booth's complaints but had no provision for recovery of money damages. Before resorting to federal court, Booth filed an administrative grievance, but did not seek administrative review after the prison authority denied relief. Booth's failure to appeal administratively led the District Court to dismiss the complaint without prejudice for failure to exhaust administrative remedies under § 1997e(a). The Third Circuit affirmed, rejecting Booth's argument that the exhaustion requirement is inapposite to his case because the administrative process could not award him the monetary relief he sought (money then being the only relief still requested).

Held: Under 42 U. S. C. § 1997e(a), an inmate seeking only money damages must complete any prison administrative process capable of addressing the inmate's complaint and providing some form of relief, even if the process does not make specific provision for monetary relief. The meaning of the phrase "administrative remedies . . . available" is the crux of the case. Neither the practical considerations urged by the parties nor their reliance on the dictionary meanings of the words "remedies" and "available" are conclusive in seeking congressional intent. Clearer clues are found in two considerations. First, the broader statutory context in which Congress referred to "available" "remedies" indicates that exhaustion is required regardless of the relief offered through administrative procedures. While the modifier "available" requires the possibility of some relief for the action complained of, the word "exhausted" has a decidedly procedural emphasis. It makes no sense, for instance, to demand that someone exhaust "such administrative [redress]" as is available; one "exhausts"

processes, not forms of relief, and the statute provides that one must. Second, statutory history confirms the suggestion that Congress meant to require procedural exhaustion regardless of the fit between a prisoner's prayer for relief and the administrative remedies possible. Before § 1997e(a) was amended by the 1995 Act, a court had discretion (though no obligation) to require a state inmate to exhaust "such . . . remedies as are available," but only if they were "plain, speedy, and effective." That scheme is now a thing of the past, for the amendments eliminated both the discretion to dispense with administrative exhaustion and the condition that the remedy be "plain, speedy, and effective" before exhaustion could be required. The significance of deleting that condition is apparent in light of *McCarthy v. Madigan,* 503 U. S. 140. In holding that the pre-amended version of § 1997e(a) did not require exhaustion by those seeking only money damages when money was unavailable at the administrative level, *id.,* at 149–151, the *McCarthy* Court reasoned in part that only a procedure able to provide money damages would be "effective" within the statute's meaning, id., at 150. It has to be significant that Congress removed the very term, "effective," the *McCarthy* Court had previously emphasized in reaching the result Booth now seeks, and the fair inference to be drawn is that Congress meant to preclude the *McCarthy* result. Congress's imposition of an obviously broader exhaustion requirement makes it highly implausible that it meant to give prisoners a strong inducement to skip the administrative process simply by limiting prayers for relief to money damages not offered through administrative grievance mechanisms.

206 F.3d 289, affirmed.

SOUTER, J., delivered the opinion for a unanimous Court.

PORTER
V.
NUSSLE

534 U.S. 516; 122 S. CT. 983; 152 L. ED. 2D 12 (2002)

CERTIORARI TO THE UNITED STATES COURT OF APPEALS FOR THE SECOND CIRCUIT

No. 00–853   Argued January 14, 2002—
Decided February 26, 2002

Without filing a grievance under applicable Connecticut Department of Correction procedures, plaintiff-respondent Nussle, a state prison inmate, commenced a federal-court action under 42 U. S. C. § 1983, charging that corrections officers, including defendant-petitioner Porter, had subjected him to a sustained pattern of harassment and intimidation and had singled him out for a severe beating in violation of the Eighth Amendment's ban on "cruel and unusual punishments." The District Court dismissed Nussle's suit, relying on a provision of the Prison Litigation Reform Act of 1995 (PLRA), 42 U. S. C. § 1997e(a), that directs: "No action shall be brought with respect to prison conditions under section 1983 . . ., or any other Federal law, by a prisoner . . . until such administrative remedies as are available are exhausted." The Second Circuit reversed, holding that exhaustion of administrative remedies is not required for a claim of the kind Nussle asserted. The appeals court concluded that § 1997e(a)'s "prison conditions" phrase covers only conditions affecting prisoners generally, not single incidents that immediately affect only particular prisoners, such as corrections officers' use of excessive force. In support of its position, the court cited legislative history suggesting that the PLRA curtails frivolous suits, not actions seeking relief from corrections officer brutality; the court also referred to prePLRA decisions in which this Court distinguished, for proof of injury and mens rea purposes, between excessive force claims and conditions of confinement claims.

Held: The PLRA's exhaustion requirement applies to all inmate suits about prison life, whether they involve general circumstances or particular episodes, and whether they allege excessive force or some other wrong. Cf. Wilson v. Seiter, 501 U. S. 294, 299, n. 1.

(a) The current exhaustion provision in § 1997e(a) differs markedly from its predecessor. Once within the district court's discretion, exhaustion in § 1997e(a) cases is now mandatory. See Booth v. Churner, 532 U. S. 731, 739. And unlike the previous provision, which encompassed only § 1983 suits, exhaustion is now required

for all "action[s] . . . brought with respect to prison conditions." Section 1997e(a), designed to reduce the quantity and improve the quality of prisoner suits, affords corrections officials an opportunity to address complaints internally before allowing the initiation of a federal case. In some instances, corrective action taken in response to an inmate's grievance might improve prison administration and satisfy the inmate, thereby obviating the need for litigation. Id., at 737. In other instances, the internal review might filter out some frivolous claims. Ibid. And for cases ultimately brought to court, an administrative record clarifying the controversy's contours could facilitate adjudication. See, e. g., ibid.

(b) Determination of the meaning of § 1997e(a)'s "prison conditions" phrase is guided by the PLRA's text and context, and by this Court's prior decisions relating to "[suits by prisoners," as § 1997e is titled. The pathmarking opinion is McCarthy v. Bronson, 500 U. S. 136, in which the Court construed the Federal Magistrates Act's authorization to district judges to refer "prisoner petitions challenging conditions of confinement" to magistrate judges. This Court concluded in McCarthy that, read in its proper context, the phrase "challenging conditions of confinement" authorizes the nonconsensual reference of all prisoner petitions to a magistrate, id., at 139. The McCarthy Court emphasized that Preiser v. Rodriguez, 411 U. S. 475, had unambiguously placed cases involving single episodes of unconstitutional conduct within the broad category of prisoner petitions challenging conditions of confinement, 500 U. S., at 141; found it telling that Congress, in composing the Magistrates Act, chose language that so clearly paralleled the Preiser opinion, 500 U. S., at 142; and considered it significant that the latter Act's purpose-to lighten overworked district judges' caseload-would be thwarted by allowing satellite litigation over the precise contours of an exception for single episode cases, id., at 143. The general presumption that Congress expects its statutes to be read in conformity with this Court's precedents, United States v. Wells, 519 U. S. 482, 495, and the PLRA's dominant concern to promote administrative redress, filter out groundless claims, and foster better prepared litigation of claims aired in court, see Booth v. Churner, 532 U. S., at 737, persuade the Court that § 1997e(a)'s key words "prison conditions" are properly read through the lens of McCarthy and Preiser. Those decisions tug strongly away from classifying suits about prison guards' use of excessive force, one or many times, as anything other than actions "with respect to prison conditions." Nussle misplaces principal reliance on Hudson v. McMillian, 503 U. S. 1, 8–9, and Farmer v. Brennan, 511 U. S. 825, 835–836. Although those cases did distinguish excessive force claims from conditions of confinement claims, they did so in the context of proof requirements: what injury must a plaintiff allege and show; what mental state must a plaintiff plead and prove. Proof requirements, once a case is in court, however, do not touch or concern the threshold inquiry at issue here: whether resort to a prison grievance process must precede resort to a court. There is no reason to believe that Congress meant to release the evidentiary distinctions drawn in Hudson and Farmer from their moorings and extend their application to § 1997e(a)'s otherwise invigorated exhaustion requirement. It is at least equally plausible that Congress inserted "prison conditions" into the exhaustion provision simply to make it clear that preincarceration claims fall outside § 1997e(a), for example, a § 1983 claim against the prisoner's arresting officer. Furthermore, the asserted distinction between excessive force claims and exhaustion-mandatory "frivolous" claims is untenable, for excessive force claims can be frivolous, and exhaustion serves purposes beyond weeding out frivolous allegations.

(c) Other infirmities inhere in the Second Circuit's disposition. See McCarthy, 500 U. S., at 143. In the prison environment, a specific incident may be symptomatic of a systemic problem, rather than aberrational. Id., at 143–144. Nussle urges that

his case could be placed in the isolated episode category, but he might equally urge that his complaint describes a pattern or practice of harassment climaxing in the alleged beating. It seems unlikely that Congress, when it included in the PLRA a firm exhaustion requirement, meant to leave the need to exhaust to the pleader's option. Cf. Preiser, 411 U. S., at 489–490. Moreover, the appeals court's disposition augurs complexity; bifurcated proceedings would be normal thereunder when, for example, a prisoner sues both the corrections officer alleged to have used excessive force and the supervisor who allegedly failed adequately to monitor those in his charge. Finally, scant sense supports the single occurrence, prevailing circumstance dichotomy. For example, prison authorities' interest in receiving prompt notice of, and opportunity to take action against, guard brutality is no less compelling than their interest in receiving notice and an opportunity to stop other types of staff wrongdoing. See id., at 492.

224 F.3d 95, reversed and remanded.
GINSBURG, J., delivered the opinion for a unanimous Court.

WOODFORD
V.
NGO

548 U.S. 81; 126 S. CT. 2378; 165 L. ED. 2D 368 (2006)

ON WRIT OF CERTIORARI TO THE UNITED STATES COURT OF APPEALS FOR THE NINTH CIRCUIT

No. 05–416   Argued March 22, 2006— Decided June 22, 2006

The Prison Litigation Reform Act of 1995 (PLRA) requires a prisoner to exhaust any available administrative remedies before challenging prison conditions in federal court. 42 U. S. C. §1997e(a). Respondent filed a grievance with California prison officials about his prison conditions, but it was rejected as untimely under state law. He subsequently sued petitioner officials under §1983 in the Federal District Court, which granted petitioners' motion to dismiss on the ground that respondent had not fully exhausted his administrative remedies under §1997e(a). Reversing, the Ninth Circuit held that respondent had exhausted those remedies because none remained available to him.

Held: The PLRA's exhaustion requirement requires proper exhaustion of administrative remedies.

(a) Petitioners claim that a prisoner must complete the administrative review process in accordance with applicable procedural rules, including deadlines, as a precondition to bringing suit in federal court, but respondent contends that §1997e(a) allows suit once administrative remedies are no longer available, regardless of the reason. To determine the correct interpretation, the Court looks for guidance to both administrative and habeas corpus law, where exhaustion is an important doctrine. Administrative law requires proper exhaustion of administrative remedies, which "means using all steps that the agency holds out, and doing so *properly.*" *Pozo* v. *McCaughtry*, 286 F. 3d 1022, 1024. Habeas law has substantively similar rules, though its terminology is different.

(b) Given this background, the Court is persuaded that the PLRA requires proper exhaustion.

  (1) By referring to "such administrative remedies as are available," §1997e(a)'s text strongly suggests "exhausted" means what it means in administrative law.

  (2) Construing §1997e(a) to require proper exhaustion also serves the PLRA's goals. It gives prisoners an effective incentive to make full use of the prison grievance process, thus providing prisons with a fair opportunity to correct their own errors. It reduces the quantity of prisoner suits. And it improves the quality of those suits that are filed

because proper exhaustion often results in creation of an administrative record helpful to the court. In contrast, respondent's interpretation would make the PLRA's exhaustion scheme totally ineffective, since exhaustion's benefits can be realized only if the prison grievance system is given a fair opportunity to consider the grievance. That cannot happen unless the grievant complies with the system's critical procedural rules. Respondent's arguments that his interpretation would filter out frivolous claims are unpersuasive.

  (3) As interpreted by respondent, the PLRA exhaustion requirement would be unprecedented. No statute or case purports to require exhaustion while at the same time allowing a party to bypass deliberately the administrative process by flouting the agency's procedural rules. None of his models is apt. He first suggests that the PLRA requirement was patterned on habeas law as it existed between 1963 and 1977 when, under *Fay v. Noia*, 372 U.S. 391, 438, a federal habeas claim could be procedurally defaulted only if the prisoner deliberately bypassed state remedies. That would be fanciful, however. The PLRA was enacted contemporaneously with the Antiterrorism and Effective Death Penalty Act of 1996, which gave federal habeas review a structure markedly different from what existed before 1977. Furthermore, respondent's interpretation would not duplicate that scheme, for it would permit a prisoner to bypass deliberately administrative review with no risk of sanction. Respondent next suggests that the PLRA exhaustion requirement is patterned on §14(b) of the Age Discrimination in Employment Act of 1967 and §706(e) of Title VII of the Civil Rights Act of 1964, but neither provision is in any sense an exhaustion provision.

(c) Respondent's remaining arguments regarding §1997e(a)'s interpretation are also unconvincing.

403 F. 3d 620, reversed and remanded.

ALITO, J., delivered the opinion of the Court, in which ROBERTS, C. J., and SCALIA, KENNEDY, and THOMAS, JJ., joined. BREYER, J., filed an opinion concurring in the judgment. STEVENS, J., filed a dissenting opinion, in which SOUTER and GINSBURG, JJ., joined.

JONES
V.
BOCK

549 U.S. 199; 127 S. CT. 910; 166 L. ED. 2D 798 (2007)

CERTIORARI TO THE UNITED STATES COURT OF APPEALS FOR THE SIXTH CIRCUIT

No. 05–7058   Argued October 30, 2006— Decided January 22, 2007

The Prison Litigation Reform Act of 1995 (PLRA), in order to address the large number of prisoner complaints filed in federal court, mandates early judicial screening of prisoner complaints and requires prisoners to exhaust prison grievance procedures before filing suit. 42 U. S. C. §1997e(a). Petitioners, inmates in Michigan prisons, filed grievances using the Michigan Department of Corrections (MDOC) grievance process. After unsuccessfully seeking redress through that process, petitioner Jones filed a 42 U. S. C. §1983 suit against six prison officials. The District Court dismissed on the merits as to four of them and as to two others found that Jones had failed to adequately plead exhaustion in his complaint. Petitioner Williams also filed a §1983 suit after his two MDOC grievances were denied. The District Court found that he had not exhausted his administrative remedies with regard to one of the grievances because he had not identified any of the respondents named in the lawsuit during the grievance process. While the court found Williams's other claim properly exhausted, it dismissed the entire suit under the Sixth Circuit's total exhaustion rule for PLRA

cases. Petitioner Walton's §1983 lawsuit also was dismissed under the total exhaustion rule because his MDOC grievance named only one of the six defendants in his lawsuit. The Sixth Circuit affirmed in each case, relying on its procedural rules that require a prisoner to allege and demonstrate exhaustion in his complaint, permit suit only against defendants identified in the prisoner's grievance, and require courts to dismiss the entire action if the prisoner fails to satisfy the exhaustion requirement as to any single claim in his complaint.

Held: The Sixth Circuit's rules are not required by the PLRA, and crafting and imposing such rules exceeds the proper limits of the judicial role. Pp. 10–24.

(a) Failure to exhaust is an affirmative defense under the PLRA, and inmates are not required to specially plead or demonstrate exhaustion in their complaints. There is no question that exhaustion is mandatory under the PLRA, *Porter* v. *Nussle*, 534 U. S. 516, 524, but it is less clear whether the prisoner must plead and demonstrate exhaustion in the complaint or the defendant must raise lack of exhaustion as an affirmative defense. Failure to exhaust is better viewed as an affirmative defense. Federal Rule of Civil Procedure 8(a) requires simply a "short and plain statement of the claim" in a complaint, and PLRA claims are typically brought under 42 U. S. C. §1983, which does not require exhaustion at all. The fact that the PLRA dealt extensively with exhaustion, but is silent on the issue whether exhaustion must be pleaded or is an affirmative defense, is strong evidence that the usual practice should be followed, and the practice under the Federal Rules is to regard exhaustion as an affirmative defense, including in the similar statutory scheme governing habeas corpus, *Day* v. *McDonough*, 547 U. S. ___, ___. Courts should generally not depart from the Federal Rules' usual practice based on perceived policy concerns. See, *e.g., Leatherman v. Tarrant County Narcotics Intelligence and Coordination Unit*, 507 U. S. 163 Those courts that require prisoners to plead and demonstrate exhaustion contend that prisoner complaints must be treated outside of the typical framework if the PLRA's screening requirement is to function effectively. But the screening requirement does not—explicitly or implicitly—justify deviating from the usual procedural practice beyond the departures specified by the PLRA itself. Although exhaustion was a "centerpiece" of the PLRA, *Woodford* v. *Ngo*, 548 U. S. ___, ___, failure to exhaust was notably not added in terms to the enumerated grounds justifying dismissal upon early screening. Section 1997e(g)—which allows defendants to waive their right to reply to a prisoner complaint without being deemed to have admitted the complaint's allegations—shows that when Congress meant to depart from the usual procedural requirements, it did so expressly. Given that the PLRA does not itself require plaintiffs to plead exhaustion, such a result "must be obtained by ... amending the Federal Rules, and not by judicial interpretation." *Leatherman, supra,* at 168.

(b) Exhaustion is not *per se* inadequate under the PLRA when an individual later sued was not named in the grievance. Nothing in the MDOC policy supports the conclusion that the grievance process was improperly invoked because an individual later named as a defendant was not named at the first step of the process; at the time each grievance was filed here, the MDOC policy did not specifically require a prisoner to name anyone in the grievance. Nor does the PLRA impose such a requirement. The "applicable procedural rules" that a prisoner must properly exhaust, *Woodford, supra,* at ___, are defined not by the PLRA, but by the prison grievance process itself. As the MDOC's procedures make no mention of naming particular officials, the Sixth Circuit's rule imposing such a prerequisite to proper exhaustion is unwarranted. The Circuit's rule may promote early notice to those who might later be sued, but that has not been thought to be one of the leading purposes of the exhaustion requirement. The court below should determine in the first instance whether petitioners' grievances otherwise satisfied the exhaustion requirement.

(c) The PLRA does not require dismissal of the entire complaint when a prisoner has failed to exhaust some, but not all, of the claims included in the complaint. Respon-

dents argue that had Congress intended courts to dismiss only unexhausted claims while retaining the balance of the lawsuit, it would have used the word "claim" instead of "action" in §1997e(a), which provides that "[n]o action shall be brought" unless administrative procedures are exhausted. That boilerplate language is used in many instances in the Federal Code, and statutory references to an "action" have not typically been read to mean that every claim included in the action must meet the pertinent requirement before the "action" may proceed. If a complaint contains both good and bad claims, the court proceeds with the good and leaves the bad. Respondents note that the total exhaustion requirement in habeas corpus is an exception to this general rule, but a court presented with a mixed habeas petition typically "allow[s] the petitioner to delete the unexhausted claims and to proceed with the exhausted claims," *Rhines* v. *Weber*, 544 U. S. 269, 278, which is the opposite of the rule the Sixth Circuit adopted, and precisely the rule that respondents argue against. Although other PLRA sections distinguish between actions and claims, respondents' reading of §1997e(a) creates its own inconsistencies, and their policy arguments are also unpersuasive.

No. 05–7058, 135 Fed. Appx. 837; No. 05–7142, 136 Fed. Appx. 846 (second judgment) and 859 (first judgment), reversed and remanded.

ROBERTS, C. J., delivered the opinion for a unanimous Court.

ALI
V.
FEDERAL BUREAU OF PRISONS

552 U.S. 214; 128 S. CT. 831; 169 L. ED. 2D 680 (2008)

CERTIORARI TO THE UNITED STATES COURT OF APPEALS FOR THE ELEVENTH CIRCUIT

No. 06–9130   Argued October 29, 2007—Decided January 22, 2008

The Federal Tort Claims Act (FTCA) waives the United States' sovereign immunity for claims arising out of torts committed by federal employees, see 28 U. S. C. §1346(b)(1), but, as relevant here, exempts from that waiver "[a]ny claim arising in respect of the assessment or collection of any tax or customs duty, or the detention of any . . . property by any officer of customs or excise or any other law enforcement officer," §2680(c). Upon his transfer from an Atlanta federal prison to one in Kentucky, petitioner noticed that several items were missing from his personal property, which had been shipped to the new facility by the Federal Bureau of Prisons (BOP). Alleging that BOP officers had lost his property, petitioner filed this suit under, *inter alia*, the FTCA, but the District Court dismissed that claim as barred by §2680(c). Affirming, the Eleventh Circuit rejected petitioner's argument that the statutory phrase "any officer of customs or excise or any other law enforcement officer" applies only to officers enforcing customs or excise laws.

Held: Section 2680(c)'s text and structure demonstrate that the broad phrase "any other law enforcement officer" covers all law enforcement officers. Petitioner's argument that §2680(c) is focused on preserving sovereign immunity only for officers enforcing customs and excise laws is inconsistent with the statute's language. "Read naturally, the word 'any' has an expansive meaning, that is, 'one or some indiscriminately of whatever kind.'" *United States v. Gonzales*, 520 U. S. 1, 5. For example, in considering a provision imposing an additional sentence that was not to run concurrently with "any other term of imprisonment," 18 U. S. C. §924(c)(1), the *Gonzales* Court held that, notwithstanding the subsection's initial reference to federal drug trafficking crimes, the expansive word "any" and the absence of restrictive language left "no basis in the text for limiting" the phrase "any other term of imprisonment" to federal sentences. 520 U. S., at 5. To similar effect, see *Harrison* v. *PPG Industries, Inc.*, 446 U. S. 578, 588–589, in which the Court held that there was "no indication

whatever that Congress intended" to limit the "expansive language" "'any other final action'" to particular kinds of agency action. The reasoning of *Gonzales* and *Harrison* applies equally to 28 U. S. C. §2680(c): Congress' use of "any" to modify "other law enforcement officer" is most naturally read to mean law enforcement officers of whatever kind. To be sure, the text's references to "tax or customs duty" and "officer[s] of customs or excise" indicate an intent to preserve immunity for claims arising from an officer's enforcement of tax and customs laws. The text also indicates, however, that Congress intended to preserve immunity for claims arising from the detention of property, and there is no indication of any intent that immunity for those claims turns on the type of law being enforced. Recent amendments to §2680(c) restoring the sovereign immunity waiver for officers enforcing *any* federal forfeiture law, see §2680(c)(1), support the Court's conclusion by demonstrating Congress' view that, prior to the amendments, §2680(c) covered *all* law enforcement officers. Against this textual and structural evidence, petitioner's reliance on the canons of statutory construction *ejusdem generis* and *noscitur a sociis* and on the rule against superfluities is unconvincing. The Court is unpersuaded by petitioner's attempt to create ambiguity where the statute's structure and text suggest none. Had Congress intended to limit §2680(c)'s reach as petitioner contends, it easily could have written "any other law enforcement officer *acting in a customs or excise capacity*." Instead, it used the unmodified, all-encompassing phrase "any other law enforcement officer." This Court must give effect to the text Congress enacted.

204 Fed. Appx. 778, affirmed.

THOMAS, J., delivered the opinion of the Court, in which ROBERTS, C. J., and SCALIA, GINSBURG, and ALITO, JJ., joined. KENNEDY, J., filed a dissenting opinion, in which STEVENS, SOUTER, and BREYER, JJ., joined. BREYER, J., filed a dissenting opinion, in which STEVENS, J., joined.

Appendices

APPENDIX I

AMENDMENTS TO THE UNITED STATES CONSTITUTION

Articles in addition to, and amendment of, the Constitution of the United States of America, proposed by Congress, and ratified by the legislatures of the several states, pursuant to the Fifth Article of the original Constitution

AMENDMENT I

Congress shall make no law respecting an establishment of religion, or prohibiting the free exercise thereof; or abridging the freedom of speech, or of the press; or the right of the people peaceably to assemble, and to petition the Government for a redress of grievances.

AMENDMENT II

A well regulated Militia, being necessary to the security of a free State, the right of the people to keep and bear Arms, shall not be infringed.

AMENDMENT III

No Soldier shall, in time of peace be quartered in any house, without the consent of the Owner, nor in time of war, but in a manner to be prescribed by law.

AMENDMENT IV

The right of the people to be secure in their persons, houses, papers, and effects, against unreasonable searches and seizures, shall not be violated, and no Warrants shall issue, but upon probable cause, supported by Oath or affirmation, and particularly describing the place to be searched, and the persons or things to be seized.

AMENDMENT V

No person shall be held to answer for a capital, or otherwise infamous crime, unless on a presentment or indictment of a Grand Jury, except in cases arising in the land or naval forces, or in the Militia, when in actual service in time of War or public danger; nor shall any person be subject for the same offence to be twice put in jeopardy of life or limb; nor shall be compelled in any criminal case to be a witness against himself, nor be deprived of life, liberty, or property, without due process of law; nor shall private property be taken for public use, without just compensation.

AMENDMENT VI

In all criminal prosecutions, the accused shall enjoy the right to a speedy and public trial, by an impartial jury of the State and district wherein the crime shall have been committed, which district shall have been previously ascertained by law, and to be informed of the nature and cause of the accusation; to be confronted with the witnesses against him; to have compulsory process for obtaining witnesses in his favor, and to have the Assistance of Counsel for his defence.

AMENDMENT VII

In Suits at common law, where the value in controversy shall exceed twenty dollars, the right of trial by jury shall be preserved, and no fact tried by a jury, shall be otherwise re-examined in any Court of the United States, than according to the rules of the common law.

AMENDMENT VIII

Excessive bail shall not be required, nor excessive fines imposed, nor cruel and unusual punishments inflicted.

AMENDMENT IX

The enumeration in the Constitution, of certain rights, shall not be construed to deny or disparage others retained by the people.

AMENDMENT X

The powers not delegated to the United States by the Constitution, nor prohibited by it to the States, are reserved to the States respectively, or to the people.

AMENDMENT XI

The Judicial power of the United States shall not be construed to extend to any suit in law or equity, commenced or prosecuted against one of the United States by Citizens of another State, or by Citizens or Subjects of any Foreign State.

AMENDMENT XII

The Electors shall meet in their respective states and vote by ballot for President and Vice-President, one of whom, at least, shall not be an inhabitant of the same state with themselves; they shall name in their ballots the person voted for as President, and in distinct ballots the person voted for as Vice-President, and they shall make distinct lists of all persons voted for as President, and of all persons voted for as Vice-President, and of the number of votes for each, which lists they shall sign and certify, and transmit sealed to the seat of the government of the United States, directed to the President of the Senate;—The President of the Senate shall, in the presence of the Senate and House of Representatives, open all the certificates and the votes shall then be counted;—The person having the greatest Number of votes for President, shall be the President, if such number be a majority of the whole number of Electors appointed; and if no person have such majority, then from the persons having the highest numbers not exceeding three on the list of those voted for as President, the House of Representatives shall choose immediately, by ballot, the President. But in choosing the President, the votes shall be taken by states, the representation from each state having one vote; a quorum for this purpose shall consist of a member or members from two-thirds of the states, and a majority of all the states shall be necessary to a choice. And if the House of Representatives shall not choose a President whenever the right of choice shall devolve upon them, before the fourth day of March next following, then the Vice-President shall act as President, as in the case of the death or other constitutional disability of the President.—The person having the greatest number of votes as Vice-President, shall be the Vice-President, if such number be a majority of the whole number of Electors appointed, and if no person have a majority, then from the two highest numbers on the list, the Senate shall choose the Vice-President; a quorum for the purpose shall consist of two-thirds of the whole number of Senators, and a majority of the whole number shall be necessary to a choice. But no person constitutionally ineligible to the office of President shall be eligible to that of Vice-President of the United States.

AMENDMENT XIII

SECTION 1. Neither slavery nor involuntary servitude, except as a punishment for crime whereof the party shall have been duly convicted, shall exist within the United States, or any place subject to their jurisdiction.

SECTION 2. Congress shall have power to enforce this article by appropriate legislation.

AMENDMENT XIV

SECTION 1. All persons born or naturalized in the United States and subject to the jurisdiction thereof, are citizens of the United States and of the State wherein they reside. No State shall make or enforce any law which shall abridge the privileges or immunities of citizens of the United States; nor shall any State deprive any person of life, liberty, or property, without due process of law; nor deny to any person within its jurisdiction the equal protection of the laws.

SECTION 2. Representatives shall be apportioned among the several States according to their respective numbers, counting the whole number of persons in each State, excluding Indians not taxed. But when the right to vote at any election for the choice of electors for President and Vice President of the United States, Representatives in Congress, the Executive and Judicial officers of a State, or the members of the Legislature thereof, is denied to any of the male inhabitants of such State, being twenty-one years of age, and citizens of the United States, or in any way abridged, except for participation in rebellion, or other crime, the basis of representation therein shall be reduced in the proportion which the number of such male citizens shall bear to the whole number of male citizens twenty-one years of age in such State.

SECTION 3. No person shall be a Senator or Representative in Congress, or elector of President and Vice President, or hold any office, civil or military, under the United States, or under any State, who, having previously taken an oath, as a member of Congress, or as an officer of the United States, or as a member of any State legislature, or as an executive or judicial officer of any State, to support the Constitution of the United States, shall have engaged in insurrection or rebellion against the same, or given aid or comfort to the enemies thereof. But Congress may by a vote of two-thirds of each House, remove such disability.

SECTION 4. The validity of the public debt of the United States, authorized by law, including debts incurred for payment of pensions and bounties for services in suppressing insurrection or rebellion, shall not be questioned. But neither the United States nor any State shall assume or pay any debt or obligation incurred in aid of insurrection or rebellion against the United States, or any claim for the loss or emancipation of any slave; but all such debts, obligations and claims shall be held illegal and void.

SECTION 5. The Congress shall have power to enforce, by appropriate legislation, the provisions of this article.

Amendment XV

SECTION 1. The right of citizens of the United States to vote shall not be denied or abridged by the United States or by any State on account of race, color, or previous condition of servitude.

SECTION 2. The Congress shall have power to enforce this article by appropriate legislation.

Amendment XVI

The Congress shall have power to lay and collect taxes on incomes, from whatever source derived, without apportionment among the several States, and without regard to any census or enumeration.

Amendment XVII

The Senate of the United States shall be composed of two Senators from each State,

elected by the people thereof, for six years; and each Senator shall have one vote. The electors in each State shall have the qualifications requisite for electors of the most numerous branch of the State legislatures.

When vacancies happen in the representation of any State in the Senate, the executive authority of such State shall issue writs of election to fill such vacancies: Provided, That the legislature of any State may empower the executive thereof to make temporary appointments until the people fill the vacancies by election as the legislature may direct.

This amendment shall not be so construed as to affect the election or term of any Senator chosen before it becomes valid as part of the Constitution.

Amendment XVIII

SECTION 1. After one year from the ratification of this article the manufacture, sale, or transportation of intoxicating liquors within, the importation thereof into, or the exportation thereof from the United States and all territory subject to the jurisdiction thereof for beverage purposes is hereby prohibited.

SECTION 2. The Congress and the several States shall have concurrent power to enforce this article by appropriate legislation.

SECTION 3. This article shall be inoperative unless it shall have been ratified as an amendment to the Constitution by the legislatures of the several States, as provided in the Constitution, within seven years from the date of the submission hereof to the States by the Congress.

Amendment XIX

The right of citizens of the United States to vote shall not be denied or abridged by the United States or by any State on account of sex.

Congress shall have power to enforce this article by appropriate legislation.

Amendment XX

SECTION 1. The terms of the President and Vice President shall end at noon on the 20th day of January, and the terms of

Senators and Representatives at noon
on the 3d day of January, of the years
in which such terms would have ended
if this article had not been ratified; and
the terms of their successors shall then
begin.
SECTION 2. The Congress shall assemble
at least once in every year, and such
meeting shall begin at noon on the 3d
day of January, unless they shall by law
appoint a different day.
SECTION 3. If, at the time fixed for the
beginning of the term of the President,
the President elect shall have died,
the Vice President elect shall become
President. If a President shall not have
been chosen before the time fixed for the
beginning of his term, or if the President
elect shall have failed to qualify, then the
Vice President elect shall act as President
until a President shall have qualified; and
the Congress may by law provide for the
case wherein neither a President elect
nor a Vice President shall have qualified,
declaring who shall then act as President,
or the manner in which one who is to act
shall be selected, and such person shall
act accordingly until a President or Vice
President shall have qualified.
SECTION 4. The Congress may by law
provide for the case of the death of any
of the persons from whom the House of
Representatives may choose a President
whenever the right of choice shall have
devolved upon them, and for the case
of the death of any of the persons from
whom the Senate may choose a Vice
President whenever the right of choice
shall have devolved upon them.
SECTION 5. Sections 1 and 2 shall take effect
on the 15th day of October following the
ratification of this article.
SECTION 6. This article shall be inoperative
unless it shall have been ratified as
an amendment to the Constitution by
the legislatures of three-fourths of the
several States within seven years from
the date of its submission.

AMENDMENT XXI

SECTION 1. The eighteenth article of
amendment to the Constitution of the
United States is hereby repealed.

SECTION 2. The transportation or
importation into any State, Territory,
or Possession of the United States for
delivery or use therein of intoxicating
liquors, in violation of the laws thereof,
is hereby prohibited.
SECTION 3. This article shall be inoperative
unless it shall have been ratified as
an amendment to the Constitution by
conventions in the several States, as
provided in the Constitution, within
seven years from the date of the
submission hereof to the States by the
Congress.

AMENDMENT XXII

SECTION 1. No person shall be elected to
the office of the President more than twice, and
no person who has held the office of President,
or acted as President, for more than two years of
a term to which some other person was elected
President shall be elected to the office of the
President more than once. But this Article shall
not apply to any person holding the office of
President, when this Article was proposed by
the Congress, and shall not prevent any person
who may be holding the office of President,
or acting as President, during the term within
which this Article becomes operative from
holding the office of President or acting as
President during the remainder of such term.
SECTION 2. This article shall be
inoperative unless it shall have been ratified
as an amendment to the Constitution by the
legislatures of three-fourths of the several
States within seven years from the date of its
submission to the States by the Congress.

AMENDMENT XXIII

SECTION 1. The District constituting the seat
of Government of the United States shall
appoint in such manner as Congress may
direct:

A number of electors of President and
Vice President equal to the whole number of
Senators and Representatives in Congress to
which the District would be entitled if it were
a State, but in no event more than the least
populous State; they shall be in addition to
those appointed by the States, but they shall
be considered, for the purposes of the election
of President and Vice President, to be electors

appointed by a State; and they shall meet in the District and perform such duties as provided by the twelfth article of amendment.

SECTION 2. The Congress shall have power to enforce this article by appropriate legislation.

AMENDMENT XXIV

SECTION 1. The right of citizens of the United States to vote in any primary or other election for President or Vice President, for electors for President or Vice President, or for Senator or Representative in Congress, shall not be denied or abridged by the United States or any State by reason of failure to pay any poll tax or other tax.

SECTION 2. The Congress shall have power to enforce this article by appropriate legislation.

AMENDMENT XXV

SECTION 1. In case of the removal of the President from office or of his death or resignation, the Vice President shall become President.

SECTION 2. Whenever there is a vacancy in the office of the Vice President, the President shall nominate a Vice President who shall take office upon confirmation by a majority vote of both Houses of Congress.

SECTION 3. Whenever the President transmits to the President pro tempore of the Senate and the Speaker of the House of Representatives his written declaration that he is unable to discharge the powers and duties of his office, and until he transmits to them a written declaration to the contrary, such powers and duties shall be discharged by the Vice President as Acting President.

SECTION 4. Whenever the Vice President and a majority of either the principal officers of the executive departments or of such other body as Congress may by law provide, transmit to the President pro tempore of the Senate and the Speaker of the House of Representatives their

written declaration that the President is unable to discharge the powers and duties of his office, the Vice President shall immediately assume the powers and duties of the office as Acting President.

Thereafter, when the President transmits to the President pro tempore of the Senate and the Speaker of the House of Representatives has written declaration that no inability exists, he shall resume the powers and duties of his office unless the Vice President and a majority of either the principal officers of the executive department or of such other body as Congress may by law provide, transmit within four days to the President pro tempore of the Senate and the Speaker of the House of Representatives their written declaration that the President is unable to discharge the powers and duties of his office. Thereupon Congress shall decide the issue, assembling within forty-eight hours for that purpose if not in session. If the Congress, within twenty-one days after receipt of the latter written declaration, or, if Congress is not in session, within twenty-one days after Congress is required to assemble, determines by two-thirds vote of both Houses that the President is unable to discharge the powers and duties of his office, the Vice President shall continue to discharge the same as Acting President; otherwise, the President shall resume the powers and duties of his office.

AMENDMENT XXVI

SECTION 1. The right of citizens of the United States, who are eighteen years of age or older, to vote shall not be denied or abridged by the United States or by any State on account of age.

SECTION 2. The Congress shall have power to enforce this article by appropriate legislation.

AMENDMENT XXVII

No law, varying the compensation for the services of the Senators and Representatives, shall take effect, until an election of Representatives shall have intervened.

APPENDIX II

SELECTED FEDERAL STATUTES

§ 1983. CIVIL ACTION FOR DEPRIVATION OF RIGHTS

Every person who, under color of any statute, ordinance, regulation, custom, or usage, of any State or Territory, subjects, or causes to be subjected, any citizen of the United States or other person within the jurisdiction thereof to the deprivation of any rights, privileges, or immunities secured by the Constitution and laws, shall be liable to the party injured in an action at law, suit in equity, or other proper proceeding for redress.
R.S. § 1979.

28 U.S.C. § 1915. PROCEEDINGS IN FORMA PAUPERIS

(a) (1) Subject to subsection (b), any court of the United States may authorize the commencement, prosecution or defense of any suit, action or proceeding, civil or criminal, or appeal therein, without prepayment of fees or security therefor, by a person who submits an affidavit that includes a statement of all assets such [person] prisoner possesses that the person is unable to pay such fees or give security therefor. Such affidavit shall state the nature of the action, defense or appeal and affiant's belief that the person is entitled to redress.

(2) A prisoner seeking to bring a civil action or appeal a judgment in a civil action or proceeding without prepayment of fees or security therefor, in addition to filing the affidavit filed under paragraph (1), shall submit a certified copy of the trust fund account statement (or institutional equivalent) for the prisoner for the 6-month period immediately preceding the filing of the complaint or notice of appeal, obtained from the appropriate official of each prison at which the prisoner is or was confined.

(3) An appeal may not be taken in forma pauperis if the trial court certifies in writing that it is not taken in good faith.

(b) (1) Notwithstanding subsection (a), if a prisoner brings a civil action or files an appeal in forma pauperis, the prisoner shall be required to pay the full amount of a filing fee. The court shall assess and, when funds exist, collect, as a partial payment of any court fees required by law, an initial partial filing fee of 20 percent of the greater of—

(A) the average monthly deposits to the prisoner's account; or.

(B) the average monthly balance in the prisoner's account for the 6-month period immediately preceding the filing of the complaint or notice of appeal.

(2) After payment of the initial partial filing fee, the prisoner shall be required to make monthly payments of 20 percent of the preceding month's income credited to the prisoner's account. The agency having custody of the prisoner shall forward payments from the prisoner's account to the clerk of the court each time the amount in the account exceeds $10 until the filing fees are paid.

(3) In no event shall the filing fee collected exceed the amount of fees permitted by statute for the commencement of a civil action or an appeal of a civil action or criminal judgment.

(4) In no event shall a prisoner be prohibited from bringing a civil action or appealing a civil or criminal judgment for the reason that the prisoner has no assets and no means by which to pay the initial partial filing fee.

(c) Upon the filing of an affidavit in accordance with subsections (a) and (b) and the prepayment of any partial filing fee as may be required under subsection (b), the court may direct payment by the United States of the expenses of (1) printing the record on appeal in any civil or criminal case, if such printing is required by the appellate court; (2) preparing a transcript of proceedings before a United States magistrate in any civil or criminal case, if such transcript is required by the district court, in the case of proceedings conducted under section 636(b) of this title or under section 3401(b) of title 18, United States Code; and (3) printing the record on appeal if such printing is required by the appellate court, in the case of proceedings conducted pursuant to section 636(c) of this title. Such expenses shall be paid when authorized by the Director of the Administrative Office of the United States Courts.

(d) The officers of the court shall issue and serve all process, and perform all duties in such cases. Witnesses shall attend as in other cases, and the same remedies shall be available as are provided for by law in other cases.

(e) (1) The court may request an attorney to represent any person unable to afford counsel.

(2) Notwithstanding any filing fee, or any portion thereof, that may have been paid, the court shall dismiss the case at any time if the court determines that—

    (A) the allegation of poverty is untrue; or.

    (B) (the action or appeal—

        (i) is frivolous or malicious;

        (ii) fails to state a claim on which relief may be granted; or

        (iii) seeks monetary relief against a defendant who is immune from such relief.

(f) (1) Judgment may be rendered for costs at the conclusion of the suit or action as in other proceedings, but the United States shall not be liable for any of the costs thus incurred. If the United States has paid the cost of a stenographic transcript or printed record for the prevailing party, the same shall be taxed in favor of the United States.

(2) (A) If the judgment against a prisoner includes the payment of costs under this subsection, the prisoner shall be required to pay the full amount of the costs ordered.

    (B) The prisoner shall be required to make payments for costs under this subsection in the same manner as is provided for filing fees under subsection (a)(2).

    (C) In no event shall the costs collected exceed the amount of the costs ordered by the court.

(g) In no event shall a prisoner bring a civil action or appeal a judgment in a civil action or proceeding under this section if the prisoner has, on 3 or more prior occasions, while incarcerated or detained in any facility, brought an action or appeal in a court of the United States that was dismissed on the grounds that it is frivolous, malicious, or fails to state a claim upon which relief may be granted, unless the prisoner is under imminent danger of serious physical injury.

(h) As used in this section, the term "prisoner" means any person incarcerated or detained in any facility who is accused of, convicted of, sentenced for, or adjudicated delinquent for, violations of criminal law or the terms and conditions of parole, probation, pretrial release, or diversionary program.

USCS § 1915A SCREENING

(a) Screening. The court shall review, before docketing, if feasible or, in any event, as soon as practicable after docketing, a complaint in a civil action in which a prisoner seeks redress from a governmental entity or officer or employee of a governmental entity.

(b) Grounds for dismissal. On review, the court shall identify cognizable claims or dismiss the complaint, or any portion of the complaint, if the complaint—

    (1) is frivolous, malicious, or fails to state a claim upon which relief may be granted; or

    (2) seeks monetary relief from a defendant who is immune from such relief.

(c) Definition. As used in this section, the term "prisoner" means any person incarcerated or detained in any facility who is accused of, convicted of, sentenced for, or adjudicated delinquent for, violations of criminal law or the terms and conditions of parole, probation, pretrial release, or diversionary program.

42 U.S.C. § 1997 CIVIL RIGHTS OF INSTITUTIONALIZED PERSONS

§ 1997. Definitions

As used in this Act—

(1) The term "institution" means any facility or institution—

(A) which is owned, operated, or managed by, or provides services on behalf of any State or political subdivision of a State; and

(B) which is—

(i) for persons who are mentally ill, disabled, or retarded, or chronically ill or handicapped;

(ii) a jail, prison, or other correctional facility;

(iii) a pretrial detention facility;

(iv) for juveniles—

(I) held awaiting trial;

(II) residing in such facility or institution for purposes of receiving care or treatment;
or

(III) residing for any State purpose in such facility or institution (other than a residential facility providing only elementary or secondary education that is not an institution in which reside juveniles who are adjudicated delinquent, in need of supervision, neglected, placed in State custody, mentally ill or disabled, mentally retarded, or chronically ill or handicapped); or

(v) providing skilled nursing, intermediate or long-term care, or custodial or residential care.

(2) Privately owned and operated facilities shall not be deemed "institutions" under this Act if.

(A) the licensing of such facility by the State constitutes the sole nexus between such facility and such State;

(B) the receipt by such facility, on behalf of persons residing in such facility, of payments under title XVI, XVIII, or under a State plan approved under title XIX, of the Social Security Act [42 USCS §§ 1381 et seq., §§ 1395 et seq., or §§ 1396 et seq.], constitutes the sole nexus between such facility and such State; or

(C) the licensing of such facility by the State, and the receipt by such facility, on behalf of persons residing in such facility, of payments under title XVI, XVIII, or under a State plan approved under title XIX, of the Social Security Act [42 USCS §§ 381 et seq., §§ 1395 et seq., §§ 1396 et seq.], constitutes the sole nexus between such facility and such State;

(3) The term "person" means an individual, a trust or estate, a partnership, an association, or a corporation;

(4) The term "State" means any of the several States, the District of Columbia, the Commonwealth of Puerto Rico, or any of the territories and possessions of the United States;

(5) The term "legislative days" means any calendar day on which either House of Congress is in session.

§ 1997a. Initiation of civil actions

(a) Discretionary authority of Attorney General; preconditions. Whenever the Attorney General has reasonable cause to believe that any State or political subdivision of a State, official, employee, or agent thereof, or other person acting on behalf of a State or political subdivision of a State is subjecting persons residing in or confined to an institution, as defined in section 2 [42 USCS § 1997], to egregious or flagrant conditions which deprive such persons of any rights, privileges, or immunities secured or protected by the Constitution or laws of the United States causing such persons to suffer grievous harm, and that such deprivation is pursuant to a pattern or practice of resistance to the full enjoyment of such rights, privileges, or immunities, the Attorney General, for or in the name of the United States, may institute a civil action in any appropriate United States district court against such party for such equitable relief as may be appropriate to insure the minimum corrective measures necessary to insure the full enjoyment of such rights, privileges, or immunities, except that such equitable relief shall be available under this Act to persons residing in or confined to an institution as defined in section 2(1)(B)(ii) [42 USCS §

1997(1)(B)(ii)] only insofar as such persons are subjected to conditions which deprive them of rights, privileges, or immunities secured or protected by the Constitution of the United States.

(b) Discretionary award of attorney fees. In any action commenced under this section, the court may allow the prevailing party, other than the United States, a reasonable attorney's fee against the United States as part of the costs.

(c) Attorney General to personally sign complaint. The Attorney General shall personally sign any complaint filed pursuant to this section.

§ 1997b. Certification requirements; Attorney General to personally sign certification

(a) At the time of the commencement of an action under section 3 [42 USCS § 1997a] the Attorney General shall certify to the court—

(1) that at least 49 calendar days previously the Attorney General has notified in writing the Governor or chief executive officer and attorney general or chief legal officer of the appropriate State or political subdivision and the director of the institution of—

(A) the alleged conditions which deprive rights, privileges, or immunities secured or protected by the Constitution or laws of the United States and the alleged pattern or practice of resistance to the full enjoyment of such rights, privileges, or immunities;

(B) the supporting facts giving rise to the alleged conditions and the alleged pattern or practice, including the dates or time period during which the alleged conditions and pattern or practice of resistance occurred; and when feasible, the identity of all persons reasonably suspected of being involved in causing the alleged conditions and pattern or practice at the time of the certification, and the date on which the alleged conditions and pattern or practice were first brought to the attention of the Attorney General; and

(C) the minimum measures which the Attorney General believes may remedy the alleged conditions and the alleged pattern or practice of resistance;

(2) that the Attorney General has notified in writing the Governor or chief executive officer and attorney general or chief legal officer of the appropriate State or political subdivision and the director of the institution of the Attorney General's intention to commence an investigation of such institution, that such notice was delivered at least seven days prior to the commencement of such investigation and that between the time of such notice and the commencement of an action under section 3 of this Act [42 USCS § 1997a]—

(A) the Attorney General has made a reasonable good faith effort to consult with the Governor or chief executive officer and attorney general or chief legal officer of the appropriate State or political subdivision and the director of the institution, or their designees, regarding financial, technical, or other assistance which may be available from the United States and which the Attorney General believes may assist in the correction of such conditions and pattern or practice of resistance;

(B) the Attorney General has encouraged the appropriate officials to correct the alleged conditions and pattern or practice of resistance through informal methods of conference, conciliation and persuasion, including, to the extent feasible, discussion of the possible costs and fiscal impacts of alternative minimum corrective measures, and it is the Attorney General's opinion that reasonable efforts at voluntary correction have not succeeded; and

(C) the Attorney General is satisfied that the appropriate officials have had a reasonable time to take appropriate action to correct such conditions and pattern or practice, taking into consideration the time required to remodel or make necessary changes in physical facilities or relocate residents, reasonable legal or procedural requirements, the urgency of the need to correct such conditions, and other circumstances involved in correcting such conditions; and

(3) that the Attorney General believes that such an action by the United States is of general public importance and will materially further the vindication of rights, privileges,

or immunities secured or protected by the Constitution or laws of the United States.

(b) The Attorney General shall personally sign any certification made pursuant to this section.

§ 1997c. Intervention in actions

(a) Discretionary authority of Attorney General; preconditions; time period.

(1) Whenever an action has been commenced in any court of the United States seeking relief from egregious or flagrant conditions which deprive persons residing in institutions of any rights, privileges, or immunities secured or protected by the Constitution or laws of the United States causing them to suffer grievous harm and the Attorney General has reasonable cause to believe that such deprivation is pursuant to a pattern or practice of resistance to the full enjoyment of such rights, privileges, or immunities, the Attorney General, for or in the name of the United States, may intervene in such action upon motion by the Attorney General.

(2) The Attorney General shall not file a motion to intervene under paragraph (1) before 90 days after the commencement of the action, except that if the court determines it would be in the interests of justice, the court may shorten or waive the time period.

(b) Certification requirements by Attorney General.

(1) The Attorney General shall certify to the court in the motion to intervene filed under subsection (a)—

(A) that the Attorney General has notified in writing, at least fifteen days previously, the Governor or chief executive officer, attorney general or chief legal officer of the appropriate State or political subdivision, and the director of the institution—

(i) the alleged conditions which deprive rights, privileges, or immunities secured or protected by the Constitution or laws of the United States and the alleged pattern or practice of resistance to the full enjoyment of such rights, privileges, or immunities;

(ii) the supporting facts giving rise to the alleged conditions, including the dates and time period during which the alleged conditions and pattern or practice of resistance occurred; and

(iii) to the extent feasible and consistent with the interests of other plaintiffs, the minimum measures which he believes may remedy the alleged conditions and the alleged pattern or practice of resistance; and

(B) that the Attorney General believes that such intervention by the United States is of general public importance and will materially further the vindication of rights, privileges, or immunities secured or protected by the Constitution or laws of the United States.

(2) The Attorney General shall personally sign any certification made pursuant to this section.

(c) Attorney General to personally sign motion to intervene. The Attorney General shall personally sign any motion to intervene made pursuant to this section.

(d) Discretionary award of attorney fees; other award provisions unaffected. In any action in which the United States joins as an intervenor under this section, the court may allow the prevailing party, other than the United States, a reasonable attorney's fee against the United States as part of the costs. Nothing in this subsection precludes the award of attorney's fees available under any other provisions of the United States Code.

§ 1997d. Prohibition of retaliation

No person reporting conditions which may constitute a violation under this Act shall be subjected to retaliation in any manner for so reporting.

§ 1997e. Suits by prisoners

(a) Applicability of administrative remedies. No action shall be brought with respect to prison conditions under section 1979 of the Revised Statutes of the United States (42 U.S.C. § 1983), or any other Federal law, by a prisoner confined in any jail, prison, or other correctional facility until such administrative remedies as are available are exhausted.

(b) Failure of State to adopt or adhere to administrative grievance procedure. The failure of a State to adopt or adhere to an administrative grievance procedure shall not constitute the basis for an action under section 3 or 5 of this Act [42 USCS § 1997a or 1997c].

(c) Dismissal.

(1) The court shall on its own motion or on the motion of a party dismiss any action brought with respect to prison conditions under section 1979 of the Revised Statutes of the United States { 2 U.S.C. § 1983), or any other Federal law, by a prisoner confined in any jail, prison, or other correctional facility if the court is satisfied that the action is frivolous, malicious, fails to state a claim upon which relief can be granted, or seeks monetary relief from a defendant who is immune from such relief.

(2) In the event that a claim is, on its face, frivolous, malicious, fails to state a claim upon which relief can be granted, or seeks monetary relief from a defendant who is immune from such relief, the court may dismiss the underlying claim without first requiring the exhaustion of administrative remedies.

(d) Attorney's fees.

(1) In any action brought by a prisoner who is confined to any jail, prison, or other correctional facility, in which attorney's fees are authorized under section 2 of the Revised Statutes of the United States (42 U.S.C. § 1988), such fees shall not be awarded, except to the extent that—

(A) the fee was directly and reasonably incurred in proving an actual violation of the plaintiff's rights protected by a statute pursuant to which a fee may be awarded under section 2 of the Revised Statutes; and
B

(i) the amount of the fee is proportionately related to the court ordered relief for the violation; or
(ii) the fee was directly and reasonably incurred in enforcing the relief ordered for the violation.

(2) Whenever a monetary judgment is awarded in an action described in paragraph (1), a portion of the judgment (not to exceed 25 percent) shall be applied to satisfy the amount of attorney's fees awarded against the defendant. If the award of attorney's fees is not greater than 150 percent of the judgment, the excess shall be paid by the defendant.

(3) No award of attorney's fees in an action described in paragraph (1) shall be based on an hourly rate greater than 150 percent of the hourly rate established under section 3006A of title 18, United States Code, for payment of court-appointed counsel.

(4) Nothing in this subsection shall prohibit a prisoner from entering into an agreement to pay an attorney's fee in an amount greater than the amount authorized under this subsection, if the fee is paid by the individual rather than by the defendant pursuant to section 2 of the Revised Statutes of the United States (42 U.S.C. § 1988).

(e) Limitation on recovery. No Federal civil action may be brought by a prisoner confined in a jail, prison, or other correctional facility, for mental or emotional injury suffered while in custody without a prior showing of physical injury.

(f) Hearings.

(1) To the extent practicable, in any action brought with respect to prison conditions in Federal court pursuant to section 1979 of the Revised Statutes of the United States (42 U.S.C. § 1983), or any other Federal law, by a prisoner confined in any jail, prison, or other correctional facility, pretrial proceedings in which the prisoner's participation is required or permitted shall be conducted by telephone, video conference, or other telecommunications technology without removing the prisoner from the facility in which the prisoner is confined.

(2) Subject to the agreement of the official of the Federal, State, or local unit of government with custody over the prisoner, hearings may be conducted at the facility in which the prisoner is confined. To the extent practicable, the court shall allow counsel to participate by telephone, video conference, or other communications technology in any hearing held at the facility.

(g) Waiver of reply.

(1) Any defendant may waive the right to reply to any action brought by a prisoner confined in any jail, prison, or other correctional facility under section 1979 of the Revised Statutes of the United States (42 U.S.C. § 1983) or any other Federal law. Notwithstanding any other law or rule of

procedure, such waiver shall not constitute an admission of the allegations contained in the complaint. No relief shall be granted to the plaintiff unless a reply has been filed.

(2) The court may require any defendant to reply to a complaint brought under this section if it finds that the plaintiff has a reasonable opportunity to prevail on the merits.

(h) Definition. As used in this section, the term "prisoner" means any person incarcerated or detained in any facility who is accused of, convicted of, sentenced for, or adjudicated delinquent for, violations of criminal law or the terms and conditions of parole, probation, pretrial release, or diversionary program.

§ 1997f. Report to Congress

The Attorney General shall include in the report to Congress on the business of the Department of Justice prepared pursuant to section 522 of title 28, United States Code—

(1) a statement of the number, variety, and outcome of all actions instituted pursuant to this Act including the history of, precise reasons for, and procedures followed in initiation or intervention in each case in which action was commenced;

(2) a detailed explanation of the procedures by which the Department has received, reviewed and evaluated petitions or complaints regarding conditions in institutions;

(3) an analysis of the impact of actions instituted pursuant to this Act including, when feasible, an estimate of the costs incurred by States and other political subdivisions;

(4) a statement of the financial, technical, or other assistance which has been made available from the United States to the State in order to assist in the correction of the conditions which are alleged to have deprived a person of rights, privileges, or immunities secured or protected by the Constitution or laws of the United States; and

(5) the progress made in each Federal institution toward meeting existing promulgated standards for such institutions or constitutionally guaranteed minima.

§ 1997g. Priorities for use of funds

[(a)] It is the intent of Congress that deplorable conditions in institutions covered by this Act amounting to deprivations of rights protected by the Constitution or laws of the United States be corrected, not only by litigation as contemplated in this Act, but also by the voluntary good faith efforts of agencies of Federal, State, and local governments. It is the further intention of Congress that where Federal funds are available for use in improving such institutions, priority should be given to the correction or elimination of such unconstitutional or illegal conditions which may exist. It is not the intent of this provision to require the redirection of funds from one program to another or from one State to another.

§ 1997h. Notice to Federal departments

At the time of notification of the commencement of an investigation of an institution under section 3 [42 USCS § 997a] or of the notification of an intention to file a motion to intervene under section 5 of this Act [42 USCS § 997c], and if the relevant institution receives Federal financial assistance from the Department of Health and Human Services or the Department of Education, the Attorney General shall notify the appropriate Secretary of the action and the reasons for such action and shall consult with such officials. Following such consultation, the Attorney General may proceed with an action under this Act if the Attorney General is satisfied that such action is consistent with the policies and goals of the executive branch.

§ 1997i. Disclaimer respecting standards of care

Provisions of this Act shall not authorize promulgation of regulations defining standards of care.

§ 1997j. Disclaimer respecting private litigation

The provisions of this Act shall in no way expand or restrict the authority of parties other than the United States to enforce the legal rights which they may have pursuant to existing law with regard to institutionalized persons. In this regard, the fact that the Attorney General may be conducting an investigation or contemplating litigation pursuant to this Act shall not be grounds for delay of or prejudice to any litigation on behalf of parties other than the United States.

8 U.S.C. § 3626 (1997) APPROPRIATE REMEDIES WITH RESPECT TO PRISON CONDITIONS

(a) Requirements for relief.

(1) Prospective relief.

(A) Prospective relief in any civil action with respect to prison conditions shall extend no further than necessary to correct the violation of the Federal right of a particular plaintiff or plaintiffs. The court shall not grant or approve any prospective relief unless the court finds that such relief is narrowly drawn, extends no further than necessary to correct the violation of the Federal right, and is the least intrusive means necessary to correct the violation of the Federal right. The court shall give substantial weight to any adverse impact on public safety or the operation of a criminal justice system caused by the relief.

(B) The court shall not order any prospective relief that requires or permits a government official to exceed his or her authority under State or local law or otherwise violates State or local law, unless—

(i) Federal law requires such relief to be ordered in violation of State or local law;

(ii) the relief is necessary to correct the violation of a Federal right; and

(iii) no other relief will correct the violation of the Federal right.

(C) Nothing in this section shall be construed to authorize the courts, in exercising their remedial powers, to order the construction of prisons or the raising of taxes, or to repeal or detract from otherwise applicable limitations on the remedial powers of the courts.

(2) Preliminary injunctive relief. In any civil action with respect to prison conditions, to the extent otherwise authorized by law, the court may enter a temporary restraining order or an order for preliminary injunctive relief. Preliminary injunctive relief must be narrowly drawn, extend no further than necessary to correct the harm the court finds requires preliminary relief, and be the least intrusive means necessary to correct that harm. The court shall give substantial weight to any adverse impact on public safety or the operation of a criminal justice system caused by the preliminary relief and shall respect the principles of comity set out in paragraph (1)(B) in tailoring any preliminary relief. Preliminary injunctive relief shall automatically expire on the date that is 90 days after its entry, unless the court makes the findings required under subsection (a)(1) for the entry of prospective relief and makes the order final before the expiration of the 90-day period.

(3) Prisoner release order.

(A) In any civil action with respect to prison conditions, no court shall enter a prisoner release order unless—

(i) a court has previously entered an order for less intrusive relief that has failed to remedy the deprivation of the Federal right sought to be remedied through the prisoner release order; and

(ii) the defendant has had a reasonable amount of time to comply with the previous court orders.

(B) In any civil action in Federal court with respect to prison conditions, a prisoner release order shall be entered only by a three-judge court in accordance with section 2284 of title 28, if the requirements of subparagraph (E) have been met.

(C) A party seeking a prisoner release order in Federal court shall file with any request for such relief, a request for a three-judge court and materials sufficient to demonstrate that the requirements of subparagraph (A) have been met.

(D) If the requirements under subparagraph (A) have been met, a Federal judge before whom a civil action with respect to prison conditions is pending who believes that a prison release order should be considered may sua sponte request the convening of a three-judge court to determine whether a prisoner release order should be entered.

(E) The three-judge court shall enter a prisoner release order only if the court finds by clear and convincing evidence that—

(i) crowding is the primary cause of the violation of a Federal right; and

(ii) no other relief will remedy the violation of the Federal right.

(F) Any State or local official including a legislator or unit of government whose jurisdiction or function includes the appropriation of funds for the construction, operation, or maintenance of prison facilities, or the prosecution or custody of persons who may be released from, or not admitted to, a prison as a result of a prisoner release order shall have standing to oppose the imposition or continuation in effect of such relief and to seek termination of such relief, and shall have the right to intervene in any proceeding relating to such relief.

(b) Termination of relief.

(1) Termination of prospective relief.

(A) In any civil action with respect to prison conditions in which prospective relief is ordered, such relief shall be terminable upon the motion of any party or intervener—

(i) 2 years after the date the court granted or approved the prospective relief;
(ii) 1 year after the date the court has entered an order denying termination of prospective relief under this paragraph; or
(iii) in the case of an order issued on or before the date of enactment of the Prison Litigation Reform Act [enacted April 26, 1996], 2 years after such date of enactment.

(B) Nothing in this section shall prevent the parties from agreeing to terminate or modify relief before the relief is terminated under subparagraph (A).

(2) Immediate termination of prospective relief. In any civil action with respect to prison conditions, a defendant or intervener shall be entitled to the immediate termination of any prospective relief if the relief was approved or granted in the absence of a finding by the court that the relief is narrowly drawn, extends no further than necessary to correct the violation of the Federal right, and is the least intrusive means necessary to correct the violation of the Federal right.

(3) Limitation. Prospective relief shall not terminate if the court makes written findings based on the record that prospective relief remains necessary to correct a current and ongoing violation of the Federal right, extends no further than necessary to correct the violation of the Federal right, and that the prospective relief is narrowly drawn and the least intrusive means to correct the violation.

(4) Termination or modification of relief. Nothing in this section shall prevent any party or intervener from seeking modification or termination before the relief is terminable under paragraph (1) or (2), to the extent that modification or termination would otherwise be legally permissible.

(c) Settlements.

(1) Consent decrees. In any civil action with respect to prison conditions, the court shall not enter or approve a consent decree unless it complies with the limitations on relief set forth in subsection (a).

(2) Private settlement agreements.

(A) Nothing in this section shall preclude parties from entering into a private settlement agreement that does not comply with the limitations on relief set forth in subsection (a), if the terms of that agreement are not subject to court enforcement other than the reinstatement of the civil proceeding that the agreement settled.

(B) Nothing in this section shall preclude any party claiming that a private settlement agreement has been breached from seeking in State court any remedy available under State law.

(d) State law remedies. The limitations on remedies in this section shall not apply to relief entered by a State court based solely upon claims arising under State law.

(e) Procedure for motions affecting prospective relief.

(1) Generally. The court shall promptly rule on any motion to modify or terminate prospective relief in a civil action with respect to prison conditions. Mandamus shall lie to remedy any failure to issue a prompt ruling on such a motion.

(2) Automatic stay. Any motion to modify or terminate prospective relief made under subsection (b) shall operate as a stay during the period—

(A) (i) beginning on the 30th day after such motion is filed, in the case of a motion made under paragraph (1) or (2) of subsection (b); or

(ii) beginning on the 180th day after such motion is filed, in the case of a motion made under any other law; and

(B) ending on the date the court enters a final order ruling on the motion.

(3) Postponement of automatic stay. The court may postpone the effective date of an automatic stay specified in subsection (e) (2) (A) for not more than 60 days for good cause. No postponement shall be permissible because of general congestion of the court's calendar.

(4) Order blocking the automatic stay. Any order staying, suspending, delaying, or barring the operation of the automatic stay described in paragraph (2) (other than an order to postpone the effective date of the automatic stay under paragraph (3)) shall be treated as an order refusing to dissolve or modify an injunction and shall be appealable pursuant to section 1292(a) (1) of title 28, United States Code, regardless of how the order is styled or whether the order is termed a preliminary or a final ruling.

(f) Special masters.

(1) In general.

(A) In any civil action in a Federal court with respect to prison conditions, the court may appoint a special master who shall be disinterested and objective and who will give due regard to the public safety, to conduct hearings on the record and prepare proposed findings of fact.

(B) The court shall appoint a special master under this subsection during the remedial phase of the action only upon a finding that the remedial phase will be sufficiently complex to warrant the appointment.

(2) Appointment.

(A) If the court determines that the appointment of a special master is necessary, the court shall request that the defendant institution and the plaintiff each submit a list of not more than 5 persons to serve as a special master.

(B) Each party shall have the opportunity to remove up to 3 persons from the opposing party's list.

(C) The court shall select the master from the persons remaining on the list after the operation of subparagraph (B).

(3) Interlocutory appeal. Any party shall have the right to an interlocutory appeal of the judge's selection of the special master under this subsection, on the ground of partiality.

(4) Compensation. The compensation to be allowed to a special master under this section shall be based on an hourly rate not greater than the hourly rate established under section 3006A for payment of court-appointed counsel, plus costs reasonably incurred by the special master. Such compensation and costs shall be paid with funds appropriated to the Judiciary.

(5) Regular review of appointment. In any civil action with respect to prison conditions in which a special master is appointed under this subsection, the court shall review the appointment of the special master every 6 months to determine whether the services of the special master continue to be required under paragraph (1). In no event shall the appointment of a special master extend beyond the termination of the relief.

(6) Limitations on powers and duties. A special master appointed under this subsection—

(A) may be authorized by a court to conduct hearings and prepare proposed findings of fact, which shall be made on the record;

(B) shall not make any findings or communications ex parte;

(C) may be authorized by a court to assist in the development of remedial plans; and

(D) may be removed at any time, but shall be relieved of the appointment upon the termination of relief.

(g) Definitions. As used in this section—

(1) the term "consent decree" means any relief entered by the court that is based in whole or in part upon the consent or acquiescence of the parties but does not include private settlements;

(2) the term "civil action with respect to prison conditions" means any civil proceeding arising under Federal law with respect to the conditions of confinement or the effects of actions by government officials on the lives of persons confined in prison, but does not include habeas corpus proceedings challenging the fact or duration of confinement in prison;

(3) the term "prisoner" means any person subject to incarceration, detention, or admission to any facility who is accused of, convicted

of, sentenced for, or adjudicated delinquent for, violations of criminal law or the terms and conditions of parole, probation, pretrial release, or diversionary program;

(4) the term "prisoner release order" includes any order, including a temporary restraining order or preliminary injunctive relief, that has the purpose or effect of reducing or limiting the prison population, or that directs the release from or nonadmission of prisoners to a prison;

(5) the term "prison" means any Federal, State, or local facility that incarcerates or detains juveniles or adults accused of, convicted of, sentenced for, or adjudicated delinquent for, violations of criminal law;

(6) the term "private settlement agreement" means an agreement entered into among the parties that is not subject to judicial enforcement other than the reinstatement of the civil proceeding that the agreement settled;

(7) the term "prospective relief" means all relief other than compensatory monetary damages;

(8) the term "special master" means any person appointed by a Federal court pursuant to Rule 53 of the Federal Rules of Civil Procedure or pursuant to any inherent power of the court to exercise the powers of a master, regardless of the title or description given by the court; and

(9) the term "relief" means all relief in any form that may be granted or approved by the court, and includes consent decrees but does not include private settlement agreements.42 U.S. §2000cc.

42 U.S.C. § 2000CC RELIGIOUS LAND USE AND INSTITUTIONALIZED PERSONS ACT

(a) Substantial burdens.

(1) General rule. No government shall impose or implement a land use regulation in a manner that imposes a substantial burden on the religious exercise of a person, including a religious assembly or institution, unless the government demonstrates that imposition of the burden on that person, assembly, or institution—

(A) is in furtherance of a compelling governmental interest; and

(B) is the least restrictive means of furthering that compelling governmental interest.

(2) Scope of application. This subsection applies in any case in which—

(A) the substantial burden is imposed in a program or activity that receives Federal financial assistance, even if the burden results from a rule of general applicability;

(B) the substantial burden affects, or removal of that substantial burden would affect, commerce with foreign nations, among the several States, or with Indian tribes, even if the burden results from a rule of general applicability; or

(C) the substantial burden is imposed in the implementation of a land use regulation or system of land use regulations, under which a government makes, or has in place formal or informal procedures or practices that permit the government to make, individualized assessments of the proposed uses for the property involved.

(b) Discrimination and exclusion.

(1) Equal terms. No government shall impose or implement a land use regulation in a manner that treats a religious assembly or institution on less than equal terms with a nonreligious assembly or institution.

(2) Nondiscrimination. No government shall impose or implement a land use regulation that discriminates against any assembly or institution on the basis of religion or religious denomination.

(3) Exclusions and limits. No government shall impose or implement a land use regulation that—

(A) totally excludes religious assemblies from a jurisdiction; or

(B) unreasonably limits religious assemblies, institutions, or structures within a jurisdiction.

P.L. 105–277, DIV A, § 101(B) [TITLE I, § 127], 112 STAT. 2681–74, OCT. 21, 1998, NON-DISCLOSURE OF INFORMATION RELATING TO PRISON EMPLOYEES ACT

Notwithstanding any other provision of law, in any action brought by a prisoner under section 1979 of the Revised Statutes (42 U.S.C. 1983) against a Federal, State, or local jail, prison, or correctional facility, or any employee or former employee thereof, arising out of the incarceration of that prisoner—

(1) the financial records of a person employed or formerly employed by the Federal, State, or local jail, prison, or correctional facility, shall not be subject to disclosure without the written consent of that person or pursuant to a court order, unless a verdict of liability has been entered against that person; and

(2) the home address, home phone number, social security number, identity of family members, personal tax returns, and personal banking information of a person described in paragraph (1), and any other records or information of a similar nature relating to that person, shall not be subject to disclosure without the written consent of that person, or pursuant to a court order.

Index

Note: Page numbers in **bold** indicate a table on the corresponding page.